THE PAPERS OF ULYSSES S. GRANT

THE PAPERS OF

ULYSSES S. GRANT

Volume 23:

February 1–December 31, 1872

Edited by John Y. Simon

ASSISTANT EDITORS
William M. Ferraro
Aaron M. Lisec

TEXTUAL EDITOR
Dawn Ruark

———

SOUTHERN ILLINOIS UNIVERSITY PRESS

CARBONDALE AND EDWARDSVILLE

Library of Congress Cataloging in Publication Data (Revised)

Grant, Ulysses Simpson, Pres. U.S., 1822–1885.
  The papers of Ulysses S. Grant.

  Prepared under the auspices of the Ulysses S. Grant Association.
  Bibliographical footnotes.
  CONTENTS: v. 1. 1837–1861.—v. 2. April–September 1861.—
v. 3. October 1, 1861–January 7, 1862.—v. 4. January 8–March 31,
1862.—v. 5. April 1–August 31, 1862.—v. 6. September 1–December 8,
1862.—v. 7. December 9, 1862–March 31, 1863.—v. 8. April 1–July 6,
1863.—v. 9. July 7–December 31, 1863.—v. 10. January 1–May 31,
1864.—v. 11. June 1–August 15, 1864.—v. 12. August 16–November 15, 1864.—v. 13. November 16, 1864–February 20, 1865.—v. 14.
February 21–April 30, 1865.—v. 15. May 1–December 31, 1865.—
v. 16. 1866.—v. 17. January 1–September 30, 1867.—v. 18. October 1,
1867–June 30, 1868.—v. 19. July 1, 1868–October 31, 1869.—v. 20.
November 1, 1869–October 31, 1870.—v. 21. November 1, 1870–
May 31, 1871.—v. 22. June 1, 1871–January 31, 1872.—v. 23. February 1–December 31, 1872.

  1. Grant, Ulysses Simpson, Pres. U.S., 1822–1885. 2. United
States—History—Civil War, 1861–1865—Campaigns and battles—
Sources. 3. United States—Politics and government—1869–1877—
Sources. 4. Presidents—United States—Biography. 5. Generals—
United States—Biography. I. Simon, John Y., ed. II. Ulysses S. Grant
Association.
E660.G756 1967   973.8'2'0924   67–10725
ISBN 0-8093-2276-5 (v. 23)

The paper used in this publication meets the minimum requirements
of American National Standard for Information Sciences—Permanence
of Paper for Printed Library Materials, ANSI Z39.48-1992. ⊗

Published with the assistance of a grant from the National Historical
Publications and Records Commission.

Contents

Introduction

THE ISSUE OF A second term as president loomed over Ulysses S. Grant in 1872. Mixed emotions troubled him as he looked toward the political future. He would gladly have relinquished the burdens of the presidency and reluctantly accepted unanimous renomination by the Republican Convention at Philadelphia in June. But he remained committed to Republican policies. "I do now, as I did four years ago, sincerely believe that the interests of the whole country demand the success of the Republican party." Grant also wanted to complete his own initiatives to strengthen the economy, to improve foreign relations, and to ease conflicts among whites, blacks, and Indians. "My desire is to see harmony, concord and prosperity exist everywhere in our common country."

In the end, increasingly vicious accusations of ineptness and misuse of power from political opponents who organized under the name Liberal Republicans escalated the campaign from a typical partisan struggle to a serious personal challenge. "The opposition in this canvass seem to have no capital but slander, abuse and falsehood." Grant revealed the depth of his feelings to a friend: "So far I have been blessed with a constitution that has stood all climates and other strains upon it without any yiealding. The severest test I have had to undergo has been slanderous and false abuse with hands and tongue tied. I do hope this mode of warfare will soon end." Determined to defend his good name, Grant battled against Liberal Republican presidential candidate Horace Greeley, Senator Carl Schurz, Senator Charles Sumner, and other foes. Election returns vindicated Grant's optimistic predictions of electoral

xi

success over Greeley's tenuous coalition of Democrats and "Soreheads & thieves who have deserted the republican party." Grant magnanimously attended Greeley's funeral in New York City only weeks after the election to pay public respect to his defeated rival.

Grant had legitimate reasons for ambivalence toward a second presidential term. Patronage pressures besieged him. Particularly embarrassing or awkward predicaments involved Grant's brother Orvil and the Chicago Customhouse, Grant's former staff officer George K. Leet and the New York City Customhouse, and powerful politicians interested in appointments for United States attorney for the Southern District of New York and Philadelphia postmaster. Civil Service reforms provided some defense against less aggressive or influential aspirants, but Grant knew only too well the weaknesses in this line: "Heretofore federal offices have been regarded too much as the reward of political services. Under authority of Congress rules have been established to regulate the tenure of office and the mode of appointments. But without the more direct sanction of Congress these rules cannot be made entirely effective, nor have the rules adopted entirely proven satisfactory." Federal officials in Dakota Territory and Florida engaged in political disputes or outright criminality embroiled Grant in additional patronage dilemmas.

The *Alabama* Claims negotiations tested Grant's foreign policy and his confidence in the steady guidance of Secretary of State Hamilton Fish. The high stakes involved in preparing and presenting the United States case against Great Britain before the Geneva tribunal caused Grant considerable worry. Furthermore, Fish maneuvered Grant into selecting Charles Francis Adams, a man Grant passionately disliked, to represent the nation at Geneva. But the move paid off, and the final award of $15,500,000 to the United States and the establishment of lasting principles of neutrality vindicated the long and tedious diplomatic process. Elsewhere, difficulties with Spain over political oppression, slavery, and atrocities in Cuba led to the temporary recall of United States minister Daniel E. Sickles. Grant's eagerness to promote an isthmian canal encouraged political adventurers and financial schemers in Central America. The promising beginnings of relations with Japan, manifested in the celebrated tour of the Iwakura delegation, dissipated in confusing trade negotiations. A proposal to annex Samoa foreshadowed future intrigue and signaled a shift in focus from the Caribbean to the Pacific.

Domestic policies in place since early in Grant's first term showed tentative rather than solid progress. Concerted actions between federal judicial officers and United States Army detachments had checked the rampant Ku Klux Klan violence of the previous year. Grant received appeals to withdraw his agents and to pardon those imprisoned for Klan activities, but he also learned of sporadic outbursts of violence against blacks and Republicans in the South. Grant expressed a genuine desire "that all citizens, white or black, native or foreign born, may be left free, in all parts of our common country, to vote, speak & act, in obedience to law, without intimidation or ostrasism on account of his views, color or nativity." He reiterated the point to a delegation of Philadelphia blacks: "All citizens undoubtedly in all respects should be equal."

Indian relations challenged Grant's resolve frequently as he struggled to maintain his peace policy in the face of mounting objections from both civilians and army officers. "If any change takes place in the Indian Policy of the Government, while I hold my present office, it will be on the humanitarian side of the question." Grant also used his presidential office to call attention to unlawful or unethical treatment of laborers and immigrants, prompting at least some meaningful steps toward reform.

Growing personal demands on Grant likewise contributed to his ambivalence toward a second term. In his roles as husband, father, son, and guardian of the children and estate of John A. Rawlins, Grant balanced a welter of responsibilities and conflicting emotions. In his willingness "to do whatever is the best" for his friend Rawlins's widow and children, Grant coordinated discussions among others interested in their welfare, managed the family's financial assets, and occasionally furnished money. The widow's remarriage further complicated an already awkward situation.

Grant's father's failing health necessitated visits to Covington, Kentucky, that did not fit comfortably with official duties or personal preference. Grant's three older children traveled overseas during much of 1872 and were sources of both pride and concern to their parents. Grant doted on his only daughter, Ellen (Nellie): "She has been all her life so much of a companion of her mother that I feared she would want to return by the first steamer leaving Liverpool after her arrival. But she writes quite the reverse of being homesick."

Grant's own finances were not in good shape. His farm near St. Louis was unprofitable despite his best efforts to direct its manager. "Another place like it would break me." Neighboring property owners resisted construction of a railroad through the area, denying Grant the lucrative prospect of selling off unproductive land. An investment in a Maryland quarry never returned promised earnings, and Grant grudgingly accepted a loss when continued association with the company meant becoming mired in political scandal. He complained bitterly before the forced sale of his stock that all the scandal "is in the imagination of Sore Head Republicans and Democrats because I own an interest." As in the past, Grant found rest and relaxation in a circle of trusted friends whom he visited and constantly urged to come to the White House or to his summer cottage in Long Branch, New Jersey.

When Harvard University presented him an honorary degree, Grant expressed thanks for the approval of his "efforts to serve our beloved country both in time of War and in time of peace. It will be my effort to continue to deserve that confidence." In the midst of political and personal obligations, Grant retained a commendable sense of equanimity and humility. Admittedly susceptible to indulging a friend or relative with a favor, and often confessing to being indolent or lazy, Grant's human weaknesses overshadowed his efforts to act with fairness as president during a time of unprecedented challenges. As 1872 ended, Grant knew that he would have four more years to lead the nation and, with renewed optimism, believed that better results were in store.

We are indebted to Timothy Connelly and Michael T. Meier for assistance in searching the National Archives; to Harriet F. Simon for proofreading; and to Joni Eberhart, David Gerleman, and Steve Swearingin, graduate students at Southern Illinois University, for research assistance.

Financial support for the period during which this volume was prepared came from Southern Illinois University, the National Endowment for the Humanities, and the National Historical Publications and Records Commission.

JOHN Y. SIMON

October 21, 1998

Editorial Procedure

———

1. Editorial Insertions

A. Words or letters in roman type within brackets represent editorial reconstruction of parts of manuscripts torn, mutilated, or illegible.

B. [. . .] or [——— ———] within brackets represent lost material which cannot be reconstructed. The number of dots represents the approximate number of lost letters; dashes represent lost words.

C. Words in *italic* type within brackets represent material such as dates which were not part of the original manuscript.

D. Other material crossed out is indicated by ~~cancelled type~~.

E. Material raised in manuscript, as "4th," has been brought in line, as "4th."

2. Symbols Used to Describe Manuscripts

AD	Autograph Document
ADS	Autograph Document Signed
ADf	Autograph Draft
ADfS	Autograph Draft Signed
AES	Autograph Endorsement Signed
AL	Autograph Letter
ALS	Autograph Letter Signed
ANS	Autograph Note Signed
D	Document

DS	Document Signed
Df	Draft
DfS	Draft Signed
ES	Endorsement Signed
LS	Letter Signed

3. Military Terms and Abbreviations

Act.	Acting
Adjt.	Adjutant
AG	Adjutant General
AGO	Adjutant General's Office
Art.	Artillery
Asst.	Assistant
Bvt.	Brevet
Brig.	Brigadier
Capt.	Captain
Cav.	Cavalry
Col.	Colonel
Co.	Company
C.S.A.	Confederate States of America
Dept.	Department
Div.	Division
Gen.	General
Hd. Qrs.	Headquarters
Inf.	Infantry
Lt.	Lieutenant
Maj.	Major
Q. M.	Quartermaster
Regt.	Regiment or regimental
Sgt.	Sergeant
USMA	United States Military Academy, West Point, N.Y.
Vols.	Volunteers

4. Short Titles and Abbreviations

ABPC	*American Book Prices Current* (New York, 1895–)
Badeau	Adam Badeau, *Grant in Peace. From Appomattox to Mount McGregor* (Hartford, Conn., 1887)

CG	*Congressional Globe.* Numbers following represent the Congress, session, and page.
J. G. Cramer	Jesse Grant Cramer, ed., *Letters of Ulysses S. Grant to his Father and his Youngest Sister, 1857–78* (New York and London, 1912)
DAB	*Dictionary of American Biography* (New York, 1928–36)
Foreign Relations	*Papers Relating to the Foreign Relations of the United States* (Washington, 1869–)
Garland	Hamlin Garland, *Ulysses S. Grant: His Life and Character* (New York, 1898)
Julia Grant	John Y. Simon, ed., *The Personal Memoirs of Julia Dent Grant* (New York, 1975)
HED	*House Executive Documents*
HMD	*House Miscellaneous Documents*
HRC	*House Reports of Committees.* Numbers following *HED, HMD,* or *HRC* represent the number of the Congress, the session, and the document.
Ill. AG Report	J. N. Reece, ed., *Report of the Adjutant General of the State of Illinois* (Springfield, 1900)
Johnson, Papers	LeRoy P. Graf and Ralph W. Haskins, eds., *The Papers of Andrew Johnson* (Knoxville, 1967–)
Lewis	Lloyd Lewis, *Captain Sam Grant* (Boston, 1950)
Lincoln, Works	Roy P. Basler, Marion Dolores Pratt, and Lloyd A. Dunlap, eds., *The Collected Works of Abraham Lincoln* (New Brunswick, 1953–55)
Memoirs	*Personal Memoirs of U. S. Grant* (New York, 1885–86)
Nevins, Fish	Allan Nevins, *Hamilton Fish: The Inner History of the Grant Administration* (New York, 1936)
O.R.	*The War of the Rebellion: A Compilation of the Official Records of the Union and Confederate Armies* (Washington, 1880–1901)
O.R. (Navy)	*Official Records of the Union and Confederate Navies in the War of the Rebellion* (Washington, 1894–1927). Roman numerals following *O.R.* or *O.R.* (Navy) represent the series and the volume.
PUSG	John Y. Simon, ed., *The Papers of Ulysses S. Grant* (Carbondale and Edwardsville, 1967–)

Richardson	Albert D. Richardson, *A Personal History of Ulysses S. Grant* (Hartford, Conn., 1868)
SED	*Senate Executive Documents*
SMD	*Senate Miscellaneous Documents*
SRC	*Senate Reports of Committees.* Numbers following *SED, SMD,* or *SRC* represent the number of the Congress, the session, and the document.
USGA Newsletter	*Ulysses S. Grant Association Newsletter*
Young	John Russell Young, *Around the World with General Grant* (New York, 1879)

5. *Location Symbols*

CLU	University of California at Los Angeles, Los Angeles, Calif.
CoHi	Colorado State Historical Society, Denver, Colo.
CSmH	Henry E. Huntington Library, San Marino, Calif.
CSt	Stanford University, Stanford, Calif.
CtY	Yale University, New Haven, Conn.
CU-B	Bancroft Library, University of California, Berkeley, Calif.
DLC	Library of Congress, Washington, D.C. Numbers following DLC-USG represent the series and volume of military records in the USG papers.
DNA	National Archives, Washington, D.C. Additional numbers identify record groups.
IaHA	Iowa State Department of History and Archives, Des Moines, Iowa.
I-ar	Illinois State Archives, Springfield, Ill.
IC	Chicago Public Library, Chicago, Ill.
ICarbS	Southern Illinois University, Carbondale, Ill.
ICHi	Chicago Historical Society, Chicago, Ill.
ICN	Newberry Library, Chicago, Ill.
ICU	University of Chicago, Chicago, Ill.
IHi	Illinois State Historical Library, Springfield, Ill.
In	Indiana State Library, Indianapolis, Ind.
InFtwL	Lincoln National Life Foundation, Fort Wayne, Ind.
InHi	Indiana Historical Society, Indianapolis, Ind.
InNd	University of Notre Dame, Notre Dame, Ind.
InU	Indiana University, Bloomington, Ind.

KHi	Kansas State Historical Society, Topeka, Kan.
MdAN	United States Naval Academy Museum, Annapolis, Md.
MeB	Bowdoin College, Brunswick, Me.
MH	Harvard University, Cambridge, Mass.
MHi	Massachusetts Historical Society, Boston, Mass.
MiD	Detroit Public Library, Detroit, Mich.
MiU-C	William L. Clements Library, University of Michigan, Ann Arbor, Mich.
MoSHi	Missouri Historical Society, St. Louis, Mo.
NHi	New-York Historical Society, New York, N.Y.
NIC	Cornell University, Ithaca, N.Y.
NjP	Princeton University, Princeton, N.J.
NjR	Rutgers University, New Brunswick, N.J.
NN	New York Public Library, New York, N.Y.
NNP	Pierpont Morgan Library, New York, N.Y.
NRU	University of Rochester, Rochester, N.Y.
OClWHi	Western Reserve Historical Society, Cleveland, Ohio.
OFH	Rutherford B. Hayes Library, Fremont, Ohio.
OHi	Ohio Historical Society, Columbus, Ohio.
OrHi	Oregon Historical Society, Portland, Ore.
PCarlA	U.S. Army Military History Institute, Carlisle Barracks, Pa.
PHi	Historical Society of Pennsylvania, Philadelphia, Pa.
PPRF	Rosenbach Foundation, Philadelphia, Pa.
RPB	Brown University, Providence, R.I.
TxHR	Rice University, Houston, Tex.
USG 3	Maj. Gen. Ulysses S. Grant 3rd, Clinton, N.Y.
USMA	United States Military Academy Library, West Point, N.Y.
ViHi	Virginia Historical Society, Richmond, Va.
ViU	University of Virginia, Charlottesville, Va.
WHi	State Historical Society of Wisconsin, Madison, Wis.
Wy-Ar	Wyoming State Archives and Historical Department, Cheyenne, Wyo.
WyU	University of Wyoming, Laramie, Wyo.

Chronology

February 1–December 31, 1872

FEB. 3.   USG and Vice President Schuyler Colfax visited Baltimore to attend an orphan asylum fair.

FEB. 4.   USG expressed anger at his brother Orvil L. Grant's alleged influence over the collector of customs at Chicago.

FEB. 22.   USG attended a Philadelphia reception for John W. Forney, recently resigned as collector of customs.

FEB. 23.   USG and cabinet interviewed Charles Francis Adams, U.S. arbitrator on the *Alabama* Claims tribunal at Geneva.

MAR. 1.   USG discussed Mormon troubles with James B. McKean, chief justice, Utah Territory.

MAR. 1.   USG signed a bill creating Yellowstone National Park.

MAR. 2.   USG met C. F. Daniels, who recently had married John A. Rawlins's widow.

MAR. 4.   USG welcomed a Japanese delegation sent to negotiate a treaty with the U.S.

MAR. 6.   USG wrote to Maj. Gen. John M. Schofield concerning Brig. Gen. Oliver O. Howard's authority as "commissioner to study the present condition of Indian affairs in Arizona."

MAR. 7.   USG, Julia Dent Grant, and Ellen Grant left for Philadelphia, to attend the wedding of Anthony J. Drexel's daughter, returning March 11.

MAR. 13.   USG appointed a commission to study possible canal routes across Central America.

MAR. 14.   USG met a delegation of Chippewas from Mich. and later hosted a dinner for the Japanese delegation.

MAR. 21. USG received a Cherokee delegation.

MAR. 28. USG discussed with a Tex. delegation Indian raids launched from Mexico.

APRIL 2–4. USG visited New York City to see his daughter Ellen depart for Europe.

APRIL 16. USG issued new civil service rules as recommended by an advisory board.

APRIL 17. USG told a delegation of black Methodists that he hoped they would soon enjoy all rights of citizenship.

APRIL 19. USG recalled Daniel E. Sickles, minister to Spain.

APRIL 19. USG wrote to the House of Representatives concerning Ku Klux Klan violence in S.C.

APRIL 27. On his birthday, USG objected to a *New York Herald* article attacking Secretary of State Hamilton Fish.

APRIL 30. USG welcomed Russian minister Baron d'Offenberg, who replaced Constantin de Catacazy, recalled at U.S. request.

MAY 1–3. The Liberal Republican party convened at Cincinnati and nominated Horace Greeley for president.

MAY 11. USG issued a proclamation reaffirming the eight hour day for federal laborers, workmen, and mechanics.

MAY 14. USG requested legislation to protect immigrants during and after their passage to the U.S.

MAY 18. USG and Julia Grant left for a weekend at Elkton, Md., as guests of Postmaster Gen. John A. J. Creswell.

MAY 21. USG appointed a commission to investigate raids into Tex. from Mexico.

MAY 22. USG sent to the Senate a proposal for a U.S. naval station in the Samoan Islands.

MAY 28. USG asked Red Cloud and other visiting Oglala Sioux to consider relocating to the Indian Territory.

MAY 31. U.S. Senator Charles Sumner of Mass. attacked USG in a lengthy speech on the Senate floor.

JUNE 1. USG proclaimed the removal of most political disabilities imposed by the Fourteenth Amendment.

JUNE 4. The Senate ordered the printing of its report on alleged fraud in the New York City Customhouse. Investigation, begun in Jan., elicited testimony from several men close to USG, including his secretaries Horace Porter (Mar. 4) and Orville E. Babcock (Mar. 6).

JUNE 6.   The Republican party convention in Philadelphia unanimously nominated USG for a second term. U.S. Senator Henry Wilson of Mass. secured nomination for vice president.

JUNE 10.   USG formally accepted his renomination.

JUNE 10.   USG signed a bill appropriating $10,000 for a statue of John A. Rawlins.

JUNE 11.   USG and family left for their summer home at Long Branch.

JUNE 18–20.   USG at Washington, D.C.

JUNE 24–28.   USG and Julia Grant visited Boston. On June 26, USG received an honorary degree from Harvard. USG and Julia Grant attended a musical jubilee featuring Johann Strauss as conductor.

JULY 2–4.   USG at Washington, D.C. On July 3, USG met an Apache delegation and ordered Howard to inspect Indians in New Mexico Territory.

JULY 6.   USG and Julia Grant visited New York City to see their son Ulysses S. Grant, Jr., depart for Europe.

JULY 9.   The Democratic party convened at Baltimore and nominated Greeley.

JULY 16.   USG wrote to Fish expressing hope for a trade treaty with Japan, despite difficult negotiations. Talks ended July 22.

JULY 24.   USG ordered the seizure at Newport, R.I., of the *Pioneer*, engaged in supplying Cuban insurgents.

JULY 28.   USG wrote privately to Gerrit Smith concerning the merits of pardoning prisoners convicted of Ku Klux Klan activities. During 1873, USG pardoned many of these prisoners.

JULY 29–AUG. 10.   USG and family toured upstate N.Y., visiting U.S. Senator Roscoe Conkling of N.Y. at Utica, and the St. Lawrence River summer home of George M. Pullman.

AUG. 16.   At Washington, D.C., USG received the new minister from Nicaragua.

AUG. 26.   USG predicted privately that Greeley would not carry a single northern state.

AUG. 28–29.   USG at Washington, D.C.

SEPT. 7.   In a private letter, USG promised to ask Jesse Root Grant to resign as postmaster, Covington, Ky.

SEPT. 11–12.   USG at Washington, D.C.

SEPT. 14.   The tribunal at Geneva awarded the U.S. $15.5 million for damages caused by the *Alabama* and other C.S. raiders.

SEPT. 19–20.   USG attended the N.J. State Fair and visited an industrial exhibition at Newark.

SEPT. 26.   USG and Porter attended a reception given by Philadelphia merchants.

SEPT. 27.   USG and family returned to Washington, D.C.

OCT. 8.   Early elections presaged Republican victory in Nov.

OCT. 10.   William H. Seward died.

OCT. 20–23.   USG and Julia Grant traveled to New York City. On Oct. 22, Ellen Grant returned from England.

NOV. 4.   USG won election to a second term, carrying 31 of 37 states.

NOV. 8–12.   USG at Philadelphia. On Nov. 11, USG attended the funeral of Maj. Gen. George G. Meade, who had died Nov. 6.

NOV. 15.   USG told a Pa. delegation that he would follow civil service rules in nominating the Philadelphia postmaster.

NOV. 26.   USG told a delegation of Philadelphia blacks that he supported the idea of equal rights for all citizens.

NOV. 29.   Greeley died.

DEC. 1.   Porter resigned as USG's secretary.

DEC. 2.   USG submitted his fourth annual message to Congress.

DEC. 3.   USG nominated Ward Hunt to succeed Samuel Nelson as U.S. Supreme Court justice.

DEC. 4.   USG attended Greeley's funeral in New York City.

DEC. 10–11.   USG, Julia Grant, and Ellen Grant visited Philadelphia for the wedding of Emily Borie.

DEC. 12.   The House of Representatives began to investigate the Crédit Mobilier scandal.

DEC. 20–24.   USG and son Jesse visited Jesse Root Grant at Covington, Ky.

The Papers of Ulysses S. Grant
February 1–December 31, 1872

To Joseph Medill

Washington D. C. Feb: 1st 1872.

HON: J. MEDILL
DEAR SIR:

Your letter of the 21st ult: tendering your resignation as a member of the Advisory Board on Civil Service was duly received. No action has been taken in the matter heretofor because I did not care to act without consulting the other members first.

An opportunity of doing so has not occured until now. The result of conference is that we agree that your resignation should not be accepted. All appreciate the reasons for your absence from the sittings in the past and for the future, but believe that your name is valuable as a member of the board, and that the labor can be performed in the future as in the past with occasional correspondence to insure your concurrence in the work performed. It is my intention that Civil Service reform shall have a fair trial. The great defect in the past custom is that Executive patronage had come to be regarded as the property of individuals of the party in power. The choice of Federal officers has been limited to those seeking office. A true reform will leave the offices to seek the man.

So many people are waiting to see me that I will close without saying some things which I might like to say. Mrs: Medill and daughter arrived here Tuesday evening,[1] well, but somewhat fatigued, some nine hours behind time. They are now fully rested however and seem to be enjoying themselves as well as could be expected.

Very truly yours
U. S. GRANT.

Copy, DLC–USG, II, 1. Joseph Medill, born in 1823 near St. John, Canada, raised in Ohio, was admitted to the Ohio bar (1846), and became a Cleveland journalist. A founder of the Republican party, he became part owner of the *Chicago Tribune* (1854) and then its editor. See *PUSG*, 19, 176; *ibid.*, 22, 299; letter to Joseph Medill, April 9, 1873.

1. Jan. 30. Medill had married Katharine Patrick in 1852. She had been active in the U.S. Sanitary Commission.

To James E. McLean

———

Washington, D. C. Feby 4. *18672*

DEAR SIR:

I am just in receipt of your letter of the 1st inst. wherein you give me copies of letters from Mrs. O. L. Grant.[1] I regret exceedingly that anything so unpleasant should have occurred. I appointed you Collector of the Port of Chicago because I beleived you the fittest person for the place among all those who aspired to it or were recommended for it. As a matter of course while you and my brother were engaged in business I supposed you would make your own arrangements as to the compensation he should receive for attending to it alone. When your private partnership ceased all obligation on your part to pay anything out of the receipts of your office ended. I really regard it as a serious matter to farm out offices between incumbents and those of supposed outside influence, and in every instance where it has been intimated that such arrangements existed I have refused to appoint the applicant.—If you hope to hold your present place you must annull all obligations to pay for it. I did not dream that such obligation existed.

Yours truly
U. S. GRANT

JAS. E. MCLEAN ESQ
COL. PORT OF CHICAGO.

Copy, USG 3. See letter to Hamilton Fish, July 16, 1872. On March 13, 1877, William Penn Nixon and William Henry Smith, Chicago, wrote to U.S. Senator John Sherman of Ohio. "*Personal.* . . . If you will pardon us the presumption we would like to make some suggestions of a general character in Regard to the Government appointments here— The Republican party in Chicago has been greatly demoralized and many of its most valuable and Respected members disgusted for the last four or five years—Many businessmen have been driven from us and others held to the party only by the exigencies of National affairs. This has been effected largely if not almost entirely by the manner and form in which the patronage of the General Government has distributed—The offices have been generally given to persons who were the favorites of some one in power without Regard to their fitness for the positions or the desire of the Representative men of the party or of the business community—Of course such officials were devoted to the personal fortunes of the individuals influential in giving them place—The good name of the administration and duty owed to the public were secondary considerations—Their influence at primary meetings & nominating conventions was very important; but in elections before the people they were inefficient and in more cases than one were weights upon the party & heavy ones at that—We wish it understood that we do not make this charge against President Grant—The appointments he made here of personal friends were several of the better class of officials . . ." LS, OFH. Smith alone continued the letter. "Note: My acquaintance runs further back than Nixon's, & while I join him there is one or two points I wish to particularize: When I came to Chicago bet. 7 & 8 years ago the Collector was J. McLean a partner in the leather business of Orville Grant, with whom the salary was divided. In nearly all of the other offices were members of the Galena ring, or bummers. Hence the public disgust. 2. There is a strong clause in the Inaugural about the determination of the Administration to require pub. officers to give their time to Gov. business. At present Geo. S. Bangs is Sub. Treasurer while holding a position in Am. Express Co. wh. requires his attention at Cinti. J. Russell Jones is Collector of Customs to which office he does not devote a half hour a day. He is Prest of a R. R. Co. and gives his attention there." AN (initialed), *ibid.* See letter to James E. McLean, May 30, 1872; *Chicago Tribune*, Jan. 28, 29, 1872.

1. See *PUSG*, 19, 93.

To John W. Forney

Washington D. C. Feby. 12th 1872:

COL. J. W. FORNEY:
COL: PORT OF PHILA.
MY DEAR COLONEL:

Your letter of the 10th inst: tendering your resignation of the office of Collector of the Port of Philadelphia to take effect on the 1st of March, prox. was duly received. I regret that you have found this course necessary because your appointment to that place gave general, almost universal, satisfaction when it was made, and since, your services have been appreciated and approved quite as generally. I appreciate however the reasons which you assign for the course taken and hope for your continued success as a journalist and citizen. I will be highly gratified if successful in procuring as your suc-

cessor one enjoying the same confidence of the public and Administration and who will administer the Office as well as you have done.

With high regards

Your obt: Svt:

U. S. GRANT.

Copy, DLC-USG, II, 1. On Feb. 10 and 11, 1872, John W. Forney, Washington, D. C.,
wrote to USG. "When you did me the honor to tender me the appointment of Collector
of the Port of Philadelphia I accepted it most reluctantly because I apprehended it would
seriously interfere with my business, and especially with my independence as a journalist.
Ten months' experience have so entirely confirmed this impression that I find myself constrained to send you this my resignation of that office to take effect on the First of March
next. I shall then return to my profession as a far more congenial field of usefulness, and
devote all my ~~energies~~ efforts to my newspaper, and to the energetic support of the principles of the great republican party. Most earnestly thanking you for your kindness and
consideration, . . ." ALS, ICHi. "I thank you for your expressed wish to see me, as kindly
conveyed by Judge Kelley; but I *must* go home ~~to-night~~ at 5-40. I take this occasion to
add that you have no more honest or disinterested friend than I am, however I may have
been misunderstood or misrepresented because I have attachments to those who oppose
you, and because of my opposition to local and selfish politicians who use your great name
as their shield. The Custom House was making me poor both ways. I had to pay out my
salary and to ~~to as~~ pay more than that for talent to do my work on my paper. I do not forget your kindness to me, nor, while life lasts, your services to our Country." ALS, USG 3.
See *PUSG*, 21, 241. On Feb. 12, 1872, a correspondent reported: "The President to-day
stated that he should not say who will be appointed Collector of Customs at Philadelphia,
but would send the nomination to the Senate, where the name would be made public."
Philadelphia Public Ledger, Feb. 13, 1872.
    On Feb. 18, Cornelius A. Walborn, Philadelphia, wrote to USG. "*Confidential* . . .
Having held the Position of Post Master of this City by appointment of the Lamented Lincoln and having during my Administration given very General Satisfaction to the Goverment, the People, and the *Several Interests* of the Republican Party—And believing that I
might be of Service to your Administration at *this present time*—I take the liberty to offer
you my name (Confidentialy) for the office of *Collector* of this Port   Should you entertain
the offer & desire an Interview I refer for character & Capability to the *Senators* & Members of Congress from Pennsylvania" ALS, DNA, RG 56, Collector of Customs Applications. A letter recommending Thomas M. Rellen is *ibid.*
    On Feb. 19, J. Gillingham Fell, Philadelphia, wrote to USG. "The temper of the Pub-
lic Mind at this time will not accept the average run of Candidates. The Collector should
be a Merchant of Philada of such position, that the mention of his name would meet with
immediate approval—First on my list, I place Edward C Knight—He is a thorough Phil-
adelphian, a Merchant of wide experience and great industry—He has large means,
therefore the salary is not an object to him, but his own honour and the honour of the
Republican Party is everything to him—He is a sugar Refiner and imports some of the
goods which he converts,   This may be a difficulty, but I am inclined to think that if
the place is offered to him, that he could arrange to take it—Mr Borie agrees with me in
what I have said—I am authorized to say so—My next man is Stephen A Caldwell of the
firm of Stokes Caldwell & Co—a first rate man—not so well known in a general way as

Mr Knight but unimpeached and of first class ability—Next, Seth J Comly late President of Corn Exchange, in the flour Com. business, a first rate man, of well known character— These men are outside of Rings, stand upon their own merits and will do honour to your Administration   Excuse my abrupt way of writing, our times are limited—" ALS, *ibid.*

On Feb. 20, Forney, Philadelphia, wrote to USG. "*Private* . . . If Mr. D. F. Houston, Deputy Collector cannot be appointed Collector of the Port of Philadelphia I would most earnestly present to you the name of Seth J. Comly, late President of the Commercial Exchange. He is not an applicant but upon inquiry you will find him eminently qualified for the post—energetic, of independent fortune, honest and thoroughly Republican. He belongs to no faction, is not an importer, and I believe would carry out the programme I have inaugurated. Please find enclosed an editorial from the Press of to day" LS, *ibid.* The enclosure urging harmony among Republican factions is *ibid.* On Feb. 26, Horace Porter wrote to Secretary of the Treasury George S. Boutwell. "The President directs me to request you to have prepared, by twelve o'clock to day, a nomination for Seth J Comly to be Collector of Customs at Philadelphia." Copy, DLC-USG, II, 1. On the same day, Edward C. Knight & Co. and Isaac Jeanes & Co., Philadelphia, telegraphed to USG. "We think the appointmen[t] of Seth J Comly a Collector for this Port will give entire Satisfaction to the Commercial Community" Telegram received (at 12:15 P.M.), DNA, RG 56, Collector of Customs Applications. On Feb. 27, Forney telegraphed and wrote to USG. "Your independent action in appointing Mr Comly collector of the Port meets the universal approbation of our People   I have never known any of your Selections who more heartily and honestly approved   I again return you my thanks for your generous response to my suggestions" Telegram received (at 12:30 P.M.), *ibid.* "*Private* . . . I have just telegraphed you that public opinion universally approves the appointment of Mr. Comly, and I now write to say that I am quite sure you will never regret your action in this respect. He is a plain, honest, upright Republican—your devoted personal friend—wholly removed from faction—belonging to no sect or section—independent in his circumstances, and my warm, attached friend. We shall cooperate together in maintaining the good feeling which now exists among our merchants and politicians. As the appointment is your own—precisely as my appointment was yours—and is therefore untrammelled by any of the local and selfish cliques that have so long afflicted our party in Pennsylvania— Mr. Comly will make it a point, I am sure, to consult your interests in every step he takes. My object however in writing this note is not so much to thank you for this new mark of your consideration as to state that yesterday I had a visit from an immediate friend of Mr. Greeley of the New York Tribune, and I have consented to meet Mr. Greeley on Friday next for a friendly consultation at the Continental Hotel in this city. I told his friend that I thought it was quite time for Greeley to accept the certainty of your nomination, and to do so in one of his best articles, at the earliest day. I also suggested to him to make that declaration an eloquent appeal for harmony in new York—to cast behind him all personal feeling, and to set an example of toleration and forgiveness which I had no doubt would be responded to in all quarters. I added that I believed you—if I knew you at all— would be proud to recognize such an act on the part of our oldest Republican Journalist. Mr. Greeley's friend is a member of his editorial staff, with whom I have had several conferences, and who is most anxious to place Mr. Greeley in his old political relations with your administration. I said he could not expect the President of the United States to give assurances as to what he may do in the future between the factions in New York, unless Mr. Greeley initiated a complete reconciliation by an act of bold and manly magnanimity on his own part. I trust, Mr. President, in taking this step I have done nothing that will meet your disapproval. My entire object is that what remains of my life shall be devoted to the harmony of our organization and its perpetuity. Every day I live more and more convinces me that in a great party made up of so many different interests and individuals we must look alike not simply to the rights of our political leaders, but also to their prejudices and peculiarities. You have a most burdensome office, and a thankless one. If I can in any way as a journalist contribute to lighten your load, and lessen your difficulties, you have only to command me. Asking nothing for myself, and once more in the ranks, a private soldier—full of devotion to our cause, and attachment to you, alike as a gentleman and the chief magistrate—. . ." LS, USG 3.

On Feb. 21, USG had written to Adolph E. Borie. "Gen. Porter will be in Phila. probably to-morrow or the day after. I gave him the name of some men who have been suggested for the Collectorship in your City and some names that suggested themselves to me, to enquire about. I am desirous of making a selection that no one can attack successfully. . . . I would like to have a suggestion from you on the subject of Collector. Come down and spend a few days here. It will do you good to hear the debates in Congress . . . P. S. I will add the names of Richard Peterson as one to be considered for Collector." Robert F. Batchelder, Catalog 50 [1985], no. 141. In this letter, USG also mentioned William McMichael as potential collector. *Ibid.* See letter to John W. Forney, Feb. 17, 1872.

On Feb. 14, George W. Draper, "Pennsylvania Hospital for the Insane," had written to USG. "Desirous of receiving an appointment under your Administration of the United States Government I respectfully offer my services as Collector of the Port of Philadelphia to your consideration Believing myself capable of performing the duties of the above named appointment to the entire satisfaction of your Excellency and all the parties concerned . . . I will conclude my letter by stating that I have received no money for many services up to this date & wish to be at Liberty." ALS, DNA, RG 56, Collector of Customs Applications. On March 10, 1869, Draper had written to USG offering his "services as Ambassador to England France Russia or Spain Secretary of State for the United States Director of the United States Mint Collector of the Port or Postmaster for the city of Philadelphia . . ." ALS, *ibid.*, RG 59, Letters of Application and Recommendation. Related papers are *ibid.* No appointments followed.

On Feb. 15, 1872, H. R. Blakiston, Philadelphia, wrote to USG. "I Would respectfully suggest to you sir the Name of Mr E. A Souder, For the Collector of the Port of Philadelphia. Mr. S. has been for many years a Well known and highly respected shipping Merchant of this City. An Active member of the Union League Board of trade and other associations conducted for the Public Welfare. The correspondents of Mr. S have been the Prominent and influential Merch[a]nts of Our Principal sea Ports. Inquiry Will more than Confirm the Above statements Without the authority of Mr. S." ALS, *ibid.*, RG 56, Collector of Customs Applications. On Feb. 16, Benjamin H. Brewster, Philadelphia, wrote to USG. "With some surprise & pleasure I learned to day that Mr Edmund A Souder is named to you as a suitable person for the place of Collector of this Port. I have known him all of my life. He is a Merchant of very high standing and an unflinching Republican   He is a man of unquestioned integrity and posesses great executive ability and is far far above any little association with mean men who follow politics & place hunting for a living   I really believe you could not take a gentleman whose name would give more satisfaction to the public or who could better fill the place   This letter is written of my own motion & without his knowledge. Written because I wish to serve you & secure the public & the party a good officer" ALS, *ibid.*

On Feb. 15, William P. Hacker, Philadelphia, had written to USG. "The Collectorship' of the Port of Philadelphia. having been made vacant by the resignation of the Hon. John W Forney I take the liberty of presenting myself to your consideration as an applicant for the place,   I can furnish unquestionable references. as to integrity and ability, and having been an Importer of Foreign M'dze for some thirty Years I have been qu.te familiar with. the workings of the Custom House. I have not written to any member of Congress for they have many applications, but the members from the City all know me and I believe I can safely refer to them for my status &c as a citizen and as an undeviating Republican." ALS, *ibid.* On Dec. 22, 1869, Anthony J. Drexel *et al.*, Philadelphia, had petitioned USG to nominate Hacker as appraiser, Philadelphia. DS (11 signatures), *ibid.*, Appraiser of Customs Applications.

On Feb. 15, 1872, William Larzdere, Philadelphia, wrote to USG. "Allow me to address you upon a matter in which every Merchant Importer & Broker in Philadelphia is, Somewhat interested and that is who is to be the successor of the present Collector Col John W Forney, in whom the entire community had confidence, at least not one ever expressed any dissatisfaction and it is to be hoped his successor may have equeal ability in that department, and permit me to name Mr Benjamin Huckel the present auditing Deputy Col, who is personally known to our Hon L: Myers, W D Kelly & A Harmer, with these few remarks I refer you to our Members of Congress" ALS, *ibid.*, Collector of Customs Applications.

On Feb. 16, Edmund A. Souder *et al.*, Philadelphia, petitioned USG. "We the undersigned Importers. Merchants, and business men of the City of Philadelphia, respectfully present for your favorable consideration the name of David. F. Houston for the position of Collector of this port. We know Mr Houston as a faithful. efficient. and industrious officer, and one who in his position of Deputy Collector of this Port has given general satisfaction to the business community, and has endeavoured while carrying out the regulations of the Department, to forward the interests of those having business to transact with the Custom House." DS (7 signatures), *ibid.* Related papers are *ibid.* On Feb. 17, a correspondent reported: "Early this morning, a delegation of Philadelphians, headed by Colonel James, visited the Executive Mansion, in company with Judge Kelley, who introduced them to the President. The delegation informed the President that they appeared for the purpose of urging the appointment of the present Deputy Collector of the Port of Philadelphia (Houston) to be Collector of the Philadelphia Custom House. They presented a petition in behalf of Mr. Houston, which is signed by 269 prominent merchants of Philadelphia. The President said he would receive the paper and consider it in connection with other applications." *Philadelphia Public Ledger*, Feb. 19, 1872. On Feb. 19, another Philadelphia delegation visited Washington, D. C., to recommend David F. Houston. *Ibid.*, Feb. 20, 1872.

On Feb. 16, William B. Mann, Philadelphia, wrote to USG. "As I have heard the name of Col Wm McMichael mentioned in connexion with the Collectorship of this Port, I desire to express to your Excellency my opinion that his appointment would give general satisfaction to the Republican Party here, and would be regarded as a most excellent and proper selection—" ALS, DNA, RG 56, Collector of Customs Applications. Morton McMichael, father of William, also was considered for collector of customs, Philadelphia. *Philadelphia Public Ledger*, Feb. 15, 1872.

On Feb. 16 and 19, Francis Wells, Philadelphia, wrote to USG. "Since our interview yesterday I believe I have ascertained that Mr. Stephen A. Caldwell is *not* an importer; but that his business is wholly a domestic one. His selection would be an eminently happy one. He is peculiarly fitted in every particular for the post, and occupies such an enviable position in this community as a prominent merchant, a most valuable citizen, a staunch Republican, and a man of large business experience & ability, and of unspotted integrity, that I am sure that his acceptance of the position would reflect the highest credit upon the Administration, and accomplish *everything* that could be effected by the selection of a first-class man at this time—He would be *cordially* endorsed everywhere, except among a few disappointed politicians, who are at this time so far below par with our people as to be of no possible consequence. . . . P. S. Since writing above I have ascertained positively that Mr. Caldwell's house is *not* an importing one—He is therefore eligible" "I saw Mr. Fell after my return, & told him that we had discussed the possibilities of having him accept the Collectorship. He appreciated the compliment highly; but said that neither his business nor his taste would fit him or allow him to accept it. His own first choice is for Mr. Knight, if eligible; but he expressed the warmest approval of Mr Caldwell, with the opinion that it would require positive pressure to induce him to undertake it. I see no others named as yet whose appointment, in my judgmt, would be equal to either one of these two gentlemen." ALS, DNA, RG 56, Collector of Customs Applications. On Feb. 15, Wells had met USG with a delegation from Philadelphia pressing for a new post office building. *Philadelphia Public Ledger*, Feb. 16, 1872.

On Feb. 17, Thomas Fitzgerald, Philadelphia, wrote to Porter. "(*Entirely Private.*) . . . I see by the papers, that you have twenty applicants for the Collectorship. Good! 'The more, the merrier.' Mrs. Fitzgerald, (*my best friend,*) thinks you had better make it twenty-one, by putting my name in the hat! The President ought to have a zealous friend in the place,—a speaker, writer, and general worker,—a man of energy and courage. But, if this note is calculated to embarrass, in the least, do not present it. 'You know how it is yourself!'" ALS, USG 3. On Oct. 25, 1873, Charles H. T. Collis, city solicitor, Philadelphia, wrote to USG. "I am informed that Thomas Fitzgerald, the proprietor of a newspaper here called 'The All Day City Item', has been appointed a Special Inspector in the Philadelphia Custom House—I deem it my duty to inform you that this person has been ejected from my office for endeavoring to levy black mail against me as the Head of this Department,—and I therefore most respectfully but earnestly protest against the appointment." ALS, DNA, RG 56, Letters Received. A related petition is *ibid.*

On Feb. 19, 1872, Charles Adams, Philadelphia, had written to USG. "My name may possibly be unknown to *you*, but I am well known in Philada being a resident of fifty years standing. Originally a Whig, and one of the first Republicans taking an active part in the election of A. Lincoln, being at the time Vice President of the Republican Club in the Fourth District. I am not connected with any 'ring' or 'clique', and if appointed would endeavor to satisfy our merchants, and at the same time do all in my power to *sustain your Administration* and *unite* the Party: I have not mentioned this to *any one*, or *asked* for influence, but can refer you to Genl Cameron, Leonard Myers, A. C. Harmer, J. W. Forney G. W. Childs, Wm S. Stokley (Mayor) E. C. Knight, G. H. Stuart, E. A. Souder, W W Harding, Judge Peirce, Geo H. Earle. Wm. V. McKean &c. Our late Marshall J. Ely, was an intimate friend of mine: I inclose a printed slip, taken from the newspapers, ten years ago. when I was urged to ask a nomination, but was beaten by Mr Harmer, for Recorder of Deeds—I *have never held office.*" ALS, *ibid.*, Collector of Customs Applications. The enclosure is *ibid.* On Dec. 22, 1869, Adams had written to USG. "A vacancy having occurred in the office of Appraiser here, I take the liberty of applying for the position   I was, after the first election of Mr. Lincoln, urged for Post Master here, with testimonials of the highest order from members of the Society of Friends, (of whom I was a member,) as well as many other, first class citizens: Having been connected with the mercantile interests of Phil. for a number of years, & well acquainted with Mdze generally I flatter myself I could discharge the duties satisfactorily. I am well known here as an old and *unwavering* Republican but consider this more of a *business*, than a *political* office—I was also an old friend of the late & lamented John Ely whom you so properly appointed Marshal here, over the 'political ring.'" ALS, *ibid.*, Appraiser of Customs Applications.

In Feb., 1872, James Hunter *et al.*, Philadelphia, petitioned USG. "We the undersigned citizens of Philadelphia respectfully recommend the appointment of Richard Peterson Esq as Collector of the Port of Philadelphia. He is a gentleman in every way capable and worthy and his appointment would give universal satisfaction" DS (16 signatures), *ibid.*, Collector of Customs Applications.

To Senate

To THE SENATE OF THE UNITED STATES

In answer to the Resolution of the Senate of the 8th instant, I transmit a Report from the Secretary of State and the copy of the case of the United States presented to the Tribunal of Arbitration at Geneva which accompanied it.

U. S. GRANT

WASHINGTON, FEBRUARY 13TH 1872.

DS, DNA, RG 46, Presidential Messages. *SED*, 42-2-31. On Feb. 13, 1872, Secretary of State Hamilton Fish wrote to USG transmitting a printed copy of the U.S. case against Great Britain involving the *Alabama* and other claims. LS, DNA, RG 46, Presidential Messages. Submitted to the Geneva tribunal on Dec. 15, 1871, the U.S. case aroused British indignation because it included the so-called "indirect claims," which alleged that British support for the C.S.A. had prolonged the war. Under these claims the U.S. held Great Britain responsible for the cost of the war after the battle of Gettysburg, arguing that C.S. offensive operations ceased after that date except at sea. The British, who protested that the Joint High Commission of 1871 had tacitly agreed to set aside these claims, ultimately threatened to withdraw from the Geneva arbitration. See *SED*, 42-2-31, 188–90; J. C. Bancroft Davis, *Mr. Fish and the Alabama Claims: A Chapter in Diplomatic History* (Cambridge, Mass., 1893), pp. 86–96; Nevins, *Fish*, pp. 518–37; Adrian Cook, *The Alabama Claims: American Politics and Anglo-American Relations, 1865–1872* (Ithaca, N. Y., 1975), pp. 207–16.

On Feb. 3 and 6, 1872, Sir Edward Thornton, British minister, Washington, D C., wrote to Lord Granville. "I had the honour to receive from Y. L. this day at 5 P. M. the following Tel. in cypher dated Feb. 3 /72. 'Inform Mr Fish confidentially that I have written a letter to Genl Schenck of a friendly character in wh. H. M. Govt declare that they hold that the indirect claims are beyond the province of the Geneva Arbitration." "Confidential . . . Immediately after the receipt of Y. L. Tel. of the 3rd Inst. I called upon Mr Fish at his private residence, & repeated to him without any comment whatever the words of that Tel. wh. were evidently quite new to him & entirely unexpected. He made a gesture of vexation, & after being silent for a moment, said that there was an end of the Treaty & that he might have saved himself the trouble of spending so much time the day before on the fishery question, alluding to the interview wh. he had had with the Committee on Foreign Relations of the House of R. R. He went on to say that he considered it to be the undoubted right of the U. S. Govt to present its case in whatever terms it thought proper, & that not all the powers of Europe should force it to do otherwise; he looked upon it as a suit before a Court of law, where the plaintiff was entitled to put forward whatever pleas it he chose. He added that if Y. L. Tel. meant what it said, there was an end to Arbitration & in his opinion the U. S. Arbitrator & Counsel would be withdrawn as soon as ever H. M. Govt might wish it. . . . I did not think it wise, seeing the irritation & disappointment wh. Mr Fish evidently felt, then to enter into any arguments with regard to his view of the subject. He told me that he had not yet recd any Tel. upon the subject from Gen. Schenck, & as I got up to go away, he begged me to remember that whatever he had said, was the expression of his individual & private opinion & that of course he could have no idea of the views of the President upon the subject. I have not since had any opportunity of seeing Mr Fish. . . . Mr Morton, who resides at N. Y. & is a partner of Sir J. Rose recd a tel. from the latter on the 3rd Instant respg. the question wh. has arisen about the indirect claims. He came here on the following day & has seen both the President & Mr Fish. He tells me that he is convinced from what he hears from all sides that neither the President nor Congress will consent to abstain from presenting the indirect claims to the Tribunal of Arbitration, & they will be supported by the people. But Mr Morton seems to have suggested first to Mr Fish, & with his consent, then to the President, a possible arrangement by the payment by England of a gross sum, in the manner proposed to H. M. High Commrs during the negotiation of the Treaty. Mr Fish, whilst he declared his the determination of his Govt not to withdraw the indirect claims, acknowledged his belief that the Tribunal would never adjudge anything on their account to the U. S. But he approved of Mr Morton's idea of a gross sum being agreed upon betw. the two Countries & the Arbitration being consequently given up altogether, & began to discuss the amount with that Gentleman. He began by saying that the U. S. could not accept less than from 8 to 10 millions sterling, but concluded by reducing the sum to from four to five millions Sterling. Mr Morton subsequently made a similar suggestion to the President who expressed himself in favour of it, but by him no mention was made of the possible amount. . . ." Copies, Thornton Letterbooks, ICarbS. See letter to Levi P. Morton, May 27, 1872; Robert McElroy, *Levi Parsons Morton: Banker, Diplomat and Statesman* (New York, 1930), pp. 59–67.

On Feb. 6, Tuesday, Fish wrote in his diary. "The British excitement over the Alabama Case, is discussed . . . The President does not seem to have given much consideration to L. P. Mortons proposition for a lumping payment—says if they think fit to make payment of a good sum he would not object—I think that he regards it less favorably than he was inclined to on Sunday—The Cabinet is unanimous that no part of the claim can be withdrawn. I mention that I told Thornton on Saturday, decidedly, but unofficially, that we would accept any consequences, even war, rather than withdraw—that the Tribunal might decide against us, but and we should accept the decision—The validity of the claim for incidental damages was discussed. Boutwell refering to Art X of the Treaty, thinks they cannot be maintained. I quote Article VII, which allows a gross sum to be awarded, under which they may be allowed—at the same time expressing the opinion that they will not be awarded. While the subject is being discussed Schenck's telegram of 5 inst with copy of Granvilles note of 3d sent to him, is brought in, & read. Prsdt at first thinks, that it need not be answered, 'barely an acknowledgment' is reminded that it is a letter to Schenck which he says he has acknowledged & informed Granville that he refers it to his Government. After some discussion he hands me a paper, as follows 'Lord Granville's note of __ inst. to you received—This Govt sees no reason for a change of its presentation of claims against the British Govt   It is for the Geneva Commissioners to decide what claims are valid under the Treaty and to determine amount of awards'—which he says is about the substance of what he would send—. . . In the evening, returning from dinner at Atty Genl Thornton calls (about 11½ oclk.) & reads to me confidentially an extract from the Queens Speech on the treaty & the question of 'indirect damages'—He remains until near one oclk is told that we cannot withdraw. I read him a Mem. which I think of sending Schenck" DLC-Hamilton Fish. Fish copied this memorandum into his diary. "An independent party to a submission submits its case, & its claims in its own way, and in its own interest—It is the sole judge on that point—Its claims, its arguments may be controverted by facts, by reason, by Arguments. The selected tribunal must judge between the parties, & their respective arguments—There can be no withdrawal of any claim, or any argument advanced by either of the sovereign powers to a submission to Arbitration—we ask none—we can make none—You may state that in form, or in substance at your discretion but in a friendly way—we mean to abide by the reference to which we have agreed, but must control the management of our own case—(this was drafted 'for consideration' as a despatch to Genl Schenck—& shewn confidentially to Thornton)" *Ibid.*

On Feb. 3, Granville had written to Robert C. Schenck, U.S. minister, London, objecting to the indirect claims but stressing the importance of providing "an example to the world how two great nations can settle matters in dispute by referring them to an impartial Tribunal. . . ." Copy, DNA, RG 59, Diplomatic Despatches, Great Britain. On Feb. 23, Fish had written in his diary. "The Cabinet having all assembled, except Robeson, who entered while I was reading, I read Granvilles note to Schenck of 3 Feb. & the draft of my reply. . . . the question again came up, on my desire to have the criticisms, or views of the Cabinet on the reply—Boutwell thought the reference to the presentation of the Confederate Cotton debt, before the Claims Commission, weakens the Case—Delano thinks it will strike the public mind more strongly than any other point—Williams concurs—President says he 'dont see that the paper can be improved—it is splendid'—I desire very thorough scanning, & criticism of the language as well as the ideas—before it leaves here—for it will get it abroad—President thinks there is no occasion for haste in sending the reply—that a week from now will be early enough—suggests that I consult one or two discreet members of the Committee on F. R. of both houses—not to give them copies, but to read it to them—thought adviseable to have it printed Confidentially for the use of the Cabinet. Belknap says he can have it thus printed in the War Dept—" DLC-Hamilton Fish. On Feb. 24, Fish wrote to Secretary of War William W. Belknap. "By the President's direction, I enclose a printed copy of a paper read in presence of the Cabinet, yesterday—You are respectfully requested to consider and Keep it as *confidential* from all persons except the President and the Cabinet." LS, NjP. The enclosure is *ibid.*

On Feb. 27, Fish wrote to Schenck. ". . . You will receive herewith a despatch of the same date with this, giving the opinion of this Government on the question suddenly and abruptly raised by Her Majesty's Government, and presented by Earl Granville nakedly and without any argument. Although no reply is invited by the note of the British Government, the settlement of all causes of difference between the two countries, and the successful example of the mode of settling international differences established by the Treaty, are so earnestly desired by this Government, that we accept the friendly assurances of the British note, disregarding its bold and sudden announcement of an opinion which we think unsustained by the history of the negotiations between the two Governments, or by the events which gave rise to the claims, and for which we see no logical foundation in the Treaty itself. You will therefore read the despatch referred to to Lord Granville, and may leave with him a copy, in case he desires it." Copy, DNA, RG 59, Diplomatic Instructions, Great Britain. On the same day, Fish addressed to Schenck a lengthy defense of the U.S. decision to include the indirect claims. "... The United States seek not to be Judge in their own case. The course which they pursued afforded a happy solution to what might have been a question of embarrassment. They desire to maintain the jurisdiction of the Tribunal of Arbitration, over all the unsettled claims, in order that being judicially decided, and the questions of law involved therein being adjudicated, all questions connected with or arising out of the Alabama Claims or 'growing out of the acts' of the cruisers may be forever removed from the possibility of disturbing the perfect harmony of relations between the two countries...." Copy, *ibid.*

On Feb. 28, Benjamin Moran, secretary of legation, London, wrote in his diary about a visit to Cyrus W. Field. "He says we have lost all the warm English friends we had during the rebellion, and that such men as the Duke of Argyll, John Bright and Tom Hughes are now among our enemies. They look upon this claim for consequential damages as dishonest and as confirming the popular English opinion, which they never heretofore entertained, that we are a tricky people. I tried to argue him out of his sympathetic views with them, but failed, and as he is ill, I did not persist in trying to change his opinions. He lays great stress upon the fact that Gen'l Schenck was present in the House of Lords when Lords Granville and Ripon explicitly stated that these indirect claims were expressly excluded, that he reported this home, & that no objection was taken to this declaration either by him or the Govt., but that the ratifications of the Treaty were exchanged by him a few days after with this British construction ringing in his ears. But I told him that this line of argument was unfair, and that Gen'l Schenck could only act on the instructions he received and not assume to prevent the exchange of the ratifications of a Treaty because its had been construed in a certain sense in a debate in which he could not take part...." DLC-Benjamin Moran.

On March 10, Orville E. Babcock wrote to Adam Badeau, consul gen., London. "Your good letter came in good time and afforded much satisfaction—I gave it to the President and Gen Porter to read. I think your views on the Treaty quite correct. Your letter deserved an early answer, but in all the busy time I have neglected it. Our govt cannot recede from its position, especially on the eve of a bitter campaign. In the language of the old story it is no time to swap horses—If England backs out all our people will stand by the President. If she stands by the treaty, all will say 'it is because Grant stood firm.' Of course this is a view on this side. If England throws up the treaty, it will make no war, nor speck of war. Gen Grant need only ask Congress to issue bonds to pay the american claim (that puts the people right.) and then say let the matter rest until the people wish it taken up. Like San Domingo leave it with the people. I for one rather hope they will back out. These views are mine—but I know many who entertain the same veiws—...." ALS, MH. On March 8, Badeau had written to USG. "Mr. Dudley, the Consul at Liverpool, who as you probably know, is more intimately acquainted with what took place in England in-connection with the Alabama and similar claims, blockades,-running, Confederate supplies and sympathy, than any other American now here—has just been to see me in a state of great anxiety, about the counter claims to be presented at Washington. He states that claims to the amount of 5 millions have been presented at his office for verification within the last week; that he has no doubt the entire amount of claims will be at least $50,000,000: that men who were prominent here as rebel agents during the war, are among the claimants; for instance Prioleau of the firm of Frazer Trenholm & co; Lafone, his agent, and even representatives of Laird the builder of the Alabama. Lafone has put in a claim for 5 millions for blockade-runners, and for 5000 bales of cotton destroyed by Sherman. Battersley of Manchester, who was engaged in sending army clothes and stores to the rebels, claims $1.500,000; even arms that were captured are included among the articles that should now be paid for. Southerners who owned cotton have now made fraudulent transfers, to Englishmen, ante-dating them, and these English present their claims. Charles Hill, a famous blockade runner brings a claim for $200,000. At my consulate, about twenty five claims have been presented within a fortnight, and since I began this letter two such for nearly half a million; both for blockade runners, captured by us, and *condemned*, the decision being appealed from and confirmed by the Supreme Court of the United States. Dudley says he spoke to Cushi[n]g about such cases, and Cushing sa[ys] that *under the treaty, the decisions of the Supreme Court are liable to reversal by the Commissioners at Washington.* Dudley says every blockade runner captured & condemned, every bale of cotton burnt, every piece of arms or clothing sent from England to the Rebels will be brought before this Tribunal. Another claim has just come into my office for cotton destroyed; and on looking at his claim the account of the blockade runner, I find it is presented by two persons of the name of *Gurney*, and my Vice Consul says they are relatives of the British Commissioner. Bates, the owner of the Georgia, boasts to Dudley that he will be paid for that vessel; says he knows it positively and directly, that Gurney the British Commissioner absolutely told his (Bates's) lawyers so.—Dudley says the claimants are loud in their assertions that they will be successful; they declare that they know this. He says they will bribe freely; that he has been approached in one case, and made to know that if a claim for $3,000,000 is passed, he can have $500,000. This shows what these people are prepared to do. He was so earnest that I thought you ought to know how he feels. (A third memorial comes in while I write, claiming $3.600,000 for cotton destroyed in Savannah). Some months ago, Dudley came to me (before he was in America), and said that he had refused to certify to the identity of the magistrate before whom claims of this character were sworn, he did not think an American official's seal should cover any such document; I approved his action, and reported my approval to the State Department, which overruled my decision; so of course since then, such certifications have been made by the various Consuls. But in view of the character and large amount of these claims, and Dudley's intimate knowledge of the subject, and of the men themselves who bring the claims, he now suggests to me that I issue a circular requiring the Consuls, before certifying, to demand copies of the documents, and send them to me; and that then I forward them to him, so that he can examine them, and give our government any information he may have in regard to any particular case. Unless this is the last day for presenting the memorials for certification (of which I am in doubt) I think I shall take the responsibility of doing this, and of course notify the State Department of my action. Perhaps you will be so good as to shew this letter to Gov. Fish. I did not intend to write to you on this branch of the subject, and as you know never approach you direct on the subject of my official duties. But this matter slipped off my pen unawares. I should like Gov. Fish to see the entire letter. As the British are making such a row about unfair and indirect claims 'tis a pity all this should not be known. Perhaps 'twill be quite as well, if such claims on their side are to be considered, to let them withdraw from the treaty, if they choose." ALS (press), NjR. On April 11, Badeau wrote to Thomas H. Dudley, consul, Liverpool. "I have just received a letter from Gen Porter in which he says that my letter about claims (that suggested by you) has come to hand and its contents are regarded as of *very great* importance. The President read it and handed it to Gov. Fish, who took it away from Cabinet meeting.— Porter also tells me that Miss Nellie Grant, the Presidents only daughter was to sail for

Europe by the Algeria on the 3d, under the care of the Hon A. P. Borie late Secretary of
the Navy, and his family. . . ." ALS, CSmH. See *PUSG*, 19, 424–25.

To John W. Forney

Washington, D. C. Feb.y 17th 18~~67~~2

My Dear Colonel:

I am just in receipt of your letter of yesterday inviting me to be
present at your reception on Thursday evening next. Nothing
would afford me more pleasure, but I do not see how I can leave in
the middle of the week whilst Congress is in session. If I feel it possible to go however, when the time comes, I will go, and will advise
you by telegraph in advance.

Yours Truly
U. S. Grant

Col. J. W. Forney,
Col. Port of Phila Pa

ALS, PHi. On Feb. 15, 1872, John W. Forney, collector of customs, Philadelphia, wrote to
USG. "I took the liberty of inviting you to my reception on Thursday evening next and
now beg to add that if you could come possibly you would meet some men that you have
not yet met in Philadelphia, and many of your old and sincere friends. I write this to express the hope that you will be able to do me the honor of being present on that occasion."
LS, USG 3. On Feb. 22, USG and Orville E. Babcock attended Forney's reception. "Given
at the close, or near the close, of Colonel Forney's brief, but conspicuously successful, administration of the office of Collector of the Port, during which he placed himself in close
communication with the commercial, mercantile and business activities of Philadelphia,
without regard to party or interest, he was surrounded last evening by a constellation of
the men who make up the living enterprise of Philadelphia to-day, of all parties and shades
of political opinion. . . . In the midst of them all, however, was the President of the United
States, his secretary, General Babcock, and the Secretary of the Interior, Mr. Delano, who
had come from Washington expressly to attend it; and we think it may be said truly that
no one present seemed to enjoy the unique, artistic, musical and exquisitely humorous entertainment to which a part of the evening was devoted, more than the President." *Philadelphia Public Ledger*, Feb. 23–24, 1872. See letter to John W. Forney, Feb. 12, 1872.

To Henry S. Hewit

———

Washington, D. C. Feb. 19th 1872

Dear Doctor:

Your letter of the 27th of Dec. in relation to the apt. of your son to West Point was duly received. I intended answering it immediately but not having time just then the letter got concealed in a pile of other letters.—You understood Mrs. Wallen[1] in regard to the matter. I said to her that it would afford me pleasure to appoint a son of yours to the Military or Naval Academy. Your son Augustine however is not elegible for the Military Academy at this time. The law requires Cadets entering the Military Academy to be between the ages of 17 & 22 years, and at the Naval Academy between 14 & 18 years. He is elegible for the Naval Academy to enter in June. Please let me know whether you will let him go there, or if you have an older son who you would like to send to West Point.

Very Truly
your obt. svt.
U. S. Grant

Dr. H. S. Hewit

ALS, ViU. See *PUSG*, 4, 229; *ibid.*, 11, 396. On Sept. 3, 1873, Nathaniel Hewit, Jr., New York City, wrote to USG, Long Branch. "My father, Dr. Henry S. Hewit, formerly on your staff, died very suddenly in this City on the 19th ult. Being the eldest son, the cares and responsibilities of the family necessarily devolve upon me. I believe my father had the promise of an appointment as Cadet at West Point for my brother, Augustine F. Hewit, and had for the last year kept him in preparation for the academy. May I beg that I be informed when it will be your pleasure to confer the appointment upon him, as he will be seventeen in October next. By replying to my inquiry you will confer a lasting obligation . . ." ALS, DNA, RG 94, Correspondence, USMA. On Sept. 6, USG endorsed this letter. "Refered to the Sec. of War. I did promise to make this appointment and wish, if possible, that it should be made for next year in case of failure of any at present apt'd." AES, *ibid.* On Nov. 20, Augustine F. Hewit, Bridgeport, Conn., wrote to USG on the same subject. ALS, *ibid.* On Nov. 22, USG endorsed this letter. "Refered to the Sec. of War. This is an appointment I wish to make." AES, *ibid.* See letter to Ellen E. Sherman, Nov. 17, 1873. Hewit graduated USMA in 1879.

In an undated letter, USG had written to John A. Dix. "I enclose to you a letter I recd from an old friend and acquaintance of mine, Dr H S Hewit, which explains itself better than I can do. The Dr was an old army surgeon—that is, he entered the regular army as

Asst Surgeon a good many years ago—& resigned to enter into private practise in California in the early days of the settlement of that state—Subsequently he moved to New York City, where I believe he has practised his profession ever since, except during the rebellion—He was a war democrat and offered his services early to his Country—serving as a surgeon throughout the war, a portion of the time directly with me—I know the Dr. well personally, and can vouch for his professional qualifications, his integrity and his ability out side of his profession—I do not wish to embarrass you with recommendations, knowing from my own experience how much trouble you will have in that way, but in the case of Dr. Hewit, I can say what I have here without reserve, believing that if he should receive the appointment he asks for, that he will fully sustain the reputation I give him"
Copy, ViU.

1. Laura Wallen, wife of Lt. Col. Henry D. Wallen. See *PUSG*, 1 passim.

To Elihu B. Washburne

Washington, D. C. Feb.y 22d *1867*2

DEAR WASHBURNE:

Your letter of the 2d inst. in relation to your quarry stock, purchased for you by H. D. Cook,[1] is just rec'd. As I start for Phila in ten minuets I will confine myself in this letter to simply telling you what I know about the matter, though there is much just now which I would like to write you.

I have no doubt but Cooke thought he was making a good investment for you though I much doubt his judgement in this particular instance. This however does not justify his neglecting your querries on the subject.—In /67 I was induced, against my judgement, to take $10.000 00/100 worth of stock in that Quarry. It has been able to sell all the stone that could be got out since that and with a demand probably five times greater than the supply, although that looks unlimited under proper management. I have never yet had a dividend except a stock dividend and under present management doubt whether any ever will be made. All the ring there is for selling this stone is in the imagination of Sore Head Republicans and Democrats because I own an interest.[2] As a matter of fact, as stated before, the company do not supply one fifth the demand, and no govt. contract has ever been made for any of the stone that I am aware of. It is a beautiful article and some of it has been purchased to lay the pavement about the Treas. building because it is cheaper, better and much more beautiful than the gray stone heretofore used for that purpose.—I think, but do not know, that the management is bad. With good management the property should pay from 25 to 40 pr. ct. on the investment. No doubt, after a while, the stockholders will tire out of the present management and will insist upon honest business men being put in charge.

Present Mrs. Grant's and my kindest regards to Mrs. Washburne and the children. I will endeavor to find time in a few days to write you a letter on other topics.

Yours Truly
U. S. GRANT

ALS, IHi. On Feb. 2, 1872, Elihu B. Washburne, Paris, had written to USG. "*Private &*
Confidential . . . Some three or four years ago I had several thousand dollars in the hands
of Jay Cooke & Co. the proceeds of my pine lands. I asked Henry D. Cooke if he would not
invest the amount for me in some good dividend paying Stocks. He advised me afterwards
that he had bought me shares of the Maryland Free Stone Quarry Company, which was
an excellent Stock and would pay large dividends. Not receiving any dividends, I wrote
him in the spring of 1870, and he wrote me in June of that year in reply that they would
make a 'cash dividend at the close of the season's business.' Getting neither dividend nor
any information on this subject I wrote Mr. H. D. Cooke in June 1871 asking information.
He never deigned to reply to my polite and courteous letter.—When Mr. Huntington was
here last September on his return from St. Peterbourg, I spoke to him about the matter,
and he made a memorandum of it and pledged his word that he would write me fully in
regard to the matter on his return to Washington. I waited and waited but heard nothing
from him, and so on the 14th of November last I wrote him calling attention to his promise and asking him to write me. He has made no reply. It is evident, therefore, that it is not
intended that I shall have any information, and I need not say to you, that I do not like this
business at all. I relied upon Mr. C. as an old friend and as an honorable man, as I believe
him, to make an investment for me in a solid, interest paying Stock. I have no dividends,
and what is worse, I see that this corporation is very much criticized as being run by a
ring of officials, who use their influence to sell the Stone to the Government. I write to
you on this subject because I believe you are in the same position as I am, Mr. C. having
invested your funds in the same way as he did mine.—It was an injustice to us both, though
not so intended, to invest our funds in non-interest paying stock, but a greater injustice
to interest us in a corporation the management of which has so challenged public criticism.—As I have no friend now in Washington to whom I care to write on this subject, I
have ventured to address you, hoping that you may find a moments' time to give me what
light you may have in this matter. It may be, and I hope it is, all right, but I confess I do
not like to be kept in the dark all the time. Pray excuse this long letter . . ." ALS (press),
DLC-Elihu B. Washburne. On the same day, Washburne wrote to Levi P. Luckey. "Please
place this letter in the hands of the President *yourself*. . . ." ALS (press), *ibid.* On April 5,
Washburne wrote to USG. "*Private.* . . . I am very much obliged to you for the trouble you
took to write me about that Quarry stock, though I confess it is not a very encouraging

showing. It seems you knew what you was going into. I did not. I had my money in Mr. Cooke's hands and I trusted entirely to his good faith to make a paying investment for me. I had known him from the time we gave him the binding of books for the 34th Congress and our relations had always been most friendly and I felt entirely safe in trusting my interests in his hands. If it shall turn out, as I hope it may not, that this stock is comparatively worthless, and that having it on hand he put my money into it, it would be such a fraud as the courts would redress. If I go home to vote next fall, I will go to the bottom of the matter: What little I have ought to be productive.—With all the economy I could practice, it has cost me very nearly two thousand dollars a month to live for the last six months which is at the rate of $6.500 a year more than my salary. I can only make the two ends meet by shutting up my house and sending my family to the country half the year. Mrs. W. will go to Bonn, on the Rhine, before a great while with the children in order to have them learn German. They all speak the French very well. We are all in pretty good health. Two weeks ago Mrs. Washburne returned from a trip to Italy, which occupied nearly eight weeks. She visited Nice, Leghorn, Rome, Naples, Florence, Venice, Milan, &c. She met Fred at Rome and Naples   You will appreciate the interest I now feel in the political situation at home. I have been well nigh appalled at the torrent of abuse and defamation that has been rolling over the administration. Yet I had seen the same thing before. So far as you are concerned, even to a much greater extent. The universal howl after Shiloh was followed by the universal plaudits after Vicksburg. As I wrote friends, I jumped six feet into the air when I read of our triumph in New Hampshire, and now it is followed up by the overwhelming route of the copperheads and Possums in Connecticut. I should take a judicious pleasure in now seeing those 'Knights of the Rueful Countenance', Sumner and Schurz, and that pure and immaculate 'Reformer' Lyman Trumbull.— What an outrage to have our noble State, with its 50.000 republican majority crucified in the Senate. And then how badly Palmer has behaved, ploughing with Gratz Brown, and the whole sorehead gang, and then fraternizing and colluding with the copperheads in the Legislature to censure the gallant Sheridan. I am delighted to see the House butchering the land grabs and subsidy jobs. But the most unblushing attempt at plunder is the Goat Island Steal. The people are aching for a regular old Jackson veto, and if that job get through in *any shape*, I hope you will put the knife to it, even up to the hilt. Mrs. Washburne and Gratiot, are at my side as I write, and they both desire kindest regards to yourself and family." ALS (press), *ibid.* On April 22, Luckey wrote to Washburne. "Your letter of the 5th instant came to hand last Friday—the 19th.—I placed the enclosure in the President's hands immediately after its receipt. I am very glad you speak so kindly of my letter, & that it contained matter which was interesting. We are all well, both here at the Mansion—and also in my own little home. The President was quite sick for two or three days a week ago. He took a dose of blue-mass and did not physic it off and it gave him quite a serious turn, though Dr Norris brought him right around again. I think he & Mrs Grant both miss Nellie a great deal. I presume you see the New York daily papers & keep posted on the Cincinnati 'movement'. I believe it attracts a great deal more attention here in Washington, and among politicians than with the people. I believe the Democrats will help the thing along all they can, & when the breach is as wide as they can make it they will hold their convention & nominate their candidates, and the Cincinnati Reformers will thereupon drop immediately out of sight. They are mostly disappointed office seekers. That reminds me to tell you of Charley Royce. Charley is a 'sore head,' or else getting crazy. He has been writing to me, & sent one or two letters to the President. He thinks that the party is not doing anything for the hard-workin[g] farmers of the West, because you don't sent French capital to built cotton manufactories on Rock River at Oregon. His letter may amuse you, so I will send it—I stuck it in a pigeon hole & preserved it for the purpose. Logan does not openly join the Liberal movement, but I learn from several sources that his most particular friends in Chicago & elsewhere are working for Cincinnati. I hear Oglesby wishes to be Gov. again. I wish you would come home in the Fall & let the Illinois people elect you to the Senate next Winter. It is about time our State had a Senator, within the meaning of the term, is it not? I have heard the thought suggested several times. I suppose I wish it because I should like so well to see you living here again, for in your case such a move might be going backwards instead of forwards. Gen Logan has missed a splendid chance to make himself the leading man in Illinois, and has thrown it away. The President lost all confidence in him, I think, over a year ago, when he attacked the President about Seneca stone, in a speech in the House. Last Fall he had his friends come here & assure the President of his friendly feeling towards the Administration, but he certainly has not shown it, and has allowed himself to be classed among his enemies without any particular denial. I don't trust him. . . ." ALS, *ibid.*

On May 6, 1876, Frederick W. Jones, D. C. attorney, testified before the House Select Committee on the Freedman's Bank. "Q. Have you at any time had any business connection with the company commonly known as the Seneca Stone Company?—A. I was elected secretary of the company in the spring of 1874, and I continue to hold that office. Q. Have you the stub-book of the company, showing to whom and at what times stock was issued to the several persons appearing as stockholders in said company? . . . Look at that book, and say whether the stock issued to General U. S. Grant is receipted for in his own name or by some other person.—A. I have looked through the stock-book, and I find but two certificates issued to General U. S. Grant. The first, No. 12, dated November 22, 1867, for 200 shares, is receipted for by William S. Huntington. The other, No. 91, January 21, 1870, for 120 shares, (being the dividend stock,) is receipted for by U. S. Grant. I cannot say that this is his signature, but it is just like one to a proxy of his which I have. I never saw him write, and do not know his signature. . . . Q. Who is the attorney mentioned in the proxy of General Grant?—A. Henry D. Cooke. . . . Q. Do you or not know that that stock of Mr. Washburne's was subscribed for without his authority, and that his funds were issued to pay for it by Mr. Cooke?—A. I have no knowledge on the subject. Q. Does that stock still stand in the name of E. B. Washburne?—A. It does, so far as these books show. . . ." HRC, 44-1-502, 176–77. See *ibid.*, pp. viii–ix, 24–28, 57–65, 92–95, 115–16; SRC, 46-2-440; Walter L. Fleming, *The Freedmen's Savings Bank: A Chapter in the Economic History of the Negro Race* (Chapel Hill, 1927), pp. 77–81.

1. Henry D. Cooke, born in 1825 in Sandusky, Ohio, graduated from Transylvania University (1844), studied law in Philadelphia, and then became a journalist and financial partner of his brother Jay. He edited the *Sandusky Register* and *Ohio State Journal* before moving to Washington, D. C., at the beginning of the Civil War to conduct family business, including the First National Bank and National Life Insurance Co. On Feb. 27, 1871, USG nominated Cooke as governor, D. C. See *PUSG*, 19, 412; *ibid.*, 21, 194.

On Jan. 15, 1880, Cooke testified before the Senate Select Committee on the Freedman's Savings and Trust Company. "Question. Mr. Cooke, I will ask you to state to the committee what relations you sustained to the late Freedman's Saving and Trust Company?—Answer. I was a member of the board of trustees for several years; . . . and I was also a member of the committee on finance. . . . Q. I will ask you to state to the committee what you know of the so-called Seneca Sandstone Company. Loans were made to that company from time to time, and we would be glad to have you state what you know of them?—A. That was a company doing a large business and employing a large number of hands, who were principally residents of Washington and Georgetown, although they worked up there. . . . I gave what time I could in assisting this company in its development and its growth and its success for a long time, until they were overtaken by these hard times, which impaired and destroyed the value of its securities, as well as of itself, its standing. . . . Q. You were not one of the original corporators of the company, then?— A. No, sir—O, of the Seneca Company; yes, we bought the property and organized the company. . . ." *SRC*, 46-2-440, 51–53.

2. On Nov. 1, 1871, the *Washington Evening Star* reported that USG had written to John L. Kidwell, president, Seneca Stone Co., "requesting the latter to dispose of his (President Grant's) stock in that company."

Endorsement

The hour named within will suit me for receiving Mr. Adams.

U. S. GRANT

FEB.Y 23D /72

AES, DLC-Hamilton Fish. Written on a letter of Feb. 23, 1872, from Secretary of State Hamilton Fish to USG. "Mr Chas Francis Adams is in the City & proposes to call upon you this morning—If it will suit your convenience to receive him at half past Eleven I will accompany him at that hour" ALS, *ibid.* Also on Feb. 23, Fish wrote in his diary. "~~CB~~By appointment I call for Mr Adams & accompany him to the Presidents—an interview of half an hour before the Cabinet assemble—Mr Adams very cautiously & reservedly gives his views ~~of~~ as to the position of the questions with G. B. in connection with the Claims Submission—he evidently wished to be drawn out, rather than volunteer, but clearly answered all questions—of which there were many, as the Members of the Cabinet appeared—on my way to the Presidents he handed me a paper of 'points suggested' which he had prepared at my request—In the interview, which lasted about an hour & a half, he manifested his apprehension that the Treaty was in danger, the difficulty in which the Brit Ministry had become involved by the newspaper publications, & more particularly by Mr Gladstones' imprudent & intemperate speeches—thinks it important to disabuse the public mind of Gt Britain & of Europe of the impression produced by the publications that have been made that we have made an extravagant claim—" *Ibid.* See *PUSG*, 22, 81.

On April 19 and 20, Fish wrote in his diary. "As Mr Adams is to sail on Wednesday next the President thinks that I had better see him in NY, or request him to come here— & express to him the views of the Govt   As the Cabinet was adjourning Boutwell mentions that he is going to Boston, to leave tomorrow—it was therefore agreed that I telegraph Adams to know if he can meet Boutwell in Boston on Monday at 11—" "Gov Boutwell calls at my house early in the morning, to speak about his proposed interview with Chas Frans Adams—He subsequently came up to the Department—the object of the interview is to ascertain Adams precise views as to the liability of a Govt for indirect or consequential damages—he having intimated when here some weeks since that he did not consider G. B. liable, & ~~that~~ assenting to the statement which I made that it was not the interest of the U. S. to have the rule established that a State is liable for the indirect con-

sequences of an act of violation ~~of its~~ or of failure to observe its neutral obligations—. . ."
DLC-Hamilton Fish. On April 22, Monday, Secretary of the Treasury George S.
Boutwell, Boston, wrote to Fish. "Personal. . . . I met Mr Adams according to the appointment made by you and I have telegraphed *Interview Satisfactory*. . . . Mr. Adams said
that while he felt bound to keep his mind free until further consideration of whatever
might be presented his impressions were in entire accord with the suggestion; and further
that he had nearly reached the conclusion that he would take the responsibility of giving
the British authorities so to understand. . . ." ALS, *ibid.* See George S. Boutwell, *Reminis-
cences of Sixty Years in Public Affairs* (New York, 1902), II, 200–202; Martin B. Duber-
man, *Charles Francis Adams 1807–1886* (Boston, 1961), pp. 343–51, 360.

Endorsement

———

Respectfully refered to the Sec. of State. If vacancy exists, and no
promise made, attention may be specially called to this application.

U. S. GRANT

FEB.Y 24TH /72

AES, DNA, RG 59, Letters of Application and Recommendation. Written on a letter of
Feb. 24, 1872, from Thomas P. Robb, Washington, D. C., to USG. "I have the honor to
make application for an appointment in the Foreign Consular Service of the United States.
My late experience as Collector of the Port of Savannah, Ga. will enable me to perform
the duties appertaining to such a position, I trust, to the satisfaction of my government,
and with credit to myself. I would respectfully refer you to the Hon Simon Cameron,
Chairman Foreign Relations Committee—Senators Kellogg Logan and Morton." ALS,
ibid. Born in 1819 in Bath, Maine, Robb operated a wholesale grocery in Chicago (1838)
and moved during the Gold Rush to Sacramento where he continued as a merchant and
served as mayor. Returning to Ill., he was maj. on the staff of Governor Richard Yates and
later inspector gen. with the rank of col. and responsibility for medical affairs. As a Ga.
cotton agent, he became president, Board of Tax Commissioners, and postmaster, Savannah (1867–69). See *PUSG*, 19, 309–11; Proclamation, May 21, 1872.

On Feb. 27, 1871, U.S. Senator Richard Yates and U.S. Representative John A. Logan
of Ill. and U.S. Senator William P. Kellogg of La. wrote to USG. "We hope it will be consistent with your wishes to retain Col. T. P. Robb in his place as Collector of Customs at
Savannah Georgia" DS, DNA, RG 56, Collector of Customs Applications. About the
same date, Samuel A. Young and many others had written to USG. "Learning that efforts
are being made to effect the removal of the Hon. T. P. Robb from the office of Collector of
Customs at Savannah, we Georgia (Colored) Republicans do hereby respectfully protest
against the said removal, and earnestly request that he be retained in his present
office, . . ." Copy, *ibid.* On March 22, Washington Booth, Baltimore, wrote to USG. "The
object I have in addressing you will, I trust, be sufficiently apparent to warrant the liberty
I take in calling your attention to the case of Mr T. P. Robb, the present Collector of Customs for the port of Savannah—Ga—The writer is President of a line of SteamShips run-
ing between this port & Savannah & has had opportunities of judging, as well as ascertaining the opinion of Merchants doing business at latter in regard to the able manner,

impartiality and courtesy that Mr Robb exercises in discharging the duties of his office—
Many of the principal Merchants of Savannah will, so I am informed, recommend that he
be continued in Office—The opposition to him is exclusively political—Mr Robb has
been and is still, one of the most firm & active supporters of your Administration that is
to be found in any of the Southern States, & in proportion to his means he has made as
great sacrifices as any other individual—In the organization of the Republican Party in
Georgia, he was most prominent—he invested almost every dollar that he possessed in
establishing the 'New Era' at Atlanta—the first newspaper in the state of Georgia that advocated your claims for the nomination for President—being elected a delegate to the
Chicago Convention his Voice & his Vote aided in securing that nomination—For the Republican Party he has labored faithfully, and to remove him now from Office would in my
opinion, not only operate prejudicially to the interest of the Party, but also be doing a
wrong to Mr Robb—. . ." LS, *ibid.*

On March 3, Thomas P. Saffold, Madison, Ga., wrote to USG. "If it is deemed advisable to change the Officer of Collector of customs at Savannah, I would like to have the
appointment. I refer you to attorney Gen Akerman, and Messrs Hill and Miller as to my
qualifications and claims for the office. With the best wishes for your health and the success of your administration, . . ." ALS, *ibid.* On Nov. 23, Safford telegraphed to USG. "Seeing Col Robb is to be removed permit me to Call Your attention to my written application
of March last" Telegram received (at 3:54 P.M.), *ibid.*

On July 10, Isaac Seeley, Savannah, had written to USG. "I have the honor to submit
the following facts for your attention and immediate action   1st That in April 1868, being chairman of the Republican Executive Committee for the first Congressional District
of Ga, and needing funds to carry on the campaign for the ratification of the new Constitution, for the election of Governor, members of Congress and members of the Legislature, and county officers, I called upon T P Robb to contribute he being Postmaster of Savannah at a salary of $4000 pr year, but he refused to give any thing for that campaign . . .
5th In August 1870 he was appointed Chairman of the Republican Executive Committee
of Chatham county, but refused to sign a handbill calling a mass meeting of Republicans
for the county, said Committee under his Chairmanship not even raising a dollar to elect
the Republican ticket which was defeated,   He subscribed $25 on an outside subscription,
but has never paid it, although he receives about $6000 pr year as collector of Customs,
Such is the kind of republican and such the political unworthiness of the man now enjoying the most lucrative government office in Ga, and *being* such, it is obvious how utterly
impossible it is for sincere republicans to co'operate with him, & also to what extent he
stands in the way of the success of the Republican in Savannah, by destroying that unity
which is essential to success,   The present situation therefore is pregnant with peril to
the party, and assures defeat in the future as in the past and requires the immediate removal of the Collector of Customs" ALS, *ibid.* In Nov., Seeley again wrote to USG. "I have
the honor to submit a few encouraging facts, to show that the republican cause is *not hope-
less* in the State of Georgia,   In the election of 1867 the vote *for* Convention, was 32.000
white, and about 48.000 colored, Total 80.000   In April 1868 the vote for ratification,
Governor &c, was about 36.000 white, and 54.000 colored, Total 90.000   In the Presidential election of 1868 the total white *and* colored vote for General Grant was 55.000,
This shows a falling off, of 35.000 from the previous vote   Sixteen counties in the '*black
Belt*', (the republicans being nearly all colored) which gave 25.000 for Bullock, only gave
5.000 for General Grant,   While in fourteen counties in the '*White Belt*' (the republicans
being nearly all white) the vote for General Grant was just equal to the vote for Bullock,

This shows that the falling off, of 35.000 votes was almost entirely from the colored—that the *colored* vote for President was not more than 25.000, and the white vote about 30.000; that the white republican vote is more uniform and reliable than the colored vote, and constitutes ⅗ of the numerical strength of the party in Georgia,   The whole vote of the state is 220.000—120.000 white, & 100.000 colored, 30.000 of the white are republicans, which leaves but 90.000 white democrats, to 130.000 white *and* colored republicans, being 40.000 republican majority,   Admit that 30.000 colored will not vote at all, we still have 10.000 republican majority,   Now in order to poll this vote, three things are necessary, 1st Crush out, or demoralize the K K,   2nd Unify the leadership of the party,   3d Organize and unite the masses,   But we cannot unite the *masses*, while their *leaders* are divided,   The first step therefore is to harmonize the leaders,   To accomplish this, we now bend every effort, and subordinate every interest, and to *this end* we ask, *earnestly ask*, the assistance and co'operation of your Excellency,   And while all extend their hearty thanks for the appointment of Wilson and Clark at Savannah, we entreat your Excellency not to turn a deaf ear to the *united* voice of the party, for the removal of Collector Robb, and the appointment of James Atkins—Permit us to offer a few facts and reasons which render it impossible for leading republicans, and Collector Robb, to work in harmony,   While the working men of the party in April 1868, went forth with their lives in their hands battling for reconstruction and victory, *he*, sat in his easy chair, secure from danger at $4000 pr year, and not only refused to give a cent, not only refused to strike a blow for victory, but was welcomed to the bosom of the enemy by being appointed delegate to a democratic Convention,   No one knows better than your Excellency, how impossible it is for *true* republicans to work in harmony with a two faced political hypocrite, . . ." ALS, *ibid.*

On July 12, Richard W. White *et al.*, Savannah, had written to USG. "We the undersigned Republicans of Chatham County, state of Georgia, having heard that representations were being made to you of the disorganized condition (or want of organization) in our party, would most respectfully represent that such statements are entirely unfounded. . . . Col T. P. Robb as our chairman did not confine the workings of his committee to this county exclusively, he saw the want of organization in the other twenty eight (28) counties of this congressional district, when he appointed canvassers who visited many of the counties, effected organizations, encouraging our Republican friends, to stand firm and true to our standard bearers &c. and in many instances the canvassers for their own personal safety were obliged to abandon their labour of love,   In some of the counties our friends were keep in such fear by the Rebel Democracy, they could not render assistance, and in counties with a large Republican population, we failed to poll a single vote, for the reasons stated,   Nevertheless our efforts were successfull in a portion of the Congressional district, and in many of the counties we have now strong an effective organizations, It was a noticiable fact during the canvass that Chatham was the only county properly and thoroughly organized, the credit of which is due to the unceasing efforts of our worthy chairman. We would further state, that the parties who are instrumental in reporting the want of organization in our party, are those who during the late canvass, and for a long time have stood aloof from our party organization, its labors, anxieties, and perplexities. . . ." DS (23 signatures), *ibid.*

On July 6, Robb, Savannah, had written to Horace Porter, Long Branch. "I enclose herewith a copy of a communication forwarded to the Secretary of the Treasury this day. It is lengthy, but I hope you will read it, both on account of its official and political character. I am also deeply pained and mortified to to inform you that the Deputy Collector at this Custom House, Geo B. Wellman, has, upon investigation, been found short in his cash account some 2000$. Mr W— is a Boston man, and served some 30 years in the Custom House in that City. He was Deputy Collector at Hilton Head during the War, and Deputy Collector under Ex Gov Johnson at this port. He is considered one of the most experienced customs officers on the Atlantic Coast—He was esteemed highly at the Depart, and of course, I had great confidence in him. . . . The Depart has been notified of this case, and I write you fearing that exaggerated accounts might perhaps reach you. I sincerely hope the case will not be made *public*—neither the govt or myself will sustain a loss—and its publicity will do no good—and only make food for political enemies." ALS, *ibid.*, Letters Received. The enclosure is *ibid.*

On Aug. 14, M. H. Hale, special agent, Treasury Dept., and Andrew Sloan, Savannah, wrote to USG. "The officers and members of the District Council of the National Guard of the First Congressional District of Geo. respectfully ask the removal from Office T. P. Robb the present Collector of Customs at the port of Savannah and the Appointment in his place James Atkins of Atlanta. We ask this change to be made in justice to the Republican Party of the State who almost unanimously demand it. For other reasons we ask it. It is publicly known and it cannot be controverted that Collector Robb's administration of affairs at this Custom House has been loose and disreputable, unlawful and demoralizing practices have grown up which has finally culminated in a defalcation and an attempt to cover up this defalcation by fraud in accounts and vouchers transmitted to the Treasury Department, and the discovery that the Collector while knowing of these fraudulent accounts has for months allowed them to slumber in secret, with no effort on his part towards an investigation and a correction of the fraud. We ask his removal on the further ground that he knowingly allowed the unlawful use of the public monies in his charge, and has been cognizant of other unlawful practices by his Subordinates, himself even participating in the benefits of some of them. We charge upon him also as in no manner administering the affairs of the Custom House to the benefit of the Republican Party of the State, . . ." DS, *ibid.*, Collector of Customs Applications. On Aug. 17, White and many others wrote to USG. ". . . Since Mr Hale has held his present position, he has not identified himself with the regular organization of our Party, in either of the states, he has assumed to himself a degree of Arrogance and Pomposity, that has estranged him from the masses, and leaves him today with no influence whatever. During the last Congressional Canvass in this district. he rendered us no assistance, and the principle 'Seaports' of this state, are in his district, as they are also in this Congressional, and if well managed should redound to our success,   his persistant opposition to Col T. P. Robb, Collector of Customs at Savannah, who has the confidence of the masses undivided, and no firmer friend and supporter have you in the whole Party south, one who is continually abused by the Democratic papers of this section, for his unqualified support of yourself and your administration,   Mr Hale has daily and publicly outspoken in opposition to your Re-nomination, saying 'That if you should be the candidate the Party would meet defeat,' all this at a time when unity of action should govern our councils,   such teachings from one in his position has had its demoralizing effect. We therefore in the name of the Republican Party of the First Congressional District, State of Georgia, do most emphatically recommend the removal of Mr M. Hale for the reasons stated, and that a firm supporter of your adminestration. (also for the succession) may be appointed, one having the unity and success of our party more of an object, than the present incumbent, and in return we can pledge a successful result," Copy, *ibid.*

In [*Sept.*], "the Peoples Deligat[es]" wrote to USG. "we are requested by the Voters of Chatham County, over 3000 Republicans to pray for the *removal* of P Robb from the

Coustom House in Savannah Ga for his *labors* to devide the Republican Party last November and for having in his imploy, *colored* and *white* persons who are known K K K's and have never voted with the True succesful Republicans in the First District. The People pray that you will be pleased to select from the names here presented as true Repulicans and good and strong Friends to U S Grant, for our next President. Dr James Waring native, Hon Charles H Hopkins native *or* Hon A Alpeora Bradley native. If you have any reply please send it to Dr James Waring or the Hon Charles H Hopkins Savannah Ga If you wish this backed up by a petition—we will send it, pleas do not continue to give the *childr[en's]* bred to the Dogs—who put 100 true Republicans in Jail for Voting the only Republican Ticket that ever did or can be elected in the first District of Ga. This jailing was to intimitate Voters and to gain $10 for each victam. Please remember the colored Men cast 90,000 Votes in Ga—and therefore should be regarded, as well as the 20,000 White votes in upper Ga. A hint to the wise may stop a great leak in the Ship of State." D (docketed Sept. 21, 1871), *ibid.*

On Oct. 4, Robb wrote to USG. "On my return I find two indictments against me— one for embezzlement and one for conspiracy. It is universally beleived that Mr Hale was the sole instigator and indeed I am promised the affidavits of more than one person who heard him state that his object in prosecuting Wellman was simply a blind and that it was done really for the purpose of reaching me and making me odious and notorious. Some of the men on the Grand Jury were persons relieved from office by myself and personal enemies, Mr Hale is vindictive and is determined to push me to the bitter end, to prosecute and persecute . . ." LS, *ibid.* On Oct. 11, Robb wrote to USG on the same subject. LS, *ibid.* Also in Oct., Robb wrote to USG. "Personal—. . . I hope you will pardon me, and read the lengthy letter I have, in Justice to myself, written to you—although long as it is, I feel unsatisfied with it, and crave a personal interview, well knowing I could say what I feel it my duty and privilege so to do, in fewer words, and make you to more thoroughly understand my position socially as well as politically. But you will doubtless recollect that at our late interview at Long Branch, you expressed a wish that I should not visit Washington on Ga. political, or place errands—therefore in deference to your wishes (although the case and occasion is one of such vital importance to myself and family) I refrain from going. Mr President I left you with so much hope and encouragement in regard to the future, I was enabled to infuse new life and renewed zeal among your personal friends in this City & Dist. At a great pecuniary loss (if removed) I have provided for my family for the coming year—And now this letter from the Secretary (after all his personal assurances, that all I had to do was to satisfy the President) has so disappointed me, that I feel crushed, and unfitted to write, even in Justification of myself. In addition to this wholley unexpected blow, the terrible fire now raging at Chicago has deprived me of a home for my family, and swept away every prospect for business. I actually donot know what I am to do. Mr President, if I had committed a wrong—if I had not one of the best regulated and best conducted offices on the coast, and if I could not give you more than satisfactory evidence that you have no truer friend in this State—nor one who can influence as large a colored vote as I—I would not say a word—But the deep intrest I feel in your personal success, and in the party you represent—will not permit me to stand idely by, and allow personal prejudice and Jealousy on the part of those opposing me, to discourage and wean from you, your only true friends in Ga. Finally Mr President—in behalf of my family— in behalf of the Western men—Ex Soldiers and their families residing here (God help them if I am relieved) and the colored men connected with this office, and so wholley dependent upon me, I make this personal appeal, and beg that you will not permit this Hale,

Mass. influence, in combination with the 'Anti Grant' and quasi republican ring in this State, to crush the *only* influence favorable to you personally. in this Dist. . . ." ALS, *ibid.*

On Oct. 13 and 20, White, Savannah, wrote to USG. "Understanding that certain persons in this State, who are opposed to your administration and re-nomination, are again praying you for the removal of Col T. P. Robb the present efficient collector of Customs at this port, therefore I beg of you, in-behalf of the Republicans in this District and State—and as the republican nominee for the 41st Congress in the campaign of 1870. to respectfully but earnestly protest against the removal of Col Robb for the following reasons. 1st The Gentelmen who are seeking his removal, are not, nor never have been favorable to your administration—2d They have never allied themselves openly with the republican party, but on the contrary have publicly declared their intention to oppose your re-nomination in the next National convention, And I assure you if they Succeed, in their present undertaking against Col Robb, it will greatly weaken us as a party in this State. 3d The Collector by his firm and unflinching Advocacy of your Administration and re-nomination has won the respect and confidence of the republicans of this District and State, And in my opinion it is absolutely necessary to retain him in his present position, in order to Sustain our party organization. Prominently among those opposed to your administration and re-nomination referred to in the first paragraph of this communication I regret to say is M H. Hale Special agent of the Treasury at this port, and in view of these facts I would most respectfully Suggest and reccomen'd his removal, from this District. Mr Hale by virtue of his position in this Dist is capable of doing yourself and friends much good or harm, but I am confident that he is using the powers of his office to defat your re-nomination. Should Mr Hale be removed I can assure you that it will greatly weaken and demoralize the opposing element here and unite us as a party in sending delegates to the National convention favorable to your re-nomination. In this connection I wish to add that A. A. Bradley has returned, and is now the authorized agent of the 'New York Tribune' (Daily) and is circulating it at $1[0] per year, and is also circulating a petition for the removal of Collector Robb, the colored and Northern-Men connected with the Savannah Custom House, and has already procured the Signatures of the Members of the Colored Democratic Club of this city, a class of men controled by Democratic Merchants and Politietians,   He is a bad Mischiefmaker, entirely void of principle. He Sold us out last fall for democratic Money—and defeated us, and is seeking now to do the same thing, And I hope before you entertain his petition you will give us a chance to be heard, for while he may get up a petition of a few hundred, We can get up a counter one of as many thousands . . ." "Understanding that one A. A. Bradley has fowarded your Excellency a petition, praying the removal of Col. T. P. Robb, the collector at this Port, and the most of the men now in his Employ—and asking you to appoint one G. I. Taggart Collector, &c Therefore I have thought it proper to request you to with-hold the said petition, until we are heard from through a counter petition—as we are now engaged in getting up one, and also affidavits—Showing that a very large number of those who signed the Bradley petition did so through false representations—and are not expressive of the real wish of the people, As you will see by the enclosed Affidavit of Paul Gordon—and the proceedings of the District and County Executive Committees—that will be handed you by Collector Robb. . . . P. S. The will be fowarded in a few days." ALS, *ibid.* On March 5, 1869, Grantham I. Taggart, Savannah, had written to USG. "I have the honor to herewith respectfully Solicit the appointment of Collector of Customs for the Port of Savannah Georgia.—I have been a citizen of Savannah for Four years, and served as an officer of U. S. Vols during the late Rebellion.—As I have the honor to be personally known to you, I take the

liberty simply, in addition, to refer, to the following gentlemen who have given me permission to do so.—" ALS, *ibid.* Among those named were Secretary of War John A. Rawlins and U.S. Senators Simon Cameron and John Scott of Pa., Alexander G. Cattell of N. J.,
and George E. Spencer of Ala. Related papers are *ibid.*

On Oct. 14, 1871, Yates, Jacksonville, Ill., telegraphed to USG. "Please do not act
further in case of Col Robb collector at Savannah till you see him and me" Telegram received, *ibid.* On Oct. 21, John H. Deveaux, secretary, Southern States Convention, *et al.,*
Columbia, S. C., petitioned USG. "The undersigned having confidence in Col. T. P. Robb,
Collector of Customs at Savannah Ga, as a true republican and ardent supporter of the national Administration, and believing any change in that important office, especially at this
time, would be detrimental to the republican party of Georgia, do hereby most respectfully protest against his removal. Believing your Excellency will give this your earnest
consideration . . ." DS (11 signatures), *ibid.*

On Nov. 18, John J. Weed, Savannah, wrote to USG. "As one of the Counsel engaged
in the defence of Col. T. P. Robb Collector of Customs at this place I deem it my duty to
advise you as fully as I am able of the exact situation of the case, and the influences which
led to, and still continue, to actuate and inspire the proceedings against this Officer. That
the trial of Collector Robb, will demonstrate his innocence of any official or moral wrong
in connection with the embezzelment committed by his subordinates I am fully satisfied
from a most patient and careful examination of all the facts which may be developed in the
Case. . . . This prosecution of Collector Robb, is only a struggle between '*the in's*' and '*the
outs*'—and in this case '*the outs*' have been utterly unscrupulous in regard to the means to
be used to accomplish their ends—If the Collector, had accommodated them by resigning
his Office, you would never heard of his indictment for offences of which the Secretary of
the Treasury knows, and has admitted that he is entirely *innocent*—The Secretary of the
Treasury promised the Collector to send here a competent and honest man to investigate
all the matters in any affecting Collector Robb's Official Character. This promise the Secretary did not fulfill, for I think you will be satisfied when the facts are laid before you that
the person sent here for that purpose was neither competent nor *honest.* It is true he is a
special agent of the Treasury Department, named Henry S. Martin—He arrived here last
Saturday, and was at once and during that night and the day following in close commu-
nion and fellowship with the gang of scoundrels who have instigated these prosecutions
against the Collector. I suppose this was done to prepare his mind for an *impartial* investigation of the matters wherewith he was charged   Major Ferrill, who is associated
with me in the defence of the Collector was with me when this special detective came
to the Collectors Office, and we then asked if he was authorized in any way to examine the
charges against the Collector upon which he was under indictment   He replied that he
had no authority in regard to those matters at all—and came only to examine *generally*
into the affairs of the Collectors Office—Two days latter than this, he informed ~~that~~us
that his only business here was to examine these charges—upon which the Collector was
indicted—and that he was here upon no other duty but *that.* It was then suggested to him
that there were important papers in the Collectors Office relating to those matters which
he might *profitably* examine but I am advised that he declined to examine them or give
them the least consideration whatever. He subsequent to this time and the day before he
left here told me that the proceedings instituted against the Collector would be discontinued '*if he would resign* his Office.' Do you want any stronger evidence of the fact that
he had joined the herd of slanderers, whose only purpose has been to drive the Collector
out of Office? Special Agent Hale, is now devoting his energies to the work of manu-

facturing evidence to sustain these prosecutions although in his Official reports to the Secretary of the Treasury made the same week the indictments were found he stated that after the most thorough and patient investigation, he had been unable to find any evidence in any way implicating the Collectr in the matters wherewith *at the instance* of this man Hale, he was subsequently indicted—He probably foresees that the vindication of the Collector must result in his own dismissal from Office—For I was informed by Hon Horace Maynard, whom I met here last Thursday, that from Hale's own statement of the case—without hearing anything from the Collector—he was satisfied that either the Collector *or Hale ought to be removed*, but *he* couldn't tell *which*, from Hales statement of the case. . . ." ALS, *ibid.*

On Dec. 3, Osborne A. Lochrane, Savannah, wrote to USG. "At the request of Mr. Robb and his Friend, I have the honor to communicate with your Excellency in regard to his case pending in the circuit court. Pardon the trespass of a word, in assuring your Excellency after the most patient Examination of all the facts and papers connected with the matter, that my honest opinion is, the accusation was conceived in malise and that he only awaits a trial to vindicate his course, and secure his triumphant acquittal, for which he announced himself ready some days ago—" ALS, *ibid.*, Letters Received. On Dec. 18, Robb wrote to USG. "On the evening of Saturday last, Judge Lochrane telegraphed to you the result of the trial of the indictments pending against me in the U. S. Circuit Court. He will shortly visit Washington, and if permitted an interview with your Excellency, will state to you his views as to why and in what manner these indictments were found, the nature of the facts disclosed by the investigation, and the political bearing of the prosecution. I only wish now to state that my vindication was most complete and triumphant. . . ." LS, *ibid.*, Collector of Customs Applications. On the same day, Robb again wrote to USG on this subject. ALS, *ibid.* On Dec. 21, Governor Benjamin Conley of Ga. wrote to USG. "Permit me to introduce to you Hon. O. A. Lochrane of this city, Chief Justice of the Supreme Court of this State. Previous to his appointment to the high office he now holds, Judge Lochrane occupied an important judicial position as one of the Judges of the Superior Courts of this State, and he ranks among the foremost advocates and jurists of Georgia. Though for many years before the rebellion a resident of this state, he has since the close of the war been a firm and consistent supporter of the reconstruction measures of Congress, and an earnest and unfaltering advocate of law and order in this State. The influence of his exalted station aided by his high reputation as an eloquent speaker and forcible writer has from the outset been freely exerted in this direction. Judge Lochrane will represent the views of the administration here in the statements he may make concerning the existing state of affairs in Georgia and I respectfully and earnestly request that such statements receive your consideration." LS, OFH.

On Dec. 29, A. Alpeora Bradley wrote to USG and cabinet. "A Alpeora Bradley on oath comes and says, that on the 25th day of December Thomas P Robb caused to be assembled in the U S Custom House his Government employees and agreed to send his colored employees to brake-up a public meeting being held under the call here annexed by Killing A A Bradley and others: and Fleming Butts, H Spering, Richard W White, John Deveaux, Josiah Grant and others formed a consiracy to Kill and murder the good citizens of Savannah on Christmas day, and attempted to execute their unlawful conspiracy—by coming to said meeting, with Pistols loded with powder and ball, and fired at several person and among others, two Policmen who had been ordered their by his Honor the Mayor. Nine warrents have been issued and yet these parties defy all civil law and keep the colored people of the city of Savannah and county of Chatham in great *Terror*!" ADS,

DNA, RG 56, Collector of Customs Applications. The enclosure is *ibid.* On Jan. 8, 1872, Benjamin F. Burton, Bainbridge, Ga., wrote to USG. "I want the appointment of Collector of the Port of Savannah, and ask that you turn out the carpetbagger who now has it and give the place to me. Do'nt throw this in your waste basket without thought, but consider it and let me hear from you. I can give satisfactory references and will do so when necessary" ALS, *ibid.*

On Feb. 19, Robb, Washington, D. C., wrote to USG. "I have the honor to place in your hands my resignation of the office of Collector of Customs for the Port of Savannah, Ga. to take effect so soon as my successor shall have been appointed and qualified. I am impelled to this course, from a desire to promote, so far as any act of mine can do, entire harmony in the ranks of the Union Republican Party in the State of Georgia. That there have been dissensions and divisions amongst us there, you have often been advised. I am unconscious however of having contributed in the least to those dissensions and divisions; but on the contrary, I have by every act possible for me, endeavored to promote harmony and entire agreement. It is needless that I should assure you that in the future as in the past, I shall be found an earnest advocate of the principles of that Great Party, by whose efforts the country was saved from disruption: and by whose united voice you were called to the position you have so honorably and acceptably filled. Accept my thanks for the many acts of kindness you have hitherto shown me, and for the repeated expressions of confidence you have been pleased to give me. Wishing for yourself personally, continued health and prosperity—. . ." ALS, *ibid.* On the same day, James J. Waring and three others, Savannah, telegraphed to USG. "We signed the bond of Collector Robb cheerfully, and voluntarily, and have no desire to withdraw our names there-from. If it is represented that deception was practiced by him we are not aware of the fact," Telegram received (on Feb. 20), *ibid.* On Feb. 21, Orville E. Babcock wrote to Secretary of the Treasury George S. Boutwell. "The President directs me to transmit the accompanying letter of Resignation of Col: Robb, as Collector of Customs at Savannah, Ga. & request you to have a withdrawal made out, to go to the Senate to day, of the nomination of Mr. James Attkins, which was sent in yesterday 'Vice Robb to be removed,' in order that that he may again be nominated 'Vice Robb resigned.'" Copy, DLC-USG, II, 1.

On July 20, 1871, Charles H. Prince, Augusta, Ga., had written to USG. "Judging from reports that reach me through the press, and from other sources, I am led to believe there may be a change in the office of Collector of Customs for the port of Savannah. Should a change be made, I desire to recommend the appointment of *Col. James Atkins* as the successor of the present incumbent for the following reasons: First—*Col. Atkins* is a man of the strictest integrity, of excellent business reputation, and as well fitted, I believe, to perform the duties of so responsible a position as any man that could be selected. Second—He is a Native Georgian, possessing sound republican principles, an ardent worker in our cause, and, I think, free from prejudice against colored, and Northern, men. Third—I believe that *Col. Atkins*, on account of his reputation for honesty, his high social standing among the people of this State, his outspoken advocacy of the principles of our party, and *warm support* of the policy of the present administration, could do more to strengthen the Republican party here by uniting our friends, and securing accessions to us from the ranks of the enemy, than any other man in Georgia. For these reasons, I earnestly recommend his appointment." ALS, DNA, RG 56, Collector of Customs Applications. On Sept. 28, Samuel F. Gove, Prince, *et al.*, Atlanta, wrote to USG. "The undersigned, Republican citizens of Georgia, respectfully ask that your Excellency will remove Col. T. P. Robb from the office of Collector of Customs at the Port of Savannah and appoint Col. James Atkins to that position. . . . Col. Atkins is one of the most influential Republicans in the State. He assisted in the organization of the party, and has spent his time and money to promote its interests. He was the Republican candidate for Congress in the 7th Congressional District in the campaign of 1868, and his popularity was so great, that he reduced the Democratic majority in that strong Democratic District to about twenty five hundred votes, thus enabling the Republicans to carry the State. He is an able man, is also a man of property, and enjoys the confidence of all who know him whether Republicans or Democrats. In our opinion Georgia would be a Republican State, if we could poll our entire vote: That we may do so, it is in our opinion necessary that our party shall be thoroughly reorganized. An effort is now being made to that end, and we believe the change in the Savannah Custom House which we suggest will greatly aid us in the effort to carry the State in 1872. At that time, in addition to the election of Electors of President and Vice-President, we shall elect seven members of Congress; a Governor for four years; members of the General Assembly—the House of Representatives for two years and half of the Senate for four years—and county officers in 137 counties for two and four years. Believing that you desire to do all in your power to strengthen the Republican party of this and other States, we, therefore, earnestly entreat that you will make the appointment which we request." DS (6 signatures), *ibid.* On Dec. 20, A. D. Rockafellow, Atlanta, wrote to USG. "I have the honor of calling your attention to the fact. that there is now a movement on foot. to have Col T. P. Robb the Collector of customs of the Port of Savannah. removed and have Col James Atkins of Atlanta appointed in his Sted. I have only to say that this change is uncalled for. Col Robb has done more for the Republican party in Georgia two to one then Col James Atkins the man they want appointed—We have as evidence. he Col Atkins is now the Revenue Collector at this place. and he aids the Republican party by appointing Democrats to office. . . ." ALS, *ibid.*

To George S. Boutwell

Washington, D. C. Feb.y 26th 1872,

Hon. Geo. S. Boutwell,
Sec. of the Treas.
Dear Sir:

This will introduce to you Rev. Dr. J. Lanahan, of the Methodist Book Concern, New York City, who desires some information from the Sub Treasurer in New York City. I do not know the propriety or impropriety of giving the information sought, which the Dr. will explain, but refer the matter to you.

Your obt. svt.
U. S. Grant

ALS (facsimile), USGA. In Sept., 1869, John Lanahan had publicized controversial charges of fraud and mismanagement at the Methodist Book Concern, a large New York City publishing house. See Lanahan, *The Era of Frauds in the Methodist Book Concern at New York* (Baltimore, 1896), pp. 244–45; Robert D. Clark, *The Life of Matthew Simpson* (New York, 1956), pp. 284–85, 287–88.

Endorsement

[*Feb. 1872*]

Dr. Canisus desires to be appointed a Com. to the Worlds Fair to be held in Vienna.[1] The Dr. has served this country an Consul to Vienna and speaks the language fluently.

AE (undated), DNA, RG 59, Letters of Application and Recommendation. Written on a letter of Feb. 13, 1872, from Robert T. Lincoln, Washington, D. C., to USG. "I take the liberty of presenting to your favorable attention Dr. Theodor Canisius of Illinois—He has been known to me for a great many years as an earnest, hardworking Republican, doing great good among his German fellow countrymen—If his wishes can be gratified I should be much pleased—" ALS, *ibid.* See Lincoln, *Works*, II, 524; *ibid.*, IV, 418. On Feb. 19, USG wrote to Secretary of State Hamilton Fish. "Will the Sec. of State please see Dr. Canisus, late Consul to Vienn" ANS, Gallery of History, Las Vegas, Nev.

On April 6, 1869, Lincoln, Chicago, had written to USG. "I have the honor to present to you Dr Theodore Canisius who is one of the original Republicans of this State and of great influence among our German population—He was our Consul at Vienna from 1861 to 1866 and during that time contributed largely by his writings in the German Press to form a friendly feeling towards us in Europe—Dr Canisius desires to return to Vienna in the same Capacity and if it seems proper to you—I would be one of many who would be glad of his appointment—" ALS, DNA, RG 59, Letters of Application and Recommendation. Related papers are *ibid.*

On Dec. 8, 1874, U.S. Senator John A. Logan of Ill. *et al.* wrote to USG. "We most earnestly reccommend the appointment of Dr. T. Canisius of Chicago to a consulate in place of one of the appointments now held from Chicago, and designate the one at Barmen, Germany   The Dr. is a man of education and ability and would represent the Govt in a Creditable manner should he be appointed." LS (4 signatures), *ibid.* On Dec. 11, USG endorsed this letter. "I approve most decidedly of the removal asked, and have no objection to the appointment herein recommended." AES, *ibid.* Related papers are *ibid.* On Dec. 15, Fish recorded in his diary a conversation with USG. "I tell him that Dr Canecius being a German by birth he could not be appointed to the consulate; he remarked that he thought that it was a collectorship of Internal Revenue for which they had recommended him but that he wished a change made in the consulate at Bramen as Hoechster the present consul was acting in hostility to the administration, and authorizing me to appoint some other person than a naturalized German to the place." DLC-Hamilton Fish. On Jan. 11,

1875, USG nominated Theodore Canisius as consul, Bristol, in place of Edgar Stanton; on the same day, he nominated Stanton as consul, Barmen, in place of Emil Hoechster.

On Jan. 4, 186[9], Gustave P. Koerner, Springfield, Ill., had written to USG recommending Hoechster. ALS, DNA, RG 59, Letters of Application and Recommendation. On June 10, Charles E. Riehle, Galena, wrote to USG. "From the inclosed note of the Hon: E. B. Washburne your Excellency will see, that I have been an Applicant for a Consulate. I had every reason to hope for success, but find after all, that I have been disappointed, at least for the present. Willingly I should have borne my fate with resignation, had it not been for an article in the Ill. Staats Zeitung, which reads thus:—'Mr: Emil Hoechster, our esteemed fellow Citizen has been appointed Consul in Barmen, by the President. This is but a just recompensation for his excellent services to the party during the last Campaign.'—Now, if such services are a standard of merit, I should certainly have deserved some consideration, for Mr: Hoechster has but this *One* time rendered such services, while I have been a member of the Rep: Party from its organization and have been on the stump in every Campaign, ruining my health and injuring my practice. At the reelection of Mr: Lincoln I desired an appointment, but my hope was frustrated by his untimely death. This time I certainly hoped to succeed, for Mr: Washburne had promised me repeatedly to procure me an appointment as Consul. . . ." ALS, *ibid.* No appointment followed.

On March 13, 1873, U.S. Representative Charles Foster of Ohio, Fostoria, wrote to USG. "I have not troubled you much in the way of soliciting place for my people, and do not propose to in the future—, but I would very much like to secure a eConsulship for Mr Jules Erckner of Sandusky at some point *in* or *near* the German Empire—You will remember that I mentioned this case to you on the occasion of your last state dinner—I know this appointment would do us all good, and will certainly an officer of much more than ordinary merit—His papers are on file with Sec'ty Fish, where the case is more completely presented   Will you do me the favor to give this matter careful attention" ALS, *ibid.* On Jan. 21 and Feb. 3, Julius Erckener, Sandusky, Ohio, had written to Foster. ". . . I saw the Gentleman who lived in Chicago next door to the man, who represents us at present in Barmen, Prussia. He says that Salomon also a Jew after being made governor of Washington Ter, pushed the man & helped him most to get the appointment,   when it became known, several Papers, Germans & Americans protested & it is said that a Protest was even sent to the Senate. The gentleman here told me further that the Chacago and a Baltimore Germ. Paper accused him of having 4 wives living & that a certain Article was spoken of, published in a Paper of the City where he resides as Consul, . . ." "Since I had the pleasure to address You about two weeks ago, I have heard more about the Gentleman in Barmen; who was sent there. Mr Kromer & Jacob Neuert, the former partner of Mr Foerster told me that Hoechster used to play on the stage as Comediant was here in the City & well known,   I would not repeat what they said about his reputation   They felt surprised & very indignant when they heard that that man held the position yet as Consul. They say that our government would certainly not keep him any longer if he was better known,   they also told me that other men used to write short stump speeches for him, which he delivered not being able to do it himself.—. . ." ALS, *ibid.* No appointment followed.

1. See letter to Hamilton Fish, May 29, 1873, note 1.

Speech

———

GENTLEMEN,

I am gratified that this Country and that my administration will be distinguished in history as the first which has received an Embassy from the nation with which ~~we~~ the U. S were the first to establish diplomatic and commercial intercourse.

The objects which, you say, have given rise to your mission, do honor to the intelligence and wisdom of your Sovereign and reflect credit on you in having been chosen as the instruments for carrying them into effect. The time must be regarded as gone, never to return, when any nation can ~~so far consult its own pleasure as to~~ keep apart from all others and expect to enjoy ~~that~~ the prosperity and happiness which depend, more or less, upon the mutual adoption of improvements, not only in the science of government[1] but in those other sciences and arts which contribute to the dignity of mankind and to national wealth and power.

Though Japan is one of the most ancient of organized communities, and the United States ~~are one of~~ rank among the most recent, we flatter ourselves that we have made some improvements upon the political institutions of the nations from whom we are descended. ~~Among these, is the entire freedom which we ourselves enjoy in this country in matters of religion and which we allow to all foreigners resident among us.~~[2] ~~In the pursuit of these our policy has been~~ Our experience leads us to believe that the wealth, the power, & the happiness of a People are advanced by the encouragement of trade & commercial intercourse with other powers—by the elevation & dignity of labour—by the practical adaptation of Science to the Manufactures & the Arts—~~the~~ by increased facilities of frequent & rapid Communication between different parts of the Country—by the encouragement of emigration which brings with it the varied habits & diverse genius & industry of other lands—by a free press—by freedom of thought & of conscience, & a liberal toleration in matters of religion & ~~of polities~~ not only to Citizens but to all forigners resident among us.

It will be a pleasure to us to enter upon that consultation ~~with you~~ upon international questions in which you say you are authorized to engage.[3] The improvement of the commercial relations between our respective countries, is ~~an~~ important and desirable ~~purpose~~ and cannot fail to strengthen the bonds which unite us.

I will heartily coöperate ~~with you~~ in so desirable ~~a measure~~ an object.

Your kind wishes for me personally Gentlemen, are cordially reciprocated. I trust that ~~nothing may happen to make~~ your abode with us ~~other than~~ may be agreeable to you and ~~profitable~~. may contribute to a more intimate acquaintance & intercourse between our respective Peoples—

MARCH 4TH 1872.

Df, DNA, RG 59, Notes from Foreign Missions, Japan. USG spoke in reply to Ambassador Iwakura Tomomi. "His Majesty the Emperor of Japan, our August Sovereign, has sought since the achievement of our National reconstruction, to attain a more perfect organization in the administrative power of His government. He has studied with interest the results attained by Western nations, and having a sincere desire to establish permanent and friendly relations with Foreign Powers on a still closer footing, has commissioned us His Ambassadors Extraordinary to all Powers having Treaties with Japan. Upon the soil of your country, we first present our credentials, delivering to you personally the letter of our August Sovereign, at this public official audience. . . ." Copy, *ibid.* On Nov. 4, 1871, Emperor Mutsuhito had written to USG. ". . . The period for revising the treaties now existing between Ourselves and the United States, is less than one year distant; We expect and intend to reform and improve the same so as to stand upon a similar footing with the most enlightened nations and to attain the full developement of public right and interest. The civilization and institutions of Japan, are so different from those of other countries, that We cannot expect to reach the desired end at once. It is our purpose to select from the various institutions prevailing among enlightened nations, such as are best suited to Our present conditions and adopt them in gradual reforms and improvement of Our policy and customs so as to be upon an equality with them. . . ." Copy, *ibid.* See *PUSG*, 21, 206, 310–11; Charles Lanman, ed., *The Japanese in America* (New York, 1872).

On Jan. 3, 1872, George B. Williams, San Francisco, telegraphed to USG. "Would it not be well to instruct officers Commanding fortifications to fire proper salutes as steamships bearing Japanese Embassy to treaty powers enters this Harbor due about January sixteenth" Telegram received, DNA, RG 94, Letters Received, 20 1872. See note 1, below.

On Jan. 16 and Feb. 29, Secretary of State Hamilton Fish wrote in his diary. "Read note of Mr Mori (Japanese Chargé) announcing the expected arrival of a Japanese Embassy—The telegraph announces its arival at San Francisco—On a previous occasion on receipt of a despatch from De Long announcing their intended visit, it was thought it wd be adviseable that Congress bear their expense while here—President desires that I see the Chairmen of the Comms. on For Rels in the Senate & House of Reps on the subject—"

"Mr Mori (Japanese Chargé) brings letter of credence of the Ambassador, & a translation thereof—Says the Ambassador wd prefer waiting two or three days before being presented—Monday is suggested" DLC-Hamilton Fish.

1. See *PUSG*, 22, 37, 45, 255. On Oct. 26, 1871, Fish had written in his diary. "Mr Mori—(Japanese Chargé) refers to letter advising of the desire of his Govt to engage some person conversant with the details & system of Internal Revenue, & wishes some person recommended—I mention the name of Geo B. Williams now Dep. Commr of Internal Revenue telling him that personally ~~I kno~~ I know but little of him—but that he has been recommended by Mr Delano & Mr Douglas (the present Commr) Shew him Delano's letter, & promise to send him a copy" DLC-Hamilton Fish. On Sept. 4, Secretary of the Interior Columbus Delano had written to Fish recommending George B. Williams. LS, DNA, RG 59, Letters of Application and Recommendation. Related papers are *ibid.*

On May 2, 1872, Delano, San Francisco, wrote to USG. "I have met in this city Geo. B. Williams, who is returning to this country with the Junior Minister of Finance for Japan for the purpose of negotiating, if possible, a small loan for that Government. He has a full statement from the Privy Council of Japan of the resources and liabilities of that Empire and the showing is so creditable, and the rate of interest offered so good as to make the loan an inducement, I think, to capitalists. The stability of the Japanese Government, as the case appears to me, is the only question likely to made. If our people would take this loan it will do much towards giving to our government that controlling influence in Japanese affairs hitherto enjoyed by England. The Japanese Government desire to place the loan here for this reason more than any other. I sincerely hope the loan can be made and if the Secretary of State shall concur in this desire I trust it can be done." ALS, OFH.

On Feb. 14, 1873, James B. McKean, chief justice, and William Cary, U.S. attorney, Utah Territory, Salt Lake City, wrote to USG. "Certain facts have come to our knowledge, which, while they do not relate to affairs in Utah, we deem of sufficient importance to be laid before you. About a year ago, when the Japanese Embassy was in this city, Hiraka, the Associate Justice of the Japanese Empire, met here, and renewed his acquaintance with Dr. Charles F. Winslow, whom he had formerly known in the city of Boston, and who was then and still is here looking to some mining interests. Dr. Winslow has not only travelled extensively in Europe and in North and South America, but he is a gentleman of distinguished scientific attainments. Among his contributions to science is a profound work, published a few years since in London, entitled 'Force and Nature.' He has given much thought and study to political economy. Judge Hiraka, having learned, when in school in Boston, highly to appreciate Dr. Winslow's character and attainments, on finding him here, took the Doctor into his closest and most intimate confidence. Through Hiraka, Prince Iwakura learned of Dr. Winslow, and did the latter the honor to request a personal interview, and also for advice and suggestions in regard to the management of the internal and foreign affairs of the Japanese Empire. The Doctor complied with the request, and, in several confidential interviews, developed to the Prince, in much detail, what he deemed to be the best policy for the Japanese government in regard to its own subjects, and also in regard to other nations. The Prince expressed himself as more deeply impressed with the Doctor's views than with any thing that he had heard, and urgently and repeatedy requested the Doctor to submit to him the same views in writing, in order that he might lay them before the Mikado. With this request the Doctor also complied,—presenting to Iwakura an elaborate, and necessarily a somewhat voluminous document. We have seen a duplicate of that document, and have been greatly impressed with its statesmanlike and far-reaching views. Since leaving here, prominent members of the Embassy have written to Dr. Winslow in terms of great kindness, and have assured him of the continued gratification of Iwakura with his essay. Judge Hiraka writes him that the Prince is much attached to him. Permit us now to call your Excellency's attention to some important steps taken by the Japanese government within a few months past, and since Dr— Winslow's interviews with Iwakura. 1. That government has adopted a policy of strict economy. 2. It has established nearly 60,000 public free schools. 3. It has established compulsory education. 4. It has adopted Sunday as a day of rest throughout the Empire. Now, on reading the duplicate of the essay presented to Iwakura by Dr. Winslow, we were much gratified to find that the Doctor had recommended those very measures, and had fortified them with cogent arguments. His essay contains many other recommendations, some of which the Mikado has already adopted. Be assured, Mr. President, that nothing is further from our intentions than to presume to offer advice to your Excellency; but we have felt it to be right to lay these facts before you; and, because of Dr. Winslow's eminent attainments, and also because of his intimate relations with the distinguished men mentioned above, may we take the liberty to ask the question, whether he could not be of great service to our country were he made minister to Japan? . . . P. S. We understand that Senator Wilson and Secretary Boutwell are somewhat acquainted with Dr. Winslow." LS, DNA, RG 59, Letters of Application and Recommendation. Related papers are *ibid.* No appointment followed.

2. On March 12, 1872, U.S. Senator William A. Buckingham of Conn. *et al.* wrote to USG. "The undersigned, a committee appointed by the American Board of Commissioners for Foreign Missions, at their late meeting in Salem, Massachusetts, have been requested to approach you, as Chief Magistrate of the United States, on the subject of a new treaty with Japan, which, it is expected, may be negociated in 1872. . . . Your Excellency is aware that according to the last treaty of the United States with Japan—the treaty, namely, of July 29, 1858,—while the Diplomatic agent and Consul general from our Country may travel freely in any part of Japan, all other citizens of the United States are confined to six ports and their immediate neighborhood, and to the cities of Yedo (since 1862), and of Osaca since 1863. They are allowed to go to the distance of 10 ri, that is about 24 miles, from most of the ports which are specified, and at Nagasaki into any part of the 'imperial,' as opposed, we judge, to the feudal domain, in its vicinity. The Japanese, on the contrary, are allowed liberty of travel and of residence in all places and parts of this country. There are about a hundred of them here at this moment, engaged in the study of various sciences and mechanical arts. They have free access to our schools and colleges. They have full liberty to profess, teach, and make proselytes to, their own religion. They can any where engage in trade. They are likely, as they go home, to remain fast friends of the Americans. Many of them have avowed themselves Christians. We are credibly informed, and we beg leave to mention it to your Excellency as a proof of the increasing liberality of the Japanese government, that one of them, who became a convert to Christianity and was supported, as many are, by their government, having felt himself bound in honor and conscience to acquaint the government with his change of religion, in order that his support might be withheld, if the authorities saw fit, received for answer to his communication that he was free to choose his religion for himself, and that an increase of salary would be given to him because he had been a man of uprightness. What, now, the Committee of the American Board have to request of your Excellency is this: that, if possible, the new treaty may be constructed on the plan of complete reciprocity; that Americans, as they are now allowed to lease ground; to purchase buildings, erect buildings,

warehouses and houses of worship, and to enjoy the free exercise of their religion, so also, under the full protection of the government of Japan, so long as the same privileges shall be freely conceded by our own government, may have leave (1) to travel and settle in any part of the empire; (2) to prosecute their labors as teachers of the Christian faith, wherever they may be, without hindrance thereto; (3) to employ servants, teachers, interpreters, and assistants, whenever and wherever they shall have occasion therefor; & (4) in accordance with those principles of toleration which respect all conscientious convictions, as they have never been respected in any previous age, to gather congregations and form churches without detriment or obstruction to those who shall belong to such congregations or churches. The Committee ask for no favors which may not be conceded to all Americans, and which are not granted, as a matter of course, to all Japanese resident among us ..." DS (6 signatures), DNA, RG 59, Miscellaneous Letters. See Ivan Parker Hall, *Mori Arinori* (Cambridge, Mass., 1973), pp. 195–202. On Jan. 18, Orramel H. Gulick, Kobe, Japan, had written to Nathaniel G. Clark, secretary, American Board of Foreign Missions, describing the recent arrest of Catholics near Nagasaki. ". . . It will be remembered that immediately after the deportation of Christians, two years since, the former Prime Minister of the Japanese Government, Ewaukura, the same person whose name spelled 'Iwakura,' and who is the head of the Embassy to Europe and America, stated in the presence of his fellow Ministers, to Sir Harry Parkes, Mr. De Long, and to all the representatives of the treaty powers, that the Council of State had agreed 'to stop these proceedings against the Christians, and that an officer would leave on the morrow to suspend them.' It was afterwards claimed that this promise did not apply to those who had already been arrested, and that it was only an agreement that no more Christians would be arrested in future.—Now, what becomes of that promise formally and solemnly made to the Christian powers, 'that those proceedings would be stopped'? This matter should be known by the nations and governments to whom this high toned Embassy has been sent for the exchange of compliments, and from whom they would solicit reciprocal benefits. . . ." Copy, DNA, RG 59, Miscellaneous Letters. On March 12 and April 4, Fish wrote in his diary. "Senator Buckingham & Dr Parker were at the Presidents—to present a memorial from the American Board of Commissioners for Foreign Missions respecting the revision of the Japanese Treaties   These good people, like many other good people, think that they can manage not only their own affairs & those of this Govt but those of other Governments, better than the Govermnts themselves can." "Mr Westenberg (Holland) enquires as to progress of negotiations with Japan, & reads a letter from the Dutch Minister to Japan, on the subject of extending Japanese laws & jurisdiction over all foreigners taking the same views which ~~wh~~ we have maintained that it cannot be allowed until a '*Satisfactory*' exhibition is presented of their capacity to enact & to administer properly laws calculated to protect & preserve rights of persons & of property" DLC-Hamilton Fish.

On March 2, Horace Porter wrote to Charles E. De Long, minister to Japan, who had accompanied the Iwakura mission to the U.S. "The President extends to yourself and the Japanese Embassy an invitation to attend the Metropoliten M. E. Church to morrow morning at Eleven. If this will be agreeable the President will be obliged if you will inform him at as early an hour as possible, that word may be sent to the Church authorities to provide seats." Copy, DLC-USG, II, 1.

3. On March 12, Fish wrote in his diary. "Mr Mori (Japanese Chargé) called this morning—says the Ambassadors are convinced that they have made a mistake in coming without powers to negotiate or sign a Treaty, & that they intend to send one or more of their number back for the purpose of having such Powers given either to one of the Am-

bassadors or possibly to himself—" DLC-Hamilton Fish. On March 19, Charles Hale, asst. secretary of state, wrote to Edward Everett Hale. "*Confidential* . . . The Japanese ~~kept us all hard~~ gave us all a hard day yesterday. The Secretary had promised them one hour from 3 to 4 (as those who return, leave today.) They stayed till 5.40'. . . . the Secretary and I got away in the carriage together at about half-past six. Then he had to ascertain the President's pleasure to fix an hour to ~~see~~ receive the ambassadors who return, today—and I went to communicate it in person in the Evening. It is a pity Ito goes as he is the only one of the *Ambassadors* who speaks English, and he is one of the ablest. But they need ability to explain things in Japan I dare say more than they do here. They have a queer mixture of frank simplicity and profound skill in negotiation. . . ." AL (initialed), Smith College, Northampton, Mass. Negotiations continued while two of the ambassadors returned to Japan for consultations. See letter to Hamilton Fish, July 7, 1872; Payson J. Treat, *Diplomatic Relations between the United States and Japan 1853–1895* (1932; reprinted, Gloucester, Mass., 1963), I, 426–49; Marlene J. Mayo, "The Iwakura Embassy and the Unequal Treaties, 1871–1873," Ph.D. Dissertation, Columbia University, 1961.

To Maj. Gen. John M. Schofield

Washington D. C. March 6, 1872

GEN. J. M. SCHOFIELD
COMD'G MIL. DIV. OF THE PACIFIC.
GENERAL:

The anxiety felt by the public generally, and by myself in particular, that Indian hostilities should be avoided in the future, and a policy to civilize and elevate the Indian prove successful, has induced the sending out of a commissioner to study the present condition of Indian affairs in Arizona, and, if possible, to suggest a means for accomplishing the end aimed at. Gen. Howard has been selected as the Commissioner to visit that country. It is not proposed to interfere with any military movements ordered by proper authority. On the contrary it is hoped that symapthy of views may be entertained between the Comr and the officers under your command.[1]

Indians who will not put themselves under the restraints required will have to be forced, even to the extent of making war upon them, to submit to measures that will insure security to the white settlers of the Territories. It is not proposed that all the protection shall be to the Indian, but that if they will submit to rules and limitations laid down for them then protection by Military force shall be mutual.

> Very Truly
> your obt. svt.
> U. S. GRANT

Copy, DLC-USG, II, 1. *HED*, 42-3-1, part 5, I, 545. On March 25, 1872, Maj. Gen. John M. Schofield, San Francisco, wrote to USG. "I was very glad to get your letter of March 6th about Indian affairs in Arizona. I have taken the liberty of showing it to a few of your most influential friends here and have sent a copy of it to Genl Crook. It will go far toward correcting the erroneous impression produced by the simple fact of another Commissioner being sent to Arizona, and will be of great assistance to Genl Howard in his efforts to produce a better state of feeling among the people of Arizona in respect to the policy of the Government. I have some hope of good results from Genl Howard's mission. He will at least be able to give the Interior Dept. and the Eastern public more correct information of the real state of affairs than they have had heretofore. The Apache question is one of great difficulty, but we will all do the best we can to solve it in a satisfactory manner." ALS, OFH. On Feb. 29, Secretary of the Interior Columbus Delano had written to Secretary of War William W. Belknap. "Referring to our conversation, in which allusion was made to the desire of this Department to send some suitable person to Arizona, to coöperate with the military authorities in preserving peace and inducing the Indians to settle, and remain permanently, upon reservations, I have the honor to inform you that Genl O. O. Howard has consented to accept the appointment, on condition that he may be ordered, by the War Department to go, and that he be permitted to take with him a member of his Staff, Lieut: M. C. Wilkinson. From a conversation I had with the President, last evening, on this subject, I am encouraged to hope that the Order suggested, will be given. It is very desirable that Genl Howard proceed immediately upon this mission: I beg, therefore, respectfully to invite your attention to this subject and to express the hope that he may receive orders to leave, at once, provided there be no reason to the contrary." LS, DNA, RG 94, Letters Received, 2465 1871. On March 6, AG Edward D. Townsend wrote to Schofield. "The President of the U. S. has selected Brig. General O. O. Howard, U. S. A. as an agent under the Department of the Interior to visit Arizona; and in conference with the military authorities to use every endeavor to induce the Indians there to yield to the 'peace policy,' which this administration has been endeavoring to establish, and has in many cases already succeeded in establishing. The President and Secretary of War are fully aware of the difficulties attending the proper conduct of military relations toward the Arizona Tribes, and have given heed to the reports, through your headquarters of the threatening attitude assumed by them. But the Secretary is greatly embarrassed by many circumstances, among the most prominent of which is the want of funds for conducting a war, in a section of country where it would be unusually expensive, as in Arizona. While, therefore, he is entirely in accord with yourself and General Crook in your plans, and views, he assents to the policy of sending General Howard with full powers from the Department of the Interior, to make a determined renewed effort to influence the Indians for their own good and that of the country. General Howard is not authorized to interfere with, or control in any manner the military authorities—They will of course afford him all proper aid and protection. But his duty will be to endeavor to enlist the favor of the citizens of the Territory in behalf of the Government policy, as well as to reach the Indians themselves. It is expected he will give more deliberate attention to the matter, and act more immediately in concert with General Crook than any agents who have heretofore visited Arizona—The Secretary hopes you will discover from this explanation the motives which actuate the administration; and that the visit of General Howard if unhappily productive of no other good, will serve to convince the people of Arizona, that the administration, while consistently pursuing its benovelent policy towards the Indians, is yet determined to the extent of the ability which congress places at its disposal, to restrain the savages from depredations upon the whites, while it will also discourage unjustifiable war upon the former by the latter. General Howard is fully authorized to suggest any change in the locality of the Reservations lately declared for the Indians, and is instructed to persuade them if possible to accept Reservations farther East, in New Mexico." Copy, *ibid.*, Letters Sent. On Feb. 17, Vincent Colyer, former emissary to the Apaches, Washington, D. C., had written to USG. "I have the honor to herewith tender my resignation as a member of the Board of Indian Commissioners   Permit me to say that, until yesterday, I was not aware of the precise contents of the letter of the Hon Secretary of the Interior of the 12th ultimo, although aware at the time of my resignation of the Secretaryship that some such letter had been received   I trust that this will be a sufficient apoligy for my delay in retiring from the Board   Thanking you for your kindness to me . . ." ALS, *ibid.*, RG 48, Appointment Div., Letters Received. See *PUSG*, 22, 90–91; *HED*, 42-3-1, part 5, I, 446–47, 482–83, 533–59; *CG*, 42–2, 1433–37.

On Nov. 9, 1871, Gen. William T. Sherman had written to Schofield. "I now enclose you copies of a correspondence between the Secretary of the Interior & War Department, on the subject of the policy that is to prevail in Arizona with the Apache Indians. The Secretary of War wishes you to give all the necessary orders to carry into full effect this policy, which ~~in effect~~ is the same that prevails in the Indian Country generally, viz to fix and determine (usually with the assent expressed or implied of the indians Concerned,) ~~of~~the Reservations within which they may live, and be protected by all branches of the Executive Govermt, but if they wander outside they at once become objects of suspicion liable to be attacked by the troops as hostile. The three Reservations referred to in these papers, and more particularly defined in the accompanying map seem far enough removed from the White settlements to avoid the dangers of collision of interest. At all events these Indians must have a chance to escape War, and the most natural way is to assign them homes and compel them to remain thereon. Whilst they remain on such Reservations there is an implied condition that they should not be permitted to starve, and our experience is that the Indian Bureau, is rarely supplied with the necessary money to ~~supp~~ provide food, in which event you may authorize the Commissary Dept to provide for them, being careful to confine issues only to those acting in good faith, and only for absolute wants. The Commanding officer of the nearest Military Post will be the proper person to act as the Indian Agent until the Regular Agents come provided with the necessary authority and funds to relieve them, but you may yourself, or allow General Crook to appoint these temporary Agnts, regardless of rank—The Citizens of Arizona should be publicly informed of these events, and that, the Military have the Command of the President to protect these Indians on their Reservations, and that under no pretence must they invade them except under the leadership of the Commanding officer having charge of them. The Boundaries of these Reservations should also be clearly defined, and any changes in them suggested by experience should be reported, to the end that they may be modified or changed by the highest Authority. After general notice to Indians and whites of this policy, General Crook may feel assured that whatever measures of severity he may adopt to reduce these Apaches to a peaceful & subordinate condition will be approved by the War Dept, & by the President." ALS, DNA, RG 94, Letters Received, 2465 1871. On Nov. 21, Schofield wrote to Townsend. "I have the honor to acknowledge receipt of your letter of Nov. 11th, enclosing letter of instructions from General Sherman and copies of correspondence between the War and Interior Departments on the subject of the policy that is to prevail in Arizona with the Apache Indians. I enclose herewith a copy of an order I have issued for the purpose of giving full effect to the policy of the government, according to the General's instructions, which I hope will meet the approval of both the War and Interior Departments. I have now more hope than ever before of a satisfactory solution of the Apache question, but I desire to suggest that, until this experiment is fully tried, it would be wise not to appoint any civilian Indian agents for the Apaches but to leave them under exclusive military control. If we succeed in localizing them and putting an end to hostilities, we will then be glad to relinquish their further care to the Interior Department. But strict military control of the Indians *on the reservations* is necessary to enable to effect the desired change in their habits. . . ." ALS, *ibid.*

On Dec. 7, 1871, and Feb. 6, 1872, Lt. Col. George Crook, Prescott, Arizona Territory, wrote to asst. AG, Military Div. of the Pacific, San Francisco. "Referring to General Orders No 10, Military Division of the Pacific, I would respectfully call attention to a matter that is of vital importance in carrying out its provisions. It seems that 'Cochise' with portions of his bands are reported as being on or near the 'Canada Alamosa' reservation in New Mexico. Whether he leaves the reservation for the purpose of committing depredations on this side of the line, or not, it is certain that large bands that have always operated under him and who recognize him as their chief are doing this constantly. They do not confine their movements to any particular locality, but depredate, as they have always done, when and where they please, and I have strong reasons for believing that he himself is not acting in good faith, but is simply making this reservation a convenience as heretofore. I wish therefore that this Indian, Cochise, either return to this side of the line where he belongs, and come upon some reservation to be designated, or that he be required to show the sincerity of his professions of peace, by joining such Troops as may be designated, in New Mexico or Arizona, for the purpose of following and punishing those bands, formerly under him, who still refuse to be peaceable. This chief should control his people for good as effectually as he has heretofore for bad. This is the only course which will secure a permanent peace with the Indians which have been so long under Cochises command. Copies of affidavits relative to the state of affairs at 'Canada Alamosa' reservation enclosed." "I have the honor to report that there is every reason to believe that the majority of the Indians lately being fed at Camps Grant, McDowell, and Verde, have been oscillating between these posts, drawing rations from each as most convenient, and saving such portions as will keep, for their Caches in the mountains. . . . When they left McDowell the last time (see accompanying report) then not only took some Stock, but showed their utter contempt for the troops by firing upon parties in the immediate vicinity of the post, within a few days afterwards. The late massacres on the Overland Stage route East, are nearly as complete in their details as the Wickenburg stage massacre, and after the 15th inst., I propose that they shall no longer make use of the reservations as sheltering places, but all who on that date are absent therefrom will only be received upon them again as prisoners of War. They have all been fully advised on these subjects, and instead of making preparations to remain on the reservation, have been melting the lead from old cans, picking up fragments of iron, steel and such ammunition as they could, and generally using the present truce *on our side* to render themselves more formidable than ever, and all who remain outside the reservations fully understand and want us to understand that by staying out they mean hostilities; and I have no doubt that the present cold weather has been the only obstruction in the way of their depredations being committed all over the country. At Camp Grant, Lieut. Whitman has not paid any attention to the provisions of G. O. No 10, 1871, from your Headquarters. I have instructed the Commanding Officer of the post to see that the provisions of the order are carried out, and thus if possible prevent the Indians from other posts drawing rations at Grant too, and otherwise preparing themselves for hostilities." LS and copy, *ibid.* On Feb. 13 and 22, Schofield telegraphed to Townsend. "Latest advices from Genl Crook states that the Apaches have become insolent & manifest contempt for those who have been feeding them   many have left their reservation and others seem on the eve of movement   Genl Crook is preparing for the active campaign which seems unavoidable & I hope Congress will provide them the necessary means" Telegram received (on Feb. 14), *ibid.* "Crook reports that the Apaches in large numbers have left their reservations carrying with them every thing they could steal & firing on the troops   they make no secret of their purpose to war against the whites under such circumstances the troops cannot avoid conflict with the Indians except by standing aloof and allowing them to prey upon the white settlers   It is of vital importance for Col Crook to have more specific instructions than is contained in Maj Whipples telegram this day forwarded   the fifteenth of this month was the day fixed by Col Crook for commencing operations   I presume he is now in the field with all his force   please inform as fully as you can what the wishes of the department are" Telegram received, *ibid.* On Feb. 24, Townsend wrote to Schofield. "The Presdt Secy of war & Secy of Intr have conferred upon your despatches & I am directed to say to you, An Indian War is much to be deprecated & should by all means be averted if it can possibly be done. The Indians should be induced by persuasive means, if possible, to return to their reservations or better, to go upon reservations in New Mexico where they can be better cared for. ~~They cannot~~ It must be impressed upon them that they cannot stay off the reservations & have peace   The citizens must be protected. In the movements to enforce this it must be borne in mind that the appropriations are almost exhausted and that the new appropriations are not available before July 1, 72   The Sec'y. of the Intr. will shortly send a new agent to visit the Arizona Department & co-operate with the Mily. authorities ~~to~~in inducing the Indians to remain on the reservations—~~The settlers~~" ADf (initialed), *ibid.* On Feb. 26, Schofield wrote to Townsend. ". . . It is the concurrent opinion of all officers and citizens familiar with the Apaches of Arizona that it is impossible to prevent those on reservations from raiding upon the white settlements, and the mail and freight lines, if they are permitted to absent themselves long enough for the purpose. Indeed this practice is that which has created such intense feeling among the white settlers and led to acts of savage retribution. I am satisfied there is no medium course. The Indians must be strictly confined to their reservations, and this can only be done by some such vigorous measures as I have prescribed. I have not even hoped that this could be done without the use of vigorous measures toward those bands who have been in the habit of going and coming, and preying upon the whites at pleasure. Those who have heretofore been friendly submit to the new regulations with perfect cheerfulness. It is the opinion of General Crook and so far as I know of every body else in Arizona, that the 'bad' Apaches must be subjugated by force; that they regard the operations of Mr. Colyer last summer as evidence of our weakness and recognition of their strength; that they think we are ever ready to beg for peace and willing to purchase it upon terms which they regard as enormously liberal. They are consequently arrogant, defiant and utterly insubordinate. They are determined to have their usual savage sport, in spite of the troops, this summer, and feel quite certain that another Commissioner will be sent out from Washington, with presents, to beg for peace, and to welcome them back upon the reservations whenever they find it convenient to come. They comprehend perfectly that there is an influence antagonistic, as they understand it, to that of the Army, which is always sure to come to their relief when they are hard pressed. These views apply of course to only a portion of the Apaches—those who have been in the habit of roaming at will through Arizona and Sonora and preying upon every body and every thing that comes in their way. A large proportion of the Apaches are peaceable, friendly and rather disposed to be industrious. These are perfectly content to remain under military restrictions so long as their wants are supplied. It is the worst only who desire any relaxation of restraint, and that for the worst purposes. This I repeat is the theory of those who, from residence or military service in Arizona, are most familiar with the Apache character; and it must be confessed the evidence is very decidedly in favor of its correctness. Yet I will not presume to say that the course which has been adopted by the Government may not be the wisest. The indian question in Arizona presents points of no little difficulty and embarrassment, and doubtless some which are less apparent at this distance from the seat of government than they are there. I will cheerfully do all in my power, and no doubt General Crook will do the same, to carry out the policy adopted in regard to these Indians. But I think it my duty to say that I believe the following is at least a strongly probable statement of what has been, and what must be done to settle this Arizona Indian difficulty viz: Last summer General Crook's operations had reduced the whole Apache nation to the verge of submission as prisoners of war. Had those operations been continued a few weeks longer the Apache question would have been settled once for all. General Crook's work having been interrupted in consequence of Mr. Colyer's mission, the whole question is now in substantially the same state that it was a year ago, except that the Indians have been better fed this winter than before and are better prepared for war. One vigorous campaign with sufficient means would teach the roving Apaches the necessity of submitting to the regulations prescribed for their government and would give a reasonable degree of peace to Arizona for the future, and that sooner or later this course must be adopted. I do not think a milder policy can possibly succeed. Yet if the Government is not prepared at this time, from want of funds or other cause, to carry out such a course, as I have proposed, it is better not to attempt it, but to limit the operations of the troops to giving such protection as they can give to the settlements and routes of travel. . . ." LS, *ibid.*

On April 20, John Holmes, "Camped 3 Miles West of Prescott A. T.," wrote to USG. "Not known anny better authority to write to then to you. Sir, And feeling much assured that I shall find re dress for my loss   In 1869, I came here from Nevada With hopes of haveing a oppurtunity of pleaseing Myself with a place. build a home on. While on the road to here, the Indians took my 2 horses from me, and left me on foot.   another time sence, they took overey thing I had, and killed my Companion.   up to this time, I had money to replace overey thing, and start anew. Now, that I am Satsified, the Indians will not let me live here, I made up my mind to leave, and go back to Nevada. I have made a start of 3 miles, to what called, the Burnt Ranch. Turned my horse out to feed. Cooks supper.   after eating Supper goes out to get my horse for the night, but the Indians have got him, have killed him and already eaten him. President, Sir, if there was anything, in the World that I loved it was my horse (a good horse too) that was all was left me in this world to care for, or live for. And still worse to think, that he severed a horiable death of it.   oh, if that bad man Colyer was with in gun shot of me at moment he would have been apt to got hurt. . . ." ALS, *ibid.*, RG 75, Letters Received, Arizona Superintendency.

1. On April 15, Howard, Fort McDowell, Arizona Territory, wrote to USG. "After a satisfactory interview with General Crook I have thought it advisable to write you directly. I am fully satisfied that General Crook has no other desire than to carry out your views, as expressed in the letter I bore from you to General Schofield. He is industrious, asks for no more force, believes in punishing the guilty, but is far from being sanguinary in his purposes or practice. I would ask for no better officer to work with me in carrying out what I understand to be your Indian policy. It is a difficult task to prevent thieving, and murder here, to establish peace and preserve it. The Officers, and soldiers appear very well at this Post. The Indians have left here, taking with them some horses,   They have offered to come in again upon conditions, and I am in hopes that they may yet be brought in, or sent to the Reservations proper. I am carefully studying this field, and may think differently, but my impression now is, that army, & citizens, & friendly Indians, can be brought to cooperate in bringing the nomadic tribes upon the reservations already established, or to punish those who *will* not behave," LS, DLC-John M. Schofield. See note to AG Edward D. Townsend, July 3, 1872; Howard, *My Life and Experiences Among Our Hostile Indians* (Hartford, 1907), pp. 9–11, 120–225; Martin F. Schmitt, ed., *General George Crook: His Autobiography* (Norman, Okla., 1960), pp. 167–79; John A. Carpenter, *Sword and Olive Branch: Oliver Otis Howard* (Pittsburgh, 1964), pp. 209–19; Jeanie Marion, "'As Long As the Stone Lasts' General O. O. Howard's 1872 Peace Conference," *Journal of Arizona History*, 35 (Summer, 1994), 109–40.

Proclamation

To all who shall see these Presents, Greeting:

Know Ye, That, reposing special trust and confidence in the Integrity and Ability of Brevet Major General Andrew A. Humphreys[1] of the United States Army, Professor Benjamin Pierce,[2] of Massachusetts, and Captain Daniel Ammen,[3] of the United States Navy, I do hereby appoint them jointly and severally to be Commissioners for the United States, to examine and consider all surveys, plans, proposals or suggestions of routes of communication by Canal or water connection between the Atlantic and Pacific Oceans across over or near the Isthmus connecting North and South America which have already been submitted or which may be hereafter submitted to the President of the United States, during the pendency of this appointment or which may be referred to them by the President and to report in writing their conclusions and the result of such examination to the President of the United States with their opinion as to the probable cost and practicability of each route or plan and such other matters in connection therewith as they may think proper and pertinent. And I do hereby authorize them and each of them, to execute and fulfil the duties of that appointment according to law and the instructions which they shall from time to time receive from the President, and to have and to hold the said appointment with all the powers and privileges thereunto of right appertaining unto them the said Brevet Major General Andrew A. Humphreys of the United States Army, Professor Benjamin Pierce of Massachusetts and Captain Daniel Ammen of the United States Navy, during the pleasure of the President of the United States for the time being.

Given under my hand at the City of Washington, the Thirteenth day of March, in the year of Our Lord one thousand eight hundred and seventy-two and of the Independence of the United States the Ninety-sixth.

U. S. GRANT

DS, ICHi. On Feb. 12, 1872, Simon Stevens, president, Tehuantepec Railway Co., New York City, wrote to USG. "The United States are deeply concerned in all movements aimed at the creation of new or the deflection of ancient lines of traffic and especially in those for the creation of an Interoceanic Ship canal across the American Isthmus at some point best adapted to the requirements of her commerce and to the commanding of the trade between western Europe and eastern Asia. Within the last few years numerous surveys and explorations have been made with this object in view, and reports with maps, plans and estimates of cost have been made in great detail and are now in the possession of the Government and will doubtless furnish an amount of data sufficient to enable a just comparison of the relative advantages of the proposed routes and to authorize, if not call for such an investigation. Being, in common with many other citizens of the United States, deeply interested in the questions involved, I have the honor to request that the President will constitute a Commission to be composed of five distinguished officers of high rank, viz two from the Army, two from the Navy and one from the Coast Survey of the United States, to which may be referred the reports and accompanying maps and documents of the several U. S. and other surveys and explorations of the American Isthmus, and that the Commission may be requested to make a careful and complete analysis of the same, and report whether or not such surveys and explorations determine the practicability of constructing at a reasonable cost a ship canal across the American Isthmus, and if so, what point or points are the most eligible for such a route and the most advantageous to the United States." LS, DLC-Hamilton Fish. Frederick A. Conkling, Horace Greeley, and others, New York City, signed a nearly identical petition, dated Feb. 27, addressed to USG. DS (19 signatures), DNA, RG 59, Miscellaneous Letters. On July 29,

1871, Stevens had written to USG. "Whereas the Government of the United States lately sent an Exploring Expedition to the Isthmus of Tehuantepec to ascertain if a sufficient quantity of water exists upon the Summit for the supply of an Interoceanic Ship Canal and Whereas, the results of the investigation of that Expedition, as well as the report of the Commissioners which co-operated with it on the part of the Mexican Government, are favorable to the Construction of such a canal, and Whereas, this company has received from the Mexican Government, its Decree, approved December 20th 1870, authorizing, in addition to its other privileges the Construction of a Ship, or navigable canal, across thate Isthmus of Tehuantepec, and Whereas, the line of the Railway, authorized to be constructed, was duly located in July 1870, has now to be modified in order that it shall become an auxiliary to the Canal; Therefore, this company desires, before proceeding further in the great works it has undertaken, to obtain such information relative to the great artificial waterways which have been constructed in other countries and to procure such other information as will be beneficial to the work of locating the line of the Canal across the Isthmus of Tehuantepec, defining the mode of its construction & preparing the plans and making the necessary estimates; With this view I have, as President of this Company, resolved to form a Commission, composed of Eminent Engineers, to whom will be refered these preliminary questions; and inasmuch as the work is recognized as one, both of high National and International importance, it has seemed proper, and desirable, that an officer, of high rank of the United States Engineers should be on the Commission—I have therefore tendered the appointment to General J. G. Barnard of the US. Engineers, and have named as his coadjutors, Colonel Julius W. Adams, vice President of the American Society of Civil Engineers, and Colonel Lorenzo Perez Castro, of the Mexican Engineers, to compose that commission & to meet in London as soon as may be convenient after the 20th of August, when & where I propose to join them with Colonel J. J. Williams Engineer in chief of the Company   I have the honor to request that General Barnard may be detailed by the Honorable Secretary of War for this duty and that he may receive the necessary orders to enable him to visit such places as the Commission may deem requisite" LS, *ibid.*, RG 77, Letters Received.

In [*March*], 1872, Elias Baker, Meriden, N. H., wrote to USG. "'Individual man is weak but associated man builds railroads and telegraphs the ocean' as I said before I have been looking over the Surveys of Charles H. Davis, Trautwine and others for a ship canal across the Isthmus of Panama and I am of the same opinion that I was when I wrote to you before that the Nicaragua route is *the* route the most feasaible one entering at Greytown following up the San Juan River to Lake Nicaragua Leon or Managua then by the map there seems to be a valley from lake Leon to the Bay of Fonseca or Conchagua which would make a *splendid* harbour according to the map   In my opinion this is the best route on the continent—I trust that you and your agents will give this route a thorough survey as I see by the papers that an expedition has been sent for this purpose . . . The Napipi route is short but a chain of mountains intervene   I have no doubt that that *could* be done with the Treasury of a nation to back it   But so far as I can see the Nicaragua route is the best . . ." AL (incomplete, docketed March 26), *ibid.*, RG 45, Miscellaneous Letters Received. See *SED*, 39-1-62. On Feb. 21, Oliver W. Easton, San Francisco, had written to USG. "By telegraph we learn that [a] new expedition is projected to Nicaragua to find if possible at that point, what the numerous [a]ttempts at the Isthmus of Panama have failed to find, a feasible practicable route for an Interoceanic Ship Canal   Having given several years [o]f study to the Topographical Geological and Orographical features of this problem am fully prepared to say that in 60 days time I can solve this problem successfully in connection with the Isthmus of Panama, upon the basis laid down by Admiral C H Davis then Superentndent—Naval Observatory at Washington in his report to Congress in Session '66 . . ." ALS, DNA, RG 45, Miscellaneous Letters Received. Easton sought unsuccessfully to be appointed geologist to the expedition. On Oct. 19, E. R. Dodge, Brooklyn, wrote to USG. "Hearing of an expedition now being fitted out for Surveying in Nicaragua, I write to see if you can appoint me to some office in the expedition. I am in my (19) nineteenth year, and out of employment at present. If there is no place vacant, I would like to get in some of the legations, in *some* foreign country. . . ." AL, *ibid.*

On May 10, Charles N. Riotte, U.S. minister, Managua, had written to Secretary of State Hamilton Fish. "I have the honor of advising you that Commander Chester Hatfield, commanding United States interoceanic canal exploring expedition, arrived here yesterday, and is staying with me at the Legation. Today at 12 O'cl. M, by appointment, I presented him to Pres. Quadra, who, together with two of his Ministers, received him with the utmost cordiality, conversed with him through my instrumentality for over half an hour and sent this evening the military band to serenade him. I was happy to learn from him that the work is going on already successfully, one party being engaged in the survey of the delta of the San Juan River, another one upon the traject Sapoa River—Salinas Bay (the Belly line) and a third one upon Col. Childs' line (Las Lajas—Brito). The sanitary condition of all the members of the expedition is excellent, not one of them being so much as unwell. Captain Hatfield seems quite sanguine of success in finding within the territory of this Republic not only a feasible but a good and not over difficult line for an interoceanic canal and he urged strongly upon me to suggest to our Government to at once enter into a contract with this Government, the ratification whereof might be deferred until any additional articles or stipulations, meeting the necessities evolved in the consecution of the exploration, had been incorporated. . . ." ALS, *ibid.*, RG 59, Diplomatic Despatches, Nicaragua. On July 16, Fish endorsed this letter. "Instruct Minister to inform Dept on what terms the contract he recommends may be made—he must be cautious in his investigation, & avoid any committal of this Govt" AE, *ibid.* See *PUSG*, 22, 197; Speech, Aug. 16, 1872; Jackson Crowell, "The United States and a Central American Canal, 1869–1877," *Hispanic American Historical Review*, XLIX, 1 (Feb., 1969), 27–52.

On July 21, 1873, Symphorien L. J. Quercy, Montgiscard, France, wrote to USG expressing interest in canal design and requesting data related to constructing a canal across the isthmus of Panama. ALS (in French), DNA, RG 45, Letters Received from the President; translation, *ibid.*

On Jan. 23, 1874, Secretary of the Navy George M. Robeson wrote to USG. "The reports of the different surveys of inter-oceanic canal-routes between the Atlantic and Pacific oceans, and the estimates relating to proposed constructions, are now completed, with the exception of actually finishing up a part of the maps of the Nicaraguan survey. The information therefore, is in such a form as to be presentable to the Commissioners whom you were pleased to appoint, to examine and report upon that subject, and awaits such action as you may consider advisable, or may direct." LS, *ibid.* On Jan. 27, Orville E. Babcock wrote to Robeson directing transmittal of all information to the commissioners. LS, *ibid.* On Feb. 7, 1876, Andrew A. Humphreys, Daniel Ammen, and Carlile P. Patterson, who had replaced Benjamin Peirce, wrote to USG. "The Commissioners appointed by you to consider the subject of communication by canal between the waters of the Atlantic and Pacific oceans across, over or near the Isthmus connecting North and South America, have the honor, after a long, careful and minute study of the several surveys of the various routes across the continent, unanimously to report:—1st—That the route known as the 'Nicaragua route,' beginning on the Atlantic side at or near Greytown, running by canal to the San Juan river; thence following its left bank to the mouth of the San Carlos river, at which point slack-water navigation of the San Juan river begins, and by the aid of three short canals of an aggregate length of 3.5 miles, reaches Lake Nicaragua; from thence across the Lake and through the valleys of the Rio del Medio and the Rio Grande to what is known as the port of Brito on the Pacific coast, possesses, both for the construction and maintenance of a canal, greater advantages, and offers fewer difficulties from engineering, commercial and economic points of view, than any one of the other routes shown to be practicable by surveys sufficiently in detail to enable a judgment to be formed of their relative merits, . . ." DS, *ibid.*, RG 59, Miscellaneous Letters. See *SED*, 46-1-15.

1. See *PUSG*, 10, 433–34; *ibid.*, 16, 262.
2. Born in 1809 in Salem, Mass., Benjamin Peirce taught mathematics, natural philosophy, and astronomy at Harvard and was appointed supt., U.S. Coast Survey, in 1867. On Nov. 30, 1874, Peirce, Cambridge, wrote to USG. "Since my retirement from the superintendency of the Coast Survey, I have found it expedient to confine myself strictly to purely scientific work. I, therefore, very respectfully request to be relieved from further service as a commissioner upon the interoceanic canals." ALS, DNA, RG 59, Letters of Resignation and Declination. USG endorsed this letter. "Accept resignation and appoint Capt Patterson of the Coast Survey" AE (undated), *ibid.* Patterson, born in 1816, had replaced Peirce in Feb., 1874, as supt., U.S. Coast Survey. On Dec. 24, USG formally appointed him to the commission to study canal routes. Copy, *ibid.*, General Records.
3. See *PUSG*, 10, 133–34; Daniel Ammen, *The Old Navy and The New* (Philadelphia, 1891), p. 463. On Feb. 6, 1872, Ammen, Washington, D. C., had written to USG. "Enclosed is the photograph that I mentioned and that I beg to present. As an instantaneous picture it has great merits besides setting aside all doubts of the truthfulness of the effect that a torpedo is capable of producing." ALS, ICHi. On Dec. 8, 1871, USG had nominated Ammen as chief, Bureau of Navigation; on May 6, 1872, he nominated Ammen for promotion to commodore. On Nov. 7, Robeson wrote to USG. "I have the honor to submit, herewith, for your signature the appointment of Commodore Daniel Ammen as Acting Chief of the Bureau of Ordnance during the temporary absence of Rear Admiral A. L. Case." Copy, DNA, RG 45, Letters Sent to the President.

To Roscoe Conkling

Washington D. C. March 13th *1872*

MY DEAR SENATOR:

This will introduce to you Hon. Geo. H. Yeaman, now a resident of New York City, formerly from Ky. and representative of this Govt. to Denmark. Mr. Yeaman will explain the nature of his business. I can only say that while I abstan from recommending for office persons who others must be responsible for, I entertain a high opinion of Mr. Yeamans ~~as to his~~ fitness, in every way, for the place he asks.

Very Truly Yours
U. S. GRANT

HON. ROSCOE CONKLING U. S. S.

ALS, DLC-Roscoe Conkling. Born in 1829 in Ky., George H. Yeaman practiced law before serving as U.S. Representative from Ky. (1861–65) and minister to Denmark (1865–70). See *PUSG*, 19, 162–63; *ibid.*, 20, 69. On March 14, 1872, Yeaman, New York City, wrote to USG. "Sincerely thanking you for your kindness to me when I saw you at Washington yesterday, I now desire to say that later, on the same day, I saw Mr Atty Genl Williams; and after a pleasant and obliging interview with him, I adopted his suggestion of seeing Judge Davis, the U. S. District Atty here. There is needed more working force in his office, and another assistant or Depty Atto could be very well employed; but there is a difficulty as to the amount at present allowed for the expenses of the office. This obstacle is probably under the control of the Atty Genl, and in writing to him about it, I have taken the liberty to suggest that you would cheerfully approve a plan of enlarging the force and providing for its payment. This position would suit me, *would be a very great advantage to me*, would be no sinecure, but one of great labor, which I am more than willing to perform. I hope I have too much respect for you, and the Attorney General, and for myself, to ask that any place be created for my benefit. But this work is *needed*, and as it would go so far in *securing* my own professional future, I am sure you will excuse me in asking for it your favorable consideration, should the matter come before you." ALS, DNA, RG 60, Letters from the President.

To William Elrod

———

Washington D. C. March 15th *1872.*

DEAR ELROD:

I shall not be able to send you any horses from here this Spring; but I think you had better purchase a pair of large strong mares. They could be put to the horse and still do full work this year. If all should breed then next year more would have to be bought; but it is not likely that all will.—I think it advisable now to stop sheep raising. Sell all the lambs in the Spring and Summer, and as the old sheep find a market as Mutton sell them. I would have none on hand for next Winter. If you can not raise the money to buy two mares I will spare you $200 00/100 towards it.

Have you used any lime yet? I am anxious to see the effect particularly on clover.[1] Clover hay should never be fed to horses particularly horses that have any work or exercise. It is very bad for the wind. Hence I hope you have enough timothy for the horses and will get it in as fast as possible.

You may if you think proper take out license and stand young Hambletonian,[2] on the farm, this Spring. I would not have him go to exceed fifteen or twenty mares, besides mine, and would set the price at $30 00 the season for this year, pasturage extra. If, when you begin to sell in the Spring & Summer, have any spare cash put it into additional cows. I think too you should raise a few acres of carrots & turnips to feed to cattle and colts in the Winter.

I think it doubtful whither I shall get to the farm this year though I may for a day or two in June.—Will you have fruit this year?

AL (signature clipped), Illinois Historical Survey, University of Illinois, Urbana, Ill.

1. See *PUSG*, 21, 94; *ibid.*, 22, 237.
2. See *ibid.*, pp. 97, 196.

To C. F. Daniels

————

[*Washington, D. C., March 20, 1872*]
. . . In regard to the arrangement made for the children of Gen. Rawlins it is entirely satisfactory to me . . . After the adjournment of Congress I will visit them and either provide for them . . . or resume engagements for them where they are. In regard to the purchase of Mr. Daniel's interest in the real estate left by Gen. Rawlins, I doubt the propriety of it under present arrangement . . . when I proposed this purchase I was under the supposition that I could make Mrs. Daniels no allowance except the one fourth of what was left by Gen. Rawlins himself. To purchase it I would be obliged to sell registered bonds to get the money . . . also to pay the balance due on the Danbury house . . . I would suggest that the Washington

house be not sold now. It would not bring $10,000.00 at this time but I think will enhance in value . . . next Summer I will make a final arrangement but in the mean time will remit regularly one fourth of the income of Gen. Rawlin's estate to Mrs. Daniels . . .

Charles Hamilton Auction No. 41, April 23, 1970, no. 88. On March 2, 1872, William S. Hillyer "and Mr. C. F. Daniels, of New York, whose recent marriage to the widow of Gen. Rawlins, was announced, had interviews with the President." *Washington Evening Star*, March 2, 1872. See *PUSG*, 22, 372; letter to William S. Hillyer, July 12, 1872; letters to William D. Rawlins, June 22, July 30, 1872.

To William S. Hillyer

Washington D. C. March 27th 1872

DEAR HILLYER;

Your letter of the 20th inst. making inquiry as to the time you left the rear of Vicksburg, in 1863, was duly received. If I were to answer from memory I would say that as soon as you heard of the investment of Vicksburg you left Memphis, or wherever you were at the time, to join me; that you remained ~~there~~ with me a few days or a week and then left and did not return again during the siege. But I would not pretend to say that my memory on this subject is ~~entirely~~ accurate.

I find on examination a letter to Gen. Hurlbut, dated, "Near Vicksburg, May 31st 1863"[1] of which you were made the bearer. ~~of~~ ~~f~~From ~~which~~ this I infer that you left, to go North, on that day. I have no recollection of your returning afterward. If however anything can be found in the records to shew that you did return again you certainly are entitled to it and shall have the benefit of it.

Yours Truly
U. S. GRANT

ALS, ICarbS. On March 20, 1872, William S. Hillyer, New York City, had written to USG. "I do not wish to annoy you about personal matters. But Captain Dunn seems to have done me gross injustice in stating that I left the army on the taking effect of my resignation   Of course you know that he was mistaken. I do not suppose that you have any data to fix the exact time at which I left, but you will remember it was after I returned from Memphis with the troops you sent me for—Those reinforcements arrived about the middle of June—From letters to my wife and a letter I have from Dana in which he regrets not being able to bid me good bye and stating that he encloses me a small amount of money which he owed me, I think the day I left was the 21 or 22 of June. Danas letter is dated June 22—I wrote today to Judge Dunn recommending that his son should see you or some one else knowing the facts and satisfy himself that he was mistaken and correct his testimony—I might readily be mistaken as to whether I knew Leet at Vicksburg but I could not be mistaken as to my being there during the greater part of the siege. If Dunn does not call on you I submit to your own sense of right and propriety whether you can write me a letter to be submitted to the Committee stating the facts in this case   I have brought all this annoyance on myself by ~~attempting to vindicate~~ my vindication of you from the effort of your enemies to show complicity on your part in these Custom House transactions—" ALS, USG 3. On June 30, 1863, Hillyer, St. Louis, had written to USG that he had been home for ten days. *PUSG*, 8, 219–20.

Beginning in Jan., 1872, the Senate Committee on Investigation and Retrenchment probed alleged fraud and influence-peddling in the New York City Customhouse. A principal target was the firm of Leet and Stocking, run by former USG aide George K. Leet, which held the so-called general-order business, a lucrative concession to warehouse imported goods. See *PUSG*, 10, 161; *ibid.*, 19, 157–58; *ibid.*, 22, 243–44. On Feb. 3, 1872, Hillyer testified before the committee that he had met USG in Jan. and discussed Leet and the customhouse. *SRC*, 42-2-227, II, 449–50. On March 6, Orville E. Babcock testified that Leet and Wilbur F. Stocking had visited USG in Feb. *Ibid.*, III, 197–98. On Feb. 2, Hillyer had testified. "My first acquaintance with Mr. Leet was when he was detailed as clerk at headquarters, at Vicksburgh. I was then a member of General Grant's staff. . . . I left on the fall of Vicksburgh. . . . Q. What rank had Mr. Leet when he was assigned as a clerk at General Grant's headquarters at Vicksburgh, in 1863?—A. He was a clerk detailed from a Chicago battery. I think he was detailed on the recommendation of General Porter. . . ." *Ibid.*, II, 428. On March 4, Horace Porter disputed Hillyer's account. ". . . The siege of Vicksburgh lasted during the months of May and June, and the surrender occurred on the 4th of July. General Hillyer had left the Army and gone to Saint Louis to practice law, I believe. He resigned on the 15th of May, 1863. . . . He may have come back there, and paid a visit to the Army in the fall; but that is not the most important part of it. Here is the order detailing Colonel Leet first from the Chicago battery as a clerk to General Grant's headquarters, dated on the 28th of July, nearly a month after Vicksburgh was captured. Colonel Leet had never seen anybody connected with General Grant's headquarters—General Hillyer or anybody else—until he arrived on the 29th of July, 1863; he was serving in his battery until then. It is a known fact that Colonel Leet never saw General Hillyer until a year or two afterward, when he met him in Washington City. . . . General Hillyer, in his testimony, says, '. . . I think he was detailed on the recommendation of General Porter.' I was serving in the Army of the Cumberland, and never saw anybody connected with those headquarters until several months afterward. General Hillyer was not there, Colonel Leet was not there, and I was not there." *Ibid.*, III, 131. On [March 9], Hillyer wrote to U.S. Senator William A. Buckingham of Conn., committee chairman. ". . . Months before the siege of Vicksburg began, in compliance with a promise made to my family and an express understanding with Gen. Grant I announced my intention of retiring from the army upon the fall of Vicksburg . . . at the special request of Gen. Grant and in conformity with my own preferences I remained with him until the latter part of June. . . . I know nothing of the date of Mr. Leet's detail. I know that it was not customary at our headquarters to make a permanent detail of clerks until their fitness was tested by trial. . . . The date of the detail therefore cited by Gen. Porter is no evidence to my mind that that was the time Mr. Leet joined headquarters, on the contrary it is evidence that he was at headquarters on trial for some time before—. . . I stated in my testimony that my impression was that Leet was detailed upon the recommendation of Gen. *Parker*—If the stenographers reported me as saying Gen. Porter they misunderstood me—I never saw or heard of Gen. Porter until he joined the staff of Gen. Grant during the latter part of the war—. . ." Copy (undated), Hillyer Papers, ViU. *SRC*, 42-2-227, II, 467–68. On March 13, Capt. William M. Dunn, Jr., assigned to USG's hd. qrs. at about the end of May, 1863, testified that Hillyer had already left hd. qrs. "Q. Have you understood that some importance was attached to the contradiction of General Hillyer's testimony in regard to when he saw Leet at headquarters?—A. No, sir; Colonel Hillyer makes his statement, and I thought—I knew it was—at least I thought it was not so. I am certain it was not so. I told General Porter I would make it. I do not know anything about whether there was any importance attached to it or not. Q. And he thought you had better make it?—A. I suppose that was it. Q. Do you know who communicated your wish to the committee?—A. No, sir; I do not. Q. You did not yourself?—A. No, sir. Q. The general got the dates for you from the Army records, as you have given them here from that memorandum?—A. Yes, sir. Q. General Porter, I mean, got that for you?—A. Well, I asked him to get them, sir." *Ibid.*, III, 294–95. On March 21, John Riggin, Jr., St. Louis, wrote to Hillyer. "Yours of Mch 16th was recd yesterday ev'g—You say that an issue has been raised as to whether you were 'with the army at Vicksburg after the 16th May' and you want my testimony on the point.—I cannot recollect the exact date of yr leaving the army then investing Vicksburg, but my recollection is, that you left there about the Middle of June 1863. . . ." ALS, Hillyer Papers, ViU.

On Feb. 2, Hillyer had also testified concerning Porter and John P. Lindsay, a New York City importer. ". . . I recollect very well meeting General Porter one day, when my office was on the corner of John street and Broadway, and Mr. Lindsay's office was on John street—I recollect meeting General Porter one day in New York, on John Street, and suggesting to him that—having known him, of course, in the Army—that he should make my office his headquarters when he came to New York when he wanted to do any writing; and he said to me that Mr. Lindsay had been kind enough to offer his office, and he had been making that his headquarters. . . ." *SRC*, 42-2-227, II, 427. On Feb. 7, Hillyer wrote to Porter. "Your letter of the 5th reached me yesterday and I should have answered it immediately, but I had no report to refer to—I mean of my testimony—My recollection of the conversation is that in response to my offer, you replied 'Thank you I have already accepted Mr Lindsays proposition to make his store my headquarters.' Now after such a lapse of time I would not pretend to swear as to the exact language, but ~~that~~ the impression left on my mind, that you assigned as a reason for declining my offer that you had previously accepted a similar proposition made to you by Mr Lindsay is too strong to admit of any alteration of my testimony on that point. The impression is further strengthened in my mind, because ~~shortly after the Mudgett affair some one I think it was~~ Mr Mudgett stated to me that you had said you did'nt know Lindsay, to which I replied that he had misunderstood you for that you had told me what I have above stated. You can see therefore that ~~impropriety~~ I cannot modify my testimony. I dont think I spoke of a 'place of business.' If so I meant nothing more, than a place where you received and wrote your letters or met parties by appointment ~~or rendezvoused~~ or made your general stopping place when ~~down town~~ in the city and away from your hotel   My explanation as to 'headquarters' is so ample that I cannot be misunderstood [*on that point.*]" ADfS, Hillyer Papers, ViU. On March 4, Porter testified on this matter. "Q. . . . Did you ever make any effort to induce a witness who had testified here to correct or change a portion of his testimony?—A. Yes, sir; one; not induced him to. I communicated the circumstances to him, thinking that he was in error, and, by reference to circumstances, could correct himself. That was General Hillyer. I didn't think he had any object in making the mis-statement at all, and that upon reflecting upon it he could correct it. . . . Q. Did you write to him at once about it, sir?—A. At once. I thought it was a mere error of his memory, and that he would be very glad to correct it when the circumstances were recalled. . . . It was to the mere form of expression, I will say, used in regard to going in Lindsay's store. He testified that I said I was going to make Lindsay's store my headquarters and my place of business. As I never had any business to transact in New York, and was there but a short space of time, I thanked him for his invitation to his office, which was on the same street— John street—and said, 'I am going down to Lindsay's store.'" *SRC*, 42-2-227, III, 155–56. See Elsie Porter Mende, *An American Soldier and Diplomat: Horace Porter* (New York, 1927), pp. 117–22.

On Feb. 13, Secretary of State Hamilton Fish had written in his diary. "President directs Secr of Treasury & Atty Genl to give instructions for the prosecution of all persons in New York, who have testified that they gave bribes to Govt Officials, or against whom evidence has been given that they either gave such bribes, or being Officials received them—Williams enquires whether it may be made public that the order for such prosecutions has been given—I suggest that the announcement of such order may be misconstrued by opponents of the Administration, if if made public pending the investigation, as an intimidation to witnesses further to appear & testify—The General Order business is referred to. Robeson asks if orders have been given for its discontinuance—Boutwell says 'yes'—& the plan of a substitute is under consideration—Robeson & Williams think the public should know that it has been determined to discontinue, or modify the system—" DLC-Hamilton Fish.

On Feb. 16, Grenville M. Dodge, Washington, D. C., had written to "General," presumably USG. "*Private* . . . I enclose a letter with extract that I want you to read—I have no fear myself in relation to the question but Mr 'Carnagies' views are worth knowing; You know he makes most of the negotiations Financially for the Penn. Central and its interests   I go to Penn. New York and East tonight   I intended to see you, and say breifly what I must write for want of time   1st I am satisfied that you should make a *written order* signed by yourself—that can be used and published doing away—with the 'Gen Ordr buisness' in New York. I say this as I have been told you propose to change or abolish it 2d Seems to me. we should get, from the from the defensive policy now being used in the county and in *Congress* to the *aggressive*   The raid against 'Grant' is now a raid upon the Republican party and if some *Strong Senator* who has not taken part so far—should sound the *alarm*—and place all these investigations and attacks where they belong—and show that they are for purpose of defeating the party—the response would astonish all—3d I feel anxious about 'Illinois'   If *Logan* could be induced to sound the alarm of danger to the party and in that way come heartily in with us it would do great good—I know the difficulties in this but it is worth an effort—and I think you should make it yourself— With the orginization we are makeing and this help from you seems to me we would be safe—" ALS, CSmH. On Feb. 23, Edwin D. Morgan, New York City, wrote to USG. "I think it of the utmost importance, that what is known as the 'General Order business,' should be changed without any delay. I cannot doubt but we all agree, that the change is *soon* to be made. But situated as we are with Elections in two states immediately before us, both of which must of necessity be close, *time* is every thing." ALS, OFH. Both Morgan, as chairman, and Dodge served on the Republican National Executive Committee.

    1. *PUSG*, 8, 297.

To George W. Childs

————

Washington D. C. Apl. 1st *1872.*

My Dear Mr. Childs,

    This will introduce to you Col. Holloway,[1] of the Ia. Journal, a brother-in-law ~~of~~to Govr. Morton. The Col. will explain to you the nature of his business. I give him this letter of introduction not knowing but you may know newspaper men who wish to invest in the line of their business when they are in all human probability certain of a fair return for their investment, with a prospect, owing to the rapid growth of Indianapolis, and the state of Ia, of a very large return.

Yours Truly
U. S. Grant

ALS, PHi.

    On May 20, 1871, Horace Porter telegraphed to William R. Holloway, postmaster, Indianapolis. "Letter of 10th very important. Get all the facts and figures about that paper, and come here for consultation. Postmaster General will authorize your trip." Copy, DLC-USG, II, 5. On April 23, Sept. 30, and Oct. 28, 1872, Porter wrote to Holloway. "I am very glad to hear what you say. I hope you have seen your way clear by this time to obtain the control of the paper. It will do immense good. Let us know the result of your negotiations." "Your letter of the 16th is recd. Delano is attending to Ohio. The State has been neglected heretofore, but our folks are now actively at work. Eakin has been appointed in Hoyt's place and I hope this may be of great service to you. In haste, . . ." "Yours of 19th instant received. You covered yourselves all over with glory a foot thick in Indiana, and I have no doubt can double up considerably in November. We are trying to push matters as hard as possible to make the victory in November overwhelming. Only one more week to work." LS, InHi.

    On July 23, 1875, Holloway wrote to "General," presumably USG. "Senator Morton has written the Secy of War, requesting the use of a piece of artillery from the arsenal at this place, for a Soldiers re-union at Rockville Ia. during the first week in Sept. Also, the use of some damaged tents from the U. S. Q. M. Depot at Jeffersonville   The Senator is anxious they should at least have the cannon, for the reason that Gov. Hendricks refused to let them have one belonging to the State—but would like the tents also—They will be responsible for them—Please aid us in this matter and oblige . . ." ALS, DNA, RG 156, Letters Received.

    1. Born in 1836 in Richmond, Ind., Holloway learned printing from his father, worked on the *Cincinnati Times* (1852–57), read law with Oliver P. Morton, was Morton's private secretary (1861), served as Ind. state printer (1861–63), and purchased the *Indianapolis Journal* (1864). Holloway had married Eliza Burbank (1858), a sister of Morton's wife. On April 2, 1869, USG nominated Holloway as postmaster, Indianapolis.

    Holloway later wrote an inaccurate unpublished account (InHi), "How Gen. Grant came to be An Indiana Soldier," that portrays Morton as offering USG a commission as col. of an Ind. regt.

Speech

[*April 5, 1872*]

Admiral: I heartily reciprocate the wish which you express on behalf of your sovereign and of the Spanish government, that the friendly relations which have always existed between the United States and Spain may not only be maintained unbroken, but may daily be strengthened. It is hoped that your disposition to promote this policy may lead to results not yet accomplished, but which for some time past have earnestly been sought by this government in its diplomatic relations with yours. You may be assured that for this purpose I shall co-operate by all the means which may be in my power.

Washington Evening Star, April 5, 1872. USG spoke after Admiral José Polo de Bernabé presented his credentials as Spanish minister. *Ibid.*

    On April 19, USG wrote to King Amadeo I of Spain. "I have received the letter which Your Majesty was pleased to address to me on the 17th of February last, acquainting me that you had judged it expedient to terminate the functions of Señor Don Mauricio Lopez Roberts, who has for some time resided in the United States as Your Majesty's Envoy Extraordinary and Minister Plenipotentiary. I consider it but justice to Mr Lopez Roberts to state to Your Majesty that during his residence in this country, his language and conduct have been such as to meet the unqualified approbation of this Government. On his return to Spain, he will, I am persuaded, assure Your Majesty of the invariable friendship of the United States and of their sincere desire to preserve and strengthen the harmony and good understanding so happily subsisting between the two countries. . . ." Copy, DNA, RG 84, Spain, Instructions. On March 12, Alvey A. Adee, U.S. chargé d'affaires *ad interim*, Madrid, had written to Secretary of State Hamilton Fish. "*Confidential.* . . . On receiving this morning your telegram of the 11th instant, as reported in my No 111 of this day's date, I deemed that it would not be inopportune to communicate its import, confidentially to the Minister of State, . . . Mr deBlas heard me with much attention and then replied that as the motives of Mr Roberts' recall were not apparent and might naturally be miscon-

strued, he saw no objection to acquainting me, frankly although with reserve, with the
circumstances with gave rise to the present purpose of the Government, in order that I
might communicate them to you, with equal frankness and reserve. A brother cf the
Spanish Minister at Washington, holding an official capacity at the Havana, had unfortu-
nately taken a prominent part in the late horrible affair of the young students, which he
added parenthetically he could not sufficiently condemn, and that it had been found necessary to dismiss him (*separarle*) from his post; and that apart from the odium and want
of confidence which this stain upon the family name had, perhaps unjustly but at any rate
unavoidably, reflected upon the Minister at Washington, to the detriment of his influence,
the latter had resented the course of the central government in regard to his brother, thus
impairing its relations with him to an extent which seemed to call for his removal. The
respect, however, which the government had always entertained for Mr. Roberts' high
personal character demanded that his recall should be effected with all delicacy, for which
reason it was advisable to put forth no ostensible motive for terminating his mission. . . .
In conclusion Mr deBlas repeated with great earnestness his assurances and personal
pledge that the sole object that animated the Spanish Government in its intercourse with
us was to strengthen the bonds of friendship, already he trusted indissoluble, that had ever
existed between the two countries; and that Admiral Polo had been selected to contribute
towards this end, from his great ability—which without being invidious he would state to
be far superior to that of Mr Roberts,—and from the certainty felt by himself and his col-
leagues that no fitter man could be found for so high a post. In the course of his remarks
Mr deBlas spoke freely and at some length respecting the late deplorable occurrences at
the Havana, and at my request gave me permission to inform you, in confidence, that the
pardon of the surviving students had been prepared in the Colonial office and now only
awaited His Majesty's signature, and that the most prominent delinquents, among them
the Second Chief of the Island, commanding at the Havana at the time, and the brother of
Mr Roberts, would be brought to trial for their complicity in the crime. . . ." ALS, *ibid.*,
RG 59, Diplomatic Despatches, Spain. On March 29, Fish read this letter to the cabinet.
Hamilton Fish diary, DLC-Hamilton Fish.

On April 11 and 18, Fish wrote in his diary. "Admrl Polo de Barnabe, (Spanish
Minst) desires to have the duty on manufactured Corks, reduced or abolished, says that
there is a large trade, & that numerous petitions for the reduction or abolishing of the
duty, from various parts of the U. S. are being forwarded to Congress—wishes to know
what he can do to advance the object. A conversation ensues on the general relations of
the two Govts & I complain of the delays & non performance of promises made for the reformation of abuses in Cuba, & for the absence of redress, or delay in obtaining redress for
injuries to our Citizens." "Admiral Polo (Spain) is instructed to say that his Govt will loy-
ally & earnestly' take up the case of Dr Houard, with the view to a full & candid examination: that all the facts & papers in connection therewith have been ordered from Havana
to Madrid, & should arrive there within about a week. I say, that while glad to hear this,
there are also a large number of Cases, of embargoed Estates, & of complaint of violation
of personal rights, which have frequently been brought to the notice of his predecessor,
but remain unsatisfied—that it would be very agreeable to this Govt to have them attended to as they were tending to make difficulties between the two Govts & were embarrassing to us, & a worry to our Citizens—He disclaimed knowledge as to them saying
that his recent arrival, & being away from the Legation, he had not had time to familiar-
ize himself with the details of the past negotiations—. . ." *Ibid.* See *PUSG*, 22, 314; letter
to King Amadeo I, April 19, 1872.

To Charles W. Ford

Washington, D. C. Apl. 6th 1872.

DEAR FORD:

I am in receipt of your letter in which you say that Dr. Steinhaur [1] demands large damages from the rail-road for running through his place. I am sorry to hear this for I know no land that will be benefited more by the road than his. Probably Judge Long [2] might have influence with him. For my own part I proposed, as soon as the road was spoken of, to give the right of way whereever my land was touched, both on the farm and near Carondelet, and to give five acres off the farm for a depot. Since that, at the suggestion of Mr Hays, I agreed to make the depot grounds twenty acres but to be sold in lots one half the proceeds to come to me, the other to go to the road. You are at liberty to state this to Mr. Pierce. [3]

Your Truly
U. S. GRANT

ALS, DLC-USG. On March 27 and April 18, 1872, the *Missouri Democrat* reported: "THE Carondelet branch of the Pacific railroad will be commenced in about sixty days. Some of the land owners have put their figures too high for the company, and condemnation will be resorted to." "THE Carondelet branch of the Pacific railroad is to start from Kirkwood, after all. Steps have been taken for the condemnation of the right of way. The rails will cross the Gravois road at President Grant's farm." See also *Missouri Democrat*, May 30, 1872; *St. Louis Globe*, Aug. 18, 1872.

On May 31, USG telegraphed to Charles W. Ford, St. Louis. "You can sell the Stone." Telegram received (at 12:48 P.M.), DLC-USG.

On June 4, 1873, Ford telegraphed to USG. "I find it will cost about three hundred and fifty dollars to grade the track   it is probably the best I can do,   shall I go ahead with it,   answer by telegraph as the men are ready to go to work." Telegram received, *ibid.*

On May 27, 1874, Levi P. Luckey wrote to John F. Long, St. Louis. "Your letter of the 25th is received and the President directs me to reply and say that he has given no one permission to quarry stone, and for you to do in the case exactly as if the land was your own. That you can, if you choose, make a lease to these parties if they are taking stone, if they pay a good liberal rent. Do in the matter just as you would for yourself. I mailed yesterday the 'acceptance' in the case of the road." Copy, *ibid.*, II, 2.

1. H. F. Steinhauer owned property near USG's farm. *PUSG*, 1, 44; *ibid.*, 10, 122.
2. For Long, *ibid.*, 1, 345.
3. Francis B. Hayes, president, and Andrew Peirce, gen. manager, Atlantic & Pacific Railroad, directed the Carondelet Branch of the Missouri Pacific Railroad following a con-

solidation. See *New York Times*, Sept. 21, 1884, Dec. 29, 1891; Ross L. Muir and Carl J. White, *Over the Long Term ... The Story of J. & W. Seligman & Co.* (New York, 1964), p. 101.

Endorsement

——————

Respectfully refered to the Sec. of War. If Washington & Jefferson College come up to the requirements of law I see no reason why an officer of the Army may not be detailed for that institution. If the particular applicant who I understand is very much desired by the faculty, can be spared without violations of the rules established for making these selections, I do not object to his apt.

U. S. GRANT

APL. 13TH /72

AES, DNA, RG 94, ACP, 5158 1871. Written on a letter of Feb. 9, 1872, from 2nd Lt. Daniel C. Pearson, 2nd Cav., Fort Fred Steele, Wyoming Territory, to Secretary of the Treasury George S. Boutwell. "I have the honor of recalling myself to your notice as one who received at your hands an appointment to the United States Mil'y Acad'y. The Rev. Dr. Hays, President of the Washington & Jefferson College of Pennsylvania, has tendered me a Professorship at that institution, which can be held by an army officer in conformity with an act of Congress. I am encouraged by your former kindness to take the liberty of asking your assistance for Dr. Hays, thro' whom this letter is transmitted, in obtaining from President Grant my appointment to the College. Trusting that my request is is not misplaced and that it does not presume too much upon your time and attention, . . ." ALS, *ibid.* On April 15, Secretary of War William W. Belknap wrote to U.S. Senator John Scott of Pa. that ". . . it is impossible to comply with the wishes of Lieut Pearson as it is only two years since he graduated, and the Department has invariably decided that no officer should be detailed for such duty who has not had four years experience in active service." Copy, *ibid.*, RG 107, Letters Sent, Military Affairs.

Order

——————

Washington April 16. 1872

The Advisory Board of the civil service having completed the grouping contemplated by the rules already adopted have recommended ~~the following~~ certain provisions for carrying the rules into effect.

The recommendations as herewith published are approved and the provisions will be enforced as rapidly as the proper arrangements can be made. and the 13th of the Rules adopted on the 19 day of December last is amended to read as ~~now set forth~~ published herewith

The utmost fidelity and diligence will be expected of all officers in every branch of the public service. Political assessments, as they are called, have been forbidden within the various Departments, and, while the right of all persons in official position to take part in politics is acknowledged, and the elective franchise is recognized as a high trust to be discharged by all entitled to its exercise whether in the employment of the Government or in private life, honesty and efficiency, not political activity, will determine the tenure of office.

U. S. Grant

DfS, DLC-Hamilton Fish; DS, DLC-Executive Orders. *SED*, 43-1-53, 100. On March 15 and 22, Secretary of State Hamilton Fish wrote in his diary. "The second report of the Civil Service Commission had been issued to the Members of the Cabinet, & we had been requested to come prepared to day to make suggestions &c—there was very little discussion, but the President took the copies, on which some of us had made memoranda—" "Geo. W. Curtis spent the Evenig before last with me, on the subject of his regulations for the Civil Service & left with me a draft for an Executive Order which he desires to have issued, promulgating the regulations—He had shewn it to the President—I brought it up in Cabinet—there was some discussion, the prevailing sentiment appearing to be that if any order be issued it be confined to a promulgation of the regulations—I stated that this excluded precisely the part which Curtis was most anxious to have in the order—he had said to me that 'there were just three words in his draft that he wished in the order' these were that 'honesty & efficiency *not political activity* will determine the tenure of Office' the three words 'not political activity' were the first to which exception was taken—(by Boutwell)—After discussion the President requested me on Tuesday to bring *two* drafts, one a simple promulgation, the other with Curtis pet idea & words—" DLC-Hamilton Fish. The draft Curtis gave to Fish, with emendations in Fish's hand, is *ibid.* On April 16, Fish wrote in his diary. "*Cabinet* All present except Delano who is represented by Cowen President signs Executive Order adopting the Civil service regulations having amended them by striking out the 5th & the 18th of the Regulations, & amended altered the 2d 3d & 7th—" *Ibid.* See *PUSG*, 22, 297–98; Ari Hoogenboom, *Outlawing the Spoils: A History of the Civil Service Reform Movement 1865–1883* (Urbana, 1961), pp. 107–10.

On April 11, 1872, George William Curtis *et al.*, Washington, D. C., wrote to USG. "Having been designated by you as an advisory board under the rules and regulations for the improvement of the Civil Service adopted on the 19th of December, 1871, we beg leave respectfully to submit the following report: The rules assume that the efficiency of the

Civil Service will be promoted by a more careful inquiry into the character and qualifications of those who are to be appointed to office. The report which accompanies the
rules states strongly the conviction that there has long been a practice, which has acquired
almost the force of an unwritten law, of appointing persons to the minor offices of the government because of what is called political service rather than of proved qualification. The
evils and the perils of this practice are recognized and deplored by the country, and have
often been forcibly stated in both houses of Congress. . . . We beg to repeat, in conclusion,
that the regulations which we have the honor to recommend are experimental; and we
shall not hesitate, in obedience to the rule, to suggest any change or modification of them
which may prove to be desirable. As the enforcement of any rules depends wholly upon
the pleasure of the President, their efficacy will be determined by the Executive purpose—a purpose which has been urgently declared, for which the support of Congress has
been asked, and which will be heartily sustained by every good citizen." Charles Eliot
Norton, ed., *Orations and Addresses of George William Curtis* (New York, 1894), II,
91–106. The Civil Service regulations as promulgated on April 16 are *ibid.*, pp. 107–16.

On Oct. 7, William A. Richardson, act. secretary of the treasury, wrote to USG. "I
have the honor to request that authority be granted this Department to use one thousand
(1.000) dollars of the appropriation for 'Promoting the Efficiency of the Civil Service,
1873' for the purpose of paying the expenses incident to the introduction of the Civil Service rules into the Customs and Independent Treasury Service, of this Department."
Copy, DNA, RG 56, Letters Sent to the President. See *U.S. Statutes at Large*, XVII, 82.

Endorsement

Respectfully refered to the Supt. of the Mil. Academy.[1] The Member of Congress from the 1st Dist. of New York has nominated
Mr. Murphy for West Point to fill the vacancy created by his dismissal. I will gladly appoint him if the legal disability under which
he lays is removed by the recommendation of the "Academic Board."

U. S. GRANT

APL. 18TH /72

AES, DNA, RG 94, Correspondence, USMA. Written on a letter of April 17, 1872, from
Paul St. Clair Murphy, Washington, D. C., to USG. "In compliance with your verbal directions, kindly given last evening through Senator Wilson, I have the honor to make application for permission to return to West Point, with the class to enter next June. I entered the Academy, upon the nomination of Hon Henry A Reeves with the Class of June,
1871, and at the Examination of January, 1872, was 'found deficient.' On the 8th of February last I was renominated by Hon Dwight Townsend. Owing to my age, I will not be
eligible unless I can enter this year, and I would feel very grateful Sir, if you would assist
me to return to the Academy with the class of June next. West Point has been my ambi-

tion for years, and my failure has been a bitter disappointment to me." ALS, *ibid.* On
Jan. 6, 1873, USG nominated Murphy as 2nd lt., U.S. Marine Corps. See *New York Times*,
Nov. 10, 1931.

1. Col. Thomas H. Ruger. See *PUSG*, 21, 318–19.

To J. Russell Jones

Washington. D. C. Apl. 18th 1872

Dear Jones:

I take great pleasure in introducing to you Mr. John Hoey, of
New York City, in the Winter, but of Summers a neighbor of mine
at Long Branch, N. J. Mr Hoey, with his family, visit Europe this
Summer on a tour of pleasure but expect to return in the Fall in time
to go for the Cincinnati Convention nominees as Sheridan went for
Jubel Early in the Valley of Va

Any attention shown Mr Hoey and his family will be duly appreciated by them and by me.

Very Truly Yours,
U. S. Grant

ALS, Marshall B. Coyne, Washington, D. C. See *PUSG*, 20, 259.
On Feb. 19, 1872, USG wrote to J. Russell Jones, U.S. minister, Brussels. "I take pleasure in introducing to you Mrs: Davenport, the wife of Captain Davenport of the Navy,
who purposes spending some time in Brussels. I commend Mrs: Davenport to your kind
attentions during her sojourn near you." Copy, DLC–USG, II, 1.

To House of Representatives

To the House of Representatives

In answer to the resolution of the House of Representatives of
the 25th of January last I have the following accompanied by the report of the Attorney General to whom the resolution was referred.

Representations having been made to me that in certain portions of South Carolina a condition of lawlessness and terror ex-

isted, I requested the then Attorney General, Akerman, to visit that State, and, after personal examination to report to me the facts in relation to the subject. On the 16th of October last, he addressed me a communication from South Carolina, in which he stated that in the counties of Spartanburg, York, Chester, Union, Laurens,[1] Newberry, Fairfield, Lancaster and Chesterfield, there were combinations for the purposes of preventing the free political action of citizens who were friendly to the Constitution and Government of the United States and of depriving the emancipated class of the equal protection of the laws. "These combinations embrace at least two thirds of the active white men of those counties, and have the sympathy and countenance of a majority of the other third. They are connected with similar combinations in other counties and States, and no doubt are part of a grand system of criminal associations pervading most of the Southern States. The members are bound to obedience and secrecy by oaths which they are taught to regard as of higher obligation than the lawful oaths taken before civil magistrates. They are organized and armed. They effect their objects by personal violence, often extending to murder. They terrify witnesses. They control juries in the State courts, and, sometimes in the courts of the United States. Systematic perjury is one of the means by which prosecutions of the members are defeated. From information given by officers of the State and of the United States and by credible private citizens, I am justified in affirming that the instances of criminal violence perpetrated by these combinations within the last twelve months in the above named counties could be reckoned by thousands".[2]

I received information of a similar import from various other sources, among which were the Joint Select Committee of Congress upon Southern outrages, the officers of the State, the military officers of the United States on duty in South Carolina, the United States Attorney[3] and Marshal[4] and other civil officers of the Government, repentant and abjuring members of those unlawful organizations, persons specially employed by the Department of Justice to detect crimes against the United States, and from other credible persons.

Most if not all of this information, except what I derived from the Attorney General, came to me orally, and was to the effect that said counties were under the sway of powerful combinations popularly known as "Ku Klux Klans", the objects of which were, by force and terror to prevent all political action not in accord with the views of the members, to deprive colored citizens of the right to bear arms and of the right to a free ballot, to suppress schools in which colored children were taught, and to reduce the colored people to a condition closely akin to that of slavery; that these combinations were organized and armed, and had rendered the local law ineffectual to protect the classes whom they desired to oppress, that they had perpetrated many murders and hundreds of crimes of minor degree, all of which were unpunished and that witnesses could not safely testify against them unless the more active members were placed under restraint.

U S GRANT

EXECUTIVE MANSION
APRIL 19, 1872

Copy, DNA, RG 130, Messages to Congress. *HED*, 42-2-268. On Jan. 25, 1872, the House of Representatives passed a resolution asking USG for the information "upon which he acted in exercising the power conferred upon him by the third and fourth sections of the act of Congress, approved April 20. 1871, entitled 'An act to inforce the provisions of the fourteenth amendment to the Constitution of the United States, and for other purposes'. . ." D, DNA, RG 60, Letters from the President. On the same day, U.S. Representative James B. Beck of Ky. offered an unsuccessful substitute resolution restricting the request for information to counties in S. C. where *habeas corpus* had been suspended. *CG*, 42–2, 594–99. See *PUSG*, 22, 200–201. On April 2, 1872, Secretary of State Hamilton Fish wrote in his diary. "Attorney General produces resolution of the House of Reps requesting of the President the information on which he took certain action with regard to the Ku Klux in South Carolina—I express the idea that the House has no right to call upon the President for the motives leading to his independent Executive Action, & suggest that if it be thought advisable to answer there should be some reservation, or protest of the rights of the Executive—& of the absence of right to call for such information—Delano quite earnestly agrees with me—the question seems to be a new one to Williams   Boutwell is indifferent on the question—thinks the information that will accompany the answer will be politically beneficial—Robeson inclines to reserving the right of the Executive not very strongly—Belknap & Creswell express no opinion—" DLC-Hamilton Fish. On April 19, Attorney Gen. George H. Williams wrote to USG transmitting statistics on arrests and trials in response to the House resolution. Copy, DNA, RG 60, Letters Sent to Executive Officers. On the same day, the House referred USG's message to the Joint Select Committee on the Condition of the Southern States. *CG*, 42–2, 2593. See *HED*, 42-2-268.

On Jan. 14, John C. Selvidge, former 1st lt., 2nd Tenn. (1861–63), Kingston, Tenn., had written to USG. "It has becom my Painfull Duty to apply to you as the Chief Justice of the fedral Goverment to assist me in Having the civil Law Executed: On ~~the~~ the night of the 28th of May in Garrard County Kentucky my House was broken into by a pack of Outlaws, numbering 46 men (of whome I. knew 27) and I. was taken from my House with the intention of assasination of which they thought they had Done.   they left me laying on the Ground for Dead.   they inflicted Several wounds on me with Pistoles and Sabres and their Charges against me was for Beeing a Fedral Officer in the Supression of the Rebelion   I. heard no Oather Charge than I. was *dm* Obolitionist and they Did not allow any Republicans to Stay there. I got a guard to Stay with me till I got able to travil   I. left with the intention of Returnig to Louisville to the proper Authority and having the Law inforced on them, but they found out I. knew a portion of them and I. have been warned by my friends that they Have watches for me on the Roads in Diferent places and have watches allso in Lousville So that I. Cannot safely Reach that place.   therefore it is a Duty I Owe to my Self and my Country to pray you as Chief Justice of the Goverment to Condicend to Send me aid to arest the party as fare as known and Delver them to the proper Authoritys in their District to answer the Charges against them   I. pray you Gave me 50 Regular Soldiers with one Comisioned Officer to go with me from Louden or Chattanooga Tenn to Lancaster Ky (Via, Lousville to obtain the proper papers) to asist me in aresting this party as fare as known and Delver them to the martial of the 8th District of Ky where they Can answer the Charge as the Law Directs . . ." ALS, DNA, RG 60, Letters from the President.

On Feb. 28, J. T. Smith, New Middleton, Tenn., wrote to USG. "It my suprise you to get a letter from me but with my undertakeing I know nothing better to do   I am teaching school   I am about 49 miles from Nashville   the kuklux ar here so badly that people ar indander of thir lives   tha whip some and kill some   tha killed a man a little while ago tha have left a notice for me to leave   I will not leave if tha kill me which tha are likely to d   this I can prove by 20 if you want me to do so   you do not know how badly tha tha way lay men and shoot them down   then tha can get no Justis done them   if tha go to law tha prove what tha want so yo see tha we need help worse than in the indian settlement   I mean what I say   what to do I know not   let me know what you think of it and if I can get a stats garde   some of the union men say that I can get help but I know not but I want help   I want to start four schools in here but tha tell me that tha shal not help I want and with out it schools for the Negr bust stop   some have not had schools for too years   tha burn up school houses   tha burnt six or eight here close by   write to me . . ." ALS, *ibid.*

On March 28, William S. Cheatham, Nashville, wrote to USG. "On last monday night a colored man by the name of David Jones who was charged with murdering a man by the name of Murry in this city was taken out of Jail in this city and Shot and then Dragged to the Square and a rope put a round his neck and hung until he was nearly dead and then cut down and then carried back to Jail where he died the ~~died~~ the next day—The Rebel City authorities of this city must have known that the Colored man was going to be taken out that night because it was talked about I am told all day—They the city authorities ought to have written to the military officer in charge of the united States Troops and had Troops there but nothing was done until after the Colored man was hung and had been Shot—Now Mr President I ask you in behalf of the loyal Republicans to place the State of Tennessee under Martial law and keep it under Martial law until after the Presidential election—I have given you all the facts—The Colored man Said when he was dyeing that he did not Shoot Murry—I refer you to Senator W G Brownlow and Hon Horace Maynard M C of Tennessee who know me well—The Colored man that was Shot and hung was a leading Republican and was for you for President—" ALS, *ibid.*

In a letter docketed May 29, W. D. Jenkins, Madisonville, Ky., wrote to USG. "I am a pore old afflicted man   I am as True Republican as Ever Lived   my home is in Coffee County Tenssee   I Leaves a pore afflicted wife and Daughter Behind to morne my absenc if you wil agree to protect me with soldiers I wil give you a full Detail of Clekkism & Who is the grand wizzard of the united states   they came to my hous & maid me take the oath & swore they would kill me if I Did not take the oath & then swore if I ever Betrad or told on them they would kill me sure   they have got up [— —] negrow to swear Lyes against me to my hurte & Ruin—I have I have alwais Bin a union man   I was Born a whig Raised a whige   I have never voted for a Democrat nor never wil vote for one   I wil Remain here untill I heare from you   I hav children here   I am with them   my wife at home Tucke sick   I am a miserrable man   if I tell you the whole Truth it is Deth with me unless you wil protet mee   if I had the means to pay my way I would come to see you—Tenssee should at this time Be thrown under melatery Rule . . . I hav Bin Treated offol Bad & if you wil protect me & Let me have means to come to see you I wil Repote Every thing to you in confidene   my Life is at stake   the grand wizzard have maid a mellon & a half Dollars By the Clans" ALS (undated), *ibid.*, Letters Received, Ky.

In a letter docketed Oct. 18, S. G. Ginner, Jackson, Tenn., wrote to USG. "I hope you will excuse me writing to you, but, I am a stranger in these Southern States   I am an Englishman by birth & am a Physician—&cc have lived in New York several years—and am a firm friend to your political party—For these reasons I call upon you for protection   I came to Jackson—last May, a perfect stranger in this part of the Country—I entered into the Services of a man by the name of Pendleton—a week or two after I entered his service he made overtures to me—that I could live without work if I wished to do so   I asked him how.   he told me that he was a Captain over a Band of men—, that he was in fact a Klu Klux Klan   I refused to join any such thing & told him that I had been to long in the North—to sympathize with the South—or to join any of the orders,   from this time he set upon me to do me all the injury he could   he nearly killed me with work—and when I asked him to let me go he told me it would be at my pereil—he told me that if I left his services untill his pleasure that my life should pay the penalty—For all this—I at last got away from him—on the 25th Sept., i. e. last month—nothing happened untill the 7th inst, when a party of his riders, entered—the Revd Mr Potts Church, one of them was drunk and came and fell down before the Altar, & we had to carry him out of the church—that same night when I was going home with my Partener a gentlemen by the name of Trevor we where led into the wood by one man by the name of Dick Jones then a party of Klu Klux Klan set upon me & my friend and we should have been murdered only the night was so dark & we where in the woods and they could not track us, so I made my escape in one direction & my *Business Parte* made his escape in another.   the lawyers & magistrate who I have consulted upon this subject are afraid to do any thing—my life is marked—and this Gang will kill us—the following are known to me to be amongst the Ring leaders   Dick Jones, Frank Bumpass, Jobe Bumpass—, Joe Lane,—this last named Joe Lane killed his own Father some time ago,   I believe they have been set upon me by my late employer—

A. G. Pendleton, who is a druggist in Jackson—General—I want you to save my life & the live of my friends—and you can only do so by bringing the Law down upon this gang of bad men,   I have marks & bruises upon me now from the strikes I got in the wood,   I dare not leave my house—even in open day—with-out being fully armed—and I am quite afraid to leave it at all after dark—by giving me your protection you will save to your cause—a good friend—and a good citizen—" ALS (undated), *ibid.*, Letters from the President.

On Jan. 18, T. G. W. McMeskin, Cedartown, Ga., wrote to USG. "For one so Humble in circumstances as Myself to presume to write to your Excellency for any other purpose, than from Shere necessity would be more than I would dare do. I have been living in this county, Ever since 1846, and am well acquainted with the citizens of this county, and to my certain knowledge there is a considerable number of its inhabitants have no more chance of Justice in the courts here, than if they did not live in a republican and free government. persons have been mobbed, and they have made efforts for protection and the Grand Jury. have, invariably thrown them out of court. I can send you affidavits from seven or eight persons that will swear positively, to the partieys that taken them out of their own house and whipped them, at midnight, but they can get no re dress here.   application has been made to every source except yourself.   outrages are always committed on the poor and ignorant, but persecution has wreaked its vengeance in other forms, on other persons that would dare sympathize openly with these oppressed people. I will not mail this letter in Cedar Town for fear it will never reach you, but kept at this office, and would bring more vengence on me without accomplishing any thing   the acting Post master. here at this place is also the acting Ordinary of this county. his disabilities have never been removed. manages to do the business of Post master in the name of H. May, an unnaturalized foreigner, and the office of Ordinary in the name of Francis. Clark a man that can scarcely write his name. This person's name is Stephen A. Borders as tiranical a rebble as lives on this continent. The papers here would have you and all others believe that the State Government was working all smoothly and that all persons can have Justice here the same as before the war, but a person that differs from them has no chance of Justice and this party in power and influence is far from being in the Majority, but there are thousands of both white and black that are affraid to be any thing else, and are compelled to go with this body of tyrants through fear.   this and some of the adjoining counties have been oppressed as much as any of the counties of South Carolina." ALS, *ibid.*

On March 19, Frank Rowlin, Rome, Ga., wrote to USG. "I take the orthity to write you this letter to in form you of the death of my Brother.   he was murdered by four men and three of them has had triel in our last court, and one of the party that was found with the watch and pistol that he had on was sentence to the prison for life, and the other two was equited and the other one will wil have his triel next call turm. I thought that I this to you to know if those that have bin loost as we dont think that thay thay have bin dealt fairly with.   if we cant have them tried again and as thay failed to prove whair thay stayed on that night of the Beastly mudering of them had homes.   as and sir as your very umble servont I will ask you as a favor if you woud healp ous to pay our expencies which it is four hundred and fifity three Dollars. I shall look for and answer just as soon as you get this. and sir I am requested by a friend of my and yours allso to ask a favor of you   his nam is Willima Johnson Col.   he was takeing up last june and put in prisson falsley and thay have had him to triel two ar three times and have fail to prove him giltly in eather one of his triels that he has had. and thay ar still repealing against him. and want to know if his triel

cant be heard so that he can get justess wright away   the last aco account he was in prisson in Taladiga Ala. Court is going on thair now but I dont know wether he will be tried
in this court ar not but pleas let me know just as soon as you get this what you will do for
me in eather case. I will be glad if you will hear bourth of these cases. as we poor col. people
cant get justess down here. that I woul write to you to see if you cant gave it to ous.   bourth
of these men was and is heard laboring men and men of good stand ing. . . . P. S. my Brothers Name is John Pierce Rowlin." ALS, *ibid.*

On April 20, Samuel G. Johnston, New York City, wrote to USG. "I notice by the
papers this morning that you have put Sevral Countys in S. C under martel law—I sus-
pose you Would put Robison Co. N. C. under martel law if the Outlaws ware not Nigroes
the Lowerys &C.   they have murderd about 60 of the best Citisens. of the Co—& Robed
them of all they had—I mearly mention this for your consideration." ALS, *ibid.* On
March 1, William Mitchell, *U.S.S. Iroquois,* Brooklyn Navy Yard, had written to USG. "I
have seen lately in the Papers A Reward for Lowerre and his Bandit Gang who infest
Robinson County North Carolina   I spent 3 Months in Robinson County trying to take
those outlaws which failed owing to the Swamp Fever   I had to give it up and go to Sea
to recruit my health   on arriving to New York for the want of means I was forced to join
the the Navy. Most Hon Sir I should once again like to raise a few men to go with me and
I confident that I can rid Robinson Co of those outlaws with a little assistance from the
Goverment in regards to small arms and amunition . . ." ALS, *ibid.* See W. McKee Evans,
To Die Game: The Story of the Lowry Band, Indian Guerrillas of Reconstruction (Baton
Rouge, 1971).

On May 1, Isabella D. Feemster, "Ridgeway Home (near) Columbus Miss," wrote
to USG. "You know that in the days when our Savior was upon earth ten Lepers were
cleansed and only one returned with a thank offering   I now come with mine   though
late I hope you will accept it and I shall not be left amongst the ungrateful   I first appealed to governor Alcorn for protection when acting under the Authority of the state in
teaching a Public Free school I was interrupted or forbidden to procede by the KuKlux   I
next appealed to you after about all the Free schools were stopped and numerous ofther
deeds were being perpetrated continually   I sent my appeal pr request to you enclosed
with a similar one by miss Tarzah A Randall (Now Mrs Brown) whose Husband and
Brotherinlaw are commissioned by the A M A. These letters were first sent to My sister
in Portland Indiana to be forwarded to you lest the enemy might intercept them if sent direct   You have granted our request and nobly defended our country by the Investigating
committee and U. S. Court and now our schools are going on without interruption   Now
I return you thanks as being the instrument under God of our deliverance from these
bloody persecutors   Mr Huggins to whom I begged you to give justice is now nobly
standing up for the right in our Legislature whether opposed by friend or foe and God has
blessed his almost Martyrdom to the good of his country   My Brother became acquainted with him this year at the legislature and pronounces him one of the choice men
of our generation   Mr Browns opinion of him is confirmed   He visited Mr Browns
school the evening before he was Ku Kluxed   O shall we not all thank God together for
this deliverance   But his arm alone can keep then down and unless he does elections will
be a farce here   We are a little Mission band here having been preserved through the
war here without one of my Fathers (Rev. S T. Feemster) church having takeng up
arms against our goverment: but those that were liable to Confederate service had to
forsake Father and Mother, Wife and children, houses and lands, for conscience sake

Our churches now have under their care 4 sabbath schools and 6 Free schools col and one white. Such is the confidence of the colored people in us that they have sent one of my brothers to the legislature another is Judge or Supervisor and two cousins justices of the peace but except in our own little band we have little association. Rebels and Kuklux have little sympathy or association with us either in Politics or religion . . . Had you not prevailed in subduing rebels by the KuKlux law God only knows what a situation of wretchedness our country would have been in . . . My Brother R. M. D Feemster our legislator has just returned from Jackson where he was sent a delegate to a state covention to nominate delegates to a national convention for your renomination ~~asto ourfill nex~~our next Presidential term also. Some whom we counted on going heart and soul with us Fear that you are not loyal to God and are trammeld with oaths to Secret Societies that will hinder you from administring Justice. I wish that I could get an honest, candid, free heartfelt expression of your sentiments on these heads; such as are truthful; and calculated to allay all fears and doubts of consciencious christians that we might use them with the brethren both north and south that we may be a united people and the enemy get not the advantage by our division . . ." ALS, DNA, RG 60, Letters from the President. See *PUSG*, 21, 336–37.

On May 12, Christian Mornhinveg, Opelousas, La., wrote to USG. "I take the liberty of addressing you these few lines, I am residing in the Town of Opelousas Parish of St Landry La. Since thirty five years I have strictly complied with the oath I have taken as a naturalized citizen. When the war broke out I was against it as much as any man could be, I had a great deal to suffer during the war. I had fifteen bales of cotton which were taken by the United States Army commanded by General Banks for which I had a receipt from Col. Pope—After the war was ended I got acquainted with Capt John Amrein who was acted as Provost Marshall in Opelousas and he advised me to have a petition made out for my cotton claim and being an officer of the United States I have complied to his request, and the petition have been forwarded by him to Hon. R. Yates—and it appears that those papers were lost with the receipt of Col. Pope of which a full statement in my last petition sent to Washington to Messrs. Chase, Hartman & Coleman Attorneys—from which I have never yet received an answer. I have sent several letters to Hon. C. B. Darrell. M. C. and through his kindness I found out that nothing had been done in regard to my cotton claim. During the time I was attending the Republican Convention in New Orleans as a delegate I received a Letter from him stating that the time for this cotton claim had expired and that a certain Bill might be passed in Congress extending more time and that it was necessary for me to prove loyalty; there were very few men who has suffered more than I; am ready for the strictest kind of examination but I had never had the occasion of being heard, my oldest son Thos L. Mornhinveg died in the Federal service La Regt commanded by Col. Culburn and by second son who had to go to Vicksburg and as soon as the place surrendered, I sent him in New Orleans where he had to go through the Confederate lines at the risk of his life. I wish your Excellency woud be so kind to give me a chance to be heard and if any thing can be proven against me I will submit to the judgment—Mr Thomas Lewis the lawyer employed here by the Government told me that I ought to have been paid long ago for my cotton claim, nothing has been done here for the loyal people My house has been marked with the Ku Klux brand, and if it had not been for several friends I have here, I would certainly been killed in the riot of October 1868. Your Excellency may judge what sufferings I have endured, hoping that your Excellency, who has not been informed of these facts may be so kind to give Justice to a

loyal citizen" ALS, DNA, RG 94, Letters Received, 2189 1872. Related papers are *ibid.*
Congress received bills concerning Mornhinveg's claim in 1872 and 1890. *CG*, 42–2,
3763; *CR*, 51–1, 2636.

1. On March 29, 1872, S. C. Senator Young J. P. Owens and Representatives Joseph
Crews, Harry McDaniel, and Griffin C. Johnson petitioned USG. "The undersigned, cit-
izens of the United States and of the State of South Carolina respectfully represent to Your
Excellency: That the first disturbance of any magnitude on account of political opinion,
which tooke place in that portion of South Carolina in which the operation of the Writ of
Habeas Corpus is now suspended, occurred at Laurens C. H. in the County of Laurens, in
October 1870, on the day next after the day of election, when a riot tooke place in which
the assailants were all Democrats and the victims all Republicans, many of the latter citizens of Laurens, C. H. and vicinity, being killed, injured or compelled to flee for their lives,
and some of those who were so compelled to flee have not been able to this day to return
to their homes. That there is every reason to believe, from facts which have since come to
light, that this riot was planned and executed by the Ku Klux Klan, and that encouraged
by their success at that time they were lead to commit those further crimes against the
laws of the United States in the persecution of citizens for their political opinions, which
have made the Ku Klux Klan infamous. That although a military Post was formerly established at Laurens C. H. in the County of Laurens, there is none there now. though a
state of terror still exists in that County and crime and persecution are increasing, so that
Republican citizens are not safe in life or property. We therefore earnestly pray Your Excellency to reestablish a Military Post at Laurens C. H., with a sufficient number of troops
to protect the citizens from persecution, and to assist in the arrest of those persons who
are now or shall hereafter be charged with violations of the laws of the United States." DS,
DNA, RG 94, Letters Received, 1817 1872. On April 10, Governor Robert Scott of S. C.
and five others endorsed this petition. "Laurens County has been one of the worst places
in the State, and many of the most active and wealthy Republicans of the County have been
driven from their homes, and their property left to the mercy of the Ku Klux. I would
therefore recommend that the request be granted." ES, *ibid.* U.S. Representatives Robert B. Elliott and Robert C. De Large of S. C. also favorably endorsed this petition. AES,
ibid. Related papers are *ibid.* See *PUSG*, 21, 257–58; *SRC*, 42-2-41, part 5, pp. 1302–25.
    2. See *PUSG*, 22, 176–78.
    3. On March 16, 1867, President Andrew Johnson nominated David T. Corbin as
U. S. attorney, S. C. On June 24, 1869, Scott wrote to USG. "I trust you will pardon me
for addressing you in relation to the judgship for this (4th) United States Circuit. I wish
to recommend for that high position Hon. D. T. Corbin, U. S. District Attorney for this
State. Mr. Corbin is in every way eminently qualified for the position. He has been in the
state since the close of the war in 1865, and has taken a very active part in the reorganization and reconstruction of the state. He was Solicitor to the Convention that framed the
new Constitution, and is now President of the State Senate. I can safely say, that to him,
more than any other man, is the new Government of the State indebted for its Constitution and laws. His legal attainments and natural ability, from personal observation, I can
testify to be of the highest order. Being a native of Vermont, and a soldier throughout the
war, for the Union, I conceive to be sufficient proof that judicial powers would be, so far
as loyalty is concerned, safe in his hands. I believe he would be an ornament to the bench
of the United States, and justify your highest confidence, therefore I hope he may receive

the appointment of U. S. Circuit Judge for this Circuit." LS, DNA, RG 60, Applications and Recommendations. On April 13, U.S. Senators Frederick A. Sawyer and Thomas J. Robertson of S. C. *et al.* wrote to USG on the same subject. DS (7 signatures), *ibid.* Related papers are *ibid.*; *ibid.*, Records Relating to Appointments. See Louis F. Post, "A 'Carpet-bagger' in South Carolina," *Journal of Negro History*, X, 1 (Jan., 1925), 15; Lou Falkner Williams, "The South Carolina Ku Klux Klan Trials and Enforcement of Federal Rights, 1871–1872," *Civil War History*, XXXIX, 1 (March, 1993), 47–66. See also Williams, *The Great South Carolina Ku Klux Klan Trials, 1871–1872* (Athens, Ga., 1996).

On March 1, 1871, Sawyer wrote to USG. "The undersigned respectfully recommends for re-appointment as United States Attorney for South Carolina, D. T. Corbin, who has filled the position for four years past with credit to himself, with fidelity to the government, and with satisfaction to the loyal citizens of the State. Major Corbin is a vigorous, upright, able lawyer, and a thoroughgoing Republican." LS, DNA, RG 60, Records Relating to Appointments. On March 21, USG nominated Corbin to continue as U.S. attorney, S. C.

On Oct. 22, [*1873*], Judge Hugh L. Bond, Richmond, wrote to USG. "I learned the other day that an effort was on foot in South Carolina for the removal of the District Atty, Mr Corbin. As this officer is one of the most able in my Circuit and a man of unquestioned integrity, I have determined to say as much to you and to ask that nothing be done in the matter till I can see you. I should be extremely sorry to lose so efficient and laborious officer without reason" ALS, *ibid.*, Letters from the President. On Dec. 15, 1875, USG renominated Corbin.

4. See *PUSG*, 22, 168.

To King Amadeo I

TO HIS MAJESTY AMADEO I. KING OF THE SPANIARDS—
GREAT AND GOOD FRIEND:

Mr. Daniel E. Sickles, who has for some time resided near the Government of Your Majesty in the character of Envoy Extraordinary and Minister Plenipotentiary of the United States, being about to return to his country, I have directed him to take leave of Your Majesty. Mr Sickles, whose standing instructions had been to cultivate with your Government relations of the closest friendship has been directed on leaving Spain to convey to Your Majesty the assurance of our sincere desire to strengthen the friendly intercourse now happily subsisting between the two Governments, and to secure to the People of both countries a continuance of the benefits resulting from that intercourse. The zeal with which he has fulfilled his former instructions leads me to hope that he will execute his last commission in a manner agreeable to Your Majesty.

Written at the City of Washington, the nineteenth day of April, in the year of our Lord One thousand eight hundred and seventy two and of the Independence of the United States of America the ninety sixth—

Your Good Friend

U. S. GRANT

Copy, DNA, RG 84, Spain, Instructions. On April 19, 1872, Secretary of State Hamilton Fish wrote to Daniel E. Sickles, minister to Spain. "Your return to resume the active duties of your mission at Madrid, affords an occasion to consider whether your prolonged official residence there, is likely to secure or to hasten the adoption of measures on the part of the Spanish Government, respecting which you have from time to time been instructed by this Department, and which are desired by this Government. I regret to say that the question has been decided in the negative. You have, under instructions from this Department, frequently pleaded for a more humane and christian mode of warfare in Cuba; but in vain, for although no Statesman in Spain denies the atrocities committed or professes to justify them and although you have been repeatedly promised that they should be stopped, it is notorious that prisoners are constantly garrotted or shot and that cruel punishments are inflicted on mere suspicion of sympathy with people struggling for liberty. You have tried most earnestly to persuade Spain to grant some amelioration of the severely despotic rule practiced in Cuba.... Had the things of which this Government has complained occurred in a remote country, we might have looked on with regret and disapproval, but in silence, they occurred, however, on our borders, in such close proximity to our Territory that their dangerous influence extended and spread within our limits, and has involved us in disagreeable consequences. And it was to Military service in this neighboring possession that Spain opened her Prisons, granting pardon to Convicts on condition of such service. Again and again did you remonstrate against this thing as offensive to American civilization and dangerous to us by reason of the facility and frequency with which these infamous characters may escape from Cuba to our shores. All of your remonstrances have been met with silence; no reply having been made to your complaints on the subject of this grievance.... Despite, however, this unsatisfactory state of the relations between the two countries, the President has no disposition to foment a rupture with Spain. On the contrary, he still hopes that the best understanding may be kept up with that Government. A letter announcing your recall and an office copy of the same, accordingly accompany this paper. You will apply for the appointment of a time to present the original, as soon as you can conveniently arrange your business with a view to your final return home. On taking leave of the Minister for Foreign Affairs, you will present Mr Adee as Chargé d'Affaires ad interim. If you should be asked whether this Government has an intention to appoint a successor to you, the answer may be that the question is and probably will remain for some time to come in suspense. It is certain, however, that no new Minister of the United States will be accredited to the Government of Spain, until we shall have reason to expect such a change in the disposition of the latter with reference to the measures above adverted to, as may lead to greater hope of their success. It is true that the

suspension of intercourse through a Minister at Madrid has, in part at least, been occasioned by a discouragement that if one of your acknowledged patriotism, sagacity and zeal
should not have entirely accomplished the objects of your Government, there would be
little occasion to hope for more favorable results from the appointment of another." Copy,
ibid., RG 59, Diplomatic Instructions, Spain. Sickles had been in the U.S. on leave.

On March 5 and April 25, Fish wrote in his diary. "President hands me a letter from
Sickles dated March 2 complaining of Articles published in World—Sun, Tribune, stating that Spain had requested his recall—He wishes me to answer it" "Admiral Polo (Spain)
by instructions—says that Genl Sickles, had made himself unacceptable to some of the persons now in power, by remarks made, & things written & by partizanship with others—
& his recall had consequently been requested.   he is instructed to ask if he is to return
Is told that Sickles will return, to present his letters of recall. I then disclaiming official
communication, but personaly & informally recapitulate the grievances of unfulfilled
promises &c on the part of Spain, & express the opinion that it scarcely seems necessary
for us to have a Minister in Madrid that should another be sent, he would have the same
difficulties & we have no assurance that he could effect any more, that it probable therefore that no successor will immediately be appointed to Sickles—I refer to the embargoed
estates of Mora, & Mueses, particularly, as cases of mistaken identity—to the refusal to
give information to Consul in Houard's case—to the delay in making regulations to enforce the decree abolishing slavery, the enlistment of Convicts—&c the imprisonment
&c of the Medical Students—& the pardon promised ~~them~~ & express the hope that it may
soon be granted" DLC-Hamilton Fish. See *PUSG*, 19, 236–37; *ibid.*, 22, 305–7; Speech,
April 5, 1872; telegram to Hamilton Fish, Dec. 20, 1873; *Foreign Relations, 1872*, pp. 551–
52, 566–76, 580–84.

On March 20, USG wrote to the House of Representatives. "I transmit herewith a
report dated the 20th inst—received from the Secretary of State, to whom was referred
the resolution of the House of Representatives of the 28th ultimo—" Copies, OFH; DNA,
RG 59, Reports to the President and Congress; *ibid.*, RG 130, Messages to Congress.
HED, 42-2-207. On the same day, Secretary of State Hamilton Fish answered a House
resolution seeking information "relative to the reindenture or reinslavement of Chinamen
in the Island of Cuba, by decrees lately issued by Captain General Valmaseda, and what
action, if any, has been taken by the Executive to prevent the extension of human slavery
contemplated by said decrees—. . ." Copy, DNA, RG 59, Reports to the President and
Congress.

On March 22, "a Grant Republican & a Captain & Vessel owner," Philadelphia, wrote
to USG. "Enclosed please find an article cut from the Philadelphia evening Telegraph   it
shows how an american citizen is treated in Cuba.   there has been thousands of other just
such cases & our government suffers such outrages to go on unnoticed.   even every
American vessel that enters this barbarous Island has to pay an unjust fine of from $25. to
$10.000. yet our government says nothing   our flag is insulted our Citizens imprisoned
& murdered without any cause or provocation & now it is time for this thing to stop
Cuba should be taken by the United States as our abuses have paid the price Spain asks
for it.   and now my Honorable President if you take active measures against Cuba you
will secure all the votes of Captains & vessel owners which will pour in a powerful vote at
your coming contest. . . ." AL, *ibid.*, Miscellaneous Letters. An enclosed article concerning Dr. John E. Houard is *ibid.* See *PUSG*, 22, 314.

On April 20, 1872, Margaret Ray, Owensboro, Ky., wrote to USG. "As your Country woman I feel I have a right to address you and ask your attention to a great wrong

being perpetrated upon your Country men & your subjects—Some weeks ago a New Orleans Boat took as deck hands from our little City two collored men   after arriving at N. O. they were offered by a Steam Ship fabulous wages to embark with them,   this ship gathered togather 100 collored freedmen and thus decoyed them to Cuba where the poor creatures were forced into slavery more terrible than of which they could ever have conceived. One of these men was a hansome mulatto man whom I reared from infancy and who feels to me more as a child than as a former slave—People seem to feel nothing can be done for the release of these men but I, woman as I am, could not fold my hands and believe this goverment in all its power and strength will stand by with folded arms and see its subjects enslaved by a power compared to ours, a mere mith, or shadow without the substance. Yea better go and take Cuba and wipe out the stain of her stolen slavery   Your American women could do that provided our men stand back in cowardice and have such wrongs perpetrated unresented by our government   If any other particulars are needed to bring this simple matter of justice before the proper authorities I am at your service—" ALS, DNA, RG 59, Miscellaneous Letters.

On Sept. 12, Joseph A. Ward, editor, *Lockport Daily Journal*, Lockport, N. Y., wrote to USG. "I send you to day copies of the Lockport daily Journal containig full accounts of the outrage on our correspondent by the Spanish authorities   It seems to us this matter should be attended to in such a manner as to teach Spain a lesson in the matter of illegal arrest of our citizens   Trusting that this matter will have immediate attention . . ." ALS, *ibid.* The enclosure, an account of the correspondent's week-long detention at San Sebastiàn, Spain, is *ibid.*

To Senate

TO THE SENATE OF THE UNITED STATES:

I transmit for the information of the Senate a report from the Secretary of State, and the copy of the Counter Case of the United States in the matter of the claims against Great Britain, as presented to the Board of Arbitration at Geneva, which accompanied it.

U. S. GRANT

WASHINGTON APRIL, 20, 1872

DS, DNA, RG 46, Presidential Messages. *SED*, 42-2-67. On April 20, 1872, Secretary of State Hamilton Fish wrote to USG transmitting a copy of the U.S. counter case, presented at Geneva on April 15. LS, DNA, RG 46, Presidential Messages. See message to Senate, Feb. 13, 1872; Endorsement, Feb. 23, 1872. On March 19, Charles Hale, asst. secretary of state, had written to Edward Everett Hale that he had advised against mentioning the indirect claims in the U.S. counter case. AL (initialed), Smith College, Northampton, Mass.

On April 15, Fish recorded in his diary a conversation with Italian minister Luigi Corti. "He says that he has a recent letter from Ct Sclopis who says he has examined the 'Alabama Cases' & papers on both sides, & thinks he understands them as far as presented—. . . I say that we wish a decision on the Indirect Claims, will be quite content that the Tribunal say that a State is not liable for the indirect or Consequential results of an accidental or unintentional failure to observe its neutral obligations—such a decision will be sufficient to meet our point of the right of the Tribunal to pass on the question, while it will quiets the apprehensions of G. B. & will not decide directly against the liability— but being a judgment in the abstract form, will not wound either Country—He expresses his self approval of such a decision as eminently desirable & as affording a solution of the difficulties—I caution him that I am speaking with him quite confidentially & privately & unofficially—still I think the substance of what I have said will go to Ct Sclopis—" DLC-Hamilton Fish.

On April 19, Fish wrote in his diary. "American Counter Case is recd & laid before the Cabinet   Schencks telegram asking if it can be laid before Parliament, & my answer (17th) & his further telegram of 18th were read & decided that the paper be communicated to Congress, & that afterward it may be laid before Parliament—Letter from Genl Banks Chr Comm For. AffrRels with copy of Mr Peters letter resolutions on the American Case, were read by me—& question raised   I is it adviseable that this Govt give any instruction or expression of opinion, to the Counsel at Geneva, or to the American Arbitrator, on the subject of the indirect claims—II If deemed adviseable, what instruction or opinion shall be expressed—Discussions followed in which the President, Boutwell, Robeson Creswell & Williams as well as myself take part—Opinion so far as expressed, seemed unanimous—I that the claims cannot be withdrawn—II that it is important to have a decision by the Tribunal, on the questions of law involved as to the liability of a State for indirect claims   III that the interests of the US are that it be decided that a state is not liable in pecuniary damages for the indirect consequences of a failure to observe its neutral obligations—Creswell suggested that the U. S. might say that they desire the tribunal to decide the question whether G. B. is liable for the indirect injuries, & consent to leave the question of damages for future arrangement between the two nations—Robeson says that strikes him favourably—Williams thinks that no award will be made on acct of the indirect injuries, & that no one expects it, or wishes it—All agree that the question be held as a diplomatic one, & not thrown before Congress—& the President therefore decides that I see Gen Banks instead of writing to him in answer to his note—& urge that the further consideration of the resolution be either withheld or delayed—or if that cannot be done that the resolution be amended, & the preambles rejected—. . . During the discussion in the Cabinet, the idea was thrown out that if England will agree that in the future no claims for indirect damages similar to those now pending shall be advanced on her part, in any case where she is belligerent & the U. S. neutrals, that the Govt might consider that as the basis for withdrawal of claims—it was not much discussed, but seemed to be recd as a possible basis for some agreement—I think it was suggested by Williams" *Ibid.* See message to Senate, May 13, 1872; *HMD*, 42-2-180.

On April 24 and 26, USG wrote to the House of Representatives. "In answer to a resolution of the 22d instant I transmit to the House of Representatives a report from the Secretary of State with the British case and papers which accompanied it—" "In answer to a Resolution of the House of Representatives of yesterday, I transmit a report from the Secretary of State and the copies of the British Counter Case and volumes of appendix to the British Case, which accompanied it" Copies, OFH; DNA, RG 59, Reports to the President and Congress; *ibid.*, RG 130, Messages to Congress. *HED*, 42-2-282, 42-2-324.

On April 2 and 3, Fish had written in his diary. "A telegram from Schenck recd yesterday in Cipher asking if 'there be objection to Brit—Govt. filing Counter Case without prejudice to their position in regard to consequential damages' was discussed—some exception was taken to a draft of a reply which I had prepared & taken with me, & read—I then prepared another while in Cabinet, which was approved as follows 'We understand the Brit. Govt is bound to file Counter Case, & that their so doing will not prejudice any position they have taken, nor affect any position of this Government—The rights of both parties will be the same after filing as before—Is the enquiry made at their request?'" "Govr Morton calls—wishes to see Granvilles last note—looks over it—probably not very carefully as he asks me what conclusions it reaches—He then shews me a draft of a resolution, expressing the opinion of the Senate that the question whether the indirect claims are within the province of the Tribunal is one for the Tribunal to decide—He asks my opinion as to the expediency of presenting the resolution—I advise against doing it at present—Explain that the British Ministry seems to fear a Parliamentary discussion, & that Granville & the Ministry have refused to produce papers, or answer interrogations, appealing to the silence of the Senate & House—that nothing had better be said until the time for putting in their Case (15 April) has passed" DLC-Hamilton Fish.

To Edward A. Perry

———

Washington, D. C. April 22d 1872.

DEAR SIR:

I regret that it will be impossible for me to accept your invitation to be present at the "Grand Soldiers Meeting" at Cooper Institute on the 26th inst: The object to raise funds for the erection of a monument to that great and patriotic soldier, Maj. Genl. Geo. H. Thomas, and "Four Thousand Union dead" who sleep in Cypress Hill Cemetery"—is one to be commended, and which commends itself to every lover of his country.

Though I cannot be ~~with~~ at your meeting please receive the enclosed check as a very slight expression of my appreciation of its object.

Very truly
Your obt: Svt:
U. S. GRANT.

EDW. A. PERRY
SEC'Y: &c. NEW YORK CITY

Copy, DLC–USG, II, 1. USG quoted from a resolution read at the meeting in New York City, postponed until May 3, 1872. *New York Times*, May 4, 1872. For Edward A. Perry, see *ibid.*, Jan. 22, 1889. See also *PUSG*, 20, 128–29.

Pardon

———

To all to whom these Presents shall come, Greeting

Whereas, on the 26th day of April, 1871, in the United States Circuit Court for the District of South Carolina, one Alfred Williams[1] and one L. S. Langley[2] were convicted of neglect of duty while acting as Commissioners of Elections, and were sentenced to be imprisoned for two years and to pay a fine of five hundred dollars each;

And whereas, their pardon is strongly recommended by Senator Robertson,[3] the Representatives in Congress from South-Carolina, Governor Scott,[4] many members of the State Legislature and others;

And whereas, half of their term of imprisonment has expired:

Now, therefore, be it known, that I, Ulysses S. Grant, President of the United States of America, in consideration of the premises, divers other good and sufficient reasons me thereunto moving, do hereby grant to the said Alfred Williams and L. S. Langley a full and unconditional pardon.

In testimony whereof, I have hereunto signed my name and caused the Seal of the United States to be affixed.

Done at the City of Washington, this Twenty-third day of April, A. D. 1872, and of the Independence of the United States the Ninety-sixth.

U. S. Grant.

Copy, DNA, RG 59, General Records. On April 13, 1872, Levi P. Luckey wrote to Attorney Gen. George H. Williams. "The President directs me to say that he desires that a pardon may be extended to Messrs. Williams and Langley, convicted of interfering with ballots in the De Large-Bowen contest, S. C., unless you have strong reasons against. The pardon can be issued on the ground of previous good conduct and the lenght of confinement already suffered." Copy, DLC–USG, II, 1. On April 19, USG pardoned Christopher Green, who had been imprisoned and fined in S. C. for "neglect of duty while acting as manager of elections, . . ." Copy, DNA, RG 59, General Records.

1. For Alfred Williams, born in 1843 in Newark, N. J., who served in the q. m. dept. and settled in Beaufort, S. C., see *New York Times*, March 31, 1881.

2. Born in Vt., Landon S. Langley, a mulatto, served in the 54th Mass. and 33rd U.S. Colored. Following his discharge, he lived in Beaufort County, S. C., taught in Freedmen's Bureau schools, and held local offices. See Thomas Holt, *Black over White: Negro Political Leadership in South Carolina during Reconstruction* (Urbana, 1977), pp. 125, 131, 218.

3. Born in 1823 in S. C., Thomas J. Robertson graduated from South Carolina College (1843) and became a planter. An avowed Unionist during the Civil War, he was elected Republican U.S. senator upon readmission of S. C. in 1868.

4. See *PUSG*, 16, 35, 196; *ibid.*, 18, 60–61; *ibid.*, 20, 248–51.

To William Elrod

———

Washington D. C.
April 23d 1872.

DEAR SIR:

In writing to you a few days ago I forgot to say that you might breed the two two year old filleys. If we were prepared to have them properly driven and exercised I would not have them bred. As it is they may as well be allowed to raise colts [—— —— —— ——].

[—— —— —— ——] Logan has [—— —— —— ——] horse that is worked and fed on clover hay will become more or less foundered. Straw is infinitely better for work horses than clover hay.

I shall send for Logan and the three year old in about two weeks.[1] Will send at the same time a fine Alderney heiffer, with calf. I am also negociating for ~~five~~ four heiffer and one bull calf, Holstein or Dutch Belted cattle, and the same of Alderney. If I succeed they probably will reach you in May. I think with that start I will stop the purchase of cattle.

WM ELROD, ESQ.

AL (signature clipped), Illinois Historical Survey, University of Illinois, Urbana, Ill. On May 3 and July 25, 1872, William Porter, Webster Groves, Mo., wrote to USG seeking appointment as consul. "... I was on your farm a week ago   The stock looked well & the work was fully up to the season. One of the calves, sired by the Holstein bull, was shipped from this place to a purchaser up the R. R. this morning. I should be most happy to meet you at Mr. Elrod's when you visit your farm next month. ..." "... In one of my botanical excursions last week I ~~passed~~ rambled over a portion of your farm, & called on Mr. Elrod. He was in the midst of harvest, but the frequent rains retarded his work, besides damaging the hay & oats. I saw little of the stock, but Mr. E. said it was all doing well. The vineyard is in fine order & the vines heavily loaded with fruit. Mr. E. was still hoping to see you this month. . . ." ALS, DNA, RG 59, Letters of Application and Recommendation. No appointment followed.

1. See *PUSG*, 22, 302.

To Charles W. Ford

———

Washington D. C.
April 23d 1872.

DEAR FORD:

Your letter of the 8th only reached me on Saturday. I shall send for the two colts in about two weeks. I am also negociating for some more Dutch Belted Cattle and Alderney. If I get them will send them out also. That will end my purchase of stock for the farm for the present. It ought soon to begin to have something to sell off of it. Another place like it would break me.

We shall soon see what the Cincinnati Convention is to come to.[1] It will be a large gathering of course, for the whole party will be there. My prediction is that the democratic party will attempt to hold out the idea that they will support the C nominees in hope of permanently dividing the Republican party, that is, of committing the bolters to their ticket, and then make a strait out nomination of their own. I believe such action will result in the withdrawl of the Cincinnati ticket just as the Fremont ticket was withdrawn in /64.[2] We shall see what we shall see however.

Yours Truly
U. S. GRANT

ALS, DLC–USG. See letter to Charles W. Ford, May 17, 1872.

1. The Liberal Republicans convened at Cincinnati on May 1, 1872. See letter to Charles W. Ford, May 2, 1872; letter to Elihu B. Washburne, May 26, 1872.
2. On Sept. 22, 1864, John C. Frémont withdrew as a Radical Democratic presidential candidate.

To Frederick Dent Grant

Washington D. C. April 28th *1872.*

DEAR FRED:

I learn from a Herald Correspondent at Alexandria, Egypt, that you propose leaving Gen. Sherman at Berlin and to travel through Scotland, England, and some other countrys and return home alone. I want you to travel through these countries but I doubt not but Gen. Sherman will go there. I think you had better stay with him until he returns. You will have a much better opportunity of seeing and profiting by your travels.

We have had two letters from Nelly.[1] She seems to be enjoying herself very much. Her travels will not be very extensive as she must stay with Mr. & Mrs. Borie and they have visited Europe so often that they will only go now to a few favorite place. You will no doubt meet her in Paris. Buck also will be in Europe by the middle of July. He will remain there eleven months.[2]

I expected when you left to write frequently to Gen. Sherman, but I have not done so. I am so constantly engaged seeing people, day and night, that I get but little time when I can write and then I feel disinclined, beside I must take that time to read up the papers. Say to Gen. Sherman that I watch his progress with great interest and pride at the cordial reception he receives every where. I am always glad to hear from him if I do not answer his letters.[3]

Your Ma and Jesse are well and send a greatdeal of love to you.[4]

Yours Affectionately

U. S. GRANT

ALS, USG 3. On June 5, Gen. William T. Sherman, Berlin, wrote to Ellen E. Sherman. ". . . Last night Fred arrived from Hamburg whither he had accompanied his Aunt Mrs Kramer who embarks today for home. He is now out hurrying up his sight seeing, as tomorrow we go to Leipzig,—and so on to Dresden, and Vienna, where I have promised our Minister Mr Jay to arrive on Monday next. I think the President will be disappointed that we do not see Bismark or the Emperor here, but I have no reason to know that by even delaying a day or two we would accomplish it. Fred on arrival got several letters from his father & Mother which he shewd me, in which he was advised to stick by me to the end of the trip—so you may tell Mrs Grant that Fred has seen his Aunt, and is perfectly well,—that we will pretty hastily run through Germany, Austria & Switzerland to Paris which we shall reach by July 4,—. . . Audenried & I got no letters here, though I advised Mr Stevens in London of our route of travel & times of arrival &c, but we will be in Vienna next Monday the 10, & suppose we shall find our letters there. I feel no uneasiness on that score, as Gen Grants letter of the 14 of May speaks of your dining with them the day before with Lizzie, and that Elly & Rachel came to hear the music. . . ." ALS, InNd. On June 7, Gen. Sherman, Dresden, again wrote to Ellen Sherman. ". . . Fred Grant who had been to Copenhagen to see his Aunt, and had accompanied her to Hamburg, where she was to embark, joined us at Berlin last Tuesday, but as we had fixed Thursday Morning to start for Vienna, via Leipzig & Dresden, he Concluded to stay a few days longer at Berlin & to overtake us at Vienna, where we will spend four or five days. He is of course perfectly well, and we left him with Mr Fish Secretary of Legation & son to Mr Hamilton Fish, Secretary of State. . . ." ALS, *ibid.*

On June 10, 2nd Lt. Frederick Dent Grant, Berlin, wrote to Gen. Sherman. "I write to you to say I think it will be better for me to go down the Rhine than to see Vienna so I shall leave here tonight for Brussels via of Frankfort   I shall stay in Brussels but a short time then go & see the Washburne's in Homburg then to Paris where I shall either meet Nellie or go & meet her ~~when~~ in Geneva & stay there until I can join you again   Mr Fish has been very kind and I have been able to see every thing here in Berlin   Hoping you & Col Audenried are both well and enjoying your selves very much, &c, &c, &c . . ." ALS, DLC-William T. Sherman. On June 13, Gen. Sherman, Vienna, wrote to Ellen Sherman. ". . . I notice by the Newspaper slip that you enclose for Audenried, that the papers make the most of Prince Fred—He is a good natured fellow, but cares for little. He went to see his Aunt at Copenhagen—& joined me at Berlin; but asked to stay a few days more, and at the time he was to join me, he wrote that he would go to Paris to see Nellie, and would rejoin me at Geneva, or Paris. Of course I go on my course utterly regardless of him, and dont want any one to find fault with General Grant for sending him with me, as I know Mrs Grant did it, and of course she did it as a mother, thinking herself very smart to catch the chance. . . ." ALS, InNd. On July 7, Gen. Sherman, Paris, again wrote to Ellen Sherman. ". . . Fred Grant has gone home—He is a good fellow and really feels the taunts of the newspapers, and child like thinks he can stop them by removing the cause—but the newspaper scribblers will laugh at his innocence. The truth dont enter into their calculation at all. . . ." ALS, *ibid.* See letter to Horace Porter, Dec. 1, 1872; M. A. DeWolfe Howe, ed., *Home Letters of General Sherman* (New York, 1909), pp. 381–82; *Julia Grant,* p. 181.

1. On April 6, USG had written to "Dear Sir." "My daughter sailing for Europe on Wednesday last, the 3d inst. from New York City, I requested my son, Ulysses, to meet her there at that date; hence his absence from Harvard on the 2d & 3d." ALS, IHi. See letter to Jesse Root Grant, June 2, 1872.

2. See letter to Robert C. Schenck, July 5, 1872.

3. See *PUSG,* 22, 357–58. On April 24, Sherman, Sevastopol, wrote to USG. "I hope Fred has kept you advised of matters most interesting to himself, though I fear he has not, and I have so large a list of private correspondents that I cannot possibly undertake to supply his omissions. He is perfectly well, and will profit much by his experience and observations on this trip. In the son of Mr Curtin who joined us at Constantinople, he finds a companion of congenial tastes, and he is now off [— —] with him so that I must tell you of some thing [. . . .] of which I would rather that he should write himself. On reaching Constantinople we learned that we were to be the gu[e]sts of the Sultan, and on arrival [w]e were taken on shore by the splendid caiques, and from the landing in the carriage of

the Sultan to a house prepared for us. We soon found our Minister Mr. Boker who said we must submit with the best grace possible, and that he would arrange for our presentation. This occurred the day after our arrival, on which occasion his Majesty met us at the foot of the Grand stairway, (a mark of extraordinary distinction—) when he took Fred as the honored guest, and treated him as a Prince of the first magnitude. He placed Carriages and servants at our disposal, entertained us at a State breakfast, and in a thousand ways did honor to us, but on all occasions giving Fred the preference much to the chagrin of my aid, Colonel Audenried. I confess I was relieved, as it lessened my personal obligation, as I construed his purpose to be to do honor to you through your Son. I cannot recite his man[y ac]ts of special favor, but on our inten[ded] departure East in the Regular packet, [h]e sent his Master of Ceremonies Hamde-Bey to ask us to postpone for a few days, as he desired to see us further. At the third & final interview he placed his own yacht at our disposal, and we had no alternative but to accept, and on Sunday last, accompanied by Mr Curtin and son, we embarked in the Gorgeous Steamer 'Sultanish', and as we steamed past the iron clad fleet o[f] 13 splendid Ships, anchored off the Palace in the Bo[sp]horous, every ship was dressed in her co[lo]rs, the American Flag at the Main, and the Flag Ship saluted us with 21 guns. This was a complimnt to our Country and not to me.—The whole affair was one of the most magnificent displays ever seen in that Great Harbor.—We arrived here yesterday, and in writing a note to the Captain Izzett Bey, I said I would report the fact to you that a suitable acknowledgment should be made.—We paid in Constantinople to the servants, to the Carriages and barges, about what our visit would have cost us in the best of hotels: and on our arrival here we paid the steward and servants what would have paid our passage in the Regular Steamer, but this does not lessen the compliment paid our Country through us, by the Sultan of Turkey. If you think proper I ask you to mention to the Turkish Minister at Washington the fact that I have written to you on the subject, and if you would write or cause to be written some general recognition of the politeness, I believe it will be a source of gratification to the Sultan. He has a hard task. He inh[er]its a past that he cannot ignore, and [he] is surrounded by flatterers who concea[l] all that is unpleasant, but he does [se]em to desire to put Turkey in harm[on]y with the rest of Civilized poeple—Religion seems free, and I saw American Schools in progress, without religious tests or proscriptions. Telegraphs and Railroads are encouraged, and the improvements are steady and gradual. I was also told that during our Civil War, the Sultan would never allow a Rebel privateer to have even refuge in one of his Ports, and to us he expressed the greatest admiration of our poeple. Though we never can have any political interest or connection with Turkey, and though I would much have preferred not to receive any favors, yet having been [. . . . .] in that unhappy [— — —] like to make suitable acknowledgements. Fred is now in, and promises to write fully from here, tomorrow, or the day after." ALS (mutilated), USG 3.

On May 23, Gen. Sherman, St. Petersburg, again wrote to USG. "We reached St Petersburg, all well this morning, Mr Curtin having preceded us two days from Moscow. At Moscow I got a letter from Mr Cramer saying that Mrs C would leave for home about the end of May. I had Fred to telegraph him for the exact day and his answer is June 1—so Fred must cut short his visit here, and hurry to Copenhagen, fo[r] it takes 4½ days to reach there   He is now out with young Mr Curtin, to draw some money, an[d] to make the necessary arrangemts for departure tomorrow. He may have to go by Berlin, as the steamers on the Baltic have no[t] yet begun their regular trips. Mr Curtin and our Consul here will do all that is possible to enable him to make the trip alone, for I cannot make this detour, without spoiling my own trip. I want to see Cronstadt and other objects

here and at Warsaw, and Fred can join us again at Berlin or Vienna, though he now feels inclined to hurry on from Copenhagen to Paris to see Nellie. I have fixed the 4th of July as the earliest day for reaching Paris, and hope to sail for home from Liverpool, about the end of August, so as to reach home by the time Mrs Sherman returns from her summer Qrs. We certainly have had a most interesting and instructive trip, seeing much, & hearing much—but the greatest advantage will be that hereafter we can understand history, and events as they transpire. Expenses in Russia are heavy, & this cause may force us to hurry, for spite of disclaimers I am treated as a Commandg General, and Fred as a sort of Prince. Hotel charges & Railway charges, are made to correspond. Fred is in perfect health, one of the best tempered fellows I ever saw, but I scold him sometimes for neglecting opportunities, and for not writing home as he should though he insists that he has done so.—I have so many correspondents that I cannot afford to suppliment his neglect, but when he comes home, I feel sure he will delight his mother, if not his father by his narratives and experiences—Mrs Sherman and my children often write of your visits to them, and I assure you it has been to them and me a real cause of satisfaction. I notice of course the Political Complications of the day, and fear to speak my mind, further than to assure you of my sympathy for the annoyances that must try your patience, and my hearty desire that by the practice of that patience, you may in the future, as you have in the past surmount all difficulties real or fancied. Present me kindly to Mrs Grant, . . ."
ALS, Nellie C. Rothwell, La Jolla, Calif. See Rachel Sherman Thorndike, ed., *The Sherman Letters* . . . (New York, 1894), pp. 337–38.

4. On April 10, USG had telegraphed to William W. Smith, Washington, Pa. "Will not you Emma and the children come and spend a week with us   we are all alone now" Telegram received, Washington County Historical Society, Washington, Pa.

To George S. Boutwell

[*April 29, 1872*]

Will the Secretary of the Treasury please see Col. O'Brian, with a committee of workingmen from New York City. I have stated to them that all employees of the Government are entitled to the benefits of the eight hour law so long as it stands on the statute books. I refer you to the committee for the grounds of the complaints.

U. S. GRANT.

Pittsburgh Commercial, April 30, 1872. On May 8, 1872, "The committee of workingmen from New York who recently called on the President in relation to the alleged evasion of the eight hour law, in the work on the New York post office, yesterday called on Secretary Boutwell in relation to the matter, and presented a card of reference on the subject given them by the President. Mr. Rankin, assistant supervising architect of the Treasury, was of the opinion that the present mode of labor on government buildings was 'clearly an evasion of the law,' and stated at once to the chairman of the committee that 'the right thing would be done at once in the premises.' Secretary Boutwell assured the gentlemen that orders would be immediately sent to New York to have the eight hour law enforced on the new post office and custom house work. The committee then called at the White House, took leave of the President thanked him for his action in the matter, and last evening took the train for New York. The President has directed an executive order to be prepared which shall reiterate what he said in a former order, viz: that 'the eight hour law must be enforced.'" *Washington Evening Star*, May 9, 1872. See Proclamation, May 11, 1872.

On May 1, David L. Smith and two others, Richmond, had written to USG. "We the undersigned Committee representing the interest of the Stone-cutters now employed on the U. S. new State Department Stone of said building being dressed near Richmond Va Have through Hon' N. P. Banks presented a Petition (Signed by over two-hundred Granite-cutters employed on the works) To the Hon Hamilton Fish Sec State Supposing him to be the propper person to address, Praying that the benefit of the Eight-hour-law be extended to us   This Petition being presented April 18nth 1872 April 23 we sent a note to Genl Banks to know if he could give any information regarding it but as yet have recieved no reply   So we trust by placing the matter in the hands of your Excellency That you will deal with us, we feel confident according to the Eight Hour *Law* as you have done with the men employed on Government Work of South Carolina & New York   Full particulars stated in said petition   Hoping to hear soon from you . . ." D, DNA, RG 60, Letters from the President.

On the same day, Albert E. Redstone, Washington, D. C., wrote to USG. "When it becomes necessary to make a last appeal—the Laboring men and the moral portion of the Communities feel that they have a friend in *you*—and you in position to hear and dicide I thank you in behalf of the Labor Organizations of which I am authorized representative for your answer in favor of the Eight hour Law. I also ask that you will read the inclosed printed slip, the contents of which I believe to be *true*, *know* the most of it is correctly stated and ask you to insist upon John Q. Adams Esq. & Mr. N. Collins being reinstated upon [M]are Island Navy Yard the first as foreman Laborer—the latter as Foreman S[p]ar Maker—and further that Capt T. P. Wilson than whom none did better service for the country be [a]ppointed Foreman Caulker for [th]e said yard—These men are the g[e]ntlemen referred to in the printed matter as having done service for [th]e Country—and are men of influence [a]nd *your friends*; reliable   The way that navy yards has [be]en handled by Mr. Coghlan is [a] disgrace to the civilization of [t]he Age—and country" ALS, *ibid.*, RG 45, Miscellaneous Letters Received. The enclosed clipping alleging that John M. Coghlan had replaced workers for supporting USG and Republicans is *ibid.* On March 29, F. W. Cushing *et al.*, Vallejo, Calif., had petitioned USG. "We the undersigned Officers Farragut Post No 4 G. A. R. would respectfully present to you our grievances, and earnestly [pr]ay that an effectual remedy may be applied—This Post is one of the largest in this [*Dep*]t and is mostly composed of mechanics and laboring men who have served their time at the various trades in Shipbuilding, and while we all have fought under the Stars and Stripes and helped to save this Union—we now ask you that we may be allowed to still serve the Government in whatever capacity we are fitted for at the Mare Island Navy Yard. The present officers and heads of Departments seem to be determined to proscribe all members of the G. A. R and every discharge that has been made of late they have violated Paragraph 1263 of the Naval Regulations also Circular of Jan 1st 1872 from the Navy Department. We think sir that men who served under [o]ur respected President and the gallant Generals [of] our Armies on the land and under the [la]mented Farragut on the sea, ought to [h]ave at least an equal show with those [w]ho remained at home and had steady [e]mployment at good wages. We earnestly [r]equest that the Secretary of the Navy may be [i]nstructed to issue an order that will secure us work, thereby enabling us to provide for ourselves & families—aid and assist the Widows & orphans of our deceased comrades." DS (10 signatures), *ibid.*

On July 11, Secretary of War William W. Belknap wrote to USG. "I have the honor to return, herewith, the letter of Timothy T. Manning & others, Gatekeepers, at Spring-field Armory, complaining to the President that they are not allowed the benefit of the 'Eight Hour Law'—which letter was referred to me by your endorsement of the 5th ulto. The J. A. General reports that no sufficient reason is perceived why these gate keepers should not be treated as coming within the designation of 'laborers' or 'workmen', as these terms are used in the Act of June 25. 1868, and the President's proclamation of May 19. ~~1869~~ But, the Chief of Ord. submits the reports of Major Benton, Comd'g. the Armory, showing that these men were employed under a special agreement at their own instance, by which, having been allowed, for some time previous the ten hour rate ($1.65) for eight hours work, they engaged to work as before, eleven hours, for 1.75 and the privilege of sleeping in the Gatehouse after midnight. In this view of the case, they would appear to be entitled to no more than they receive." Copy, *ibid.*, RG 107, Letters Sent, Military Affairs.

On Dec. 20, 1871, the House of Representatives had passed a bill authorizing the president to appoint a commission to study concerns involving labor and capital. *CG*, 42–1, 561, 42–2, 102–5, 217–28, 251–58. On Dec. 9, 1872, the Senate declined to consider the bill. *Ibid.*, 42–3, 75.

On Dec. 22, 1871, John Halbert, New York City, had written to USG. "I am instructed by the Committee of the International Workingmens Association to recommend to you the following men for the Commission on 'Labor investigation' for your selection. Theo' H. Banks Delegate to the Federal Council of the I. W. A. and President of the Grand Lodge of Painters. Henry Drury of the I. W. A. Boston and Gustave Pierrot also of the I. W. A. St Louis. They are men who understand the 'Labor Question' thoroughly and therefore the most fitted for that position." ALS, DNA, RG 59, Letters of Application and Recommendation. See *New York Times*, Dec. 16, 1871.

On Dec. 26, Walter Gussenhoven, "Empl in the U. P. R. R. Car Departement," Omaha, had written to USG. "I glean out of the papers that there is to be nominated Three Commissioners on the Labor Capital question without regards to Politicts and one to be nominated out of the laboring population, It is a boone and we want to make the most of it Give me the nomination, my Claims to it are That I am fully up, to the question in all its phases by seventeen years study and contact with it as a laborer in the principal parts of Europe as well as in the United States further that I will serve my fellow workmen without Renumeration or Pay, just as well as I went for Grand with head heart and wallet in 68 Never would my name have been heartt of in conection with office but this question is my hobby my Ideas are not extreme Emancipation of labor through Education the latter through Legislation. I did not forget red tape and did sent to Hon John Taffe a petition in forma the only excuse for these lines are that I know you will not hurt us working men knowingly and that would be the case by nominating a man who is not aquainted with the question in all its bearings." ALS, DNA, RG 59, Letters of Application and Recommendation.

On the same day, Philip Weitzel, Osage City, Kan., wrote to USG. "I see Congress has passed a Law authorizeing you to appoint a Commission on Labor reform Being a practical mechanic I most respectfully ask a place on that commission. . . . in support of my claim and also my apology for asking is that I have been a life long friend of your's and a Republican from principle I have never asked for an office but once and that was from

Genl Schenck asking an appointment as mail route Agent and did not get it   I served in the U. S. Army from the begining untill the close of the war and if you will examine the papers in the P. O. Dept you will find me reccommend for an appointment by the most prominent men of the 3d Congressional Dist in Ohio for the appointment above alluded to. Please take my name into favourable consideration and I will be very much obliged" ALS, *ibid.*

On Dec. 29, Charles Tompkins, Henrietta, N. Y., wrote to USG. "I would respectfully solicit an appointment on the commission to investigate 'the subject of wages and hours of labor; and the division of profits between labor and capital in the United States.' Being a mechanic myself, I am 'practically identified with the laboring interests of the country;'. . ." ALS, *ibid.*

On Dec. 30, Elijah P. Grant, Canton, Ohio, wrote to USG. "Observing that a bill has passed the lower house of Congress providing for the appointment of three Commissioners to inquire into the Labor Question, now pressed so earnestly upon public attention, I presume to address you in order to suggest myself, in the event that the bill should become a law, as one of those Commissioners. I have made the subjects they will be required to investigate almost a life study, and about a year since published a little treatise, the purpose of which is to indicate in a very condensed form, but still intelligibly as I hope, the true solution of the problem to which their attention will inevitable be directed. I send you a copy by same mail herewith. I would gladly hope that you will read it, and carefully, . . ." ALS, *ibid.* See E. P. Grant, *Co-operation; or, Sketch of the Conditions of Attractive Industry; and Outline of a Plan for the Organization of Labor.* . . . (New York, 1870).

On Jan. 1, 1872, R. M. Hicks, Waynesboro, Va., wrote to USG. "I most respectfully beg leave to recommend to you David D. Durboraw of this place for an appointment on the Commission To examine and report; on *wages* and *hours* of *labour* and divisions of profits between *labour* & *capital* in the United States, &[c.] I am well acquainted with Mr Durboraw and that he has acquired a full knowledge of labour & capital and their distinctions having been extensively engaged in the Iron business . . ." ALS, DNA, RG 59, Letters of Application and Recommendation.

On Jan. 23, Edward D. Mansfield, Aiken, S. C., wrote to William Dennison. "You will be surprised to receive this letter from me and from this place; but, I am here for a short time, for my daughters health.—By the proceedings of Congress,—I think it certain, that the 'Labor Commission Bill'—will pass Congress in a few days. The inquiries and Reports to be wholly Statistical & the work not very arduous,—& the office not permanent. Under these circumstances, I have written to several Members of Congress: Among others to Sherman & Morton,—that I should be a candidate for Commissioner. . . . I wish—(if you think proper)—that you would address a letter reccommending me to the President—. . . I am not personally acquainted with General Grant—though I doubt if any one person has done, as much,—in writing, to defend his Administration. . . ." ALS, OFH. On Jan. 27, Dennison, Columbus, Ohio, favorably endorsed this letter to USG. AES, *ibid.* On Jan. 22, Mansfield, Aiken, had written to U.S. Senator John Sherman of Ohio on the same subject. ALS, *ibid.* Sherman favorably endorsed the letter to USG. AES (undated), *ibid.* See *PUSG*, 22, 447–48.

On Feb. 20, 1872, Aurora H. C. Phelps, Boston, wrote to U.S. Representative Nathaniel P. Banks of Mass. "The Women's Economical Garden Homestead League have requested or rather instructed me to secure your powerful aid for their cause and for a request they make that one or both of two Gentlemen known and estemed by our organization may be appointed on the Board of Labor Inquiry as contemplated by Mr Hoar's bill.

I refer to the Hon Thomas J Durant now Advocate of our claims with Spain, who is the first choice of our League. He has earned not only the confidence of our Society but of all working people by his rare devotion to justice and labor. Our second choice falls upon Ira Stewart of Cambridge Mass. a working man honest and true, he is well known to the people by his labors for the Eight Hour Law. Representing a large class of laborers—with a present and affiliated membership of 100,000, linked by sympathy to all working peoples associations, we feel assured no request of ours, founded on justice and the welfare of the people, will be lightly passed over. Of your sympathy we are certain, judging by all the deeds of your past, and though we have, of ourselves, no voice or vote in public affairs, we can confidently rely on the justice and kindness of those we send to legislate in our stead. I forward you copies of our Rules &.c, . . ." ALS, OFH. On March 2, Banks endorsed this letter to USG. AES, *ibid.* For Phelps, see *New York Times*, Oct. 28, 1873.

 On April 4, 1872, U.S. Senator James W. Patterson of N. H. wrote to USG. "The bearer, Lewis Wieser desires to be made one of the Commissioners to be appointed under the 'Bill to provide for the appointment of a commission on the subject of the wages & hours of labor and the division of profits between labor & capital in the United States' Mr Wieser is an educated German who has given much thought & study to these & related subjects & I think could be of much service on such a board. I have not been long acquainted with him but I know he speaks several languages & did good service in our army during our late war. I commend him to your favorable consideration." ALS, OFH. On April 8, U.S. Senator William Windom of Minn. favorably endorsed this letter. AES, *ibid.* On May 1, Harry White, Indiana, Pa., wrote to USG. "I take pleasure in recommending Lewis Wieser, now of Washington City, in connection with the Bureau of Industry—now proposed to be established by Congress—I became acquainted with Mr Weiser as a fellow prisoner in Libby in the darkest days of the rebellion. He was captured, I believe, on the Gettysburg Campaign and went through all the tortuous rigors of rebel captivity for over twenty months. He bore himself like a faithful patriotic soldier. He is intelligent industrious &, I believe, of unquestioned integrity—As a soldier he is entitled to recognition, as a citizen he would be competent & suitable for the position indicated. I hope Your Excellency will be pleased to regard with favor Mr Weisers application for a position in connection with the proposed Bureau" ALS, *ibid.*

Speech

[April 30, 1872]

 BARON: I welcome you as the representative here of your august sovereign.

 It shall be my study to reciprocate the purpose of your mission, which, you say, is to maintain the good understanding and to tighten the bonds of friendship which have always existed between the United States and Russia The mutually kind relations between his Imperial Majesty and his Government and the Government of the United States are of long duration, and remain without abatement.

From your antecedents, there can be no doubt that you will deserve my confidence and the good will of the people of the United States.

Washington Chronicle, May 1, 1872. USG responded to Henri d'Offenberg, Russian minister. "MR. PRESIDENT: I have the honor to present to your Excellency the letters which accredit me near the Government of the United States, and likewise the letter of recall of my predecessor. The only purpose of the mission with which I am honored is to maintain the good understanding and to draw closer the friendly relations which have never ceased to exist between the United States and Russia. I shall be happy, Mr. President, if, in the fulfillment of this mission, I succeed in gaining the confidence of your Excellency, and the sympathies of the American people." *Ibid.*

For Baron d'Offenberg's predecessor, Constantin de Catacazy, see *PUSG*, 22, 130–31, 147. On May 2, 1872, Secretary of State Hamilton Fish recorded in his diary a conversation with Blacque Bey, Turkish minister. "He says the new Russian Minister tells him that Catacazy is in disgrace—that he was placed 'indisponibilite' rather than dismissed, in order that the Governmt should have control over him, & be able to impose restrictions upon him as an official" DLC-Hamilton Fish. In Aug., d'Offenberg visited Fish at his N. Y. home. "Baron Offenbergh, Russian Envoy came to Garrison to present an autograph letter from the ~~President~~ Emperor to the President in response to the letter of recall of Mr Curtin   He says that the Emperor very emphatically condemns the conduct of Catacazy—Speaking of the Perkins Claim I state that this Govt never attached any importance to it & mention the mistake which was made in a telegram I sent to Curtin in ~~Curtin~~ Sept last & which he transmitted erroneously to the Russian Govt & had only recently corrected—He says that Catacazy exaggerated the Perkins Affair—that had any discreet diplomatist been in his place there wd have been no difficulty—He says that on C's return to St Petersburgh, Gortchacow requested him (Offenbergh) to be present at his reception of Catacazy, that Weterman was also present, & that Gortchacow was very stern in his reception, & cold—& rebuked C—" *Ibid.*

On April 5, Andrew G. Curtin, St. Petersburg, wrote to USG. "Having written the Honorable Hamilton Fish Secretary of State that I desired to return to the United States and the reasons which induce me to leave Russia it is only necessary to offer formally to you my resignation of the office of Envoy extraordinary and Minister Plenipotentiary of the United States in Russia and to ask that any letter of recall be sent me not later than the first of July   The motives for my resignation are personal and I separate from you officially with the highest regard and confidence and with many thanks for the distinguished place you gave me without solicitation and the generous kindness I have received since my residence in Russia from you and the members of your Cabinet—" ALS, *ibid.* On April 12, Elihu B. Washburne, Paris, wrote to USG. "*Private* . . . Curtin has sent to me to go by the bag which leaves to-day, his formal letter of resignation to you and also a private note to the Governor. I see some speculation in the home papers as to his attitude towards the administration after his return. He talked with me very freely when I was in Nice two months ago, and he expressed great friendliness and he alledged as one reason of his resigning was to go home to take a part in the fight this summer and fall. He is a great stumper and can do us a world of good. He is now on his way to Constantinople where he expects to meet Sherman and Fred and to go with them to St. Petersburg, which city they expect to reach about the 15th of next month." ALS, IHi. On July 1, Curtin wrote to Fish. "Having taken leave of the Emperor I will leave Russia in a few days and will place the affairs of this Legation in the charge of Mr. Schuyler as you direct in your despatch enclosing my letter of recall. The Emperor in the audience he granted me referred to the recall of Mr Catacazy and the causes which induced the demand for it, and expressed his regret that the unhappy affair occurred to interrupt the friendly relations of the two governments and peoples. He said what is true that he ordered the recall of Mr. Catacazy as soon as he was informed that he had made himself disagreeable to the President, and his recall had been asked for, only delaying until his son the Grand Duke Alexis had made his visit. . . . During my interview the Emperor referred with his usual satisfaction and pleasure when the subject is mentioned, to the distinguished consideration and hospitalities shown his son the Grand Duke Alexis during his visit to the United States, but at the same time spoke of the manner of his reception at Washington. I repeated the explanation I made to Prince Gortchacoff when it occurred and communicated to you at the time, that I believed the visit of the Grand Duke to Washington was accepted as a ceremonious tender of respect and that he was doubtless expected to return, when the civilities would have been shown him by the President and the other officers of the Government. The subject seemed to me to be introduced in order to speak of, if not to explain, the fact that the Grand Duke declined an invitation to return to Washington, as he said in that connection with apparent feeling, that after all that had occurred he could not accept the invitation and that the conduct of Admiral Possieta in declining it had been approved. I regret that the Emperor spoke of the visit of the Grand Duke to Washington as it was an unpleasant subject introduced into an interview very agreeable in other respects, and I only refer to it, as I have from the beginning to the end of the Catacazy affair avoided concealment and endeavored to inform you definitely and fully of all that was done or said here in reference to it. . . ." LS, DNA, RG 59, Diplomatic Despatches, Russia. See letter to Elihu B. Washburne, Aug. 26, 1872.

On Dec. 3, Fish wrote in his diary about a conversation with USG during a cabinet meeting. "I call attention to the necessity of filling the Russian Mission—he says that he wishes to await answer from Schenck to the enquiry addressed him some weeks since as to his desire to remain in London, as he proposes in case Schenck is Coming home to name John A Bingham for Russia—but Ohio Cannot have both England & Russia—I remind him that Bingham is ineligible, by reason of his being a member of Congress during the time the salary of the Minister to Russia was raised—He then asks if some suitable Southern Man cannot be found—the name of James L Orr of S. C. is mentioned, & he directs a nomination to be at once made out—" DLC-Hamilton Fish.

Endorsement

———

Capt. Geo. B. Hoge¹ may be nominated to the Senate to fill the first vacancy occuring in the Infantry, or now if a vacancy exists, and when confirmed by the Senate he may be placed on the Army retired list.

U. S. GRANT

WASHINGTON D. C,
MAY 1ST 1872.

AES, Mrs. Walter Love, Flint, Mich. Written on a letter of March 8, 1872, from Secretary of War William W. Belknap to U.S. Representative Charles B. Farwell of Ill. "The President, at your instance, on the 21st ultimo, directed that the order wholly retiring Captain George B. Hoge, with one year's pay and allowances, be revoked, and that he be placed on the Retired list of the Army when a vacancy should occur, and instructions were accordingly given to that effect; but I regret now to inform you that, as Captain Hoge is now entirely out of service, and as the proceedings which led to that result were perfectly regular, there is no law under which he can be placed on the retired list by revoking the order wholly retiring him, and the instructions of the President have therefore been cancelled." LS, *ibid.*

    1. Born in Pittsburgh in 1834, George B. Hoge served as capt., 25th Mo., and col., 113th Ill., and joined the regular army as capt. in 1867. On Aug. 30, 1871, Hoge was retired with one year's pay because of illness. On Sept. 25, Mrs. Abraham H. Hoge, Chicago, wrote to [USG] asking that the order retiring her son be revoked. ALS, DNA, RG 94, ACP, 2508 1872. On the same day, U.S. Senator John A. Logan of Ill. favorably endorsed this letter. AES, *ibid.* On Sept. 29, USG endorsed these papers. "Refered to the Sec. of War." AES, *ibid.* On Sept. 25 and Oct. 2, U.S. Representative John F. Farnsworth of Ill. and Farwell, Chicago, wrote to USG on the same subject. ALS, *ibid.* Related papers are *ibid.* On Oct. 14, Mrs. Hoge wrote to USG. "The case of my son Capt. George B. Hoge, 12th. Inf. U. S. A. is now in your hands—In the midst of the dire calamity with which we have been visited, this pressure still adds to the weight. We are penniless—My husband sons & sons-in-law are all burnt out of homes & employment—All that we have to fall back upon is what my son the Captain may be able to do for us & he always divides with us—I ~~am~~ was sick from anxiety before the fire & now poverty at over 50 years of age stares me in the face. Should your Excellency be willing to grant the great boon, of having my son retired on his rank & pay, I should be relieved from an almost unbearable pressure on mind & body—" ALS, *ibid.* See *PUSG,* 14, 166. On Feb. 21, 1872, Belknap wrote to AG Edward D. Townsend. "The President directs that order retiring Capt. Hoge with one years pay be revoked & that he be placed on the Retired List of the Army when a vacancy occurs—" AL (initialed), DNA, RG 94, ACP, 2508 1872. On Feb. 1, 1873, USG nominated Hoge for reappointment "with the view to retirement." DS, *ibid.,* RG 46, Nominations. Reinstated on March 3, Hoge retired as of Jan. 31, 1874.

To Hamilton Fish

Washington D. C. May 1st *1872.*

DEAR GOVR.

Mr. Henry A. Bowen, of New York, is about sailing for Europe and would like to be the bearer of any despatch to any of our Ministers abroad. He does not expect compensation. If any can be given him I would be pleased to see him made the bearer of them.

Very Truly Yours,

U. S. GRANT

HON. HAMILTON FISH, SEC. OF STATE.

ALS, DLC-Hamilton Fish. On May 27, 1872, Secretary of State Hamilton Fish wrote to Orville E. Babcock. "There will be no note or despatch to Genl Schenck, except in the ordinary form of sending by mail copies of the telegrams which are being sent—Of necessity, all Communication with him on the subject of the Treaty, has to be by the Cable. Mr Bowen is mistaken in supposing there is to be any note or despatch sent to him—I return Mr Bowens telegram" AL (initialed, press), *ibid.* Henry A. Bowen was the nephew of Henry C. Bowen. See *PUSG*, 20, 143; *New York Times*, May 14, 23, June 13, 1878, Nov. 2, 1879.

On March 31, 1871, Babcock had written to Henry C. Bowen, *Brooklyn Union.* "The President directs me to acknowledge the receipt of your letter of the 29th inst: in relation to the distilleries in Brooklyn, and wishes me to express to you his sincere thanks for your kind interest in the welfare and honest administration of the government. He desires me to say that in compliance with your suggestion he has ordered the appointment of Mr. Wass and hopes it accomplish all the good which you anticipate." Copy, DLC-USG, II, 1. In 1871, Bowen wrote to USG about the "'Whiskey Ring,' etc., and the propriety of supporting U. S. Marshals with the military." William Evarts Benjamin, Catalogue No. 27, Nov., 1889, p. 5.

On May 15, Bowen *et al.* wrote to USG. "The undersigned earnest republicans and friends of the Administration, sincerely desiring to promote order, harmony and discipline in the party in the city of Brooklyn respectfully suggest to you the propriety of dispensing the patronage of the Navy Yard and the New York Custom House—so far as the same is given to this city—*only* through the 'General Republican Committee' which committee is by all republicans acknowledged to be composed of fair minded, honorable men who are respected as such by our best citizens. The present method of disposing of said patronage through individuals or factions, however worthy in themselves, has done and is now doing us much harm by dividing the party into several cliques and thereby creating jealousy and trouble in every direction. No objection whatever is made to the direct appointments of the Administration *only* so far as the same may be influenced by parties or factions not acting through the General Republican Committee   There now seems to be a general disposition to union and harmony and if directions can be given by you to ob-

serve the suggestions now made we think the party will at once be in working order" DS
(8 signatures), DNA, RG 56, Letters Received. On May 30, Horace Porter wrote to
Bowen. "The President received your letter and directs me to say in reply that he will leave
here on Thursday next for Long Branch and will remain there till the next Tuesday, when
he intends visiting West Point. He will hardly be able to get to Brooklyn though it would
give him much pleasure to do so. If you can make it convenient to run down to the Branch
and spend a night with him, it will give him an opportunity to talk to you about a number of matters which he deems important." Copy, DLC-USG, II, 1. In 1872 and 1874,
Bowen wrote to USG concerning politics. William Evarts Benjamin, Catalogue No. 42,
March, 1892, p. 5.

To Timothy O. Howe

Washington D. C. May 1st *1872.*

HON. T. O. HOWE
CH. SENATE COM ON CLAIMS;
DEAR SIR:

On the 12th of April I returned Senate Bill No 2041 for the relief of Lucy C. Baker & Mary A. Baker, children of John M. Baker.
This I did without any other knowledge than was derived from
the records of the State Dept. I wish to state now that if the same
bill receives the sanction of Congress again it will afford me pleasure to sanction it.

Very Truly Yours
U. S. GRANT

ALS, Ralph F. Brandon, M. D., Short Hills, N. J. On April 10, 1872, USG sent a veto message to the House of Representatives. ". . . The bill proposes to pay a sum of money to the
children of John M. Baker, deceased, late United States Consul at Rio de Janeiro, for services of that person as acting Chargé d'Affaires of the United States in in the year 1834.
So far as it can be ascertained, it is apprehended that the bill may have received the sanction of Congress through some inadvertence, for upon inquiry at the proper Department,
it appears that Mr Baker never did act as Chargé d'Affaires of the United States at Rio de
Janeiro, and that he was not authorized to act, but, on the contrary, was expressly forbidden to enter into diplomatic correspondence with the government of Brazil. The letter of
the 8th of February 1854, a copy of which is annexed, addressed to William L. Marcy,
then Secretary of State, to James M. Mason, Chairman of the Committee on Foreign Relations of the Senate, specifies objections to the claim which, it is believed, have not since
diminished, and in which I fully concur." Copy, DNA, RG 130, Messages to Congress.
HED, 42-2-255; *SMD,* 49-2-53, 379–80. In June, USG signed a bill providing $1666.67

for Lucy C. and Mary A. Baker. See *HRC*, 26-1-276, 34-1-335; *SRC*, 33-1-105; *CG*, 42-2, 4091; *U.S. Statutes at Large*, XVII, 706–7.

To Charles W. Ford

———

Washington D. C. May 2d *1872.*

Dear Ford:

I am just in receipt of your letter of the 29th of April, and am much obliged to you for your timely hint as to what the Republican clique will endeavor to accomplish. I will be on guard against them.

I shall be in St Louis about the middle of July probably. You may be away at that time, and when you do go East this Summer I want you to spend a few days with me at Long Branch.

I wish you would direct Elrod to have White Cloud altered. I shall be sending for him soon and I want no stallions around.

Yours Truly
U. S. Grant

ALS, DLC-USG.

To Joseph Hooker

———

Washington D. C. May 5th 1872.

My dear General.

Up to within a few minutes of the present writing it has been my expectation as it would be my pleasure to be present at the meeting of the Society of the Army of the Potomac on the 7th inst. in Cleveland Ohio,   Unfortunatly however official business of such a pressing nature is to preclude the possibility of my leaving Washington now, will deprive me of the pleasure I had anticipated both in attenting your meeting and in visiting the City of Cleveland.

It would afford me special pleasure to meet together so many companians in Arms as will be assembled there on the 7th inst: I

predict for you a happy reunion and wish that you may all live to in-
joy many more, and that in the future I may be so fortunate as to be
permitted to be with you.

> With great respect
> Your obt. Svt.
> U. S. GRANT

GENL. JOE. HOOKER
PRESIDENT SOCIETY A. OF THE P.

Copies, DLC–USG, II, 1; DLC–Society of Army of Potomac. See *Cleveland Plain Dealer*,
May 6–9, 1872; Walter H. Hebert, *Fighting Joe Hooker* (Indianapolis, 1944), pp. 294–95.

To Senate

May 7th 1872.

TO THE SENATE OF THE UNITED STATES.

I herewith, communicate to the Senate, a report from the Acting Secretary of the Interior[1] of this date, in answer to the resolution of that body adopted on the 23rd ultimo, calling for information relative to the recent affray at the Court House in Going Snake
District, Indian Territory.[2]

In view of the feeling of hostility which exists between the
Cherokees, and the United States Authorities of the Western District of Arkansas it seems to be necessary that Congress should
adopt such measures as will tend to allay that feeling, and, at the
same time secure the enforcement of the laws in that Territory.

I therefore, concur with the Acting Secretary of the Interior, in
suggesting the adoption of a pending bill for the erection of a Judicial District,[3] within the Indian Territory as a measure which will
afford the most immediate remedy for the existing troubles.

> U. S. GRANT

DS, DNA, RG 46, Presidential Messages. On May 10, 1872, USG sent the same message to the House of Representatives. *SED*, 42-2-70; *HED*, 42-2-287. On May 7, Benjamin R. Cowen, act. secretary of the interior, had written to USG. "On the 25th ultimo,
this Department received, by Executive reference, of the 23d, a Resolution of the Senate

in the following words, . . . That the President of the United States, be, and hereby is, requested if not inconsistent with the public interests, to furnish to the Senate of the United
States, copies of any papers on file, since April A. D. 1865, relating to the acts of United
States Marshals and deputy marshals in that portion of the Western district of Arkansas
now comprising the Indian Country. Also all information in the possession of the Department, relating to the late outrages at Whitmore Barron Fork, in the Cherokee Nation . . . I now have the honor to transmit herewith, copies of all papers received, to this
date, containing information in relation to the subject of said Resolution. It will be observed that there is a wide difference in the detail of the circumstances attending the riot,
as stated by the U. S. Marshal and by the reports of the Cherokee Authorities. The feeling between the U. S. Officers and the citizens of the Indian Territory is very bitter, growing out of the anomalous condition of things in that Territory. This unfortunate occurrence is but the natural result of the hostile feeling which has existed for some time
between the residents of the Indian Territory and the U. S. Authorities in the Western
District of Arkansas. Many whites have been adopted into the Cherokee Nation and the
Indian Authorities claim the same jurisdiction over such adopted citizens as is accorded
by our laws to persons of Indian blood. This right seems to be denied by the U. S. Court
having jurisdiction over the Territory, and, on account of such difference, questions of jurisdiction are continually arising which engender very bitter feeling. Some such question
seems to have been at the foundation of the recent riot. The unfortunate occurrence at Going Snake Court House, and the unmistakeably hostile feeling which has been referred to
as existing between the authorities of the Indian Territory and of the United States would
seem to call for some action by Congress to prevent a repetition of the acts of violence and
harmonize the differences between them. The bill now pending in Congress, for the erection of a Judicial District in the Indian Territory, seems to be the most practicable means
of accomplishing the purpose. It is authorized by the treaty with the Cherokees concluded
on the 19th July 1866, and I would therefore respectfully urge the passage of said Bill at
an early day" LS, DNA, RG 46, Presidential Messages. Related papers are *ibid.* On
May 17, USG wrote to the Senate. "I, herewith, transmit to the Senate, a communication,
of this date, from the Acting Secretary of the Interior, and the papers therein described,
containing information, called for in Senate Resolution, of the 23d ultimo, which was answered, in part, on the 8th instant." DS, *ibid.* Cowen's letter of transmittal and related papers are *ibid.* See *CG,* 42–2, 2674; *SED,* 42-2-70.

On Dec. 10, 1870, Richard H. Jackson, Chicago, had written to USG. "You will
please excuse me calling your attention to matters, which I think will justify it. You will
recollect that in April last I waited upon you at the Executive Mansion and applied for the
Office of U. S district marshal for the western District of Arkansas, embracing the Indian
Territory, recommended by Butler, Logan, Cobb, Yates, Parker and others, and by the
Chiefs of the Delegations of the Indian Country,   you informed me that you could not
possibly give me the Office because I was not a resident of the state of Arkansas and without the endorsement of the Arkansas republican Congressional Delegation. I respectfully
submitted that the citizens of the Western District of Arkansas were not particularly interested in the matter, that the Judicial District contained but seven small counties
sparsely inhabited, but embraced the whole of the Indian Country containing 21.000
square miles and 68.000 Indians; which furnished 75/100ths of the business of the Court,
that these Indians were frequently dragged hundreths of miles from their homes to attend
the court at VanBuren, either as witnesses or parties, perfectly ignorant why they were
arrested, simply for the pupose of increasing the fees of U. S. Officers. That there was
great complaint existing among the Indians over this treatment and the abuse of their au-

thority by the U. S. marshal and his deputies. And that I did not believe that our friendly relations with these Indians could be much longer maintained without the correction of such abuses. You replied that you were not aware of any such condition of things. I remarked, they existed nevertheless. But a short time before at the instance of the Indian Commisioner I had prepared a report and legal argument which was endorsed by him and submitted to the Secretary of the Interior Department, and by him referred to the Atty' Genl'. A long time having elapsed & nothing being heard from the Atty' Genl' upon the subject, I went with Major McCraig, (who was then in Washington as a Government Agent of the Cherokees, and who had had serious difficulty in the discharge of his official duties with the U. S. marshal and his Deputies) to the Atty' Genl's Office to learn his action in the premises,   Atty' Genl' Hoar was absent and his chief clerk could give us no information. Well, it appears by recent reports in the papers that my predictions have been lately partially verified,   it was read to me a few days ago that a reputed U. S. Deputy Marshal arrested some one in the custody of an Officer charged with some offence against the Cherokee laws and also two Cherokees for interfering in the matter and carried them all to Van Buren, which has caused great excitement in the Territory among the Indians,   knowing nought of the facts in the case, I cannot express any opinion upon it, but it is sufficient to know, that this condition of things, unless properly corrected, will result in a bloody Indian war. Peace can only be maintained between the Indian Country, the U. S. Marshal, his Deputies and the Internal Revenue Offices by a proper understanding of their relative jurisdiction in that Country. It is respectfully submitted, Mr President, that I am no longer an applicant for the Marshalship of the Western District of Arkansas, but that, if there is any special agent appointed to investigate the foregoing, I would be pleased to accept the position in the event of recovering my health,   it is also submitted that Congress will soon establish a U. S. District or territorial court in the Indian Country, which event I want the Judgeship. The Indians have said to you in their petition that they believed me to be humane, just, and able and asked my appointment to an equally responsible trust. Butler, Logan, Cobb and other distinguished Republicans have asked you for my appointment to a Western Judicial position and as your personal and political friend I expect it. . . . P. S. I have been confined to my bed for three months and am still helpless by an attack of neuralgia." D, DNA, RG 60, Records Relating to Appointments. Related papers are *ibid.*; *ibid.*, RG 59, Letters of Application and Recommendation. No appointment followed. See *ibid.*, RG 94, ACP, 191J CB 1867; *PUSG*, 14, 417, 453; *ibid.*, 15, 71–72.

On Oct. 23, 1872, Lewis Downing, "Principal Chief of the Cherokee Nation," Tahlequah, Indian Territory, wrote to USG. "Enclosed herewith I have the honor to transmit a copy from the record in the case of the Cherokee Nation v. s. Isaac Keys—charged with the murder of J. G. Kelley, a white man '*connected*' with the Cherokees by marriage and for several years a resident and citizen of the Cherokee Nation by '*adoption*'   Isaac Keys is a Cherokee Indian and a citizen of the Cherokee Nation, and he has been again indicted, arrested, and is now held for trial before the U. S. District Court for the Western District of Arkansas, for the same offence for which he was tried and acquitted by the Circuit Court of the Cherokee Nation in Coo we Scoo we District—TO WIT the killing of J. G. Kelley. The Cherokees had thought the jurisdiction of their Courts, '~~secured~~' over this class of citizens '*secured*' by terms sufficiently clear and unmistakable, by the 5th Article of the Cherokee treaty of 1835–6 which has also been confirmed and revived by the 31st Article of the Cherokee treaty of July 19th 1866; their being at the date of the first named treaty, no other class of persons that could have been discribed or by any possibility intended by the terms—'such persons as has *connected* themselves with them.'. . . The happiness and wellfare of the Cherokee poeple as well as the good faith of your Government are concerned in the enforcement of the treaty stipulations, . . ." LS, DNA, RG 60, Letters from the President. Related papers are *ibid.* See William G. McLoughlin, *After the Trail of Tears: The Cherokees' Struggle for Sovereignty, 1839–1880* (Chapel Hill, 1993), pp. 303–7.

1. Born in 1831 in Moorfield, Ohio, Cowen worked as printer and editor (1848–57) and served as army paymaster and Ohio AG, receiving a bvt. as brig. gen. An active Republican, he became asst. secretary of the interior in 1871. See *PUSG*, 22, 136.

2. On April 15, 1872, a gunfight between Cherokees and deputy U.S. marshals left dead and wounded on both sides. See *HED*, 42-3-1, part 5, I, 618–19; McLoughlin, *After the Trail of Tears*, pp. 299–301.

3. Congress passed no legislation on this subject. See *CG*, 42–2, 953, 2958, 3416–18, 42–3, 2, 204, 1133, 1779.

To Edward S. Atkinson et al.

———

Washington, D. C. May 9th 1872.

GENTLEMEN:

I am in receipt of your invitation extended to me to attend a Mass Meeting to be held for the purpose of aiding in securing civil rights for the Colored Citizens of our Country.

I regret that a previous engagement will detain me at the Executive Mansion this evening and that I shall not be able to participate with you in person in your efforts to further the cause in which you are laboring. I beg to assure however that I sympathize most cordially in any effort to secure for all our people of whatever race, ~~nationality~~ nativity or color the exercise of those rights to which every Citizen should be entitled.

I am very respectfully
U. S. GRANT.

E. S. ATKINSON[1]
F. G. BARBADOES[2]
GEO. T. DOWNING[3]
F. DOUGLASS JR.[4]
J. W. LE BARNES[5]
COMMITTEE ON INVITATION.

Copy, DLC-USG, II, 1. The meeting especially advocated admitting children to public schools without reference to race. On May 6, 1872, Edward S. Atkinson *et al.*, Washington, D. C., wrote to U.S. Senator Charles Sumner of Mass. about the meeting. L, MH. See *Washington Chronicle*, May 10, 1872; John W. Blassingame and John R. McKivigan *et al.*, eds., *The Frederick Douglass Papers. Series One: Speeches, Debates, and Interviews Volume 4: 1864–80* (New Haven, 1979), p. 300.

On April 15, 1872, John M. G. Parker, New Orleans, telegraphed to USG. "You have been fully endorsed by the national colored convention" Telegram received, Mrs. Gordon Singles, Alexandria, Va. See *New Orleans Picayune*, April 11–13, 16, 1872.

On April 17, "The members of the Baltimore Annual Conference of the African M. E. Church, now in session in this city, visited the White House at noon to-day to pay their respects to the President. . . . The President replied, saying that no one except themselves could be more gratified than he was that four millions of persons who had been held in bondage and disposed of as chattels were now free to think for themselves and worship God as they thought proper, and that civil rights for all were fast becoming recognized throughout the land. It may be some little time before they enjoyed all the rights which belong to citizens, but that day is surely coming, and he hoped it might come speedily. In conclusion, he thanked them for this call and for the expression of their good will. . . ." *Washington Evening Star*, April 17, 1872.

On Aug. 15, the Associated Press reported an interview with USG. ". . . The conversation turning on the remark of Senator Sumner to the effect that Greeley is a better friend to the black man than President Grant, the President replied that he never pretended to be, as he had repeatedly said, an original abolitionist; but he favored emancipation as a war measure. When this was secured, he thought the ballot should be conferred to make the gift complete and to place those who had been liberated in full possession of the rights of freemen. . . . On the subject of slavery his views were well known. They were expressed in letters to Washburne and others, and extensively published, and hence this was not now a matter of dispute. . . . While he had no unkind words to utter concerning Senator Sumner, he was perfectly willing to place his acts against Senator Sumner's words; and in this connection he said that Senator Sumner did not show himself such a good friend to the black man as he professed to be, when he was not willing to have a civil rights bill stand on its own merits, requiring only a majority vote but insisting on a bill of his own as an amendment to the amnesty bill, which could not be passed without a majority of two-thirds. Carpenter's civil rights bill, however, was passed during the absence of Senator Sumner, and, as the facts show, much to his surprise. The President also said that it will be seen by the Congressional Globe that Senator Sumner did not vote at all on the joint resolution recommending the ratification of the Fifteenth amendment to the Constitution. . . ." *Louisville Courier-Journal*, Aug. 16, 1872.

On Sept. 5, Charles Lenox Remond, president, and Charles E. Pindell, secretary, Convention of Colored Citizens of New England, wrote to USG. "Allow us to offer you a tribute of grateful hearts. We feel that much is due to you, when we consider that you obeyed the summons of your country in an hour when its unity was assailed by armed traitors from within. The important services you rendered your country in the long struggle which followed, have gained for you an honorable fame which ages can never destroy. We feel it our duty to teach our children to transmit to their posterity this fact, that when you drew your sword in the defence of the American Union four millions of our race were enslaved; and that when you returned that sword to its scabbard not a slave was left to lift his imploring hand to GOD for deliverance; for the last chain that bound the American

slave had by that sword been cut asunder. We are also indebted to you for urging President Lincoln to issue the Proclamation of Emancipation, which you as commander of the
loyal armies in the field, made a reality, and thus secured to us, by your successful
achievements, all the rights that we at the present day enjoy as American citizens. Again
are we in common with the nation indebted to you for its unity and power, threatened as it
was by the disloyal Andrew Johnson, who, on displacing Edw[in] M. Stanton, the efficient
Secretary of War, aroused anew the loyal element of the land, creating in them new fears
for its safety; just then you stretched forth the hand of assurance, and the nation again was
quieted. Again, we are indebted to you for urging the adoption of the Fifteenth Amendment of the Constitution of the United States, so essential to our prosperity. And we are
still further indebted to you for issuing the proclamation to Congress, requesting that
body not to adjourn until the necessary laws had by them been passed for the suppression
of the midnight murderous bands then perpetrating their atrocities upon the defenceless
loyalists of the South. For your faithful execution of that law in suppressing those bands
you have been fiercely assailed by the friends of the Ku-Klux, under the cover of State
rights, resulting in their calling the Cincinnati Convention, and their purposes may be
seen in the fourth resolution adopted by that body, which if approved by the people would
secure to them the license they seek. Again, do we thank you for appointing men of our
color Ministers Plenipotentiary, thus establishing the fact of your practical recognition of
the equality of all men before the law. And now, sir, as we cast our eyes over those regions
of our country where darkness—utter darkness—reigned in the past, the result of slavery, we behold under your free and humane administration, schools springing up and
maintained only by virtue of your recommendations to Congress; and to you we are indebted for the proper laws to defend those schools upon which the future welfare of our
race depends, and to some extent the nation's welfare—for all must admit that upon education the security of the Republic rests. To your recommendations, also, are we indebted
for that full protection of the ballot, without which the conferring upon our people in the
South of the right to vote would have been but a mockery. Thus, as we recall your acts,
conferring unnumbered blessings upon our race, we cannot but believe that it is by your
glorious deeds, surpassing expectations, rather than pretentious pledges, which too often
have proved but broken promises, that we are to learn the true feelings with which you
have regarded us. And now, Honored Sir, notwithstanding your humane and patriotic
efforts for the welfare of all, without regard to color, race or previous condition, you are
simultaneously assailed by men occupying extreme positions,—one class professing loyalty, the other class open and defiant rebels; but both making common cause against you,
the nation's deliverer. Though our sufferings may be counted by hundreds of years, still
we would count it as but gain to be permitted to receive their anathemas in such a cause,
upon our heads instead of yours; but having faith in the God of justice, we commit our
cause and you into His care and keeping, in the assurance that all will be well because you
have done well, in securing to us a country united and strong, wherein ultimately will
dwell the happiest, most prosperous and the highest type of man. Permit us to say, in view
of the disloyal elements existing in many of the States of this Union, growing out of a
thwarted attempt to destroy it, we cannot but think that Providence has assigned to you
the work of checking and controlling this disloyalty; that a large majority of our white
fellow-citizens who love their country, together with the entire race to which we belong,
will sustain you; and we believe that to do this, is to pursue the only course that will lead
to the realization of your motto, 'let us have peace.'" LS, DLC-USG, VIII. On Sept. 30, a
committee presented this letter to USG. *Washington Chronicle*, Oct. 1, 1872. See *Boston*

Transcript, Sept. 5, 1872; James M. McPherson, "Grant or Greeley? The Abolitionist Dilemma in the Election of 1872," *American Historical Review*, LXXI (Oct., 1965), 43–61.

On Sept. 19, U.S. Representative Robert B. Elliott of S. C., Columbia, wrote to USG. "Having been informed that a rumor is current in Washington, that I am hostile to your election, or at least, view your nomination with sullen coldness, I desire, in justice to you, to remove any impression that such false rumor may have created. The statement referred to, doubtless owes its origin to the fact that I was reared at the feet of the most distinguished assailant of your administration; one whom all New England long delighted to honor. I was not dazzled however by the lustre of a deservedly great name. I saw the duty and the danger of the hour, and, unhesitatingly, I performed the one and hastened to aid in rallying my race to meet the other. Had I done otherwise, I would have proved false to my record as a Republican. I had the honor of presiding over the Convention that nominated the Republican electors in this State in 1868 and have presided over every State Republican Nominating Convention that has met in South Carolina since that date. As Chairman of the delegation from this State in the Philadelphia Convention, I had the honor of supporting you and your distinguished associate by my voice and vote; and as the present Chairman of the Republican Executive Committee here, I am now engaged with my associates in organizing victory for the only columns that carry your standard in South Carolina, or that can present a front against the common enemy in this State. I need not here refer to the fact, that throughout the 42d Congress, I have sustained actively the salient measures of your administration, and having recently been renominated for Congress by the unanimous vote of my District Convention, I expect to support such measures again, assured that, in the future as in the past, they will commend themselves to my judgment, as calculated to advance the best interests of our whole country. Hence, Sir, my position cannot be mistaken. It is that of the great mass of my race in the United States. We stand by you because you have stood by us. In this we but obey that intelligent instinct of the true soldier which teaches him, when without orders, to move in the direction of the heaviest firing. We perceive too, that the heaviest firing is against you, and blazes from the guns of the same party that confronted you in 1864, and whose defeat has always signalized the advance of free government in this country. No, Mr. President, I am for the ticket which your name leads. Republicans of South Carolina, standing self-sustained without any appreciable aid from official patronage, poor and needy in purse, and confronted by the organized capital of the State, are advancing to your support with their thirty-five unpurchasable majority, as a just tribute to the man who, in the gravest conjuncture of his country's affairs, has been tried in many high trusts and has proved faithful in all and superior in every emergency. With best wishes for Your Excellency's good health, and satisfied of your assured triumph, . . ." ALS, CSmH. See Peggy Lamson, *The Glorious Failure: Black Congressman Robert Brown Elliott and the Reconstruction in South Carolina* (New York, 1973), 150–52. On Sept. 3, Elliott had written to USG accusing Maj. Lewis Merrill, commanding U.S. troops at Yorkville, S. C., of "openly interfering in the popular assemblages and Republican Party Conventions in York County, . . ." ALS, DNA, RG 94, Letters Received, 3994 1872. Gen. William T. Sherman endorsed this letter. "This paper should be referred to Maj Merrill, I dont believe a word of it" AES (undated), *ibid.* On Oct. 22, Merrill, Yorkville, wrote to AG Edward D. Townsend denying the charges. LS, *ibid.* See *PUSG*, 22, 360–62.

On Sept. 22, Edwin Prucha *et al.*, Rapides Parish, La., signed a "Petition from the Colored Poeple," asking USG "for Pertection on the Ellection Season as we wish for Peace at that time Bayonets is What we wish to See in Alexandria La Cheneville La and all

thoes Little Voteing holds . . ." DS (54 signatures), DNA, RG 94, Letters Received,
4172 1872.

1. See *PUSG*, 21, 196.

2. See *ibid.*, 19, 109.

3. Born in 1819 in New York City, George T. Downing, son of a prominent black
leader, prospered as a caterer in Providence and Newport, R. I., and pressed for civil
rights measures involving schools, suffrage, curfews, and public transportation. Shortly
after the Civil War, he assumed management of a Capitol restaurant. On May 4, 1869,
Downing, Washington, D. C., wrote to Fish offering catering services to the state dept.
ALS, DNA, RG 59, Letters of Application and Recommendation. See *PUSG*, 19, 108;
Rayford W. Logan and Michael R. Winston, eds., *Dictionary of American Negro Biography*
(New York, 1982), pp. 187–88.

On June 7, 1872, after the Republican National Convention adjourned, Downing,
Philadelphia, wrote to Sumner. ". . . a reservedness has possessed me in differing with you
as to the propriety of the colored vote being cast for Grant: Know that I felt great relief
when you Said to me and to the body of colored delegates who had the honor to wait on
you last Sunday, that you would vote for Grant, if you were convinced that the cause of the
[b]lack man would be served by [s]o doeing, it being said in connection with a doubt expressed, as to there being a probability of their [b]eing elected any man who would [se]rve
the cause better. . . ." ALS, MH. See Beverly Wilson Palmer, ed., *The Selected Letters of
Charles Sumner* (Boston, 1990), II, 585–87, 594–95.

4. Born in 1842 in New Bedford, Mass., Frederick Douglass, Jr., supported his
father's activities, recruited blacks in Miss. during the Civil War, learned typography
in Denver, and after 1870 assisted in editing the weekly *New National Era* in Washington, D. C.

5. See *PUSG*, 21, 196; James H. Whyte, *The Uncivil War: Washington During the
Reconstruction 1865–1878* (New York, 1958), pp. 123, 144, 243.

Proclamation

Whereas the act of Congress approved June 25th 1868, constituted, on and after that date, eight hours a day's work for all laborers, workmen, and mechanics employed by or on behalf of the Government of the United States;

And whereas on the nineteenth day of May in the year one thousand eight hundred and sixty-nine, by Executive proclamation it
was directed that from and after that date, no reduction should be
made in the wages paid by the Government by the day to such laborers, workmen, and mechanics on account of such reduction of
the hours of labor;

And whereas it is now represented to me that the act of Congress and the proclamation aforesaid have not been strictly observed by all officers of the Government having charge of such laborers, workmen, and mechanics;

Now, therefore, I, Ulysses S. Grant, President of the United States, do hereby again call attention to the act of Congress aforesaid, and direct all officers of the Executive Department of the Government having charge of the employment and payment of laborers, workmen or mechanics employed by or on behalf of the Government of the United States to make no reduction in the wages paid by the Government by the day to such laborers workmen and mechanics on account of the reduction of the hours of labor.

In testimony whereof, I have hereunto set my hand and caused the seal of the United States to be affixed.

Done at the city of Washington, this eleventh day of May, in the year of our Lord one thousand eight hundred and seventy two, and of the independence of the United States, the ninety sixth.

U. S. GRANT

DS, DNA, RG 130, Proclamations. *HRC*, 51-1-2606. See *PUSG*, 19, 189–91; letter to George S. Boutwell, [*April 29, 1872*].

On June 5, 1872, USG wrote to Secretary of War William W. Belknap. "Will the Sec. of War please have the legal question examined as to whether Watchmen are entitled to the benefit of the 'Eight Hour Law.'" ANS, Karpeles Manuscript Library, Montecito, Calif.

On July 8, a correspondent reported from Washington, D. C. "After President Grant had returned from Long Branch last Tuesday, he was on his way from the Executive Mansion to the Arlington for his breakfast, when he noticed quite a commotion among the laborers at Lafayette Square, who are engaged under the Commissioner of Public Buildings and Grounds. On making inquiry of one of these, he was informed that an attempt was being made to have some of them work ten hours a day. The President made no reply, but passed on and took his breakfast. He then returned to Lafayette Square, inquired who had charge of the works, and was informed that it was Mr. Benjamin. This gentleman he sent for at once, and when he arrived asked him by whose authority he had required his men to work ten hours a day? Having been apprised in this respect, the President notified Mr. Benjamin that he should never again exact above eight hours labor a day from his men, and he then passed on to the White House." *Philadelphia Public Ledger*, July 9, 1872.

On Oct. 15, U.S. Representative Henry L. Dawes of Mass., Pittsfield, wrote to USG. "The matter of the back pay to the Springfield Armorers for which provision was made in an appropriation Bill last session encounters mysterious delays in the Departments. The men are many of them poor and in great need of their pay. The delay causes great hard-

ship and discontent. They constantly write to me and I as constantly write to the different bureaus about it. I enclose one of many letters I am receiving on the subject. I take the
liberty of appealing to you that you would cause measures to be taken to secure them the
pay the law allows them without any farther delay. There doesnt seem to be any obstacle,
only those who have it in charge don't seem to understand how important it is to the poor
laborer and the consequences of this delay which I am unable to explain to them. I want
they should get their pay very soon." LS, DNA, RG 156, Letters Received. On Oct. 25,
Belknap wrote to Dawes that the delay occurred in the Treasury Dept. LS (press), *ibid.*
See *CG,* 42–2, 1480–85, 1511–12, 3094–97; *U.S. Statutes at Large,* XVII, 134.

On Nov. 23, Joseph Cardona, "Sculptor by profession but poor," Richmond, wrote to
Julia Dent Grant proposing a granite monument to commemorate USG's enforcement of
the "eight hour law." ALS, DNA, RG 56, Letters Received.

To Senate

To the Senate of the United States:

I transmit herewith, the correspondence which has recently
taken place, respecting the differences of opinion which have arisen
between this Government and that of Great Britain, with regard to
the powers of the Tribunal of Arbitration, created under the Treaty
signed at Washington, May 8, 1871.

I respectfully invite the attention of the Senate to the proposed
article[1] submitted by the British Government, with the object of
removing the differences which seem to threaten the prosecution of
the arbitration; and request an expression by the Senate of their
disposition in regard to advising and consenting to the formal adoption of an article, such as is proposed by the British Government.

The Senate is aware that the consultation with that body, in advance of entering into agreements with foreign States, has many
precedents. In the early days of the Republic, General Washington
repeatedly asked their advice upon pending questions with such
Powers.

The most important recent precedent is that of the Oregon
Boundary Treaty, in 1846.[2]

The importance of the results hanging upon the present state
of the Treaty with Great Britain, leads me to follow these former

precedents and to desire the counsel of the Senate in advance of agreeing to the proposal of Great Britain

U. S. GRANT

WASHINGTON, MAY 13TH 1872.

DS, DNA, RG 46, Reports Submitted to the Senate. See message to Senate, April 20, 1872. On April 26, 1872, and subsequently, Secretary of State Hamilton Fish wrote in his diary. "I read the following as a suggested instruction by Cable to Genl Schenck . . . ' . . . If G. B. be at liberty when a Belligerent to advance claims for indirect losses or injuries, our Claims must be maintained—But if G. B *is willing to stipulate & agree that in the future when she may be a belligerent, & this Country a neutral, should* there be any failure on the part of the U. S. to observe their neutral obligations, no reclamations shall be made for any indirect remote or consequential results of such failure the U. S will consent not to press for any award of damages before the Geneva Tribunal on account of the claims which the B. G. think not included in the submission—namely the transfer of American Shipping, the increased insurance, & the prolongation of the War' Creswell suggests that the sentence underlined above '*is willing to stipulate*' be changed so as to make it a recognition by G. B as part of '*international law*' that indirect damages be not claimed &c—President remarks that we cannot ask G. B. to establish such rule ~~with~~ as to other Powers which may not establish or recognise it toward them—Another objection is that this might require submission to the Senate—whereas as drawn it is either a promise, or a release which the Executive may consider, & may regard sufficient to induce him to adopt a certain course in the instructions for conducting the case before the Arbitrators   Richardson is anxious for a new agreement to be submitted to the Senate—After much discussion the President thinks it better that I see Thornton & tell him that if G. B. will make this proposal we will not ask damages on acct of the 'indirect claims' to which she has taken exception   In pursuance of the Presidents request I called in the afternoon on Thornton—. . . He spoke of the want of reciprocity in the suggestion that G. B. should stipulate not to make claims for indirect losses, & the U S not be likewise bound—to which I replied that the U S could not enter into such stipulation except by Treaty & that there was not time now to consider such a course—moreover that our experience wd not incline us again to make such claims, & that a decision by the Tribunal, wd have the effect of a rule of law between the two Powers—He seemed satisfied & said he would again telegraph to Granville—" "May 3 . . . Read telegram to Schenck of 27 April—& his telegrams of 30th April & yesterday & this date—& proposed reply   President suggests that it be submitted to Republican Members of Comm on F. A. of Senate & House—& he directed Genl Babcock to send notices to them to meet at Dept of State tomorrow morning at ten—" "On Saturday last May 4   The President met at the Department with Senators Harlan Morton, Hamlin, Patterson, & Representatives Banks, Meyers, Willard, Ambler, Packard, & Buell [*Duell*]—The recent telegrams (27th April to Schenck, & 30th Apl from him) were read, as also the proposed reply which I submitted yesterday to the Cabinet, with some slight alterations—Morton criticized the statement in my telegram of 27 that no demand for pecuniary damages was made on account of the indirect claims, in the 'Case'—he thinks the language used amounts to a demand—Patterson does not ~~so~~ understand the telegram in the same light, & comments on the sentence which says that if G. B. be at liberty to make claims in the future for indirect damages, we must press for compensation—Ambler approves the settlement suggested in telegram of 27th April—so does Willard   Banks disapproves, & wishes the proposed reply to contain an express withdrawal—Morton inclines in the same direction. Banks writes on the back of a copy of the American Case what he wishes added—Meyers writes also (on a sheet of paper) a proposed addition which Banks objects to as opening an opportunity to ~~accept th~~ tender the proposal suggested on 27 April—The President directs the sending of the telegram as I had prepared it, with something in the nature of Banks addition, so as to preclude the inference of a willingness now to agree to the suggestion of 27th April" DLC-Hamilton Fish.

On May 6, Robert C. Schenck, U.S. minister, London, telegraphed Great Britain's most recent proposal to Fish. ". . . Her Majestys Government are ready to engage that in the event of the Government of the United States agreeing that the Arbitrators are not to have regard in any award that they may make to the claims for indirect losses, namely:—The transfer of the American shipping, the increased premiums of insurance, and the prolongation of the war, Her Majesty's Government will on their part agree, that the view which they have heretofore presented, of such claims, shall be their principle of future action and conduct and they are ready in pursuance of the recognition of such principle to give assurance to the United States that if Great Britain should at any time hereafter be a belligerent while the United States are neutral Great Britain will never advance any claims inconsistent with that principle, such an engagement for the future being reciprocally given by both parties. The notes which are exchanged on this subject to be presented to the Tribunal of Arbitration, and entered on its records. . . ." Telegram received (copy), DNA, RG 59, Diplomatic Despatches, Great Britain. On May 7, Fish wrote in his diary. "It is agreed by all that the proposition in Schencks telegram of yesterday cannot be accepted—that no arrangement to bind the future action of the Govt can be made except by Treaty—~~I suggest that~~ The President at one time seemed inclined not to reply to this last proposal, but on the suggestion that it would throw upon this Govt the responsibility of breaking the Treaty, he immediately acquiesced, & on my saying that we might reply to the effect that the President without the assent of Congress cannot enter into an engagement to bind the future action of the Govt   that in that view the suggestion in my telegram of 27th April had been made—that he has gone to the verge of concession—but in his desire to save the Treaty will consider any proposal for a new arrangement, & if he can approve will submit it to the Senate. Robeson says it is very easy to frame a despatch in that view—whereupon I hand him a sheet of paper, & request him to draft one—he does so, & reads it—the President says it strikes him favourable, & successively asks the opinion of each Member present—each answering approvingly—Bristow however intimates a doubt whether the President has the Constitutional right to say that he will not ask for pecuniary ~~damages~~ compensation for the indirect losses—Each one present having separately approved the President authorises an instruction to Schenck in the 'spirit & general sense' of Robeson's paper—" DLC-Hamilton Fish.

On May 10, Schenck telegraphed to Fish the text of a proposed article amending the Treaty of Washington, under which both the U.S. and Great Britain agreed to the principle that neutrals should not be liable for indirect damages caused by belligerents, and the U.S. agreed not to press such claims at Geneva. Telegram received (copy), DNA, RG 59, Diplomatic Despatches, Great Britain. On May 11, USG convened an evening meeting of key senators, cabinet officers, and Speaker of the House James G. Blaine to discuss the British proposal. See Fish diary, May 11, 1872; letter to Hamilton Fish, May 16,

1872; Nevins, *Fish*, pp. 537–46; Adrian Cook, *The Alabama Claims: American Politics and Anglo-American Relations, 1865–1872* (Ithaca, N.Y., 1975), pp. 217–32.

1. On May 15, George Wilson, New York City, wrote to USG. "The Chamber of Commerce has instructed me to transmit to you the enclosed Preamble and Resolution in regard to the Treaty of Washington, adopted at a large and enthusiastic meeting held this afternoon." ALS, DNA, RG 59, Miscellaneous Letters. The accompanying resolution of the New York State Chamber of Commerce urged the ratification of the supplemental article, "which Article appears to this Chamber to be sound in principle binding the two Governments to the adoption of a beneficent rule for the future, and especially beneficial to the United States and its commerce, . . ." DS, *ibid.*

2. See *HMD*, 53-2-210, part 4, p. 449; Milo Milton Quaife, ed., *The Diary of James K. Polk During His Presidency, 1845 to 1849* (Chicago, 1910), I, 451–68; Paul H. Bergeron, *The Presidency of James K. Polk* (Lawrence, Kan., 1987), pp. 131–33.

Veto

————

TO THE SENATE OF THE UNITED STATES:

I have the honor to return herewith S. 955, entitled "An act granting a pension to Mary Ann Montgomery, widow of Wm. W. Montgomery, late Captain in Texas Volunteers," without my approval, inasmuch as the concluding phrase "and in respect to her minor children under sixteen years of age", has obviously no meaning whatsoever.

If it were the intention of the framer of the bill, that the pension thereby granted should revert to said minor children upon the re-marriage or death of the widow, the phrase referred to should read as follows: "and in the event of her re-marriage or death to her minor children under sixteen years of age." I therefore return the bill for proper action.

U. S. GRANT

EXECUTIVE MANSION, MAY 14, 1872

DS, DNA, RG 46, Presidential Messages. *SED*, 42-2-74; *SMD*, 49-2-53, 381. While in Tex. in 1863, William W. Montgomery, provisional capt., had been "seized one night by a gang of rebels and carried out of the town and hung." *CG*, 42-2, 3573. Congress overrode USG's veto. See *HMD*, 42-2-43; *CG*, 42-2, 2753, 4314–15.

On Aug. 19 and 20, 1872, Secretary of the Interior Columbus Delano wrote to U.S. Representative John Coburn of Ind., Indianapolis. "Your letter of the 3rd inst., addressed to the President was on the 17th. inst. forwarded to this Department and bears the following endorsement; 'Respectfully referred to the Sec. of the Int. for his answer to

Mr. Coburn. I do not remember the circumstance. U. S. GRANT.' In your letter you say, 'I have seen and heard the charge made by Democratic speakers, and it is used very extensively against you here, that you vetoed some pension bill of the widow of a soldier, which has passed over your veto.—It being cited as a condemnation of you by Congress.' You desire to be informed what the case is, and request to be furnished with a copy of the President's veto message. Having no recollection of such a case as that to which you refer, I have caused an examination of the records of this office to be made, with a view to complying with your request. All pension bills are referred by the President to this Department for information, as to whether any objection exists, to their receiving the approval of the Executive. An Act granting a pension to Mary Ann Montgomery, Widow of Wm W. Montgomery, late Captain of Texas Volunteers, was passed during the last session of Congress, and referred to this Department in the usual manner. . . . This is the only case that can be found upon the record in this Department where the President's approval is with-held, and the reason why the Act did not receive the Executive approval at the date of the letter, is obvious. It is presumed that when the error was corrected by Congress the Act was approved, as in all other pension cases which were referred to this Department for information as to the propriety of such action by the Executive. If this is not the case out of which the falsehood alluded to in your letter has been forged, I presume it will be found to have been uttered in regard to some other case equally easy of explanation." ". . . I have forwarded a copy of my letter to you to the President at Long Branch for his inspection, and to see if there is anything which he desires should be adde[d] to or taken from my letter. As soon as I hear from him I will telegraph you. Until you hear from me by telegram or letter, please omit to make public the letter which I have sent you." Copies, Delanc Letterbook, OHi. *The Collector*, May, 1948, listed the original letter from Coburn to USG with USG's endorsement.

To Congress

[*May 14, 1872*]

In my Message to Congress at the begining of its present Session allusion was made to the hardships and privations inflicted upon poor immigrants. coming to this country on shipboard, and upon arrival on our shores. and [a] suggestion was made favoring National legislation for a [withfor the purpose of effecting a] radical cure of the evil. Promise was made of [that] a special Message during the Session, on this subject [would be presented during the present session] should information be received [which would] warranting it. I now transmit to the two houses of Congress all that has been officially received since that time bearing upon the subject and recommend that such legislation be had as will secure first; such room and accomodation on ship board as ~~wd~~ is necessary for health and comfort; and such privacy [and protection] as not to ~~subject the~~ compell, immigrant[s] to be the unwilling witness ~~of~~ [to] so much vice and misery; and, Second: legislation to protect them [~~the emi-grant~~] upon their arrival at our Seaports from the ~~sharpers~~ [knaves who are] ever ready to despoil them of the little all which they are able to bring with them.—Such legislation will be in the ~~direction~~ [interests,] of humanity and seems ~~to me~~ to be fully justifyable. The immigrant is not a citizen of any state, or territory upon his arrival, but comes here to become a citizen of a great republic, free to change his residence at will, to enjoy the blessing of a protecting government where all are equal before the law, and to add to the National wealth by his industry. On his arrival he does not know states or corporations but confides implicitly in the protecting arm of the great free country of which he has heard so much before leaving his native land. ~~What must be the~~ [It is a source of serious] disappointment and discouragement ~~of thousand annually~~ [to those] who ~~come~~ start with means sufficient to support them comfortably until they can choose a residence and begin employment for a comfortable support to find themselves subject to ill treatment and every discomfort on their passage here, and at the end of their journey seized upon by professional friends claiming legal right to take charge of them for their protection who do not leave them until all their resources are exhausted when they are abandoned in a strange land ~~among~~ [surrounded by] strangers, ~~and~~ without employment and ~~without the knowledge how~~ [and ignorant of the means of] to secure[ing] it. Under the present system this is the fate of thousands annually. The exposures ~~of~~ [on] shipboard, and the treatment on landing ~~have~~ driven[s] thousands to lives of vice and shame who, with proper humane treatment might be[~~have become~~come] useful and respectable members. of society.

I do not advise National legislation in affairs that should be regulated by the states but I see no subject more National in its ~~nature~~ [character] than provision for the safety and welfare of the thousands who leave foreing lands to become citizens of this republic.

When their residence is chosen they ~~become~~ may [then] look to the laws of their locality for protection and guidance.

[The mass of immigrants arriving upon our shores, coming as they do on vessels under foreign flags, makes treaties with the nations furnishing these immigrants necessary for their complete protection. For more than two years efforts have been made, on our part, to secure such treaties, and there is now reasonable ground to hope for success.]

ADf, OFH (bracketed material not in USG's hand); DS, DNA, RG 46, Presidential Messages, Domestic Affairs. The final paragraph is not in the draft. *SED*, 42-2-73. On Nov. 1, 1871, J. Fred. Meyers, clerk, Treasury Dept., wrote to Secretary of the Treasury George S. Boutwell. "Under date of June 22, 1871, I had the honor to receive from the Department the following comprehensive instructions: ['] You are authorized to visit those parts of Europe which furnish the larger number of emigrants for this country, for the purpose of ascertaining and reporting upon the character of the emigrants who come to the United States; the accommodations furnished by emigrant-ships; the treatment which the emigrants receive upon the passage; whether the laws of the United States in regard to emigrant-vessels are complied with; and, in fine, to ascertain whether any changes can be made either by legislation or by regulation to facilitate and encourage the emigration of such persons as are calculated to make good citizens of the United States.['] In pursuance of these instructions I proceeded to Great Britain and Germany, and subsequently to New York city, to investigate this important subject, and to gather the documents needful to its proper consideration. These documents, consisting in part of the emigration laws of England and of Hamburg and Bremen, as well as the regulations made in pursuance thereof, projects of treaties and of laws and statistical information, will be transmitted with a special report as soon as practicable. . . ." *Ibid.*, p. 2.

On Feb. 11, 1873, Joseph P. McDonnell, New York City, wrote to USG. "I beg respectfully to draw your attention to letters of mine, on the treatment of steerage passengers on the Allantic ocean, which appeared in *The New York Herald* of monday the 27th January and Tuesday the 4th February. I pray you for the sake of Humanity to give the matter your careful consideration and to have it brought before Congress. It is an all important question and I have not the slightest doubt that if you take it up you will find the Govts of England and other countries to co-operate with you. The question will shortly come before the British Parliament. I am about to demand an investigation by the Commissioners of Emigration but if no *legal* wrongs are proved, it has been resolved to demand an amended emigration law for the removal of the moral grievances, which are a disgrace to civilization. In a short time monster meetings will be held on the subject in New York and throughout the Union and there can be no doubt that every man in the United States who has crossed the ocean will raise his voice in favor of the proposed amendment." ALS, DNA, RG 59, Miscellaneous Letters. Also in Feb., Anton Sontag. New Orleans, wrote to USG and Congress seeking a subsidy for a steamship line to serve emigrants from the "South Slavic" countries. LS (printed), *ibid.* In March, Sontag, Washington, D. C., addressed a printed circular to USG and others asking for investors in his project. *Ibid.* Also in March, a German committee in "Birstein near Hanau on the Main" petitioned USG for reforms to benefit steerage passengers. DS, *ibid.*

On Dec. 1, 1873, Helen M. Barnard submitted a "Report on Emigration" to Secretary of the Treasury William A. Richardson. "In compliance with your instructions of June 6, 1873, directing me to report upon the treatment of emigrants on board steamships, particularly to inquire into that of women and children, authorizing me to visit the ports of Baltimore, Philadelphia, New York, and Boston, in the United States; Liverpool, Havre, Brest, and Hamburg, in Europe; directing me, in order to fully understand the conduct and treatment of passengers during the voyage, to inspect the steerage as frequently as possible, both in ordinary and exceptional weather, I commenced my investigations at Castle Garden on the 10th of June. . . ." *SED*, 43-1-23, 145. Barnard's recommendations included steps to prevent overcrowding aboard ship, standardize railroad schedules and ticket prices, and create a national emigration bureau. "I cannot close this report, Mr. Secretary, without expressing my appreciation of the courtesy and consideration with which I was received, in my official capacity, by the agents of the steamship companies and railroad officials. Every facility was given me for observation and investigation, with one exception—that of the agent of the Hamburg line of steamers, at Southampton, England. This was especially gratifying to me, as the appointment of a woman being an innovation upon established customs, it proved my mission to be well founded in good sense and humanity." *Ibid.*, p. 155. Similar reports, including one by Meyers, are *ibid.*

On March 26, Vice President Henry Wilson had written to USG. "The wish has been expressed by several that a lady should be appointed as one of the commissioners to the approaching exposition at Vienna   I am (now) free to express my hearty approval of the suggestion, and my conviction that Mrs Helen M. Barnard of this city is a very suitable person to receive that appointment, and I heartily concur in the wish expressed that she may receive it" ALS, DNA, RG 59, Letters of Application and Recommendation. On the same day, Benjamin R. Cowen, asst. secretary of the interior, wrote to USG. "I have known Mrs. H. M. Barnard quite will for the past eighteen months as a writer for the press, and as an active political worker. As such She has rendered most efficient Service to the Republican cause, & her Services have been gratefully attested by our Several Committees. She is a lady of culture and fine address who would reflect high credit upon our nation if sent to the Vienna Exposition, & her appointment there would be a fitting & graceful acknowledgment of her Services, her qualifications, and the growing influence of woman in our public affairs." ALS, *ibid.* On March 27, U.S. Representative James A. Garfield wrote to USG. "The appointment of Mrs Barnard as one of the Assistant Commissioners to the Vienna Exposition, would gratify her large circle of friends—and would be a fitting recognition of the position which woman is taking in this country, in journalism and the general industries of this country—Mrs Barnard is a woman of remarkable intelligence and ability—and would most worthily and ably perform the duties of the position referred to—" ALS, *ibid.* Related papers are *ibid.* See *HMD*, 43-1-172, 43-1-208.

On May 30, 1871, Stephen G. Marcou had written to Secretary of State Hamilton Fish. "enclosed is a letter from the governor of Kansas, the state in which I reside, vouching for my respectability—I am now starting for France to lecture there about Kansas with a view to inducing immigration and as my efforts would amount to little or nothing without any recommendations I hope that you shall, on the strength of Gov—Harvey's request grant me what he asks for me . . . P. S. If you see fit to grant me that that favor, please address it at Mr Washburne's office in Paris in France where I shall find it." ALS, DNA, RG 59, Miscellaneous Letters. The enclosure is *ibid.*

On Sept. 20, Isaac Hessberg, Cincinnati, wrote to Fish. "I take the liberty to transmit to you copy of letter of Hon. Edw. Young Chief of Bureau, referring me to this Dept for information of immigration. My intention is to go in that capacity to Germany to promote such immigration, and my standing here, as well, as out there including the influence, I can bring to this country not only laboring classes, but also people of means. If I could obtain Such a Commission, I offer myself as a candidate without reference to any appropriation of Congress. My recommendations will be unexceptional, and I would ask the favor of a personal interview, if such can be had of you." ALS, *ibid.*, Letters of Application and Recommendation. On Sept. 13, Edward Young, chief, Bureau of Statistics, Treasury Dept., had written to Hessberg. "Your letter of the 5th inst, to the Secretary of the Interior, has been referred to me. In reply I have to state that there is no 'organized system for promoting immigration from Germany to the United States, regulated and sanctioned by the Federal Government,' altough many of the Western and Southern States have agencies in Europe. A Bureau of Emigration was established in the State Department and a Commissioner appointed, but it was discontinued about two years since owing to the failure of Congress to make the necessary appropriation. It may not be amiss, perhaps for you to address the State Department on the Subject. I send you a copy of my Report on Immigration" Copy, *ibid.*

On Oct. 5, 1866, William S. Rowland, commissioner, Northern Pacific Railroad Co., Washington, D. C., had written to Secretary of State William H. Seward. "Believing that with proper efforts, the 'Exposition of all nations,' at Paris can be made the means of giving a new and vital impetus to the promotion of emigration from the old world, I propose to visit Paris as a '*Special* Commissioner,' representing the states of Wisconsin, Minnesota & Oregon and the Territories of Dakota, Montana, Idaho & Washington commissioned by their respective Governors, with a view to provide a full and complete representation of their cereal and mineral productions, collecting & collating complete statistics of climate, soil &c., thereby affording to the people of Europe & especially of the Germanic countries, that education in all that pertains to our present and future as a country and people, so necessary to be understood by the emigrant before entering upon a new and untried field of life. . . ." LS, *ibid.*, Applications and Recommendations, Lincoln and Johnson. USG endorsed this letter. "I am of opinion that the Course proposed by Mr Rowland would have a tendency to encourage immigration from abroad and the settlement of the north west and west" Copy (undated), *ibid.*

On Nov. 23, 1870, a correspondent reported from the "National Immigration Convention" in Indianapolis. "One of the agents that had been most active in the inauguration of this Convention is Col. William S. Rowland, who has served the Government as foreign representative and in the late war, has long had this subject at heart. Not from opposition to any organized scheme of immigration, but for the purpose of ameliorating, in every possible way, the condition of the immigrant, and promoting increased immigration. The table of rates shows a falling off in the last ten years. The Colonel is an active, energetic worker, and, while pursuing the business of the Convention with vigor, has been singularly modest about thrusting his views before the public." *New York Tribune*, Nov. 28, 1870. Rowland attended the convention as a delegate from Minn. See *PUSG*, 20, 199.

On June 26, 1871, Horace Porter, Long Branch, wrote to Rowland. "The President directs me to acknowledge the receipt of your letter of the 22d inst. and to say that he will leave the Branch tomorrow and be absent till Saturday next. At any time after that date he will be pleased to give you an interview at any time you may find it convenient to call upon him." ALS, Wayde Chrismer, Bel Air, Md. On July 18, Fish wrote "To the Diplomatic and Consular Representative of the United States, in Europe—" "Mr W. S. Rowland visits Europe desiring to investigate the system prevailing in different Countries there for the protection of Emigrants coming to the United States—& in the hope of contributing to the melioration of the condition & treatment on their voyage of that large & valuable class of Passengers. I have to request that you will render to Mr Rowland such advice and assistance in attaining the object mentioned as may be proper and consistent with your duties—" ALS, DNA, RG 59, Miscellaneous Letters.

On Oct. 13, Fish wrote in his diary. "I read a letter from the German Society, in the City of New York complaining of Col W. S. Rowland, supposed by them to have been 'appointed' U S Commissioner of Emigration in Europe' & requesting that that 'position be given to a man of good & unblemished character'—He has not been appointed to any position—but by the Presidents express instructions, (& in spite of many remonstrances, & much hesitancy on my part,) a circular letter of introduction, & recommendation to the Dept & Consular agents of the Govt—He directs that it be recalled—(a difficult thing to do, as the man has it, & is—I know not where)   A private letter from Badeau to Davis rcd to day enquires who he is—says he has two 'hobbies—Emigration—& opposition to Erie RRoad'—" DLC-Hamilton Fish. In Sept., 1871, Adam Badeau, consul gen., London, had written to "My dear Sir," probably J. C. Bancroft Davis, asst. secretary of state. "I enclose a copy of the Circular which at Mr. Rowland's request I have addressed to the Consuls in the United Kingdom. The inquiries are his own; the rest mine. I wish to know whether I am to furnish him with a letter embodying the result of the information that may be obtained in reply: particularly in answer to his Ninth and Tenth ~~paragraph~~ inquiries. He wants me to address the letter to the Secretary of the Treasury, and furnish him a copy; but the Sec of the Treasury has not asked me for any such document, and it would be officious in me to propose one. The State Dept by its circular letter in his behalf has opened the Subject, and I should suppose if a letter were written, it should be to the State Dept; but I think I should ~~be~~ have authority before giving him a copy. He declares that the President means to issue a special message on the subject, and to lay my letter before Congress. All I want is to do whatever the President and the Department desire. Gen Schenck allows me to say *confidentially* that he knows Col R's character to be bad; which makes me still more anxious to be directly informed in the matter. I remember you took a great interest in Emigration not long since. Ham. Fish says you are likely to be out here in November. Nobody will be more glad to see you . . ." ALS, DNA, RG 59, Consular Despatches, London. The enclosed "Circular No. 8," signed by Badeau, is dated Sept. 29. ". . . NINTH:—Are you cognizant of instances of mis-information having been given to persons for the purpose of inducing them to emigrate, if so, what is its character and by whom was it given? TENTH:—Has any credible report reached you of abuse or fraud practised upon Emigrants after embarkation, and while in transit upon the seas or inland, in the United States; if so what is it? Any answers to paragraphs nine and ten may be made in a separate document, and will be considered confidential." DS, *ibid.*

On Oct. 13, Fish wrote to Robert C. Schenck, U.S. minister, London. "On the 18th of July, last, by direction of the President, a circular letter was issued from this Department recommending William S. Rowland, to the good offices of the Diplomatic and Consular Officers of the United States, especially in connection with the subject of emigration. The President desires to have the recommendation recalled. Should it be presented to you you will therefore retain it and transmit it to this Department." Copy, *ibid.*, Diplomatic Instructions, Great Britain. An editorial appeared the following day. "People in Europe should be cautious how they trust individuals professing to be agents of the United States' Government. Those who are really acting in such a capacity are able to show irrefragable proofs of the fact, in the absence of which they may safely be put down as impostors. We fear that in the latter category must be included 'Col. W. S. ROWLAND,' who is at present traveling about Europe as 'the Special Commissioner of the United States Government to examine into the whole subject of emigration.' . . ." *New York Times,* Oct. 14, 1871.

On Oct. 27, Rowland, Paris, wrote to USG. "Having concluded my investigations in Europe of the Question of emigration to the United States, especially refering to laws and regulations enforced by the various Governments of Europe for the protection of Emigrant passengers, and being this moment informed that gross attacks have recently been made upon me by individuals and through the press in the United States, I deem it a duty to the President to return to him the circular letter of the Hon the Secretary of State issued prior to my departure from the U. States   In doing so permit me to assure the President that no improper use has been made of this letter and that the information obtained by a carful study of the whole question of Emigration aided as I have been by some of the best and most inteligent men of Europe, will be at the disposal of the President at any time after the 1st of December" ALS, DNA, RG 59, Miscellaneous Letters.

In an undated letter, Pancratz Boll wrote to USG. "The wise and beneficent policy of the Government in providing for the construction of continental lines of Railway to the Pacific Ocean, and the consequent rapid reduction of our American Wilderness to a condition of Civilisation, has rendered it imperative that increased facilities shall be afforded to promote emigration to and the settlement and development of our rich agricultural and mineral lands which are thus brought into market. . . . The People of Europe are men of education and means, industrious and intelligent, skilled in agriculture, manufactures, & the Arts and Sciences. These germs of foreign industry can with safety be engrafted upon our New World. Your Memorialist therefor hopes That this important matter will meet with the careful consideration and earnest support of your Excellency" ALS, DLC-Carl Schurz. Governor John M. Palmer of Ill. endorsed this letter. "Mr P. Boll of Bond County the writer of the within is well known to me as an intelligent and honorable man who is worthy of the fullest confidence and I cordially sympathise with his views and commend him to the consideration of the governmt" AES (undated), *ibid.* On Dec. 9, 1872, USG nominated Boll as postmaster, Greenville, Ill.

To Senate

TO THE SENATE.

In answer to a Resolution of the Senate of the 28th of March, last, I transmit herewith, copies of the correspondence between the Department of State and the Consul of the United States at

Bucharest, relative to the persecution and oppression of the Israelites in the principality of Roumania.

U. S. GRANT

WASHINGTON, MAY 14TH 1872.

DS, DNA, RG 46, Presidential Messages. *SED*, 42-2-75. On May 14, 1872, Secretary
of State Hamilton Fish wrote to USG transmitting copies of correspondence between
Benjamin F. Peixotto, consul, Bucharest, and the State Dept. on the subject of a recent
pogrom in Romania. LS, DNA, RG 46, Presidential Messages. See *PUSG*, 21, 74; *Foreign
Relations, 1872*, pp. 680–98. On May 23, USG wrote to the House of Representatives. "In
answer to a Resolution of the House of Representatives of the 20th instant, requesting me
to join the Italian Government in the protest against the intolerant and cruel treatment of
the Jews of Roumania, I transmit a report from the Secretary of State relating to the
subject." Copies, DNA, RG 59, Reports to the President and Congress; *ibid.*, RG 130,
Messages to Congress. *HED*, 42-2-318. On May 22, Fish had written to USG. ". . . early
in February last, on the occurrence of the recent outrages upon the persons and property
of Israelites, the Consul of the United States at Bucharest, in common with the Representatives of other Powers, addressed a note of remonstrance to the Minister; and more recently united with the Representative of those Powers (Italy being included) in a collec-
tive note to the Princier Government, bearing date April 18, 1872 on the subject of these
recent occurrences, and pointing with marked but just severity, to the impunity which had
been enjoyed by the perpetrators of the violence which is characterised appropriately as
unworthy of a civilized Country—The action of the Consul was approved and he was
instructed not to be backward in joining any similar protest or other measure which the
foreign representatives there may deem advisable, with a view to avert or mitigate further
harshness toward the Israelites residents in or subjects of the Principalities. . . ." Copy,
DNA, RG 59, Reports to the President and Congress.

On July 30, J. Jaroslawski, New York City, wrote to USG. "The fanatical persecu-
tions of the Jewish inhabitants of Rumania, has produced a just indignation among the
leading Governments of Europe, who have lately admonished the Ruler of that Country
that the Government should in future prevent such barbarous actions by providing equal
privileges to all the people, irrespective of their Relegeous sentiments. The cause of humanity and civilization would be greatly aided, if our administration could, in accord with
the traditional policy of the Government, address a similar remonstrance to the Government of Rumania   I therefore, very respectfully present this matter to the consideration
of your Excellency and beg to favor me in reply with your views on the subject." ALS,
ibid., Miscellaneous Letters.

On Sept. 16, George P. A. Healy, Bucharest, wrote to USG. "Being called here pro-
fessionally by the reigning Sovereign of this Country, where I have been treated with high
consideration and kindness; which has made the accounts of I have heard both from English and French residing here; very painful to me, as an American citizen; viz. that the
United States Consul has taken the initiative and induced the consuls of the other Powers
to sign a note to this Government in regard to the Jews of Roumania, which is considered
highly improper and meddlesome, utterly apart from his duty as American Counsul,   this

step, has really done harm to the cause of the Jews, for advocating which, it is said he has forty thousand francs a year from the Jews of the State of Callifornia. I have been careful to be sure that thate misdemeanour complained of by our consul, is entirely true. Since writing to your Excellency from Rome, when I forwarded your son's portrait, which I hope has arrived in safety. I have had the pleasure of seeing General Shurman in Paris: which city I left the 6th of last month,   I expect to be detained in Bucarest until about the 6th of Decr   I shall return to Rome the 1st of Jany after finishing two or three work commenced in Paris. With kind regards to your family, . . .'' ALS, *ibid.* See *PUSG,* 19, 109–10. Healy had written to USG transmitting his portrait "of the unspoiled and gifted son of the man our country loves to honor." William Evarts Benjamin, Catalogue No. 27, Nov., 1889, p. 7.

To Editor, Cincinnati Gazette

———

WASHINGTON, D. C., May 14, 1872.

DEAR SIR: Your favor of the 10th inst., saying that the managers of the GAZETTE had decided to come out squarely for my nomination at Philadelphia June 5th prox., when they were met by the report that I would either decline being a candidate before the Convention, or would decline after nomination, was recieved last night, after leaving my office for the day. I caused a dispatch to be sent to you to the effect that the report was without any authority whatever.

I am not in the habit of writing letters on political subjects, and especially have I never written a letter calculated to influence a Conveniion as to who should be candidates before it, or selected by it. But your letter is of such a nature as to properly demand an answer, more particularly as you say you will treat my response as strictly confidential.

Now I will say that I never proclaimed myself a candidate, either before the Convention which meets in Philadelphia this year, nor the Convention which was held in Chicago four years ago. I have never written a line, done an act, nor, I believe I can say with truth, entertained a thought calculated to produce action by the Republican party in favor of my promotion over that of any other man in it who might be their choice.

I do now, as I did four years ago, sincerely believe that the interests of the whole country demand the success of the Republican party,   If deemed advisable, I am willing to make any sacrifice to accomplish that success. I feel that I did make a sacrifice in giving up a high position so highly prized by me—one created for me by an appreciative public, for which act I can never thank them sufficiently.

Now, if I can be of service to the party that chose me then, I shall render that service conscientiously and to the best of my ability. The personal sacrifice made four years ago can not be made now.

With great respect, your obedient servant,

U. S. GRANT.

Cincinnati Gazette, Oct. 31, 1874. Allegations that USG would seek a third term prompted this letter's publication. On Oct. 27, 1874, Secretary of State Hamilton Fish recorded in his diary. "Mr Bristow referred to a conversation with Senator Edmonds respecting the effect produced in northern New York by the prevalent excitement and aprehension of third term—. . . He referred to a speach reported to have been made by Genl Dix, in New York last night, and suggested that it might be advisable for the President to say something on the subject stating at the same time that when the matter had been spoken of a few days since, he had expressed a different opinion but had been led to change his mind in consequence of what he had learned from Edmonds and other sources—The President said that the whole thing was too absurd to be talked of, that it had been started by the New York Herald as one of its sensation and for the purpose of personal annoyance to him—That it had been dead for nearly a year but had been lately revived by the Sun, Tribune, and Democratic Press. That he had never given it a thought or spoken of it except in ridicule and contempt and he was not disposed now to do otherwise than he had done—I was appealed to as to my opinion, of the effect of the thing in New York. I thought that it was working disasterously and was endangering both the state ticket and the Legislature. And being asked whether I thought any expression now, could change the current I said—Yes! and suggested that the President might make Dix's speach of last evening, the subject of a letter to him to him expressing coincidence of views. Jewell was also of opinion that some opinion should be put forth by the President. Delano and Williams opposed thinking that any declaration at this time, would be taken as an indication of alarm, as to the results of the pending election and would be disasterous. The President concurred in this view, but authorized the repeating of any-thing he had said on the subject, adding that the only time that it lately had been brought to his notice, was in Chicago, when some strolling minstrels came into his parlor and after preforming some time retired. When his little son Jesse exclaimed, well! I am opposed to Papa's being a Candidate for the third term if he is to be subjected to such annoyances." DLC-Hamilton Fish. See *ibid.*, Oct. 28, 1874; *Cincinnati Gazette*, Nov. 2, 3, 1874.

To Hamilton Fish

Washington D. C. May 15th *1872.*

HON. HAMILTON FISH;
SEC. OF STATE;
DEAR SIR:

Mr. Savage's address is Fort Plain, N. Y. I am just in receipt of a note from him in which he says that the granting of leave of absence without pay leaves him 3000 miles from home without the means of reaching there. I think it will be well to send him the appointment agreed upon yesterday, and; if not inconsistent with law, allow him "Leave of Absence" pay sufficient time for him to reach his home, or until his pay commences in his new position.

Very Truly Yours
U. S. GRANT

ALS, DLC-Hamilton Fish. Richard H. Savage, born in 1846 in Utica, N. Y., graduated from USMA (1868) and served as bvt. 2nd lt., corps of engineers, in San Francisco until Dec. 31, 1870. He was consular clerk in Rome and Marseilles and military secretary in the Egyptian Army (1871–72). See Proclamation, May 21, 1872.

To Hamilton Fish

Washington D. C. May 16th *1872.*

HON. HAMILTON FISH,
SEC. OF STATE:
DEAR SIR:

Senator Cameron, Ch. Com. on Foreign Relations, called on me last evening to suggest the idea that all the correspondence in relation to the Washington Treaty be ordered published by the Senate, and that he would so move to-day unless notified that I would prefer that it should not be done. I should have written this to you last night but having company until late it escaped my memory.

Whether it is proper to permit the publication officially without notifying the British Gvt. first or not I have my doubts. If you deem this course advisable will you be good enough to so notify Senator Cameron and send such a dispatch to Gen. Schenck as you deem advisable.

Faithfully Yours,
U. S. GRANT

ALS, DLC-Hamilton Fish. On Thursday, May 16, 1872, Secretary of State Hamilton Fish wrote in his diary. "Sir Ed. Thornton—. . . I mention the surreptitious publication in the NY Herald of the Correspondence sent to the Senate on Monday last in connection with the Geneva Conference question, & ask if his Govt wd object now to the authorized publication of the correspondence &c. He thinks not—I say that we will not publish it if there be any objection on the part of his Govt & ask if he feel authorized to speak in their behalf on the question, or will telegraph to obtain their assent—he says that being already published, he feels justified in saying that no objection will be had to our authorized publication by the Senate, & that he will telegraph to his Govt that he has said so" *Ibid.*

On May 15, USG wrote to the House of Representatives. "I transmit herewith, for the information of the House of Representatives, the correspondence which has recently taken place respecting the differences of opinion which have arisen between this Government and that of Great Britain with regard to the powers of the Tribunal of Arbitration created under the Treaty signed at Washington May 8. 1871. and which has led to certain negotiations still pending between the two Governments." Copies, DNA, RG 59, Reports to the President and Congress; *ibid.*, RG 130, Messages to Congress. *HED,* 42-2-294. On May 17, Fish wrote to U.S. Representative Nathaniel P. Banks of Mass., chairman, Committee on Foreign Affairs. "I have the honor to acknowledge the receipt of your letter of yesterday, suggesting that the recent correspondence relating to the Alabama Claims should be transmitted for the use of your Committee. The President transmitted to the House, the day before yesterday all of the correspondence, excepting that leading to the proposal by the British Government of the new article which is now under consideration by the Senate. If you or any of the Members of the Committee desire to see this later correspondence, I shall be glad to show it to any of the Committee in confidence." Copy, DNA, RG 59, Reports to the President and Congress.

To Charles W. Ford

———

Washington D. C. May 17th *1872.*

DEAR FORD.

I have shipped this morning, man in charge, one mare and one thorough bred Alderney heiffer. The man will bring back with him the two gray colts. The mare I sent I have had for six years. She could, when sound, trot to the poll in about 2.40. I paid $2500 00 for her and mate now on my farm. This one has given out in the front feet but is otherwise sound I believe. The man (Farrier) employed by govt. at Jefferson Bks. says that he can cure her. If he succeeds I think you had better send Butcher Boy to the farm in the Fall and take the mare, provided she is not in foal at the time. I think she will not be for I put her to the horse for four years at considerable expense without getting a colt. She is perfectly kind in single or double harness. Any woman or child may drive her.

I tried to get five head more of the Dutch belted cattle to send to the farm but the price is so high, $400 00 a piece, that I declined.

Yours Truly
U. S. GRANT

ALS, DLC-USG. See letter to Charles W. Ford, April 23, 1872.

To Robert C. Schenck

Washington D. C. May 17th *1872.*

MY DEAR GENERAL:

Since Nellie's arrival in England she has written several letters home in which she speaks of the attention and kindness she received at your hands and that of your daughters.[1] Allow me on my own behalf, and that of Mrs. Grant also, to thank you and them for their attention, and to say they will ever be appreciated.

Nellie seems from her letters to be enjoying her trip very much and without, as yet any signs of homesickness. She has been all her life so much of a companion of her mother that I feared she would want to return by the first steamer leaving Liverpool after her arrival. But she writes quite the reverse of being homesick. She is however with the most estimable people, and with whom she is well acquainted.[2]

Before you receive this I have but little doubt but you will have heard that the "Washington Treaty" is in a fair way for settlement. I have been disappointed at the conduct of many of our own people in the matter, particularly those who are in the habit of visiting abroad, and those who have business connections with Europe.

Mrs. Grant joins me in kindest regards to yourself and daughters.

With great respect,
Your obt. svt.
U. S. GRANT

GEN. ROBT. C. SCHENCK
MINISTER PLEN. &C.
LONDON, ENG.

ALS, InHi. On May 14, 1872, and subsequently, Secretary of State Hamilton Fish wrote in his diary. "The new Article of the Treaty with England & its probable fate in the Senate, discussed—Morton & Chandler have declared themselves warmly in favour—Sprague & Sumner made speeches, trying to put it on the Calendar—Chandler came in during the meeting, & advises that the friends of the measure be called upon to come to its support—I write a telegram to L P Morton which is copied by others to be sent to parties in other parts of the Country—" "May 17 . . . The President mentioned that the Comm. on For. Rels of the Senate had requested that he & I attend their Comm tomorrow morning at 9—on the subject of the proposed new Article with Gt Britain—Creswell & Robeson suggest that the President do not go to the Comm. Room. but request the Comm. to meet him in his room at the Capitol—I find a note from the Prsdt (by his Secr) requesting me to attend the meeting at the Committee Room   In the Evening Frelinghuysen & subsequently Robeson call, wishing me to restrain the President from committing himself in his interview with the Committee—I think the President should not attend a Committee—if they wish to confer with him they should call upon him" "May 18—Saturday   Before going to the Capitol I drive to the Presidents, & find him in his Carriage on the point of starting for the Capitol—I say that I have come to ask whether he think it adviseable for him to attend the Committee—that as a mere matter of Etiquette & courtesy the Comm. should call upon him, not he on them—& further that his visiting the Capitol & being in consultation with the Comm. would attract attention, be commented upon by the Press, & by his opponents & be represented as an attempt to exert undue influence, & with those with whom the treaty is not recd favorably the odium would be thrown upon him—He concludes not to make the visit. I attend the Committee—. . ." DLC-Hamilton Fish. See letter to Levi P. Morton, May 27, 1872.

1. See *Julia Grant*, pp. 180–81. Widower Robert C. Schenck's three daughters accompanied him to London. See *PUSG*, 21, 99; letter to Robert C. Schenck, July 5, 1872.
2. See letter to Frederick Dent Grant, April 28, 1872.

Proclamation

TO ALL WHO SHALL SEE THESE PRESENTS, GREETING:

Know Ye; That reposing special trust and confidence in the Integrity and Ability of Thomas P. Robb,[1] of Georgia, Fabius J. Mead,[2] of Mississippi, and Richard H. Savage,[3] of California, I do hereby appoint them jointly and severally to be Commissioners under a Joint Resolution of the Senate and House of Representatives of the United States of America in Congress assembled, approved May 7, 1872,[4] to examine and enquire into depredations alleged to have been committed upon the frontiers of the State of Texas for several years past by bands of Indians and Mexicans who are alleged to have crossed the Rio Grande river into the said State of Texas; And the said Commissioners to proceed to the frontiers of the State of Texas and enquire into the extent and character of said depredations, by whom committed, their residence, or country inhabited by them, the persons murdered or carried into captivity, the character and value of the property destroyed or carried away, from what portions of said State and to whom the same belonged, And to make and transmit to the President full reports in writing of their investigations,   And do hereby authorize them and each of them to execute and fulfil the duties of that appointment according to law; And to have and to hold the said appointment with all the powers and privileges thereunto of right appertaining unto them the said Thomas P. Robb, Fabius J. Mead and Richard H. Savage, during the pleasure of the President of the United States for the time being.

Given under my hand at the City of Washington this 21st day of May in the year of our Lord one thousand eight hundred and seventy-two, and of the Independence of the United States the Ninety-sixth.

U. S. GRANT.

DS, William Roth, Lakeland, Minn. On March 16, 1871, Governor Edmund J. Davis of Tex. had written to USG. "I have the honor to enclose herewith certified copy of a Joint Resolution asking the Congress of the United States to send a joint committee to the frontiers of Texas to inquire into and report upon the number of murders and extent of the outrages committed in Texas during the last five years, and now being committed in Texas, by bands of Indians living within the territory of the United States, and harbored within the Republic of Mexico. Approved March 15th 1871." LS, DNA, RG 75, Letters Received, Miscellaneous. The enclosure is *ibid.* and printed as *HMD*, 42-1-37. In May, a delegation of Cheyenne, Arapahoe, and Wichita chiefs met USG at the White House "and stated that their people were very anxious for peace. The President called their attention, through the interpreter, to the late depredations on the Texas border, and the chiefs disclaimed any responsibility for those outrages, which they maintain were committed by half-breeds from Mexico. The Indians then asked that the boundaries of their reservations be so defined as to confine whites and Indians within their present respective limits; and the President stated that he would communicate with Congress on the subject." *Washington Evening Star*, May 23, 1871. On Oct. 2, Frank E. Macmanus, district attorney, Brownsville, Tex., wrote to USG. "The undersigned has the honor to invite your attention to the enclosed official copy of the Report of the Grand Jury of Cameron County, made at the last term of the District Court here, revealing a system of predatory warfare upon the persons and property of citizens of the United States, inhabiting the sparsely settled country between the Rio Grande and the Nueces river, by armed bands of Mexicans, organized for that purpose in the territory of Mexico, and there finding secure asylum." ALS, DNA, RG 60, Letters Received, Tex. On March 28, 1872, U.S. Senator Morgan C. Hamilton of Tex. and others spoke at length with USG "in relation to the Mexican depredations on the frontier." *Evening Star*, March 28, 1872.

On April 16, Lt. Gen. Philip H. Sheridan, Chicago, telegraphed to AG Edward D. Townsend. "Gen Augur telegraphs that a camp of armed Mexicans one hundred (100) strong was broken up by Captain Myers Company of the ninth Cavalry from Fort McIntosh   Seven (7) commissioned officers and thirty seven (37) privates were captured, The privates are discharged and parolled and officers taken to San Antonio,   Valdez who surrendered at Fort Duncan was in Command but not captured,   They are Juarists, I advise that the officers be parrolled to save trouble and expense." Telegram received, DNA, RG 94, Letters Received, 3623 1871. On April 17, Townsend wrote to Sheridan. "Yours of sixteenth received—The President says hold the prisoners for the present—The Attorney General will instruct the District Attorney and marshal as to the matter—" ADfS, *ibid.* Related papers are *ibid.*

On the same day, Judge William H. Russell, 15th District, Brownsville, wrote to USG. "I have the honor to forward to Your Excellency the report of the Grand Jury for Hidalgo County at the last term of the District Court. The people are being daily robbed, with impugnity by armed bands from the Mexican side, as far up as Laredo & above that point by Indians. I beg to assure Your Excellency that outrages herein complained of are not in the least exaggerated." ALS, *ibid.*, RG 60, Letters from the President. A copy of Russell's letter and the grand jury report, forwarded on April 30 by Benjamin H. Bristow, act. attorney gen., to Secretary of State Hamilton Fish, is *ibid.*, RG 59, Miscellaneous Letters.

On Aug. 5, T. J. Davis, Live Oak County, Tex., wrote to USG. "With leav I A Citizen of Texas Native of the United States hear By Take The Week Hand to inform you of the diss tress of Our Frunt tier Cuntry Which has Came to Such A Pass that to Wee the Sitizans of this Frunt tear Is Suffering Every Day of the Murdering & Robing of the Indians & Mexicans   Wee Hav Wated With Patiance for help but I think if Wee Get Help Wee Will haft to Help our Self   I am Aposed to Disobaying The Laws of the U S But the

Time has Came That Every Man must Look out for his Self   I have but little to Loos
except my Famele   The time has Came that Wee Air not Aload to Use our Armes Which
Gives the Indians & uther Partes All the Shoing Which tha air Uesing to Perfect tion &
I entend to use my Armes from this on to Defend my Stock & Famele and When Mr Poleas
man Wants them He Can Git them in Indian Stile if it is   Be my Brother   ef you Would
take Thoes Damd Affercans Solders you have Stroud up & down the Reogrande Put them
to Work Arm & Equip Regelar Texians Rangers to De Fend them Selves & Fameles then
Work Would Be Dun And no time Lost or Give them Authority & Powar   it Will be dun
at our Exspence   Something must Be dun   the Frunt Tiears Is Perishing every Day for
the Want of help   the U S Troops hear is the Mexacans & Indians Gide   Pleas Give us
Power To defend our Selves . . . Look Hear   Pleas Read this" ALS, *ibid.*, RG 94, Letters
Received, 3506 1872.

On Aug. 28, George G. Davis, Brownsville, transmitted to USG resolutions adopted
at a public meeting on Aug. 16. ". . . Whereas, A depredatory war has existed on this frontier, from the year 1859, up to date with occasional intermissions, and the people residing
between the Nueces and the Rio Grande, have suffered immense losses of property; That
what is worse they have had many lives sacrificed to gratify the hate or secure the safety
of the bands of mexican marauders, levying war upon a defenseless people and Whereas
the murder of Mr. Joseph Alexander on the 11th inst. is one of the most malignant and
bloody deeds which has been perpetrated during a long series of acts of violence and
bloodshed, Resolved: That in order to prevent the recurrence of such deeds we respectfully request the President of the United States to use the powers of our government, by
every means within his reach to repel or prevent the constant incursions upon our soil,
and the actual war levied upon our people, or to take such measures of policy as will secure to us the protection, which in his public utterances he has promised to every man who
owes allegiance to our flag. . . . That we hail the sessions of the Hon. Commission now in
our midst, as a harbinger of the amelioration of our condition, and as a token of the
earnestness of the Government in affording us the protection we so sorely need . . ." DS,
ibid., RG 59, Miscellaneous Letters. See *HED*, 42-3-13.

On Sept. 10, Joseph F. Haden and James A. Millican, Austin, wrote to USG. "As the
Fall election [a]re approaching, we feel it our duty to confer with you in behalf of the
voters of our section, as regards the Mexican depradations on our Frontier: to learn your
views in regard to its protection. Every one is in favor of a war, and we think that by some
decided action in the case, you could gain the majority in our State; as we know several
who are willing to vote, and even canvass, for such a President. We promise to do all in
our power for you, if you will consent to war, as nothing else will satisfy the Texas
people. By an immediate answer, you will much oblige, . . ." LS, DNA, RG 59, Miscellaneous Letters.

On Sept. 16, Archie F. McGrew, Perryville, Kan., wrote to USG. "I have the honor
to request of you a reply to a letter sent you dated August 5th 1872, with reference to the
removal of the Kickapoo and Pottawatomie Indians from the State of Coahuila Mexico to
the Indian Territory in the United States. (Application from the Indians themselves were
Enclosed)   I have received several letters from Mexico, written at the request of the
Indians making inquiries as to what we were agoing to do to expedite their removal. I have
replied that I have presented their application to Superintendent Hoag and to the Indian
Department at Washington D. C. and by letter to the President—that they will have to
await your action in the matter. You will greatly Oblige the Indians in question, as well as
myself by an Early reply." ALS, *ibid.*, RG 75, Letters Received, Central Superintendency.

On Feb. 11, 1873, Fish wrote in his diary. "President says that a Regiment of Cavalry has been orderd to the Mexican frontier: & he desires that the Mexican Govt be notified, & requested to prevent incursions of marauders from their territory, & be informed that unless they be stopped, it may become necessary to pursue them into Mexican territory— I mention that instructions were sent some time since to Nelson, to say that unless these depredations are prevented, it may become impossible to prevent retaliation—& suggest that I see Mariscal & inform him of the force sent there, & read to, or inform him of the purport of the instructions referred to—the Prsdt thinks that will be the most judicious course at the present time—" DLC-Hamilton Fish. On Feb. 13, Ignacio Mariscal, Mexican minister, told Fish ". . . that his Govt wd not be unwilling to be somewhat blind to any seemingly unintentional incursion under such circumstances, but that the hostility of the people on the frontier of Mexico toward the Texans is such that any entrance of troops on the Mexican territory would occasion much indignation—to which I reply that there is much indignation on the part of our people, at the raids made from Mexico—" *Ibid.* On Feb. 14 and March 14, Fish wrote in his diary. "The President says the Regiment of Cavalry will be there within two or three weeks—& that the orders to follow wherever they may go any marauders or Cattle thieves will be issued shortly thereafter—After some suggestions, he says they need not be issued '*immediately* after their arrival'" ". . . the Secretary of the Interior states that he is about making arrangements to send a Commission to endeavor to bring back the Kickapoo Indians, now in Mexico, to their reservations, but that there among them some freedmen and negroes with respect to whom he wishes to determine the manner in which they shall be regarded. I raise the question, whether, this band having been engaged in frequent predatory incursions and robberies in the United States may not be demanded under the Extradition Treaty. No copy of the Treaty being present the question is reserved for consideration." *Ibid.* See also Fish diary, March 25, 27, June 20, 1873. *Ibid.*

On May 30, Lt. Gen. Philip H. Sheridan, Chicago, telegraphed to Secretary of War William W. Belknap. "The prisoners captured by MacKenzie fifteen women & twenty four children have arrived at San Antonio   I will send them up to Ft Gibson in the Indian Territory where they belong Unless you otherwise direct" Telegram received, DNA, RG 75, Letters Received, Central Superintendency. On May 31, Belknap wrote to Sheridan. "I have seen the President and he approves of your disposition of the prisoners captured by Mackenzie. He will be sustained . . ." Copy, *ibid.*, RG 107, Letters Sent, Military Affairs. On Jan. 15, 1874, Fish recorded in his diary. "Mr. Mariscal . . . said he wished to approach with delicacy the subject from which he had heretofore abstained from making reference, viz. the incursion by Col. Mc.Kenzie last spring into Mexican territory— he said the Government felt very sensitive but had awaited until the Kickapoos had been removed before alluding to the subject and hoped that now that the removal was effected that they might receive some assurance to guard against any recurrence of such event. . . . I reminded him of the application which this Government had made for their consent to allow the military from the United States, in coöperation with the Mexican authorities, to remove these indians, and, that failing to obtain such assent, I had pointed out to him the risk of a necessity to take in our own hands the punishment of marauders from Mexican territory. . . ." DLC-Hamilton Fish. See *PUSG*, 16, 489; *HED*, 43-1-1, part 5, I, 537–41; A. M. Gibson, *The Kickapoos: Lords of the Middle Border* (Norman, Okla., 1963), pp. 236–52.

On April 30, 1872, U.S. Senator James W. Flanagan of Tex. had written to USG. "I have the honor to recommend for appointment as Chairman of the Commission to be appointed under resolution of Congress which passed the Senate this day authorizing a Commission to enquire into the troubles on our Mexican frontiers. Col B. F. Grafton of Jefferson Texas. Col Grafton is an able lawyer & a staunch republican." LS, DNA, RG 59, Letters of Application and Recommendation. Flanagan also recommended James M. Waide. AE, *ibid.* On Sept. 13, 1870, Waide, Denton, Tex., had written to USG. "I am requested by the friends of the Administration, living upon the frontier of Texas, to give you a few plain facts relative to our Indian troubles, facts that we are satisfied have never been communicated to you. When you was elected President your friends upon the frontier flattered themselves that our Indian troubles would soon be brought to a close, and for a short time while Gen Sheridan was in Command we had quiet upon our borders, but before and Since that time a perfect state of terror has prevailed   I will commence with James Box killed, his wife and four daughters carried off captive, two of McElroys children, Wm Freeman Son, and a Son of Thos Baily Carried off,   On the 5 Jany 68 the Kiowas killed Leatherwood, Long & Menascoe, and carried off captive Miss Carrolton, Mrs Shegog and four children,   on the 6th they killed Fitzpatrick, his wife and child and Parkhill and carried off two of Fitzpatricks little Girls (now in Washington in the care of Col Leavenworth) they burnt McCrackins house, Granery and Smoke house and Wilsons dwelling and out houses,   On the 27 Augt 68 they killed Sol Forrester, and wounded Jeff Chisum,   on the 25 Oct they carryed off about 300 head of horses   on the 30th they killed Fortinberry, Coonis, Widow Russel & 5 children and Baily,   During 69 we had but few raids   In July 70 they killed Dawson, two negroes, and Kooser and carried off Mrs Kooser and four children   In August and up to this time in this month they have made Six other raids killing Macky and two children wounded two women and carried off two children,   The number of horses stole in the last 30 months will not fall short of 4000 head,   These raids were made in Denton, Cook Montage Wise & Clay Countys, A few days ago they burnt Victoria Peak a little town in Montague Co,   I could innumerate at least twenty other raids made by Small parties of Indians,   The question daily asked is 'With Gen Grant as President, Shearman as Commander in Chief of the Armies of the U, S, and Phil Sheridan Comg the Indian Dept, all good and tried Generals, and familiar with Indian treachery, how long is this state of affairs to last? No other Class or nation of people would be allowed to commit these outrages unpunished   The Government feeds, cloths, arms & protects the Indians, why not punish them when they kill and carry off captives our Citizens,   They are allowed to bring their Captives in to the agencys and offer them for sale to the Government   a bargain is struck, the Captives are returned and that is an end of it   They go to the Comissary. draw rations amunition &c for an other raid yet no Indians are punished. We never can have peace upon our border until our Government teaches the Indians that blood means blood, and for every white man killed or captive carried off, some chief must pay the penalty just as other murderers   If the government wants to be just to her citizens, let her withhold a sufficiancy of the Indian annuity to remunerate our citizens both in life and property,   We never can have any protection until a few Companys of active Cavalry are stationed in the vicinity of where these outrages are being committed   *Let us know what our fate is to be, whether we are to have protection or abandon our homes to the Indians* . . . These Statements are made of *my own* personal knowledge, and not from hearsay,   If you doubt my veracity ask our worthy Senator J. W. Flanagan who & what I am." ALS, *ibid.*, RG 94, Letters Received, 701W 1870. Related papers are *ibid.*

On May 1, 1872, Alfred A. Green, Washington, D. C., wrote to USG. "I have the honor to make application to be appointed one of the Commissioners under the Act recently passed by Congress creating a Commission to inquire into & report upon depredations committed by Mexican & Indian marauders upon citizens living upon the frontier of Texas. I am a citizen of California & have been a member of its State Legislature, but have resided in Mexico and have a perfect familiarity with the language & habits of the people of that country and believe that I possess the other requisite qualifications to fit me for the proper & intelligent discharge of the duties of the Office to which I desire to be appointed and would respectfully refer you to the accompanying testimonials & endorsements." ALS, *ibid.*, RG 59, Letters of Application and Recommendation. U.S. Senators J. Rodman West of La. and Cornelius Cole of Calif. favorably endorsed Green's application. AES (undated), *ibid.* On Nov. 13, Green, Mazatlan, wrote to USG requesting government intervention to redress "outrages" allegedly committed by Mexican officials. ALS, *ibid.*, Miscellaneous Letters. On Aug. 5, 1874, Green, San Francisco, wrote to USG. "I have learned that Mr. Isaac S. Sisson is about giving up the Consulate of Mazatlan, and I now embrace this opportunity to comply with a request that you made to me two years ago; When you were Sending a Commission to the Rio Grande; at that time I became aware of your disposition to Send me on that Commission. I did not apply for any other position then, as you Suggested; because I did not know any office which was then vacant that I felt qualified to fill. . . ." ALS, *ibid.*, Letters of Application and Recommendation. On Aug. 11, Green again wrote to USG. "Confidential . . . Enclosed herewith, I Send you Some views of my own, tending to show that there are Strong reasons why you Should be continued in office and foreshadowing Some ideas that should be promulgated among the American people. I became aware Some two years past, when in Washington, of your desire to place me on the Commission that was Sent to the Rio Grande, and I am also aware of the influence that was brought to bear, in favor of another party. I Saw also, your card to your Secretary Genl Dent, on which was written, 'Tell Mr. Green to apply for Something else': I felt grateful to you for the offer, and although very poor (for I had been ruined by the Mexican authorities) I did not apply, for the Simple reason that I knew of no vacancy at the time that I was qualified to fill. However, if there is at the present time anything that I can do in the City of Mexico, or in any part of that Republic, I will gratefully accept it. If your late Minister to that Republic, Mr. Thos: Nelson is in Washington, he will inform you of my yielding to his desires, when I had it in my power to displace the late President Juarez and put another in his place. This I did not do because of the appeal made to my patriotism by Mr. Nelson, who Solemnly assured me that to the Juarez Government you had pledged the Support of the United States. Another favor I respectfully request. I have been waiting for Some time, as the poor only wait, with a continual longing, for a decision of my Mexican claim: a kind opportune word from you to Mr. Wadsworth, may hasten the decision, if Such a course is not incompatable with Public duty" ALS, USG 3. The enclosure likely was a letter of July 31 from Green to USG. "You will remember, that upon a certain occasion, prior to the meeting of the Philadelphia convention when I visited you at the White House, for the purpose of conversing with you upon Mexican matters, I Said 'General, you are destined by the Lord's Providence to be continued in your office another term'. My words were prophetic, altho' at that time Your Political Horizon appeared rather gloomy. . . . I will do you the justice to State, that many of the evils pertaining to Your administration, and which are charged against you, are the natural results or consequences that must inevitably flow from the belief in the doctrine that justifies rotation in office; until this is abandoned, neither the Chief Executive nor any of his Subordinates can act with full political freedom." ALS, *ibid.* On Aug. 18, 1876, Green, Washington, D. C., wrote to USG. "Having learned that the office of Vice Consul at the port of Acapulco

Mexico is now vacant by the death of the incumbent I respectfully make application to you for the appointment. . . ." ALS, DNA, RG 59, Miscellaneous Letters. No appointments followed.

On May 7, 1872, Mortimer J. Alexander, New York City, wrote to USG. "I respectfully make application to be appointed one of the Commissioners 'to enquire into the depredations on the frontiers of Texas,' recently created by joint resolution of the Senate and House of Representatives. I resided for eighteen years on the Western frontier of the State of Texas, and regard myself as familiar with the subject matter contained in the joint resolution. As to character, qualifications &c I can refer you to the leading citizens of the frontier; among others Governor Davis, and also to well-known residents of the City of New York, some letters from whom I herewith enclose. If appointed I shall direct every effort to make a report in every respect just and equitable to all parties in interest." LS, *ibid.*, Letters of Application and Recommendation. Related papers are *ibid.*

On May 8, Belknap wrote to USG. "Mr. Harlan will probably recommend to-day Genl. J. A. Williamson—late Brig. Genl. of Vols. for appointment as one of the Commissioners to the Rio Grande under act passed May 1. 1872—He will I think perform the duties, if appointed, faithfully—" ALS, OFH.

1. See Endorsement, Feb. 24, 1872.

2. Born in 1839 in Raleigh, Fabius J. Mead moved to Kankakee, Ill. (1854), served in the U.S. Army, and was collector of customs, Natchez (1866–70). On March 25, 1872, Mead, Washington, D. C., wrote to USG. "Having been informed that the mission to the Argentine Republic is now vacant, I have the honor to respectfully request the appointment at your hands" ALS, DNA, RG 59, Letters of Application and Recommendation. On the same day, U.S. Senator James L. Alcorn and U.S. Representatives Legrand W. Perce, Henry W. Barry, and George E. Harris of Miss. favorably endorsed this letter. ES, *ibid.* William W. Holden added a favorable endorsement. AES (undated), *ibid.*

On Dec. 19, Mead, Washington, D. C., wrote to USG. "I was commissioned by Senator Alcorn to say that he called yesterday, to see you but that you had gone out, and that he regreted not being able to call again, as he had to leave for Mississippi He thinks I had better not resign until he can see you on his return in January. I however enclose my resignation according to my promise, and leave my case in your hands, trusting you will not forget my circumstances in life, in dealing with my case" ANS, *ibid.*, Miscellaneous Letters. Mead's resignation, dated Dec. 17, is *ibid.*

On Dec. 28, Orville E. Babcock wrote to U.S. Senator John A. Logan of Ill. "I recd your note and spoke to the President about the matter and found that the place had been offered to a Mr. James of the Treasury, upon the recommendation of the Secty' of the Treasury, provided he desired it. The President authorized me to address the Secty and say that unless Mr James was ready to say that he desired the appointment, he (the President) had another gentleman in view who wished it and whom he would be pleased to appoint. Mr James does not desire it, and the President directs me to say to you that he will be glad to offer the place to Gen. Osborn, and that you may telegraph him to come on here as the Commission design starting for the field of their labors immediately after the re-assembling of Congress." LS, DLC-Logan Family Papers. On Jan. 7, 1873, USG appointed Thomas O. Osborn in place of Mead. Copy, DNA, RG 59, General Records.

On July 5, U.S. Senator Adelbert Ames of Miss., Natchez, wrote to USG. "I am requested by F. J. Mead of this city, to say that at any time it may suit your convenience he is now at liberty to accept a foreign appointment at your hands. He is, of course, desirous of having as lucrative a position as it is convenient for you to give him as he has at his own selection (I understand) remained up to this time here to assist in the pending canvass. Will you be kind enough to advise him of your action in the case." ALS, *ibid.*, Letters of Application and Recommendation. On Jan. 14, 1874, Mead, Washington, D. C., wrote to USG. "I regret very much that the salary is such as to preclude the possibility of my accepting the appointment to Valencia, so kindly offered me through your preference. Several years of active, and—my friends attest—efficient service and constant pecuniary contributions in the interest of the republican party in my State find me to-day, I confess, without the means to justify me in accepting an appointment at a salary of $1500—From your uniform expressions of a desire to serve me, and the assurances I had received from my entire delegation, I had no reason to doubt that I would receive a good appointment on my arrival in Washington, and, consequently, brought with me my family, library &c., ready to enter on the discharge of my duty. While I confess, Mr. President, that I have entertained the hope of receiving a more lucrative appointment at your hands, yet I deem it my duty to say, that if you will give me an appointment with a salary of $2500 or $3000, I will accept it, for aside from my urgent necessities, I feel keenly the annoyance I have given you so far, and at a time when your mind is engrossed with interests affecting the country at large, in the moulding of which, I need not add, you have my entire sympathy. . . . P. S. I have officially notified Hon Sect'y of State of my conclusion." ALS, *ibid.* See *Chicago Tribune*, Aug. 28, 1901.

3. See letter to Hamilton Fish, May 15, 1872.

4. See *CG*, 42–2, 2442–43. On Nov. 13, 1872, Edmund Davis wrote to USG. "*Personal* . . . Referring to the report of the [c]ommissioners 'to inquire into depredations [o]n the Frontiers of the State of Texas,' appoint[e]d by you under the joint resolution of Congress of May 7th 1872, which report *may* form the basis of some suggestions from you in your coming annual message, I have thought it due to truth, as well as necessary to a correct understanding by you of affairs on the lower Rio Grande, that you should be warned against full faith in some of the conclusions said to have been arrived at by those commissioners. . . . Since the Peace of Guadalupe Hidalgo, there has always infested the Rio Grande a class of Americans who live by trading in stolen property (mainly horse and mule stock) brought from Mexico. The bad conduct of these men might be found largely to give a pretence for depredations from the other side, especially as it never happens that any of them are punished according to their deserts. To a correct understanding of the condition of affairs on that River, and generally of the Mexican question, we must also remember the tendency of our people to fillibuster expeditions, and the desire to furnish a cause of war against Mexico on the part of those who covet that excitement, many of whom may *perhaps* not be unmoved thereto by the recollection that Mexico sympathized with the U. S. Government in our struggle and furnished safe asylum to many fleeing Unionists from Texas. I have to ask in conclusion, that these suggestions be duly weighed, being confident that your calm and deliberate judgment, will lead you to a correct determination and one that will be satisfactory to all just minded citizens." ALS, DNA, RG 59, Miscellaneous Letters. On Nov. 23, the commissioners talked with USG about their report, "when he asked for many explanations, taking a deep interest in it. . . ." *Missouri Democrat*, Nov. 25, 1872. On Dec. 16, USG transmitted to Congress the commission's report. Copies, DNA, RG 59, Reports to the President and Congress; *ibid.*, RG 130, Messages to Congress. See Fish to U.S. Representative James A. Garfield of Ohio, Dec. 6, *ibid.*, RG 59, Reports to the President and Congress; *HED*, 42-3-39.

To Ministers and Consuls

Washington D. C. May 21st 1872.

SIR:

I take pleasure in introducing to you Mrs: Young, of Washington who proposes traveling in Europe with her Children.

Mrs: Young is the wife of Prof. Chas B. Young of this City, a most estimable man, under whose instruction I placed my sons for several years.

I commend Mrs: Young to your kind attention and protection while she may remain in your vincinity.

Very respectfully yours
U. S. GRANT.

MINISTERS & CONSULS OF THE U. S. RESIDENT ABROAD.

Copy, DLC-USG, II, 1.

On Dec. 24, 1870, USG had written to ministers and consuls. "I take pleasure in introducing to you Mr. Alexander White, an estimable citizen of Chicago, Illinois, who proposes traveling in Europe. I commend Mr. White to all United States officials abroad and bespeak for him such attention as it may be in their power to entend to him." Copy, *ibid.* Alexander White, merchant and art collector, had lived in Chicago since 1837.

On May 10, 1872, USG wrote to ministers and consuls. "I take pleasure in introducing to you Genl. J. B. Kiddoo as a Soldier who served with distinction in the rebellion, and who now visits Europe on a tour of pleasure. I commend the General to your good offices while he remaines in your vicinity." Copy, *ibid.* On Jan. 20, 1865, Bvt. Brig. Gen. Samuel A. Duncan, Annapolis, had written to Secretary of War Edwin M. Stanton recommending Col. Joseph B. Kiddoo, 22nd U.S. Colored, for appointment as brig. gen. Copy, DNA, RG 94, ACP, 1323 1875. On June 10, USG endorsed this letter. "Respectfully forwarded to the Secretary of War, and promotion by brevet recommended" ES, *ibid.* Kiddoo was appointed bvt. brig. gen. and bvt. maj. gen. of vols. as of June 15. On May 7, 1867, Kiddoo, lt. col., 43rd Inf., Detroit, wrote to AG Edward D. Townsend requesting bvt. rank in the U.S. Army. LS, *ibid.* On Oct. 12, USG endorsed this letter. "Approved for brevet of Colonel, for assault on Petersburg, 15th June 1864." ES, *ibid.* On June 9, 1868, Bvt. Maj. Gen. John Pope, Detroit, wrote to USG recommending Kiddoo for bvt. brig. gen. ALS, *ibid.* On June 19, USG unfavorably endorsed this letter. ES, *ibid.* Kiddoo retired with the rank of brig. gen. as of Dec. 15, 1870. On July 15, 1875, Jackson S. Schultz, New York City, wrote to USG enclosing a lengthy undated appeal from Kiddoo to USG protesting his reduction from brig. gen. to col. ALS, *ibid.*; copy (printed), *ibid.* On March 22, 1876, Attorney Gen. Edwards Pierrepont wrote at length to Secretary of War Alphonso Taft ruling that Kiddoo should be restored to brig. gen. LS, *ibid.* On April 12, Taft endorsed this letter. "By direction of the President, and under this opinion, the order, under the act approved March 3. 1875, reducing the rank of Brigadier General Kiddoo to that of Colonel will be revoked." ES, *ibid.* See *New York Times,* Aug. 20, 1880.

On May 17, 1872, USG wrote to Robert C. Schenck, U.S. minister, London. "I take pleasure in introducing to you Mr. Newton T. Hartshorn, of Boston, as an artist of rare excellency and ability, who has had great success in his crayon portraits in this country & now visits England in the interest of his profession. I beg to commend Mr. Hartshorn to you and bespeak your kind interest in his success." Copy, DLC-USG, II, 1. On June 15, Orville E. Babcock wrote to Newton T. Hartshorn, care of George H. Corliss, Providence, R. I. "Mrs Grant desires me to write you and in her name convey to you her sincere thanks for the crayon portrait of the President which you were so very kind as to present to her. She wishes me to say that she thinks you have been remarkably successful in your picture and that she feels no hesitation in pronouncing it one of the best, if not the very best likeness of the President yet drawn. She sends you her best wishes for your continued success in your profession." Copy, *ibid.* See Thomas William Herringshaw, ed., *National Library of American Biography* (Chicago, 1914), III, 81–82.

On May 22, William H. Benton, St. Louis, wrote to USG. "The bearer Prof. E. M. Bowman of our City desires to Visit Europe to perfect his Musical Studies   If you Can assist him in procuring such a letter from the State Departmt as will enable him to Visit the places desired by him you will Confer a favor, by doing so, on Your friend" ALS, DNA, RG 59, Miscellaneous Letters. Charles W. Ford favorably endorsed this letter. AES (undated), *ibid.* Born in 1848 in Barnard, Vt., Edward M. Bowman was an acclaimed church organist in Minneapolis and New York City before moving to St. Louis in 1867.

On June 18, USG wrote to ministers and consuls. "It affords me much pleasure to introduce to you Mr H. A. Spaulding, of the firm of Tiffany & Co. of New York, who visits Europe partly upon business and partly upon a tour of pleasure; and to commend him as a gentleman who will fully appreciate any attention you may be able to show him while he remains in your vicinity." LS, ICarbS. On Oct. 25, 1865, Bvt. Col. Ely S. Parker, Washington, D. C., had written to Henry A. Spaulding about presenting to Julia Dent Grant jewelry that Spaulding had crafted from the Appomattox apple tree, which USG identified as "the tree under which Col Babcock found Gen Lee near the Appomattox C. H. when sent after Lee to come out of his lines and capitulate—Mrs Grant intimated to me that her husband would send you an a letter of acknowledgment of the present, which for aught I know has already been done. . . ." ALS, Gilder Lehrman Collection, NNP. See *Encyclopædia of Biography of Illinois* (Chicago, 1894), II, 374.

On July 24, 1872, USG wrote to ministers and consuls. "This will introduce to you Mr Merritt Gally, who is about to visit Europe. Mr Gally is a citizen of the state of New York who has distinguished himself by a number of ingenious inventions in the art of printing. . . ." Copy, DLC-USG, II, 1. On Feb. 12, 1873, Isaac F. Quinby, Washington, D. C., wrote to USG. "Permit me to recommend Mr Merritt Gally of Rochester N. Y for appointment as one of the Commissioners from the United States to attend the Vienna Exposition to be held this year. I take the liberty of making this recommendation with the less diffidence because you have personal knowledge of some of the qualifications that Mr Gally possesses for such an appointment   In the assurance that his claims will not thereby be weakened I will state a few circumstances in reference to him that probably have never been brought to your notice   When a lad of about 15 years Mr Gally was apprenticed to a job printer in Rochester and served out his full time becoming not only an expert in his trade but also an accomplished wood engraver. Feeling the want of a literary and scientific education at about 18 years he entered the University of Rochester and though throughout his course in that Institution he worked at his trade for his support he maintained a highly creditable standing in all his classes. After graduating at the University he studied for, and finally entered upon the ministry of the Gospel; but failing health and loss of voice in a few years compelled him to abandon the ministry and to resort to some other mode of support for himself and family. While engaged as a printer his attention had been called to many imperfections in the presses then in use but the necessities of his condition did not at that time permit him to attempt a remedy for these imperfections. When he gave up the ministry he recalled the experience of his boyhood and set his inventive genius at work on a job printing press. The result of his labor was a press of that kind which is rapidly supplanting others and which is acknowledged by competent judges to be by far the best in use. Your attention has been called to some of Mr Gally's more recent inventions and I will therefore conclude this letter by stating that he is a gentleman of culture—a most important requisite for the appointment I ask for him and, in addition, his knowledge of Machinery and the readiness with which he can analyze a complicated Machine, and discover its merits and defects, would, in my opinion, render his services, as one of the Commissioners, of great value to this Country." ALS, DNA, RG 59, Letters of Application and Recommendation. No appointment followed. On Feb. 13, Babcock wrote to Mortimer D. Leggett, commissioner of patents. "The President directs me to request you to make a special case of Mr. Gally's application and take it up out of the regular order as it is necessary and desirable that it should be acted upon at once in order to admit of its presentation before the Vienna Exposition" Copy, DLC-USG, II, 1.

On Aug. 16, 1872, USG wrote to ministers and consuls. "It affords me much pleasure to introduce to you Colonel A. Piper, an officer of highly commendable service, in the Army of the United States and to bespeak for him your kind attention, while he may remain near you." Copy, *ibid.* See *PUSG*, 13, 467.

On Oct. 12, USG wrote to George H. Boker, U.S. minister, Constantinople, *et al.* "This will introduce to you Mr Lewis M. Brown, one of my most highly esteemed neighbors at Long Branch. . . ." Copy, DLC-USG, II, 1. See *Entertaining A Nation: The Career of Long Branch* (n. p., 1940), p. 44.

On Nov. 15, Annie Wittenmyer, Philadelphia, wrote to USG. "I write to ask a letter of introduction for Miss Louisa Holmes to the American Minister at Paris. Miss Holmes is a young lady of wealth and position, *a native of this country*, and highly connected in this city. But she has spent a number of years in Paris, and expects to return in about ten days. She is a Protestant lady, and goes to Paris to devote her wealth and time, to benevolent and religious work among the lower classes and her friends are afraid of the interference of the priests, unless it is understood that she is under the protection of our Goverment. I am deeply interested in her and her mission, and knowing your willingness to aid in every good movement, I take the liberty to ask this favor. Congratulating you and the country, on the result of the recent election, which has guarenteed to us an other four years of peace and honesty, . . ." ALS, DNA, RG 59, Miscellaneous Letters.

On March 10, 1873, Babcock wrote to U.S. Representative Charles B. Farwell of Ill. "I duly received your letter of the 1st inst. enclosing Mr. Hesing's letter requesting a letter of introduction abroad for Miss. Fessel, from the President. I laid the matter before him, and he expressed himself as desiring very much to gratify you, but as the matter of letters of introduction is one for which he so frequently receives application, he early in the administration adopted the rule of never giving them where the parties were going abroad on personal business, but only to personal friends traveling for pleasure, and

Mr. Hesing's application coming under the former class he had to decline it" Copy, DLC-USG, II, 2. See *PUSG*, 20, 111.

On March 12, USG wrote to ministers and consuls. "This will introduce to you Rev. W. L. Harris, D. D.   L. L. D., Bishop of the Methodist Episcopal Church, who visits Japan, China, India, Turkey & other foreign countries in the discharge of his official duties; and I commend him to your kind offices during his sojourn in your vicinity." Copy, DLC-USG, II, 2.

On March 20, USG wrote to ministers and consuls. "I take much pleasure in introducing to you Don Juan Foster, an old and esteemed resident of California, who proposes making a pleasure tour of Europe, and in the course of his travels will present this letter to you. I bespeak for him, while he may remain in your vicinity, such attention as you may be able to extend." Copy, *ibid.* See John D. Tanner, Jr., and Gloria R. Lothrop, eds., "Don Juan Forster: Southern California Ranchero," *Southern California Quarterly*, LII, 3 (Sept., 1970), 195–230.

To Senate

To the Senate of the United States:

I transmit to the Senate for its consideration, an agreement between the Great Chief of the Island of Tutuila, one of the Samoan group in the South Pacific, and Commander R. W. Meade,[1] commanding the United States Steamer "Narragansett," bearing date the 17th of February last. This instrument proposes to confer upon this Government the exclusive privilege of establishing a naval station in the dominions of that Chief for the equivalent of protecting those dominions.

A copy of a letter of the 15th instant, and of its accompaniment, addressed by the Secretary of the Navy to the Secretary of State, descriptive of Tutuila and of other Islands of the group, and of a letter in the nature of a protest from a person claiming to be Consul of the North German Confederation in that quarter, are also herewith transmitted. No Report has yet been received from Commander Meade on the subject. Although he was without special instructions or authority to enter into such agreement the advantages of the concession which it proposes to make are so great, in view of the advantageous position of Tutuila, especially as a coaling station for steamers between San Francisco and Australia, that I should not hesitate to recommend its approval but for the protection on the part of the United States which it seems to imply. With some modification of the obligation of protection which the agreement imports it is recommended to the favorable consideration of the Senate.

U. S. GRANT

WASHINGTON, MAY 22ND 1872.

DS, DNA, RG 46, Presidential Messages. *HED*, 44-1-161, 6. On March 16, 1872, USG had written to the House of Representatives. "I transmit herewith a report dated the 16th instant received from the Secretary of State in compliance with the resolution of the House of Representatives of the 7th instant" Copies, OFH; DNA, RG 59, Reports to the President and Congress; *ibid.*, RG 130, Messages to Congress. *HED*, 42-2-201. On the same day, Secretary of State Hamilton Fish, in answer to a House request for documents "relating to the application of the inhabitants of the Navigator Islands in the Pacific Ocean to have the protection of the Government of the United States extended over said Islands," reported that no such application was on file. Copy, DNA, RG 59, Reports to the President and Congress.

On April 27, Mauga, Pago Pago, Tutuila, Samoa, wrote to USG. "I write to you to beg that you will confirm and protect the compact entered into between Captain Meade and myself in Feburary last—that this harbour shall be a Naval Station for the U. S. ships of war, but that my authority shall remain and that the U. S. Government shall respect and aid in enforcing my laws (after they have been approved) and protecting my authority. I cannot give up my authority. The Chiefs of Upolu and Savaii do as they please, but I cannot cede my government and my authority. Let me therefore beg you to be so kind as to confirm and enforce the compact formed between Captain R. W. Mede. Commander of the U. S. S. 'Narragansett' in behalf of the U. S. Government, and myself Feby 17. 1872 and then signed by us both. That is all . . . P. S. I am most willing to be guided by your advice as to what laws should be made under the new circumstances" LS (in Samoan), DNA, RG 59, Miscellaneous Letters; translation, *ibid.*

On April 9, "the chiefs and rulers of Samoa," Apia, Upolu, Samoa, had petitioned USG to annex Samoa, ". . . for our future well-being and better establishment of Christianity, free institutions, fellowship of mankind, protection of life and property, and to secure the blessings of liberty and free trade to ourselves and future generations, . . ." *HED*, 44-1-161, 4. On June 28, James B. M. Stewart, New York City, wrote to William H. Webb, New York City, asking him to present this petition to USG. *Ibid.*, pp. 3–4.

On May 7, Louis-André Elloy, Apia, wrote to USG. "Would it be allowed to the Bishop of the poor Islanders of Samoa to apply to Your Excellency in favour of his people, who are now in a great anxiety about a petition addressed to Your Excellency in the beginning of the last month, to which writing they gave their names without having a proper knowledge of its content. When it came to the notice of the Upolu, Manono and Savaii chiefs, how and in what conditions the chiefs of Tutuila Island had received the protectorate of the United States of America, on proposition made to them by Captain R Meade, commander of the U. S. S. the 'Narragansett' I openly advised the principal chiefs of our Islands to follow the same steps, and to range themselves under the protectorate of the United States of America, in the same terms proposed to the chiefs of Tutuila by the

Commander of the 'Narragansett'. Our Islanders were disposed to follow my advise, when the American Schooner 'Witch Queen' arrived in Apia harbour, having on board members of the 'Central Polynesian land and commercial co. In that same time I went myself to Tutuila in a pastoral visit. During my absence propositions have been made to the Samoan chiefs of Upolu, Manono and Savaii by members of the 'Central Central Polynesian Land and commercial company. Papers have been written, and it was explained that by signing those papers, the petition to Your Excellency and a treaty made between them an[d] the 'Polynesian land and commercial company', they would secure for their Islands the protectorate of the U. S. of America. More than thirty names of chiefs have been written without any notice given to the named persons. But besides that thos[e] of the subscribers who were present unanimously attest that in the preliminary explanation given to them, it was spoken only of a protectorate, nothing was said of an annexatio[n.] It was assured to them that the object of their present petition was the same thing which has been accepted in Tutuila; the same, was it said also, to which the Bishop had advised them to give their consent. Upon this last attestation the natives did not make any mo[re] consideration, and they signed at once without taking any notice of the content of the writings. When I came back from Tutuila in the end of Apri[l] hearing from the natives what they had done, and thinking they had a perfect knowledge of it, I congratulated them[.] But what has not been my surprise when, copies of the petition and of the treaty having been handed to me I could see that, instead of a protectorate for Samoa it was the annexation of Samoa they had petitioned fo[r.] Instead of 'preserving their independance and Soverynty and instead of 'wise laws to be made by themselves, wit[h] the assistance of wise men sent from America' as it is expressed in the address presented by Captain R. Meade, commander of the 'Narragansett', it is quite the reverse whi[ch] is contained in the 2d article of the treaty with 'Polynesian land and commercial company. It is said there that 'if th[e] the President of the U. S. of America accepts the offer of annexation of those Islands to the U. S. of America, the chiefs and Rulers bind themselves to repeal any constitution they have hitherto formed, and will adopt the constitution and common law of the U. S. of America.' As use has been made of my name to induce the natives to give their consent, and as myself I had approved what they thought have done, I considered it was required from me by justice and conscience to give to the chiefs and Rulers a proper knowledge of the true meaning of their petition and treaty. What being done, they came unanimously and asked me to frame a letter, to which they wish to put their names, to protest against the error in which they have been induced. I now humbly present that contra-petition of those poor natives, and I hope Your Excellency will not allow them to be so deeply deceived in their good feelings towards the U. S. of America; I hope nothing will be done before an investigation having been made by an officer of the U. S. government, in the presence of consciencous men, upon the true mind of these natives about the proposed annexation of their Islands and the acceptation by them of the constitution and common law of the U. S. of America. For my own part I solemly testify that nothing of the kind has ever been in their idea. The annexation of their country and the lost of their nationality would be looked upon by them as the most dreaded calamity. Your Excellency will excuse this long letter from an unknown Bishop of poor people called Savages. May the voice of a father speaking for his children not be put a side, and find a good reception in the presence of Your Excellency." ALS, DNA, RG 59, Miscellaneous Letters. The enclosed petition to USG, dated May 1, disavowed the previous petition and requested protectorate status. "... We all testify that what we say now and that only has been in our mind. Those who wrote the letter and treaty to which we put our names, did not explain any other thing to us. . . . We do not know at all what may be that 'Polynesian land and commercial company'; we know only the power of the United States of America, to that power we apply for protection for our Samoan Islands. . . ." DS (in Samoan), *ibid.*; translation, *ibid.*

On July 16 and 18, Fish had written in his diary. "Sir Ed' Thornton, at the request of Ld Granville says that rumors of the application of the Navigators Islands for Annexation to the U. S. have reached the Brit. Gvt & desires information on the subject—Is told that I think there has not been any such application for annexation—but that a convention for a port in one of those Islands was signed (without previous authority from this Gvt) by an Officer of the Navy—He appeared to be informed as to that Convention—I promise to ascertain whether there has been any thing further, & let him know when next he calls" "Sr Edward Thornton, in reference to the question asked yesterday of in relation to the Navigators Island, is told that no application for Annexation or protectorate has been received—. . . He speaks of the Agreement of Commander Meade with the Chief of the Island of Tutuila respecting the Port of Pango pango—I tell him that I have not a copy of the Agreement here—it was sent to the Senate, & not being acted upon is retained there—that it is a very informal sort of Treaty, but according to my recollection it merely gave to the U S. the exclusive right of establishing a naval Station in that Harbor—" DLC-Hamilton Fish.

On Aug. 17, Albert B. Steinberger, Washington, D. C., wrote to USG. "I beg to present to your Excellency my sincere thanksfor your kindly expressions of last night. Mr. Webb will present full facts relating to the 'Navigator's Islands.' In the interests of the Government and yourself, I wish to go thither under the mantle of authority and report personally to yourself, and can only pledge my earnestness and good faith." HED, 44-1-161, 3. On Aug. 20, Horace Porter, Long Branch, endorsed this letter. "Respectfully referred to the Secretary of State. Mr. Webb strongly recommends Mr. Steinberger as a competent person to visit the Navigator's Islands and report upon their condition. He proposes to serve without pay. Of course it is not the intention to annex these islands, but if, in your judgment, it would be well to send a commissioner to report upon their condition with a view of sending such information to Congress, you might commission Mr. Steinberger for this duty." *Ibid.* Also on Aug. 20, Webb, New York City, wrote to Robert C. Schenck, U.S. minister, London. "With the full assent of Prest Grant, I beg to lay before you some facts in connection with efforts made to establish an American Line of Steamers, between the Colonies of New-Zealand & Australia & San Francisco. . . . Up to the present time the line has been running under great difficulties, many discouragements and at a large positive loss,—The prospects are now more favorable and if not interfered with, the line will soon be on a footing, worthy of an American enterprise. There are however parties in Australia and England representing Sydney interests, inclined to oppose it, and I am informed that an Agent is now on his way to England to make efforts for the organization of an English Line. . . . The President in an interview I had with him yesterday, kindly promised to have your attention officially called to this matter with the view of your making such use of these documents, and exerting such influences as will be favorable to the enterprise, and discourage others from interfering with it . . ." LS, DNA, RG 59, Miscellaneous Letters. See *PUSG*, 17, 382–83.

On Oct. 31, James Clark *et al.*, "American citizens now residing at the Samoan Islands," Apia, petitioned USG to retain Jonas M. Coe as commercial agent, Samoa. ". . . in the present unsettled State of the political affairs of the natives who are now engaged in an internecine war, the removal of the present representative of our country who has acquired a degree of respect and influence with the inhabitants that we could hardly hope possible of attainment within even a long period by any successor; would we are persuaded be not only highly injudicious but might we fear seriously imperil the lives and Property of your Petitioners . . . an extensive Land Speculation in connection with this group of Islands has been set on foot by a Mercantile Company of San Francisco styled Collie Stewart & Coy all the published Partners of which are aliens to the United States and whose political influence and interests would be we are constrained to fear, be inimical to the interests of your Petitioners . . . your Petitioners have further reason to fear that the confidence and good esteem heretofore entertained by the natives of Samoa towards the Government and people of the United States is becoming somewhat impaired through the undue delay of the Land Company referred to in fulfilling agreements entered into for the purchase of Lands as also the terms of a 'Treaty of Peace, Commerce and protection to which from its nature the United States Government were presumed by inference to be a Party . . ." DS (12 signatures), DNA, RG 59, Miscellaneous Letters. On April 22, USG had appointed Samuel S. Foster to replace Coe; on June 16, 1874, USG nominated Foster as consul, Apia. See letter to U.S. ministers and consuls, March 31, 1873; George Herbert Ryden, *The Foreign Policy of the United States in Relation to Samoa* (New Haven, 1933), pp. 42–86; Barry Rigby, "Private Interests and the Origins of American Involvement in Samoa, 1872–1877," *Journal of Pacific History*, 8 (1973), 75–87; Rigby, "The Origins of American Expansion in Hawaii and Samoa, 1865–1900," *International History Review*, X, 2 (May, 1988), 228–33.

1. Born in 1837, the nephew of Maj. Gen. George G. Meade, Richard W. Meade graduated U.S. Naval Academy (1856), commanded ships during the blockade of Charleston, S. C., and in the Gulf of Mexico, and won promotion to commander (1868).

To Federico Errázuriz

To His Excellency Federico Errazuriz
President of the Republic of Chile
Great and Good Friend

I have to acknowledge the receipt of the letter which Your Excellency was pleased to address to me on the 20th of March last announcing the termination of the Mission of Don Joaquin Godoy as Envoy Extraordinary and Minister Plenipotentiary of Chile near this Government, and to express to you my sincere regret that Mr. Godoy's ill-health should have prevented him from continuing to act as the Representative of Chile at this Capital.

It is but justice to state to Your Excellency that the language and conduct of Mr. Godoy during his residence in this country were such as to merit the approbation of this Government, and to secure for him the respect and esteem of all who have had intercourse with

him. I am persuaded that he has already assured the Government of
Chile of the friendship of the United States and of their desire to
preserve and strengthen the harmony and good understanding so
happily subsisting between the two countries. And so I recommend
Your Excellency to the protection of the Almighty.

    Written at Washington the twenty third of May in the year of
Our Lord one thousand eight hundred and seventy two.

Your Good Friend,
U. S. GRANT

Copy, DNA, RG 84, Notes to the Chilean Foreign Office. On April 9, 1872, Secretary of
State Hamilton Fish wrote in his diary. "Mr Godoy, Minister from Chili—about to go
home on leave for a short time introduces his Secr of Legation Mr Gonzales as Chargé
d'Affaires ad interim—" DLC-Hamilton Fish.

To Elihu B. Washburne

———

Washington D. C. May 26th 1872.

DEAR WASHBURNE:

    I wrote you a long letter just before the meeting of the Cincin-
nati Convention, but as I did not complete it before that event and
as most of the letter was upon the subject of that Convention I
did not send it. The work has been done and no one is satisfied but
Greeley himself[1] and a few Tamany republicans who expect office
under him if he is elected, and who know that under no other man
could they be appointed to office.—I predict that Greeley will not
even be a Candidate when the election comes off. The democracy
are not going to take him and his following in the republican ranks
is not sufficient to make up an electoral ticket; nor is it compos[ed]
of respectibility enough to put on such a ticket. His nomination has
had a good effect however. It has apparently harmonized the party
by getting out of it the "sore-heads and knaves who made all the
trouble because they could not controll. The movement was egged
on by the democrats, the rank and file acting in good faith, until
now the effect upon them is just what the leaders intended it should
be upon the rebublicans; it is dividing their party. Many of the demo-

cratic parpers, particularly in the South, have committed themselves so ~~throughly~~ thoroughly that they will have to go to Baltimore on the 8th of July in support of Greeley. Many others will go
there to break up the Cincinnati ticket by putting one of its candidates at the tail of a new ticket and Adams, Davis or Trumbull at the
head.[2] The ~~o~~Old Hunkers will fight all such movements, and in my
judgement, will carry the day but will create great disaffection in
their ranks. We will soon see how my prediction comes out.

Nellie writes very often and speaks in warm terms of the kindness and attention she receive[s.][3] Fred I presume will be in Pari[s]
before she leaves there, and Buc[k] will meet her before he commence[s] his studies. He sails on the 6th July and will only return in
time for examination next year. His intention is to pursue his Junior
years course at Harvard some place in Germany, and return in time
for examination. He wants if possible to graduate wit[h] the class he
entered college with. Mrs. Grant joins me in kindest regards to
yourself and family.

Yours Truly
U. S. GRANT

ALS, IHi. On May 10, 1872, Elihu B. Washburne, Paris, had written to USG. "I think that
steal of Goat Island is one of the most audacious pieces of jobbery which ever got through
the House, and they have been many. It is of the same character of the attempted steal of
Rock Island some twenty years ago, which it was my good fortune to crush. That Island
being saved to the Government, the result is that National work which will be the admiration of the whole world. It seems to me an absolute crime to vote away our military
reservations, for no one can tell what the wants of the Government will be hereafter. No
matter what plausible shape they put the bill into, if the rail-road company once gets on
the Island, *they will never be got off.*—If the Senate shall pass the bill, as I suppose it will
do, I earnestly trust you will veto it. The people want to see a good healthy veto, of a corrupt job, and if you will only put the executive knife to the very heart of the bill it will be
hailed by all honest men with enthusiasm. It will be like Jackson's veto of the United States
Bank Bill, which did more to commend him to the masses of the people than any act of his
whole administration. I was, night before last, talking with an intelligent Californian on
the subject, and he says if the bill becomes a law we shall lose the State this fall, but that
if you veto it, we will have it without any trouble. He says the Island will be worth twenty
millions of dollars. I saw Nellie night before last & she is first rate. Mr. Borie is better.
Mrs. W. will come to Paris to see Nellie next week. You must tell Mrs. G. how proud we
all feel of Nellie. The whole American Colony has been in a broad grin ever since we heard
of the nomination of Greeley—'Old Meally Potatoes.' We dont know what to make of it
and await with impatience the arrival of the mails. 'On the face of the papers' the bolt in

Illinois is quite formidable. I have great fears of the German vote. . . . P. S. I have written the Governor a long letter about the new French Minister to Washington, the Marquis de Noialles—He may shew it to you." ALS (press), DLC-Elihu B. Washburne. On April 24, the House had passed a bill granting the Central Pacific Railroad use of Yerba Buena Island (also called Goat Island) in San Francisco Bay. See *CG*, 42–2, 1423–31, 2738–39. The Senate did not vote on the bill. See *SED*, 42-3-23; *SMD*, 42-3-75. On March 7, Robert B. Swain and Washington Bartlett, San Francisco Chamber of Commerce, had telegraphed to USG opposing the bill. *HED*, 42-2-195. On March 11, John A. Russell, clerk, San Francisco board of supervisors, telegraphed to USG expressing similar opposition. *Ibid.*

On April 30, Secretary of State Hamilton Fish wrote to Washburne. "Private & Personal . . . Your private letter of 15th inst. is received this day. Being Cabinet day I took it with me & shewed it to the President—His opinion concurred entirely with my own—I expressed none to him, but he remarked 'I would not prohibit it, but while he holds official position under the Govt I think he had better not lecture on the events which occurred while he has been in official employment in France'—You have only intimated to me the probability of your applying for leave to return home. You may count upon the application being granted, whenever made, unless there be reasons to the contrary which cannot now be fore seen—We are very uncertain as to the fate of the Geneva Arbitration For my own part, I am inclined to wish that G. B. take the responsibility of backing out & breaking the Treaty—Perhaps this is from weariness of the subject—But the *moral* weight of the Treaty, it appears to me, is already destroyed—Arbitration, as a mode of settlement of international differences has rcd a serious if not a fatal blow, & as to the other matters involved in the Treaty, while they are not without importance or advantages they are damaged by the hanging-fire on the main question—I am out of patience with the w[hole] matter—" ALS, DLC-Elihu B. Washburne.

1. On May 3, 1872, the Liberal Republican convention at Cincinnati had nominated Horace Greeley for president. On May 4, Eli Perkins (the pen-name of humorist Melville D. Landon), New York City, wrote to USG. "Nast and I propose to take care of Greeley in this direction. He has a splendid character for satire" ALS, ViU.

2. Charles Francis Adams, Justice David Davis, and U.S. Senator Lyman Trumbull of Ill. figured among potential presidential candidates. See Earle Dudley Ross, *The Liberal Republican Movement* (1910; reprinted, Seattle, 1970), pp. 77–85.

3. On May 3, Washburne had written to USG. "I have seen Nellie, who has jumped since I saw her from girlhood to almost woman-hood. She has improved very much and is really a charming girl who is making the most favorable impression. She will undoubtedly write you that she is well and delighted with Paris. Mrs. W. is away at the present time at Bonn with the children, but will be back here before Nellie leaves as we want to shew her some attention and introduce her to some official people. I suppose Fred will be along here before a great while. I was delighted to see Mr. Borie, though I am sorry to find him not at all well. I must say we dont exactly understand these reports that come to us from the other side in regard to the Alabama business and we are a little uneasy. We have not yet heard the result of that rabble of soreheads and office-seekers who have gathered at Cincinnati. I am prepared for a great deal of racket and noise because the whole copperhead and rebel party of the Country is behind them to yell them on. It will wake up our people for Philadelphia." ALS (press), DLC-Elihu B. Washburne. On May 6, Washburne

wrote to Foreign Minister Charles de Rémusat concerning the arrival in Paris of "Miss Grant the daughter of the President of the United States." ALS (press), *ibid.*

On June 12, Washburne wrote to USG. "I was glad to get your letter of the 26th ult. We now have N. Y. dates to the 30th. I watch everything and read everything with the greatest interest. To my mind the tendency of the old rebel democracy is to take Greeley, but I think he will be 'busted up' in the Convention by the ⅔ds rule. I should be quite content to see the party take him, for we would then have an easy victory. All the harm that he could do would be by drawing off votes from our side as an independent candidate, and that will not amount to very much when it becomes evident that he is running merely as a tender to the rotten democracy. Your nomination was always a fore gone conclusion, and I supposed that of Colfax would follow. Yet I think Wilson's nomination was wise. I cannot but believe that the ticket will go through triumphantly, though I have no doubt the canvass will be bitter and personal and vindictive to the last degree. It is unwise to underrate the strength of the enemy, in politics as well as in war. I have now been away so long and so completely out of the political rut that I do not suppose I could be of any particular service, but I want to say this, that if at any time, you should think my presence at home useful, I will immediately return, at whatever cost, inconvenience or personal sacrifice. Nellie left for Switzerland on Monday morning and her letters have been forwarded. I suppose Fred. is in Brussels and that he will be here in a short time. I suppose Nellie has written to you how cordial Mr. Thiers was to her and all the kind messages he sent. The Illinois Republican Convention was a great success and put a capital ticket in the field. But it is a mistake for Oglesby to be running for U. S. Senator and Governor both at the same time. Still, it will all come out right, I reckon   It has been 'up and down' all the time in this Alabama business and to-day it looks as if the treaty will certainly be broken by England. They have acted as badly as possible from the beginning and I am now content to see them trample their own work under foot. England is a nation of Punic Faith. The first Napoleon hit the nail on the head when he called her 'Perfidious Albion.'" ALS (press), *ibid.*

To Levi P. Morton

Washington D. C. May 27th *1872*

Dear Sir:

Your note of the 24th inst. withdrawing a former letter is received. I did not retain the letter referred to but destroyed it when read and, I believe, without any one but myself being aware of the contents.

The treaty Article, as you no doubt have learned, passed the Senate with but eight dissenting votes.[1] If there is a failure now it must be entirely the fault of the British Govt.

I feel much hope now that Congress will get through and adjourn by the 3d of June. I am anxious to get away.

Yours Truly
U. S. GRANT

L. P. MORTON, ESQ.
NEW YORK CITY.

ALS, NN. Born in 1824 in Vt., Levi P. Morton prospered as a merchant in Hanover, N. H., Boston, and New York City, where he began a second career in international finance. With his London partner, Sir John Rose, Morton helped launch negotiations that led to the Treaty of Washington on May 8, 1871. See *PUSG*, 21, 178; message to Senate, Feb. 13, 1872.

On April 27, 1872, Secretary of State Hamilton Fish had written in his diary. "The Presidents Birth day. I go to see him early in the morning find him in company with L. P Morton who leaves soon after my entering—When he had gone I refered to an Article in the NY Herald of yesterday, violently attacking me, representing that I was holding views on the Alabama question differing from the President, pursuing a policy of my own antagonistic to his & calling upon him to dismiss me—He at once said he had read the Article with great regret, had been speaking with Morton about it—that it was a very gross misrepresentation &c—I told him, that, of course, such articles were unpleasant to me, but they were more injurious to him—that as to myself, he knew I was remaining in his Cabinet against my own wishes—that he held my resignation in his hands & could act upon it at any moment—but that it was part of the policy of those opposed to him, to represent his Cabinet one by one as differing with him, & thus to weaken him in the eyes of the public by shewing distraction & division, & impairing confidence for the want of any unity of policy or of views in his Administration—told him that he alone could correct this by giving the contradiction to it himself—that the declarations of his Cabinet would not be regarded—He assented & said that he would do so—He sent for Morton, who had left the White House, had him called back, requested him to see Bennett (both Father & Son) & say that there was no differences of views &c & that such representations were injurious & calculated to produce mischief & divisions &c—Morton (who was to leave on the 12 45 train for NY) said he wd telegraph to Bennett Junr that he wd be at his house this Evening on his arrival, & wd see the Father tomorrow—. . . Sr Ed. Thornton has a telegram from Granville to the effect they are carrying on negotiations in London with Schenck, but he is without instructions &c Thornton wishes Instructions sent to Schenck—I prepare them, & carry them to the President, who reads & approves them— . . . L. P. Morton is there when I enter—& the President is reading a letter which he hands to me to read—it is from Morton to Bennett to the effect of what the President had asked him this morning to say to Bennett—Morton had rcd a telegram from Rose asking him to remain in Washington & he consequently had not gone in the midday train to NY. . . ." DLC-Hamilton Fish.

On May 29, Morton, New York City, wrote to USG. "confidential . . . I have the enclosed confidential note from Sir Edward Thornton this morning, which I enclose for your perusal and return, . . ." ALS, USG 3. On May 30 and June 1, Morton wrote to Horace Porter. "*Confidential* . . . I enclose copy of a letter which I addressed to Mr Fish on the 24th

May, also copy of his reply thereto.—It seems rather hard, after all the labor and anxiety (to say nothing of the large expenditure of money in Cable dispatches) to be held responsible for the tone of the Press upon his acts. As you are well aware the feeling was so strong, not only among the friends of the administration but with the public generally, that it was quite impossible to get any papers to attempt to sustain the position which he had taken, and for which the public hold him personally & almost entirely responsible— When the President has a few spare moments, I shall be glad if he can find time to run through this letter and the enclosures—after which please destroy them . . . P. S. II I have just learned from a reliable source that a breakfast was given at the New York Club a few days ago with the view of having Mr Greeley meet some of his new bedfellows and at which Greeley, Belmont, Thayer, (a New York Politician), and *Henry Clews* were present—A good association for the 'Financial Agent' of General Grant's Government!" "I hand you below copies of telegrams which I have sent to Sir John Rose since the passage of the Article by the Senate which I shall be glad to have you hand to the President for his perusal—Cable to Sir John Rose, Sunday, May 26th 1872 'It is of vital importance that England should accept the Article as passed by the Senate—public feeling sensitive and opposition gaining—any attempted modifications will almost certainly defeat Treaty— Morton' Cable to Sir John Rose, Wednesday, May 29th 1872 'Know the slightest modification impossible—America has done everything—responsibility now yours'— Morton'. . . I still have a lingering hope that England may accept the Article, otherwise all your valuable services and my long efforts have been in vain—Please say nothing about the Breakfast to which I alluded yesterday, as I wish to get farther information so that there may be no possibility of any doubt about the names of the people who were present" ALS, *ibid.* See *PUSG,* 22, 69; letter to Hamilton Fish, June 1, 1872.

1. On May 21 and 26, 1872, Porter had written to George M. Pullman. ". . . The chances are now decidedly in favor of the ratification, but I want to keep our people well scared, so as to make it sure. I spoke to Drexel about the bond you proposed to issue (confidentially of course) and, as you said, he is quite willing to take hold of it. Should the treaty pass the bond will undoubtedly sell several per cent higher. . . ." "Our efforts have been crowned with success in regard to the treaty. The additional article was ratified by the Senate last evening by a vote of 43 to 8—more than four-fifths. At one time a two-thirds could not be mustered, but by perseverance we improved the chances each day. Some of our people made terribly wry faces over it, but we urged them to swallow it, and then take something to remove the taste from their mouths. The additional article as amended by the Senate is in good shape for us and cannot help being accepted by England. . . . I told the President of the interest you took in the treaty, and the efforts you made in its behalf. He wishes me to send you his regards." ALS, ICHi.

Speech

[*May 28, 1872*]
I am very glad to see you here again, and to hear that you have tried so hard to carry out the promises made by you when you

were here before—to keep the peace between your people and the whites.

We regret the murder that recently took place there but we are satisfied that Red Cloud and Red Dog has nothing to do with it, and will help to punish these men who committed the act. We know that the murderers will be considered outlaws by the Indians as well as by the whites.

We want to do for you and your people all we can to advance and help them, and to enable them to become self-supporting. The time must come when, with the great growth of population here, the game will be gone, and your people will then have to resort to other means of support; and while there is time we would like to teach you new modes of living that will secure you in the future and be a safe means of livelihood.

I want to see the Indians get upon land where they can look forward to permanent homes for themselves and their children. The matter of the location of your agency we want to make agreeable to you, and also to the white people, and to regulate this you must speak to the Secretary of the Interior. I want you to have your talk with him. He tells me all that is said to him, and he speaks for me.

I do not want you and your people to go beyond the territory which has been guaranteed to you by treaty stipulations, except with your full consent; but I am going to suggest to you for your thought and reflection a movement—not for you to decide upon today, nor this year necessarily, but for you to think about taking into consideration the advantages that will be gained by it—and if you all consent I will state what we propose to do for you.

If, at any time, you feel like moving to what is known as the Cherokee country, which is a large territory, with an admirable climate, where you would never suffer from the cold and where you could have lands set apart to remain exclusively your own, we would set apart a large tract of land that would belong to you and your children. We would at first build houses for your chiefs and principal men, and send men among your people to instruct them so they could have houses for shelter. We would send you large herds of cattle and sheep to live upon, and to enable you to raise stock. To this end we would send, if you so desire, Indians who have been accustomed to live with white men, who would instruct you in growing and raising stock until you know how to do so yourselves. We would establish schools, so that your children would learn to read and to write, and to speak the English language, the same as white people, and in this way you and your people would be prepared, before the game is gone, to live comfortably and securely.

I say this only for you to think about and talk about to your people. Whenever you are ready to avail yourself of this offer, then you can talk to us, and we will do what I say. All the treaty obligations we have entered into we shall keep with you unless it is with your own consent that the change is made, or so long as you keep those obligations yourself.

Any reply that you wish to make you can make to the Secretary of the Interior. This you can put off until you have thought over the subject.

Washington Evening Star, May 28, 1872 (interpolations omitted). USG spoke in the White House to Red Cloud, Red Dog, and other Oglala Sioux. Red Cloud responded: "I have but little to tell you—a very few words. There have been many Indians in your house; but all these Indians were sent for. This is the second time I have come, and now I come without an invitation—I have come of my own will. You have told me that in thirty-five years I shall control my nation, and I have listened to you. When I went back to my people I went further north to see the missionary people, and while I was gone they put the agency across the river; they did it against my will. When they put the agency across the river I was not there. I was further north. I have decided a place for my agency. I want it on the White river, and all the people that are with me want it there. We have found a good creek, and this man (pointing to Dr. Daniels, the agent,) went with me to select that place, and we came down to let you know of it. That is the only place that is suitable for our agency. I don't wan't any other." *Ibid.* USG replied: "The place you mention is within the limits of Nebraska, and if you were to go there it would, probably, not be a great many years before the white people would be encroaching upon you, and then there would have to be another change. However, the Secretary of the Interior and Commissioner of Indian Affairs will talk to you about that matter and then talk to me. What they say I will agree to. I am glad that you have brought so many of your Braves here to pass through the country and see the number of people. They will find that the whites are in number as the blades of grass upon the hill-side and the number increases every day. They come from other countries in greater numbers, every year, than the whole number of Indians in America." *Ibid.* (interpolations omitted). Secretary of the Interior Columbus Delano then spoke: "I have the Great Father's views fully about the location of your agency, and I will hear you and your friends fully. I will settle it with you and Dr. Daniels, your agent, before you leave. I will meet and talk with you whenever you wish. The time of the Great Father will not allow him to talk any more to-day." *Ibid.* See *PUSG*, 20, 433; *HED*, 42-3-1, part 5, I, 485, 651–53; James C. Olson, *Red Cloud and the Sioux Problem* (Lincoln, Neb., 1965), pp. 144–52.

On July 24, a correspondent reported. "The Spotted Tail delegation of Indians had an interview with the President this morning, at the Executive Mansion. They were accompanied by three Indian women and by General Walker, the Commissioner of Indian Affairs, Mr. D. R. Risley, their agent, and others. Spotted Tail was in his shirt-sleeves, and wore a heavy red mantle, his hair ornamented with a feather of the same color. A large silver medal, with the raised likeness of Andrew Johnson, rested on his breast. After the usual hand-shaking by all the Indians with the President, Spotted Tail said, through the interpreter, that he was a little tired now, but would have something to tell his great father to-morrow. The President replied that they would not see him to-morrow, as he was going away, but they could talk to the Secretary of the Interior and Commissioner of Indian Affairs, who were authorized to act for him. He understood that Spotted Tail had something to say to him about the location of his agency, and requested the interpreter to say that Red Cloud was permitted to change his agency location because at the former place there was little or no water in the summer season. He did not want to drive Spotted Tail away from the present location of the agency, but he thought it would be better to remove, as a considerable sum of money, $60,000, would be saved in transportation, which would be expended for Spotted Tail and his people. Spotted Tail said that all the young Indians now present were good men, and they intended to-day to have a council among themselves as to a change of location. The President replied, 'Then let them tell the Commissioner the result.' Agent Risley said to the President that when he went among those Indians he found them all peaceably disposed and desirous of maintaining friendly relations. Spotted Tail not only exerted his counsel to this end, but always strived to impress his people with the importance of obeying the President's orders. The President expressed his gratification with this report, adding: 'We will do all we can for their benefit; we want to make them self-sustaining, and are willing to help them until they can reach that point. We want the white and red man to be on good terms, so that one as well as the other can go where he pleases without being molested.' Spotted Tail said he had something more to say to the President. I hear, he remarked, that in a few months there will be an election for a new President. I hope you may be successful. This would please me very much, for you have been very kind to my people. The President replied, however the election may result, I hope there will be no change in the Indian policy." *Philadelphia Public Ledger*, July 25, 1872. See *HED*, 42-3-1, part 5, I, 485.

On Sept. 28, a delegation of Hunkpapas, Blackfeet, and Upper and Lower Yankton Sioux met USG: "After they had shaken hands with the President he inquired if there was anything special which they desired to say to him. 'The Grass' stepped to the front, and through an interpreter said he never had anything against the white men. 'You sent for me before, but I did not like to come. You sent for me again, and I came. I have seen you; I have been pleased. We want room at our reservation, and don't want to be crowded. We will mind the Great Father and do what he tells us. Our people are all working, but are very poor.' The President inquired as to the nature of the land on which the tribe is located, and inquired if anything had been said to them about moving them into the Indian country. Secretary Cowen replied in the affirmative. The President then, addressing the Indians, said he would like to see them on fertile lands, where it would be easy for them to make a living, and when they should be willing to go on such lands the government would send them and learn them to build houses. Their young especially should be instructed. It was for them to think about it, and unless they wanted to go he did not want to make them. They could go back to their homes now, and talk the matter over this year to their people. If they would not agree to go he would not compel them. Above all things they should be at peace with the white people, who outnumbered them a great many times, and if a conflict should come it would be much worse for the Indians. He did not want to fight them, but protect them and care for them. Above all things, too, they should have their young people instructed. The white people were increasing rapidly, and in a few years it would be much worse for the Indians than now. Anything they wanted now could be asked of the Commissioner of Indian Affairs and the Secretary of the Interior, who would act for him. 'The Grass' said the land of his reservation was bad, but he was raised in that country and wanted to stay there. He knew it was not good, but he wanted to stay on it, and did not want any white man to come on it. They also wanted Mr. O'Connor, their agent, to remain there. The President assured them that no change should be made in their agent, and further that he did not want to force them from the land. He would do all he could to instruct them and protect them, and hoped their young people would grow up instructed in all the arts of civilization." *New York Herald,* Sept. 29, 1872. See *HED,* 42-3-1, part 5, I, 645–46.

To James E. McLean

Washington. D. C. May 30th 1872.

DEAR SIR:

Your letter of the 27th of May tendering your resignation of Collector of the port of Chicago to take effect at such time as your successor may be appointed and qualified, is received. I have noted on your letter "to be accepted on the 30th of June."

In pursuing this course allow me to express the appreciation I have of the efficient manner in which you have ever filled the import office entrusted to your management, and also of the kind expressions contained in your letter of resignation. In selecting your successor I only hope the Government may secure the services of an equally faithful and efficient agent.

With high regards
Your obt. Svt.
U. S. GRANT.

JAS. E. McLEAN
COLLR PORT OF CHICAGO.

Copy, DLC–USG, II, 1. On May 27, 1872, James E. McLean, Chicago, had written a letter of resignation to USG. LS, DNA, RG 56, Collector of Customs Applications. USG endorsed this letter. "Accept to take effect June 30th /72" AE (undated), *ibid.* See letter to James E. McLean, Feb. 4, 1872; *Chicago Tribune*, May 31, June 1, 2, 1872. On June 28, Wiley M. Egan, Chicago, wrote to USG. "I have been largely engaged in the vessel business since 1852 as owner and Agent, representing in both capacities nearly one hundred vessels, and now take pleasure in stating that I have never done business with a collector of customs with so much satisfaction, as I have with collector McLean, since Chicago has had a Custom House. Now, Sir, may I, as a person having a great deal to do with the Custom House, and a strong supporter of your administration presume to hope that, for the good of business generally, and as I honestly believe for your good, you will continue M'r. McLean in the position he now occupies." ALS, DNA, RG 56, Collector of Customs Applications. On the same day, J. W. Doane & Co., "a Grocery Importing House," Chicago, wrote to USG on the same subject. L, *ibid.*

On June 10, U.S. Representative Charles B. Farwell of Ill. had written to USG recommending Norman B. Judd to replace McLean. ALS, *ibid.* On Dec. 5, USG nominated Judd.

On Dec. 9, McLean wrote to USG. "Trusting that I have ever conducted myself in such manner as to merit your esteem & approbation, and remembering your kind expressions as to an interest in my future welfare,—I take the liberty of addressing you pertinent to my occupying some position of trust under Government—on such a scale as you would think my abilities would justify. I do not presume to dictate what the position may be,—but being out of business & unmarried, I have no particular interests to tie me down to any section or locality. Should you—therefore—feel disposed to favor me, the field from which a selection could be made covers a very wide range. I have noticed during the last two weeks that some unknown friends have been putting my name before the public in connection with the Consul-Generalship to Montreal;—This has been done without any knowledge or collusion on my part;—Nor do I know whether the present incumbent (Mr Dart) contemplates relinquishing the position; If however there is any prospect of a change in that quarter, or in any other equally as desirable—I would esteem it the greatest boon of you to make me a tender of the place." ALS, *ibid.*, RG 59, Letters of Application and Recommendation. On Dec. 14, USG endorsed this letter. "Respectfully referred to the Sec. of State. The writer of this is a most worthy man and would reflect credit on any position that might be given him." AES, *ibid.* No appointment followed.

To Congress

To THE SENATE AND HOUSE OF REPRESENTATIVES:

I have the honor to respectfully call the attention of Congress to an Act approved July 14 1870, directing the Secretary of War to place at the disposal of the President certain bronze ordnance to aid in the erection of an equestrian statue of the late General John A.

Rawlins; and to the facts that no appropriation of money to pay for the statue is made by the resolution; no artist is named or party designated to whom the ordnance is to be delivered.

In view of the ambiguity of the statute I would recommend that Congress signify what action is desired as to the selection of the artist and that the necessary sum required for the erection of the monument be appropriated. A board of officers should also be named to designate the location of the monument.

U. S. GRANT

EXECUTIVE MANSION
MAY 31 1872

DS, DNA, RG 46, Presidential Messages. *SED*, 42-2-84. See *PUSG*, 19, 242. On May 18, 1872, Secretary of War William W. Belknap had written to USG raising these questions. Copy, DNA, RG 107, Letters Sent, Military Affairs. On May 25, U.S. Senator John A. Logan of Ill. introduced a bill appropriating $10,000 for a statue of John A. Rawlins; on June 10, USG signed this bill into law.

On March 21 and May 1, Belknap had written to Theophilus Fisk Mills, Washington, D. C. "The President having sent me your request of the 19th instant, for the bronze donated for the equestrian statue of the late Secretary of War, General John A. Rawlins, by Congress in a Public Resolution approved July 14, 1870, I have the honor to request information as to the weight of metal that will be required for the specified purpose;— The Resolution of Congress and your communication being silent upon the subject of the weight." "I have to request that you please deliver to the Quartermaster General the plaster cast of the late General Rawlins, which, as you stated to me, is the property of the War Dept. Upon its receipt I shall confer with the President as to what further steps may be necessary to carry into effect the intention of Congress in regard to the bronze monument provided for by the Joint Resolution approved July 14 /70." Copies, *ibid.* On June 3, U.S. Senator William A. Buckingham of Conn. introduced a bill "directing the Secretary of War to deliver to Fisk Mills, sculptor, condemned ordnance to be used in the casting of the equestrian statue of the late General Rawlins, and making an appropriation for the erection of the same upon the public grounds . . ." *CG*, 42–2, 4184. The Senate did not vote on this bill. On Aug. 7, 1873, Belknap wrote to Mills. "In reply to your letter of the 1st instant relative to the bronze-metal for the equestrian statue of the late General Jno. A. Rawlins, I beg to inform you that Congress not having acted upon the Presidents recommendation of May 31, 1872 he will take no further action upon the subject at present. I respectfully return to you your receipt enclosed in your letter of the 1st instant." Copy, DNA, RG 107, Letters Sent, Military Affairs. See *SRC*, 44-1-515, 52-1-907.

On April 10, 1869, Mills had written to USG. "The undersigned, feeling anxious to again spend a few years abroad in the vicinity of Munich, Germany, a former place of residence, for the greater perfection of the art of sculpture; and feeling that his acquaintance with the language customs and people of that country would qualify him for some little service abroad, most respectfully asks an appointment as Consul to Munich, or some place adjacent." ALS, DNA, RG 59, Letters of Application and Recommendation. Mills had also studied sculpture under his father, Clark Mills. See *PUSG*, 20, 352–53.

On Dec. 29, 1872, the *New York Times* editorialized. "We are to have a statue of Gen. RAWLINS. Not satisfied with the superb treasures of the sculptor's art with which a MILLS and a REAM have enriched the Capitol, Congress recently appropriated ten thousand dollars in order to awaken the creative genius of other eminent sculptors, and so to secure a statue of RAWLINS which should be worthy to be ranked with the circus-riding WASHINGTON and the stiff-necked LINCOLN. The competitors for this sum of ten thousand dollars have sent in their models to a Committee composed of a Governor, a librarian, an architect, and a Commissioner of Public Buildings. . . . The choice of the Committee is understood to have fallen upon Mr. BAILLY; and certainly, as between MILLS, whom we do know, and the seven competitors whom we do not know, it is fortunate that the former will not be awarded the contract. Washington is a city covering a good deal of ground, but it is hardly large enough to contain another statue by CLARK MILLS. . . ." See *ibid.*, Jan. 6, 1873. Joseph A. Bailly's statue of Rawlins was dedicated in 1874. See *HRC*, 49-1-107.

On Aug. 12, 1872, David K. Hitchcock, Boston, wrote to Elihu B. Washburne, Paris, recommending that Americans there ". . . procure of the Sculptor Mr Bailly the Equestrian Statue of Gen. Grant (a duplicate) and present the same to France to be erected in Paris, as a tribute to a sister republic, and in grateful recognition of the unbounded sympathy and aid which we received through the immortal Lafayette and his countrymen in our infancy as a republic. . . . You will remember that the President sat for the statue & that the horse he rode in all his battles was exactly copied, all of which exceedingly delighted him, as I very well know. The amount to be raised is about $40,000, and it will not be difficult to secure some forty or fifty persons who would consider it a privilege to aid in securing such a compliment to one of the greatest & most illustrious Military heroes that ever lived" ALS, DLC-Elihu B. Washburne. See *PUSG*, 20, 51–52.

To George S. Boutwell

Washington, D. C. May 31st 1872.

DEAR SIR:

Enclosed I send you some dispatches received last evening in relation to the passage of the "Steamboat bill" now before the Senate. In addition to the dispatches inclosed I have received one to the same purport from Richard Smith, of the Cincinnati Gazatte, and one sent to you yesterday.

I believe it is understood that the principle opposition to the bill comes from the Treasury Dept: I feel myself that the Steamboat interest of the Country are entitled to relief from the hardship, (almost prohibition from the pursuit of their calling,) imposed by the present law. It is too late in the session to give any other relief than can be given by the passage of the bill now befor the Senate. If not perfect it can be amended at the next session of Congress, and in the mean time that great interest in our inland and coastwise waters can go on. I would suggest at least, if you can not withdraw from the position taken by the Dept: in your absence, that these dispat-dispatches, with any others that you may have received on the same subject, be laid before the Senate Committee having the matter in charge.

Very truly yours
U. S. GRANT.

HON. GEO. S. BOUTWELL
SECTY OF THE TREASURY.

Copy, DLC-USG, II, 1. Congress did not pass the bill reducing mandatory safety mea-sures on steamboats and the liability of steamboat operators against personal injury claims. See *CG*, 42–2, 1960–61, 2112–17, 2141–50, 2168–69, 3697, 3891, 4038–39, 4107–9, 4308–13, 4475–76; 42–3, 73.

1. See *PUSG*, 4, 293; *New York Times*, April 23, 1898.

Veto

TO THE SENATE OF THE UNITED STATES.

I have examined the bill entitled "An act for the relief of J. Milton Best," and, being unable to give it my approval, return the same to the Senate, the House in which it originated, without my signature.

The bill appropriates the sum of twenty-five thousand dollars to compensate Dr. J. Milton Best for the destruction of his dwelling-house and its contents by order of the Commanding officer[1] of the United States Military forces at Paducah, Kentucky, on the twenty-sixth day of March, eighteen hundred and sixty-four. It appears that this house was one of a considerable number destroyed for the purpose of giving open range to the guns of a United States fort. On the day preceding the destruction, the houses had been used as a cover for Rebel troops attacking the fort, and, apprehending a re-newal of the attack, the commanding officer caused the destruction of the houses. This, then, is a claim for compensation on account of the ravages of war. It cannot be denied that the payment of this claim would invite the presentation of demands for very large sums of money, and, such is the supposed magnitude of the claims that may be made against the Government for necessary and unavoidable destruction of property by the army, that I deem it proper to return this bill for reconsideration.

It is a general principle of both international and municipal law that all property is held subject, not only to be taken by the government for public uses, in which case under the Constitution of the United States, the owner is entitled to just compensation; but also subject to be temporarily occupied, or even actually destroyed in times of great public danger, and when the public safety demands it, and in this latter case, governments do not admit a legal obligation on their part to compensate the owner. The temporary occupation of, injuries to, and destruction of property caused by actual and necessary military operations, is generally considered to fall within the last mentioned principle. If a government makes compensation under such circumstances, it is a matter of bounty rather than of strict legal right.

If it be deemed proper to make compensation for such losses, I suggest for the consideration of Congress, whether it would not be better, by general legislation, to provide some means for the ascertainment of the damage in all similar cases, and thus save to claimants the expense, inconvenience, and delay of attendance upon Congress, and, at the same time, save the Government from the danger of having imposed upon it fictitious or exaggerated claims, supported wholly by *ex parte* proof. If the claimant in this case ought to be paid, so ought all others similarly situated;[2] and that there are many such cannot be doubted. Besides, there are strong reasons for believing that the amount of damage in this case has been greatly over-estimated. If this be true, it furnishes an illustration of the danger of trusting entirely to ex-*parte* testimony in such matters.

U. S. GRANT

WASHINGTON, JUNE 1. 1872.

DS, DNA, RG 46, Presidential Messages. *SED*, 42-2-85; *SMD*, 49-2-53, 381–82. On May 18, 1872, during debate on this bill, U.S. Representative Austin Blair of Mich. explained that plans had been made to remove—with compensation—Dr. J. Milton Best's house, situated higher than the U.S. fortifications. ". . . Then, sir, subsequently General Forrest came down on Paducah and attacked it, the report not having been completed and the house not taken down; then, just as General Paine had supposed would be the case, the rebel forces seized Best's house, filled it with sharp-shooters, used it as a fortification, and picked off the gunners in our fort. It was a most dangerous thing. The gun-boats on the river were directed to shell the house; and I will say this one thing for Dr. Best, that while the gun-boats were shelling the house he stood on the top of it, with the rebels below, and with a flag waved to the gun-boats letting them know where to fire into his own house. The insurgents were finally driven out, and the battle subsided somewhat, and the house was immediately set on fire and burned up to prevent their reoccupation of it. . . ." *CG*, 42–2, 3621. U.S. Representative James A. Garfield of Ohio also spoke in support of this bill. ". . . Any American citizen who in time of war will do what Dr. Best did with his property, under the circumstances, ought to have the best hearing the House of Representatives can give him, and I hope we shall pay this claim. I only fear that there are but few others in the country that can plead this as a precedent. I wish there were more, even if they cost the Treasury much." *Ibid.* See *ibid.*, 2252–53, 3621–24. On June 1, U.S. Senator Timothy O. Howe of Wis. spoke in response to USG's veto. "Mr. President, that message takes me somewhat by surprise. I cannot pretend that the bill which is returned with that message received the assent of the Senate without full consideration. I think every Senator will agree that that was no hasty legislation, though it might have been unwise. Still there is strong reason to believe that the Senate and the Committee on Claims committed a mistake. . . ." *Ibid.*, 4156. See *SRC*, 41-2-69, 42-2-9, 42-3-412, 43-1-126. On Dec. 3, USG nominated J. Milton Best as postmaster, Paducah.

On June 7, Elihu B. Washburne, Paris, wrote to USG. "I suppose from the telegraphic despatch that it was the bill of Dr. Best for the payment of damages resulting from the casualties of war, that you vetoed. There is no act of your administration which has afforded me more satisfaction. I early saw a tendency among the loose Congressmen to sanction that extraordinary principle and I Combatted it with all my might in Old Armes's case. You will receive the gratitude of all loyal and patriotic men in the north for thus taking the bull by the horns and squelching the most dangerous assault ever made on the public treasury. Now, if the Goat Island steal ever gets to you, I hope you will put the same knife right into its heart. At the time I write, Friday forenoon, the 7th inst we have nothing from Phila but we dont feel much interest as we have long known that the 'hash' was settled so far as you are concerned. The cable of yesterday reported that we had carried Oregon, and I pray it may be so. Among other good results it will be likely to put Judge Williams back into the Senate. I consider him one of the best men we have. Russ Jones has been making me a visit of a few days. He returns to Brussels to-night. His health is a good deal better than it used to be and he is feeling very well. He makes a most excellent and a very popular minister. He saw Nellie yesterday & found her well and so much improved. Mrs. W. is at Bonn with the children. They are learning German very fast. Hempstead is also there and he has got so he can speak German very well. It will a great thing for Buck to come out here and learn the languages. Pitt will speak French & German like a native. With kind regards to Mrs. Grant & Mr. Dent, . . ." ALS (press), DLC-Elihu B. Washburne. For the claim of Josiah O. Armes, see *CG*, 38–1, 2388–91; for Goat Island, see letter to Elihu B. Washburne, May 26, 1872.

1. Col. Stephen G. Hicks, 40th Ill.

2. On June 7, USG vetoed a similar bill to compensate Thomas B. Wallace, a Lexington, Mo., Unionist whose home had been destroyed by federal forces during battle on Sept. 13, 1861. DS, DNA, RG 46, Presidential Messages. *SED*, 42-2-86; *SRC*, 46-2-718, 48-2-917; *SMD*, 49-2-53, 382–83. See *CG*, 42–2, 3846–48.

Proclamation

Whereas, the act of Congress approved May 22, 1872, removes all political disabilities imposed by the third section of the fourteenth article of amendments to the Constitution of the United States, from all persons whomsoever, except Senators and Representatives of the Thirty-sixth and Thirty-seventh Congresses and officers in the judicial, military, and naval service of the United States, heads of Departments, and foreign Ministers of the United States;

And whereas, it is represented to me that there are now pending in the several Circuit and District Courts of the United States, proceedings by *quo warranto*, under the fourteenth section of the act of Congress approved May 31, 1870, to remove from office certain persons who are alleged to hold said offices in violation of the provisions of said article of amendment to the Constitution of the United States, and also penal prosecutions against such persons under the fifteenth section of the act of Congress aforesaid;

Now, therefore, I, Ulysses S. Grant, President of the United States, do hereby direct all District Attorneys having charge of such proceedings and prosecutions, to dismiss and discontinue the same, except as to persons who may be embraced in the exceptions named in the act of Congress first above cited.

In testimony whereof, I have hereunto set my hand and caused the Seal of the United States to be affixed.

Done at the City of Washington, this First day of June, in the year of our Lord one thousand eight hundred and seventy-two, and of the Independence of the United States of America the Ninety-sixth.

U. S. GRANT

DS, DNA, RG 130, Presidential Proclamations. See *CG*, 42–2, 3744–45.

To Hamilton Fish

Washington D. C. June 1st 1872.

Hon. Hamilton Fish;
Sec. of State;
Dear Sir:

In view of the probable failure of the "Washington Treaty" I suggest whether it is not advisable to have prepared for transmittal to the Senate, on Monday next, all the correspondence on the subject? It should be accompanied by a short message setting forth the concessions made by this Govt. to secure the benefits of a treaty equally honorable and advantageous to the two countries directly interested in the treaty, and, as an example, to the civilized world. I would also suggest in the message that at the next Session of Congress means should be provided for settlement with American Citizens who suffered by the acts of vessels illegally fitted out in English waters.

It might be well also to notice the reasons why in claims for indirect damages were presented by this govt. towit: the necessity for establishing a principle for our protection when we may be the neutral; and the fact that the indirect losses to this Govt. has been the subject of so much correspondence and public comment[1] from the time the Alabama committed her first depridations upon our commerce to the present time.

I think it important to get this correspondence before the public before the adjournment of Congress.

Very Truly Yours,
U. S. Grant

ALS, DLC-Hamilton Fish. On May 28, 1872, Secretary of State Hamilton Fish wrote in his diary. "Read Schenck's telegram recd this morning—announcing the proposed changes to the Supplemental Article suggested by Ld Granville and mention my interview with Thornton last Evening, & the answer I made him—there is a unanimous concurrence of opinion that no proposition for any further change can be entertained." *Ibid.* See Fish diary, May 29, 31, 1872. On June 2, a correspondent reported. "The President has, as he remarked to inquirers, surrendered his personal views to what he considered a proper concession, in the desire to save the Treaty in behalf of the financial and commercial interests of the United States, and to maintain peace between the two countries.

There was, he said, a point beyond which further concessions would be a sacrifice of national honor, and, as we had reached that point, it remained for England to decide whether or not the Treaty should be abandoned." *Philadelphia Public Ledger*, June 3, 1872.

On June 10, Levi P. Morton, New York City, wrote to USG. "I enclose copy of a dispatch received this day from Sir John Rose by cable, and which I have repeated to Secretary Fish in Cypher by wire—I can see no possible objection to our Government joining in a postponement of the case to give time to arrange the slight difference in the wording of the future rule—There would seem to be many advantages in such a course for us, as it would avoid any unfavorable political effect during the present canvass. I earnestly hope the Government will see its way clear to this course . . . Copy of cable dated June 10th 1872 from Sir John Rose, London to L. P. Morton, N. Y. 'I am satisfied present slight difference wording future rule can be arranged   indispensable your Government consent to English proposals about meeting & filing arguments on the fifteenth—Gladstone's defaulting certain if proceeding unconditional—most important—if arranged success assured—Situation critical'" LS, OFH.

On June 21, Friday, Fish wrote to USG, Long Branch. "Accompanying this are the telegrams from Mr Davis received on Wednesday evening.   we have had some difficulty in making them out accurately, but by subsequent telegrams think we have them now, with the exception perhaps of some few words, in a state to understand their full meaning. I enclose also a draft instruction to Mr. Davis, for your consideration and approval. I have submitted it to Judge Williams and Mr. Creswell (the only two of the Cabinet whom I have been able to consult). Should it meet your approval I would thank you to authorise Mr. Chew (who will convey the papers to you) to telegraph to me, to that effect *immediately*, in which case I will send it by Cable to Mr. Davis at Geneva. Should you desire any alterations which may be communicated by telegraph I shall be glad to receive them if possible tomorrow. If however, you desire more change than can well be directed by telegraph, Mr Chew will return tomorrow evening, so as to reach here on sunday morning, and I will delay the Cable despatch until then. I think that we can see an honorable solution of the trouble between the two Governments, and the practical attainment of what we have contended for, in the course now in contemplation. We shall have made G. B. file her Counter Case, in April, on time, and to appear in Court also on time, in June, and shall have a virtual Judgment upon the Admissibility of the indirect claims." LS (press), DLC-Hamilton Fish. See letter to Hamilton Fish, Aug. 24, 1872.

1. On April 18, Elihu G. Holland, Chicago, had written to USG. "As an American, I take the liberty of commending your firmness, in not changing in any respect the American claims before the Geneva Conference. England must now learn, what she had forgotten, that Nations are amenable to Justice, and that Retribution, in the nature of things, is as sure to overtake them as it is to overtake individuals. I would not, if the discussion of the present international difficulties were in my hands (and I doubt not, it is in far abler hands) ever use the words, 'Indirect damages,' 'Consequential damages,' and 'Inferential damages;' but I would make the word, *'Real damages'* Cover the whole ground, for there is nothing in our claims which does not honestly come under this head. . . ." ALS, NN.

On April 25, U.S. Senator William A. Buckingham of Conn. wrote to USG. "I have the honor to inclose a copy of a resolution and report unanimously adopted by The National Council of Congregational Churches of the United States at its session in November last expressing profound satisfaction with the Treaty of Washington   Assuring you that the Council were impressed with truth that you and those associated with you in the administration of the government are entitled to great honor for negotiating a Treaty so much in the interests of universal peace . . ." ALS, DNA, RG 59, Miscellaneous Letters. The enclosure is *ibid.*

On April 26, L. Gildersleeve, La Porte, Ind., wrote to USG. "If it be clear that the conference is competent to determine what claims shall be admitted, let it and it alone determine. It is of little consequence whether consequential or other damages be allowed. This is altogether incidental, and secondary. The great question is—Shall there be a disposition exhibited by both nations to deal liberally and justly and to submit their differences to peaceable adjustment on the ground of justice by a disinterested tribunal" ALS, *ibid.*

On April 30, Benjamin Bannan, editor, *Daily and Weekly Miners' Journal*, Pottsville, Pa., wrote to USG. "There is a painful rumor abroad that the Consequential Damages are to be withdrawn, or at least compromised by the Administration. This would be most unfortunate at this juncture. It is just what the enemies of your Administration desire. Far better let it go and remain unsettled than to make a move in that direction. It is not true that it is effecting our foreign commerce—because the importations are heavier now than they ever were before—and as regards the refund of our indebtedness the settling of our difficulties, or the non-settling of the same here will not effect the rates of interest. ~~unless~~ To fund them at the lower rate now of course would banish them all from the country, and while the Governmt would be benefitted a little it would not change the rates of interest at hand on capital engaged in the productive interests of the country. All ~~the~~ our Bonds could have been refunded wthout costg the Gvmnt any thing but the expenses of issg new bonds, and the expense of exchange if the Gvmnt had not taken the advice of the traffickers and the money changers instead of the producing classes. I know of but two Republicans disaffected to you in Schuylkill County now—but if the Consequential damages are withdrawn or comprised in a manner that the epithet *craven* could be applied to the Administratn it is hard to tell what the effect would be upon the people. I know this that when the charge was made in the Tribune on Friday last the people would not believe it—and they felt rejoiced when they saw it contradicted in a despatch from Washington as havg come from yourself—but I find by the city Papers this evening that it re-newed again under the head of Compromise. Pardon one who has so little acquaintance—but has been an editor for upwards of 42 years on the same paper   I felt that I would not be doing my duty if I did not drop you these lines on the subject" ALS, *ibid.*

On May 7, William H. Hicks, Boston, wrote to USG. "Please do not give up our claim for consequential damages at Geneva. It would be disastrous to the Country and disastrous to the Republican party. 25 years would not repair the damage to our prestage if we yield. Better lose all damages, even in a money point of view, than this. Our claim is true and just, we do not expect any money award, but we do claim the right to present it   We can not back out with honor, and money is not to be compared with honor. I predict that if we take a firm stand on this point, not pressing for damages, but our right to present the claims, Great Britain will find a way for the treaty to proceed." ALS, *ibid.*

On May 14, Rodney K. Shaw, Marietta, Ohio, wrote to USG. "Is not the position of the English Government in relation to the Geneva Arbitration wholly untenable. The Arbitrators constitute a special equitable tribunal instituted by the agreement of the two nations. They are from the nature of their selection and manner of proceeding, sole judges of the law and the fact   To their finding there can be no exception, and from their deliverance there can be no appeal   The Agreement of submission gives them jurisdiction, of the *scope* and *extent* of which they are the sole judges   It is not the province of one party to *protest* against the presentation by the other, of any claim arising out of the matters in dispute   If a party denies the jurisdiction of a claim presented by the other, they must meet it by *argument* addressed to the Arbitrators and ask their opinion whether the claim be within the scope of the submission or not and a finding upon this is as binding as upon any other point—The Arbitrators have to pass first upon the fact whether the English Government was guilty of any neglect or wrong   If this point be found in the affirmative, then they assess the extent and character of the damages   A matter which it is peculiarly their province to determine by their opinion of public law   The protest is a denial of the right of the United States to present its view of public law, as applied to the facts, an implied admission of an existing wrong, which the English Government are unwilling to have adjusted by an impartial tribunal and an impeachment of its intention to do equity . . ." ALS, *ibid.*

On May 18, Alfred H. Love, president, Universal Peace Union, Philadelphia, wrote to USG. "Deeply impressed with the importance of the consummation of the Treaty of Washington, we feel drawn at this time to urge, that it is important for the sake of humanity, for the sake of peace and for the true glory of the nations interested, and the enlightened age in which we live. We approved and applauded the spirit which dictated and ratified it; and our confidence in the principle of Arbitration is by no means lessened, because of the diversity of views respecting the claims to be submitted, but it is greatly strengthened by the various propositions emanating from those high in power looking to a settlement and which we are confident would result satisfactorily to both nations. and most likely to the establishment of a permanent High Court of Arbitration, were time, patience and charity liberally extended. . . ." ALS, *ibid.* On June 3, Love led a delegation to present this letter to USG. *Washington Chronicle*, June 4, 1872.

To Jesse Root Grant

Washington D. C. June 2d *1872.*

DEAR FATHER;

Hearing from home frequently as I do through persons coming from there and through occasional letters I scarsely ever think of writing. Hereafter however I will try to write oftener or have Jesse write. The children might all write to you for that matter. We hear occasionally from Fred. direct and very often through the papers. He has enjoyed his European trip very much and I think will be much improved by it. Nellie writes very often and a very much better writer than either of the boys. Her composition is easy and fluent, and she writes very correctly. She seems to have made a very good impression where she has been.—Buck sails for Europe on the 6th of July. He will travel but little however. He expects to study his third year Harvard course in some quiet German villege, and return in June next in time for his examination. In this way he expects to graduate at the same time he would if he did not go abroad. The object is to acquire a speaking knowledge of both the German & French languages, both of which he is now quite a good scholar in.

I received a letter from Mary a short time since. She said that she would leave for home about the first of June. You may expect her home by the twentyeth no doubt.

Julia & Jesse are well and send much love to you and mother.

Sincerely yours
U. S. GRANT

JESSE R. GRANT, ESQ.
COVINGTON KY.

ALS, Dartmouth College, Hanover, N. H.

Proclamation

Whereas Congress has adjourned without granting the necessary supplies for sundry civil purposes; and whereas, in the absence of such supplies, it will be impossible to make suitable provision for the Courts, Juries Light-Houses, Coast survey &c., and the Government will thus be deprived of the means of discharging several of its most important functions, and an extra . . . Done at the City of Washington, the tenth day of June in the year of our Lord one thousand eight hundred and seventy-two, and of the Independence of the United States the ninety-sixth

U. S. GRANT

DS (incomplete), Mrs. Walter Love, Flint, Mich. This proclamation, never issued, would have extended the Congressional session to counter a threatened Democratic filibuster of an appropriations bill. See *New York Times*, June 11, 1872.

To Thomas Settle et al.

Washington D. C. June 10th, 72

Thos. Settle Pres. Nat. Rep. Com. Paul Strobach, Elisha
Baxter, C. A. Sargent, and others, V. Prs. Gentlemen

Your letter of this date, advising me of the action of the
Convention held in Phila Pa on the 5th & 6th of this month, and of
my unanimous nomination for the Presidency by it, is received. I
accept the nomination, and through you return my ~~most~~ heartfelt
thanks to your constituents for this mark of their ~~support~~ confidence and ~~confidence in me after a three years incumbency of the
office.~~ support.[1]

If elected in November, and protected by a kind Providence in
health and strength to perform the duties of the high trust confered,
I ~~can~~ promise the same zeal and devotion to the good of the whole
people for the future of my official life, as shown in the past; ~~and no
more, though~~ pPast experience may guide me in avoiding mistakes
inevitable with novices in all professions and in all occupations.

When relieved from the responsibilities of my present trust, by
the election of a successor, whether it be at the end of this term
or next, I hope to leave to ~~my successor~~ him, ~~the~~ as executive ~~of~~ a
country at peace within its own borders, at peace with outside nations, ~~and without~~ with a credit at home and abroad, and without
embarassing questions to threaten ~~our~~ its future ~~safety.~~ prosperity.

With ~~an~~the expression of a desire to see a speedy healing of all
bitterness of feeling between ~~parties.~~ Sections, parties or races of
Citizens, and the time when the title of *Citizen*[2] carries with it all
the protection ~~to~~ and privileges to the ~~most~~ humblest, that it does
to the most exalted, I subscribe myself,

Very respectfully
your obt. svt.
U. S. Grant

ADfS, DLC–Benjamin H. Bristow. On June 10, 1872, Thomas Settle *et al.*, Washington,
D. C., wrote to USG. "In pursuance of our instructions, we the undersigned, President and
Vice Presidents of the National Republican Convention, held in Philadelphia on the 5th

and 6th inst; have the honor to inform you of your nomination for reelection to the office of President of the United States—As it is impossible to give an adequate idea of the enthusiasm which prevailed, or the unanimity which hailed you as the choice of the people, we can only add that you received the entire vote of every State and Territory. Regarding your reelection as necessary to the peace and continued prosperity of the country, we ask your acceptance of the nomination" DS (44 signatures), USG 3. Settle, a former N. C. judge who had recently resigned as U.S. minister to Peru, led a delegation to the White House to present this letter to USG. USG responded. "Well, gentlemen, I am not ready to respond to your letter at present, but in the course of a few days will prepare my reply, which I suppose I must forward to Judge Settle in North Carolina." *Washington Evening Star*, June 10, 1872. "Soon after receiving the presidents and vice presidents of the national republican convention yesterday afternoon, the President left for the Capitol, arriving there a few minutes before three o'clock. He at once went to his room on the Senate side, and sitting down at a table read over carefully the letter notifying him of his nomination. After reading the letter he took up a lead pencil and began writing his reply on a half sheet of letter paper, . . . The President wrote rapidly, and when he had finished the letter read it aloud to those present, upon which they all expressed themselves highly pleased with it. A verbal alteration, suggested by one of the gentlemen present, was accepted by the President, but with this exception the original draft of the letter bore no erasures. After press copies had been made, the President gave the original draft to Solicitor General Bristow, at the latter's request. The first copy of the letter was sent to Judge Settle and the Associated Press, and the morning papers were furnished with copies at about seven o'clock last evening." *Ibid.*, June 11, 1872.

On June 6, 12:32 P.M., William Orton, president, Western Union Telegraph Co., Philadelphia, had telegraphed to USG. "Your nomination has just been announced, and was received with an enthusiasm which language cannot fitly describe. The display surpasses that at Chicago, four years ago. Accept my warmest congratulations." *Ibid.*, June 7, 1872. On the same day, Orton telegraphed to USG. "First ballot, Colfax 312 Wilson 386 Scattering—" Telegram received (at 3:40 P.M.), USGA. On June 13, at Long Branch, a reporter asked USG: "'How do you like the substitution of Wilson for Colfax on your own ticket?'" USG responded. "'The idea seems to have been to have the two candidates from different sections of the country. Otherwise there is no preference between the two men. Personally I have a great affection for both Wilson and Colfax. Mr. Colfax, so far through our term, has been a firm friend, and we have always entertained the most affectionate relations toward one another.'" *New York Herald*, June 14, 1872. See Willard H. Smith, *Schuyler Colfax: The Changing Fortunes of a Political Idol* (Indianapolis, 1952), pp. 338–63.

On June 6, Edwards Pierrepont, New York City, wrote to USG. "The wild enthusiasm with which your name was hailed at Phila is most gratifying and is the harbinger of a November victory—The nomination of Wilson is well—It gives new life by awakening new hopes—you may remember what I said to you on that subject when we met last at the Fifth Avenue Hotel. People like change and they must have new hopes or they will not work—*Announce* that no changes would be made by you in the next four years and you would see the effect right soon. The chief strength of the Greeley movement lies in this, that in the expected changes, new hopes arise—A great effort will now be made to indorse Greely at Baltimore, it will be earnest from this day forth. Believe not those who tell you that it will be well to have him thus indorsed, and that such course would make our victory easy—it is not true; and if he is indorsed you will surely agree with me before Sept. We ought not to aid in that indorsement. I am glad that Colfax was not nominated, tho' I like him; I am glad simply because it proves to the people that all will not run in the same old ruts—new life, new hopes this people need, and if they were in Paradise, they would demand something that looked like progress & novelty—The Democratic Party is dissolved, as truly so as was the old Whig Party before the Republican Party was formed—we ought to secure large fragments from it, and we can do it—we can carry this City by bold & sagacious combinations—Greeley & Hoffman are trying to unite; the price to Hoffman is the United States Senate in place of Conkling—we ought to secure the entire O'Brien influence, most of the German & all the enemies of Hoffman which are legion—it must be done by address, and by applying the forces which influence human actions; not all are moved by the same things, you know. I write this letter at the hour of your greatest exaltation—I write it because I am your *friend*, and because I wish the result in November to justify what I have so often asserted; and because much experience in lesser contests ~~haves~~ proved how many good causes have been *lost* by just a little neglect, which over-confidence has caused" ALS, PHi.

Also on June 6, Grenville M. Dodge, Philadelphia, wrote to USG. "*Strictly Private* . . . On last Sunday—I met accidentally at the house of Horace F. Clark—*Commodore Vanderbilt* a warm friend of yours—Incidentally I heard him state the case of the New York Central ~~Pacific~~ R R—He spoke of his visit to you—your decision the action of the commission you appointed and the subsequent action of the Commissioner of *Internal Revenue*—What the merits of the case are I do not kno—He thinks the goverment has treated him *badly* but beleives it is done *without your knowledge* as he says it is in *direct violation of your order in case*—He feels the matter keenly—says if he should go to you about it at this time it would be misconstrued and he prefers to *pay*—than that ~~you~~ he should do anythg that could hurt you in the campaign—I intended befor I went south to see you and say what I write—It seems to me that there is a misunderstanding—and that the action taken by Internal Revenue Dept is a mistake especially at this time—My only reason for saying a word is the kindly feeling exhibited towards you by *Vanderbildt* and *Clark* and the *very evident* anxiety of former in the case—and his evident disapointment and surprise at the presnt action of Government   It seems to me—that a *halt* should be made in this case until you get an opportunity to examine it personally or until shuch time as you have a chanc to hear personally their undestanding of the question, and of your order in the cases—They certainly ~~have~~ think they have cause—to be aggreived—and I do not think the 'Commodore' cares a *fig* for the *Tax* only the action Govt has taken after his agreement with them—I write this upon my own responsibility without their knowledge—but it is due to you—that I should state it as I heard it   If you undestnd the case fully no harm is done   if you do not this will give you their feelings in the matter—I *dont want to see as good a friend* to you as the Commodore—feel as he does without reason . . . The Convention was—the ablest and best I ever attended—all were Earnest and mean victory but we have got *hard work* if the other Elements combine—I noticed but *one feature in convention* that *was significant* that was the *almost entire absence* of the *German Element*,—They seem to stand aloof now—I believ if we are prudent we will get them almost entirely—Your endorsemnts were spontaneus—as much so as when—you were greeted fresh from your victories and it argues well for the cause—you would have been gratified if you could hav seen as much as were your friends—I have no doubts of your election" ALS, CSmH. See Stanley P. Hirshson, *Grenville M. Dodge: Soldier, Politician, Railroad Pioneer* (Bloomington, Ind., 1967), pp. 186–88. On April 7, 1873, William H. Vanderbilt, New York City, wrote to USG. "When I saw you in this city last week, you stated you would take an opportunity to look over the statements connected with the Tax claimed of The New York

Central Rail Road Company, and said I might send them to you for that purpose—. . . I must apologize for trespassing upon you, but I am extremely desirous that our position should be fully understood by you as the Chief Executive of the government. I said to you on a former occasion, and I now repeat, that we want *only* what is *right*—we are willing to submit the matter to the Courts for adjudication—a course authorized by the Tax Law, and one that *now* involves no question of precedent—and which was (as I am informed) recommended by Mr Smith (now Asst. Attorney General) when he was counsel to the Department, and before the Commission was appointed." Typescript, USGA. See *SED*, 41-3-9, 46-2-216, 50-1-257; *SMD*, 46-2-97.

On June 7, 1872, Governor John W. Geary of Pa. wrote to USG. "Please accept my most Sincere and hearty congratulations upon your unanimous renomination to the Presidency. May your election be equally triumphant" ALS, OFH. On the same day, John P. Newman, Albany, N. Y., wrote to USG. "I was in this old Dutch city yesterday, when a hundred guns announced your renomination. The feeling which followed was confident & joyous. Although the result was no surprise to me, yet I fully shared the joy expressed by others. So far as I can learn, public sentiment is against Mr Sumner's course, & were it not for the sins he commits in so doing, we might wish him to make a few more such speeches, for they help you & injure him. The future of our country brightens evry day. God bless you, my dear friend & give you grace in the future as in the past! We are now the guests of Captain Baker of Troy, who with his lady send their compliments. Remember us to Mrs Grant." ALS, ICHi. On June 8, Brig. Gen. John Pope, Fort Leavenworth, wrote to USG. "I cannot deny myself the pleasure of telling you how much we are all gratified here at your nomination at Philadelphia—The result was expected, but the unanimity & enthusiasm with which the nomination was made, has been peculiarly gratifying to us & has no parallel in the history of the country—The result of the election no man really doubts however much may be openly said to the contrary—I am sure I need not tell you that I rejoice with all my heart, not only from personal regard for you, but because I believe that the election of any other man at this time would be next to fatal to the best interests of the country—The atrocious speech of Mr Sumner has been deeply felt & resented by all who served under your command—It is felt as a personal insult by every one of them & will secure you thousands of votes which for political reasons, might have been given to another candidate—I only regret that any of your friends in the Senate thought it necessary to reply to such a Speech—It carried it's own answer with it & not a word need to have been said on the subject, nor could any thing be said, that would add to the profound indignation which is everywhere felt at that speech—" ALS, OFH. On May 31, U.S. Senator Charles Sumner of Mass. had attacked USG in a lengthy speech, accusing him of nepotism and autocratic rule. *CG*, 42–2, 4110–22. For rebuttals, see *ibid.*, pp. 4147–50, 4154–55, 4172–73, 4282–83. Sumner published his speech in pamphlet form as "Republicanism vs. Grantism. The Presidency a Trust; Not a Plaything and Perquisite. . . ." See David Donald, *Charles Sumner and the Rights of Man* (New York, 1970), pp. 547–51.

On June 14, George H. Clower, Forsyth, Ga., wrote to USG. "for the fist time I have under taken to salie you in relation to the political sisation of the state of Georgia   I am Glad to know that you Was renominated   sir it made Glad our hartes When We here that you Was renominatid againe for president of the united states   We muste organized in this state and it Will tak the Best speeker that We have to do it Bothe Whit and Colord to do it   Dear sir I am one of the Leader of the republican party in this state   I have all Ways Work for the party all Ways Will all Ways Carred my party in this district   I am

Going to Work for the state   I have Got seavrel speeker under me to Go in to the Grate Work and I Will say to you that We must Go to Work right now if We Expecte to Beate the Democrats party   Dear president if you Will help me I Will Go to Work Writ away   no man of my Colard can do more Good for the party then I Can   if you Want to know ask Hon Thomas. J. Speer Hon. R. Whitly Hon John. T. Costin Hon. J. F. Long Hon. Henry. P. Farrow Hon. A. T. Akerman Hon. Benjamin Conley and meney cuther and they Will tel all about me   I am very poor and are not abel to do much for the party the Democrate party have offar me $3000.00 and told me I can Get ten $1000.00 if I Will Go in to the Feald and Go to Work for them But I am republican Expect to Live and die one   I am a Member of the Legislature and have been for. 4. years   Dear sir if you Will let me have some Money I Will do as much Good to organized as a man in the state I am also a member of the stat senral Committe   Dear sir pleas Help. me if you can right away and I Will Go to Work for the presidenal Campe Paine   pleas let me here form you soon   Excuse bad Writing as I am a colard man" ALS, OFH.

On June 18, S. S. Guthrie, Buffalo, wrote to USG. "It affords me great pleasure to congratulate you on your unanimous renomination, by the great Republican party, to the Candidacy of the Office, which you have, under such trying circumstances, during the past four years, so nobly filled. Your Administration has had an unusual number of office seekers, consequently more than an ordinary number of disappointments. Among these, are many 'Sore heads,' who now appear Leaders in the 'new departure.' Some of them are here, and have a zeal surpassed only by their desire for Office. The coming campaign, and November Election will defeat their highest aims, and *prove the triumph* of our glorious party. Wishing you every success, and *determined* to do what I can to advance the cause . . ." ALS, *ibid.*

On June 26, Thomas H. Nelson, U.S. minister, Mexico City, wrote to USG. "I beg leave to tender my cordial congratulations upon your unanimous nomination by the National Republican Convention, for re-election to the Presidency of the United States— a nomination, which I feel confident will be sustained by a large majority of our people. With my best wishes for your health and happiness—and the continued prosperity of our Government and people under your Administration, . . ." ALS, ICHi.

On June 8, Adam Badeau, consul gen., London, had written to USG. "I wish to congratulate you most heartily upon your re-nomination having been made in the same manner (by acclamation) as your first. I cannot forget that I was by your side when you received the news of the first, and though the Second was as fully expected as the other, it is none the less acceptable news. I am as confident of the later result as of the former, and do not doubt your endorsement at the polls will be as triumphant in 72 as in '68. The ridiculous show of opposition in the Republican party will be seen not to extend beyond some who think themselves leaders, but are not; and the great mass of the people will evince their satisfaction with your course in civil matters, as before they did in military ones. I trust the worst trouble about the treaty is over. I cannot think that the British government will be so stupid as to refuse the Senate Amendments. They dare not say to the world that all their outcry against the principle of indirect damages was insincere. They dare not withdraw from the arbitration on that ground. The British people would not sustain them. And yet the extension of the rule of excluding such claims in future, will be a great diplomatic triumph for us; equal to that of the original treaty. I wish very much, if the treaty is absolutely ratified, you and Gov. Fish would consent to my writing an article for Harpers Magazine on the history of the negotiation, and public opinion in its fluctuations here. I think I could make it very serviceable to the administration and a good campaign document. It would be indispensable that my name should be withheld absolutely— perhaps from the publishers. But the article could be offered through Mr. Curtis, and Harpers would be sure to publish it. I would submit it here to General Schenck, and then send it to Gov. Fish, so that any thing could be omitted, which you or he disapproved of. Please remember I am *not* in the Diplomatic corps   I could write it in a few days, if he would telegraph me permission. Will you please consider this. I regard the whole subject as one that can be shown to redound greatly to the honor and reputation of the government and its agents. Sir Stafford Northcote's letter to Lord Derby shews our honor intact; and if you'll let me, I'll put the ability and diplomatic success so that they shall be equally clear. The administration ought to have the credit with the people which it deserves in this matter. Gen Schenck has been admirable nobody could have done better here in this crisis. He maintains (outside I mean of diplomatic correspondence) which you of course know all about) the dignity of his country. He is courteous and liked, but *never* knuckles or toadies. His daughters too are thoroughly American   They were delighted with your letter about Nellie.—I am hard at work on the Appomattox chapter   Porter of course told you, why I take that next. It will be ready in August. I mean ready then to appear in America. I hope you liked the Wilderness chapter. Please make my best compliments to Mrs. Grant and Jessee, . . ." ALS, DLC-Hamilton Fish. See letter to Robert C. Schenck, May 17, 1872; letter to Adam Badeau, July 14, 1873. On June 29, 1872, Horace Porter wrote to Secretary of State Hamilton Fish. "The President directs me to enclose Badeau's letter, and to say that he will leave the decision entirely to you. If you approve of such an article, please telegraph Badeau permission to write it. The President thinks it might do some good if written in the ~~write~~ right spirit, and with a proper knowledge of the facts." ALS, DLC-Hamilton Fish. On Aug. 27, Badeau wrote to Fish. "Private & *Confidential* . . . I got my article done some days ago, but Gen Schenck was away, and I was obliged to keep it for his inspection. He sat up late with me last night, and went over it all. He says it is *sharp*, but telling, and he approves it's appearance without omitting the bitter passages. Of course, it would not be proper for me to publish it here, or any where as an emanation from the Consul General at London; but for use at present in America, and without any name he regards it justifiable.—It came out bitterer, than I expected; but I believe every word of it. In fact I think I *know* every word of it to be true. I leave it however entirely to your judgment to say whether it shall appear in its present state; or whether the passages marked in red ink should be omitted. If they are, the article will be about one fourth shorter; and will be confined to a documentary history. It will be complete in its way (I dont mean in treatment or style, but in design) but less popular less likely perhaps to be readable. In either event, it seems to me that it may be useful   It ought to reach you in time for its appearance in Harper's Monthly for October; or any other periodical that may be selected. The Oct. No. of Harper appears on the 20th of September, so there would be six good weeks for it to operate. Articles for that No. can appear if they reach the publisher by the 10th of Sept. Other magazines dont require matter so long in advance. I have written to Gen Porter on the subject, but dont know if he has made any arrangement. Of course I can do nothing in this matter myself, as my name is not to appear. Perhaps Mr Hale would be willing to take some steps. I dont know whether he knows Mr. Curtis, but presume he does of course. The article as it stands is rather stronger against England's course than I fancy Mr. Curtis feels. It occurred to me that if it first appeared in some periodical, it might *afterwards* be published as a campaign document by the Committee; but if by the Committee first, it would have vastly less effect; seeming to have been written for a purpose. I think it will print about twenty five or thirty pages of Harper. It is difficult to cut it down, except in the way I have suggested; and if some of the questionably politic passages are omitted, all should be; (I think), to preserve a uniform character. I leave it however *altogether in your hands.* I have marked this confidential, but should like the President or Gen Porter to see it, or Mr Hale if you have no objections. It occurred to me that if Gen Woodhull were supposed to be the author, the supposition would have many grounds of probability? He was here while the discussion and panic were at their height, and might be supposed to have known every fact, public or private that is mentioned. I have however said nothing that printed documents given to the world could not furnish to any one—and a little observation. I have taken the liberty of telegraphing you in advance I have said I leave all in your hands, but I beg particularly that any epithets I may have applied to the American Secretary of State or his productions may remain unchanged." ALS (press), NjR. See "The Treaty of Washington," *Harper's New Monthly Magazine,* XLV, CCLXX (Nov., 1872), 913–32. On Feb. 3, 1873, Fish described in his diary a conversation with USG, during which Fish offered to remain in the cabinet. "I then say that there is another matter, which is very unpleasant, & as I think tending to injure his Administration—refering to an Article which appeared in the NY Times of 28th ult. He had not read it—I shew him the Article. He says the displeasure of the Times arises from an expression in An Article in Harpers Magazine (Badeau's article) which (he adds) 'I suppose never attracted your notice'—I tell him that it did not, & recount the history of the publication of a despatch of Mr Davis, & of Badeaus article, each of which were sent to the Press at his (the Presidents) request—I say that I think he should regard an attack upon any member of his Cabinet, as an assault upon the integrity of the Cabinet, & thus upon himself, & his Administration—that the Times claims to be the especial supporter & friend of his Administration, & while I regard the Article as personally offensive to me, I think it calculated to weaken his Administration—that a few words from him would stop such things, but they should be decided words—I name Murphy & Geo. Bliss as among those to whom he might speak. He says the Times is hostile to Bliss & was much opposed to his appointment as Dist. Attorney—that this desire of some persons in N. Y. to have a Secr of the Treasury from N. Y. is at the bottom of the feeling, & not hostility personal to me— He says that he will speak to Crounse (the Correspondent of the Times) & request him to write to Jones (the Publisher) that a repetition of such attacks will be regarded as evidence of hostility   Mr Davis suggests the fact that Jennings, the Editor is jealous of Crounse, & thinks Crounse may supercedeed him—" DLC-Hamilton Fish. The diary incorporates a brief *New York Times* clipping, dated Jan. 28, concerning Fish and J. C. Bancroft Davis.

1. On May 20, 1872, Ethan A. Allen, New York City, had written to USG. "I take the liberty of sugjesting to you that the best interests of our country require you should be the candidate of the Republican party at the Philadelphia convention. I feel a deep interest in this, my country and I hope you will not *allow* that convention to take any candidate other than yourself. I beg leave to inform you that there is an Ethan Allen in this City (who was at one time assistant District Attorney) & now an advocate of Mr Horace Greeley   This man Allen is *no connection whatever* of mine. I am a Grand-son of Col Ethan Allen of Revolutionary memory. My Father graduated at West Point in 1806. & my Uncle Hannibal in 1804. I am the only living Grand-Son of Col Allen.   the Col Ethan Allen Hitchcock formerly of the U. S. Army who Died in Georgia about a year ago was a Grandson of Col Allen   Wishing you success in Philadelphia . . ." ALS, OFH.

On May 25, Charles J. Meng, Hopkinsville, Ky., wrote to USG. "It is a remarkle fact in the history of this Nation. We have been in existance as a Government upwards of 90 years and during that time no man was ever elected to the Presidency from the North except Mr Lincoln and he did not live 60 days after his inauguration. My advice to you is not to think of running for a reelection as you may Share the fate of Mr Lincoln." ALS, *ibid.*

2. On May 4, Victoria Woodhull had written to USG. Parke-Bernet Sale No. 2235, Dec. 3, 1963, no. 226. In this letter, or more likely another of Nov. 9, 1874, Woodhull wrote: "Unless the Republican Party does something commensurate with its necessities for salvation, nothing is more certain than that it will be wiped out of existence in the next presidential election. . . . The fate of the Party lies in you hands. It must have the votes of Women at its next general election, or else it will be buried beyond any future resurrection." *Ibid.*

Probably in 1872, Isabella Beecher Hooker wrote to USG. "I have seen recently a Memorial addressed to you, by Dr Horace Dresser on the subject of the immediate admission of women of the U. S. to their electoral rights, ~~through the~~ by proclamation of the President to the officers of elections. ~~by the President~~. Permit me to say that I have for some time past been of the opinion that the women of the several States should claim their right & ~~perform their duty~~ exercise it at the coming pres. election, ~~leaving these officers~~ dealing with these officers personally in the attempt to persuade them that they should not dare assume the responsibility of denying ~~the to~~ any citisen so fundamental a right as that of the ballot, but should accept the vote of all citisens alike, leaving the question of the legality of the votes of women to the legislatures of the several States, precisely as ~~they~~ do ~~cases of contested~~ in the case of male voters whose votes are contested. If you will kindly read the enclosed abstract of an argument on this point recently made by myself before our legislature you will perceive that ~~the~~ the ground is perfectly tenable & that Dr Dresser's proposition simply goes a step farther & in urging that the Chief Executive shall ~~simply~~ assist women ~~in this their plain privilege & duty~~ to their liberty by a proclamation similar to the one issued by Mr Lincoln ~~in regar for the benefit~~ in behalf of the black race. Need I say to you Sir, who know full well the subjection of the women of our country to laws they have had no voice in making & taxes whose imposition ~~is~~ has been without ~~consultation even~~ their consent, that he who should speak theis last word of emancipation to ~~twenty million~~ these loyal millions ~~would rank must lay up for himself a~~ would rank among the world's deliverers second to none—& prove himself a loyal son indeed to the mother who bore him. It is with motives like these that I would urge you to give the subject the most serious consideration rather than ~~from considerations to press~~ by suggestions of a purely partisan character. But I cannot forbear adding that ~~the~~ in my judgment ~~the days of~~ the republican party is doomed not only to present defeat but to absolute disintegration & extinction except it become once more the instrument in the divine hand to break chains & let the oppressed go free. Should it refuse to enforce Constt. Amt. of the plainest liberating quality ~~passed~~ created by itself ~~for~~ in its hour of need ~~for~~ to secure the fealty its black men, ~~in to~~ in the case of *black women* (more intensely loyal alway than their dusky mates) it would deserve ~~its~~ its doom—how much more if faithless to the white women of the whole land ~~who~~ through whom alone the successes of the war were made possible. That you may be guided into just judgment & speedy action is the prayer of your sincere friend." ADf, Stowe-Day Foundation, Hartford, Conn. Hooker addressed Julia Dent Grant in the same letter. "In the enclosed you will find an appeal to your husband to do justice, love mercy & walk humbly with his God. It seems to me, that I know that this is an opportunity such as will come to no man again on this earth. Liberty, we women are to have—& responsibility we ~~are to accept~~ must assume & that right speedily—perhaps by ourselves alone we are to fight this great battle & win the everlasting victory, which shall redeem a race. . . ." ADf, *ibid.* See *SRC*, 42-2-21.

To Ministers and Consuls

—————

Washington, D. C. June 10. 1872.

Dear Sir:

I take pleasure in introducing to you Mr. Thomas Ochiltree a prominent Citizen of Texas who proposes traveling in Europe.

I commend Mr. Ochiltree to your good office during his sojourn in your vicinity.

Very respectfully
U. S. Grant.

To. U. S. Ministers and Consuls abroad.

Copy, DLC-USG, II, 1. See *PUSG,* 18, 241; *ibid.,* 19, 296.

On Feb. 1, 1872, Governor Edmund J. Davis of Tex., New York City, had written to USG. "When in Washington I mentioned the names of persons for appointment as U. S. Marshall for the Western Dist. of Texas, in the event of removal of present incumbent, (which I hope will be made without delay). I would then have mentioned the name of Major Thos. P. Ochiltree, had I known he would accept. I now wish to present his name as my first choice for that position. I am sure Maj. Ochiltree will make an energetic and efficient Marshall and further believe that his appointment will have a beneficial influence in the District. Maj Ochiltree has, since he surrendered to the Union arms, been a faithfull and true supporter of the Government—through good and evil report. I cannot speak too highly of him in this respect." ALS, DNA, RG 60, Records Relating to Appointments. On Feb. 22, U.S. Senator James W. Flanagan of Tex. wrote to USG on the same subject. LS, *ibid.* U.S. Representative William T. Clark of Tex. favorably endorsed this letter. AES (undated), *ibid.*

On March 25, 1873, Clark, postmaster, Galveston, Washington, D. C., wrote to USG. "The only Foreign Mission charged to Texas is Nicaragua held for several years by Charles N. Riotte, appointed by Prest. Johnson—I am authorized by Senator Flanagan and every Republican of prominence in Texas, to say that the removal of the present Minister Resident and the appointment of Mr Thomas P. Ochiltree will give entire satisfaction to them—Major Ochiltree deserves the place as his strong endorsements prove—" ALS, DNA, RG 60, Records Relating to Appointments. On the same day, William E. Chandler, secretary, Republican National Committee, Washington, D. C., wrote to USG. "I desire to commend for suitable recognition by you *Col. Tom. P. Ochiltree* of Texas. Col. Ochiltree, an officer in the Confederate service, has since the rebellion acted nobly and patriotically in connection with the work of reconstruction. He has also, as a member of the Republican party, rendered efficient political service both north and south. During the late presidential campaign he spoke eloquently and effectively in Pennsylvania and other states. Whatever recognition you may extend to him will, I am sure, be approved and appreciated by the Republicans and the people of Texas" ALS, *ibid.*

On March 12, USG had nominated incumbent William E. Parker as marshal, Eastern District, Tex.; on April 15, he suspended Parker. On April 29, Davis *et al.* petitioned USG. "The undersigned Republicans, citizens of Texas and devoted to our sState's welfare and interests, as also your political friends and supporters, beg leave most respectfully to invite your attention to the following facts in the removal of Capt. Wm E. Parker, as U. S. Marshal for the Eastern District of Texas—. . . . Captain Parker is a native of Texas, reared in the State; and when a young man immigrated to California where he was at the outbreak of the late civil war—Unlike many others of his section then in that State, who cast their fortunes with the so called confederacy, Mr Parker promptly enlisted in the cause of the Union; entering a cavalry regiment which was consolidated subsequently with one from Massachusetts, and accredited to that State, he rose from the ranks to the position of a captaincy—He was with General Sheridan in the valley of the Shenandoah and did good service for which he is known and esteemed by his superior officers—Honorably discharged at the close of the war, Capt. Parker returned to his old home in Galveston, where the lamented General Griffin recognizing his fidelity to the Union and his army service, appointed him in 1867 as the registrar of Galveston, the most important county in the State—Executing faithfully his official duties in this regard—In the following year 1868 Capt. Parker was one among the few zealous and trustful Republicans of our State who supported your nomination and would have performed service in the cause had Texas then been deemed eligible to vote—In 1869 after your inauguration, at the solicitation and request of our Governor Davis and other prominent State Republicans, you nominated, and the Senate confirmed Capt. Parker as U. S. Marshal for our Eastern District—For four years in the discharge of his duties he has given hearty satisfaction to our people and especially to the loyal portion hereof—And when he was again nominated and confirmed at the beginning of your excellency's present term the act was gratefully appreciated by our people and the Republicans of Texas—During the late campaign Capt. Parker was active and mindful in your support, contributing his time and money for the success of the National and State ticket. When at the opening of the campaign the opposition to the National Republican party in Texas were all sanguine and many Republicans in this State were depressed because of the force of the Greeley movement, Capt. Parker pointedly demonstrated his position by posting in his office your portrait with the words, 'our next President' over his own signature—His position thus assumed was stoutly maintained during the canvass. A man of few words, but a man of action and fidelity, we have particularly felt that with Marshal Parker in his district, we had an official who was at all times reliable and honest. We regret that he has been removed—We know Major Ochiltree, and esteem his advocacy in behalf of our, the Republican party; but we most respectfully deprecate his appointment at the expense of Captain Parker, and what we believe to be the best interests of our community and people.—With this, not too lengthy, we trust, statement we respectfully leave the subject for your careful consideration—" DS (13 signatures), *ibid.* On Aug. 26, Davis and S. G. Newton wrote to USG introducing Parker. LS, *ibid.* On Jan. 26, 1874, Parker, Washington, D. C., wrote to Lt. Gen. Philip H. Sheridan. ". . . Thus far I have been unable to give any satisfactory explanation of the matter to my friends, and have failed to receive any explanation of or cause for my removal, and in consequence am under a cloud of suspicion in the community where I live, and have come on here for the purpose of seeing President Grant with a view of haveing the situation explained to him so that he will make some statement which can be used to clear the matter up, so that I can set myself aright before the community in which I reside. Since I saw the announcement of your arrival in the city, it has occured to me that, if I could obtain the honor and support of an introduction to President Grant from yourself, that it would materially strengthen my cause and facilitate me in obtaining a satisfactory interview with the President, and a solution of my present trouble. Trusting that you will find it convenient to grant my request, and appoint a time when it will please you to do so, . . ." ALS, *ibid.*, Letters from the President. On Feb. 17, Sheridan endorsed this letter. "Respectfully forwarded to Genl. O. E. Babcock, Secretary to the President, for his information: without remark." AES, *ibid.*

On June 28, 1873, Thomas P. Ochiltree, Galveston, had written to USG. "It has been stated here that Gov Davis would ask my suspension from the position of US Marshal, I cannot believe that he will do so, because up to within a few days the kindest relations have existed between us; I am sorry to say that a most unfortunate, and, I think, uncalled for division exists inside of the Republican party at the present time; I have refused to take any part whatever, either on the one side or the other, as will be seen by the enclosed note; I have only to say to Your Excellency that I shall continue to discharge my duties to the Government, *and maintain my fealty strictly and unfalteringly to the Administration*; I respectfully request that if any attempt is made to disturb my relations to yourself & the Govt, I may be advised thereof." ALS, *ibid.*, Records Relating to Appointments. An enclosed clipping is *ibid.* On Dec. 2, USG nominated Ochiltree as marshal, Eastern District, Tex.

On Nov. 3, 1874, George Flournoy *et al.*, Galveston, petitioned USG asking Ochiltree's retention. DS (35 signatures), *ibid.* A similar petition dated Nov. 4 is *ibid.* On Oct. 29, USG had suspended Ochiltree from office.

In an undated letter, J. W. Reed and L. P. Sawyer wrote to USG. "We the undersigned Citizens of Texas before the Reblion & Since; now in this City learning that there was about being a change of Marshall in the Eastern District of Texas, would most respectfully recommend the appointment of Mr Angie M Hobbs to the position Mr Hobbs was a citizen and actively engaged in business for ten years before the war in that State, and being an earnest Union man he had to escape from the State during the War at a great pecuniary Sacrifice He is a man of the strictest integrity, every way qualified for the position, an earnest Republican and has the entire confidence of the leading legal & business men of both parties in the State. And if time allowed could procure there endorsement We know that his appointment would give great satisfaction to Senator Morgan Hamilton and the leading Republicans of the State as well as to that class of Union Democrats' who Support the Government" LS, *ibid.*

On Dec. 14, USG nominated Lemuel D. Evans to replace Ochiltree. On Feb. 16, 1875, Boulds Baker, chairman, Republican Executive Committee of Tex., Washington, D. C., wrote to USG. "Personal & Private . . . The delay in the confirmation of Judge Evans as Marshall vice Ochiltree removed is not occasioned by factious opposition: but I am satisfied that Judge Edmonds and other Senators are conscientious in the opinion that legally he is inellegible to the position owing to his deficit with the Government. This I regret but viewing it as a fact, would it not be best that he be withdrawn and saved the mortification of defeat and our party in Texas a precedent of having appointed techinally a defaulter when others were removed for the same fault to the State Government of Texas Under great difficulties I have labored for the confirmation of all the Texas appointments and I make this modest suggestion in the interest of the Republican party of my State the destiny of which is somewhat in my hands—In the place of Judge Evans I would propose [t]he name of an unexceptional Gentleman whose appointment would be entirely satisfactory to *all* of the Republican party and respected by the democracy—Judge Sam Dodge of Galveston Texas for near six years the Criminal Judge of that district is the party I would be pleased for you to name for the position—He was a union Soldier for the entire war afterwards settled in Galveston and so conducted himself officially and socially as to win the good favor and respect of the entire community   As you will observe by the enclosed recommendations after having served that people in so delicate a position they irrespective of party and unanimously petitioned the present Governor to reappoint him—being a republican he was not continued in the position—This appointment would give strength to our party and great satisfaction to the people" ALS, *ibid.* On Feb. 24, the Senate failed to confirm Evans. Renominated on March 8 when a new Senate convened, Evans was confirmed on March 9. See *PUSG*, 18, 302; *ibid.*, 19, 325; Janet L. Coryell, *Neither Heroine nor Fool: Anna Ella Carroll of Maryland* (Kent, Ohio, 1990).

To Virginia Grant Corbin

Long Branch, N. J.,
June 13th, 1872.

DEAR SISTER:

We got here Tuesday evening[1] and are now pretty well settled. Can we not expect Mr. Corbin, you, Mary and two children down to spend a few days with us as soon as the latter arrives? If Mary does not come now, it is not probable that she will get East again this summer. You can see just as much of her here as you could at your own house; so I think the best arrangement will be for you to come immediately here and all spend the time together at the Branch. I will go up to meet you in the harbor if informed in time.

Yours truly,
U. S. GRANT.

P. S. I learned from a letter from St. Petersburg[2] that Fred. hurried off to Copenhagen to meet Mary before she left, which was to be the 1st day of June. I infer from this that she should be here in two or three days from now.

J. G. Cramer, p. 117.

1. June 11, 1872. See *New York Herald*, June 14, 1872. On June 18, Horace Porter wrote to Attorney Gen. George H. Williams. "In order that the records of the Executive Mansion may be complete and for the purpose of reducing the number of separate packages forwarded by mail the President requests that all papers for his signature be sent to the Executive Mansion, whence they will be forwarded to his address and returned to the proper Department through this office." LS, DNA, RG 60, Letters from the President. Porter sent similar letters to the other cabinet members.

2. See letter to Frederick Dent Grant, April 28, 1872, note 3.

To Manning F. Force

———

Long Branch, N. J.
June 17th 1872.

My Dear General:

Your favor of the 15th inst. urging me to attend the meeting of the Society of the Army of the Tenn. on the 5th & 6th of July next, is received. It has been my determination to attend that meeting and I feel very much disappointed at not being able to do so. But my son, who is now at Harvard, will return on the 28th of June, and he has taken passage for Europe on the Steamer leaving New York City on the 6th of July, to be absent a year. As I can not take him with me West I do not see that I can very well leave home just at the only time I can have him with me. Later however I will see and if I can possibly attend the next meeting of the Society I will do so.

Should I not be present you may assure the Society that the disappointment is much greater to me than it possibly can be to them. It is largely composed of men whos first Military service was with me and men who have earned lasting renown for services rendered their country in times of trial, and, some times, of almost despair.— Should I not be present at your meeting express my great regret thereat, and my hope that you (they) will have a happy reunion, and that there may be many more of them when I may be fortunate enough to be present.

Faithfully Yours
U. S. Grant

Gn. M. F. Force
Cincinnati, O.

ALS, DLC–USG, IC. See *Report of the Proceedings of the Society of the Army of the Tennessee, at the Sixth Annual Meeting, . . .* (Cincinnati, 1877); *Chicago Tribune*, July 4, 1872.

On May 31, 1872, Governor Cadwallader C. Washburn of Wis. wrote to USG. "The City Govt of Madison having extended to you an invitation to be present at the meeting of the Army of the Tennessee, on the 3rd & 4th July I beg leave to reinforce their invitation by urgently requesting you to accept of it. The prospect now is for a large assemblage of your old soldiers, & you need no assurance of a cordial welcome from the people of the State of Wisconsin—. . ." Copy, WHi. On [*June*] 17, USG, Long Branch, telegraphed to Washburn. "It will be impossible for me to attend the meeting at Madison

July fourth—my son returns from college the last June and sails for Europe July sixth to be gone a year" Telegram received (at 5:45 P.M.), *ibid.*

To Robert C. Winthrop

—————

Long Branch, N. J.
June 17th 1872.

HON. ROBT. WINTHROP;
DEAR SIR:

Your favor of the 15th is just received. Mrs. Grant and myself will leave here for Boston next Monday morning. If we reach New York City in time for the morning train to Boston we will go on that day and arrive in Boston in the evening. Otherwise we will take the evening boat, via Fall River, and arrive in Boston on Tuesday morning. It will afford me pleasure to dine with you on the day of the meeting of the trustees,[1] Mrs. Grant with me. I expect to return the following day to New York.

Faithfully yours,
U. S. GRANT

ALS, MHi. Robert C. Winthrop chaired the board of the Peabody Education Fund. See *PUSG*, 17, 48–49. On Feb. 7, 1871, Orville E. Babcock had written to Governor John H. Clifford of Mass. "The President directs me to write you and acknowledge the receipt of your letter of the 5th inst. and say that he will be perfectly willing to be upon such a committee as suggested by Mr Winthrop. He will not be able to be present at the meeting of the Trustees on account of his public duties, but wishes me to say that any resolution which you may prepare upon the subject will be acceptable to him and he will concur in its report." Copy, DLC-USG, II, 1.

1. The trustees of the Peabody Education Fund met on Wednesday, June 26, 1872, following graduation ceremonies at Harvard, where USG received an LL.D. D, MH. See *Boston Transcript*, June 26, 27, 1872; letter to Charles W. Eliot, Nov. 30, 1872.

While in Boston, on June 25 and 26, USG and Julia Dent Grant attended "The World's Peace Jubilee and International Musical Festival," organized by bandleader Patrick S. Gilmore. See *Boston Transcript*, June 25–27, 1872. On Aug. 5, 1871, USG, Long Branch, had written "To U. S. ministers and consuls in Europe." "I hereby commend Mr. P. S. Gilmore to Ministers and Representatives of the United States in Europe, and his plans for a Universal Musical Jubilee to be held in this Country in 1872. The kind offices of our Representatives abroad, in behalf of the enterprise which Mr Gilmore has so

much at heart, and which he is so eminently qualified to carry out, are respectfully solicited." Copy, DNA, RG 84, Austria, Miscellaneous Letters Received. *Boston Transcript*,
June 17, 1872. On Jan. 9 and 15, 1872, Secretary of State Hamilton Fish wrote in his diary. "*Cabinet*.... After the adjournment I read to the President Jays N 386 (Vienna Decr 7)
touching the application of P. S. Gilmore for assistance in securing the presence of a military musical Band of Austria at an 'International' (!) festival to be held in Boston—It
seems that the President had given to Gilmore a letter addressed to the Ministers & Consuls of the U. S in Europe commending Gilmore & his plans, & soliciting their kind offices
in his behalf (Gilmore applied to me, & I refused to give him a letter or endorsement of
any kind—& when I spoke to the Prsdt about it told him it would lead to enquiry &
trouble)—The Austrian Min. of For—Affairs to whom Gilmores application has been
presented, & his circular, in which, it seems that he has printed a programme or Circular
in which he calls attention to the Presidents recommendation—& that he has made application to the Austrian Govt to send a Band—The Minister of For. Affs requests information in regard to the personal position of Mr Gilmore & the character of the Festival contemplated by him   On reading the despatch the Prsdt laughs & says that he dont write
any more such letters—that he did not intend that such use as has been made of it should
have been—that Gilmore is an enthusiast, & he merely intended to commend him to the
Ministers &c—So that I have to write to Jay, saying in the best way that I can, that the
Presidents good nature got the better of his caution, & of the reserve which his position
should have imposed upon him—but that is not the way in which it will be put on paper—
I wish the President had sooner come to the determination to write no letters of introduction &c" "I read to him my draft reply to Jay's 386, about the note given by the President to Gillmore—he approves the draft saying it is exactly right—and he equaly
approves the letter on same subject prepared to be sent to other Ministers in Europe,
which I also read to him—" DLC-Hamilton Fish. On Jan. 15, Fish wrote to John Jay, U.S.
minister, Vienna. "... Beyond the desire which the President has for the success of every
enterprise tending to develope aesthetic habits, the cultivation of the arts, and the gratification of refined tastes, neither he nor the Government of the United States has any interest in the proposed Jubilee...." Copy, DNA, RG 59, Diplomatic Instructions, Austria.
For Gilmore, see H. Wiley Hitchcock and Stanley Sadie, eds., *The New Grove Dictionary
of American Music* (London, 1986), II, 223–25.

To William D. Rawlins

———

Long Branch, N. J. June 22d /72

DEAR SIR:

Your favor of the 19th inst. is received. It is true that
Mrs. Daniels has given up the charge of Gen. Rawlins children.[1]
Befor doing so she placed them at good Boarding Schools in
Connecticut, where I have paid all the charges up to the present,

and for Jimmie,[2] if my memory serves me right, (all the correspondence, receipts &c. are in Washington) up to the end of September or later.—I was so impressed with the importance of having the children near friends that would take an interest in them that I got Mr. Felt to see Col. Rowley whether he would not relieve me of the guardianship. He declined however.—The children have a competancy so they will not be a pecuniary charge to any one, and I will be glad to do whatever is the best for them. I will endeavor to see Mrs. Daniels soon and when a settlement is made with her will write to you again and probably ask you to come East to take the children with you.

Very Truly Yours,
U. S. GRANT

W. D. RAWLINS, ESQ.
CHICAGO ILL.

P. S. As I am not certain that I make out your initials correctly please let me know if you get this letter.

ALS, Steven C. Rawlins, Evanston, Ill. Born in 1845, fourteen years after his brother John A. Rawlins, William D. Rawlins was the youngest of nine children. See letter to C. F. Daniels, March 20, 1872; letter to William D. Rawlins, July 19, 1872.

1. See *PUSG*, 20, 97–99.
2. On April 15, May 31, June 21, and July 2, 1872, Orville E. Babcock wrote to A. S. Jarvis, Weston Boarding School, Weston, Conn. "The President directs me to acknowledge the receipt of your letter containing your bill for tuition and other expenses of James B Rawlins, amounting to $331 25/100 and to forward to you the enclosed draft drawn to your order for $112.50/100, being the balance at present remaining in his hands, which may be applied to this account.—He desires me to say that the funds available for this purpose are, derived from the rent of Genl: Rawlins House in this City and as he receives the rent he will remit you out of each months rent $56 25/100 until the 1st of July when there will be a sufficient amount of funds accruing from interest upon bonds belonging to the Estate to enable him to remit you in full of any balance which may remain due to you upon that date. Hoping this may prove satisfactory to you, and requesting an early acknowledgment of the enclosed draft—. . ." "The President instructs me to send you the enclosed draft for one hundred and fifty dollars. He wishes that you will make out a new bill up to July 1st, including the one already furnished, and he will then remit you the balance due up to that time. Please acknowledge the receipt of the draft sent herewith." "The President directs me to enclose herewith a Draft on New York to your order for sixty eight 75/100 dollars the balance remaining due on your bill of $331.25/100 rendered in April last which please acknowledge. Your letter was duly rec'd containing re-

ceipts for $112.50 & $150. The President wishes me to say that he is perfectly agreeable to the arrangement you propose of rendering the next bill on Oct 1. and that he will send you the $125, on account, on July 1st as you request, and would suggest that you remind me of it by letter on the 1st of July." "The President desires me to write you and say that he will soon know whether he shall leave Genl: Rawlins son at school with you or place him under the charge of one of his relatives. He wishes me to say that, if such a change is made he will then settle the amount of your bill up to such time as he leaves you, and if he remains at your school, he will remit you such amount as you may desire upon the present half year." Copies, DLC-USG, II, 1.

To Charles H. Rogers

Long Branch, N. J. June 22d 1873[2]

CHAS. H. ROGERS, ESQ.
MY DEAR SIR:

We are now settled at Long Branch where Mrs. Grant and myself will be pleased to have a nice long visit from you and Mrs. Rogers, and Miss Post. On Monday[1] we go to Boston, to return about Friday, expecting to have The Sec. of the Navy & wife,[2] and my son Ulysses, with us. On Saturday, the 6th of July, Ulysses sails for Europe. After that we will be glad to see you at any time.

Mrs. Grant & myself will go to the City on the 6th of July to see Ulysses off and will return in the evening. Can not you and the ladies come with us that evening?

Mrs. Grant sends a great deal of love to the ladies and desires to be remembered to you.

Very Truly Yours
U. S. GRANT

ALS (misdated), DLC-USG. On July 5, 1872, USG, Long Branch, telegraphed to Charles H. Rogers, New York City. "Will be glad to meet you & miss Post on steamer adriatic tomorrow three Pm" Telegram received, *ibid.* See *PUSG*, 21, 77.

1. June 24.
2. On Jan. 23, USG and cabinet members had attended the wedding of Secretary of the Navy George M. Robeson and Mary Aulick. See *New York Herald*, Jan. 24, 1872.

Endorsement

———

Forwarded to the ~~Sec. of the Int~~. Atty. Gen. I think the appointment of Mr. Burdick[1] would be a good one if the vacancy of Marshal exists in Dakotah, or if the present incumbent[2] is unfit for his place.

U. S. GRANT

JUNE 30TH 72

AES, DNA, RG 60, Records Relating to Appointments. Written on a letter of June 22, 1872, from James H. Burdick, Yankton, Dakota Territory, to USG. "You were kind enough to say to me on the 8th inst that you would appoint me United States Marshal of Dakota Territory, requiring me to make the application in writing stating the reasons why the present incumbent should be removed. My application was immediately reduced to writing and was endorsed by Gen Beadle, Surveyor General of this territory and placed in the hands of one of the gentlemen in Gen Dents room to be laid before you. If still agreeable to your excellency to make the appointment, I would be pleased to have it made at an early day, as I have other important business interests which must be given up entirely if I receive the appointment. Should you require further endorsement as to my qualifications for the position, or that my appointment would be acceptable to the republicans of the territory I will have pleasure in forwarding them." ALS, *ibid.* On June 8, Burdick, Washington, D. C., had written to USG. "In accordance with the conversation granted by your favor, I respectfully request my appointment as U S Marshal of Dakota Territory, in place of L H Litchfield the present incumbent. I express the opinion and most earnest wish of a large number of the people of Dakota that Mr Litchfield be removed. He has held the office for several years prior to your administration, and since by reappointment. He is now and for a long time has been grossly intemperate in habits, reaching public indecency; he is known as addicted to gambling; his office is extavagant and beleived to be corrupt, costing the Government a vast amount for fees of deputies and witnesses unnecessarily. At the last term of the U S Court at Vermillion D. T. his conduct and that of his assistants was most extraordinary bringing down general and even newspaper criticisms upon the intemperance gambling, long delay of business, unnecessary use of money and the subpoenaing without apparent need women of disreputable reputation. He has by these and other means tended and labored to divide and bring odium upon the party while he is opposed by all the soldiers and best men of the Territory." ALS, *ibid.* On the same day, William H. H. Beadle, surveyor gen., Dakota Territory, Washington, D. C., endorsed this letter. "Judge Burdick is a citizen of Dakota and widely & most favorably known for his high christian and civil character. I heartily concur in his request, and join with him in the statements in regard to Litchfield, which are either known to me personally or stated upon the best authority." AES, *ibid.* USG endorsed these papers. "Atty Gn" AE (undated), *ibid.* On Sept. 27, George A. Batchelder, Yankton, wrote to USG. "Mr. Litchfield U. S. Marshal for this Territory died today   It is hoped here that no appointment will be made until you can be seen—The undersigned states lest he may not be misunderstood that he is *not* an applicant" ALS, *ibid.*, Letters from the President.

On Oct. 7, Beadle, Yankton, wrote to U.S. Senator James Harlan of Iowa. "Rev. J. T. Walker informs me that he addressed you personally in reference to Judge J. H. Burdick of this place, and has recently written you about his appointment as U. S. Marshall—A movement is on foot here by a few, and these not the most worthy in the party, to transfer Gen. E. S. McCook from the Secretaryship to Marshallship; then to transfer W. A. Pound from Postmastership at Yankton to Secretaryship; and then have another man apptd Postmaster—Such arrangements, rings and successions meet with general disapproval. Judge Burdick should be appointed Marshall; . . ." ALS, *ibid.*, Records Relating to Appointments. On the same day, Harlan wrote to USG. "I take the liberty of enclosing herewith a letter from Rev. J. T. Walker. Pastor M. E. Church at Yankton Dakota, recommending the appointment of Hon J. H. Burdick to the position of Marshall of Dakota Territory—for your perusal—I believe Mr Walker to be thoroughly reliable— Will you be good enough after reading his letter. to return it to me." LS, *ibid.* On Sept. 30, Jefferson P. Kidder and Wilmot W. Brookings, associate justices, Dakota Territory, Yankton, had telegraphed to USG. "Our united States Marshall T, H, Litchfield is dead. Court begins next week, and successor should be immediately appointed   Genl Edwin S. McCook is best man for place and full and strong endorsements will go by mail,   we urge his immediate appointment" Telegram received (on Oct. 1), *ibid.* On Oct. 1, U.S. Senator Oliver P. Morton and U.S. Representative John Coburn of Ind., Indianapolis, telegraphed to USG. "If marshall for Dakota must be appointed immediately beg leave to recommend Genl Ed. S. McCook present secy. & William Pound for secy   see Pounds recommendation on file for secretary" Telegram received, *ibid.* On Oct. 2, McCook *et al.* petitioned USG. "We the undersigned citizens of Dakota Territory would respectfully ask for the appointment of William Pound to the position of Secretary of said Territory, in case said office should be made vacant by the appointment of Gen'l E. S. McCook to the position of United States Marshal. Mr Pound has been a resident of this Territory for three years, and during his residence here has gained the confidence and esteem of the community to an unusual degree. . . ." DS (16 signatures), *ibid.*, RG 59, Letters of Application and Recommendation. Papers recommending Laurens J. Joyce, Amos F. Shaw, and B. C. Yates as marshal, Dakota Territory, are *ibid.*, RG 60, Records Relating to Appointments. On Oct. 14, Horace Porter wrote to Attorney Gen. George H. Williams. "The President directs me to request you to bring with you to Cabinet meeting to-morrow, all recommendations for U. S. Marshal and U. S. Attorney of Dakota Territory." Copy, DLC-USG, II, 1. On Dec. 2, USG nominated Burdick as marshal, Dakota Territory.

On Feb. 1, Batchelder had written to USG. "I have the honor to respectfully present my resignation as Secretary of the Territory of Dakota   thanking for your uniform kindness . . ." ALS, DNA, RG 59, Letters of Resignation and Declination. On the same day, USG endorsed this letter. "Accepted ~~Jan.y~~ Feby 1st 1872" AES, *ibid.* On Jan. 29, Orville E. Babcock had written to Secretary of State Hamilton Fish. "The President directs me to say that, he understands that Senator Hamlin has in his possession the resignation of the Secretary of Dakota Ter. and he will be pleased to have you obtain it, as a change must soon be made in the office there." Copy, DLC-USG, II, 1. On Feb. 6, USG nominated Edwin S. McCook as secretary, Dakota Territory.

On May 9, 1870, U.S. Senators Hannibal Hamlin of Maine, Henry Wilson and Charles Sumner of Mass. had written to USG. "We recommend to your favorable consideration Col. Geo. A Batchelder for the place of Secretary of the Territory of Dakota. The Col did good Service in the late war, and is a gentleman well qualified for the place" LS, DNA, RG 59, Letters of Application and Recommendation. On May 10, USG nominated Batchelder as secretary, Dakota Territory.

On Oct. 2, 1871, Andrew J. Sweetser *et al.* petitioned USG. "We as Citizens of the City of Yankton. the capitol of the Territory of Dakota. most respectfully submit: that we are personaly acquanted with Geo. A. Batchelder. the seceretary of Dakota; that we have known him since taking charge of said Office; that his course as an Official has not commanded respect and confidence; and that his private conduct has been reckless, dissipated and licentious   Therefore we earnestly petition for the removal of the said Geo. A. Batchelder. from the seceretaryship of this Territory." DS (63 signatures), *ibid.* On Oct. 27, U.S. Delegate Moses K. Armstrong of Dakota Territory, Yankton, wrote to USG. "I am informed that Geo A. Batchelder, Secretary of Dakota is about to resign or be removed from his position. Differing somewhat with the present Administration in politics, I do not claim any right to dictate appointments in Dakota, but I would like to be *consulted* when the interests of my people are jeopardized. . . ." ALS, *ibid.* On Oct. 31, Fish recorded in his diary. "*Cabinet*—All present—. . . President speaks of Batcheldre Secr of Dakotah against whose general conduct there are complaints, & requests for his removal—Senator Hamlin (B's Father in Law) requests that he be not removed before his return to Washington—when if on examination the complaints are well founded he will either cause him to resign or consent to his removal—" DLC-Hamilton Fish.

On Oct. 16, U.S. Representative James N. Tyner of Ind., Peru, had written to USG. "If a vacancy shall occur in the office of Secretary of Dakota Territory, I respectfully recommend the appointment of Will Pound to fill it. Mr. Pound was for a long time the Indiana corespondent of the Cincinnati *Gazette.* He has fine ability as a writer, good business habits and great tact. He is sober, industrious, honest, and a gentleman in all respects. You couldn't give the place to a more worthy man." ALS, DNA, RG 59, Letters of Application and Recommendation. On the same day, Governor John A. Burbank of Dakota Territory, Yankton, wrote to USG. "Learning of the possibility of a change in the office of Secretary of Dakota Territory, I desire to recommend for appointment to the position, in that event, William Pound, Esq. of this Territory. . . ." LS, *ibid.* On Nov. 2, Vice President Schuyler Colfax, South Bend, Ind., wrote to USG. "I understand that there may be a vacancy in the office of Secretary of Dakota, with the concurrence of Senator Hamlin, whose son-in-law is the present incumbent. *If Mr. Hamlin does concur in the retiracy of the present Secretary, but not otherwise,* I cheerfully join with Gov. Burbank in recommending the appointment of *Wm Pound of Dakota.* I knew him & his services to the cause, in years past, when he resided in this State; & can vouch for his worth & qualifications." ALS, *ibid.* Related papers are *ibid.*

On Oct. 17, U.S. Senator George G. Wright of Iowa, Des Moines, wrote to USG. "I am advised that a vacancy does or soon will exist in the office of Secretary of Dakota Territory. For this vacancy I do most earnestly, strongly & personaly urge the name of *Col Robert Smyth,* of Linn Co. in this State. Col Smyth, was in the service from Iowa. He has served several years, before & since the War, in the General Assembly (Senate & House) of our State. He is a brother of the late Hon Wm Smyth, one of Iowas ablest Representatives in Congress—and is a gentleman of the highest moral character & religious integrity. I know of no man in our State or elsewhere who would more acceptably & ably fill the place named. . . ." ALS, *ibid.* On Oct. 16, Harlan, Mount Pleasant, had written to USG on the same subject. ALS, *ibid.* Related papers are *ibid.*

On Nov. 23, Speaker of the House James G. Blaine, Augusta, Maine, wrote to USG. "I join very cordially with others in recommending the appointment of Frank E. Frye as Secretary of the Territory of Dakota—Mr. Frye is a native of Maine and a resident of Nebraska—a man of high character, a sound Republican—I am well assured that his appointment would be popular & acceptable in the Territory—and when the vacancy occurs I earnestly hope that you may find it agreeable to appoint Mr Frye" ALS, *ibid.* Also in 1871, Grenville M. Dodge wrote to USG concerning the secretary, Dakota Territory. William Evarts Benjamin, Catalogue No. 48, Jan., 1893, p. 5.

On Feb. 20, U.S. Delegate Solomon L. Spink of Dakota Territory and Burbank, Washington, D. C., had written to USG. "Notice of contest for the seat of Delegate of the Territory of Dakota has been served upon Moses K Armstrong Delegate elect to the 42d Congress by Walter A Burleigh contestant and in the answer he Armstrong charges said Burleigh with having bought votes to secure his Burleighs election and in the investigation of the Legislative Committe on Elections which was said to have been a very thorough and impartial one it was found that said Walter A Burleigh did buy many votes in order to enable him to secure said election. A copy of said notice of service and answer as also the report of the Legislative Committee on Elections is herewith enclosed and it appears by said notice upon said Armstrong that Warren Cowles Esq U. S. Attorney for Dakota Territory is acting for Burleigh as his advocate and attorney—in said contest, see page 6   And it also appears by record: that said Cowles appeared before the Territorial board of Canvassers in behalf of and as the Attorney of said Burleigh for the certificate to the seat now in contest. And it is a fact that said Cowles not only *voted for* but used all the influence his position as U. S. Attorney gave him in behalf of Burleighs election by addressing political meetings and otherwise: and has been very bitter in denouncing those who differd with Burleigh politically. By an Act of Congress approved May 31, 1870 entitled an Act to enforce the rights of citizens of the United States to vote in the several States of the Union and for other purposes see Section 19 of this Act page   . It becomes the duty of the U. S. Attorney Cowles to prosecute all persons who have or may violate said act in Dakota Territory. Will Mr Cowles be likely under such circumstances to mentain and protect the interests of the Goverment and the purity of the Ballot Box by prosecuting faithfully and impartially all persons who may or have violated said Act? We believe not, and therefore urge that some able and reliable Attorney be appointed in his stead." LS, DNA, RG 60, Records Relating to Appointments. The enclosure is *ibid.* On Feb. 22, Spink and Burbank again wrote to USG. "Reposing full faith in the integrity and the ability of William Pound of Yankton Dakota (formerly of Indianapolis Indiana,) We take pleasure in recommending him for the position of United States District Attorney for Dakota Territory. . . ." LS, *ibid.* Related papers are *ibid.* On March 22, USG nominated William Pound as postmaster, Yankton.

On Aug. 28, 1872, Warren Cowles, Vermillion, Dakota Territory, wrote to USG. "I hereby tender you my commission as United States Attorney of Dakota Territory, being no longer worthy to fill the duties of that office. . . . P. S. After writing the foregoing letter, and being about to mail it, I met Judge Kidder, showed him the letter which he read. He used many arguments to induce me to recede. I finally did recede to the extent of adding the proviso that my resignation shall not be accepted until the first day of Oct. next. This was to enable me to accompany Judge Kidder to Pembina to hold Court there. Judge Kidder said he was ignorant of his duties there, but understood they were arduous, and with an Attorney equally ignorant to go up the public interests would suffer. I yielded to his arguments as appears. These observations must explain the difference of dates between the date of this letter and that which the Post Master will affix when he sends it to you." ALS (stamped as received Aug. 31), *ibid.*, Letters Received, Dakota Territory On Aug. 29, Kidder, Vermillion, wrote to USG. "I announce to you, in sorrow, the death of Warren Cowles, Esq., U. S. Attorney for this territory. Mr. Cowles was an able lawyer &

a good man. He departed this life yesterday. I am informed that since he has been sick he has sent to you his resignation. I deem it my duty to say to you, that he has been sick only about one week, & during all that time, I have seen him several times each day, & he has been insane the most of the time; therefore, I am of opinion that as regards his resignation, the subject was not properly considered. I name this that his record in this regard may be more properly appreciated. I start to day for Pembina, to hold a term of the court there, at the request of the Attorney General—This last paragraph is intended for his eye, as I suppose this letter will be referred to him." ALS, *ibid.*, Letters from the President. On Aug. 31, Batchelder, Yankton, wrote to USG. "I have the honor to suggest that in the appointment of U. S. Attorney to fill the vacancy made by the death of Hon. W. Cowles that it be made from the East   my observation & knowledge teaching that a Satisfactory appointment cannot be made from this Territory it would be better politically & in every other way" ALS, *ibid.*, Records Relating to Appointments. Letters recommending H. A. Copeland and Calvin J. B. Harris, Yankton, and Carter H. Winsor, Canton, Dakota Territory, are *ibid.*; *ibid.*, Letters from the President. On Dec. 2, USG nominated Pound as U.S. attorney, Dakota Territory. On Dec. 13, 1876, Morton wrote to USG. "William Pound of Yankton, desires to be reappointed United States District Attorney for Dakota. Having recommended his appointment and fully assured that he has performed his duties with great credit, I take pleasure in asking his reappointment." LS, *ibid.*, Records Relating to Appointments. On Jan. 5, 1877, USG renominated Pound.

1. See *PUSG*, 13, 480–81. On Dec. 16, 1873, Burdick, Yankton, telegraphed to Babcock. "Reported removed from dakota Marshalship   is it true   see president   please answer" Telegram received (at 9:55 P.M.), DNA, RG 60, Letters from the President. On Dec. 15, USG had nominated Herman Silver as marshal, Dakota Territory, to replace Burdick. USG authorized withdrawal of Silver's nomination in an undated note. AN, Omaha Public Library, Omaha, Neb. On Jan. 7, 1874, Levi P. Luckey wrote to Williams. "The President directs me to inform you that he withdrew from the Senate on the 5th inst. the nomination of Herman Silver to be U. S. Marshal of Dakota Territory." ALS, DNA, RG 60, Letters from the President. On Feb. 22, 1869, Gustave P. Koerner, Belleville, Ill., had written to USG. "My friend Mr. Herman Silver of Ottawa Ill is an applicant for the office of Consul to one of the German Seaports. He has been engaged in mercantile business until he was elected by the People Clerk of Circuit Court of Lasalle, which office he held to the great satisfaction of the Public until last fall. . . ." ALS, *ibid.*, RG 59, Letters of Application and Recommendation. Related papers are *ibid.* Silver later served as assayer in charge at the U.S. mint, Denver.

   On Oct. 28, 1875, Burdick wrote to USG. "I am informed that measures have been, and are being taken, for my removal as United States Marshal of this Territory, and that to this end, numerous charges against me have been sent to the Attorney General and yourself. Permit me to say, that any charges affecting my integrity, and faithful and fearless discharge of my duty, are without any foundation in fact. You did me the honor during the late war, to place me upon your Staff as Ordnance officer in charge of Ordnance Stores for your Army, whilst operating against Vicksburg, and you have done me the honor to state officially that I 'discharged the duties of his position with promptness, fidelity and ability.' and I beg to assure you that I have discharged the duties of Marshal of this Territory with as much fidelity as I did my military duties,   I found the expenses of the Courts as shown by the Reports to Congress of the Atty General $67000—per annum, I have reduced them below $40000—and that in the face of a large increase of business in the Courts, I found wicked wilful extravagance and waste of public money the rule, I have made *honesty* the rule, I found dissapation the chief characterstic of Juries, I have found and selected *sober* men, I found the Territory with a large Republican majority so divided by factions that we were represented by a Democrat, I have labored with others to accomplish a union of the party, and respectfully submit that *no man* has done more than myself in uniting the party, and electing a Republican as Delegate to Congress in the person of Hon J P Kidder. I only ask that in any matter affecting my integrity, or ability as an officer, I may be heard, and should I fail to vindicate myself will at once give way to one more worthy." ALS, *ibid.*, RG 60, Records Relating to Appointments.

On Oct. 9, 1876, John L. Taylor, Yankton, wrote to USG. "The enclosed letter was mislaid at the time it was written & therefor not sent, at that time, and it just now coming to hand, I have further to add, That the term of office of the accused being about to expire, I have to ask that this matter be looked into before he be reappointed, as I am informed he expects to be. Burdick is a *Thief* a *defrauder* of the Government, and a *perjuror* & I defy him to show to the contrary, by other testimony than his own I do not think it will be for the interest of the Republican party here that this man be reappointed, and I would respectfully ask that you consider these charges before acting in the matter. I stand upon what I have said, and written, and defy proof to the contrary. I hope you will not pass this matter over lightly. Please inform me as soon as possible whether you will give the subject due consideration or not." ALS, *ibid.* The enclosure of July 12 from Taylor to USG denigrating Burdick is *ibid.* On Jan. 5, 1877, USG renominated Burdick.

2. Probably in March, 1869, Walter A. Burleigh and six others petitioned USG. "The undersigned respectfully solicit your Excellency to appoint Hon Laban H Litchfield Marshal of the United States for the District of Dakota Territory. Mr Litchfield was appointed to that Office in 1865 by Abraham Lincoln, and has discharged its duties for the past four years in a very acceptable manner to the Courts—bar, and the people generally. He is an Earnest, intelligent and active Republican, and has been identified with the Republican Party since its organization. The emoluments of the Office are inconsiderable and Mr Litchfield's familiarity with the Character of the people and of the District Dakota, render him specially qualified to perform the duties of marshal in a very satisfactory to the Government, and we Earnestly hope you will be pleased to continue him in that office." DS (undated), *ibid.* Related recommendations are *ibid.* On April 3, USG renominated Laban H. Litchfield as marshal, Dakota Territory.

To Julia Dent Grant

Washington D. C. July 2d *1872.*

DEAR JULIA:

I find very important business requiring my personal attention which cannot be attended to until to-morrow owing to the absence of Judge Ferris,[1] of the Claims Commission from the city. He returns this evening. I will not therefore be back until Thursday noon. Tell Will Smith that he must stay until Buck sails for Europe.

The business refered to requires the auditing of some very important accounts by the Claims Commission and my signature to the warrant before it can be drawn from the Treas.

Love & kisses,

ULYS.

ALS, USG 3. On July 2, [1872], USG telegraphed to Julia Dent Grant. "Important business will detain me until tomorrow night have written you by mail" Telegram received, *ibid.*

1. Orange Ferriss, Southern Claims Commission. See *PUSG*, 21, 218.

To AG Edward D. Townsend

————

The Adj. Gn. will issue the necessary order to have Gn. Howard return to the Indian country. He will suggest the form of the order which may include any officer[1] who he may choose to have accompany him.

U. S. GRANT

JULY 3D /72

ANS, DNA, RG 94, Letters Received, 2465 1871. On July 3, 1872, a correspondent reported from Washington, D. C. "The President, this afternoon, gave an audience to the Apache delegation of Indians, at the Executive Mansion. They were accompanied by Secretary Delano, Commissioner of Indian Affairs Walker, and General Howard. The Indians expressed their desire to live at peace with the whites, and want houses, farms, and to be educated at schools. Santa, one of the chiefs, asked for a suit of clothes like the President's, and a cane, pistol, sword, and a horse to ride, so as to show his consequence at home. The President told them he was anxious to promote their comfort, but to that end it was necessary for them to keep the peace, and he would do everything in his power to protect them from bad white men. He thought they would have a better home in the Indian Territory, where attention could be paid to their improvement. They would be assisted in farming, and school houses would be built for them, and mechanics teach them how to work, and other benefits rendered them. Miguel said that at one time he was on bad terms with the whites, not knowing whether they were Americans or Mexicans; but as soon as he learned they were Americans, he buried all his badness, and was now their friend. Several other Indians addressed the President, declaring their determination hereafter not only to live at peace among themselves, but towards the whites." *Philadelphia Public Ledger*, July 4, 1872. On July 8, Brig. Gen. Oliver O. Howard, Washington, D. C., wrote to AG Edward D. Townsend. "Will you have the kindness to issue a supplemental order to the special order sent me on Saturday, directing me to return to my station in this city, after my special inspection in New Mexico, shall have been completed. This will enable me to cover my travelling expenses, and preserve my station here 'till ordered to some other post." LS, DNA, RG 94, Letters Received, 2465 1871. In late July, Howard, Santa Fé, telegraphed to USG, Long Branch. "News Direct from Sierra Blanca and Camp Grant arizona report apaches were Quiet & contented   Several hundred more at Grant than when I left   the Indians Generally In new mexico behaving well   some small Roving parties are Troublesome.   please confirm Tularosa reservation Immediately forty miles by fifty" Telegram received (on July 29), *ibid.*, RG 75, Letters Received, Arizona Superintendency; copy, Howard Papers, MeB. See letter to Maj. Gen. John M. Schofield, March 6, 1872; *HED*, 42-3-1, part 5, I, 485–86, 559–62.

On Sept. 29, Col. Gordon Granger, Santa Fé, wrote to Asst. AG, Dept. of the Mo., Fort Leavenworth. "I have the honor in connection with my telegram of yesterday to enclose a copy of General Howard's last communication. You will see from its contents that all our efforts for the establishment of the Apaches on the Tulerosa Reservation and their retention there being frustrated, and that the Indians being allowed to roam pretty much as they choose or as heretofore. You will please observe the instructions given by the President, the Lieutenant General and Department Commander to place them on the Reservation and compel them to remain thereon have been virtually annulled by the special commissioner for Arizona and New Mexico, General Howard. I will thank the Department Commander to inform me, if my original instructions or the modified instructions of the Special Commissioner are to be my guide in future." Copy, DNA, RG 94, Letters Received, 2465 1871. On Oct. 12, Lt. Gen. Philip H. Sheridan, Chicago, endorsed this letter. "Respectfully forwarded, inviting attention to this as only one case of the confusion constantly being produced in Indian Affairs." ES, *ibid.*

On Oct. 28, Brig. Gen. John Pope, Fort Leavenworth, wrote to Sheridan. "The action of General Howard as reported by the commander of the District of New Mexico, seems to have determined the complete abandonment of the Tulerosa Reservation by the Indians, and either their location elsewhere, or the privilege of wandering over the country at will, with papers from him. As Tulerosa Valley would never have been selected as the site of a military post, and as the virtual abandonment of the Reservation, by the authority of General Howard, does away with the expediency of posting troops there, I suggest to you whether the expenditure of twenty-thousand ($20.000) dollars, for a post there, had not better be suspended, or entirely given up? I would be glad to know your views about it soon as the troops will go on at once with the building if not otherwise ordered. It is to be regretted that a consistent and stable course had not been pursued, in the matter of the Tulerosa Reservation. Many Indians had been located there, and I have little doubt that most of the New Mexico Apaches could in reasonable time have been brought there. This unexpected action has, I think, greatly prejudiced any future undertaking of the kind by impairing the confidence, both of whites and Indians, in the adherence of the authorities to any plan whatever." LS, *ibid.* On Nov. 7, Sheridan endorsed this letter. "I am at a loss how to answer General Pope on the subject of this communication, and refer it to the General of the Army in hopes that he may ascertain in some way the intentions of the Indian Department. I cannot at present estimate the great expense to which we have been put and labor we have performed in moving Indians to the Tulerosa Valley, under the positive orders of the President of November 11th, 1871. The admirable system of civilizing and providing for the wild tribes is constantly being thrown into chaos by the impracticable, unbusinesslike actions of some of the men engaged in carrying it out. The settlement of these Indians on the Tulerosa Reservation was in process of successful accomplishment under the direction of Lieut. Colonel Devin, a good and fair man, when interrupted by Gen. Howard. I wish to know if he had authority to interfere with the positive Presidential order under which we were acting. Our desire to carry out the wishes of the President and the Indian Department makes us hesitate to do our obvious duty, even in cases where the mismanagement of Indian affairs is heartrending." ES, *ibid.* On Nov. 27, Howard, Washington, D. C., endorsed these papers to Secretary of War William W. Belknap. "A total misapprehension seems to exist as to what I did in New Mexico—I did not have General Sheridans order, based on that of the President in my hand, yet I did not really violate it. I found a small party of Indians under Poncè some one hundred miles from any reservation. Poncè had never been to Tularosa, but was willing to take his people there as soon as I was done with him. I could not have communicated with the wild Indians without him, as he was my interpreter from Indian into spanish. I provided for them temporarily, while I went for Cochise. I expected then to find the latter in New Mexico, & that Poncè would very soon return & move his people to Tularosa or to Fort Stanton . . . efficient aid, to do so. It is thus plain that *I* did not cause the 'chaos' and that the good work of the officers was interrupted before my arrival. Except that permission of a temporary delay at Cochillo Negro of some forty or fifty Indians, and that was allowed because I had no trusty officer, or other person to take the charge of them, & because they came from Fort Stanton, and not from Tularosa. I have not conflicted with the letter or spirit of the orders to which General Sheridan refers, and I did carry out literally the orders of the Secretary of the Interior, the Secretary of War, and the President. Hoping my brother officers will grant me a little indulgence for the embarassing position in which I was placed, and for striving to put *peace* before *war*, as the President and *all* the officers desire, . . ." ES (incomplete), *ibid.* Related papers are *ibid.*

On Dec. 9 and 11, Secretary of the Interior Columbus Delano wrote to Belknap. "I have the honor to acknowledge the receipt of your letter of the 16th ultimo, relative to the occupation, by certain Apaches under Sancho, of Cañada Alamosa under authority of Brigadier General O. O. Howard, U. S. A. Special Indian Commissioner, and asking whether the Reservation at Tulerosa is needed for their use or residence. Your letter was referred to the Commissioner of Indian Affairs, who reports by letter, dated the 7th instant, that it is not intended to reoccupy Cañada Alamosa as an Indian Reservation. If the Indians, now remaining there with the permission of General Howard, fail to observe their stipulations or are guilty of depredations or outrages they should be promptly returned to the Tulerosa Reservation where it is intended they shall be permanently stationed." "I have the honor to state that, in the opinion of this Department, the interests of the Indian service in the Territories of Arizona and New Mexico would be subserved if the Indians, located upon the White Mountain and Chiricahua Reservations, in Arizona, were placed under the charge and supervision of the Superintendent of Indian Affairs for New Mexico. It would not be advisable to do this, however, unless Camps Apache and Bowie, situated within the limits of said Reservations, respectively, were also transferred to the Department of New Mexico. I therefore respectfully request, if it is practicable, that your Department have this transfer made, and that the same be done as early as possible. This request is made pursuant to the conclusion arrived at to this effect, during a recent conversation on the subject between the President, the Honorable Secretary of War, and myself. I enclose, herewith, a map for your guidance in making the necessary order, as desired by you." LS, *ibid.* On Dec. 17, Gen. William T. Sherman wrote to Belknap.

"I have the honor to acknowledge the reference of the Communication of the Hon Secretary of the Interior to you, recommending such a change of the boundaries of the Departments of Arizona, and Missouri, as that the White Mountain and Chiricahua Indian Reservations may fall within the latter, instead of as now in the former. By an inspection of the map that accompanies the letter of the Hon. Secretary of the Interior you will see that these reservations are very irregular, that they extend west of the Mountain Range, that is the natural boundary of the Valley of the Rio Grande, that in great part they lie in the Valley of the River Gila, and wholly within the Political Territory of Arizona, that the two Military Posts embraced viz Camps Apache and Bowie more naturally belong to the Group of Posts which constitute the Departmt of Arizona, and that their seperation from this Departmt would much embarrass the official administration of the Dept Commander Lt Col Crook. These Boundary lines though plain on the map are extremely indefinite in an unsettled, mountainous and barren country, so that if this change be made we will be necessitated to assume some fictitious line North and South including the two named Reservations, and I feel sure this will rather complicate than improve the actual relations of the Indians with their white neighbors. Moreover the HeadQuarters of the Departmt of the Missouri are at Fort Leavenworth more than twelve hundred miles from Camp Bowie, whereas the HeadQrs of the Dept of Arizona are at Prescott, within the Territory of Arizona. I feel absolutely certain if this change be made, a clamor will at once arise on the part of the white settlers of Arizona, who will charge the Reservation Indians with all sorts of murders and depredations, and then the Commanding officer of the Departmt Col Crook, will be unable to protect them, or even to investigate the truth of the charges, because the Indians will be outside of his jurisdiction. I beg therefore a suspension of action till a copy of these papers can be sent to General Pope on the one hand, and Colonel Crook on the other, for an expression of their better judgmt." ALS, *ibid.* On Dec. 19, Belknap endorsed this letter. "By direction of the President, action in this matter is suspended. Send copies of these papers to Genl. Pope & Genl. Crooke for an expression of their views, and notify the Secretary of the Interior of this action." AE (initialed), *ibid.*

On Dec. 11, Pope had written to Sheridan. "I have the honor to ask instructions concerning the course I am to pursue in relation to the Apaches in southern New Mexico, for whom the Reservation at Tulerosa was established. A large number of these Indians had, after great labor and considerable expense been placed on this reservation—and Colonel Devin, 8th Cavalry, in charge of the movement on the part of the military authorities, reported favorable prospects of its successful completion. About this time General O. O. Howard, arrived in the Territory, as Special Commissioner under the Interior Department. The character of his instructions, and the extent of his authority are not known to me, nor, so far as I know, to any of the military authorities concerned,—but he gave permission to a number of these Indians, an indefinite number as I understand, to go to Canada Alamosa or elsewhere, and at once arrested the movement of Colonel Devin to compel them to go on the Reservation at Tulerosa according to the order of the President. His permits in writing were worded, as I learn, about as follows: 'Such and such an Indian, with his band,' is permitted &c, &c, &c. How many Indians his band consisted of no one, I suppose, exactly knows. The result has been to put a stop to the removal of the Indians to the Tulerosa Reservation as ordered, and the practical abandonment of the whole plan. It has also necessitated the re-occupation of Fort McRae, near the Canada Alamosa, where many of the Indians still remain, as is understood, by General Howard's permission. The worst effect, however, is that it has destroyed confidence both in whites and Indians of any stability in the action of the Government. This reservation at Tulerosa was established by the Government with the utmost formality and decision. The Indians were required to go on it and remain there. A sufficient time was given them for this purpose, after which the troops were ordered to remove those who did not go, by force and to treat all as hostile who were found absent. Protection by the military was to be given to the Indians on the Reservation of Tulerosa and whilst en-route there, and all citizens were warned not to molest the Indians in this movement, or on the Reservation. All these requirements and assurances were given by order the utmost publicity and for a time every body concerned rested in the certainty that this was a final arrangement which the Government would enforce. How completely their confidence has been overthrown by the unexpected, and what I must consider the unfortunate action of General Howard, need not be enlarged on. What I wish to know now, is what I am to do in the matter. I cannot order the troops to attack or use force to parties of Indians having the passes of General Howard or any other official agent of the Interior Department, but unless I do so, I cannot enforce the order of the President to place these Indians on the Reservation at Tulerosa. As matters now stand, there is uncertainty and apprehension—justified by hostilities already committed by some of these Indians—and the condition of affairs as regards the Indians in southern New Mexico is not satisfactory." LS, *ibid.* On Dec. 16, Sheridan endorsed this letter. "Respectfully forwarded. This case seems to require the action of the President, or of the Commissioner of Indian Affairs. I would also state that the sum of $20,000 00 was authorized for quarters at Tulerosa." ES, *ibid.* On Dec. 19, Sherman endorsed these papers. "Respectfully submitted to the Secretary of War—for instructions. Is the Tularosa Reservation to be given up, by the Apaches? and to which of the Reservations are these Indians to go—" AES, *ibid.*

On Dec. 13, Lt. Col. George Crook, Camp Grant, Arizona Territory, had written to Asst. AG, Military Div. of the Pacific, San Francisco. ". . . The whole peace System among the Apache here has been a fraud, not only have there been more Indians issued rations to than were found by actual count & the quantity of the ration larger than the Indian could consume, but a great proportion of the depredations here have been committed by Indians useing these reservations as a rendezvous—In my judgement had the provisions of Gen. O. No 10 of Mil. D. of the P. of 1871 been carried into immediate effect a great loss of life & property would have been saved—I shall defer the enforcement of this order on Cachise's Band until I have so far subjugated the other Indians that in case he is disposed to give trouble I can emply a strong force against him immediately—Cachise's Indians still continue their depredations in Sonora since their talk with Gen. Howard, and the mere fact of their not having depredated on our people since then, proves nothing, as it is Apache tactics, after they have thoroughly aroused a neighborhood by their depredations to cease ~~their~~ operations in that loca[l]ity until the unwary citizen is thrown off his guard, when they will commence their outrages with renewed vigor. The Reservation set apart for Cachise contains two of the most rugged chain of mountains in the Territory & in addition being on the confines of Mexico & New Mexico, affords great facilities for his outrages. In my opinion there will be constant trouble so long as he is allowed to occupy it. There is an abundance of room on the other Reservations here & he should be compelled to go on them" ALS, *ibid.* On Dec. 26, Maj. Gen. John M. Schofield, San Francisco, wrote to Townsend. "I have the honor to forward herewith a report from Brevet Maj Genl Crook, Commanding the Department of Arizona, dated Dec. 13. 1872, which appears to me to require special attention. Genl Crook uses very strong language in speaking of 'the peace system among the Apaches', but there seems no room for doubt of the general correctness of his unfavorable judgement; and I apprehend there is but little room for hope of improvement under the present system of divided responsibility. In respect to the reservation set apart by Genl Howard for Cachise, I desire to suggest, in addition to the objections mentioned by Genl Crook, that it appears to be, to say the least, a breach of good neighborhood toward Mexico to give to our common enemy peace and protection on our side of the border where he can with the greatest facility continue his war on the other side." ALS, *ibid.* On Jan. 8, 1873, Sherman endorsed these letters. "Respectfully submitted to the Secretary of War, who is invited to represent the matter to the Hon Secretary of Interior in connection with his recommendation to take the Eastern part of Arizona out of General Crooks control, to place it in the Dept of Missouri. General Crook is now actively at war with Indians who have again & again agreed to live at peace on Reservations, and as often have deceived & trifled with the Govt   If let alone, as I hope will be the case I feel certain he will bring these indians to a sense of their dependance on the agents charged with their support, and supervision" AES, *ibid.*

On Dec. 17, 1872, and Jan. 6, 1873, Howard, Washington, D. C., wrote to Schofield. "I keep getting letters from 'Camp Apache' complaining of the cruelties practiced upon the Indians. They are not even allowed to go beyond a mile from the military post on pain of death! They were forced to abandon their cows, corn &c. and come in without apparent cause. Capt. Brown acting in the name of Gen. Crook is said to be doing this and under the cover and by reason of your order to count the Indians every day—This rule it is reported to me will be applied to Cachise—Surely it will result there in driving at once every indian off the reservation. I am sorry sorry I could not have talked with you. There has been no bloodshed or depredation in the south of Arizona since I was there. I fear it is already to late to stop the mischief—This Capt. Brown does not, cannot represent General Crook. He is upsetting and destroying all the President has tried to do through me. Do please write Gen. Crook or send one of your good officers there to stop all mischief, that may arise from a positive misunderstanding of the President's wishes. Surely those Indians who are doing just as they agreed are not to be punished for the sins of others with which they are in no way connected." "Your letter of the 6th ultimo is just received. I have done simply what I was *ordered*; You could do no less. I have made my report, and of the last expedition my report was copied and sent to the General in Chief. I know it would have been better to have sent you word through the War Department. But I felt that I did not do what I ought when in San Francisco on account of your illness. The Governor, Mayor of Tucson, and other citizens, are now rejoicing in the apparent peace. I never gave Cachise permission to raid in Mexico. On the contrary took measures to prevent it. I reported to Maj. Sumner and through him, and also, directly, to General Crook what I did with Cachise. The Agent is with them, the Indians, all the time and can make the daily count that you require. The double headed action does not come from me. The War Department and Interior Department may be in conflict but no one but the President can harmonize them. I will endeavor not to trouble you or disturb the work committed to your charge." Copies, *ibid.* Related papers are *ibid.* See *HED*, 42-3-1, part 2, I, 72, 78–80, part 5, I, 681–82, 690–91, 695–706, 711–12; 43-1-1, part 5, I, 643–44, 654–61.

On Dec. 14, 1872, Benjamin R. Cowen, act. secretary of the interior, wrote to USG. "I submit herewith a report dated the 11th instant, from the Commissioner of Indian Affairs, requesting, in accordance with the recommendation of Brigr General O. O. Howard, U. S. A. Special Commissioner to negotiate with the Indians in Arizona and New Mexico—that an Executive Order be issued, setting apart for certain Apache Indians in

Arizona, two several tracts of country to be known as the 'Chiricahua Indian Reservation,' and the 'San Carlos Division of the White Mountain Indian Reservation,' respectively— and restoring to the public domain the reservation heretofore set apart for certain Apache Indians in Arizona, known as the 'Camp Grant Indian Reservation' The order is respectfully submitted for the signature of the Executive." Copy, DNA, RG 48, Indian Div., Letters Sent. On the same day, USG signed this order. DS, *ibid.*, RG 75, Orders. *HED*, 45-3-1, part 5, I, 731–32, 47-2-1, part 5, II, 309–10, 49-2-1, part 5, I, 518; *SED*, 48-2-95, 213; *SD*, 57-1-452, 812–13. USG subsequently authorized several boundary changes for this reservation. DS, DNA, RG 75, Orders. Printed in sources listed above. See D. C. Cole, *The Chiricahua Apache 1846–1876: From War to Reservation* (Albuquerque, 1988), pp. 111–31.

1. For 1st Lt. Joseph A. Sladen, Howard's aide, see Edwin R. Sweeney, ed., *Making Peace with Cochise: The 1872 Journal of Captain Joseph Alton Sladen* (Norman, Okla., 1997).

To Robert C. Schenck

———

Long Branch, N. J.
July 5th 1872,

MY DEAR GENERAL,

This will introduce to you my Son, U. S. Grant, Jr. who goes to Europe to spend a year, and who will probably spend a day or two in London on his way to the Continent. He will be pleased to meet our legation in London but will not have the time, and I know not the inclination, to be further presented while there.—He proposes to settle down in some German town and prepare himself in his Jr. years course at Harvard so as to go on next year at the University with the class that he entered with. This will leave him but little time for travel or social recreation.

Please present Mrs. Grant's and my best respects to your daughters to whom ~~Mrs.~~we feel under many obligations for their kind attention to Nellie while she was in England.

With great respect
your obt. svt.
U. S. GRANT

HON. ROBT. C. SCHENCK
MIN. PLEN. &c

ALS, Bates College, Lewiston, Maine. On July 6, 1872, Ulysses S. Grant, Jr., departed from New York City "by the steamship Baltic, of the White Star line. The President, Mrs. Grant, Collector Arthur, Mr. Van Valkenburg and a few friends of the President escorted the scion of the house of Grant to the White Star line dock. . . . The youthful passenger is in charge of Mr. Drexel, the well-known banker of Philadelphia." *New York Herald*, July 7, 1872.

On Nov. 4, 1872, Secretary of State Hamilton Fish wrote to Robert C. Schenck, U.S. minister, London. "*private* . . . When you accepted the position of Minister to Great Britain, the President understood you to say that you would not be willing to hold it for any length of time—Your very able & discreet management of the Legation during a period of great difficulty, & delicacy has given very great satisfaction and receives the warmest & most cordial acknowledgment of the President & of the Department—He feels, as I do, that the Legation could not be in better hands, & he desires me to say that it would be his wish that you remain at the Post where you have done such valuable service, & have reflected so much credit both upon yourself, & on the Country—It is however, important that if you desire, or contemplate the relinquishment of your position, that the President be early informed thereof—& in advance of the fact coming to the knowledge of the public. . . ." ALS, OFH. On the same day, Fish wrote in his diary that USG suggested this letter "be not sent until the result of tomorrows election be definitely announced—" DLC-Hamilton Fish. On Oct. 18, Fish had written in his diary, "I shew to the President a note from L. P. Morton of NY—dated Octr 16 marked 'Confidential' remonstrating against Judge Pierreponts being brought into the Cabinet, saying 'the Judge is looked upon ~~here~~ as a time serving politician & does not enjoy the Confidence of our best citizens'—In handing him the letter I remark that though addressed to me, it could only be intended to be shewn to him—After the Cabinet separated he requested me to remain—referred to the letter—said that Pierrepont 'was dying for a place in the Cabinet'—that Judge Williams having declined the Oregon Senatorship wd probably remain in the Cabinet & he was glad to have him, & he believed that he gave general satisfaction there—that the Atty Genlship, was the only place in the Cabinet towhich he would be willing to appoint Pierrepont—who was he believed a good lawyer, & the place was professional—he did not think him safe for the State Dept—Asked if Schenck or Bancroft said any thing about resigning—the he would like in some way to 'gratify Pierreponts vanity'. . ." *Ibid.*

On Nov. 6, Schenck, Rome, wrote to "My dear General." "*Private* . . . Pardon the familiarity of the address. I feel too happy just now to formally write 'Mr President '— I have this moment received the news of yesterday's work at home, telegraphed from London. I hasten to congratulate you, & to congratulate our country—to congratulate Truth, Decency & Principle; for all have triumphed. I have not permitted myself for a moment ever to doubt the result; but a mere majority would not have satisfied me, nor should it have satisfied our honest people. It was fit & necessary that your reelection should be so overwhelming a success—as it appears by the intelligences to have been— that it will serve as a crushing, demolishing blow to a most unprincipled coalition, & serve as a lesson for the future against the employment of infamous slander & fraud, such as that with which you & all your best friends have been ruthlessly assailed throughout this extraordinary campaign. Looking on anxiously at the contest from a distance, it has seemed to me that, through all the canvass, unable to assail the public policy & conduct of your Administration, the whole fight against you by this 'Unholy Alliance' has been a warfare of scandalous falsehood & personal abuse. I regard with especial content also the *collat-*

eral benefits of this Republican success. We get happily rid—& I hope for a long time to come—of the Sumners, the Schurtzes, the Banks,—that whole class of men who are ever putting their own selfish objects, personal griefs, disappointments & spleen before any attachment to principle or a common cause. But I must stop. I sat down to send my hearty congratulation, not to write a political homily. Please remember me in this jubilation also to Mrs Grant & to Miss Nellie. My daughters, who are all with me, unite warmly in the joy, & send their affectionate congratulations. We have just taken our dinner & indulged in the extravagance of the best bottle of Champaign our hotel affords, with bumpers in honor of the occasion." ALS, ICN. On Dec. 10, Orville E. Babcock wrote to Schenck, London. "The President desires me to acknowledge the receipt of your kind letter of congratulation and convey to you his sincere thanks for your cordial expressions. He appreciates highly the interest felt by our Americans abroad in the gratifying result, and especially your own which you so kindly express." ALS, OFH.

To Hamilton Fish

Long Branch, N. J.
July 7th 1872

Dear Governor:

I enclose you a cipher dispatch which Gen. Porter has just received from Gen. Babcock.[1] You will see that it should be treated confidentially.

When I was in Washington last General Myer[2] told me that the Japanese were growing very impatient at their long delay here, without results, and that their Govt. was complaining very much of it. He stated further that some of the legations in Washington were trying to discourage them.

Would it not be well to close up all business with the Japanese with as little delay as practicable, and to deal with them generously enough to insure the negociation of a treaty? It looks so to me. We ought if possible secure their confidence above that of all other nations. Please let me hear from you.

Very Truly Yours
U. S. Grant

Hon. Hamilton Fish
Sec. of State

ALS, DLC-Hamilton Fish. On July 8, 1872, Secretary of State Hamilton Fish, Garrison, N. Y., wrote to USG. "Your letter was handed to me this afternoon—too late to answer by the Afternoon Mail—The delay in the Japanese negotiation comes from no fault of ours—For weeks I was urging them, & they delayed, at length they submitted a draft very different from what we had been discussing—they submitted it at the time when we were in the very thickest of the Arbitration correspondence, & were told that negotiation must then be suspended—I then took up & prepared a counter draft, which was submitted to them some four weeks ago, or more—A time was appointed for an interview, & discussion—they were not ready, & sent word requesting a postponement   They were told that I was about to be absent until about the middle of July—they were satisfied saying the delay was on their account & that they had not yet received *their powers*—they had not received them & were not ready, as they told me, the day before I left Washington—I do not wonder that Genl Myers is tired of his Elephant—I had intended to return to Washington on Monday next—if you think it important that I should do so sooner I will change my plans, & leave this week—The story of the Prime Minister and 'hari-kari' I had heard directly from Japan—but the assigned cause was not the delay, but the necessity of granting powers to execute a Treaty without the limits of the Empire—If you think it important that I hasten my return (before Monday) & go on the latter part of this week please telegraph me, & I will endeavour to make arrangements accordingly—altho' it will interfere with some plans which I had made." ALS, USG 3.

On July 10, USG telegraphed to Fish. "After seeing the Japanese at West Point you can judge whether it is necessary to return to Washn earlier than you had proposed   I should think not   If you deem it advisable for me to be there at the same time, please inform me" Telegram received, DLC-Hamilton Fish. On the same day, Fish wrote in his diary. "Mr Iwakura, Japanese Ambassador, accompanied by Mr Schioda (Interpreter) Mr Fougoutise (Secretary) & Genl Myers, come to Glennclyffe   Mr Iwakura, referring to the return of his Associates Ito, & Okubo, for the purpose of obtaining full powers to the Ambassadors to negotiate a Treaty, said that these Powers had not been recd but that his Government, for some reasons, decided to send them to meet them in Europe, & that he was instructed to ask that this Government send a 'Delegate' empowered to sign a Treaty at some point in Europe, not yet determined   He was told that the proposal was entirely out of the question—it was inconsistent with the dignity of this Govt to appoint a travelling Agent to attend on the Embassy & to sign a Treaty, wherever the Embassy might think proper to designate—. . . After two hours conversation I told him, that I would mention the subject to the President, who, I am convinced will take the same views that I have expressed, & will not entertain the proposition" *Ibid.* See Speech, March 4, 1872; letter to Hamilton Fish, July 16, 1872.

1. On July 6, Orville E. Babcock, Washington, D. C., had telegraphed to USG, Long Branch. "*Confidential* . . . Gen. Myers says Japanese embassy very anxious to finish treaty. They expected to see Sec. of State here by (first?) of July. If not here by the eighth they expect to go to West Point to see him before leaving the country. Last mail from Japan reports much dissatisfaction with long delay without results. Prime Minister has offer to commit hari-kari on account of dissatifaction   This must remain a strict secret. Do you know positively when sec. of state will return here. Hale says not until the sixteenth. Myers does not wish to interfere, but he gets this information confidentially, and thinks he ought to communicate it." Copy, DLC-Hamilton Fish.

2. Maj. William Myers, bvt. brig. gen. On Feb. 6, Fish had written in his diary. "The appropriation of $50.000 for the entertainment of the Japanese Embassy having passed, I request that an officer of the Army be detailed to take charge of the Embassy & to make arrangements for them, & to make the proper contracts—&c at first the President suggested Commr Ammen but subsequently Genl Meyers, of the Quarter Masters Dept was agreed up & the Secr of War writes to him to report for duty" *Ibid.* See *PUSG*, 9, 152; *ibid.*, 17, 421–22.

Endorsement

Respectfully returned to Senator Cameron. The sentiments here expressed are highly honorable to Mr. Bassett and equally ~~complimentary~~ flattering to me. I acknowledge the compliment and thank him for it.—I agree that his coming home to take the stump would prove as prejudicial, from the fact of his holding a Federal office, as his eloquence of speech and pen would prove beneficial. I would therefore say "not to come' at this time.

U. S. GRANT

JULY 9TH /72

AES, DLC-Simon Cameron. Written on a letter of June 21, 1872, from Ebenezer D. Bassett, U.S. minister, Port-au-Prince, to U.S. Senator Simon Cameron of Pa., Harrisburg. "PRIVATE. . . . I trust you will pardon me for troubling you with a request for advice. I am very desirous of serving, in some way commensurate with my ability, the Republican Party during the Presidential Campaign. I am of course for Grant, first, last and always. Now if I were to visit the United States for the purpose of speaking and writing in behalf of the Philadelphia ticket, would not the influence of anything I might say be in part neutralized by the general cry that it was only the shriek of an office holder? If, on the other hand, I can send from my limited means some funds to aid in the canvass, could I not effect just as much in a more quiet and unseen way? The real fact is though, Senator, that I should like to follow both the courses here indicated. But I wish to act discreetly in the matter. I am in doubt; and I take the liberty to lay the subject before you, the Senior Senator from my State, feeling that your own keen sense of the party's needs, and that the far seeing advice which you are ever ready to give to the young men of our great State, will alike prompt you to pardon the liberty I take and give me the counsel I need." ALS, *ibid.* Cameron had endorsed this letter to USG. AE (initialed, undated), *ibid.* On Oct. 18, Bassett wrote to Cameron. "CONFIDENTIAL. . . . Following your suggestion, I sent nearly $400 to the State Republican Committee (Mr. Errett) for the canvass in our state, and also something to the National Committee sitting in New York. As I want to send at least enough to about cover the expenses of one good canvasser, and as our State is now beyond all doubt, I think I had better send my further contributions to the National Committee (Mr. Morgan). . . ." ALS, *ibid.* See *PUSG*, 20, 9–12; *ibid.*, 21, 125–27; *ibid.*, 22, 28–29.

On Aug. 16, 1872, Orville E. Babcock wrote to Cameron. "*Personal* . . . Your favor of yesterday reached me this morning and pleased me much. I have read it to the President and all of the Cabinet present Gov Cooke & other friends. It does us all good, and each friend who has read the letter says so. I let Senator Chandler read it. I agree with you that if we carry Pa in Oct the fight is won—I agree with you about the patronage but it has not been, as you know, to oppose you and your friends—but to prevent Mr Forney from having any cause for opposing the party. I shall have no anxiety about about Pa in the future. I assure you there has been no feeling against you or your friends here—The President and Gen Porter go back to Long Branch tonight. The President will bring his family here the middle of Sept. . . ." ALS, DLC-Simon Cameron.

On Nov. 23, Bassett wrote to Secretary of State Hamilton Fish about the mixed response in Haiti to USG's reelection. "(Confidential). . . . For myself, as a citizen of the United States not altogether wanting I trust in patriotism, and as a man of color, I cannot refrain from expressing my almost unbounded satisfaction and joy at the result of the long and somewhat acrimonious presidential campaign. The eminent citizen whose sword saved a nation from disruption and wrested a race from bondage, is now to give us four years more of that rare statesmanship which has never failed to conserve the liberties of the people, to vindicate the rights of a once oppressed race, and to bless the whole nation. May God bless protect and defend him and our country forever!" ALS, DNA, RG 59, Diplomatic Despatches, Haiti.

To Roscoe Conkling

Long Branch, N. J.
July 9th 1872.

DEAR SENATOR;

Two weeks from Monday next, the 29th of July I think that will be, I propose to start for "Thousand Islands," in the St Lawrence. Can you not, with Mrs. Conkling & daughter,[1] come one week before and spend the time until we start with us and all return together? I will have for the party a special car by the Erie road, and a new route branching off from it, to Syracuse. From there we will work our way East as far as Utica over the Central as best we can.

The Baltimore Convention[2] is now in incubation. Before *she* hatches, and we see what the offspring looks like, or rather how it is received by its parents, it is hard to judge how much fondling it will receive. I have no doubt but it will look like a full moon, with spectacles on the man in it, but whether it will be caressed as much after hatching as during incubation I doubt much.—But I wont write politics. I only want to know if you and Mrs. Conkling can come and spend a week with us at the time specified? If you have engagements then say so, and at what time you can come, or come then and attend to your engagements and leave Mrs. C. to Mrs. Grant's care. I know during this warm weather she will find no more pleasant place than at Long Branch.

Mrs. Grant joins me in kindest regards to Mrs. Conkling, daughter & yourself.

yours Truly
U. S. GRANT

HON. ROSCOE CONKLING, U. S. S.

ALS, DLC-Roscoe Conkling. See letter to Roscoe Conkling, July 15, 1872.

1. Julia C. Seymour married Roscoe Conkling in 1855. Eliza, or "Bessie," was their only child. See *PUSG*, 19, 234; *New York Times*, Oct. 19, 1893, Nov. 25, 1931.
2. The Democratic Convention began in Baltimore on July 9, 1872, and nominated the Liberal Republican ticket of Horace Greeley and B. Gratz Brown. In 1872, John Codman wrote to USG concerning Greeley's nomination. William Evarts Benjamin, Catalogue No. 27, Nov., 1889, p. 6.

To Margaretta W. Pierrepont

Long Branch, N. J.
July 9th 1872

MY DEAR MRS. PIERREPONT,

Can you not find it convenient to pay Mrs. Grant and myself the long promised visit of a week commencing on Monday next?[1] If it is not convenient to come on that particular day come as early in the week as you can. Mrs. Grant & myself will be delighted to see you and will endeavor to make the time pass as pleasantly as possible.

I should expect the Judge but I know he has sailed for Europe.

With kind regards of Mrs. Grant & myself to you and family,

your obt. svt.
U. S. GRANT

P. S. Jesse will be delighted to have Eddie come with you.[2]

ALS, University of Kentucky, Lexington, Ky. Margaretta Willoughby had married Edwards Pierrepont in 1846.

On Nov. 10, 1872, Edwards Pierrepont, New York City, wrote to USG. "you seemed to know what would happen long before any of us saw it; But I think that even you did not expect a result so overwhelming   Hereafter we shall look to you to make political prophecy never doubting the fulfillment. The country will now start upon a new career of advancement and you can have an administration of such glory & success as has not happened in our history—God bless & guide you—" ALS, USG 3. On Dec. 4, Orville E. Babcock wrote to Pierrepont. "The President desires me to convey to you many thanks for your kindness in sending him the 'Emperor's Wine,' which has arrived safely; and also to assure you of Mrs. Grant's appreciation of your thoughtful attention." Copy, DLC-USG, II, 1.

On Dec. 6, Julia Dent Grant wrote to Margaretta Pierrepont. "I was hoping my dear Mrs Pieerepont, to accept your very kind invitation to our Jesse. But as the Genl intends visiting his Father, at Covington Ky during the holidays & will take Jesse with him. as Mr Grants Father wishes to see Jesse (who is his name sake)   I think it will be rather a doleful visit   But still he has to go I suppose,   The old gentleman is quite feeble & has been for a year past,   I was quite disappointed that outr invitation to dinner did not reach judge P. in time   We had a pleasant party & would liked to have had him—Hoping to have the pleasure of meeting you soon . . ." ALS, Dr. Walter A. Ostromecki, Jr., Encino, Calif.

1. July 15.
2. Edward W. Pierrepont, born in 1860.

Endorsement

Reply to [~~Sen?~~] ~~Pomeroy~~ [+]8 ~~Wall St. N. Y.~~
Respectfully refered to the Atty. Gen.

Senator Pomeroy [1] desires an answer from me of the rights and privileges of the Cable Co. of which he is V. Pres. under the Act. of Congress. If the Atty. Gen. will return to me answer to the within I will forward it, with indorsement, or will answer as I may deem advisable.

U. S. GRANT

JULY 10TH /72

AES, DNA, RG 60, Letters from the President. Written on a letter of July 9, 1872, from U.S. Senator Samuel C. Pomeroy of Kan. to USG. "This is to represent, that the American, Atlantic, Cable Telegraph Company, organised under an Act of Congress, approved, Mach 30th 1867, has been for more than Four Years, in active operations, in securing means to lay Cables, and in acquiring the necessary rights from European Govern-

ments, And that they have so far progressed, as that they have already secured the necessary concessions, And more recently, have enlisted capitalists, to furnish means to complete their work, And also have a *Contract*, made and executed, with the best parties in Europe, to manufacture and lay one Cable between America and Europe, thus giving our
Government and people *one line*, over which they can have full control in any exigency of
public affairs—And now at the moment of success, the Act of Congress above refered to
is doubted, as confering upon this Company any *special rights*,   I therefore in behalf of
this interest, and as an officer of said Company, thought proper to call your attention to
this Act of Congress, And to assure you, (as one having full knowledge of all the facts) that
the Company, by neglect or otherwise, have forfeited no rights given in said Act of Congress,—And to ask of you such concurrence, with the aim and object of this Company, and
such an expression of what you judge to be their rights in the premesis, as will facilitate
this work, and add for America, one line, at last, of communication between between the
nations, A work which is especially in harmony, with the progress, and sentiments of the
age in which we live—" ALS, *ibid.* On July 10, Pomeroy, New York City, wrote to
Attorney Gen. George H. Williams. "*Unofficial* . . . While at Long Branch, today, and in
conversation with the President upon our Cable project, I handed him a letter which he
refered to you, for your advise, as to the rights of our Company under the Law—That act,
you will observe passed one *year after*, the Law, authorising any company to run lines of
Telegraphs—ovver and among the States—and the rivers bays &c, to promote the
telegraping *among the State*, . . . my hope is, you will give the President such advise as to
the Law of this case, as will justify us in proceding to lay a cable—" ALS, *ibid.* On July 22,
Williams wrote to USG. "I have had under consideration the communication addressed to
you on the 9th inst by the Hon S. C. Pomeroy, Vice President of the American Atlantic
Cable Telegraph Company, which you were pleased to refer to me for my views upon the
subject to which it relates. In that communication I do not find any particular point or
question presented, other than what is contained in a request on the part of the writer for
the expression of an opinion as to the rights generally of the aforesaid Company under the
act of March 29th 1867 (15 stat 10)—. . . I do not however construe that act as giving to
the Company exclusive rights and privileges, so as to preclude Congress from at any time
conferring similar rights and privileges upon any other Company. Indeed that body has
expressly reserved the power to alter amend or repeal the Act at pleasure. . . ." Copy, *ibid.*,
Opinions. *Official Opinions of the Attorneys-General*, XIV, 62–65.

1. Born in Southampton, Mass., in 1816, Pomeroy moved to Kan. as financial agent
of the New England Emigrant Aid Co. and was elected Republican U.S. senator in 1861.
For corruption charges against Pomeroy, see *SRC*, 42-3-523.

To William S. Hillyer

Long Branch, N. J.
July 12th 1872.

DEAR GENERAL:

I very much doubt my being able to go to New York City on Monday.[1] Should I not go I wish you would say to Mrs. Daniels that I would like to have from her distinctly what she wishes to do with the property left by Gen. Rawlins—the Washington house and so much as has been paid for on the house in Danbury.[2] I do not know whether the latter is rented or how it stands, nor positively how much is still due upon it. In regard to the trust fund left in my hand I propose to place that in the hands of some substantial monied corporation in New York City, with directions to pay one fourth of the interest as it accrues to the order of Mrs. Daniels, as long as she lives, and three fourths to the order of whoever may be appointed guardian of the children in my place. I propose to give that up, but to see that they have a proper guardian. This arrangement is dependent of course on Mrs. D's surrendering the guardianship.

Why can not Mrs. Daniels and husband come to Long Branch on Monday? It looks now as if I should be compelled to go to Washington on the evening of that day. But I shall be here until six even if I do have to go.

Yours Truly
U. S. GRANT

GN. W. S. HILLYER,
NEW YORK CITY,

P. S. Mrs. Grant received Mrs. Hillyers invitation to accompany me on Monday next and desires me to thank her but say that she has company which she cannot leave.

Please present Mrs. Grants and my kindest regards to Mrs. Hillyer and the children.

U. S. G.

ALS, Goodspeed's Book Shop, Inc., Boston, Mass. See letter to C. F. Daniels, March 20, 1872; letter to William D. Rawlins, July 19, 1872.

1. July 15.
2. See *PUSG*, 21, 185–86.

To Roscoe Conkling

Long Branch, N. J.
July 15th 1872.

My Dear Senator:

I regret that we shall not have the pleasure of your & Mrs. Conklings company next week but suppose we must wait to a later day. We will go however, if nothing happens to prevent, at the time indicated in my former letter. Our route will be by Syracuse, and our arrival in Utica will be probably Tuesday evening.[1] My son who has been with Gen. Sherman for the last six months will be with us.

My judgement is that it will be better that I should not attend any convention or political meeting during the Campaign. It has been done, so far as I remember, by but two Pres. candidates heretofore and both of them were public speakers, and both were beaten. I am no speaker and don't want to be beaten.[2]

From Utica our route will be by Watertown & Cape Vincent thence thence down the St. Lawrence, leaving Utica as early as the trains leave on Friday Morning.[3]

If you have any engagements, or if Mrs. Conkling has, which make it inconvenient to have us visit you at the time indicated pray do'nt hesitate to say so.

Mrs. Grant joins me in kindest regards to Mrs. Conkling, Miss Bessie & yourself.

yours Truly
U. S. Grant

Hon. Roscoe Conkling
U. S. S.

ALS, DLC-Roscoe Conkling. See letter to Roscoe Conkling, July 9, 1872.

1. Departing Monday evening, July 29, from the Erie Railroad depot in Jersey City, USG's traveling party stopped frequently before reaching Utica, N. Y., on July 30. USG, Julia Dent Grant, Frederick Dent Grant, Jesse Root Grant, Jr., and Horace Porter stayed at the Conkling residence. For USG's visit in Utica, see *New York Herald,* July 31, Aug. 1–3, 1872.

2. On July 12, USG, Long Branch, had spent "several hours" with U.S. Senators Henry Wilson of Mass. and Oliver P. Morton of Ind. "discussing the political situation." *Ibid.,* July 14, 1872. On July 17, USG spoke at length about politics with a *New York Herald* correspondent. *Ibid.,* July 18, 1872.

3. On Aug. 2, 11:30 A.M., USG's party left Utica on a special train and arrived in Watertown, N. Y., at 2:30 P.M. USG responded to a welcome from city officials: "It gives me sincere pleasure to visit the county of Jefferson. Many years ago, when a young man, I was stationed here, and then localities and persons were familiar to me. Coming back after a long absence, I am glad of the privilege to look for the faces I knew and to see again the places associated with many pleasant recollections. I beg you, Mr. Mayor and gentlemen, to accept for yourselves and fellow-citizens my grateful acknowledgment for your cordial assurances of welcome." *Boston Transcript,* Aug. 3, 1872. USG also addressed a crowd from the balcony of the Woodruff House. "After an absence of more than twenty years I fail to recognize a single one of all the faces I now see before me as familiar to me then. Your city has altered very much, indeed, since I last saw it. At that time I was a lieutenant stationed at Sackett's Harbor, which place I expect to see before I return." *New York Herald,* Aug. 3, 1872. For a variant version of this speech, see *Washington Chronicle,* Aug. 3, 1872. At 4:30 P.M., USG's party left for Cape Vincent, N. Y., and George M. Pullman's summer residence. *New York Herald,* Aug. 3, 1872. For USG's visit along Alexandria Bay, where Lt. Gen. Philip H. Sheridan joined the group, see *ibid.,* Aug. 5–6.

At a public reception on Aug. 5, USG spoke to a correspondent about the recent N. C. election and his reelection. ". . . I was not anxious to be President a second term, but I consented to receive the nomination simply because I thought that was the best way of discovering whether my countrymen, or the majority of them, really believed all that was alleged against my administration and against myself personally. The asperities of an election campaign will give my political opponents and my personal enemies an opportunity and an excuse to say all that can be said against me. That opportunity I do not grudge them, and I depend on the people to rebuke or to indorse me, as they see fit. All those who have treated me unfairly have now a chance to declare themselves. . . . The mere fact of my having occupied the position I have already enjoyed was an honor to me, which, I trust, I shall duly appreciate. But attacks were made upon me long before I had fulfilled my term and before I had ever thought of a second term. I reluctantly consented to enter upon this second struggle, and I would not have done so at all if I did not feel a desire to know whether the majority of my fellow citizens were willing to aid my enemies in fastening slanders upon me. Besides I am anxious to ascertain whether the republican party, whose choice I again happen to be, is to have its policy sustained or not." *Ibid.,* Aug. 6, 1872.

After visiting Ogdensburg, Lake George, Burlington, Vt., Glens Falls, N. Y., Saratoga, and Albany, USG's party returned to Long Branch on Aug. 10. *Ibid.,* Aug. 9–10, 1872.

To Hamilton Fish

Long Branch, N. J.
July 16th /72

DEAR GOVERNOR,

Your letter of the 11th I did not see until late last night, and then by accident. I receive a great many [n]ewspapers by mail which I do not get an opportunity of opening sometimes for a week. Your letter had been placed accidentally among such papers.

I shall not go to Washington this week unless there should seem to be a necessity for it.[1] If you see such necessity do not hesitate to telegraph me and I will start at once.

The proposition of the Japanese to have us send an Agt. to Europe, to negociate a treaty there, is one that cannot be entertained for a moment. I should be glad however if we could negociate a treaty with them before they leave the country. I am anxious that our country should be the pioneer in the trade & commerce between Japan, China and the balance of the world.

Unless there is special reason for it I prefer not to fill any of the foreign appointments until after the election. In the case of the Argentine Republic there may be reason for filling it at once. I do not think of any one to suggest for the place. It might do to send Julius White[2] there and thus kill two birds with one stone.

Yours Truly
U. S. GRANT

HON. HAMILTON FISH.
SEC. OF STATE

ALS, DLC-Hamilton Fish. On July 11, 1872, Secretary of State Hamilton Fish, Garrison, N. Y., had written to USG. "Mr Iwakura was here yesterday—In the course of an interview of more than two hours, he stated that his Government had given full powers to the Ambassadors, jointly and severally, to execute a Treaty, but that for certain reasons they desired that this Government should appoint a 'Delegate' to accompany the Embassy, or to meet the Embassy at some place in Europe, and execute the Treaty there—This, I told him, was entirely out of the question—that it was not consistent with the dignity, & self respect of the Government to send a representative, to negotiate a Commercial Convention, with another Power, elsewhere than to the territory & within the Jurisdiction of that Power,—that Japan had voluntarily sent an Embassy to this Country, & long negotiations

had been had, and drafts & counterdrafts exchanged & that the proposition, now, to abandon what had thus been entered upon on the invitation of Japan, could not be regarded
with favour—that the effect, if not the design of the proposal would be to make the terms
of our Treaty, to suit the interests of their negotiation with European Powers—that the
United States had always declined *joint* negotiations in connection with other Powers—
that the relations of this Country with Japan, whether commercial or political, differed
entirely from those of Japan with the European Powers—that we were prepared to make
the most friendly arrangements with them, & that as we had none of the political questions with them, which existed between them & several of the European Powers they
would find it to their interest to have a Treaty with the U. S concluded before they began
their negotiations with the Powers of Europe. I observed some prevarication, & the usual
amount of Oriental cunning and reserve—The Ambassador pressed his object with a
great deal of ingenuity and perseverance—Finally I told him, that I would mention to you
his proposal but that he must not expect any other answer than that which I had given
him—that I was confident that you would not entertain the proposition—He then acquiesced, & produced, & left with me, a counter draft, to my last projet of a Treaty—The interview was altogether very friendly & pleasant and he admitted that the answer he received was not unexpected—I told him that I would be in Washington next week, & if
necessary would remain until we conclude a Treaty—But I question if they intend to sign
one—The Argentine Minister passed a morning with me,—is very urgent for the appointment of a Minister to his Country—is apprehensive of the Aggressive policy of
Brazil, & thinks that the appointment of 'a first rate man' as Minister would do much to
protect the interests of the Republics in South America which he thinks are threatened by
the Ambition of Brazil—Genl Hurlbut has sent in his resignation—& Genl Logan urges
very strongly the appointment of Genl Julius White of Illinois—I do not know him, but
think it desirable to gratify Logan—Telegrams from Sickles & from the Consul at Cadiz,
state that Houard was placed at liberty, the night before last—I shall go to Washington
on Monday night—If you are to be there on Tuesday will you come to my house—I shall
be able to give both you & Porter a room and have arrangements to get our meals, (I hope)
comfortably—Should you go to the White House to sleep, will you come to my House,
for your meals—I will order breakfast on Tuesday morng at *Eight* oclk." ALS, USG 3. See
letter to Hamilton Fish, July 7, 1872. On July 22, Fish wrote in his diary. "The Japanese
Ambassadors came by appointed—Mr Iwakura stated that his associates Ito, & Okubo
had arrived—with instructions from their government—That the Govt had determined
to sign treaties outside of the Empire, but only in one place, in Europe, & therefore they
desire this Govt to send a delegate, to the place which may be determined for the Conference—this was declined—they were asked if they could not proceed to complete the
Treaty which we have been negotiation—they reply that they regret that their Instructions will not allow them to do so—I regret the failure, & state that I will report to the
President—" DLC-Hamilton Fish.

1. On July 16, Fish wrote in his diary. "Returned to Washington this Morning. . . .
At noon went to the Presidents House expecting a Cabinet Meeting—He has not returned
from Long Branch—Babcock has either a letter or telegram from Porter, saying that the
Prsdt does think it necessary to come until next week—I wish that he had written thus to
me—He led me to understand that he wd be here to day—in fact told Hale so—& I have
written to him assuming that I was to meet him here   He made no dissent & has allowed
me to come expecting him—Cresswell & Delano came expecting a Cabinet Meeting—

I saw Williams afterward, he is unwell & on that account not wishing to go out unless necessary, had sent to ascertain if the President had returned—He expressed surprise—Returning to the Office I find a telegram from the President saying he will not be in Washington this week unless sent for If the Democratic papers get hold of this, they will make capital out of it—" *Ibid.*

2. On July 6, U.S. Senator John A. Logan of Ill., Chicago, had written to Fish. "I see that the Hon S. A. Hurlburt of this state Minister to Bogota, has been nominated on the rep ticket for Congress, presuming that he has resigned his position at Bogota I most respectfully *ask* that Genl Julius White of this state may be appointed to fill such vacancy. Gnl White would give general satisfaction and would make an efficient Officer. This appt. I most earnestly desire should be made." ALS, DNA, RG 59, Letters of Application and Recommendation. On Dec. 3, USG nominated Julius White as minister to Argentina. See *PUSG*, 22, 99, 353.

In [*March, 1869*], Nathan Mears and others had petitioned USG. "The undersigned who are directly interested as owners, agents, or masters of shipping on the Western Lakes, or frequent shippers of cargoes, respectfully recommend General Julius White as Collector of Customs at the Port of Chicago, for the following reasons: *First,* he is and has been for twenty five years past familiar with the laws, usages and conventionalities of our Lake Commerce. *Second.* This knowledge enabled him, during the brief period he held the office in 1861, to introduce many reforms in the conduct of the business, which greatly facilitated the commerce of the Port. *Third.* He resigned the office in 1861 after holding it but three months, raised a regiment and kept the field three and a half years in the country's service: and we think should be restored to the office, if for no other reason than the patriotism he then manifested." DS (undated), DNA, RG 56, Collector of Customs Applications. Horace White, J. Russell Jones, Charles L. Wilson, Joseph D. Webster, and U.S. Representative Norman B. Judd of Ill. favorably endorsed this petition. ES (undated), *ibid.* On July 24, Secretary of the Interior Jacob D. Cox wrote to Julius White, Chicago. "Private. . . . Yours of 21st reached me this morning and I lose no time in reassuring you on the subject of its being welcome. The respect I acquired for you in our brief service together in the East Tennessee campaign, and the honorable position as an officer which I know you had in the opinion of the army there, would make me always glad to serve you in any matter within my power. As to the Harper's Ferry controversy I can sympathize with the feelings you must have, when, conscious of having acted magnanimously in carrying out what you had reason to believe was the wish of the supreme authority in the Army, you find your enemies using your self-devotion to reproach you. I am obliged to you for the account contained in the newspaper slip, as it enables me to do fuller justice to your motives & conduct on that occasion than my imperfect knowledge had before enabled me to do. As to the Appointment of the Collector by the President, I happen to know what will in part, at least, relieve your mind on that subject. I heard the President express himself on the subject of that appointment, and know that he waived all questions in any way affecting the claims of the candidates not appointed, simply putting his action on the ground of the *affirmative* merits & claims of the gentleman to whom the commission was given. I think that his mind was made up from his personal acquaintance with the appointee, & being satisfied that he was a proper person to appoint, he did not in any way intend to pass upon the merits of others or listen to objections urged against them. As your letter is one you have no occasion to be ashamed of in any way, I shall be glad to call the President's attention to it on his return, and shall most cheerfully do anything I can to secure for you the recognition which you naturally & properly desire—Assuring you again of the satisfaction I have myself taken in our acquaintance both in the Army & out of it: . . ." ALS (press), Cox Papers, Oberlin College, Oberlin, Ohio. USG had appointed James E. McLean, business partner of Orvil L. Grant, as collector of customs, Chicago. AN (undated), DNA, RG 56, Collector of Customs Applications. See letter to James E. McLean, Feb. 4, 1872.

On Nov. 20, 1871, White, Chicago, wrote to U.S. Representative John L. Beveridge of Ill. "When President Grant was last here, I spoke to him about directing an abstract of the testimony relative to the surrender of Harpers Ferry, to be made for his own examination. He very kindly said he would cheerfully make such an examination, and express in writing his approval or disapproval of the finding of the Military Commission before whom the evidence was taken—Of course it will only be necessary to refer to that portion of the testimony relating to my own official action on the occasion. This with a copy of the paper read in my own behalf by myself, which forms a part of the record, will be all that will be necessary to enable him to form an opinion. I will thank you to ask him to direct such an abstract to be made, when you can conveniently call for the purpose." ALS, *ibid.*, RG 94, Letters Received, 4349 1871. USG endorsed this letter. "Will the Sec. of War please give abstract to me." AE (initialed and undated), *ibid.* On Dec. 20, Secretary of War William W. Belknap wrote to Beveridge. "The President has directed me, in reply to the letter of Genl Julius White of the 20th November, to send you the following extract from the report of a military Commission ordered to investigate the circumstances attending the defense and surrender of Harper's Ferry, Sept. 15th 1862 and to further say that so much of said report as refers to the military ~~character~~ conduct of General White, on that occasion meets with his approval: . . ." Df, *ibid.*

On Nov. 11, 1872, White wrote to USG. "Permit me to congratulate you—not upon your re-nomination, and election to the Presidency—for *that* was not necessary to your present happiness, nor to your position in history. But it is a matter over which your friends may well rejoice, that the most powerful combination of eminent men, and influential press, ever organized in this Country for the overthrow of a political party, has been buried under the largest majority ever cast for a Presidential Candidate, in the electoral college, and in the popular vote, by one, who relying upon the rectitude of his acts and intentions, refused to ask for the office, or to respond to the torrent of slander which has been poured upon upon his name. With sincere wishes for your continued good health, and happiness . . ." ALS, USG 3.

On June 9, John G. Nicolay, Springfield, Ill., had written to USG. "Senator Harlan has done me the honor to lay before you the letter from Hon. S. M. Cullom of this place presenting my name for appointment as Minister Resident to Bogota, upon the resignation of Gen. Hurlbut, if it shall be deemed fitting and proper by yourself. In addition thereto I have the honor to forward testimonials in support of said application from sundry prominent and leading citizens of Springfield, and also from Hon. C. B. Farwell, M. C., Ex-Governor Wm Dennison, and G. W. Fishback Esq editor of the Mo. Democrat." ALS, DNA, RG 59, Letters of Application and Recommendation. On July 6, U.S. Representative James A. Garfield of Ohio, Hiram, wrote to USG. "Permit me to commend to your favorablye consideration the application of Jno: G. Nicolay Esq. for appointment as Minister to Bogota—in place of Gen. Hurlburt—recently nominated to Congress—& who will resign soon—You will remember Mr. Nicolay as the able and faithful Private Secy of President Lincoln—and afterwards as Consul gGeneral of the U. S. at Paris—I saw him in Paris in 1867, and had occasion to know of his ability & efficiency in the Consulate   I believe he is every way qualified for the place he seeks—" ALS, *ibid.* Related pa-

pers are *ibid.* In Dec., Nicolay was appointed marshal, U.S. Supreme Court. See Helen
Nicolay, *Lincoln's Secretary: A Biography of John G. Nicolay* (New York, 1949), pp. 267–68.

On Dec. 20, 1871, USG had written to U.S. Senator Roscoe Conkling of N. Y. "Will
Senator Conkling please see Mr. Scroggs, Ed. of the Atlanta New Era?" ANS, DLC–
Roscoe Conkling. On Dec. 5, 1872, USG nominated William L. Scruggs as assessor of Internal Revenue, 4th District, Ga. On Feb. 21, 1873, USG nominated Scruggs as minister
to Colombia.

To Matthew H. Carpenter

Long Branch, N. J.
July 16th 1872

DEAR SENATOR;

I was glad to learn from your letter of the 15th, rec'd last night
after the last train had left Long Branch, that Mrs. Carpenter &
children with yourself would visit on Wednesday[1] even if your stay
must be so short. Of course we will be glad to see the little boy although I neglected, through inadvertency, to include him in the invitation. He can have two rooms to himself if he w[ants] th[em.]

There being delay sometimes in the delivery of letters I will
telegraph you to-day to ascertain what train we may expect you on.

Yours Truly
U. S. GRANT

HON. MATT. CARPENTER U. S. S.

ALS, Robert L. Markovits, Middletown, N. Y. U.S. Senator Matthew H. Carpenter of
Wis., who had married Caroline Dillingham in 1855, had two surviving children: Lillian,
born in 1857, and Paul D., born in 1867. See *PUSG*, 19, 67.

On Sept. 23, 1872, Carpenter, Milwaukee, wrote to USG. "We are daily meeting 'the
Enemy' and daily, they are ours—as the Bishop in confirmation says *'more and more.'* The
bottom is out of the Greely movement. Had the Election taken place on the 1. Augt I believe Greely would have carried Wisconsin. But the 'sober second thought of the people,'
which is 'always right,' has set in, and today you would carry Wisconsin by ten thousand
majority; & in Nov, your majority may reach fifteen or twenty thousand. When I got
home, I was astonished at the state of things. The constant blowing of Sumner, Trumbull,
Schurz &c &c to which Administration men had paid too little attention, had wrought
upon the popular mind; and even in Wisconsin, it required effort to stay the progress of
the defection and *right the Ship.* My colleague pitched in & did good service until his health
failed him, and he is now sick in bed; since which I have been doing double duty filling both

his appointments & mine, but we 'have got them right'; Wisconsin is all right & *Howe* will be returned. With congratulations upon the auspicious omens which cheer us, and with the highest respect & devotion . . ." ALS, PHi.

1. July 17. See *New York Herald*, July 19, 1872.

To William D. Rawlins

Long Branch, N. J.
July 19th 1872

Dear Sir:

If convenient for you I wish you would come to Long Branch immediately on the receipt of this. On Monday week[1] I expect to leave here to be absent for two weeks. I would like to see you before that time and have you visit your brothers children and make arrangements for them for the future.

Your Truly
U. S. Grant

W. D. Rawlins, Esq,
Chicago, Ill.

I have proposed, as I understand it is my province to do, to place the funds presented to Gen. Rawlins widow & orphan children in the hands of some strong moneyied institution, with directions to pay over one fourth of the income to the orders of Mrs. Daniels, the three fourths to the guardian, or acting guardian of the children, for their use. This is based on the suposition that Mrs. Daniels surrenders the guardianship of the children entirely. I wish you to enquire also into the present status of the house in Danbury, purchased, so far as payments have been made, out of the pay of Gn. Rawlins, voted by Congress after his death, and which is the equal property of Mrs. Daniels & the children. This property was purchased at the particular request of Mrs. Daniels and is not entirely paid for. This house, with the house in Washington occupied by Gn. R. comprises the estate ~~which is~~ left by will to the widow & orphans equally. ~~and Mrs~~ Mrs. Daniels & myself are left executors of that will. I would be glad to have Mrs. Daniels indicate what should be done with this property, particularly the house in Danbury. It is not all paid for and I cannot concent now that it should be paid for out of the children's income.[2]

See Mrs. Daniels. Ascertain her wishes in regard to the disposition of property left by Gn. Rawlins. Get her consent to give up all controll of the children. See the children and let me know how they are situated and how they feel about the change which you propose—As a lawyer I would like you to arrange the agreement with Mrs. Daniels, so that it will be legal when signed by both of us.

ALS (with enclosure), Steven C. Rawlins, Evanston, Ill. See letter to William D. Rawlins, July 30, 1872.

1. July 29, 1872.
2. See *PUSG*, 22, 372–73.

Speech

[*July 24, 1872*]

MARQUIS—I am happy to receive you as the Minister of the French republic. We are confident not only that you will endeavor to make yourself acceptable, but there is every reason to believe that you will succeed in that effort. You may be assured that on our part there will be nothing omitted which may tend to make your stay here agreeable to you. Your allusion to the origin and depth of the friendship of the people of our respective countries is based upon indisputable fact, with which your own name has agreeable associations.[1] The instructions which you say you have to cherish this sentiment will, I trust, be easily carried into effect. You may be certain that I shall endeavor to facilitate them by all the means which may be in my power.

New York Herald, July 25, 1872. USG spoke in response to an address by the Marquis de Noailles highlighting the friendship between the U.S. and France that dated "from the glorious epoch of American independence." *Ibid.* Two drafts of this address (in French) are in DNA, RG 59, Notes from Foreign Legations, France. See Hamilton Fish diary, July 21, 1872, DLC-Hamilton Fish.

1. Vicomte de Noailles, ancestor of the new French minister and brother-in-law of Lafayette, served on the commission that negotiated the British surrender at Yorktown in 1781.

To James H. Coggeshall

To the Marshal of the District of Rhode Island,[1]
Greeting:

Whereas, satisfactory information has been communicated to me that a vessel called the "Pioneer," now lying and being in the waters of said District is a vessel in which, within the limits of the United States, a military enterprise has been set on foot by— Francis L. Norton, and other persons, who were knowingly concerned in fitting out said vessel with the intent that she shall be employed in the service of a foreign people, claiming to be the Republic of Cuba, to commit hostilities against the subjects of Spain, a nation with whom the United States are at peace, contrary to the provisions and prohibitions of an Act of Congress approved April 20, 1818, entitled "An act in addition to the Act for the punishment of certain crimes against the United States, and to repeal the Acts therein mentioned."

These are, therefore, in the name of the United States of America, to command and empower you to take possession of and detain such vessel, her tackle, apparel, and furniture, and all the materials, arms, ammunition, and stores belonging to or found upon her; and to employ such part of the land or naval forces of the United States as may be necessary therefor, in order to the execution of the penalties and prohibitions of said Act.

The authority and power hereby given to be held and exercised during the pleasure of the President of the United States.

In testimony whereof, I have caused the Seal of the United States to be affixed.

Given under my hand at the City of Washington, the Twenty-fourth day of July, in the year 1872, and of the Independence of the United States the Ninety-seventh.

U. S. GRANT.

Copy, DNA, RG 59, General Records. See *New York Tribune*, July 29, 1872. On Aug. 3, 1872, James H. Coggeshall, U.S. marshal, R. I., executed the order. *Ibid.*, Aug. 5, 1872. On July 12 and 20, Fish wrote in his diary. "~~B~~Admiral Polo de Barnabe (Spanish Minister) comes to Glenclyffe—He refers to the alleged Cuban Privateer 'Pioneer' which has been brought into Newport. He speaks with much feeling of the continued flying of the 'Cuban' flag, from the vessel, while in an American Port, & in charge of the Govt . . ." "A card was brought in 'Captn Norton, Cuban Navy'—A person entered in full Naval uniform, & introduced himself, saying 'I am Capt Norton of the Cuban Navy'—I immediately replied, 'I cannot receive or recognize you as an Officer in the service of a alleged Governmt not known to or recognized by the United States;' as an individual—a private Gentleman, I can receive, & converse with you—. . . He said what I claim is this—several of the South American republics have recognized Cuba as an independent Power. ~~her~~this recognition must be admitted by other Powers who have not themselves recognised Cuba, & gives her the right to carry her flag on the High Seas—the Pioneer goes out in the same way that the U. S. during the Revolution sent out Paul Jones, the U. S. being then recognized by France, but not by G. B. or the Powers generally—It was under this understanding that I accepted a Commission from Cespedes 'the President of the '*so called Republic* of Cuba'—Great care has been taken not to violate the neutrality laws of the U. S. Nothing has been done within their jurisdiction . . ." DLC-Hamilton Fish. See Nevins, *Fish*, p. 623; *New York Herald*, July 10–12, 14, 1872. On Nov. 18, 1875, Francis L. Norton wrote to USG from "debtors' or Ludlow St. Jail," New York City, alleging that a conspiracy between U.S. and Spanish officials had resulted in "a snap judgment" against the *Pioneer* to avoid "recognition of the Cuban Flag." LS, DNA, RG 59, Miscellaneous Letters. Norton claimed to have helped Spanish agents resolve the *Virginius* controversy.

1. On Feb. 3, 1871, USG nominated Coggeshall as marshal, R. I. On Jan. 27, U.S. Senator Henry B. Anthony of R. I. had written to USG recommending Coggeshall "to fill the vacancy caused by the resignation of Robert Sherman, Esq." LS, *ibid.*, RG 60, Records Relating to Appointments.

To Gerrit Smith

———

Long Branch, N. J.
July 28th 1872.

DEAR SIR:

Your letter of the 9th inst. in relation to your visit to the Ku Klux convicts in the Albany Penetentiary was duly received. I should have acknowledged the receipt of it, and of the copy, or copies, of your admirable speech to your neighbors,[1] of the 22d of June, earlyer. I shall send your letter to the Atty. Gen. with directions to send some one to Albany to visit those prisoners and from the report made, together with the testimony against them, in his possession, submit such recommendation in regard to them as he may think proper.[2] Any pardon now, before the North Carolina election,[3] would be misinterpreted. I therefore should not like to act now. But if any innocent persons are being punished, or any whose punishment is not calculated to spare innocent persons for the future from the acts of the K. K. I have no desire to keep them longer in confinement. My oft expressed desire is that all citizens, white or black, native or foreign born, may be left free, in all parts of our common country, to vote, speak & act, in obedience to law, without intimidation or ostrasism on account of his views, color or nativity. With these privileges secured there is no political offence that I would not advocate forgiveness and forgetfulness of, so far as the latter is possible.

I thank you very kindly for giving me the result of your observations during your visit to these prisoners, and also for the many kind words I have read of your utterance towards my official acts.[4]

With great respect,
your obt. svt.
U. S. GRANT

HON. GERRETT SMITH,

ALS, DLC-USG. On July 31, 1872, Orville E. Babcock wrote to Gerrit Smith. "The President desires me to acknowledge the receipt of your letter of the 9th inst, and convey to you his thanks. He wishes me to say that he has referred the matter to the Attorney Genl. with directions to have a thorough examination, & report made." LS, Syracuse University, Syracuse, N. Y. On Aug. 26, Horace Porter, Long Branch, wrote to Smith. "I received your letter enclosing applications for the pardon of Ku Klux prisoners, and have handed the petition to the Attorney General, who is daily in receipt of many similar ones, but who thinks with you, that such pardons should be few and far between. Please accept my thanks for your kindness and thoughtfulness in sending copies of your letter. The President has read, with great interest, all you have uttered in regard to the present campaign, and has been deeply touched by the kind mention you have made of him. It really seems now that honest men ~~were~~ are arranging themselves on our side and knaves on the other; and during Gen. Grant's next four years he will not only not be likely to appoint any rascals to office, but none of them will have sufficient political affiliation with him to be in a condition to ask him for office." ALS, *ibid.* On Aug. 19, Smith, Peterboro, N. Y., had written to "a gentleman" in New York City explaining his pardon requests. ". . . So far from my believing that a majority of the Kuklux prisoners now confined at Albany are innocent of any crime, I do not believe that even one of them is innocent. I take it for granted that they all had fair trials and were justly convicted. There is among those prisoners a youth who, because he is hopelessly sick, I should like to have pardoned, and also a man past middle age, who because of his weak intellect, I would commend to the President's clemency. There is also an aged man who perhaps, but only perhaps, should be left in prison not more than a year or two longer. For no others have I any plea to offer. I can have no part in whitewashing Kukluxism. I deem it the greatest crime on earth, and the party that upholds it and is identified with it as the cruelest and worst party on earth." *New York Times,* Aug. 24, 1872. See *ibid.,* Aug. 15, 1872.

On May 29, Jacob R. Davis, Washington, D. C., had written to USG. "The undersigned respectfully petitions your Excellency in behalf of suffering innocent *women,* and helpless *children,* To pardon their *husbands fathers,* and Sons who are known as Ku Klux. The offenses they are charged with grew out of the War—Congress in its wisdom has thought proper to pardon the instigators of the War, and you to your thanks, without loss of time endorsed the Same. Could you not now consistant with your kindness of heart— pardon the poor doops, tools only of those who Congress has so recently reileved. A general pardon to all offenders known as Ku *Klux* up to this date, would do more to restore harmony, than all other acts that has been passd in reference to the States late in Rebellion. . . . I have resided in the South (Georgia) since the fall of 1829, and mixed in the Polatics of the Country generally since 1832 the days of Nulafication, was then a Union man and have been ever since, was opposed to the late War. Was President of the first Loyal League in Georgia, was the first citizen Clerk in the Freedmen Beureau soon after the War.—Was U. S. Commnr for the Southern Dis of Georgia, which Comn I held untill I came to this city where I have been Clerk in the Census Bureau up to a few Days since, when I was granted leave of absence to the 1st of June at which time my services could be dispensed with. I voted for President Grant at the last Election and feel a deep interest the perpetuity of the Republican Party, and the success of our present chief Magistrate at the coming Election—.   as a Political move, setting a side all other claims, the pardoning of the Ku Klux at this time would be a *ten strike.* It would make your triumph doubly certain.—Let it come to them and upon the public, as a clap of *Thunder in a clear Sky.* . . . This move on your part, would disspate all doubt as to the success of the Republican party this fall, If there be any doubt—Should you conclude to pardon the poor creatures now in prison at Albany—I respectfully ask to be appointed bearer of the dispatch to them, Grant this petition   in doing so you will give the lie, to assertions constantly made in the South that the President is opposed to the South—*Hesitate not dear chieftain—As an Hero & Statesman you can afford to be Magnanimous*—" ALS, DNA, RG 60, Letters from the President.

On Aug. 2, Alexander N. Wilson, collector of Internal Revenue, Savannah, wrote to USG. "Afew days ago, I wrote you, stating that I believed to pardon the ~~pardon the~~ parties convicted under the 'Ku Klux' Act would have a good effect upon the convicts, and also upon the Southern people generally. From recent disturbances in this city, I am satisfied the lawless element of society is determined to make itself felt, and I desire you to consider my former letter as withdrawn." ALS, *ibid.*

On Aug. 6, Alexander H. Stephens, Crawfordville, Ga., wrote to USG. "Of my own accord I make an appeal to your Excellency for clemency and mercy in behalf of all those prisoners now suffering in Penitentiaries under sentence of courts in several states of the union for a violation of the act of Congress generally known as the Ku Klux act—or for violation of the Enforcement acts of Congress under prosecutions founded upon the last named act—Not a single one of those parties is known to me—nor am I acquainted in the slightest degree with the nature or character of the charges brought against them nor with the facts upon which the conviction of a single one of them was founded—My appeal is simply for clemency and mercy—It is founded upon these considerations— 1st My impression from what I have seen in the news papers is that all these convictions rest upon prosecutions for offenses committed before the passage of the Ku Klux act—It is I beleive well known that I was utterly opposed to all those combinations known as Ku Klux organizations—I have all my life been for law and order—without therefore saying anything about outrages of this sort, either in extenuation or condemnation, befcre the passage of the act of 1871 for their suppression by the Federal authorities I repeat that my impression is that *no one* in whose behalf I make this application committed an cffense for which he is now suffering *after* the passage of this act—This view of the case it seems to me should have weight with your excellency—2. The purpose of the Goveret it seems to me has been accomplished—I believe that no one now has any serious apprehensions of any further disturbances of this sort—Indeed as said before now as I believe none occurred since the passage of the act for their suppression by Federal authority— 3. When the object of punishment upon the individual and upon Society is accomplished lenity should be the Rule with all Governmts   4. Many of these parties, I understand are infirm, a few of them old—Several of them have families dependent upon them—all of them have suffered severely—for these reasons I ask you by the authority vested in you to grant them one and all a general pardon—I will present you with no view founded upon the unconstitutionality of the act under which they are suffering—or even of its doubtful constitutionality—but appeal to you to do as Mr. Jefferson did with those who were imprisoned under the Alien act of 1798   Give them a release under the pardoning Power wisely lodged in such cases in the hands of the Executive—If my Dear Sir this petition can not be granted I trust it will not be deemed obtrusive—Let it be attributed soley to my deep sympathy for all who are in prison—This appeal I shall put in the hands of others who I hope may after giving it their indorsement forward it to you—" ALS, *ibid.* On Aug. 8, J. Henly Smith, manager, *Atlanta Sun*, wrote to James F. Dever, collector of Internal Revenue, 4th District, Ga. "Mr Stephens has sent me the inclosed petition to Gen Grant, asking the pardon of those convicted of violations of the KuKlux and Enforcemt acts of Congress, which I hereby place in your hands and ask you to forward to His Excellency the President. . . ." ALS, *ibid.*

On Oct. 9, "H. K. Thurber & Co., Importers and Wholesale Grocers," New York City, wrote to USG. "While the returns come rolling in showing that the patriotism of the *people* is stronger than the plots of the politicians, we desire to suggest to the administration the immediate pardon of the Ku Klux prisoners, now confined at Albany. They are no longer dangerous, and such action taken by the administration *now* would be the final nail in the liberal Coffin.—We as business men doing a trade South as well as North have steadily supported your administration and we Know from daily personal cortact with the better class of Southern merchants that such action would make many support your administration as the one most likely to give them in the end prosperity to all their main interest—There can be no doubt, but that some portions of the South have suffered greatly from theiving Carpet-baggers and that *real grievances* exist which your administration, so great in acts for the public good, can to a very great extent remove; therefore permit us, as your staunch friends and steadfast supporters, to ask your earnest consideration of this our request, which we feel sure would be concurred in by the majority of the Merchants of NewYork—" L, *ibid.*

1. On June 22, 1872, Smith spoke at Peterboro. "The Democratic Party is my dread. The Republican Party is my hope. . . . Let President Grant, who so faithfully executes the laws against Kukluxism, withdraw his repressing hand for only a single week, and the flames of hell would again burst out there as furiously as ever, and the whip and halter and bullet be again as busy as ever. It is true that thirty-six persons, convicted of Kuklux crimes, were sent a few days ago to the Albany Penitentiary, and that hundreds and more nearly thousands of others are now under indictment for such crimes; but the spirit of Kukluxism will not die out so long as the Democratic Party exists to sympathize with that spirit. Let us not be deceived by the representation that Kukluxism is confined to the 'low whites' of the South. Many of the influential Southern Democrats are involved in it. No small proof of this is that not a few of them fled the country as soon as President Grant undertook to enforce the laws against the murderous scoundrels. No wonder that he is unpopular with these scoundrels, and that they prefer for President some softer person than this iron and invincible soldier. . . . But it is said that President Grant should retire at the end of his term, and give place to another. Common sense, however, argues that his having been a good President once is a strong reason why he should be President twice. Thus did common sense argue when it re-elected Washington, the first savior of his country. Thus did it argue when it re-elected Lincoln, the second savior of his country; and thus does it now argue when it is about to re-elect Grant, the third savior of his country. It is said, too, that President Grant has made mistakes. In beautifully modest terms does he himself confess it and hope to learn from experience. All men make mistakes. Not even Presidents are exempted from the aphorism that 'to err is human.' Some of his appointments have turned out badly. So was it with a larger proportion of the appointments of a part, if not, indeed, of all his predecessors. One thing more—all the efforts (and they have been as malignant as incessant) of President Grant's enemies to charge him with money-making motives, or with any other corrupt motives in his appointments, has signally failed. But he has given offices to his relatives. Yes, it is true that of the scores of thousands of offices in the gift of the Administration, some half dozen or a dozen have gone to his relatives. He has even allowed his old father to continue to be what a previous President made him, Postmaster of a little town in Kentucky. If President Grant has given offices to relatives simply because they were his relatives, he has done wrong. But if it were mainly because being his relatives he could judge better of their qualifications, then, surely, no great blame should attach to him in this matter. Another charge against the President is that during his Presidency he has accepted presents. The charge is untrue—though in saying so I do not admit that there would necessarily have been moral wrong in his accepting them. It is true presents were made to him as well as to other successful Generals, to express the gratitude and admiration of those who made them: and it is also true that to single him out for blame in the case proves that Gen. Grant is a basely-persecuted man . . . Let us, my neighbors, instead of disparaging President Grant, and dwelling on the few errors in his Administration, be thankful that he makes us so wise and safe a President. . . ." *New York Times*, July 10, 1872. See also Beverly Wilson Palmer, ed., *The Selected Letters of Charles Sumner* (Boston, 1990), II, 597–601; Ralph Volney Harlow, *Gerrit Smith: Philanthropist and Reformer* (New York, 1939), pp. 475–76.

2. See Pardon, Aug. 22, 1872.

3. On Aug. 7, Secretary of War William W. Belknap telegraphed to USG, Alexandria Bay, N. Y. "Settle telegraphs that North Carolina has elected the entire Republican State Ticket by majorities ranging from 1500 to 2000." ALS (telegram sent), DNA, RG 107, Telegrams Collected (Bound).

4. See *PUSG*, 22, 129–30. On Nov. 13, 1872, Smith had written to USG. "My congratulations on your re-election are none the less warm & sincere because coming so late. I delayed sending them, for the reason that you must have been deluged with letters immediately after the Election. I rejoice in your re-election for your own sake—for the sake of its ample vindication of your assailed wisdom & assailed integrity—but I rejoice in it more for our country's sake. What our country most needs is not prosperity in business, the speedy payment of her great debt & the increase of her wealth. Far more than this & than all things else she needs the cordial recognition & full protection of the equal rights of all her children—the black & red as well as the white. In the light of what you have already done to this end, I believe that, ere the close of your next Presidential term, this recognition will be gained & this protection enjoyed. Then & not till then shall we be a favored nation. For then & not till then will can God be at peace with it. May His wisdom continue to guide you!" ALS, Syracuse University, Syracuse, N. Y.

To *William D. Rawlins*

Utica N. Y.
July 30th 1872.

DEAR SIR:

Your letter of the 28th inst. is received. You are authorized to take the children of Gen. Rawlins with you West and to make the disposition of them proposed. I am confident they will be happier, and their interests morally and otherwise, better cared for among relations than they could be among strangers. You may also settle for interest and repairs on the Danbury house charging Mrs. Daniels her share [of] the amts which will be deducted from the rent of the house in Washington as it is paid in.

The money I gave you at Long Branch is all that is now in hand belonging to the children. No more will be coming in until the first of Jan.y, except $[75] pr. month—one fourth of that to Mrs. D— out of which probably two months rent will be expended in repairs & painting.[1]

I am satisfied to keep the Danbury house as long as Mrs. Daniels thinks it advisable.[2] It should however, if retained, be rented so as to bring something in.

You do not give any address except where you write from. I therefore address you to the care of Mrs. Augusta Smith.[3] Please drop me a line to Alexandria Bay, N. Y. so that I may know you receive this.

Yours Truly
U. S. GRANT

WM D. RAWLINS, ESQR.

ALS, Steven C. Rawlins, Evanston, Ill. See letters to William D. Rawlins, June 22, July 19, 1872.

1. On June 21, 1872, Orville E. Babcock wrote to Mary E. Daniels, South Norwalk, Conn. "The President directs me to enclose herewith drafts on New York drawn to your order for three hundred and forty five dollars, the sum being made up as follows: ¼ of $1155 interest received (coin draft) 288.75   ¼ of rent for Apr. May & June 56.25 $345.00 and request that you will acknowledge their receipt. He wishes me to say that there will be no rent available from the house for a few months, as he is going to have it repainted and repaired, it being greatly in need thereof. At the time it was built it only received one coat of paint, and has never received any since." Copy (tabular material expanded), DLC-USG, II, 1.

2. See *PUSG*, 22, 372–73; letter to William S. Hillyer, Oct. 20, 1872.

3. On June 20 and July 2, Babcock wrote to Augusta Smith, Southport, Conn. "The President directs me to say that if you will please send a bill of whatever is due, for clothing & schooling &c. up to the 1st of July next, for the little daughter of Gen. Rawlins, he will send you a draft for the amount." "The President directs me to enclose you herewith a draft on New York for three hundred and ninety 78/100 dollars, the amount of your bill of June 24. for the tuition, clothing, boarding &c. of Miss Jennie & Emily Rawlins. The President desires me to say that he intends in the Fall to make permanent arrangements for the little girls, and at that time will settle for the remainder of the Summer." Copies, DLC-USG, II, 1. The bill from Smith, dated June 15, is in USG 3. See letter to C. F. Daniels, March 20, 1872.

To Samuel Bard et al.

———

UTICA, N. Y., July 31. [*1872*]

GENTLEMEN: I have the honor to acknowlege the receipt of the resolutions of the Board of Mayor and Aldermen, and of the Board of Trade of the City of Chattanooga, extending to myself and Cabinet an invitation to spend a portion of the Summer vacation in their city and on Lookout Mountain. I am not prepared at present to accept, either on my own part or on the part of the Cabinet, but I will in a very few days lay the invitation before the gentlemen embraced in it, and will then give his Honor the Mayor, a definite answer. It would afford me very great pleasure to visit the people and City of Chattanooga, and I return my sincere thanks to the Mayor, Aldermen and the Board of Trade for the invitation, which they have given me to do so.

With great respect, your obedient servant.

U. S. GRANT.

New York Times, Aug. 7, 1872. On Aug. 15, 1872, Samuel Bard met USG concerning the invitation to visit Chattanooga. *Washington Evening Star*, Aug. 15, 1872; *New York Tribune*, Aug. 16, 1872. See letter to Josiah J. Bryan, Aug. 16, 1872.

On March 6, 1873, Samuel Bard, Nashville, wrote to USG. "Your inaugural is well received here by nearly evry class of our citizens. The following is from the 'Republican (Democratic) Banner,'—which indicates a *decided improvement* upon the *Past*." ALS, USG 3. A clipping is *ibid.*

On March 14, Thomas Settle, Washington, D. C., wrote to USG. "I beg leave to say that Govr Bard has rendered most efficient service in behalf of good government in the Southern States. He was an active and influential member of the National Convention which assembled in Philadelphia last June, and his many friends would be much gratified to see his merits recognised, by the bestowal of some good appointment, under your administration." ALS, OFH. On March 17, John Pool, Washington, D. C., wrote to USG. "I take pleasure in recommending Govr. Saml. Bard to your favor & consideration. By his character, ability, & services to the Republican cause in the Southern States, he deserves much of the party. He is qualified to fill some position of importance, & I hope it will be found within the power of the administration to confer such position upon him." ALS, *ibid.* Endorsements from prominent Republicans are *ibid.* See *PUSG*, 20, 285–86, 289–91.

To William D. Rawlins

Utica, N. Y.
July 31st 1872.

DEAR SIR:

My letter of yesterday from this place I think answers your letter of the 29th. I have no objection to your putting the Danbury house in the hands of a real estate agt. for sale with the consent of Mrs. Daniels.—I know of no papers that it is necessary that I should sign before my return to Long Branch. When you get West please drop me a line and let me know how the children seem pleased with the change. What you do in regard to selling the property in Danbury, or paying up interest &c. I would like to be informed of. I did not think when assigning to you the draft for the money on hand, belonging to the Gens children, of taking a receipt for it. Please send a receipt to Gen. Babcock (at Washington) who keeps the act. of all disbursements from that fund.

Yours Truly
U. S. GRANT

W. D. RAWLINS, ESQ.

ALS, Steven C. Rawlins, Evanston, Ill.

Endorsement

Respectfully forwarded to the Sec. of the Treas: The dispatches and letters received in favor of Sup.r McDonald are so numerous, and from people of such standing and responsibility that I do not know but that his name had not better be substituted for retention in place of Emory's,[1] or any othe[r] whom you may think can be best spared.

U. S. GRANT

AUG. 1ST /72

AES (facsimile), John McDonald, *Secrets of the Great Whiskey Ring* (Chicago, 1880), p. 75. Written on a letter of July 26, 1872, from Chester H. Krum, U.S. attorney, St. Louis, to Secretary of the Treasury George S. Boutwell, asking that John McDonald be retained as supervisor of Internal Revenue. *Ibid.*, pp. 73–74. See *PUSG*, 19, 253; *ibid.*, 20, 149–50. On June 6, USG had signed a bill reducing the number of supervisors from 25 to 10. *U.S. Statutes at Large*, XVII, 241. On July 23, USG discussed with Boutwell and John W. Douglass, commissioner of Internal Revenue, "the proposed list of supervisors of internal revenue. Emery, of Tennessee, was dropped and Cobb, of Texas, substituted. Secretary Boutwell earnestly recommended the retention of Presbrey, but the President remarked that he was not useful enough to the politicians, and had been opposed by prominent members of Congress, which only made trouble and did not profit the party at elections. This led to a plain expression of Boutwell's opinion of one of the Supervisors which the President had resolved to retain, and without continuing the discussion the further consideration of the subject was deferred until tomorrow." *New York Herald*, July 24, 1872.

On Aug. 12, Horace Porter wrote to William A. Richardson, asst. secretary of the treasury. "The President directs me to say that he has only signed nine commissions of Supervisors of Internal Rev. and desires that you will bring over with you a commission for McDonald & he will discuss that apt." LS, DNA, RG 56, Letters Received.

On Nov. 3, 1871, Boutwell had written to Douglass. "I enclose what purports to be copies of affidavits published in the 'Weekly Arkansas Gazette' of Oct, 17th 1871, affecting the personal and official character of John McDonald Supervisor of Internal Revenue. The charges are of such a character that enquiry should be made in to their truth, if your office is not already fully advised." Copy, *ibid.*, Letters Sent. See McDonald, *Secrets of the Great Whiskey Ring*, pp. 61–70.

In Aug., 1872, McDonald served on a commission to negotiate land rights with the Ute Indians in Colorado Territory. See *U.S. Statutes at Large*, XVII, 55; *Missouri Democrat*, Aug. 12, 1872.

1. On Sept. 12, 1872, Richardson wrote to George W. Emery accepting his resignation as supervisor. Copy, DNA, RG 56, Letters Sent. On June 8, 1875, USG appointed Emery governor of Utah Territory. DS, Utah State Archives, Salt Lake City, Utah. See Thomas A. McMullin and David Walker, *Biographical Directory of American Territorial Governors* (Westport, Conn., 1984), pp. 304–6.

To *William D. Rawlins*

————

Alexandria Bay, N. Y.
Aug. 3d 1872.

DEAR SIR:

I will reach Long Branch probably Friday noon. If Mrs. Daniels will see me there on Saturday I will be at home. There will be no trouble however if she should not see me about having one fourth of the income of the bonds belonging to Gn. Rawlins set apart for her benefit. The sale and division of the estate shall be subject to her wish, though, as suggested by me before, I think the Washington house should not be sold now. It would not bring to exceed $10.000 00/100 while it cost and should bring much more.[1]

Yours Truly
U. S. GRANT

W. D. RAWLINS, ESQ.

ALS, Steven C. Rawlins, Evanston, Ill.

On Jan. 2, 1873, Orville E. Babcock wrote to William D. Rawlins, Chicago. "Enclosed please find a draft on New York for $264.35 currency; also a gold draft for $770.00

and the President's check for $107 80/100 in currency. The President directs me to forward you these funds with the following explanation: The currency draft on New York for $264 35/100 is the ¾ interest of the children of Gen. Rawlins in the rent of the building in this City belonging to the estate, of which rent account the following is a statement: . . . The President to-day drew the interest on the bonds belonging to the estate, which amounted to $1155.00/100 in gold. At the same time he procured the draft for $770.00 gold, being ⅔ of the $1155.00, thinking at the time that it was the childrens' proportion. After procuring the draft, and upon arrival at his office he discovered that he had made a mistake, and should have procured a draft for ¾ of the $1155.00/100 which would have been $866.25/100 gold, leaving a difference of $96.25/100 gold to be sent you in addition to the draft already procured. He therefore drew his own check for $107 80/100 currency, being the $96 25/100 gold reduced to currency at twelve per cent premium for gold—the market rate to-day. The following would then be a statement of the Interest account. The President as Trustee of the Rawlins Estate   Dr. To interest on bonds, collected Jan. 2d '73 $1155.00 gold of which the ¾ share of the children of Genl. Rawlins is—$866 25/100 gold which is herewith enclosed made up of gold draft for $770.00 and check for $107 80 currency representing at 12 pr. ct. premium an amount gold of 96.25 $866.25 gold The remaining one fourth of the rent account remaining in the President's hands belonging to Mrs Daniels is to-day $88.11 currency, and the remaining one fourth of the interest account belonging to her, remaining in his hands to-day, is—$288.75 gold." Copy (tabular material expanded), DLC-USG, II, 1. On July 11, Levi P. Luckey wrote to Francis E. Spinner, U.S. Treasurer. "The President directs me to acknowledge the receipt of your letter of the 7th inst. enclosing check on the Asst. Treasurer at New York; (Number 10791) for $1155. coin; being interest due on the 1st inst. on bonds held in trust by him for the family of the late Genl. Rawlins. He desires me to say that he will call upon you upon his return to the city." Copy, *ibid.*, II, 2.

1. See letter to William S. Hillyer, Oct. 20, 1872.

To Cyrus B. Comstock

Long Branch, N. J.
Aug. 13th 1872

My Dear General:

Mrs. Grant is just in receipt of your note informing her of your great berievement. Sincerely do we sympathize with you. Will you not come and spend a week or so with us away from the scene of your irreparable affliction? It will give both Mrs. Grant and myself great pleasure to contribute in any way we can to your comfort.

Faithfully Yours
U. S. Grant

Gn. C. B. Comstock U. S. A.

ALS, WHi. Elizabeth B. Comstock died during childbirth on Aug. 6, 1872; her daughter, Elizabeth Marion, died on Aug. 9. See *PUSG*, 21, 319.

On Nov. 23, 1873, Julia Dent Grant wrote to Maj. Cyrus B. Comstock. "It gave me a great deal of pleasure dear Genl to hear from you I have just read your note to Genl Grant. You send your regards to Papa—he is very very feeble is confined to his bed all the time now. It is not long since he was enquiring for you   Were you not sorry to hear [Lisa] Sands had gone into the Convent? I have not seen any of your friends (the Blairs) since I came home, & cannot tell you any thing about them. My Buckie is still at Cambridge & will graduate next summer   Fred is with Sheridan & is engaged to my little pet Kate Cook, (but you must not tell any one)   Jesse is at school near Phila at Cheltenhills. will be at home on Thankgiving—yesterday a committee of The K. F. R. club called on me to learn at what hour The Club with honarary members might call & pay their respects to Jess. Jesse's trip to Calefornia did him a great deal of good   He is very much grown. Jess had been on his road to Calefornia some two days when your invitation came for him & we started just then for the West also & was only at home a week when we went to Long Branch, & with all this coming & going I neglected to answer your kind note for Jesse.   you are coming to Washington this Yule won't you?—Do come & be our guest whilst you are here we would like to have you so much. I expect Kitty & Susie Felt to make us a visit soon. I think you would enjoy meeting Miss Kattie again. Mrs Sharpe is keeping house in the cunningist little house, (Dr Sharp[e] purchased) you ever saw. I have come to the end of my paper & must close with kind reguards in which all join me" ALS, WHi. On Aug. 12, 1874, Julia Grant, Long Branch, wrote to Comstock. "Your note from Detroit was received this morning—It is only a day or two since that I was asking The Genl to write for you to come & visit us—. Can you not come down from N York & stay for a few days? Do come please. Jesse & Buck are out at Cousin Willie Smiths. They walked out, only think of that! Jesse has entered collage & without a condition. Do you not think that is doing pretty well? Having been tieded to my apron string all his life? (as his papa says.) I send you my Nellies address with much pleasure & hope you will have time to run down to see her. I think she *is* in her owne house. She expected to get in be in a few days when she last wrote me. Should we not have the pleasure of seeing you before you sail (but I hope we will) let me wish you a pleasant voyage & safe returne to your friends of whome none are truer than . . ." ALS, DLC-Cyrus B. Comstock.

Speech

[*Aug. 16, 1872*]

MR. BERNARD: You are welcome as the diplomatic representative of your country. I trust that the favorable anticipations with which you say you have entered upon your mission will not be disappointed by anything which may happen during your abode here. There is nothing, so far as I am aware, in the relations between the United States and Nicaragua to occasion apprehension that they may not be maintained upon a footing of the utmost cordiality. The endeavors which you may make for that purpose shall be heartily reciprocated by me.

Washington Chronicle, Aug. 17, 1872. USG responded to Emilio Benard, Nicaraguan minister. "MR. PRESIDENT: I have the honor to hand to your Excellency the credentials which accredit me as Minister Resident of Nicaragua to the Government of the United States of America. His Excellency the President of Nicaragua could not have distinguished me in a more grateful manner than by conferring upon me the honorable mission of making more intimate, if this be possible, the cordial relations which fortunately exist been the two countries; and certainly, Mr. President, nothing will be more satisfactory to me than to accomplish the noble object which my country has in view." *Ibid.* See Speech, June 5, 1874.

On Aug. 30, 1872, Secretary of State Hamilton Fish wrote in his diary. "Mr Emilio Benard, (Minr Rest of Nicaragua), is anxious to negotiate a Treaty, for a Canal route—says his Govt is favourably disposed—that their Congress which meets biennially will convene in January, the Session lasting three months to end of March—Has no instructions from his Govt as to terms, &c—would like to know the views of this Governmt to which I reply that this Govt is very anxious to ascertain the best practical route for Ship Communication between the two oceans—& to secure the construction of a Canal—that we are ready to enter into negotiations with that object—I am not prepared to enter into particulars but will at a future day consider the details of a Convention—" DLC-Hamilton Fish.

On Oct. 4, Fish wrote to Benard. "I have the honor to acknowledge the receipt of your note of the 9th ultimo, relative to a proposed Convention between the United States and Nicaragua on the subject of an inter-oceanic Canal through the territories of that Republic. In reply, I have the honor to state that, although the object is an important one, the necessity, on the part of this government, of a Convention for carrying it into effect, in advance of the completion of the preliminary surveys to which your government has kindly given its consent, does not seem to be apparent or to be made clear by the remarks which you offer in its favor. A work of such magnitude, involving the investment of a large capital, should be entered upon with caution and deliberation; but its completion might be hastened and secured by a suitable Convention between the two governments. If therefore you will do me the favor to furnish a draft of such an instrument as your government may wish, it shall be taken into consideration. If it should not be convenient to conclude it here within the period which you indicate as advisable, the Minister of the United States in Nicaragua may be instructed to negotiate upon the subject. . . ." Copy, DNA, RG 59, Notes to Foreign Legations, Central American States. On Oct. 10, Fish had written in his diary. "Mr Benard (Nicaragua) would like this Govt to make a declaration of the terms on which it desires to negotiat a Treaty for an interoceanic Canal—is told that we are not prepared to say that a Canal by way of Nicaragua is practicable—that it is moreover for Nicaragua to indicate the terms on which she proposes to make a Concession—It turns out that he has no authority to negotiate on the subject—& he tells me (somewhat confidentially) that he belongs to a party in his Country which desires progress, & that he wants some overture from this Country, really to advance the interest of progress—would like instructions sent to our ~~He asks if~~ Minister—I agree to instruct the Minister to receive any proposals on the subject, & to communicate them to this Govt" DLC-Hamilton Fish.

On Oct. 19, Charles N. Riotte, U.S. minister to Nicaragua, León, wrote to Fish. ". . . When I received your dispatch of July 17, No 78, instructing me 'to sound this Government and ascertain, in an informal manner to what terms of an agreement on an interoceanic canal it would probably accede'—I was already afflicted with the deseases—

dissentery and fever,—which prostrated me for more than two months, and for whose cure I am now sojourning here. To my great sorrow I was therefore incapacitated from bestowing upon the subject the attention and diligence it so much deserves and which, in better health, I would have be happy to give it. Still, I took occasion at the visits of the President and Ministers to touch the subject as one of ordinary amicable conversation and, without being able to induce them entering into details, the invariable remark met me: 'we will do everything that may be asked, for the canal is the question of life or death for us.' Yet, I take it that the remark is a little to general to be satisfactory, and especially in the mouth of people of Spanish origin may mean as little as when they assure you that 'all what they possess is yours and they and their entire family at your service.' Nor do I ascribe much significance to those answers. They are given as an empty façon de parler and to avoid showing their ignorance and little good will in entering more minutely upon the subject, and, more yet, to compromise themselves on one point or the other. The only one person, whose unconditional reply is of value is the President, not alone because he means what he says, but also because he better than any of his countrymen is able to survey the import thereof and more willing to convey its fullest meaning . . . At this moment and probably for some months to come the question whether Nicaragua or Darien may be selected by our Government for the canal will remain an open one. Shortly after Capt. Hatfield's departure and in consequence of his and his associates, perhaps a little too freely, promulgated opinions on the value of the Nicaragua lines this people felt quite sure of the canal and they began to grow very big and to think of the nice bill they would make out for U. S. This congenial dream was suddenly interrupted by the news that, simultaneously with the second expedition to this country, another one was to leave for Darien. Then again their liberal offers came out. Now, there is not the remotest doubt to my mind that if my Governments waits with the negotiation of a contract until the location of the canal be settled in favor of this Isthmus, Nicaragua's demands will be exorbitant and the negotiations will occupy years. These people know as little of fairness in their private and public transactions, as of equity in their laws. While if we now take advantage of the incertainty still prevailing we will be able to conclude terms fair to both countries and in a short time. . . ." ALS, DNA, RG 59, Diplomatic Despatches, Nicaragua. For the expedition of Commander Chester Hatfield, U.S. Navy, to survey possible canal routes through Nicaragua, see *SED*, 43-1-57.

To Josiah J. Bryan

Washington D. C. Aug 16, 1872

HON. J. J. BRYAN
MAYOR OF CHATTANOOGA, TENN.
SIR:

At the hands of Gov. S. Bard I received the kind invitation of the Board of Mayor and Aldermen, and the Board of Trade of the City of Chattanooga for myself and Cabinet to visit your City and Lookout Mountain sometime during the present Summer.

I have delayed final answer to this invitation to consult with the Cabinet on the subject. I am compelled most reluctantly after this consultation, to inform you that it is not practicable for us to accept. I assure you however, and through you the gentlemen to whom we are indebted for this invitation, that I, on my part, highly appreciate the compliment; doubly because it is independent of political or party predilections, at a time too when party feeling runs high.

I should enjoy a visit to Chattanooga under any ordinary circumstances, and particularly so as the guest of the Citizens without respect to party. My desire is to see harmony, concord and prosperity exist everywhere in our common country.

With renewed assurances of my appreciation of the invitation to visit your City, and with my best wishes for its future prosperity, I subscribe myself

> Very respectfully
> your obt svt
> U. S. GRANT

HON J. J. BRYAN

Copy, DLC-USG, II, 1. Josiah J. Bryan, former C.S. soldier, served as mayor *pro tem* of Chattanooga. See letter to Samuel Bard *et al.*, July 31, 1872; Johnson, *Papers*, 4, 450; James W. Livingood, *A History of Hamilton County Tennessee* (Memphis, 1981), p. 231.

To Edwin D. Morgan

> *Long Branch, N. J.*
> Aug. 20th 1872

MY DEAR GOVERNOR:

Some one who called here last evening, I have forgotten now who, said that you had asked them to enquire whether I would be at home on Thursday next;[1] that you proposed coming down and spending the day if I would be. I shall be here on that day and will be glad to meet you then or at any time. But I have an engagement to dine with Mr. Gerard at five on Thursday to meet a few friends, and as I would like to have you dine with me the day you spend here

I write to ask if you cannot come on Friday or Saturday, and stay with me over Sunday, just as well.—Please telegraph me boat you leave on so that my carriage may meet you at the depot.

Yours Truly

U. S. Grant

Hon. E. D. Morgan,

ALS, New York State Library, Albany, N. Y. See James A. Rawley, *Edwin D. Morgan, 1811–1883: Merchant in Politics* (New York, 1955), pp. 239–45.

On Sept. 12, 1872, USG wrote to Edwin D. Morgan. "Will Govr Morgan please see Dr. Schmidt. The Dr. is one of our most earnest workers in the republican cause, and is probably better acquainted with the influential Germans of the country than any other man connected with the Govt. having during the last four years ~~having~~ had occasion to travel the country over in connection with his official duties." ANS, Cincinnati Historical Society, Cincinnati, Ohio.

1. Aug. 22.

Endorsement

If there is no reason for keeping the Consulship at Para, Brazil, open I see no objection to the apt. of Mr. Travis to that place. I understand the apt. is desired in the interest of the inauguration of a new line of commerce between the United States and Brazil.

U. S. Grant

Aug. 21st /72

AES, DNA, RG 59, Letters of Application and Recommendation. Written on a letter of Aug. 21, 1872, from Lewis Wallace, "Ocean House," Long Branch, to USG. "The parties associated with me in promoting the commercial enterprise on the Amazon river, the outlines of which were explained to you some months ago, consider it a point of the highest importance that they should not be antagonised by an unfriendly consul at Pará. To avoid such a possibility, therefore, I respectfully solicit the appointment to that consulship of Mr. Charles M. Travis, of Crawfordsville, Indiana. Mr. Travis was a soldier from the beginning to the end of the rebellion. Upon being discharged, he educated himself, and, after graduation at a respectable college, studied law, and is now one of the most promising young lawyers of Indiana. His character is unimpeachable. Indeed, I know few men more fit and competent in every respect for the place in question. As stated, the appointment is very necessary; and in the connection permit me to add, it is equally essential that it should be made quickly as possible, as our further action in the enterprise referred to must suffer delay without information most certainly obtainable from a friendly official at Pará.

The consulship I understand is now vacant." LS, *ibid.* On Jan. 27, U.S. Senator Oliver P. Morton of Ind. had written to Secretary of State Hamilton Fish. "Permit me to call attention to an application, forwarded by me to your department some time since, of Chas M. Travis of Crawfordsville Ind. for a consulship—the name of the particular place being left blank in the application, and to request that when a vacancy occurs you will give him an appointment if you can do so." LS, *ibid.* Earlier, Morton, Henry S. Lane, and Joseph Milligan had written a recommendation. "We would respectfully recommend Mr. Charles M. Travis, of Crawfordsville Indiana, and request his appointment Mr. Travis enlisted in Co. "E." 12th Ills. Infty. when 16 years of age, and served three years faithfully as a private soldier. Upon the recommendation of all his Officers, including Lieut. Gen. Sherman, he was appointed as cadet to West Point Military Academy, but having entered the Academy from the field, he was unable to stand the examination. Since the war he has acquired a fair education; and we take great pleasure in recommending him for the above named appointment, as a faithful and trustworthy young man. We believe he can be relied upon under all circumstances, and will perform his whole duty where ever placed." DS, *ibid.* On Dec. 3, USG nominated Charles M. Travis as consul, Pará, Brazil, in place of James B. Bond.

On Sept. 6, 1869, Cyrus J. B. DeBigot, Pará, had written to USG. "It is not without pain and regret that I am obliged to complain to you of the United States Consul at Pará— James B. Bond—who is a shame and a disgrace to his Country and Government. He offers protection to no American citizens, either with or without a passport, unless he was a Southerner and a rebel; and although he makes an open profession of loyalty to the Union, for the sake only of holding office, he is by his actions an enemy to the lawful Government of the United States. He is wound up in business transactions with the government in this country, and sacrifices duty and justice rather than offend it by demanding for it just and legal proceedings towards Americans. He has sanctioned my arrest by the Roman Catholic bishop of this city—and has been foremost in trying to get me condemned: furthermore, he has allowed them to keep me in confinement, after the president of this Province declared officially in the 'Jornal do Pará' of May last, that the proceedings against me were illegal. He has refused to consider me an American citizen, and would not even look at my passports, which I received on the 22nd of January last, from Washington, and bears the number 40,203, and signed by William H. Seward. My case is not the only one—it is but one example of how American Citizens, (who are not rebels,) are allowed to be treated in this city. I humbly beg, as a loyal citizen of the U. S. and a native of Boston, Mass. that my country will grant me protection against the tyranny and illegality of this barbarous government. I have the honour to be, Most Honored and Beloved President, a loyal and true citizen of the glorious Union." ALS, *ibid.* On Sept. 28, E. Peshine Smith, solicitor, State Dept., wrote an opinion questioning DeBigot's claims and exonerating Bond. ADS, *ibid.* On Feb. 27, 1871, Joseph Whitmore wrote to USG. "Referring to the audience, to day given, to my friend the Hon. John W. Caldwell and myself; and, to your remark, that Mr Secretary Fish, on such information as was incidentally given to you, would promptly remove the consul: I now respectfully ask the removal of Mr Bond, the present incumbent, and the appointment of Mr George Eaton, a graduate of Harvard College, ex-member of the Legislature of Massachusetts, and now a resident of Para, in Brazil, as U. S. Consul at that place." ALS, *ibid.* Related papers are *ibid.* For Bond's overseas career, see *New York Times*, Sept. 26, 1889.

On June 13, 1872, Wallace, Washington, D. C., wrote to USG. "I have submitted propositions to gentlemen in Philadelphia based upon the consulate at Santarem. That I may have time to consider acceptance of the appointment, I take the liberty of suggesting that the Sec. of State be notified, (if he has not already been,) of the tender of the place.

The precaution may prevent a troublesome slip." ALS, DNA, RG 59, Letters of Application and Recommendation. On Nov. 16, Wallace, Crawfordsville, Ind., twice wrote to USG. "Private. . . . You will be kind enough, doubtless, recall the explanation I made to you of the passage by Congress of the Act establishing a consulate at the city of Santarem, on the south bank of the river Amazon; also, my explanation of the application for the appointment of Chas. M. Travis, Esq., as consul at Pará. I stated that certain gentlemen of St. Louis had it in mind to inaugurate an American commercial and navigation enterprise in that region; that the two consulates were considered important to the project; and that, if the enterprise could be begun on a scale to justify me in accepting it, I would, after the election, formally apply for the appointment to Santarem. We have diligently inquired for data to serve as a basis for an estimate of the capital required for the business; but without success. As a consequence, the gentlemen interested decline to engage themselves to put boats upon the river; and, in the absence of sufficient knowledge of the condition of trade in that part of the world, they are certainly justified in doing so. They offer to assist me if I will descend the river and collect information; but, as they will not obligate themselves to any action, and as the expedition would consume seven or eight months, I do not think I can afford to give that time upon such an uncertainty. I have, therefore, concluded to change the application to that of Minister to Bolivia. A residence in that country, about to be opened to direct trade by a railroad around the falls of the Madeira river, will give me ample opportunity to post myself and the American public upon what is to day really a sealed book—I mean commercial affairs in the Amazon valley. Of course, I understand fully the difference between the duties and proprieties incident to a mission and a consular appointment. It is only necessary to add in the connection that, if you should give me the appointment to Bolivia, I should have in mind my own credit and the interests of my country. As to Mr. Markbreit, the present incumbent, his predecessor, Mr. Caldwell, of Cincinnati, informed me that the republicans of Ohio four years ago, presented his name for the place to satisfy Mr. Hausaureck, whom you may know as editor and proprietor of a German newspaper published in Cincinnati—the same who, in the recent contest, modestly demanded of the National Rep. Com. $30.000 for his influence and paper, and failing to get it, turned over to the enemy, and deluged you with abuse. As it is, I do not think Mr. Markbreit could complain if I make application for his place or you choose to grant it. This I write in private explanation. Elsewhere I send you a formal application, and accompany it with letters recommendatory from Gov. Morton, Senator Pratt and Gen. Coburn. I have also written to Governors Jewell and Hawley, of Connecticut, and Mr. Bartlett Brent, Chairn of the Rep. Cent. Com. of that state, requesting them to furnish me letters, and forward them to Gen. Porter for submittel to you. The letter, sent herewith, from Gen. Hawley will explain why I count on their recommendation." "I respectfully apply to be appointed minister from the United States to the Republic of Bolivia, South America. Herewith please find letters recommendatory from Senators Morton and Pratt, and Gen. Jno. Coburn, of my State: others of like purport could be readily obtained; these, however, allude to services rendered in the late canvass, and, I think, sufficiently indicate that the appointment would be agreeable to the republicans of Indiana." ALS, *ibid.* On Nov. 9, U.S. Representative John Coburn of Ind., Indianapolis, and Morton, wrote to USG recommending Wallace for minister to Bolivia; on Nov. 13, U.S. Senator Daniel D. Pratt of Ind., Logansport, wrote a similar letter. ALS, *ibid.* For USG's subsequent nomination of John T. Croxton as minister to Bolivia, see *PUSG*, 19, 263–66.

On Nov. 30, 1875, Travis, Crawfordsville, wrote to Fish. "For the first time in my life I am seeking promotion upon my own representations. The cause that impels me to do this is selfish, yet one that, I believe, can be urged on the ground of merit. I have been U. S. Consul at the port of Pará, Brazil, S. A. since September 1872. The Consulate, as you know, is one of that class in which the officer is allowed to transact business. I went to my post three years ago in the interests of an enterprise, (of which you have doubtless heard from Gen. Lew Wallace), to institute a line of Steamships between New Orleans and the coast of Brazil. The enterprise failed in the 'financial crisis' of 1873, and left me in a most embarrassed condition. I had had the yellow fever, and passed through that terrible ordeal of becoming acclimated *under the Equator,* so I *stuck* to my post until March, last, when I came home on leave of absence. I came home impoverished in every thing except experience. That experience as a Consular and qua-si diplomatic officer has, I believe, qualified me for a higher trust. . . . I will write Senators Morton, and Logan, and other political friends for their indorsement of my application for promotion, or transfer to a more responsible and profitable post." ALS, *ibid.*

Pardon

——

To all to whom these Presents shall come, Greeting:

Whereas, on the 22d day of September, 1871, in the United States Circuit Court for the District of North Carolina, one Amos Owens, one William Teal, one David Collins and one William Scruggs were convicted of conspiracy, intimidation &c, and were sentenced the said Owens to be imprisoned for six years and to pay a fine of five thousand dollars; the said Teal to be imprisoned for three years and to pay a fine of five hundred dollars,—the said Collins to be imprisoned for four years and to pay a fine of five hundred dollars,—and the said Scruggs to be imprisoned for three years and to pay a fine of five hundred dollars;—

And whereas, H. C. Whitley, Esq, Chief of the Secret-Service Division, who was ordered by the President to examine into and make report upon the matter, recommends their pardon.[1]

Now, therefore, be it known, that, I Ulysses S. Grant, President of the United States of America, in consideration of the premises, divers other good and sufficient reasons me thereunto moving, do hereby grant to the said Amos Owens, William Teal, David Collins and William Scruggs, a full and unconditional pardon.

In testimony whereof, I have hereunto signed my name and caused the Seal of the United States to be affixed.

Done at the City of Washington, this Twenty-second day of August, A. D. 1872, and of the Independence of the United States the Ninety-seventh.

U. S. Grant.

Copy, DNA, RG 59, General Records. On Aug. 23, 1872, USG signed a warrant authorizing this pardon. DS, Gilder Lehrman Collection, NNP. This group pardon was not issued. See letter to Gerrit Smith, July 28, 1872; Allen W. Trelease, *White Terror: The Ku Klux Klan Conspiracy and Southern Reconstruction* (New York, 1971), pp. 415–16 USG subsequently pardoned Amos Owens (Dec. 10, 1873), William Teal (Oct. 23, 1872), David Collins (Jan. 3, 1873), and William Scruggs (July 30, 1873). Copies, DNA, RG 59, General Records.

On July 10, 1872, USG had pardoned Peter Z. Baxter, Henry Baxter, and T. O. Lackey, each sentenced to one year imprisonment with a fifty dollar fine. ". . . many citizens of North Carolina have recommended the pardon of said parties on the ground that they voluntarily abandoned the Ku Klux organization and rendered efficient service to the prosecuting officers of the Government by communicating valuable information touching said organization. . . ." Copy, *ibid.* For the "Peter Baxter crowd," see *SRC*, 42-2-41, part 2, pp. 373–74, 377.

On Sept. 17, John F. Ficken, Charleston, S. C., wrote to USG. "Enclosed I send the petitions of two unfortunate men now confined in the penitentiary at Albany N. Y. They were prepared before the removal of the prisoners from this city and hence were addressed originally to the Secretary of the Interior. They have been retained here awaiting the action of the Secretary on a similar petition and as that was returned disapproved, at their request I enclose the petitions of Gilbreth Hambright and of William Lowry directly to Your Excellency. The power which the Attorney General is of opinion does not vest in him, most undoubtedly lies in the Chief Executive of the Government. Trusting that a favorable reply will be given, and knowing that whatever course is pursued will be in accordance with strict convictions of duty, . . ." ALS, DNA, RG 60, Letters from the President. The enclosures are *ibid.* On Jan. 9, 1873, USG responded to petitions from "many citizens of South Carolina" and pardoned Galbraith Hambright, convicted of conspiracy and sentenced to two years in prison with a five hundred dollar fine. Copy, *ibid.*, RG 59, General Records. On Feb. 6, USG pardoned William Lowry, convicted of conspiracy and sentenced to two years in prison. ". . . Hon. A. S. Wallace, M. C., District Attorney Corbin, and Major Lewis Morrill, recommend his pardon, in view of the helpless condition of his family, and believing that he was not an active participant in the unlawful acts of the organization with which he was connected; . . ." Copy, *ibid.*

In a letter mailed from Richmond and docketed as received Oct. 3, 1872, "Radical" wrote to USG. "The leaded part of this communication is from the Wilmington Star. If the statements in the stern part be true it rather strikes me as a case where you could come in with a full hand" L (undated), *ibid.*, RG 60, Letters from the President. The enclosed clipping contained a letter of Sept. 14 from a professor at Wake Forest College calling for the pardon of a former student arrested in "the hall of his debating Society" and imprisoned at Albany for alleged night riding in Cleveland County, N. C. On Jan. 9, 1873, USG pardoned David Ramseur, sentenced to eight years in prison with a one hundred dollar fine. ". . . District Judge Bryan, of South Carolina, recommends that he be pardoned—believing that such action would be consistent with justice, and the proper vindication of the law; . . . Hon: W. W. Holden urges the interposition of clemency in his behalf, as an act of mercy—in consideration of his extreme youth." Copy, *ibid.*, RG 59, General Records.

On May 23, 1872, Anna O. Knox, Montgomery, Ala., wrote to USG. "Will you pardon the liberty an obscure citizen takes in address you. An article in this mornings edition of the Advertiser & Mail prompted me to do an act of common charity, to visit some young men confined in our common jail for an alleged crime called Ku klux. Having known something of their case from the Physician who made a post mortem examination of the burnt man Jackson & his wife I was inclined to doubt whether these young men were guilty & the article above refered to put me in mind to visit them. I herewith enclose you my application for admission to them. Judge Busteed is residing in my house though not my guest, & I made a visit to him after the Sheriff brought me the enclosed, & asked the Judge to allow me to see them. He He told me Genl Healy was the person to grant my request—I went to the jail and was shown an order to the Sub Sherif countermanding the order of Genl Healy which had not been presented by me until then. I was refered by Genl Healy to Judge Busteed   I went again to ask him & he was very much excited & told me I should *not* see them. I know of the outraged feeling of the citizens at seeing a Company of U S Soldiers stationed to defend the *jail* when there is not the shaddow of a shade of reason for their being here to prevent the escape or release of those prisoners. Genl Grant I know you are brave may I ask you to *ask* Judge Busteed to let me see these unhappy men. . . ." ALS, *ibid.*, RG 60, Letters from the President. On June 6, Robert W. Healy, U.S. marshal, Montgomery, telegraphed to USG. "Gov Lindsay has made demand, upon the United States district Judge for the possession of the prisoners now upon trial for violation of the Enforcement Acts. I am not advised whether he intends to use force to get them, but to guard against the emergency, such additional military aid, as can be spared, should be sent to our assistance at once,   I send this telegram with the approbation and at the suggestion of the district Judge, and district Attorney," Telegram received, *ibid.*, RG 94, Letters Received, 2186 1872. On the same day, Orville E. Babcock endorsed this telegram to Secretary of War William W. Belknap. "The President requests you to consult with the Atty Genl. before complying with request" ES, *ibid.* On June 7, AG Edward D. Townsend endorsed this telegram to Brig. Gen. Alfred H. Terry. "The President gives no special instructions in the matter." AES, *ibid.* On June 14, Terry endorsed this telegram. "Respectfully returned to the Adjutant General of the Army, inviting attention to the enclosed copies of communications written respectively by the Governor of Alabama, and the Hon. R. Busteed, Judge US. District Court, and the report made by Captain Mills, 2nd Infantry, commanding at Montgomery. Captain Mills is an excellent officer, and one in whose judgment I place great reliance. In the event of more troops being required I can send at short notice and have them at Montgomery in ample time." AES, *ibid.* On June 8, Capt. William Mills, 2nd Inf., Montgomery, had written to asst. AG, Dept. of the South. "I have the honor to transmit herewith, a copy of the correspondence to date, between the Governor of Alabama and Judge Busteed U. S. District Judge explanatory of the demand of the Governor for the surrender of U. S. prisoners to the State authorities. It was reported here yesterday that the Governor intended to enforce his demand by force if necessary, and I was notified by the Judge and the United States Marshal, that any such action of the Governor would be resisted with Military aid. I have no idea the Governor will take any such action, if anything of the kind should occur I will advise you by telegraph. I would state that I have seen a telegram sent to the President of the United States by Judge Busteed in which he applies for a strong Military force at this place. I consider I have force enough here to render the Marshal all the aid he will require. I will forward copies of any further correspondence that may take place." Copy, *ibid.* The enclosures are *ibid.* On June 6, Judge Richard Busteed, U.S. District Court, Montgomery, had written to USG transmitting copies of his correspondence with Governor Robert B. Lindsay of Ala. ALS, *ibid.*, RG 60, Letters from the President. On Nov. 2, USG pardoned George Peace, convicted of conspiracy, fined two hundred dollars, and sentenced to three years in prison, "on account of his extreme youth" and recommendations from Lindsay, Busteed, and John A. Minnis, U.S. attorney. Copy, *ibid.*, RG 59, General Records; DS, Gallery of History, Las Vegas, Nev. On Nov. 27, USG pardoned Reuben G. Young, sentenced to ten years in prison with a five thousand dollar fine, because "offences such as his appear to have entirely ceased in his District," and "in consideration of his age, and his feeble health." Copy, DNA, RG 59, General Records.

On Jan. 13, 1873, Silas F. Smith, Syracuse, N. Y., wrote to USG and Attorney Gen. George H. Williams enclosing a clipping that questioned "the expediency of Pardoning the K. Klux Prisoners, imprisoned at Albany." ALS, *ibid.*, RG 60, Letters from the President. The enclosure is *ibid.* On Feb. 17, S. Worthen, Toronto, wrote to USG. "I see by the N. Y. papers that you have pardened some of the KuKlux I presume you considered them exceptional cases I hope you will not grant it to many in the section where I reside (that is) in Rutherford & McDowell Counties North Carolina The bad men holding government mails and some other Offices; with the KuKlux comunity made it anything but A desirable place for A northern man to live. By the arests we got the worst ones away. But I assure you some of the men that hold U. S. Mail offices are desperate characters. Such men as you come in contact with Gen Clingman Judge Merriman and Gov Caldwell are of course good men. But when you come to the rest of the comunity matters are different. And unless punishment folows crime no northern man can stay there. I assure you that I never was in A fight of any kind since A Boy But I have been obliged to resort to pistols knives & Clubs since I have been in North Carolina My worst offence against the KuKlux was that I kept and protected A man that had been hunted by the KuKlux ten days, as he was to testify at Raleigh, against them. Since then evry thing that could be done has been done to injure my business and my character By telling that I kept A negroe woman and that I run away from Canada for burning A Barn. then my duck, were shot in the River; and my Cows were Shot. and Saw & Grist mill was burned, than charged it to us northern men. This was all done before the arests. I am here trying to induce some Setlers down to my place so to make it more comfortable for my family. But if those men should be pardened I dont think there is anything that would induce them to stay. I hear nothing but curses against you and the government among the common class of people. I am quite sure the government have been too lenient with them. I assure you I am A strong goverment man I lost A noble Boy in the U. S. Army; who died at Andersonville My Grandfathers were both Captains in the Revolutionary war agaist England. I could give you by seeing you or by writing considerabl information in regard to the state of the country where I live" ALS, *ibid.*

1. On Aug. 9, 1872, Hiram C. Whiteley, "Chief of the Secret Service Division," had reported to Williams. "I have the honor to acknowledge the receipt of a communication from your Department, under date of the 2d inst., inclosing a copy of a letter from Gerrit Smith, addressed to the President, in relation to those convicts in the Albany Penitentiary who were convicted for violations of the Enforcement act, and requesting me to go to Albany, make a thorough investigation into the condition of those persons, and

report to the Department my views as to the expediency of exercising Executive clemency in regard to any of them. . . . The prisoners were mainly frank and communicative. Some of them are very poor and unlearned, and have left large families behind them, and while acknowledging that they were members of the various orders of the organization known under the general head of Kuklux Klan, and that they had been justly sentenced as such, plead in extenuation that they had joined the Order without a full knowledge of its aims and objects, and had been incited to deeds of violence by their leaders, who had managed to escape from the country, leaving them to bear the responsibility and the punishment of their misdeeds. A number of them stated that they had been compelled to join the Order to save themselves and families from a visitation of the Klan. Others had entered into its ranks under the supposition that it was a society organized for mutual protection, but learned subsequently that its real designs were the extermination of the negro race and the driving out of such of the whites as were in favor of the political equality and social elevation of the blacks. These severally expressed the heartiest contrition for their misdeeds, stated that the organization was one inimical to the best interests of society, and that the Government was fully justified in breaking it up. . . ." *New York Times,* Aug. 14, 1872.

To Lucius S. Felt

Long Branch, N. J.
Aug. 23d /72

My Dear Mr. Felt.

I am in receipt of your letter of the 16th inst. *enclosing me ~~the~~ notice of the expiration of the insurence on my house in Galena.* I enclose check to you for amount required for renewel and will ask of you the favor to attend to it for me. *After the 5th of Nov. I will be able to say whether I shall ask you also to superintend repairs to the house preparitory to its occupation four months later.*

Please present Mrs. Grant's and my kindest regards to Mrs. Felt and family. We were in hope of seeing some of you this way this summer.

Yours Truly
U. S. Grant

ALS, James F. Ruddy, Rancho Mirage, Calif. On Jan. 20, 1872, Orville E. Babcock had written to Lucius S. Felt, Galena. "Your letter with $1300. to the President came to him in due time. He requests me to send many thanks for your kindness. He will be pleased to have you pay his taxes and draw on him for the same. The family are all well. Mrs. Babcock joins me in sending regards to Mrs. Felt and the other friends in Galena." Copy,

DLC-USG, II, 1. On Dec. 18, 1875, Levi P. Luckey wrote to Felt. "The President directs me to enclose his check for $276 80/100 and he wishes me to say that the letter of Nov. 20th must have been entirely overlooked in some way and he regrets that the matter was not attended to until after the receipt of your letter of the 6th inst." Copy, *ibid.*, II, 3. See *PUSG*, 19, 276–77.

To Hamilton Fish

Long Branch, N. J.
Aug. 24th 1872

Dear Governor:

I did not inform you when I intended leaving for Washington the last time because I did not know of anything requiring your presence there, and did not want to take you from home unnecessarily. I shall go again next week and although I do not think of anything requiring your presence, I will telegraph you as soon as I determine upon the time of leaving. I received your note reciting a paragraph from a private letter from Bancroft Davis. I was not much surprised—would not wonder if the whole case, except the Alabama, went against us. Would we not be better off if it did? We do not want to be bound by to strict rules as neutrals.[1]

Mrs. Grant and I would be very much pleased to have a visit from Mrs. Fish, yourself and Miss Edith any time after the first of Sept. All the company who have accepted invitations will be away by that time.

Yours Truly
U. S. Grant

Hon. Hamilton Fish
Sec. of State

P. S. The Brazilian Minister[2] called on me yesterday with the Duke of Saxe[3] & his brother, but introduced them so indistinctly that I was not aware of who they were until after they left. Your letter of the 21st had not reached me yet, or at least I had opened the mail in which it came. I however afterward sent invitations to the Minister, ~~and~~ Duke & brother to dine with me in the evening. Hav-

ing an engagement in Phila they declined.—The Duke expressed a
desire to stop over a day or two—on the plains somewhere and
wished a letter to Gen. Sheridan to secure him proper attention.
Will you be kind enough to write him a letter of introduction and
send it direct to Gen. S. or give it to the Duke while he is at West
Point on $Monday next.

U. S. G.

ALS, DLC-Hamilton Fish. On Aug. 19 and 26, 1872, Secretary of State Hamilton Fish,
Garrison, N. Y., wrote to USG. "I did not know of your intention to be in Washington
on Friday, or I should have gone—although I must confess that it would have been at
some sacrifice, as I was not well. Enclosed I send a letter received from Judge Read.—
Govr Curtin may be expected here within a week or two, & the Judge's letter is important as suggesting Curtin's position, & what he wants. It is important to secure him—
the October election in Pennsylvania, if carried for the Republican ticket, will make
easy work throughout the Country, in November—On Saturday I received a telegram
from Mr Davis, from Geneva, saying 'Adam's lead off of this morning in opinion relieving
England from liability in "Georgia"—Cockburn and neutral Arbitrators accepted his
opinion without discussion and decided the case against us.' The Arbitrators have requested the strictest confidence to be observed with regard to their proceedings until they
make an official announcement—In a second letter Mr Davis expresses the opinion that a
conclusion will be reached by the Tribunal by the middle of September—The depredations committed by the 'Georgia' were less extensive than those of either of the Cruisers
fitted out in England—her career was *comparatively* short—but she did a large amount
of damage, and I cannot understand the ground on which Mr Adams has given the opinion in favour of England, in the case of the Georgia—I thought it as bad as any—"
"Telegrams from Mr Davis state that the Tribunal has substantially decided in our favour
in the cases of the Alabama, the Florida and of the Shenandoah after she left Melbourne.
The great amount of destruction by the Shenandoah was after she left Melbourne. Davis
also says that the Tribunal will probably proceed immediately to the question of 'charges.'
I infer that this means, of an estimate of amount of damages—Will you have the good-
ness to let me know when you expect again to go to Washington—The nomination of
Dix in this State, will, I think greatly help us, except perhaps in Westchester, where
Robertson's friends are disappointed. The 'Times' irritated them unnecessarily, & they
are cross—" ALS (press), *ibid.* On Sept. 14, the Geneva tribunal awarded the U.S.
$15.5 million for damages caused by the *Alabama, Florida,* and *Shenandoah.* See Nevins,
Fish, pp. 552–66; Adrian Cook, *The Alabama Claims: American Politics and Anglo-
American Relations, 1865–1872* (Ithaca, N. Y., 1975), pp. 233–40.
    On Sept. 23, Robert Marsden Latham, president, Labour Representation League,
et al., London, wrote to USG. "We have the honour to forward you the accompanying
copy of a resolution passed unanimously on Friday evening last at a meeting of this
League—a society representing a large number of the artizans of this country and whose
prospectus we enclose—" DS (3 signatures), DNA, RG 59, Miscellaneous Letters. The
resolution expressed the League's "approval of the Geneva Award without however expressing any opinion as to the equity of the amount awarded in a merely commercial point
of view—. . ." *Ibid.* The enclosure is *ibid.*

1. Interviewed at Long Branch on July 17, USG discussed the indirect claims. "... It is of greater importance to the United States than to any other country in the world that the rights and duties of neutrals shall be distinctly ascertained and definitely settled, and settled precisely as they have just been. ... We will be the neutrals in the next war and for all the future, and it might be England's turn, if that declaration had not been made by the Geneva Conference, to present us with a long bill for indirect damages inflicted on her commerce and power by privateers escaped from our ports without the knowledge or consent of this government. ..." *New York Herald,* July 18, 1872.

2. On Oct. 9, 1871, Fish had written in his diary. "Present to the President Counsellor Borges—E. E & Min Plen from Brazil, who presents his credentials & the letter, of recall of Mr Magalhaens   After the presentation & the formal ~~replies~~ addresses, the President, in conversation, introduced the subject of Paraguay—enquired into its condition—referred to its depopulation of males inhabitants, & ~~its~~ the importance of quiet, & of exemption from unnecessary burdens, for the restoration of its means & the development of its commercial & agricultural interests; & expressed the interest of this Govt & people in its future success & prosperity, & coupled its interests with the policy of ~~the~~ Brazil & the Argentine Republic—" DLC-Hamilton Fish. See *PUSG,* 19, 154; *ibid.,* 20, 144.

3. Born in 1845 into the ruling family of Saxe-Coburg-Gotha, Prince Ludwig August, Duke of Saxony, had married Princess Leopoldina, daughter of Emperor Pedro II of Brazil, in 1864. See Fish diary, Aug. 20, 21, 1872; *New York Times,* Aug. 24, 1872.

To John A. Dix

Long Branch, N. J.
Aug. 24th 1872.

MY DEAR GENERAL.

I congratulate you upon the unanimity and enthusiasm of the Utica Convention on the occasion of your nomination for the honorable and responsible position of Governor of the great state of New York. Specially do I congratulate the citizens of that state, almost irrespective of party, upon your nomination. I believe you will receive the active support of the great majority of the best people of the state, and the secret sympathy of thousands who may be so bound up by party ties and pledges as to force them to support your opponent.

There can be no doubt about your election. With it will necessarily follow reforms in the state which all acknowledge have been much needed for years.

No one acquainted with the political history of New York for the last eight years will claim that all the abuses of legislation are due to democratic rule but members, or at least pretended members, of both political parties share the responsibility of them.

When I read the proceedings of the convention of the 21st inst. and of the unanimity of feeling in favor of you, and your associates on the state ticket, I felt that victory and reform had been inaugurated in the state of New York.

Again I congratulate you, not upon the prospect of being Governor but upon having it within your reach to render such service to your state.

It is a happy day when Conventions seek Candidates, not Candidates nominations. This dream has been realized in the action of the convention of the 21st inst. at Utica New York.

> I have the honor to be General
> Your very obt. svt.
> U. S. GRANT

GEN. JOHN A. DIX.
NEW YORK CITY.

ALS, Columbia University, New York, N. Y. On Aug. 29, 1872, John A. Dix, West Hampton, N. Y., wrote to USG. "I am very thankful to you, for your kind letter of congratulation on my nomination for the office of Governor of this state. You are, no doubt, aware that I declined it before the Convention was held. I am deeply sensible of the honor conferred on me, especially by the manner, in which it was tendered. But my objections to the acceptance of the nomination are so strong that I would not think of it a moment were it not for the deep concern I feel in the result of the election and the great public interests at stake.—I expect Mrs. Dix to arrive from Europe on the 2nd or 3rd prox. and as soon as I can confer with her, I shall reply to the letter of the President of the Convention advising me of my nomination." ALS, USG 3. See Henry Clews, *Fifty Years in Wall Street* (New York, 1908), pp. 304–305.

On Nov. 29, Dix, New York City, wrote to USG. "I have waited for the official canvass of the votes given in this state at the late election to Congratulate you on the triumphant majority you have obtained—53,525. When last I had the pleasure of seeing you and we were speaking of the extraordinary appeal of Governor Seymour to his political friends to vote for Mr. Kernan because he was a Roman Catholic, I remember you said it was a two-edged sword and that the gain would be more than compensated by the loss of Protestant votes. Your prediction is verified; and I think the difference, which is inconsiderable, between your vote & mine, is to be accounted for from this cause. O'Brien, who was expected to sustain you, had his name associated with Mr. Greeley's where-ever he thought he could gain votes for himself. I do not think we need regret that he did so, for he has no claim on us; and he might, if he had acted in good faith, have been trouble-some.—In your letter from Long Branch regarding my nomination and in mine accepting it, we put the issue of the election in this State on the ground of political reform. I regard the strong expression in your favor, as well as mine, to be an acceptance of the issue by the people; and it will give me great pleasure to sustain you in any measures to carry out the popular will in this respect by conforming to it in my administration of the affairs of this state." ALS, DLC-USG. See *PUSG*, 19, 85.

To Elihu B. Washburne

Long Branch, N. J.
Aug. 26th 1872

DEAR WASHBURNE,

Your confidential letter relating to the probable position of Curtin was received during my last visit to Washington He, Curtin, probably arrived in New York City yesterday, Sunday: but there is no communication between this and the outside world on Sunday except by telegraph, so that I do not know positively. I expect him to come and see me as soon as he does arrive, though I know he will be met on arrival and everything possible will be offered him to corrupt him. The Greeleyites will be as liberal in their offers to him as Satan was to our Savior, and with as little ability to pay.—Curtins defection would probably cost us the state of Penna in October, so far as the Govr and legislature is concerned; but without him the Congressmen, at large, three of them, and Judge of the Superior Court and other officers on the State ticket would be elected, and we would carry the State in November. I do not often indulge in predictions, but I have had a feeling that Greeley might not even be in the field in Nov. If he is I do not think he will carry a single Northern State. In the South I give him Tennessee & Texas with Va W. Va Md. Ky. Ga. Fla. & Ark. doubtful, with the chances in our favor in all of them except Md. Mo. might also be added to the doubtful states. This is the way matters look now but they may be modified before Nov.[1] We "shall see what we shall see" before long.

Fred is at home much pleased with his trip to Europe. Nellie writes every week giving glowing accounts of her trip. She will return in October. Buck writes cheerfully but he has not seen much of the country nor is he likely to.

The opposition in this canvass seem to have no capital but slander, abuse and falsehood. Some of the campaigners have come to grief already. Doolittle[2] & Killpatrick[3] for instance. They have learned that people who live in glass houses should never throw stones. The saintly Trumbull & Schurz ought to see the same thing; but their hides are thick and their impudence is sublime.—Poor old Sumner is sick from neglect and the consciousness that he is not all of the republican party. I very much doubt whether he will ever get to Washington again. If he is not crazy his mind is at least so effected as to disqualify him for the proper discharge of his duties as Senator.[4]

Please give Mrs. Grants and my best regards to Mrs. Washburne and the children.

Very Truly Yours

U. S. GRANT

ALS, IHi. On July 24, 1872, Elihu B. Washburne, Boulogne-sur-Mer, France, had written to USG. "[Co]nfidential . . . I was at Carlsbad for three weeks taking the waters & Mrs. W. was with me. As I could not stay out of France any longer the Dr. sent me here for my 'after Cure,' as they call it, leaving Mrs. W. at C. to finish her full cure. I received Luckey's despatch at Carlsbad. Curtin had all sorts of delays in getting away from St. Petersburg, and only arrived at London a week or ten days ago. He promised to come over here to see me, but as he was likely to be delayed some on account of treatment to his eyes, I concluded to run over to see him. I therefore went over *incognito* last Saturday and hid myself away in the suburbs in the rooms of McKean who is now living in L. I had many long and confidential interviews with the Gov. and the result sums up about this, that, while he remains true to the party and should vote for Grant & Wilson he feared that the State politics had got into such a situation that he had no power to change things—that Cameron had waged such a relentless warfare on everybody in the party who would not bow down to him that there was the greatest disposition on the part of vast numbers of the best republicans in the State to let the State ticket go by the board and to devote themselves to electing an anti-Cameron legislature—that Cameron, by his position in the Senate, controlled the patronage of the State, and no matter how good a Grant man and republican a man might be, yet if he was not a Cameron man he was marked for Slaughter. Hence so many republicans were determined to rid themselves of such a tyrannous control—that under his dictation there was no future for them in the republican party—that if he were to have control in future as in the past that he and all his friends were to be utterly proscribed. That Cameron tried to have his appointment recalled after it was made—that he had done all in his power to prejudice you and Fish against him and to Crown all, had put himself, as chairman of Foreign Relations, in Communication with Catacazy to get him to write to Russia to attack him before the Russian Government, which he did. That Cameron had so operated, on Fish, as to cause him to treat him with great indifference, paying no attention whatever to either his official despatches or private letters; and he is not certain that he would not have been recalled had he not resigned. Such is the situation. I may say to *you*, General, what I will admit to no one else. I am not without great alarm as to the situation at home   If I were at home and mixed up with excitements of the canvass, I might feel differently, but out of the reach of the thing, with little to do and reading most of our leading papers, with my anxieties for the success of the party and the prosperity and happiness of the country and the intense interest I feel in your personal triumph, I confess to great uneasiness. As I wrote you, that in my judgment Pennsylvania is the battle ground, and there is where the whole force of the campaign should be brought, and in such a campaign I would adopt that maxim of war of the Great Napoleon—'that nothing is done, while anything remains undone.' I know the strength, the power, the magnetic force which Curtin has in the State. I know how much he did for us in 1868 and how much he can do for us now. In this crisis I want to see him actively, earnestly, enthusiastically for us. I have talked to him confidentially and discreetly and have urged him to go home. He has consented to do so and will leave at the earliest moment he can get a passage. He will visit you at once and explain his views of the situation in the State and what he thinks can be done to save it. I have assured him that you will cordially receive him and will co operate with his views so far as you find them practicable. I have no doubt you can fully conciliate him and all his friends and get their support for the ticket. I should not even despair of Forney, for he is a very placable man. If we can get our party united by the first of September with the men brought back to us who have been driven off, with the forces which the National Committee should send into the State, I believe we can take it in October. Your *personal* influence with Curtin, Forney and others can do more than all else. You may have to take personal Command in the campaign and your head quarters ought to be at Washington. Of course once people are fully alive I am confident that we will have the 'first blood' in North Carolina in a week from to-morrow and that will do good. The battle in Illinois for November ought to be fought in Penn. before the October election. Dick Oglesby, Jack Logan Steve Hurlbut, Bob Ingersoll ought to spend a month in Pa. If we carry that State in October our Illinois election will run itself after that. All my friends write me not to come home to be part of this Canvass, because I could do no good and might only subject me to attacks as being away from my post. But I intend to go home in season to put in a vote for you. I shall hope to meet you in Galena on the day of the election. That is the place to get *good returns.* Excuse this long letter; read and destroy . . ." ALS (press), DLC-Elihu B. Washburne. On July 21, Levi P. Luckey had written to Washburne. ". . . Pennsylvania is placed in a peculiar position by the party quarrels, and Forney is trying to lose the election for us in Oct. I guess. He is a sorehead anyway. The work has not commenced in earnest & I suppose will not till after the N. C. election, though the National Com. is getting everything in good order & will make an earnest fight. One of our friends went to London confidentially to meet Curtin & forestall any plans of the other side in that direction, & telegraphed yesterday that it was all right. I presume Gov. Curtin can exert a great influence as his friends, many of them, are making most of the trouble. . . ." ALS, *ibid.* In 1872, U.S. Senator John A. Logan of Ill., Chicago, wrote to USG. "The political aspect here is brightening. Our majority in this state will be large if the October elections go for us. We will win anyhow, but we may lose the Legislature." William Evarts Benjamin, Catalogue No. 42, March, 1892, p. 14.

On June 15, Washburne, Paris, had written to USG. "*Private. . . .* There are electoral votes—366. Necessary for a choice 184. Please look at this calculation. *certain for Grant.* Arkansas 6 California 6 Connecticut 6 Florida 4 Illinois 21 Iowa 11 Kansas 5 Louisiana 8 Maine 7 Massachusetts 13 Michigan 11 Mississippi 8 Minnesota 5 Nebraska 3 N. Hampshire 5 N. Carolina 10 Ohio 22 Oregon 3 R. Island 4 S. Carolina 7 Vermont 5 Wisconsin 10   Total 180   *Probable opposition.* Alabama 10 Delaware 3 Georgia 11 Indiana 15 Kentucky 12 Maryland 8 Missouri 15 Nevada 3 N Jersey 9 N. York 35 Tennessee 12 Texas 8 Virginia 11 West Virginia 5   Total 157   For Grant 180—wanting four votes For opposition 157   For Pennsylvania 29   Total vote 366   You will see that I have not included Pennsylvania in this calculation. I have put Indiana and N. Y. in the opposition column. We only carried Indiana at the October election in 1868 (which was the test election) by less than _ thousand majority, and we have lost the State since. I am afraid, therefore, that we will be obliged to concede the State to the opposition. As to N. Y. I have little faith in carrying it, as there will be a complete coalition between two of the most corrupt elements ever known in politics—the Tammanites and the Greeleyites. I, therefore, consider Pennsylvania the key of our position. We only carried the State in October 1868 by less than 10.000 majority and at a time when we were all united and enthusiastic, and then only by Super human exertions. Now, at this distance, I dont like the looks of things there. There seems to be a deep seated disaffection at our nomination for Governor and several prominent republican papers are said to be openly opposing him. Buckalew is a strong candidate for the opposition. It is a most dangerous and fatal assumption that we can lose our Governor in October and carry the State for you in November. I dont know what can be done in that State. I see Forney is demanding a new ticket, but the Cameron influence which nominated Hartranft will not consent to that. I see that is charged that Cameron wants to drive all the prominent men, opposed to him out of the party. I think our wise and controlling men in the party should address themselves with great earnestness to the Pennsylvania situation. It is my deliberate judgment that if we lose the State in October we lose the Presidential election. Being on the spot and fully posted you may find things very different from what they appear to me from this distance. But every effort ought to be made for harmony and conciliation. When I saw Gov. Curtin in Nice last winter he was very friendly and said he should resign to go home to take the stump for the party. I learn that he has since received a letter from Mr. Fish complaining of his action in the Catacazy matter which has made him very sore. He thinks, however, that you have never seen the correspondence and know nothing about it. We ought to have the Governor earnestly with us in the campaign for he is a power in the State—very popular with the soldiers and a great stumper. I have no reason to suppose he is going to join the soreheads, but I could wish him enthusiastically engaged in the canvass. While he gave up the Russian Mission, as being out of the world, I have no doubt he would next year like some other European mission, say Berlin. This is, however, only guess work, for I have not talked with him on the subject. It is, perhaps, a matter worthy of consideration. I shall see him when he comes from St. Petersburg, but it will be before I could get a letter from you on this subject, even if you supposed it worth while writing about. Should you think it desirable that I should assure him of your friendship and confidence in the sense in which I have written, you might have Mr. Luckey telegraph me simply the word, 'yes,' which I should understand. You may consider me unduly anxious and not justified by the political situation at home.

If so, I know you will excuse me, and in any event tear up this letter and consider its contents as strictly confidential." ALS (press, tabular material expanded), DLC-Elihu B. Washburne. See Speech, April 30, 1872; William E. Chandler to Washburne, Aug. 16, 26, 29, 1872, DLC-Elihu B. Washburne; *New York Times*, Oct. 10, 29, 1872.

On Sept. 16, Frederick T. Dent wrote to Henry H. Bingham, postmaster, Philadelphia. "Do you get the last cash—you know what I mean. There is treachery in the camp somewhere and the President says he thinks Pennsylvania is lost. Work, man, work. Money you can have all you want only work." The Jenkins Co., Catalogue 208, r.o. 250. On Oct. 8, 10:00 P.M., U.S. Senator Simon Cameron of Pa., Harrisburg, telegraphed to USG. "We are going over last year in nearly every part of the State, and the majority can not be less than 20,000." *Washington Chronicle,* Oct. 9, 1872. On the same day, 10:45 P.M., James D. Cameron, Harrisburg, telegraphed to USG. "This city gives Hartranft 700 majority, a gain of 750 over Geary in 1869. The majority in this county will be over 2,000. The tidal wave is moving." *Ibid.* Also on Oct. 8, J. Gillingham Fell, Philadelphia, telegraphed to USG. "The Union League of Philadelphia congratulates the President on Pennsylvania's glorious victory. General Hartranft carries Philadelphia by about 20,000 majority, and the returns from all parts of the State show large Republican gains. The Republican party is stronger than ever by reason of the few defections that have rallied the masses to the full performance of their duty." *Ibid.*

1. See letter to Elihu B. Washburne, Oct. 25, 1872.

2. James R. Doolittle served in the U.S. Senate from Wis. as a Republican (1857–69), but supported Horatio Seymour in 1868. As Democratic candidate for Wis. governor in 1871, Doolittle lost to Cadwallader C. Washburn. See *New York Times*, Aug. 15, 16, 21, 1872.

3. On April 15, 1872, former gens. Henry A. Barnum, Judson Kilpatrick, and William F. Bartlett, Washington, D. C., had written to Lewis Wallace, Crawfordsville, Ind. "The undersigned have conferred with many representative veterans of the late war and find a general concurrence of opinion that they should raise their voice in protest against the further progress of the alarming disintegration of the Republican Party which has taken place under the administration of General Grant. To effect this the names of representative veterans of the several States who hold these views are desired for the purpose of being appended to a call a national convention of soldiers & sailors to be held in New York city some time in May proximo, which convention shall formally, by resolution or otherwise, call upon the Phila. Convention to nominate a candidate for President other than Grant, and one who will unite the party and lead it to victory. If you concur in this movement please so inform us by letter within a few days, and also give us the names of other representative veterans which we may be at liberty to likewise use" LS, USG 3. On April 24, Wallace wrote to Horace Porter. "I enclose you a letter recd yesterday, which will speak for itself. As ~~the~~ it does not appear confidential, I thought best to let you know what is going on. I'm not so sure but it is more important to one in the President's position to know his enemies than his friends. What is the matter with Kilpatrick? . . . I answered the letter. See copy enclosed." ALS (ellipses in original), *ibid.* Porter drafted a reply. "Recd—thank,   The letter of Barnum Kilpatrick &c has since been published as you have doubtless seen,   after Such responses as yours I think that convention will not be held" ADf (undated), *ibid.* See *New York Times*, Aug. 8, 19, 1872.

On Aug. 30, Luckey wrote to Washburne. ". . . Everything has worked against the Greeley party so far. The elections in N. H., Conn, Oregon, N. C., and W. Va. have given them no encouragement. They expected Schurz could carry the German vote, & he cannot do it. They depended upon Sumner to control the Negro vote; and as the boy says, it don't control worth a cent. Sumner was so cut by his old republican friends & followers in Boston upon his return there a short time since, that it made him sick in bed. He was surrounded by the bummers he has always despised, & congratulated upon the course he had taken. It was too much for him. Greeley made himself ridiculous during his trip through New England. Gratz Brown's visit to New Haven was a very bad investment. Doolittle and Kilpatrick have been stumping for them in New England, & the N. Y. Times has shut them up. . . ." ALS, DLC-Elihu B. Washburne.

    4. See letter to Thomas Settle *et al.*, June 10, 1872; David Donald, *Charles Sumner and the Rights of Man* (New York, 1970), pp. 554–55.

To J. Russell Jones

Long Branch, N. J.
Sept. 5th 1872.

DEAR JONES;

    I enclose you some papers which explain themselves. It looks to me like a "blackmailing" opperation. I have made no answer to the man nor will I until I hear from you.[1]

    I see by your last letter, just received, that you are quite uneasy about the result of the election. There has been no time from the Baltimore Convention to this when I have felt the least anxiety. The Soreheads & thieves who have deserted the republican party have strengthened it by their departure. If the election was now Greeley would ~~probably~~ carry Tennessee & Texas, and probably Maryland, West Va Geo. & Ark. & Florida doubtful with the chances in his favor; Va. Ala. Ky. & Mo. somewhat doubtful with the chances largely in our favor. Whether Greeley will get any state in Nov. depends upon ~~the~~ no changes ~~that may take place~~ for the worse between now and then. The few Greeley republicans buzzed like so many Musquetoes immediately after the nomination, giving the impression to the hearer that there was a great many more of them than there was. There was to much time between nomination and election to keep it up.

    Give my kindest regards to Mrs. Jones and the children.

Yours Truly
U. S. GRANT

ALS, H. Bartholomew Cox, Oxen Hill, Md. On Oct. 14, 1872, Horace Porter wrote to Secretary of State Hamilton Fish. "The President wishes me to say that Jones, at Brussels, is anxious to come home to vote, provided he can obtain a leave to do so without loss of pay. The President would be glad to have his wishes complied with if it can be done without violating the law, as he has probably used up his leave for the year. If you will advise me I can telegraph him in a manner which he suggests, and which will be understood by him only." ALS, DLC-Hamilton Fish. On the same day, Fish wrote to Porter. "There is no difficulty in granting *leave of absence* to Mr Jones—but the Statute . . . provides that no Diplomatic Officer shall receive salary for the time during which he may be absent from his post (by leave or otherwise) beyond the time of sixty days in any one year—*but* it also allows the time equal to that usually occupied in going to & from the U. S, *in case of return on leave* in addition to the sixty days—. . ." ALS, Babcock Papers, ICN. On [Nov. 6, 1872], J. Russell Jones, minister to Belgium, "White House, Wednesday morning *1 o clock,*" wrote to his wife Elizabeth S. Jones. ". . . It is peculiarly gratifying to me, of course to receive such a cordial welcome—nearly all the Members of the Cabinet have been here this eve'g, & all seemed to know all about me—though I had never seen many of them—It appears the Prest has read my letters ~~to him~~ *at Cabinet meetings*!! He is unchanged. He & Mrs Grant kissed Rosie, & seemed real glad to see her. It was peculiarly clever in him (the Pres't) to send Babcock to N. York to meet me—Everybody on board the ship stared when they saw a Govt. vessel come out & take us off. There are a dozen or more men, & as many ladies here now as I write, and I cannot of course write much—but know I shall not have a moment tomorrow—Kiss all the children for me . . . P. S. Wednesday AM 10. OC.   all right this morning—The result is a perfect Waterloo—The Prest is going to Cin day after tomorrow & has invited [u]s to go with him. Think we shall do so." ALS, ICHi. See George R. Jones, *Joseph Russell Jones* (Chicago, 1964), pp. 71–73.

On Sept. 26, Orville E. Babcock had written to William E. Chandler, New York City. ". . . I send you a check for $500—our Minister to Brussels J R. Jones. sent me $500 some time since—with authority to give to the committee. and I gave it to Senator Chandler. He soon after authorized me to draw on a friend of his in Chicago for $500—if I thought he should pay it. I have drawn the money and think you need it so send it—will you please acknowledge receipt to Hon J R Jones U S Minister Brussels Belgium. In addition to the $1000 Jones has helped the *boys* in Chicago—he is a brick,   I am sorry your committee is in such a bad way financially and I think it is too bad you have to ~~have~~ be annoyed in this matter and hope it will be all right in the end—. . ." ALS, DLC-William E. Chandler.

1. On July 30, 1872, Secretary of the Interior Columbus Delano had written to USG. "I have the honor to return herewith a letter addressed to you on the 22d instant by Eric U. Norberg, of Toulon Illinois, and referred to this Department. It appears to have no reference to public lands, but relates to a private matter, concerning a tract of land near Chicago, that has been conveyed to you. The subject would appear to require your personal attention or that of some competent attorney near the land described." Copy, DNA, RG 48, Lands and Railroads Div., Letters Sent. On Aug. 30, Jones, Brussels, wrote to Babcock. "I have yours of the 15th inst., inclosing a communication to the President from Mr. NORBERG, of Toulon, Ill., in regard to some land purchased by me in 1866 from the Bishop Hill Colony. The facts in regard to the matter are as follows: In Dec., 1866, Mr. P. MUNSON, then my Deputy Marshal, purchased of the Bishop Hill Colony fifty-two acres in section 15, town 39, at about $150 per acre, being an undivided half of a tract of one hundred and four acres, the other half belonging to Mr. B. F. SHERMAN, an old resi-

dent of Chicago and a large real-estate owner. The fifty-two acres were divided equally between Mr. MUNSON and myself, and I let Gen. JOHN E. SMITH have half of my twenty-six acres at just what I paid for it. In January, 1869, I bought SHERMAN's undivided half, together with ten acres he owned in the same section, making sixty-two acres purchased of SHERMAN, for which I paid him $350 per acre, and it was this latter purchase of sixty-two acres from SHERMAN which I divided with Gen. GRANT, who has nothing whatever to do with the purchase from the Bishop Hill Colony. On the 12th of January, 1869, I charged Gen. GRANT on my books with $10,850 62 for 30 955-1000 acres, and March 16, 1869, with $291 22 for interest and other expenses and assessments, and drew on him in favor of N. CORNISH [*Corwith*], who collected the draft through Coolbaugh's Bank for $11.141 84. When I left home, Mr. MUNSON still retained the twenty-six acres, and I presume owns it; if so, the fifty-two acres purchased of the Bishop Hill Colony is now owned by MUNSON, Gen. SMITH and myself." *New York Times*, Sept. 16, 1872. On Sept. 4, Babcock wrote to Eric U. Norberg. "Your letter of the 28th ult: is received and will be forwarded to the President. Your other letter was also received, and as I supposed, was acknowledged at the time. The President directed me to forward the letter to Mr. Jones, which I did." Copy, DLC-USG, II, 1. On Sept. 21, Jones wrote "*To the Editor of the New-York Tribune.*" "My attention has been called to an article in your paper of the 3d inst., in regard to what you call a grave accusation made in the Chicago *Tribune* 'against the personal and official integrity of the President in the matter of the Swedish Colony lands' and with which my name is connected. I had seen the original article in the Chicago *Tribune*, but so long as the publication of the libel was confined to that paper and in a part of the country where its infamous character is so well known, I did not think it necessary to pay any attention to it. But as you see fit to give the calumny the wide publicity of your journal, I deem it but just to the President to notice it. The suggestion and inuendo are that the President accepted from me a deed for a valuable piece of ground in Chicago for the nominal compensation of one dollar; that I had 'obtained this land in an alleged illegal manner from the Trustee of the Swedish colonists who owned it;' and is further added that the suspicious character of the transaction is that I was appointed Minister to Belgium 'about the same time.' What is charged, or intended to be conveyed by the article, is—1. That I gave a tract of land to the President of the United States for a nominal consideration. 2. That this tract of land was illegally obtained from the Trustee of the Swedish colonists, who owned it; and, 3. That the transaction was 'about the same time' that I was appointed Minister to Belgium, and the insinuation is that my appointment was in consideration of my transfer of the said tract of land to the President. Now I ask space in your columns to denounce each of these charges and insinuations as utterly false and atrocious, and a willful and malicious libel on the President. There was a land transaction between Gen. Grant and myself in December, 1868, or early in January, 1869, before he became President, the circumstances of which were as follows: In December, 1868, I wrote to Mr. B. F. Sherman, for many years a resident of Chicago, though at that time residing at Buffalo, N. Y., to ascertain what he would take for the sixty-two acres of land he owned in section fifteen west of the Chicago City limits, and received a letter from him saying he would sell at $350 per acre. I telegraphed him accepting his proposition, and just as I was sending off the telegram, Gen. Grant came into my office and I told him about the purchase I was making. He asked me if I did not want a partner, to which I replied that I would gladly let him have a half interest in the purchase, and that he could pay me when he sold his house in Washington, and it was then agreed that if I got the land he should have thirty-one acres at $350 per acre. Mr. Sherman, on receipt of my telegram, came to Chicago, and the matter was closed and the money paid him on the 12th of January, 1869, and on that day I charged Gen. Grant on my books with $10,850 for thirty-one acres at $350 per acre. On the 9th of March, 1869, I charged him with $28 21 for his portion of a fee paid Mr. George Scoville, an attorney of Chicago, who examined the title, and on the 16th of the same month I charged him with $70 99 for an assessment which had been made on the land for park purposes, and with $192 64 for interest on $10,850, from Jan. 12 to March 16, '69, and drew on him March 16, '69, for $11,141 84 in favor of Mr. Nathan Corwith, of Chicago, who collected the draft through the banking-house of Mr. W. F. Coolbaugh. Both Mr. Corwith and Mr. Coolbaugh will gladly verify the fact that the draft was paid (on presentation in Washington) by President Grant. At the time this transaction took place both Gen. Grant and myself supposed that the land would probably be sold within a short time, and it was agreed that the title should remain in me until a sale was made, when I should account to him for his share of the profits, and it was only when I determined to come abroad to remain for an indefinite time that I decided to quit-claim to him an undivided half of the sixty-two acres. . . ." *New York Times*, Oct. 12, 1872. See *ibid.*, Sept. 7–8, 1872; *PUSG*, 19, 110; Jones, *Joseph Russell Jones*, pp. 68–70.

To Shadford Easton

Long Branch, N. J.
Sept. 7th 1872

MY DEAR MR. EASTON,

Your letter of Sept. 4th tendering your resignation of the office of Special Agt. of the P. O. Dept. is received, with your reasons therefor. Please allow me to ask you to reconsider. I regret that my father should in any way interfere with the management of the office and will ask him to desist and send in his resignation. He can never be fit to take charge of the office again.

Very Truly Yours
U. S. GRANT

ALS, James F. Ruddy, Rancho Mirage, Calif. Shadford Easton, listed as a merchant in the 1871 Covington, Ky., city directory, was appointed special agent at the Covington post office as of Jan. 24, 1872. See *PUSG*, 22, 147. According to Easton, Jesse Root Grant had written to USG recommending Easton's appointment. A Nov. 23, 1872, altercation between Easton and Grant led to the publication of USG's letter. *Cincinnati Commercial*, Nov. 25, 1872.

On March 1, Easton, Covington, had written to USG asking an army commission for his nephew, George S. Easton. ALS, DNA, RG 94, Applications for Positions in War Dept. On Sept. 27, George Easton, Cincinnati, wrote to USG on the same subject. ALS, *ibid.*, ACP, 5110 1872. No appointment followed.

To L. Edwin Dudley

Long Branch, N. J.
Sept. 9th 1872

COL. L. E. DUDLEY,
SEC. SOLDIERS VET. NAT. COM.
DEAR SIR:

I am in receipt of your letter of the 4th inst. extending to me, by your Committee, a pressing invitation to attend the Grand Mass Convention of Veteran Soldiers, to be held in the City of Pittsburg on the 17th inst.

My desire to attend and meet again so many old companions in arms is very great. But my judgement tells me to leave the celebration entirely to those whose motives cannot be misunderstood.

I know of no class of citizens better entitled to meet in Convention, and to have weight accorded their views on all national matters there expressed, than the Veteran Soldiers who risked their lives for the honor and perpetuity of their Country. I am sure your councils will be marked by wisdom and patriotism, and that the meeting of so many comrades will be a joyous and an advantageous one.

I wish for you all that you expect from your meeting of the 17th inst. and only regret that I cannot be with you on that occasion.

With great respect,
your obt. svt.
U. S. GRANT

ALS, William N. Dearborn, Nashville, Tenn. See *PUSG*, 16, 479, 547–48.

On Dec. 5, 1872, USG nominated L. Edwin Dudley as superintendent of Indian affairs, New Mexico Territory. On June 24, 1874, Dudley, Santa Fé, telegraphed to USG. "*Personal* Congress abolished my office Please remember me for some other place army pay master if possible." Telegram received, DLC–USG, IB. No appointment followed.

To George H. Stuart

Washington D. C. Sept. 11th *1872*

MY DEAR MR. STUART,

Your dispatch of Sept. 4th asking if Maj. Hodges might not be pardoned under the circumstances of his extreme suffering in health was duly received. I should have answered it but I received another from you the following morning saying that the report of his ill health was a mistake. I was really very much relieved on the receipt of the second dispatch. Under all the circumstances I could not have pardoned Maj. Hodges, and it is unpleasant to deny such a request where the prisoner is seriously suffering in health and has a family of such respectability suffering outside.

I hope your own health is improving by your Summer vacation and visit to the Springs.[1] So far I have been blessed with a constitution that has stood all climates and other strains upon it without any yielding. The severest test I have had to undergo has been slanderous and false abuse with hands and tongue tied. I do hope this mode of warfare will soon end.

With kindest regards to Mrs. Stuart and yourself, I remain,
Very Truly,
Your obt. svt.
U. S. GRANT

ALS, DLC-George H. Stuart. On Sept. 10, 1871, Maj. John L. Hodge, paymaster, had written to Paymaster Gen. Benjamin W. Brice. "I have to inform you that I am unable to close my accounts, and that I owe the frightful amount of about $450,000, which sum I have lost during the last few years in stock speculations, going deeper and deeper, in hope of retrieving myself. . . ." *Washington Evening Star,* Sept. 14, 1871; *New York Times,* Sept. 15, 1871. On Sept. 26, Hodge was sentenced to 10 years in prison and ordered to pay back $445,406.60. On Oct. 9, USG approved the sentence. Copy (printed), DNA, RG 94, Letters Received, 4173 1871; *ibid.,* 3250 1871. On Nov. 25, 1872, USG pardoned Hodge. Copy, *ibid.,* RG 59, General Records. George H. Stuart subsequently wrote to thank USG for the pardon. William Evarts Benjamin, Catalogue No. 27, Nov., 1889, p. 9. In Oct., 1874, Hodge testified for the U.S. against the firm of Polhamus & Jackson, his former brokers, in an unsuccessful suit to recover the money. *New York Times,* Oct. 29–31, 1874. See *PUSG,* 22, 319.

On Nov. 18 and Dec. 4, 1871, Secretary of War William W. Belknap had written to Brice. "It is the Presidents' intention to retire you from active service, and he directs me to inform you to that effect." "The President adheres to his decision,—announced to you in my letter of the 18th November,—as to your retirement from active service,   He has directed me, this morning, to inform you to that effect immediately—" Copies, DNA, RG 107, Letters Sent, Military Affairs. On Sept. 16, a newspaper had reported. "General Brice, in a letter to the Adjutant General of the Army reporting the defalcation and the arrest of Major Hodge, says: 'The first, and to me the most important, inquiry suggested is: How could these frauds be perpetrated and continued through a succession of years without a knowledge or suspicion of their existence being disclosed in the Paymaster General's office through his accounts and statements? The answer is, first, an unwavering confidence in the man. But that confidence was not the sole or the fatal cause of a failure to detect his crimes in their very inception. . . .'" *Washington Evening Star*, Sept. 16, 1871. On Dec. 4, U.S. Senator Roscoe Conkling of N. Y. introduced a resolution of inquiry into the Hodge case; on Dec. 11, he argued for its passage, ". . . to the end that the Committee on Military Affairs may proceed to ascertain whether in truth it ought to report some bill rendering it impossible to take by embezzlement such a sum of money, . . ." *CG*, 42–2, 48. Brice was retired as of Jan. 1, 1872. On June 4, USG nominated Maj. Benjamin Alvord as col., paymaster gen. See *PUSG*, 1, 163; *ibid.*, 11, 422–23; *ibid.*, 15, 106–7.

On Dec. 16, 1873, Brice, Baltimore, wrote to USG. "Permit me respectfully to ask for the appointment 'at large' as a cadet in the U. S. Mily Academy for the Class of 1875. of my adopted son *Benjamin W. Brice Jr.* He is a native of Ohio and will be seventeen years old next August" ALS, NNP. On Feb. 9, 1875, Brice wrote to USG on the same subject. ALS, DNA, RG 94, Correspondence, USMA. Benjamin W. Brice, Jr., entered USMA in 1875 but did not graduate.

1. USG addressed Stuart at Clifton Springs, N. Y.

To Abel R. Corbin

―――――――――

Long Branch, N. J., Sept. 13, 1872

I have just returned from Washington and find your letter . . . I met Mr. Clark on the boat at New York City . . . to see whether I would attend the State Fair. It was arranged that I should go on Thursday next, taking the . . . train from here, and meet Messrs. Ward & Clark at the landing and all go to Elizabeth by the first train. In the evening I am to return to Newark and attend the exposition there. If I can go to Elizabeth afterwards I will do so and remain there to take the 4 o'clock boat the next day for Sandy Hook.[1]

When I left Julia promised to write to Jennie the next day. Whether she did it or not I do not know. I venture not. She is a dead even match with Jennie in regard to putting off answering letters until they answer themselves.—Mrs. Grant will not go with me to Elizabeth. We return to Washington the first of the week following my visit and she will be busy superintending packing up.

Nellie sails from Liverpool on the 12th of Oct. on her return. She writes the most interesting letters home. Her letters are infinitely better, as to composition and substance, than either of her older brothers can write. I have read some of her letters to Mr Childs the publisher, and he says that she ought to write a book of her travels. Of course she will do no such thing.—Fred left last Monday week for Dakotah, Montana Utah and Wyoming, with Sheridan, on an inspecting tour.[2] He will return the latter part of October and spend a week or two with us before joining his Regt. in Northwest Texas. Fred. is a splendid fellow and I think not the least spoiled yet. He seems to be a little bit susceptible and may someday get married before he is quite ready. I hope not however . . .

AL (partial facsimile), R. M. Smythe & Co., 1995, No. 145, pp. 45–46.

1. On Thursday, Sept. 19, 1872, USG visited the N. J. State Agricultural Fair at Waverly, then traveled to Newark to attend an industrial exhibition, returning to Long Branch the following day. *New York Times*, Sept. 20, 21, 1872. USG's party included Amos Clark, Jr., of Elizabeth, N. J., and former N. J. governor Marcus L. Ward, of Newark, both successful Republican candidates for Congress in 1872. On Sept. 14, USG had written to Ward. *ABPC*, 1902, p. 599.

2. On Sept. 5, Lt. Gen. Philip H. Sheridan, Chicago, telegraphed to USG. "Fred reached here last night and is well. We leave to-morrow evening." Copy, DLC-Philip H. Sheridan.

To Josiah L. Keck

———

LONG BRANCH, N. J., Sept. 13, 1872.

DEAR SIR: I regret not being able to accept the kind invitation extended by the citizens of Cincinnati, Ohio, through you, to attend the Exposition now being held there. I have been obliged to decline

a number of similar invitations[1] to visit different parts of the country, on the ground that I shall be engaged in official labors, prepara-
tory to the meeting of Congress.

Last year I had the pleasure of visiting your Exposition, and
should be glad to be able to do so again if it were possible, particularly as it would afford me an opportunity to meet again many of my
old associates of early years.

Please convey to the Committee who have honored me with this
invitation my regrets at not being able to accept it, and best wishes
for the success of the Exposition now being held in Cincinnati. Very
truly yours,

U. S. GRANT.

J. L. PECK [*Keck*], ESQ., CINCINNATI, OHIO.

New York Times, Sept. 23, 1872. See *ibid.*, Sept. 19, 1872.

1. On July 26, 1872, U.S. Representative James A. Garfield of Ohio had written to
USG urging him to accept an invitation to the Northern Ohio Fair. ALS (press), DLC-
James A. Garfield.

To William Elrod

———

Long Branch, N. J.
Sept. 16th /72

DEAR ELROD:

While in Washington last week I received a letter from you saying among other things that you proposed going to Ohio this
month if I should not be visiting the farm. I will not go West this
fall. There is nothing therefore that I know of to prevent your visit.
Mrs. Casey with her three children have gone to St. Louis, by advice of their physician, they having been in New Orleans during the
entire hot Summer, to spend a few weeks. If they should want to go
to the farm to spend a portion of the time I hope you will be able to
accomodate them. These would not prevent your absence nor the absence of any portion of your family that might wish to go with you.

I think I would not work the two two year old colts together in hawling milk? Or at least I would not send them to the depot every day. I thought you might work Beauty against them alternate days; or if Mary got out from the Barracks you might work her and Beauty or her and first one then the other of the colts.

Yours Truly
U. S. GRANT

ALS, Marjorie Stairs, Point Pleasant, Ohio.

To Charles W. Ford

———

Long Branch, N. J.
Sept. 16th 1872

DEAR FORD;

Enclosed I send you a letter just received from John P. Gillespie. I do not distinctly call to mind the interview he alludes to but presume I must have seen him. I deny however having answered "YES, YOU SHALL," to the application to be appointed Local Supt. of Public Buildings in St. Louis. I should have been very suspicious of any one making a direct application who sought his interview through Congressman Welles. Secondly I had previously advised the Sec. of the Treasury who makes these appointments, that I thought Walsh [1] was the proper man to appoint. I deny as emphatically ever having said what Mr. Gillespie ascribes to me as he says I made it.

If Walsh has not been appointed, and there is any reason to believe that he has made the assertion attributed to him of having $40.000 to controll the appointment, I wish you would let me know it.

Yours Truly
U. S. GRANT

ALS, DLC–USG. On Nov. 7, 1872, Charles W. Ford, St. Louis, wrote to USG. "I give you my most hearty congratulations on your triumphant re-election—and the country, that it has a guarantee for four years more of peace & prosperity—I am very much disappointed at the result in our state—but, I dont give it up yet. Eight thousand registered voters in this city, did not vote. It is safe to say ¾ths of them were Republicans,   It may be attributed, in part, to local nomminnations, which in some respects were objectionable, and in part to the defection of the Mo Democrat, which used its influences to defeat some of the nominees, so that, Republicans—feeling sure your re-election was safe beyond doubt—& taking no interest in the squabble of local candidates, stayed away, rather than to spend the time necessry to putting in their votes. However much we may lament our own local mistakes and partial defeat—the general result has been glorious—and espe-cially so to yourself—as it nails to the ground all the villianous lies, that have been sent broadcast over the land, by such papers as the New York Sun, and, it has taught a lesson to such renegade politicians as Schurz—Sumner Banks &co that future political aspirants wont be apt to imitate. A word about myself & I'll stop. I have been nearly 20 years in the Express. and have the feeling that I would like a change & what I want to say is—that in the changes likely to be made—that if it met your approbation, I should be glad to have you make me, 2d Assistant Post Master Genl. You know my qualifications pretty well and will justify me in saying—that I could bring to the office a good knowledge of Rail Roads, & transportation over the various routes of the country—with an average of Executive and business ability—and a cordial endorsement of every man who knows me. Thisat is as much as I can say for myself. It is quite *a draw on my modisty* to say as much. but, I pref-ered to say it and make this application myself, under the circumstances, than to have all my friends join in. If you take a favorable view of this & will indicate any steps for me to take—I shall only be too happy to comply—On the other hand—if you dont take *my view* of the case—or that it will, in any way, embarrass any arrangements made or to be made, pleas drop me out and consider I have not said a word on the Subject. If you desire it, I could take a little run down to Washington & spend a day or two—where I could tell you more fully of matters here than the limits of this already Extended letter admits . . . P. S. I send this by Chester Krum. who is to leave here this P. m. He knows nothing of its con-tents." ALS, USG 3. See letter to Charles W. Ford, Feb. 22, 1873.

1. On Nov. 24, 1874, John M. Krum *et al.*, St. Louis, wrote to USG. "We most re-spectfully ask the position of Supervising Architect of the Treasury Department for Thomas Walsh the present Superintendent of the New Custom House in this city, as we know him to be competent, reliable and trustworthy. We therefore ask his appointment as a personal favor to us—in case of a vacancy—" LS (9 signatures), DNA, RG 56, Ap-pointments Div., Treasury Offices, Letters Received. On Nov. 26, U.S. Representative Erastus Wells of Mo., St. Louis, wrote to USG on the same subject. ALS, *ibid.* Related pa-pers are *ibid.* No appointment followed.

To Orville E. Babcock

Long Branch, N. J.
Sept. 23d /72

DEAR GENERAL:

My Sec. to sign Patents, Mr. Jos. Parish died yesterday. I wish to appoint Judge Williamson of Va in his place butand do not remember his initials. Will you please see Dr. Sunderland[1] about it and ascertain from him his full name and whereabouts and allow the Sec. of the Int. to make out his apt. if he still wants it. I will be in Washington on Friday.[2]

Yours Truly
U. S. GRANT

GN. O. E. BABCOCK

ALS, Robert M. Merritt, Miami, Fla. See *PUSG*, 20, 452. On Dec. 5, 1872, USG nominated Samuel D. Williamson to succeed Joseph Parrish. See *ibid.*, 19, 317–18.

On July 22, John Corson, Washington, D. C., had written to USG. "I respectfully ask at your hands the appointment of 'Presidents Secretary to sign Land Patents.' The present incumbent Mr J. Parrish, is in feeble health, and may not return to Washington again; I ask this appointment in the event of a vacancy occurring, Mr Parrish is a very estimable man." ALS, DNA, RG 48, Appointment Div., Letters Received. On July 29, Corson wrote to USG on the same subject. ALS, *ibid.* See *PUSG*, 18, 483.

On July 9, 1875, Levi P. Luckey wrote to Williamson. "The President duly received your letter of the 3d inst., and directs me to write you that he understood that you can receive a clerkship in the Office of the Attorney General, and that it is his wish that you accept it and leave the position you now hold to be filled by him." Copy, DLC-USG, II, 2. On Dec. 8, USG nominated David D. Cone to replace Williamson.

1. On April 13, 1871, Orville E. Babcock had written to John Bailey, Washington, D. C. "The President desires me to acknowledge the receipt of your letter of the 11th instant and enclose you his check for $100 00 the amount of his Subscription to the fund for the purchase of a house for Dr: Sunderland." Copy, *ibid.*, II, 1. In 1873, Byron Sunderland, pastor, First Presbyterian Church, Washington, D. C., wrote to USG. William Evarts Benjamin, Catalogue No. 42, March, 1892, p. 21. See Sunderland, *A Memorial Sermon on the Death of General Ulysses S. Grant, . . .* (Washington, D. C., 1885).

2. Sept. 27.

To Nathaniel Niles

Washington D. C. Oct. 1st 1872.

COL. N. NILES,
DEAR COL.

Enclosed I send check for $15 00 which please pay over to Mr. Ries of your city.[1] Until I received your letter enclosing Mr. Rs receipt for $12 30/100 I was not aware of owing one cent to any man living in Mo. I remember of purchasing lumber from the firm, and of paying the bills from time to time when I was building on my farm in St. Louis Co. and supposed all had been paid.

I should not like to explain the cause of Govr Koerner's complaint.[2]

Yours Truly,

U. S. GRANT

ALS, Belleville Public Library, Belleville, Ill. Born in 1817 in N. Y. and educated at Princeton College, Nathaniel Niles moved to Belleville, Ill. (1842), practiced law, edited a Republican newspaper, and served as col., 130th Ill. On June 1, 1867, USG favorably endorsed a letter recommending Niles for bvt. promotion. ES, DNA, RG 94, ACP, 110N CB 1867. On Sept. 7, 1868, Niles wrote to someone unspecified, probably Adam Badeau, concerning USG's election as president. ALS, USG 3.

On July 15, 1869, U.S. Representative John B. Hay of Ill., Belleville, wrote to USG. "Some time in the latter part of last April, as you doubtless remember, Col Niles of this place, was appointed Consul to Victoria Vancouver's Island. The only pay of the office is derived from such fees as he can make in the discharge of the ordinary duties of the office. Owing to the high import duties imposed on all things imported therein, the trade and commerce of the Island have greatly declined, and it has become very much depopulated. In fact the fees of the office amount to very little. Secretary Fish has given Col Niles till the first of August to start for Victoria. Col Niles would like to get a consular appointment that would pay better than the one he has now, and inasmuch, as the consulship to Santiago de Cuba, has become vacant by the recent death of Mr. Stedman, the Col would be glad to be honored with the appointment to that place." ALS, DNA, RG 59, Letters of Application and Recommendation. On April 17, USG had nominated Niles as consul, Victoria. No other appointment followed.

1. Valentine Ries had operated a lumber business in St. Louis during the 1850s, and his sons continued the business in Belleville.

2. Gustave P. Koerner, German emigrant and influential Ill. politician, ran for governor as a Liberal Republican in 1872. See Thomas J. McCormack, ed., *Memoirs of Gustave Koerner 1809–1896* (Cedar Rapids, Iowa, 1909), II, 527–76.

To J. & J. Dobson et al.

———

Washington D. C. October 2d 1872

GENTLEMEN:

Your very kind letter of the 20th of Sept. inviting me to visit your respective manufactories at such time during the month as I might designate only came to hand yesterday.

I hasten to respond and to express my regrets that I did not receive your invitation earlier, although my engagements were such from the 20th of Sept. to the end of the month that it is doubtful whether I could have accepted. At a later day however when the excitement of a political campaign has passed, I will take great pleasure in visiting your manufactories, should it suit your convenience to have me do so.

I feel a very great interest in the success of the manufacturing interests of the country, and their developement, looking upon this growth as necessary to the solvency of the Nation by keeping down the balance of trade against us, and in dignifying labor and making it remunerative. You have my best wishes for the success of your respective interests and the interest of all manufacturers and producers the land over, until our productions by home labor, for export exclusive of promises to pay, equal our importations, or exceed them.

Very respectfully
Your obt. svt.
U. S. GRANT

J. & J. DOBSON, A CAMPBELL & CO., R PATTERSON & CO.,
J, LONG BROS & CO., M. BAIRD & CO., & OTHERS
MANUFACTURERS OF PHILADELPHIA, PA.[1]

Copy, DLC-USG, II, 1. On Sept. 26, 1872, USG visited Philadelphia with Horace Porter and spoke in the evening. "GENTLEMEN AND MERCHANTS OF PHILADELPHIA: You have made much better speeches to-night than I could make if I were so inclined. I am very glad to see you, and am pleased to hear that you have been to hear such fine speeches and how you have been engaged to-night." *Washington Chronicle*, Sept. 27, 1872.

In 1872, John Wanamaker wrote to USG. "Doing a large business, I have never given much time to politics, but any influence I may have as a merchant or a young man, I will be glad to contribute at this time to make a tremendous majority in November. If the success is to be a grand one there is hard work to be done, and you may be free to command me for any service I can render." William Evarts Benjamin, Catalogue No. 42, March, 1892, p. 22.

1. John Dobson, born in 1827 in England, and his brother James, operated a large carpet factory. The Campbell firm manufactured cotton and woollen goods. Robert Patterson, born in 1792 in Ireland and an officer in the Mexican and Civil Wars, owned several cotton mills. See *PUSG*, 21, 280. James Long, born in 1822 in Ireland, managed textile factories and railroads. Matthew Baird, born in 1817 in Ireland, manufactured locomotives.

Endorsement

Refered to the Atty. Gn. I have withheld the apt. of Marshal and now understand that the man to be aptd. is not a resident of the state.¹ If the new Dist. Atty. has not assumed his duties he may be notified not to until the matter is further investigated.²

U. S. GRANT

OCT. 7TH /72

AES, DNA, RG 60, Records Relating to Appointments. Written on a telegram of Oct. 4, 1872, from Edward M. Cheney, chairman, Republican State Executive Committee, and Alva A. Knight, Jacksonville, Fla., to USG. "Removal of Conant and Bisbee gives four electoral votes to Greeley and Florida to the democrats   Can removal be suspended until ~~further~~ facts are laid before you" Telegram received (on Oct. 5), *ibid.* On Oct. 5, U.S. Representative Josiah T. Walls of Fla., Gainesville, telegraphed to USG. "You *Loose* four electors & a Republican state Government in florida by the removal of Conant & Bisbee" Telegram received (at 10:00 P.M.), *ibid.* On the same day, M. H. Hale, special agent, Savannah, telegraphed to Oscar D. Madge, supervising special agent, Treasury Dept. "I fear the removal of Bisbee is a great mistake   his successor is a partner with one of the bitterest Democrats in Florida   he is not admitted to practise in the United States Court and I cannot hope for success in any cases I may put in his hands. Bisbee is an honest upright and fearless man and a true Republican. There must be some misunderstanding in the matter. I have seen him in positions where he has been tested. I know him to be a man of unimpeachable integrity. ɨOf Cowlam who succeeds Conant United States Marshal, I do not hesitate, on my own knowledge, to pronounce a fraud. ɨThe evidence of his blackmailing the late John N Muller of this City was developed in a trial in this city in the United States District Court; he is well known here and his appointment to those who know him is a great surprise. Unless these appointments are stopped at once Florida will go Democratic. You can show this to the Secretary" Telegram received (at 1:45 P.M.), *ibid.* On Oct. 6, William P. Dockray, Jacksonville, wrote to USG. "It seems it has been your pleasure to suspend from office Sherman Conant. United States Marshal, and H. Bisbee Jr U. S. District Attorney,   I am persuaded you would not have made these suspensions at this Critical time in politics. both State & National, unless the strongest kind of assurances had been given you that the interests of the Republican party demanded it, especially as they both, are the best Officers. the U. S. has had in this State since the War,   I speak from personal knowledge, of all the Government Officers, that have held Office in this state since the Rebellion, Myself assiting in the Organization of the U. S. Courts and being Clerk of them 3 years—placed me in a position to judge of their qualifications, and abilities; Conant, is a man of extraordinary executive ability, & has plied himself faithfully to the duties of his office, and to the entire satisfaction of the Court. and most of the people, and has always been a zealous hard working. Radical Republican,   the Democrats here have always said. he furnished the brains for the party. Much the same character is Col Bisbee,   The hatred to both. by their enemies. arises from the fact of their persistence in the prosecution of Corrupt men, of either party: They have pursued even the Governor of this State, for his Corruption & villany, hence his animosity towards them. I am fully aware that the most gross misrepresentations has been made to you in regard to these two faithful Officers, and that you have been as grossly imposed upon by those who made them, Their removal was without a doubt concocted by Harrison Reed. (in name) the Governor of Florida, for the purpose of electing the Democratic State ticket with the promise of the Democrats to send him to Congress; In order to accomplish such a result, Reed, would resort to any means—through his tool Tyler, and one or two others; Reed, well knows he cannot control 1000 votes in the state, not even enough to be elected to the Legislature from Duval County, in which he resides. Hence this fraud upon yourself, and the Republican party   His word is not worth the breath that gives it utterance, such is his character here for truth and veracity; neither has Reed any political influence in the State, But this one act of the President has done more to demoralise the Republican party here than all Reed & the Democrats could have otherwise effected for under its thorough Organization by Conant, Cheney, and others of like stamp the State ticket. was sure of 23000 Majority for the Republicans, and 3000 for Grant & Wilson, and unless what has been done, is speedily undone by the President, it will be the means of giving the State to the Democrats, and also of completely upsetting the Republican party here for all time—I take the liberty of presenting for your consideration the foregoing facts, in the interest of the great Republican party, and for the ReElection of your honored self and the Honored Senator Wilson—I belong to no ring or clique and have no interest. in those two gentlemen. Conant & Bisbee other than they should be reinstated, for the benefit of the great National Republican party, the welfare of which and its triumphant success. I have deeply at hart   I fought for its existence, & as I am 60 years of age I do not wish to see it buried before I shall have passed away   My Honored sir I hope and trust, you will never again allow yourself to be imposed upon, as you have been, by anything emenating from Harrison Reed, or, his emisaries   My sir, I told that man before he was Governor, I, would not beleive him under Oath, and although I have met him almost daily, I never recognised him, I not only regard him in the highest degree untruthful, but *as dishonest* as *a man can be*" ALS, *ibid.* On Oct. 7, Robert Meacham, president, Republican State Executive Committee, Monticello, Fla., telegraphed to USG. "The removal of United States Marshall Conant, and District Attorney Bisbee, we are satisfied defeats the National and State tickets" Telegram received (at 1:00 P.M.), *ibid.* Related papers are *ibid.* On Oct. 8, Frank N. Wicker, Key West, telegraphed to Frederick T. Dent. "Confidential   united states marshal and District Attorney for northern district Removed   They are the brains of the party and the presidents strongest friends in the state   Can any thing be done   answer" Telegram received (at 10:15 P.M.), ICarbS.

On Sept. 24, William E. Chandler, New York City, had written to USG. "Govr Harrison Reed of Florida recommends the appointment of F. B. Bassnet Esqr as United States District Attorney in place of H. H. Bisbee and Charles Cowlam as U. S. Marshal in place of Sherman Conant. From my knowledge of affairs in Florida I am confident Govr Reed's recommendations should be carried out and I respectfully request that you will give careful consideration to the papers presented by the Governor and make the appointments as requested by him. Mr Cowlam is personally known to me as an energetic and capable person who will make an officer of unusual ability." LS, DNA, RG 60, Records Relating to Appointments; ADf, DLC-William E. Chandler. On Oct. 5, John S. Adams, collector of customs, Jacksonville, wrote to Horace Porter. "Having just learned of the new appointments in the offices of Marshall and Dist Attorney in this District, and beg leave, through, you to congratulate the Administration upon the satisfactory changes thus effected   The unity and harmony of the Republican party in this State have been seriously disturbed and its efficiency nearly destroyed through the persistent and malignant hostility shown by Messrs Conant, Bisbee and others towards the administration of Governor Reed, now drawing to its close. This malignancy and its causelessness are fully shown by a Resolution of the last Republican State Convention, tendering the thanks of the Convention to Gov Reed for his ability, integrity & faithfulness carried through by men nominated to office by that Convention, who had upon their legislative oaths three times tried without success to impeach him of 'high crimes and misdemeanors' The effect of this constant struggle of the State Government to sustain itself against the of its political friends, at the instigation mainly of Federal Officers, has tended to dis-integrate and demoralize the party in the State. And all this time, Gov Reed has been a firm and steadfast supporter of the Gen. Administration, and an indefatigable and efficient worker in the common cause. It is no wonder then that the apparent neglect of the Gen Govt and the selection here of a State ticket of personal enemies of Reed, should have discouraged his friends; and such, in fact has been the case to an extent that jeopardized the general result—But these official changes seem to to the friends of the existing State Government like a rift in the clouds and inspired those already with new courage and hope. The very quarrels of Republicans may have jeopardized the State ticket possibly beyond recovery, but the Governor and his friends look upon the changes made as practically endorsing him and will take hold with new zeal, and I can now say with a good degree of confidence that the State may be counted safe on the National ticket though the State ticket may fail. But we confidently expect to secure the election of a Republican Senator in place of Mr Osborne & two Republican Congressmen; and I will add that in writing as I do, I express the feeling & wishes of all the Federal officers of the State outside of the clique or ring of Senator Osbornes special friends—" ALS, DNA, RG 60, Records Relating to Appointments.

On Oct. 10, Knight wrote to USG. "As the head of the Grant & Wilson Electoral Ticket for the State of Florida, allow me to thank you for your prompt action in reinstating District Attorney Bisbee and United States Marshal Conant. We will give you 5000 majority, and our state ticket 3000 majority on the Fifth of November next." ALS, *ibid.* On Oct. 31 and Nov. 1, Governor Harrison Reed of Fla. telegraphed to USG. "I am privately informed that military forces are demanded by the marshall for service at the polls on election day there is no County in the state where there is any violence or disorder threatened save in or two Counties where there is an effort by the marshall & his friends to defeat republican Candidates for the legislature who are friendly to me if troops are sent I wish them ordered to report or to act in Conjunction with the state officers in enforcing the laws & I can induce the withdrawal of the Greeley electoral ticket entirely if I can assure the people that after the election the marshall & attorney surveyor general & Collector of the internal revenue will be removed and honest republicans known to yourself appointed instead if the military are placed at my disposal I can answer for the peace of the state & the election of the republican electors by five thousand majority answer as soon as possible" "Please yet ans ours yesterday" Telegrams received (the first at 6:00 P.M., the second at 2:00 P.M.), USG 3. On Nov. 1, USG telegraphed to Reed. "Your despatch of yesterday was received. It is of so remarkable a nature coming from the Executive of a state that I decline further answer." Copy, DLC-USG, II, 5.

On Nov. 9 and 13, John Tyler, Jr., assessor of Internal Revenue, Tallahassee, wrote to USG. "Permit me to add my congratulations to the thousands which you have, doubtless, received from other sources, upon the Magnificent triumph which has attended you throughout the Nation; and to enclose to you my Editorial in the Sentinel on the occasion, which, I trust, will not compare very unfavourably with what may have been said by the leading Journalists of the Country. Your Electors in Florida have run ahead of the State & Congressional ticket, and are unquestionably elected. My impression, moreover, is that Judge Hart is elected Governor, and that we have carried the Legislature. As for the rest more doubt exists, but the chances are that all are elected, although the final count will be necessary in the case of one or two. In this central & heavy county the Bishop Pearce ticket for the State Senate & Legislature have quite a large majority. The Congressional ticket if saved at all, has been only saved by the force of the first elections in Ohio, Pensylvania & Indiana. I am particularly gratified that my friends & relatives in Virginia responded nobly to my call upon them almost to a man, and stood faithfully by you. . . . P. S. There never has been so quiet peaceable & orderly an election in Florida, either as State, or Territory. The nineteen Counties to be heard from are Democratic and will draw down the Republican Majorities as they stand." "I may now venture to say that the Republican Federal & State tickets in Florida are elected, by a small, but decisive Majority. In the Nation your triumph is complete, your revilers are overwhelmed, and your friends rejoice. Among the latter I have the honor to subscribe myself . . ." ALS, USG 3. See Jerrell H. Shofner, *Nor Is It Over Yet: Florida in the Era of Reconstruction, 1863–1877* (Gainesville, 1974), pp. 275–87.

1. See *PUSG*, 20, 352. On Jan. 24, 1870, Reed wrote to USG. "The following federal office holders are now gathered here & have formed an alliance with the Democratic party to impeach & suspend me & turn the State Government over to the ememy's of Republican government. The colored men are quaking in fear & alarm & much excitement exists, but I am happy to say that I have no fear of overthrow. Still I deem it due to the Republican party of the State & Nation that these men be removed at once & honest repub-licans be appointed in their stead: Geo. E. Wentworth, U. S. Marshall   M. L. Stearns, U. S. Surveyor General   F. A. Dockray, Collector at Jacksonville   Hiram Potter, Jr Collector at Pensacola   C. R. Mobley, U. S. Dist. Atty at Key West. Horatio Jenkins, Jr. U. S. Collector, Int. Revenue.   LeRoy D. Ball, Clerk U. S. Dist. Court & Deputy Collector Int. Rev.   Sherman Conant Deputy U. S. Marshall & Asst assessor Int. Revenue." ALS, DNA, RG 60, Letters Received, Fla. On Jan. 29, U.S. Senator Abijah Gilbert of Fla. endorsed this letter. "I fear the federal office holders in Florida are pursuing a course which is endangering the republican party & republican government in our State—but I am expecting my brother soon from Florida and would prefer to wait a day or so before giving my entire endorsement to their removal." AES, *ibid.* In [*Feb.*], U.S. Senator Thomas W. Osborn of Fla. telegraphed to USG. "Be so kind as to withhold any appointments in Florida until I can see you   I think representations of internal matters there to you have been absolutely erroneous. Senator Gilbert concurs in the request," Telegram received, *ibid.*, RG 107, Telegrams Collected (Bound). On March 15, 1871, Attorney Gen. Amos T. Akerman wrote to USG. "In answer to the note of General Porter, of this date, I have the honor to inform you that the Sherman Conant nominated yesterday as U. S. Marshal for the Northern Dist. of Florida is the same person who was nominated June 29, 1870, for U. S. Judge of the Southern District of that State—which nomination was afterwards withdrawn by you." Copy, *ibid.*, RG 60, Letters Sent to Executive Officers. On March 14 and 15, Porter had written to Akerman. "The President directs me write you and request you to have prepared a nomination of Sherman Conant of Fla. as U. S. Marshal Northern Dist. of Fla. and withdrawal of the name Chas. M. Hamilton, nominated for that position on the 10th inst." "The President desires me to ask you if the

Sherman Conant, nominated yesterday for U. S. Mar. U. Dist of Fla is the same man who
was nominated June 29. 70. for U. S. Judge of S. Dist. of Fla. and afterwards withdrawn
upon charges preferred against him." LS, *ibid.*, Letters from the President. On March 17,
the Senate confirmed Sherman Conant as marshal, Northern District, Fla. Born in N. H.,
Conant had served as capt., 3rd U.S. Colored Inf.; clerk, U.S. District Court; and chairman, Fla. Republican Executive Committee.

    On Sept. 28, 1872, Clement H. Hill, act. attorney gen., wrote to Charles Hale, act.
secretary of state. "I am directed by the President to request you to issue a commission
appointing Charles Cowlam Marshal of the United States for the Northern District of
Florida, in place of Sherman Conant suspended agreeably to the enclosed Executive Order." LS, *ibid.*, RG 59, Acceptances and Orders for Commissions. The enclosure is *ibid.*
Porter endorsed the enclosure. "Cancelled Oct 10th 1872 By direction of the President."
ES (undated), *ibid.* On Oct. 7, Charles M. Hamilton, Washington, D. C., wrote to USG. "I
have the honor respectfully to solicit the reappointment as United States Marshal for the
Northern District of Florida. Permit me to call to your mind a similar application at the
close of my second term in Congress—March 1870—which you kindly granted me, honoring me with the appointment, which you afterwards withdrew from the Senate in favor
of the late incumbent, Sherman Conant, whom you have properly removed. Permit me
further to represent that the successor whom you have appointed to Mr. Conant—Charles
Cowlam—is scarcely known in Florida, is a non-resident of the state, has rendered no
service toward Reconstruction there, and his appointment will be unsatisfactory and detrimental in many regards. No selfish interests prompts these representations, for rather
than to have the present appointment perfected—should my claim not meet your favorable consideration—I trust some one else may be appointed who is identified with the interests of Florida, and known to the people. I have been absent attending the Veteran Soldiers Convention at Pittsburgh—the only delegate present from Florida—the Member
of the National Committee from that state—and I am desirous to return there, at this
important juncture, in a capacity which will enable me to render efficent service both in
the interest of the Republican party, the state and the General Government. Hoping
the claims you once deemed best to pass over may now be favorably considered." ALS,
ibid., RG 60, Records Relating to Appointments. On Dec. 6, 1871, USG had nominated
Hamilton as postmaster, Jacksonville; on Feb. 5, 1872, the Senate rejected this nomination. See letter to George William Curtis, March 26, 1873.

    In [*Oct., 1871*], Fla. Representative W. K. Cessna had written to USG. "I write with
might mind and strength to protest against the removal of Sherman Conant as United
States Marshal for the Northern District of Florida, for the following reason—1st He is
The best Marshal we have had for years—2nd He is the only man man the KuKlux
Democracy fear   3rd His removal is to license fraud, intimidation—and violence at the
Polls—4th His Removal is to open a 'Bloody chasm' to be filled with the bodies of Loyal
men—5th A new man—however—well qualified cannot put the machinery of the office
in order in the time to elapse between now and election day—6th It is clear that the
influence brought to bear to secure his removal is rotten to the core—7th It is done to secure defeat the Regular Republican ticket and to elect Bloxham—Democrat,—governor
in the vain hope of securing a seat in the U. S. Senate for Harrison Reed—a man who is
so fearfully corrupt that he would not hesitate to sell his Country for a mess of pottage
8th. Rebels rejoice over the removal and are jubilant and hopeful and I assure you not
without cause—one boasted in my presence—not an hour ago—that they—the Democrats—were masters of the situation as they would now control the Polls—9th Because

it is bad policy for the 'boss tanner' to swap horses in the middle of the river on the word of a treacherous bandit Reed—our unfortunate Governor—is one who favors the Removal—Is he (Reed) doing anything to secure the State to our friends? No. He is running around the State from County to County trying to get men nominated to the Legislature who will favor or vote for his election to the United State Senate. Conant is laboring night and day to carry the state in the interest of law and order—and Republicanism—Reed openly boast that he is working for himself only—Conant has done all in his power to execute the law—Reed—by his faithlessness and 'want of a Policy' has failed to do anything save squander the States money—Reed's own friends Osborn and Randel have frequently said to me that he (Reed) was a man without executive ability—and possess of a poor judgement and of little and or no political sagacity—Major Conants special recommendation is his executive power—& positiveness a quality essential in the officer in this County—and of his political foresight I have yet to hear complaint—Reed is wise in low Cunning & Chicanery—and cannot do or touch a thing without the appearance, at best—of fraud and corruption—That he is corrupt none doubts—He once offerred me $500 to defeat one Col. Jenkins—I was clerk of the Circuit Court at the time—Again he paid one Keene and an other $400 a piece to vote against his Impeachment in 1870 and that is the way he defeated impeachment—And again while Special Agent of the Post Office Department for this State &c he would *enter into partnerships* with mail contractors and divide the spoils—a direct violation of law—This as the lawyers say—I am 'ready to verify' Messrs ~~Halladay~~ Tyler, Gibbs, Adams & Randal are his Co-adjutors—They have little or no influence—Mr. Tyler is a notorious 'drunken sot'—who has been picked upon the streets of Tallahassee and dumped into a wheelbarrow and wheeled like so much litter to his office and dumped out—There are charges similar to those resting against Gov. Reed again the most of them—All are doing little or nothing excepting to fight the Regular Republican nominations—10th It is bad generalship to exchange 'organized victory' for doubt and darkness just before the battle. If Conants removal be insisted upon—a new Convention will have to be called and a new set of electors put in the field—for the present ones will most surely withdraw and I think the Candidates for Congress will stop the Canvass for the present—at least—as their plans are thwarted—Believe me or not—but I assure you, General—Conant with the Marshalship is to the Republicans of Florida what Genls Sherman and Sheridan were to you in the armies of the Tennessee and the Valley of Virginia—General I regard your election as almost essential to secure and and perpetuate the grand results growing out of the late unholy war—They must be moulded into our Institution and become a part of the whole nation—you are best canculated for the great work hence I rite you when I see you are doing just what is best Calculated to defeat yourself and those measures—I know little or nothing of our Senators but will take the liberty to say you can rely upon anything Mr. Walls says or does—He an Conant are spirit of the present Canvass," ALS (docketed as received on Oct. 12), DNA, RG 60, Records Relating to Appointments.

2. USG restored Horatio Bisbee, Jr. Born in 1839 in Canton, Maine, Bisbee graduated from Tufts (1863) following service in the 5th Mass. and 9th Maine. He studied law in Ill., beginning practice in Jacksonville, Fla. On Dec. 16, 1868, President Andrew Johnson nominated Bisbee as U.S. attorney, Northern District, Fla. On March 19, 1869, Osborn, Gilbert, and U.S. Representative Charles M. Hamilton of Fla. wrote to USG. "We the Senators and Representatives of the State of Florida have the honor to request the reappointment of Horatio Bisbee Jr. of Jacksonville Florida for the office of United States District Attorney for the Northern District of the State—Mr. Bisbee is the present in-

cumbent of the office and has to the best of our knowledge filled it with honor and ability He is a republican, posseses ability and considerable reputation as a lawyer, is honest in the prosecutions of his dutis. He was an officr during the war, served with credit and was mustered out as Colonel. We make this recommendation beleving that Mr. Bisbee is an excellent officer and request that he be retained—" DS, *ibid.* On Feb. 19, 1870, Reed telegraphed to USG. "I ask the immediate removal of Horatio Bisbee Jr U. S. District Atty for Northern District of Florida   he is vicious and incompetent and uses his office for malicious purposes is now threatening indictments against the men for sustaining me and the Republican administration" Telegram received (at 11:40 P.M.), *ibid.* On Sept. 28, 1872, USG suspended Horatio Bisbee, Jr. DS, DNA, RG 60, Letters from the President. Porter endorsed this document. "Cancelled Oct 10th 1872   By direction of the Presid[en]t" ES (undated), *ibid.* On Jan. 6, 1873, USG nominated Knight as U.S. attorney, Northern District, Fla., to replace Bisbee, whose term expired on Jan. 4.

To William H. Seward, Jr.

———

Dated Washington DC Oct 14 *1872*

To Gov W H Seward

I condole with you and the Nation in the loss of a kind father and an eminent Statesman   His services to the country have baecome a part of its history   I regret that I cannot attend the funeral and participate in the last earthly honors to the remains of the distinguished Patriot & statesman

U S Grant

Telegram received (at Auburn, N. Y., 2:00 P.M.), NRU. William H. Seward died on Oct. 10, 1872. Frederick W. Seward and William H. Seward, Jr., telegraphed to USG. "We have the honor to acknowledge the receipt of your communication of this date, and in behalf of all the members of the family of our father we return you our heartfelt and sincere thanks for your expression of sympathy with them in this great affliction." *New York Times*, Oct. 15, 1872. Born in 1839, Seward, Jr., a banker, had served in the Civil War as lt. col., col., and brig. gen.

On April 11, 1873, Levi P. Luckey wrote to N. Y. Senator John C. Perry. "The President directs me to acknowledge the receipt of your letter of the 9th inst. conveying an invitation from the Senate and Assembly of the State of New York, to be present upon the occasion of the memorial discourse to be delivered in honor of the late Hon. Wm H. Seward on the 18th instant by Hon Charles Francis Adams, and to convey to you his regrets that it will be impossible for him to attend upon the invitation at that time owing to other engagements already made." Copy, DLC-USG, II, 2. See *New York Times*, April 19, 1873, April 15, 1884.

On Jan. 26, 1874, Orville E. Babcock wrote to Richard Schell, New York City. "Enclosed please find the President's check for one hundred dollars, payable to the order of the Farmers' Loan & Trust Co. of New York—the amount of his subscription to the Seward Monument fund. If you please you might acknowledge receipt of the remittance" Copy, DLC–USG, II, 2. See *New York Times*, July 18, 1873, Aug. 20, Sept. 28, 1876, Nov. 11, 1879.

To Abel R. Corbin

Washington D. C. Oct. 16th *1872*

MY DEAR MR. CORBIN;

Your letter of the 14th is just received. Mrs. Grant and I go on to New York City on Monday[1] night to meet Nellie and bring her home. It is not probable that the vessel in which she sailed will reach New York City before Tuesday morning so that we will be in the city from Monday morning until Tuesday night. If Jennie was at home I do not know but we might go as far as Elizabeth on Saturday and remain over Sunday.—I am much obliged to you for the offer of your kind offices. Likely it will be pleasant for you to meet us on Tuesday on the vessel that brings Mr. Borie and party home. What arrangements will be made I do not know; but in all probability a Rev. Cutter will be put at my service and I will be allowed to meet the vessel in the Harbor below the City. In that case I would be glad of your company down the bay.

My family are all very well.

Yours Truly
U. S. GRANT

ALS, Abraham Lincoln Book Shop, Chicago, Ill. USG, Julia Dent Grant, and others met Ellen Grant in New York City upon her return from Europe on the *Scotia.* See *New York Times*, Oct. 21–24, 1872; *Philadelphia Public Ledger*, Oct. 22–23, 1872.

On Oct. 17, 1872, Julia Grant wrote to Emma Childs. "I have concluded not to stop on my way to New York. We will be at the Fifth Avenue Hotel . . . and will expect you all to meet us there. . . . Genl. Porter has written . . . in regard to the hunt and I think we will have a pleasant day. The Lieut. left us on Monday night for a visit to our cousin W. W. Smith of Washington, Pa. and did propose making a short visit to you. . . . The visit to you seems to have been an engagement he made before leaving Long Branch. . . ." The Rendells, Inc., Catalogue 136 [1978], no. 45.

1. Oct. 21.

To William S. Hillyer

———

Washington D. C. Oct. 20th 1872

GENERAL:

As I am obliged to leave Washington City t[his] evening to meet my daughter in New York City, who is about returning from Europe, I will not be able to aide you in person in obtaining for Mrs. Daniels (late Mrs. Gen. Rawlins) the sum of money which she requires for the trip prescribed by her physician as necessary for her health. I therefore give you this letter explaining the interests which she has within my keeping which can be bound for the payment of any debt she may contract. First: a house and lot, S. E. Cor. of 12th & M. St. Washington City, now rented at $75 00/100 pr month which is one fourth hers, in her own right, and one fourth of the income from $38.500 00/100 registered U. S. 6 pr. ct. bonds, interest payable Jan. & July.—If Mrs. Daniels authorizes I will see that her interest in the above goes to the liquidation of any loan she may contract to the amount of $2000 00/100[1] and I also authorize as joint Executor with her of the Will of the late Gen. Rawlins a mortgage of her interest in the said Washington City property.[2] With legal authority from Mrs. Daniels to pay from her interest in the estate of Gen. Rawlins I will agree to become the payer of such a loan negociated payable the First of January 1873. Otherwise I will accept a draft or order upon me (payable January 1st 1874) by Mrs. Daniels ~~giving at the same time~~ for the s[um *of*] $2000 00/100 with interest from date.

Yours Truly
U. S. GRANT

GEN. W. S. HILLYER ATTY. AT LAW

ALS, University of Oregon, Eugene, Ore. See *PUSG*, 21, 185–86; letter to C. F. Daniels, March 20, 1872; letters to William D. Rawlins, Aug. 3, 1872, June 18, 1873.

1. On Jan. 2, 1874, Levi P. Luckey wrote to Mary E. Daniels, New York City. "The President directs me to say that he has to-day taken up your note given Oct. 22, 1872, in favor of George G. Pride for $2.000. and has applied your one fourth of the interest of

$1155. gold, (which has been sold for $1273.38/100 currency) towards its payment, and will so credit your share of any moneys coming in from the estate. The note amounted, with the interest, $167.22, to $2.167.22. He wishes me to say that he thinks it would be well to sell the Danbury house, and if a fair price can be realized for the house here it would be better to sell it also. He would be glad to know your opinion in the matter." Copy, DLC-USG, II, 2. On April 26, 1873, Culver C. Sniffen had written to F. S. Wildman, president, Savings Bank of Danbury, Conn., transmitting $143.27 to pay interest on the mortgage of the Danbury house. Copy, *ibid.* On Dec. 30, 1873, Luckey wrote to Mary Daniels. "The President directs me to say that he has received a letter from Lyman Platt, Collector of Taxes at Danbury, Conn. enclosing bill of $115 33/100 for taxes on the Danbury property and that he has remitted him a draft for the amount." Copy, *ibid.*

On Jan. 12, 1874, Luckey wrote to Mary Daniels, Danbury. "The President directs me to say that he received your letter of the 7th inst. and as you do not speak of receiving his letter of the 2d inst. which I wrote by his direction, he directs me to enclose you a copy with this. He wishes me to say that he would strongly urge the sale of the Danbury house, and recommends that it be advertised for private sale until a certain time and then if not disposed of to be sold at auction subject to the mortgage, with, say one third of the purchase down and the remainder in equal payments in one and two years. He suggests also that the furniture be sold at auction unless you desire to keep it for yourself. He would like your opinion upon these suggestions, and hopes they will meet with your sanction. The President has been obliged to take up the Pride note out of his own private funds and does not feel that he can afford to lose it, but must let your share of interest &c. coming due apply to its payment. This would deprive you of such amounts and he thinks it much better to dispose of the house there, and also, if a good price can be obtained, the house here. The taxes and improvements against the house here will use up the rents for months to come." Copy, *ibid.* On Oct. 26, Luckey wrote to H. Horton Smith, New York City. "The President directs me to enclose you his check for $2,500. to pay the difference in the trade of the Danbury house for Brooklyn property. He will have to sell bonds to replace it, but advances the money that you may complete the trade. I enclose a memorandum receipt which please return." Copy, *ibid.* On Nov. 14, Luckey wrote to David B. Booth, Danbury. "The President directs me to acknowledge the receipt of your letter of the 11th inst, and return you the application for the sale of the property, signed as requested." Copy, *ibid.*

2. On April 12, 1873, Luckey wrote to Col. William D. Whipple. "The President directs me to say that Mr. Hubard may have the Rawlins' house now occupied by you, at the rent named—$75.—per month, to commence the 1st of next June; for one year, with the privilege, should he desire it at the expiration of one year, of renewing the lease for another year, unless the house should be sold. Mr. Hubard may, in his letter of acceptance of the offer, make his own election whether he shall pay the rent monthly or quarterly." Copy, *ibid.* On April 10, 1874, Luckey wrote to James R. Hubbard, Washington, D. C. "I enclose you the receipt for rent for January, February, March and April ($300.) The President directs me to say that you can relinquish the house at the end of this month if you choose, or remain through May, or until another tenant is secured. In any event he will take the furnace of you, for it is required for the house, and that he cannot think of allowing you to sacrifice any thing upon it. Please let me know if we shall notify the Agent to announce it for rent on May 1st or June 1st . . ." Copy, *ibid.*

On Feb. 4 and 20, Luckey had written to Mary Daniels. "The President directs me to say that he has offered the house here for sale and it has been appraised at $13.000 by the real estate men in whose hands he placed it, and they say they can get $12.000. for it, and probably no more. He thinks, under the circumstances, if you and Mr. Smith approve, that he had better purchase from you, for the children, out of their means, your one fourth of it. If this is done, it will pay your note, which he has taken up out of his own funds (with borrowed money) and leave you about $1.200 or $1.300, ready cash for the present. After that you will continue to receive your one fourth of the interest on the bonds. Of course, after the purchase, the income from the house will belong wholly to the children. He wishes me also to say that he is perfectly willing that the Danbury house shall be sold on such terms as you and Mr. Smith may agree upon." "The President directs me to acknowledge the receipt of the deed which arrived a day or two since, and to send you the following statement of account. I send you a separate statement of the rent since July 1, 1872—at which time it was balanced and settled,—showing the receipts and disbursements of that fund up to this time. This shows a balance due you of $88.86. There is an assessment for special improvements against the property of $829.58, one fourth of which you will see is charged to you in your personal account. I think that this assessment can be paid with a certain class of bonds issued by the District Government and which are at a discount. If this is so, and they can be procured, whatever discount is saved the President will remit you your one fourth of it as well as your one fourth of the rent for last month and the first third of this (up to day of sale) which is payable on the 1st of April . . . Enclosed you will please find the President's check for $1.374.76 the balance in currency and also check for $288.75 in gold for the balance in coin. He sends this check for coin as he did not at the time of drawing the interest in coin sell your one fourth, but left it on deposit. I see that the ¾ sold at the time on account of the children was sold at a premium of 12 per cent, which is slightly below the current rate to day. I enclose a receipt in full to date, which please sign and return to the President, who would be glad to know as early as possible of the safe receipt of the checks." Copies, *ibid.* On Feb. 4, Luckey had written to Smith, Goshen, N. Y. "The President wishes me to write you and say that under the will of the late Gen Rawlins, of which Mrs Daniels and himself are the Executors, the property left was equally divided between ~~Mrs Daniels~~ the widow and the children; that with Mrs Daniels consent, he has offered the house here in Washington for sale and it is appraised at $13.000.—less than cost—but he agrees with the real-estate men who value it that its value will be enhanced if kept longer. The President proposes, but desires to consult ~~Mrs Daniels & yourself~~ you first, to buy for the children, Mrs Daniels' one-fourth interest in the house. To do this he will have to sell about $3.000 of the bonds. Under the instructions of the donors of that fund for the children of Gen. Rawlins, he has a perfect right ~~to make this disposition of a part of it~~ to do this, but desires first your opinion and advice." ADfS, *ibid.* On Dec. 31, Luckey wrote to B. Lewis Blackford, Washington, D. C. "The President directs me to enclose you his check for $20.00/100 the amount of the renewal of the policy of Insurance on the Gen. Rawlins' house." Copy, *ibid.*

Speech

[*Oct. 25, 1872*]

Mr. Dardon: I am happy to receive you as the Envoy Extraordinary and Minister Plenipotentiary of Guatemala. The several Republics of Central America are such near neighbors of the United

States that it is desirable we should cultivate the most friendly relations with their respective Governments. This can best be done by an interchange of diplomatic agents well disposed for that object. The purpose which you express for promoting it shall be heartily reciprocated by me.

Washington Chronicle, Oct. 26, 1872. USG responded to remarks by Vicente Dardon, Guatemalan minister. On May 8, 1872, Guatemalan Provisional President Miguel Garcia Granados had written to USG introducing Dardon. DS (in Spanish), DNA, RG 59, Notes from Foreign Legations, Central America; translation, *ibid.* On Feb. 13, 1874, Dardon presented his credentials to USG as minister from Salvador, while continuing to represent Guatemala. *New York Times*, Feb. 14, 1874.

On July 9, 1872, Charles Hale, act. secretary of state, wrote to Silas A. Hudson, U.S. minister, Guatemala City. "Your *despatch* No. 59, of the 30th of May last, has been received. You report that General Barrios, then supreme in authority at Guatemala, was exercising his powers in an arbitrary manner. You consequently ask for instructions which will warrant your interference in behalf of foreigners who are not represented there and of natives who may come under the displeasure of that government. In reply, I have to inform you that it is not deemed expedient to comply with your request. It is a cardinal principle with this government, to abstain from interference in the internal affairs of other countries, as we would frown upon any such interference here by the representatives of foreign powers. . . ." Copy, DNA, RG 59, Diplomatic Instructions, Central America. On April 12, 1869, USG had nominated Hudson, his cousin, as minister to Guatemala. See *PUSG*, 6, 186. On Oct. 17, 1872, Hudson addressed to Fish a lengthy description of Guatemala. ALS, DNA, RG 59, Diplomatic Despatches, Guatemala; *Foreign Relations, 1873*, I, 440–47.

To Elihu B. Washburne

———

Washington D. C.
Oct. 25th 1872.

DEAR WASHBURNE:

Your letter of the 11th of Oct. is just received and I hasten to answer as you request. I think it very doubtful about my going to Galena for the election though I may do so. My judgement now is that the prediction which I made to you about the result of the Nov. election will prove nearly right.[1] Maryland West Va Ky. Tenn. Ga.[2] & Texas[3] will probably ca[st] their votes for Mr. Greeley. Mo. may do the same thing[;] it would not if we could have a fare election throughout the state.[4] Some counties in that state are as bad as any portion of Georgia and may loose us the electoral vote. Va. is also a possible state for Mr. Greeley though the chances are in our favor.[5]

Nellie arrived in New York last Tuesday looking well and much pleased with her trip. The family are all well.

Yours Truly

[U. S.] GRANT

ALS (frayed), IHi. On Oct. 11, 1872, Elihu B. Washburne, Paris, had written to USG. "If I can get my postage treaty with the French Government, on which I am at work, sufficiently along, I intend to start for home early next week. I shall make but little stop in N. Y. but will hurry out to Galena in order to make a speech or two before the election. I have made a speech on the Saturday evening before election at Council Hill for the last twenty years, and I dont want to fail this year. I really hope you will go home to vote and reach Galena say on Saturday night the 2d November. You no need to be gone from Washington more than a week. Will you write me a line, care of C. & G. Woodman No. 30 Pine Street, N. Y. City telling me about this so that I can get it on my arrival. It is no use to tell you that we have had a 'high old time' here since we began to get the news of Tuesday's work. It is safe to say that five out of every six Americans abroad are your friend. In fact, 'Old mealley potatoes' is nowhere. My family left for Bonn yesterday and will be back when I return from the United States. My children are all learning German splendidly. Kind regards to Mrs. Grant and the children. . . . PS. I tried to get Jones to go over, but could not succeed." ALS (press), DLC-Elihu B. Washburne. On the same day, Washburne telegraphed to USG. "Truth is omnipotent and public justice certain." ALS (press, telegram sent), *ibid.*

On Sept. 26, Washburne had written to USG. "I now intend to go home to vote and I hope you will meet me at Galena about election time. It is a very proper thing for you to go to your residence to vote and your action cannot be challenged in that regard and your trip will do the party a great deal of good. You will take Mrs. Grant and the children and go out. The Galena friends will have your house all ready for you, and I think you can pass a week most pleasantly there. And then if Old 'Meally Potatoes' is to be your successor it will be a good place to receive the news. I must confess I am a little selfish in this matter, for I am afraid if I do not see you in Galena I shall not see much of you, for if I visit Washington at all it will not be until December, when Congress will be in session and at a time when you will be very busy. I have written to Col. Stephenson to have your name registered as a voter in East Galena and if you will either let him or Felt know that you will go, out, every thing will be ready for you at your house and you will receive a cordial welcome. My family is all in Paris at the present time, and we are all very well. We have had the pleasure of seeing considerable of Buck and Nellie. They are such splendid children and Nellie has grown so much and improved so much since she has been out here. I duly received your letter of the 26th inst. I think your prophecy will become a historic fact. My glorious Old State of Maine has done the business. Mrs. Washburne and the children all want to join me in kind remembrance to Mrs. Grant and yourself and Uncle Jesse." ALS (press), *ibid.*

1. See letter to Elihu B. Washburne, Aug. 26, 1872. USG carried 31 of 37 states, losing Tex., Mo., Ky., Tenn., Ga., and Md.

2. In Sept., anon., St. Marys, Ga., had written to USG. "I beg to call your attention to the following facts   The colored friends of 'Grant & Wilson' muster some six or seven

thousands in this County (Camden)—Many, perhaps the majority of them, will most surely be overawed & deterred from voting during the coming election by the influence for evil of two white men of the lowest type: both rabid enemies of the government & the dread of all colored citizens in this vicinity. Their names are Cray Pratt, & Stephen Register   It is well known that these two men shot down in cold blood three colored men whom they found hunting at a place in Camden Co—known as 'Black Point'—This they did since the Rebellion—It is true that no direct proofs can be adduced: nevertheless it is well understood in the Rebel community in which these men live that they did the cruel deed—These men should be removed from a position where they stand as living obstacles in the path of improvement of the colored race & that summarily. To depend on any local official would be a waste of time—All of these have local interests & also great fear of the men in question—A skillful detective by gradually approaching such influential colored men as William Richards & George Lucas can learn enough of the matter to warrant the arrest of Register who being an arrant coward will probably confess—Pratt who is a desperate character will never divulge   For the interests of the Republican Party as well as Humanity these miscreants should be prevented from doing further deeds of crime—As I do not wish to be assassinated I merely subscribe myself A Republican" AL, DNA, RG 60, Letters from the President. On Sept. 19, Joseph Morris, Macon, telegraphed to USG. "I want you to send protection to Wilkeson County" Telegram received, *ibid.*, RG 94, Letters Received, 3811 1872.

3. On Aug. 4, W. H. Howard, Austin, had written to USG. "As a friend and fellow northern Republican—one who is anxious for your reélection—I deem it an imperative duty to inform you that the officers of the U. S. Dist., Court at this place, (excepting Th's. F. Purnell, Marshal) are to a man strong Greeleyites; some of them open & persistant in the denunciation of your administration, and recommendation of his (Greeley's) election, and others of them none the less persevering, denunciatory and energetic, though they are doing so in a quiet and underhanded manner, and which manner I know, from a four years experience with rebel converted Republicans, to be quite characteristic. . . . It is scarcely necessary to tell your Excellency that A. J. Evans recently appointed U. S. Dist Atty for this District is a sound Republican and one of your true friends.—Excuse my having forgotten to mention this *only* other exception, in the body of this letter" ALS, *ibid.*, RG 60, Letters from the President.

4. On Aug. 9, Jacob Mitchell, Ebenezer, Mo., had written to USG. "A band of armed men Came to the residence of *Mrs Maria S. Mitchell* in this place recently and taken her son *Axley Mitchell* from his home and Subjected him to the most shameful treatment assigning no reason for so doing and *Axly Mitchell* has left his home through fear of being killed and I believe it my Duty to Inform you that this Insignificant band has a positive organization and speaks of the civil Law now in force as something of no significance or Resposibility   Speedy Action on your part will do much to allay the excitment fast spreading among our people at the over bearing conduct of those *out Laws*   Excuse this hasty and I am afraid almost unintelligible letter as I have been writing under the most unfavrable circumstances" ALS, *ibid.*

On the same day, Lawrence A. Hudson, "*Comg K. K. K. S. Mo.* . . . Near Mexico," Mo., wrote to Attorney Gen. George H. Williams. "[NOT PRIVATE.] . . . From your bold, defiant, and mistaken, advocacy of the despot, (Nero) U. S. Grant, I notify you and him, and all his corrupt adherents, that, from all his violated pledges, he had best retire from the campaign without undue delay, lest a Brutus, or Charlotte Corday, or a J. Wilks Boothe relieve both him and his distracted country. We are not afraid of his authority *now*. He could not *to-day* make *one effective* arrest of the most humble citizen of the broad State of Mo. I fully know 'whereof I affirm.' This is the new Revolution, and I can exclaim with Patrick Henry: 'If this be treason, then make the most of it!'" ALS (brackets in original), *ibid.*, Letters Received, Mo.

5. On Aug. 8, Benjamin F. Ross, Fredericksburg, Va., had written to USG. "I take the present opportunity to inform you, that in our County (Spottsylvania) we have work to do, in the Republican ranks. I served under your command, two and a half years. Was a member of Co. K, 54th Mass. Vol. I did my duty as a soldier faithfully, and I am not disposed to be idle in the impending struggle, therefore I wish to canvass the county for Grant and Wilson. We need men who are fearless and bold. There ought to be a Grant and Wilson Club, in every precinct. But as you have done work here in former days, I need not describe the 'position.'" ALS, DLC-William E. Chandler. On the same day, Michael J. Griffith, postmaster, Fredericksburg, endorsed this letter. "Mr. B. F. Ross is an active colored republican. He would make an efficient canvasser. He has done good service for the party in this county heretofor" AES, *ibid.*

On Sept. 14, U.S. Senator John F. Lewis of Va., Lynnwood, wrote to USG. "... I think Va will vote for Grant & Wilson by from 5 to 10000 majority. I am in daily receipt of letters giving the most encouraging accounts of the canvass, nothing can lose us the State but want of harmony, & I think there is a better feeling amongst our friends than has been for sometime. ..." ALS, DNA, RG 60, Records Relating to Appointments.

To George H. Stuart

Washington D. C. Oct. 26th *1872.*

My Dear Sir:

Your favor of the 24th inst. saying that a change in the Indian Policy of the Administration is reported to be contemplated, is just received. Such a thing has not been thought of. If the present policy toward the Indian can be improved in any way I will always be ready to receive suggestions on the subject.[1] But if any change is made it must be on the side of the Civilization & Christianization of the Indian. I do not believe our Creator ever placed different races of men on this earth with the view of having the stronger exert all his energies in exterminating the weaker.—If any change takes place in the Indian Policy of the Government, while I hold my present office, it will be on the humanitarian side of the question.

Very Truly Yours,
U. S. Grant

Geo. H. Stuart, Esq,
Phila Pa

ALS, DLC-George H. Stuart. See *PUSG*, 22, 81; Endorsement, Dec. 7, 1872; Robert Ellis Thompson, ed., *The Life of George H. Stuart, Written By Himself* (Philadelphia, 1890), pp. 239–48.

On Sept. 28, 1872, USG had advised a visiting Indian delegation "to cultivate the land and build houses for themselves. Above all things, he urged them to be at peace with the whites, who greatly outnumber them, and to have their young people instructed so that they might learn the arts of civilization." *Philadelphia Public Ledger*, Sept. 30, 1872. On Oct. 11, USG received a separate delegation of "Kiowas, Comanches, Apaches, Caddoes, Arraphoes, Wichitas, Wacos, Keechies, Towoccaroes and Delawares." "The President, through the interpreter, informed the Indians that the wish and effort of the Government toward them was to advance them in civilization and preserve their lives, by encouraging them in industrial pursuits and making them comfortable homes. The white people are now so numerous and increasing so rapidly as to crowd the Indians, and therefore it was necessary that the Indians should no more lead a roving life, but have fixed places of abode. The sooner they understood and valued this fact, the better for them and their children. The President remarked that he had nothing more to say, except through the Secretary of the Interior. The Indians listened attentively, but no invitation was given them to respond." *Ibid.*, Oct. 12, 1872. On Oct. 16 and Nov. 2, Alfred H. Love, president, Universal Peace Union, Philadelphia, wrote to USG. "Grateful for thy recent reply to my suggestions on Indian Affairs I now desire to ask thy influence to have the delegation of Indians now in Washington in charge of Cap Alvord visit our city. This being the home of Edward Parrish who died among them, we especially wish them to meet in Friends' Meeting House & understand our feeling towards them. I believe it will greatly further the object we all so much desire. Our friends will be willing to give them clothing, as some among them need it & in many ways a visit will be beneficial." "We are very much obliged for thy letter to our late meeting, recd thro' our friend Geo H Stuart in reference to the policy of the Govt towards the Indians. It was read to some 2000 of our best citizens & every sentence loudly applauded. As I had charge of the Delegation of Indians ‡while here, I wish to testify to their uniform excellent behaviour & they left us deeply impressed with our kindness & advice, & they assured us of their sincere determination to live peaceably & to endeavour to bring their different tribes into the walks of civilization. We shall continue to advise with them, & to send them such articles as will be useful to them. I took them to our Schools, Manufactories &c & they were deeply interested to learn all they could. A few of the chiefs have medals presented them under President Buchanan's administration, representing on one Side a Scalping scene by the Indians. They very much desire to have these re-coined & the beautiful emblem adopted on the other medals given under thy adminstration—Say thy profile & the words 'Let us have peace' &c, substituted. Some of them have been trying to rub off the Scalping scene, & when I presented the two medals to the meeting & said I was about to make an effort to have them re-coined, it recd the hearty applause of the meeting. Indeed these two medals mark the progress of civilization & is a great compliment to thee. I have asked James Pollock the Director of our Mint to re-coin them, & while he would be glad to do so, says he cannot without a special order to that effect from the Govt   I think this is so beautiful in the Indians & will tell so well for thy policy, that I urge this order being given. Please let me have it & we will pay all necessary expenses. I know it will greatly please these Chiefs & will aid our great work. This interchange of visits is in itself a wonderful peace agent. Let us encourage it. I forcibly presented the value of the Rail-road to them, in thus enabling them to make this visit & they go home favorable to such improvements." ALS, DNA, RG 75, Letters Received, Central Superintendency. See *HED*, 42-3-1, part 5, I, 513–17, 532–33;

Thomas W. Kavanagh, *Comanche Political History: An Ethnohistorical Perspective 1706–1875* (Lincoln, Neb., 1996), pp. 431–35.

On Nov. 14, Loring S. Williams, Glenwood, Iowa, wrote to USG. "You may perhaps remember a private interview with which you favored me, at the Tremont House in Chicago, on Monday before the great fire. I called then, and write now, because of my deep interest in your humane policy towards the Indian tribes   Your late letter, expressing an unwavering purpose to 'make no changes except in the direction of humanity and religion,' has called forth fervent thanksgivings from multitudes who believe that 'God has made of one blood all the nations of earth.' Dear Sir, you surely need not either fear or envy those who would insist on indiscriminate extermination. 'Go teach all nations—preach the gospel to every creature—and lo! I am with you always.' Moved by the Divine command, and encouraged by His promise, I left my home 56 yrs. ago, and located first at Chickamauga & Mission Ridge in Tenn. as a missionary among the Cherokee Indians. With them, and with the Choctaws in Miss. and also in the Indian Territory, I spent more than twenty years of incessant toil and privation. But it was *not* labor lost. God set his seal of approbation; and I was witness to a glorious, and extensive change in nearly everything desirable. Many hundreds, yea thousands were hopefully converted to christianity, and took a high stand for civilization. And, had it not been for the war of the rebellion, the fruits of our mission would have been much more conspicuous and permanent. I say not this boastingly, but to stimulate, if possible, to still further efforts in behalf of the *remnants* of the Aboriginal tribes. I know they are capable of improvement, and susceptible to kind treatment. Were the whole truth known concerning the positive evils imposed upon them by white men, we should hardly wonder at their present unfriendliness and degradation. One word, dear Sir, from an obsure individual, in addition to the abundant and hearty congratulations which you have received, for the glorious and unprecedented victory achieved on the 5th inst. I believe it was in answer to prayer in your behalf, and that of our beloved country. Excuse this brief encroachment upon your prcious time." ALS, DNA, RG 75, Letters Received, Miscellaneous. On Jan. 18, 1873, Williams wrote to USG requesting appointment as Indian inspector. ". . . My 20 years Missionary acquaintance with three of the southern tribes, and my intense desire that the whole truth might be known, *and the right prevail*—may be somewhat in my favor. But if, on the other hand, my advanced age, or other reasons should, in your judgment, be objectionable, it will be all right. Could I have the privilege of one more attempt at greater usefulness—at least for a few months trial, I should be thankful." ALS, *ibid.*, RG 48, Appointment Div., Letters Received. No appointment followed. See Grant Foreman, *The Five Civilized Tribes* (Norman, Okla., 1934), pp. 37–43.

1. On Nov. 28, 1872, Felix R. Brunot, chairman, and eight other members of the Board of Indian Commissioners, Pittsburgh, wrote to USG. ". . . The measures which seem to us the most important to the welfare of the Indians, and the success of the efforts for their advancement, are—1st. The enactment of a law under which the President may, by proclamation, when he shall deem expedient, extend the civil law of the United States for the punishment and prevention of crimes against each other over any civilized, or partly civilized tribe. 2d. A more stringent law to prevent the selling or giving intoxicating drinks to the Indians, or else to secure the better enforcement of existing laws; and to make Indians coming from the British territory, and selling liquor to Indians, liable to the same penalties as white men. The evil sought to be remedied in the last clause is most felt at Puget Sound, but may be anticipated all along the northern border. 3d. A more strin-

gent law for the punishment of trespassers upon Indian reservations, and some effective mode by which it may be enforced. Also, to make Indian testimony lawful in all courts of the United States. 4th. As of great importance to maintain and perfect the system of reform in the Indian service, we recommend a board of inspectors, not less than five in number, to be selected by the President from such persons as shall be recommended by the annual meetings of the various religious denominations of the United States, who shall see proper to make such recommendation, to hold office during good behavior, or until removed by the President. They shall be charged with the duty of visiting each tribe at least once a year, to examine into the accounts, mode of doing business, and the conduct and management of the officers and employés of the Government; see that treaty stipulations are kept by the United States, adopt such measures as will preserve the peace, examine into the educational progress of the Indians, hear their complaints, and right their wrongs, and witness the proper delivery of their annuities. They should have power to suspend agents or employés, subject to the President's approval, making immediate report of such suspension; to administer oaths, examine and report on claims for depredations, eject trespassers or improper persons from reservations, and call upon the military for aid when necessary. The board should be constituted of men of high character and ability, and should be paid a proper compensation, and give their exclusive attention to their duties. In connection with this, it is also recommended that the superintendencies, most of which we deem to be of doubtful utility in any case, be discontinued. The work of promoting peace with each other among the various tribes; protecting them in the possession of their reservation lands; securing to them a fair consideration for such parts of their reservations as they may desire to sell, and seeing that they get it; encouraging and supervising the removal to the Indian Territory of such as are willing to go; providing for giving lands in severalty to tribes fitted for and willing to receive them; instilling the idea of individual property interests, without which even the white man will not work; and other similar measures which are deemed necessary for the advancement of the Indian in civilization, would naturally rank among the duties of the board of inspectors. . . ." *Fourth Annual Report of the Board of Indian Commissioners to the President of the United States* (Washington, 1872), pp. 19–20. On Feb. 14, 1873, USG signed a bill that authorized the president to appoint up to five Indian inspectors. *U.S. Statutes at Large*, XVII, 463. See *CG*, 42–3, 471–81, 915–17, 1079–81, 1098.

On Jan. 15, John J. Henry, Washington, D. C., wrote to USG. "Four years ago I made an application to you for a Consulship—In the time have troubled you with two five minute calls and two letters—Lately seeing the Consul's office at Aspinwall was vacated by the death of the incumbent I wrote you asking that it might be given to me; which, as that was a less position than I thought I was entitled to, I was almost sure of getting it, but did not—And now Mr. President I most respectfully ask that you will assign me some position by which I can support my family—I have had quite large possions in the state of Delaware, but during the war lost all my property and am now too poor to go into business—I helped to organize the Republican Party in Delaware and have been an earnest worker for it ever since, as my letters on file will show—they are from *every* prominent republican in Delaware—the most of them written to President Lincoln & Sec. Seward— they gave me the appointment to Liberia which, because of the climate, I declined—I feel competent to perform satisfactorily the duties of any place that may be given me, and knowing my party services entitle me to some recognition in this my time of need I most respectfully make this last appeal to you—I would like a Consulship, but would be glad to have any thing the pay of which is not less than say $3,000—An Amendment to the Indian Appropriation bill was made providing for the appointment of five commissioners to look after the distribution of the fund:, I would be most happy to have one of these—I can procure in two days the recommendations of several members of Congress for the position—Mr. President please be plain with me, and if it be not asking too much, have this hastily written communication answered, so that I may know how it is considered by you—" ALS, DNA, RG 59, Letters of Application and Recommendation. Related papers are *ibid.* On Feb. 5, U.S. Representative Charles St. John of N. Y. wrote to USG recommending Henry's nomination as Indian inspector. ALS, *ibid.*, RG 48, Appointment Div., Letters Received. USG endorsed this letter. "Int. I think it will be well to give this application special attention." AE (undated), *ibid.* On Feb. 19, Orville E. Babcock wrote to Secretary of the Interior Columbus Delano. "The President directs me to call your attention to the name of John J. Henry, of Del. who, he thinks, will be a good appointment for one of the Indian Inspectors." Copy, DLC-USG, II, 1. On April 15, 1874, Henry, Washington, D. C., wrote to USG. "You were pleased to compliment me by offering me the consulship at Jamaica some weeks ago—I unfortunately failed in examination. Now, Mr. President I feel and believe that I am fully capable of discharging the duties incumbent upon such an officer, and most respectfully ask that if it be not entirely irregular I may be given the position or at least have another trial before the examining Board. I have been a member of many state and County Republican Conventions in Delaware—have usually been on the Committee to prepare business and often drawn with my own hand the whole of the resolutions &c. which have composed the party platform during the campaign—Have been for several sessions a member of the state legislature and chairman of its most important committees—Have been by many who know me best urged as a candidate for Congress and Governor of my state and thus far have never to my knowledge had my capacity questioned. . . ." ALS, DNA, RG 59, Miscellaneous Letters. On Dec. 9, 1875, USG nominated Henry as register of the land office at Fair Play, Colorado Territory.

On Jan. 15, 1873, Richard Yates, Jacksonville, Ill., wrote to USG. "An amendment to the Indian Appropriation Bill authorizing the President to appoint five or more Commissioners to visit the Indian Agencies has been or probably will be adopted. I desire to recommend to you as one of these Commissioners the Rev. Dr Norman W. Wood of this place. . . ." ALS, *ibid.*, RG 48, Appointment Div., Letters Received. On May 29, Norman N. Wood, Jacksonville, wrote to USG. "Col. James Dunlap of this city, my father-in-law, joins with me in desiring to recall to your recollection and favorable consideration his personal application to you, accompanied and seconded by Senator Logan, for my appointment as one of the Inspectors of Indian Affairs—. . ." ALS, *ibid.* See *The Biographical Encyclopædia of Illinois of the Nineteenth Century* (Philadelphia, 1875), p. 158.

On Jan. 21, U.S. Representative-elect Lloyd Lowndes, Jr., of Md., Cumberland, wrote to USG. "Maj T. F. Lang, formerly of West Virginia, but for the past seven years residing in the city of Baltimore desires to be appointed as one of the Inspectors of 'Indian Affairs.' In the past Maryland, has had but very few Government Appointments. Now that the Republican party is gaining headway in this State, and will have two Representatives in the next Congress, it is due to her Citizens that they should have a fair share of the patronage. . . ." LS, DNA, RG 48, Appointment Div., Letters Received. On May 8, Theodore F. Lang, Baltimore, wrote to USG. ". . . My native state is West Va. but at the close of the war I removed to this city for the purpose of practicing my profession, but seven years of incessant toil has demonstrated that the returns of my profession are not sufficient to even modestly provide for my family, . . ." ALS, *ibid.* No appointment followed.

On Jan. 29, Andrew P. Daughters, Moores Hill, Ind., wrote to USG. "Pardon my intrusion but allow me to say that I see by an act of Congress passed of late that you are authorized to appoint five persons to be inspectors of Indian agentes   Now I earnestly desire to be one of those inspectors   If you can consider me worthy of such a position, I will refer you to the Hon O P Morton Gen Ben Spooner, or my Army record, which you will find in the record of the famous old 18th Ind Inft under the Hon H D Washburn   I was at first made first Lieutenant then Asst. Surgeon and lastly Surgeon of the regiment, I was with the regiment at Vicksburgh and saw you several times was in the terrible charge on the 22d of May and on duty from early dawn till Midnigh without food or rest. At the close of the siege you accepted my resignation found upon Surgeon's certificate of actual disability that disability being Chronic diarrhoea brought on by exposeures incured while we lay at Millikens bend and greatly ~~agr~~ aggravated by exposures during the siege. I am nothing but a plain blunt man and know nothing of the maner of obtaining appointment consequently I apply to you direct   I am not a politician but have always been an uncompromising republican   All I ask is to be given a trial and if I done fill the bill oust me at once. Hoping no offence at my blunt manner of application . . ." ALS, *ibid.* No appointment followed.

On Jan. 31, James H. Wilson, New York City, wrote to USG. "I take great pleasure in commending Genl Jonathan Biggs of Westfield, Ills as a gentleman in every way qualified for and entitled to the appointment of Inspector in the Indian Bureau. Genl Biggs served under my command during the closing events of the War, was badly wounded in the assault & capture of Selma, and showed himself upon all occasions to be an officer of the highest merit. He will doubtless be able to present the most satisfactory testimonials from the leading citizens of Illinois, & I hope may be appointed." ALS, *ibid.* A related letter is *ibid.* No appointment followed.

On Feb. 5, John S. Abbey, Salem, Neb., wrote to USG. "Havng served my Country for over three years with you at your Head Quarters as your Orderly Seargent of Co. A 4th Reg of Ill Cavalry I feel like asking a faver at your Hands   If the amendment concerning Indian Inspector has been made a Law I would like to make an application for an appointment as one of the Inspectors, . . ." ALS, *ibid.* No appointment followed.

On Feb. 6, Attorney Gen. George H. Williams wrote to USG. "I have the honor to recommend for one of the Indian Inspectorships lately created by Congress Daniel Cram now of Boise City Idaho Territory   I have known Mr Cram for more than twenty years & from personal knowledge endorse his fitness for the place—. . ." ALS, *ibid.* On the same day, Secretary of War William W. Belknap favorably endorsed this letter. AES, *ibid.* No appointment followed.

On Feb. 11, David R. Locke, editor, *Toledo Blade*, wrote to USG. "Dresden W H Howard of Fulton Co Ohio. will be an applicant for th position of Indian Inspector under th act of Feb 4 '73. Mr. Howard at this time represents th Toledo District in th State Senate. and is one of th oldest and best citizens of Northwestern Ohio   He has especial fitness for th position   From his boyhood he was an Indian trader (up to th date of their leaving this Country,) and—*Mirabile dictu*—an honest one. He possessed their full confidence for he always dealt with and treated them as human, responsible, beings   He could always control them when evry body else failed. Mr. Howard is a man of th hghest character and of splendid business qualifications, and will, if appointed, discharge th duties of th place faithfully and well. His appointment would give general satisfaction in North Western Ohio where he is well known . . ." ALS, *ibid.* On Feb. 16, John E. Hunt, Toledo, wrote to USG. "Knowing your intimacy with my Brother Major C. C. P. Hunt and my

Brother in Law Mr Soulard of Gallena Illinois I presume to address this letter to you in behalf of the Honerable D. W. Howard a member of the ohio Senate who is an applicant for the office of Inspector of Indian Affairs. I have been acquainted with him for upwards of Therty five years, and knowing his kind and intimate acquaintance with Indians, I do not hesitate to recommend him to your most favourable consideration for the appointment." ALS, *ibid.* Related papers are *ibid.* No appointment followed.

On Feb. 17, Judge William McKennan, U.S. Circuit Court, Washington, Pa., wrote to USG. "I am informed that the name of Thomas B. Searight Esq. of Fayette Co., will be presented to you in connection with some Federal office—I do not know what specific office is desired for him, but I take pleasure in commending the effort in his behalf to your most favorable consideration—. . ." ALS, *ibid.* Speaker of the House James G. Blaine endorsed this letter. "The office specially requested fr Col: Searight is one of the five Inspectorships of Indian affairs—The Secry of the Interior has been urged to recommend the appointment—Senator Cameron specially desires it" AES (undated), *ibid.* On June 25, McKennan again wrote to USG concerning Thomas B. Searight. ". . . Although comparatively young he occupied for many years a leading and influential position in the Democratic party, is a most energetic and indefatigable man, and has a large following in the Dem. party in Fayette Co—I am most reliably assured that the large reduction of Buckalews majority, and the overwhelming vote cast for you in Fayette Co, last fall, were mainly due to his efforts and influence, and that the proposed recognition of him will enable him, by the good will with which it will inspire his friends, to detach many of them permanently from the Dem. party, and so perhaps reverse the majority in the County. . . ." ALS, *ibid.* On March 15 and Oct. 19, McKennan wrote to USG on the same subject. ALS, *ibid.* On Dec. 2, USG nominated Searight as surveyor gen., Colorado Territory.

On Feb. 21, Levi P. Luckey wrote to Delano. "The President directs me to enclose you the accompanying card of Col Hampton B. Denman, and say that it is the name of the gentleman submitted for one of the Indian Inspectors, by Father Deshon, on the part of the Catholic Church." Copy, DLC-USG, II, 1. No appointment followed.

On March 12, U.S. Senator George E. Spencer of Ala. wrote to USG. "I take greate pleasure in recommending the Hon C. W. Buckley to be appointed *Indian Inspector.* Mr Buckley's distinguished services in Congress, and in Alabama justly entitle him to this appointment. I do not think the South has a single appointment in the Indian Bureau. This appointment would give great satisfaction to the party in Alabama." ALS, DNA, RG 48, Appointment Div., Letters Received. Related papers are *ibid.* Charles W. Buckley ended his term as U.S. Representative on March 3; he became probate judge of Montgomery County, Ala., in 1874.

On March 14, 1873, U.S. Representative Mark H. Dunnell of Minn. wrote to USG. "I would respectfully recommend for Indian Inspector Hon. Stephen Miller Ex.-Gov. of Minnesota, now a resident of Worthington, Minn. . . ." ALS, *ibid.* See *PUSG*, 20, 418.

On March 22, Albert E. Redstone, president, National Labor Council, Albert W. Puett, and one other, Washington, D. C., wrote to USG. "The Committee of the National Labor Council would respectfully present the name of Albert W. Puett for the position of Indian Inspector—Mr Puett posesses high qualifications in every particular—has a thorough knowledge of the Customs and habits of the Indian having spent 18 years—of his life in the West—he is a graduate of the Western Military College of Drennon Springs Kentucky, and was highly recommended for Superintendent of Indian affairs for the Territory of Montana in 1869—by Dr Bowman President of Indiana Asbury University—(now Bishop) and by the Board of Home and Foreign Missionaries of Cincinnati, besides

other letters—of personal recommendation, all of which are on file at the office of the Interior—Mr Puett is a member of the National Labor Council—and of the National Executive Committee of United Working Men of America and a man of temperate habits—"
LS, DNA, RG 48, Appointment Div., Letters Received. On March 11, Redstone and Puett
had written to U.S. Senator Simon Cameron of Pa. "A committee of the National Labor
Council have waited upon the President—and filed a request—that they be permited to
select, and present for appointment—one of their own Members of the Labor Council, for
the position of Indian Inspector, the Law creating said Inspectors. provides that, they shall
visit the Indian Agencies and Superintendencies, throughout the Country. We therefore
wish to have one of our members, who shall be a highly qualified man in every particular,
that we may be able to establish a thorough system of communication with the working
people through our Labor Journals—with a view of Planting Colonies upon the public Lands—in the Western and South Western Territories—as to climate, soil—and the
most available points for agricultural purposes, we would have knowledge through our
representative. If it is in your power to assist us in this matter, and the movement meets
with your approval, we should hold ourselves under obligation to you—" LS, *ibid.* On
March 12, Cameron forwarded this letter to USG. ES, *ibid.* On March 11, U.S. Senator
George G. Wright of Iowa forwarded a letter on the same subject to USG. AES, *ibid.* No
appointment followed.

On March 24, USG endorsed Lt. Gen. Philip H. Sheridan's recommendation for
William M. Dye, USMA 1853. "Refered to the Sec. of the Int. I would give special attention to this application when Indian Inspectors are appointed. The services and education
of Gen. Dye specially fit him for such a position." AES, *ibid.* No appointment followed.

On March 25, Mary C. Geary, Harrisburg, Pa., wrote to USG. "Enclosed find letters
received since Gov Geary's decease pertaining to the appointment of his brother the
Rev Edward R Geary of Oregon as Inspector of Indian Affairs. Any thing you can do for
him would be most acceptable to me" ALS, *ibid.* Related papers are *ibid.* See *Portrait and
Biographical Record of Western Oregon* (Chicago, 1904), pp. 128, 131.

On March 27, U.S. Senator Arthur I. Boreman of West Va. wrote to USG. "Having
communicated with you personally, on behalf of General A. C. Jones, of West Virginia, soliciting for him the appointment of an Inspector of Indian Agencies, an office recently created, I desire herewith to make formal application for the same, . . ." LS, DNA, RG 48,
Appointment Div., Letters Received. On the same day, Spencer favorably endorsed this
letter. AES, *ibid.* On March 31, U.S. Representative Charles Hays of Ala. wrote to USG
recommending Alexander C. Jones as Indian inspector. ALS, *ibid.* In an undated letter,
Thomas P. Ochiltree wrote to USG on the same subject. ". . . Genl Jones bore a conspicuous part in the Confederate service, but, since the war, has acted the *role* of a good citizen . . ." ALS, *ibid.* No appointment followed.

On April 19, Henry T. Blow, St. Louis, wrote to USG. "Maj Wright informs me that
he has applied (for one of the appointments under the recent law) for Indian Inspector—
I take pleasure in stating therefore that your old friend and neighbor, has earned more
than ever the confidence and esteem of all classes of our fellow Citizens, and from his business experience and great natural adaption, is peculiarly fitted for the position" ALS, *ibid.*
Recommendations from John W. Noble and Chester H. Krum for Henry C. Wright are
ibid. On Dec. 7, 1874, USG nominated Wright as appraiser, St. Louis.

On April 30, 1873, Krum, St. Louis, wrote to USG. "I beg leave to recommend to
your favorable notice, my personal and intimate friend Colonel Charles Doty of Illinois.
The Colonel is, I believe an applicant for appointment as an Inspector in the Indian Bu-

reau. I presume he was known to you, during the war, through his connection with the Departments of Tennessee and of the Missouri. Of late, Colonel Doty has paid special attention to his farm in the neighborhood of Alton, and, although a thorough Republican has, in this way been less active in Politics. . . ." ALS, *ibid.* William H. Benton, Charles W. Ford, and six others favorably endorsed this letter. ES (undated), *ibid.* An undated letter of application from Charles Doty to USG listing prominent persons as references is *ibid.* Doty later served as asst. superintendent, Supervising Architect's Office, St. Louis.

On March 8, Governor Cadwallader C. Washburn of Wis. had written to USG. "I am informed that my friend of 30 years ago, & ever since, Gen. Wm Vandever of DuBuque is being pressed by his friends for a Federal appointment—I think that you personally know Genl V—but I wish to join my request with that of his many friends & to express the hope that he may receive some appointment, that shall accord with his merits, as a gentleman & a soldier." ALS, PHi. On March 27, 1869, William Vandever, Dubuque, had written to USG. "At the risk of being considered importunate I address you—Senator Harlan writes me that the Iowa delegation have agreed to ask for my appointment as Governor of one of the Territories   I know that the preasure must be great for positions of that kind—and I only desire to express the hope that you will consider the matter favorably—You know enough about me to determine whether I am worthy of such a trust." ALS, DNA, RG 59, Letters of Application and Recommendation. On Dec. 2, 1873, USG nominated William Vandever, Jonathan D. Bevier, Jared W. Daniels (see Warren Upham and Rose Barteau Dunlap, *Minnesota Biographies 1655–1912* (St. Paul, 1912), p. 160), Edward C. Kemble (see *New York Times*, Feb. 11, 1886), and John C. O'Connor (see *ibid.*, Feb. 11, 1892) as Indian inspectors.

On Feb. 15, 1873, Benjamin F. Lee, Harrisburg, had written to USG seeking appointment as Indian inspector. ALS, DNA, RG 48, Appointment Div., Letters Received. On April 3, Alexander L. Russell, Pa. AG, wrote to USG. ". . . Col. Lee, is a brother-in law of the late Ex Govr Jn. W. Geary, has filled important & responsible positions, in both civil and military life—is largely connected and acquainted throughout Penna, and, I am confident, his appointment would afford great gratification to a large circle of acquaintances & friends—" ALS, *ibid.* Related papers are *ibid.* On Dec. 9, 1874, USG nominated Lee as Indian inspector following O'Connor's resignation. The Senate never voted on Lee's nomination, presumably because USG signed a bill on March 3, 1875, that reduced the allowable number of Indian inspectors from five to three. See *CR*, 43–2, 464–65, 1539; *U.S. Statutes at Large*, XVIII, part 3, pp. 422–23; *HED*, 44-1-1, part 5, I, 517.

In an undated letter, George J. Mortimer wrote to USG. "I beg leave respectfully to renew my application (originally made in 1873) for the position of Indian Inspector. At that time I submitted recommendations of which the following is a summary: 1—From the entire Republican delegation in Congress from Mississippi;. . . Letters from James Lynch Sectr of State—Mr Revels formerly U S Senator—John R Lynch M C and a number of other prominent Colored men . . . At different times you were pleased Mr President to make the following endorsements in my behalf: (1) 'I suggest that the name of this applicant be one that is submitted to the Peace Commissioners as a suitable person for one of the Indian Inspectors! Feb 1st 1873 (Signed) U S GRANT.' (2) 'When Indian Inspectors are appointed I wish special attention given to this recommendation. (signed) U S GRANT.' For reasons with which I am unacquainted my former application was not successful   I now renew it in the hope that a more favorable result will ensue and that I may have your kind assistance in the matter. . . ." ALS, DNA, RG 48, Appointment Div., Letters Received. On May 8, 1875, Mortimer, New York City, wrote to USG. ". . . I have been here now nearly a month trying to effect a negotiation in Southern Lands (of which we own many thousand acres) but so far have had no success—I was a heavy looser in property by The War a competency acquired by hard-work and close application   If the position I ask for, is filled, Can you not provide some place for me in which I Can Creditably maintain myself & family and be useful to The Government? . . ." ALS, *ibid.* No appointment followed. Papers from other unsuccessful applicants for nomination as Indian inspector are *ibid.*

To Jesse Root Grant

WASHINGTON,
November 3, 1872.

DEAR FATHER: I am in receipt of Mr. Brent's letter, dictated by you expressing a wish to see me, if possible, before the meeting of Congress. I think it will be possible for me to go this week, probably leaving here on Thursday[1] or Friday next. I would like as far as possible to avoid meeting people while there. I hope, therefore, you will say nothing about my coming. Probably Julia, Fred, Nellie, and Jesse will accompany me. You probably have not room enough in the house for us all; but that will make no difference. Fred and Jesse can stay at the hotel. All are quite well.

Yours truly,
U. S. GRANT.

M. J. Cramer, *Ulysses S. Grant: Conversations and Unpublished Letters* (New York, 1897), pp. 126–27. See letter to Frederick Dent Grant, Dec. 31, 1872.

1. Nov. 7. See following letter.

To Gen. William T. Sherman

Washington, D. C. Nov: 6. 1872

MY DEAR GENERAL

I had already received a dispatch announcing the death of Genl. Meade when your note enclosing one to the same effect reached me. I would like to see you in the morning to make proper arrangments of sympathy and respect for so distinguished and gallant a soldier

Yours Truly

U. S. GRANT

GENL. W. T. SHERMAN U. S. A.

Copy, DLC–William T. Sherman. On Nov. 7, 1872, Gen. William T. Sherman telegraphed to Brig. Gen. Irvin McDowell. "Go to Philadelphia, see Mrs Meade and make all suitable arrangements for General Meade's funeral at the cost of the United States. You are charged with conducting the funeral ceremonies. The President will order and approve a reasonable bill of expenses. He wants to attend the funeral but had arranged to start with his whole family to visit his old father at Covington. . . ." Copy, DNA, RG 94, Letters Sent. Sherman wrote an undated note to USG. "You will see Mrs Meade wants the funeral next Monday—will that change your determination. It is almost impossible to reason with persons in affliction. Shall I delay the Detachmt 1st. Arty. it will involve expense" ANS, *ibid.*, Letters Received, 4474 1872. Sherman endorsed this note. "Ansd—by letter of the Prsidt" AE (undated), *ibid.* On Nov. 7, Sherman wrote to Col. Richard C. Drum. "General McDowell is charged with the funeral of General Meade at the cost of the United States. Please see Mrs Meade, and ascertain all her wishes which shall be sacred. The President will write her to day. . . ." Copy, *ibid.*, Letters Sent. USG drafted a response to an invitation to a "Memorial Meeting in honor of the late Maj. Gen. Meade today . . . only received this moment. Although my public duties would prevent my attending, had the invitation been received in time. I take this occasion to express my appreciation of the high character, great virtues, and public services of the deceased. . . ." Parke-Bernet Sale No. 2235, Dec. 3, 1963, no. 104. USG attended the funeral on Nov. 11. See *New York Times*, Nov. 11, 12, 1872. On Jan. 27, 1873, USG wrote to David McConaughy, Gettysburg. "I am in receipt of your letter of the 24th inst. requesting me to serve as an Associate member of the Meade Memorial Executive Committee, and in reply I beg to assure you of my hearty cooperation in the commendable work undertaken by the Committee, and my best wishes for its success." Copy, DLC-USG, II, 1.

On Nov. 9, 1872, U.S. Senator Lot M. Morrill of Maine, Augusta, telegraphed to USG. "To remind the President of an interview in which I urged the promotion of General Pope as eminently fitting and to repeat it now that opportunity offers." Telegram received, DNA, RG 94, ACP, 5013 1883. On the same day, Rutherford B. Hayes, Richard Smith, Manning F. Force, and Andrew Hickenlooper, Cincinnati, telegraphed to USG. "It would greatly gratify us if you can find it consistent with your views of duty to promote General John Pope," Telegram received, *ibid.* In an undated letter, U.S. Senator Matthew H. Carpenter of Wis. wrote to USG. "The death of Genl Mead makes a vacancy which I hope will be filled by appointing Genl Pope, who, in my judgmt was the *worst used* general of the war. He has ability and energy; is sound in mind & body and was always earnest and zealous in loyalty to the flag." ALS, *ibid.*

On Nov. 11, 1872, Brig. Gen. Oliver O. Howard, Washington, D. C., wrote to Sherman. "After much reflection and consultation with my near friends I have resolved to withdraw my application to be retired from the Army. Should the President promote me and then immediately retire me it would look as if it was simply a riddance and not a re-ward of service—'We will make you a Major General if you will retire' will be to most men, particularly in the Army, the actual interpretation of the President's action most kindly intended on his part. . . ." ALS, DLC-William T. Sherman; Df, MeB. On Nov. 12, Sherman wrote to Howard. "I have received your note of yesterday, and have been over to the President, to whom I read your letter at length. I have, therefore fully complied with your request—and must leave him to exercise his own office. . . ." Copies (2), DLC-William T. Sherman.

On the same day, Lt. Gen. Philip H. Sheridan, Washington, D. C., wrote to Sherman. ". . . I saw the President who has made up his mind I think to take the Head of the list & let McDowell go to the Dept of Dakota Howard if he goes at all will go to the lakes. I spoke about Howard as I said I would. The President saves all annoyance & trouble by taking the Head of the list. . . ." ALS, *ibid.* On Nov. 16, Sherman wrote to Sheridan. "(*Confidential*) . . . Yesterday I saw the President and talked with him about the changes incident to General Meade's death, and I think the following will result as soon as General Belknap comes, but as some slip may occur, please keep it profoundly secret, as I would not, for the world, have the matter get out through me. You are entitled to this confidence, for it conforms quite nearly to what you advised in your note of the 12th received same evening. 1st Cooke is to be promoted and retired and Howard is to be ordered to the Dept. of the Lakes. 2d McDowell to be promoted and ordered to command the Department of the South, and Division of the South; Terry to go to Dakota. 3d Hancock to go to New York to command the Military Division of the Atlantic and the Department of the East. I have recommended this in writing because it will reconcile Hancock, without putting him in the South, and it will put the three Major Generals on an equal footing like Schofield. . . ." Copies (2), *ibid.* See Sheridan to Sherman, Nov. 18, ALS, *ibid.* On Dec. 2, USG nominated McDowell as maj. gen.

On Dec. 9, William Dennison, Columbus, Ohio, wrote to USG. "I have been asked by a friend of Col. W B Hazen to join in the application made or about to be made for the promotion of the Col. in view of the Army vacancies which I am informed now exist, which I cheerfully do, because of my high appreciation of the Colonel's character & Army services. . . ." ALS, DNA, RG 94, ACP, H1207 CB 1863. No promotion followed.

Endorsement

Respectfully refered to the Atty. Gen. I approve the apt. of Wm Patrick as Dist. Atty. for the Eastern Dist. of Mo. and think the commission had better be sent without delay.

U. S. GRANT

NOV. 12TH /72

AES, DNA, RG 60, Records Relating to Appointments. Written on an undated petition from Fidelio C. Sharp *et al.* to USG. "The undersigned members of the Bar of the

City of StLouis, feeling well satisfied that he will make a competent and faithful officer, respectfully join in recommending Wm Patrick Esq for appointment as United States Attorney for the Eastern District of Missouri, made vacant by the resignation of Chester H. Krum Esq." DS (32 signatures), *ibid.* On Oct. 25, 1872, John McDonald, supervisor of Internal Revenue, St. Louis, wrote to USG. "I have the honor to recommend William Patrick Esq. of this City for the position of United States District Attorney for the Eastern District of this State. I have known Mr. Patrick personally for many years and can truthfully say that he is a young man of fine ability, remarkable energy & sterling honesty. . . ." LS, *ibid.* On Nov. 8, Chester H. Krum, St. Louis, wrote to USG. "I have the honor to recommend William Patrick Esq for appointment as US. Attorney for this District. Having been in daily intercourse with Mr Patrick for the last two years, I can and do assure you, that he is well qualified for the position. He is well known here as a lawyer and citizen. He has been my ɐAssistant, during my entire term of office. He is familiar with all of the duties and the routine of the position   Mr Patrick stands as well at the Bar here, as any of the younger members. In Criminal Law, I believe, that he is as well versed as any member of our Bar. Above all other things, I assure you, that he is an honest and fearless man. There is no such thing as double-dealing in his composition. I am sure, that his appointment will give general satisfaction." ALS, *ibid.* Related papers, including favorable endorsements from Charles W. Ford and William H. Benton, are *ibid.* On Dec. 2, USG nominated William Patrick as U.S. attorney, Eastern District, Mo. See *PUSG*, 20, 313–15.

On Oct. 17, U.S. Senator George F. Edmunds of Vt., Burlington, wrote to USG. "I am informed that Henry H Denison Esqr of St Louis is a candidate for District Atty. U S. at that place. While I do not, of course, wish to interfere in respect to appointments in Misso, I am glad to feel at liberty to bear testimony to the high character of Mr Denison while he was a citizen of Vermont. His family is among the oldest and most respected in our state; and before his removal west he held with credit places of trust and honor under our laws. So far, then, as it is lawful for me to have a wish on the subject, it is most heartily that he may have the post he is proposed for." ALS, DNA, RG 60, Records Relating to Appointments. Related papers are *ibid.* No appointment followed.

On Oct. 22, Thomas C. Fletcher, St. Louis, wrote to USG. "The Office of U. S. District Attorney for the Eastern District of Missouri, is about to become vacant by the resignation of Chester H Krum Esqr, the present incumbent whom we have nominated, and will certainly elect as a Judge of the Circuit Court of St Louis County. I have done the State some service and devoted more time to the interests of the party than was consistent with duty to my own interests, hence I am prompted by my necessities to become a beggar for an office. If you will give me the appointment of U. S. Dist' Atty' to fill the vacancy to occur by Krum's resignation, I will gratefully accept it and discharge its duties in a manner creditable to your Administration as well as to myself as a lawyer. That my appointment would be satisfactory to the party in Mo' I refer to Mr Blow, chairman of the State Central Committee, or to Mr McKee or any of the well informed and leading republicans of our State." ALS, *ibid.* On March 5, 1869, Fletcher had written to USG seeking appointment as minister to Switzerland. ALS, *ibid.*, RG 59, Letters of Application and Recommendation. No appointments followed. See *PUSG*, 16, 282–86, 415–18.

To Benjamin H. Bristow

———

Washington. D. C. Nov. 15th 1872

DEAR SIR:

In accepting your resignation of the office of Solicitor General this day tendered, permit me to express the regret I feel at severing official relations with one who has filled his trust with so much zeal and ability.

Being the first Solicitor General under the Government of the United States it has been your privilege, though accompanied by arduous labor, to organize that department. All who have come in official contact with you bear witness to the efficiency with which the service of organizing and managing the affairs of the office has been conducted.

In the new field of labor laid out for yourself you take with you assurances of my best wishes for your future success, and confidence that you cannot fail.

I thank you heartily for the kind words contained in your letter of resignation toward me, personally, and my administration of the office entrusted to me by a people to whom I shall ever feel grateful[1]

With high regard
Your obdt svt.
U. S. GRANT

HON B. H. BRISTOW, SOLICITOR GENERAL

Copy, DLC–USG, II, 1. On Nov. 1[5], 1872, Benjamin H. Bristow wrote to USG. "Pursuant to the purpose communicated to you verbally some months ago, I now tender my resignation of the office of Solicitor General, to take effect upon the qualification of my successor. Be assured, Mr. President, that in retiring from the office to which I was called by your generous confidence, I take with me a most grateful remembrance of your personal and official kindness during my term of office. I beg to tender my congratulations upon your reëlection to the Presidency by so large a majority of your fellow citizens. I trust that your administration for the next term may be free from many of the cares that I know have attended the first, and I have no doubt that its close will find the country satisfied with its results." LS, DNA, RG 60, Letters from the President. See *PUSG,* 22,

311; Ross A. Webb, *Benjamin Helm Bristow: Border State Politician* (Lexington, Ky., 1969), pp. 110–12. On Dec. 2, 1872, USG nominated Samuel F. Phillips to replace Bristow. See *PUSG*, 21, 331.

On Nov. 2, 1872, Henry H. Wells, U.S. attorney, Eastern District, Va., Richmond, had written to USG. "I should be glad to recieve the appointment of Solicitor General, made vacant by the resignation of General Bristow." ALS, DNA, RG 60, Applications and Recommendations. On Nov. 21, Wells wrote to USG resigning his office. LS, *ibid.*, Letters Received, Va. On Dec. 3, USG nominated Henry H. Wells, Jr., to replace his father. On Dec. 8, 1873, Wells, Jr., Richmond, wrote to USG resigning his office. LS, *ibid.*, Letters from the President.

On Dec. 12, 1872, Robert Bolling, Washington, D. C., wrote to U.S. Senator George F. Edmunds of Vt. "I desire to reduce to writing the statement I made to you yesterday in the presence of Ex: Gov. H. H. Wells & Hon Jas H. Platt Jr of Virginia, in reference to charges of intemperance brought against H. H. Wells Jr, before your committee— I have known Mr Wells for many years have been officially connected with him in Richmond for two years, and have never known, or heard of his being intemperate, or at any time under the influence of ardent spirits or wine—The first time that I ever heard of such a charge was in your presence—I make this statement as a matter of simple justice to one whom I think has been unjustly assailed." ALS, *ibid.*, RG 46, Nominations. USG wrote. "Look up papers from Robt. Bolling relating to Va office holders." AN (undated), Omaha Public Library, Omaha, Neb. On Dec. 11, 1869, Secretary of War William W. Belknap had forwarded to USG a letter of Nov. 29 from Bolling, Richmond, "suggesting the passage of a bill relieving all persons from political disabilities imposed by the Reconstruction Acts." Copy, DNA, RG 107, Orders and Endorsements. On May 12, 1871, USG nominated Bolling as assessor of Internal Revenue, 2nd District, Va. See *New York Times*, Sept. 1, 1868.

On Nov. 11, 1872, Richard Smith, Cincinnati, telegraphed to USG. "The appointment of R M Corwine to position of Solicitor General would be satisfactory to political friend[s] here." Telegram received, DNA, RG 60, Applications and Recommendations. On Oct. 10, 1870, Richard M. Corwine, Cincinnati, had written to USG disavowing those who then urged his appointment as solicitor gen. LS, *ibid.* No appointment followed.

1. On Nov. 6, 1872, Simeon B. Chittenden, New York City, wrote to USG. ". . . Aside from my great regard for you, I rejoice in the issue of the canvass as a crowning testimony to the sagacity and intelligence of the people. I hear it said on all hands that you are much stronger than the Republican party: that the democrats and sore heads *might* have elected *Mr* Adams: that you have been right handsomely vindicated, and now have an independent position with high authority to do that which seems to you right. With my best respects and warm congratulations to Mrs Grant, . . ." ALS, USG 3. On Nov. 8, Judge Philip B. Swing, U.S. District Court, Cincinnati, wrote to USG. "I hope you will pardon my expressions of gratification in your full, and complete, vindication by the American People, and in the glorious triumph of the Party, and principles, of which you are, the representative. . . ." ALS, *ibid.* On Nov. 9, Judge William McKennan, U.S. Circuit Court, Washington, Pa., wrote to USG. "Now—that the Presidential election has resulted so auspiciously, I beg to offer you my congratulations—Precluded, by the proprieties of my position, from any active participation in the canvass, I have not been insensible of its momentous import, or an uninterested observer of its progress—From the beginning I felt confident it could only terminate as it has done; but that confidence grew into assurance

when your adversaries, from Sumner down, proclaimed that it was to be a personal one, and instituted a carnival of calumny, unequaled, in coarseness and malignity, in political contests, since the time of Washington. . . ." ALS, *ibid.* On Nov. 20, Chambers Baird, Ripley, Ohio, wrote to USG. "Allow me, who knew you when a school-boy in our Town, to sincerely Congratulate you on your triumphant re-election, & the vindication by the people of the United States, of your public administration, & your private character. May God's. blessing be with you, in public & in private. I have faith that you will administer the affairs of the Nation honestly & faithfully. Accept my kindest regards & best wishes." ALS, *ibid.* On the same day, John F. Long, St. Louis, wrote to USG. "If not too late, Allow me to congratulate you on your extraordinary vote,—the largest ever obtained in America— both *Electorial* and *popular.* May your Second Term prove as great and glorious as your first. God Speed you." ALS, *ibid.*

On Nov. 6, Mayor Thomas B. Carroll of Troy, N. Y., wrote to USG. "Allow me to add my congratulations to the ~~pleasure~~ I assurances I had the pleasure of giving you in our pleasant meeting at Burlington last summer. This strong 'democratic city' gives you a handsome majority (500) over the 'Liberal' confederation. I now desire to see you add San Domingo to your San Juan triumph, and shall be happy to contribute towards the achievement." ALS, *ibid.* On Nov. 14, Mayor Simon S. Davis of Cincinnati wrote to USG. "I most heartily Congratulate you upon the recognition by the American people of the merits of your Administration—in the great majorities at our late election—but I regret exceedingly that Hamilton co Ohio did so badly. . . ." ALS, *ibid.*

On Nov. 6, Samuel M. Isaacs, *Jewish Messenger,* New York City, wrote to USG. "Permit me to add my congratulations to the hundreds showered upon you. Four years more of peace and good will are secured to our country by your reelection. With the blessings of God upon your administration, . . ." ALS, *ibid.* On Nov. 12, Wesley Prettyman, "Presiding Elder of North Georgia District, Methodist E Church" and postmaster, Marietta, Ga., wrote to USG. ". . . The execution of the laws, in the arrest of those who committed the atrocities at Macon, during the October election, I have regarded as a sublime exhibition of moral courage. Considering that the Presidential election was just at hand, it was one of the heroic features of yr Administration. Without those arrests, intimidation and violence would have made the November election a sham, in Georgia, and human life itself would have been largely sacrificed. This fidelity of yr administration has so happily effected the public mind that men voted in comparative security, and, as you have learned, the Democratic majority was reduced from that of the October election, more than fifty thousand. It promised greater quiet and safety, in this and all neighboring counties, to bring the colored voters to the county towns, and beyond our hopes, they voted solid, everywhere, for the General of the Armies who freed them. . . ." ALS, *ibid.* On the same day, "The Sisters of the Young Ladies' Academy," Dubuque, Iowa, wrote to USG offering "humble, but heartfelt congratulations" and appealing for a building donation. L (initialed), *ibid.*

On Nov. 6, Harry Atwater, Cranford, N. J., wrote to USG. "Do you remember My little Ponies at Long Branch   well they worked auful hard all day yesterday   I took 23 men to the Box who voted for you and I drove them there with My Ponies 12 of them were black man   The man at the Box laughed at me and would not let me vote because I am only 8 years old but when I am 21 I will vote for you   The Ponies had little flags and ribbons all over them and every body said they looked splendid.   they have not got sick yet and they can trot auful fast." ALS, *ibid.* On Nov. 9, W. R. Johnson, Jr., Tuscola, Ill., wrote to USG. "excuse me for taking the liberty of writing you a few lines. I congratalate you very much on being again elected the head of the Nation. I was not old enough to give you a vote but you had a few hundred thousand to spare so it did not make aney difference. . . ." ALS, *ibid.* On Nov. 11, Bancroft G. Davis, San Francisco, wrote to USG. "I am very glad that you are ellected President again. I did not think that Greeley had any chance, from the first. Nearly all the boys that I know are Grant boys, and my little sister Frederica said if she went for any body she would go for Grant; she is three years old, and thought it very hard because she could not vote. I am only eight years old and it will be a a good while before I shall be able to vote, but when I am, I shall vote for you.   when you come to San Francisco, I hope I shall have the pleasure of seeing you." ALS, *ibid.* On Nov. 25, John J. Cronan, House of Refuge, Cincinnati, wrote to USG. "Please pardon the freedom of a Refuge boy in addressing you by letter, as I do this in behalf of the boys to congratulate you on your reelection to office. If we are Refuge boys we have lots of fun. We heard through the papers that you were soon to visit Kentucky. We should be happy to have you pay our Institution a visit some time when you come this way. We have boys who will make voters in a few years, and we are now learning the Constitution of the United States—which we do not fancy very much—to prepare ourselves for voting. I think you have not forgotten when you were a school boy and tried to shrirk your lessons once in a while. . . ." ALS, *ibid.* This letter closed with a request that USG send a Christmas contribution.

On Nov. 6, Nellie Witherspoon *et al.*, Rochester Female Academy, N. Y., wrote to USG. "We have heard of your election with great joy and although we are not any of us believers in 'woman's rights' in regard to voting, we have been about as much excited over this election as the voters themselves. . . ." LS (34 signatures), *ibid.* On the same day, Kittie Dovel, Marshall College, Huntington, West Va., wrote to USG. "I am so overjoyed that you are going to be elected that I thought I would write you a letter of congratulation. I am a small girl only thirteen years of age and I am going to school at the state normal school of West Va.   my home is in Ironton Ohio.   my Father and two brothers and all of my kin folks are republicans and I just preach politices to evry one I see. I have the name of Grant girl in Ironton. All of the students here are for Greeley and I just argue with them all of the time I get. Our Professor is a republican and the other teacher is for Greeley and I think I have just about run him crazy   he says he thinks I will be another Mrs S. B. Anthony she is in for womans rights and she makes speeches. The boys all make fun of us and tell us that next year they are going to send us out to make stump speeches. I tell them that is honorable. It is a very bad night to night it is raining very hard. They tell me that you are a democrat and have just lately turned to be a republican is it so. I did not believe it and they tell me that you put all of your poor kin into offices that is none of their business a president has a right to put in office who he pleases. . . ." ALS, *ibid.* Also on Nov. 6, Jennie Richey, Marshall College, wrote to USG. ". . . I am a little girl nearly ten years old. My Papa was killed in your army. I go to school here at College in West Va. but my home is in Ohio.   all the other scholars here ecsep Kitty my room mate are for Greeley. I am so glad they can't vote. Mr President do you think the women will ever get to voteing. The boys laugh at us for being for Grant, but we, Kitty and I don't care, we don't like Rebels, nor Horace Greeley, but we love *you* and always will. I haven't got any brothers, but if I had I expect they would all vote for you. Mr President please don't let them kill you as they did President Lincolin. You must be most awful careful. . . ." ALS, *ibid.*

On Nov. 7, 1872, Governor Edward F. Noyes of Ohio had written to USG. "Please accept my hearty congratulations upon your triumphant election to the Presidency once more. The personal endorsement which your magnificent majorities proclaim must be very gratifying to you. It has been demonstrated that personal abuse, villification and falsehood are not good arguments for a political campaign,—that private hate and the desire for revenge on account of offended vanity, will hardly constitute a solid platform for a great party. We think Ohio,—notwithstanding it was the head quarters of Liberalism,—will give you about the majority of four years ago—We all rejoice in the result." ALS, *ibid.* Governor John W. Geary of Pa. (the same day) and Governor Marshall Jewell of Conn. (Nov. 14) also wrote congratulatory letters to USG. ALS, *ibid.* On Nov. 19, Speaker of the House James G. Blaine, Augusta, Maine, wrote to USG congratulating him on reelection while urging a friend's appointment as territorial judge. ALS, DNA, RG 60, Records Relating to Appointments. Joseph R. Hawley and Richard J. Oglesby wrote to USG in 1872 acclaiming his victory. William Evarts Benjamin, Catalogue No. 42, March, 1892, pp. 12, 16.

On Nov. 7, Michael J. Griffith, postmaster, Fredericksburg, Va., wrote to USG. "As one of your Army clerks, it affords me much pleasure to congratulate you upon your triumphant vindication by your countrymen, and the overwhelming majority in favor of peace, progress, prosperity and sound principles. . . ." ALS, USG 3. On Nov. 23, Josiah Deloach, postmaster, Memphis, wrote to USG. "I have intended to write and congratulate you on the result of the Election on 5 inst   We the republicans carried the City by a large majority for you—and the Congressional district by the Election of Judge Barbour Lewis over Landon C Haynes by a majority of 3,600 votes,—Haynes was the pet of the appeal and Secession democracy, with a majority under the Gerremandering of the last legislature which gave him according to the vote of 1870 a majority of 2,500.—Yet we overcame his advantage and have elected a full and unequivocal republican Judge Lewis your most ardent friend and Supporter—this result is a full and perfect endorsement of you and your Administration, I rejoice it is so, and flatter myself I have aided in bringing about this glorious result—In one week more we could have carried the state for Grant & Wilson—. . ." ALS, *ibid.*

On Nov. 7, C. H. S. Williams, Brooklyn, wrote to USG. "Amid congratulations, I proffer a word from the vanquished. I do not pretend to *represent*, yet I am a fair specimen of the Liberal Republicans who opposed you without personal grievances. In our State Convention we were compelled to nip in the bud the schemes of Mr. Fenton. We took about the view of your course set forth in enclosed article from the 'Nation.' We reverenced Horace Greeley's power as a worker for the people—though often questioning his methods. So we who were not politicians did what we could to rally the people in a new party. We have failed. Beyond all other explanations, the people prefer to trust you to care for the rights of all. The masses of the Dem. decline to join in the new movement. Thus we are left without party ties. Now as patriots we hope that you will disappoint our fears & criticisms. We have no claim on you. We expect no consideration at the hands of your advisers. The weakness of your party now is that it is *too strong*. We shall be honestly glad to approve your policy, for we have honestly doubted its tendency. Help us to be disinterestedly satisfied with your second term. If you appreciate the spirit in which I speak, you will not take this as an impertinence. Once, when my father & family were leaving your camp hospitality at City Point, I said a few words, expressive of pleasure, which I thought you deemed presumptuous in one of my age. Fresh from the Adj. Gen's Office of this State, & trained to observation, they were not so. Now I speak as one who has made public affairs a lifelong study, yet never strays from law into politics except at rare calls of public need—as this fall. I bear sincere testimony that among the educated Reps who have *just voted for you* there is a widespread feeling that the criticisms of the 'Nation' have much foundation. (By the way I do not know who wrote the article.) It is not likely that you hear much of this. I beg you therefore to accept this as from one who has done what he could to defeat you, but who hopes that since the people choose you, you may do the best possible for the people. Of course I expect no reply." ALS, *ibid.* The enclosure, a newspaper clipping entitled "Grant's Character" that reprints "The Second Presidency of General Grant," *The Nation*, XV (Nov. 7, 1872), 292–93, is *ibid.* On Nov. 10, Logan U. Reavis, St. Louis, wrote to USG. "I opposed your election, I was for Horace Greeley, but as I am not a politician nor an office seeker, and without means, I was unable to do much for the election of Mr. Greeley. ~~and to defeat you~~. The election now over it becomes us as American people to set a good example to man kind, and sink the partisan into the patriot, and strike for our country's cause. . . ." ALS, *ibid.* On Nov. 11, Democratic U.S. Representative Smith Ely, Jr., of N. Y., New York City, wrote to USG. "I congratulate you, very sincerely, upon your re-election to the chief Magistracy of our country. Permit me to say that this result is not due to the efforts of politicians or party organisms, but to the general contentment of the people, who are satisfied with the material prosperity of the community, with the reduction of the public debt, and with the amicable adjustment of our foreign complications. Accept the assurances of my respect and esteem." ALS, *ibid.*

On Nov. 12, John C. Webster, "Professor of Rhet. & Logic in Wheaton College," Wheaton, Ill., wrote to USG congratulating him on reelection. "Though I have one brother, Gen. J. D. Webster, who has had the honor of a somewhat intimate relationship to yourself, & another whom you have been pleased to appoint Consul to Sheffield, England, I have no sinister motive or purpose in addressing you. It is at the suggestion of Major E. P. Smith, a longtime acquaintance of mine, whom I was happy to meet at the recent meeting of the American Missionary Association at Racine Wisconsin, & with the simple design of congratulating you on you Indian Policy—I think it would have gratified you exceedingly to have heard the most hearty commendations of your course with reference to the much wronged aborigines of the country by so many decidedly christian men from different & distant parts of our land. . . ." ALS, *ibid.* Other congratulatory communications are *ibid.*

On Dec. 4, Stewart L. Woodford, Albany, N. Y., wrote to USG. "It has just been my pleasant duty, as chairman of the Electoral College of this State, to announce the formal vote of New York for your re-election. Without an added word, I feel that you know how grateful to my feeling has been the performance of this duty. Sincerely wishing you the largest success in your high office, . . ." ALS, Babcock Papers, ICN. On Dec. 9, Orville E. Babcock wrote to Woodford acknowledging his letter. Copy, DLC-USG, II, 1.

To Thomas J. Wood

Washington, D. C., November 19, 1872.

DEAR GENERAL:

Your letter of the 11th inst., covering a notice of the meeting of the *Society of the Army of the Cumberland,* to take place on the twentieth and twenty-first days of November, 1872, at Dayton, Ohio, and inviting my presence, is received. I do not remember receiving the former notice and invitation mentioned in your letter, and which I certainly should have answered, had I received it.

It would afford me very great pleasure to attend your Reunion, were it possible; but I am now busily engaged in preparing for the meeting of Congress, which will prevent my leaving Washington for the present.

It has been a matter of much regret with me, that I have been so often deprived of the pleasure of meeting my old comrades in arms at these Annual Reunions, attended, as they are, with a revival of old associations and sympathies, formed in such trying times.

Express to the meeting my regrets for not being able to be present at the Reunion of the *Society of the Army of the Cumberland* on this occasion, and also my wish that the Reunion may prove a profitable and happy one to all.

The noble deeds of the *Army of the Cumberland,* under its brave commander, GENERAL THOMAS, have now passed into history, not to be blotted out by time.

With great respect,
Your obedient servant,
U. S. GRANT.

GENERAL T. J. WOOD, *Dayton, Ohio.*

Society of the Army of the Cumberland Sixth Re-Union, Dayton, 1872 (Cincinnati, 1873), pp. 107–8. On Nov. 19, 1872, USG telegraphed to Thomas J. Wood. "Invitation to meet the *Society of the Army of the Cumberland* just received. Answer and regrets sent by mail." *Ibid.,* p. 108.

Speech

_____

[*Nov. 26, 1872*]

Gentlemen of the League—In your desire to obtain all the rights of citizens I fully sympathize. That you should have what other citizens have, I know; and I wish that every man in the United States would stand in all respects alike. It must come. A ticket on a railroad or other conveyance should entitle you to all that it does other men; I wish it to be so. I think, gentlemen, your very earnest recommendation, however, belongs more properly to the next Administration. All citizens undoubtedly in all respects should be equal. Gentlemen, I thank you for the compliment you have paid me.

Louisville Courier-Journal, Nov. 27, 1872. USG spoke to "a delegation of negroes from Philadelphia" who had recommended "a new civil rights bill like Sumner's." *Ibid.* See also *New York Times,* Nov. 27, 1872.

On Nov. 6, 1872, Mrs. Polly Shorter, Buffalo, had written to USG. "I feel so thankful to god And that you should be Again Elected our President of the nation   oh what a comfort to all and of my people i sincerly hope that kind Providence may spare you and protect you and your family—I am a poor lame woman for three years now but through your kind laws i have bin cared for   god bless you in all you may do and Prosper you Please Acept this from A poor colerd woman   what joyful news" ALS, USG 3. On Nov. 7, M. P. H. Jones, Cincinnati, wrote to USG. "Allow me to congratulate you on your late *brilliant success.* I thank God that He has permitted me with eight hundred thousand other colored men to cast our first vote for a President who so well deserves our undivided support" ALS, *ibid.*

On Nov. 8, Charles T. Brown, Little Rock, wrote to USG. "we as a Commite of the City of LittleRock the State of Arkanansa do here by Congratulate you on your sucess wich you have gaine in the State of Arkanasa an through out the United States,   we had no fere what you would be our nex President though the Democrat try to by our votes but on the 5 of November we stood by the name of Grant, we no your name.   we stood by you in the time of war and now in the time of pece stand by us as your maine Surport.   when this Ship of State reel and stager smitten by thunderbolts dashing upon rock and the America Flag allmost in the dust. the Corled Troops of America rally to your Surport and planted the Flag of the nation on Capital of Richmon and through out the Southerin State,   we have trusted you in war and we have tride you for President and by the help of God we will try you againe   the Demoracy is dead and we truse to the God of Battles she may never rise frome her grave not as a long as the Sun ries in the East and set in the West,   we have elected a Republican Governer and the whole Republica ticke   we have fet the lash and we have and smell power and we have tasted freedom and we have resolve to stand by the President of the United States And the Republica Party   I thought at one time that we would be defeated but the same God who watch the Republica Party in the time has not forgooton us and on the 5th November H smile upon the Republicans with such splender that it sunk the Demorcay into oblivion   may the name of U. S Grand and Willson and Baxter stand written in the Halls of Congress and in blazon charicters of gold in the Hall of the Brittish Parliment for our young and rising generation to see when we are dead and gone,   I trust Sir that you will excuse my writing and we as a Commite wish to here from you soon" ALS, *ibid.*

On Nov. 20, J. H. D. Payne, Cambridge City, Ind., wrote to USG. "Permitt me to congradulate you as a newly enfranchised citizen of the American republic.   though born under the dominions of slavery, but freed early in life by giving good leg bail for security, I hope you will not take any offence at these few congradulatory remarks which I offer here. It is to the end that you may know that though we are not all educated, yet we are in possession of an intellect full of self culture, and therefore beg leave to congradulate your honor, as a common man of self culture: Suffer me to say after watching your actions as a general in the field; and myself a soldier under you, your first movement upon Lee's Army at the Rapidan on the 4th of may, I think it was in 1864, I cheerfully spoke to my colored companions in arms, and told them that in the sound of our chieftain's guns there was victory. . . . N. B. I here present you some campaign songs, of my own composition, which we sang during the campaign." ALS, *ibid.*

To Hamilton Fish

Washington, D. C.
Nov. 29th 1872

MY DEAR GOVERNOR:

Under the circumstances, Mr. Greeley having died this afternoon, Mrs. Grant, Nellie and myself send our regrets for not attending Mrs. Fishs party this evening.

Very Truly Yours
U. S. GRANT

HON. HAMILTON FISH, SEC. OF STATE

ALS, DLC-Hamilton Fish. See *New York Tribune*, Nov. 30, 1872. On Dec. 1, 1872, Mayor A. Oakey Hall of New York City telegraphed to Secretary of the Navy George M. Robeson. "Having the honor of your personal acquaintance, I telegraph you to say that the civic authorities will join the private societies and citizens in a public funeral on Wednesday, from the City Hall, to the late Mr. Greeley, and the idea is universal that should the President attend, and the authorities hereby respectfully invite him, his attendance would popularly be regarded the most magnanimous, graceful, and faction-assuaging event of the country." *Ibid.*, Dec. 3, 1872. On Dec. 2, Robeson telegraphed to Hall. "Your telegram was received last night. The President had determined as early as last Saturday to attend Mr. Greeley's funeral, if the day fixed should be one on which he could properly be absent from the Capitol. He is still of the same mind, and will attend on Wednesday if his public duties, growing out of the assembling of Congress, will permit." *Ibid.* USG attended the funeral on Dec. 4 and left New York City without attending a reception honoring Elihu B. Washburne. "Gen. Babcock sent two dispatches saying that the President would attend this reception. When he was first spoken to about it, at the time of the arrival of Miss Nellie Grant, he thought very much of it and was enthusiastic about it. When he was spoken to about it yesterday he said 'I would better go back now. I came here really to attend Mr. Greeley's funeral. I do not want any misapprehension about it. If I stayed here to Mr. Washburne's reception, it might be misinterpreted.'" *Ibid.*, Dec. 5, 1872.

On Dec. 6, Sinclair Tousey, New York City, wrote to USG. "... I desire to thank you for the respect shown by you to Mr. Greeley on his deathbed, and for the great respect you paid his character and memory by your attendance on his funeral. . . ." *Washington Chronicle*, Dec. 8, 1872.

On Dec. 2, James B. Swain, New York City, had telegraphed to USG. "IN ACCORDANCE WITH INSTRUCTIONS. I HAVE THIS DAY FORWARDED THE FOLLOWING DISPATCH TO THE SECRETARY OF STATE OF THE SEVERAL STATES THAT VOTED FOR GREELEY." Telegram received, DLC-USG, IB. The enclosure is a telegram of the same day from Ethan Allen, chairman, Liberal Republican National Committee, New York City. "IN ACCORDANCE WITH THE VIEWS EXPRESSED IN THE TRIBUNE OF THIS MORNING THE PRESIDENTIAL ELECTORS CHOSEN IN THE SEVERAL STATES WHO HAVE BEEN CHOSEN TO VOTE FOR GREELEY AND BROWN. IT IS RESPECTFULLY SUGGESTED SHOULD CAST THE VOTE OF THEIR RESPECTIVE STATES FOR ULYSSES S. GRANT FOR PRESIDENT AND B. GRATZ BROWN FOR VICE PRESIDENT." Telegram received, *ibid.* See *New York Times*, Dec. 3, 1872.

To Charles W. Eliot

Washington, D. C. Nov. 30th 18~~6~~72

CHAS. W. ELIOT ESQR
PRESIDENT HARVARD UNIVERSITY:
DEAR SIR:

Your very kind and complimentary letter of the 26th inst. with the diploma confering on me the degree of Doctor of Laws by Harvard University is just received. Permit me to thank the faculty of Harvard, through you, for this mark of their approval of my efforts to serve our beloved country both in time of War and in time of peace. It will be my effort to continue to deserve that confidence.

Be assured that I shall ever hold in high esteem the parchment, and your letter accompanying it, as marked testimonials of that approval.

> With great respect,
> Your obt. svt.
> U. S. GRANT

ALS, MH. On Nov. 26, 1872, Charles W. Eliot, president, Harvard University, wrote to USG. "I have the honor to transmit herewith the diploma of the degree of Doctor of Laws which was conferred upon you by this University at the Commencement in June last in recognition of your distinguished public services both in war and peace,—in war, in preserving the integrity of the national territory and the national institutions,—in peace, in strengthening the national credit, lightening the public burdens, reforming the civil service, and settling by arbitration grave disputes of long standing between this country and Great Britain." ALS, Smithsonian Institution. The diploma is *ibid.* See letter to Robert C. Winthrop, June 17, 1872, note 1.

To Horace Porter

―――――

WASHINGTON, D. C., Dec. 1. [*1872*]

MY DEAR GENERAL: Your letter of this date, notifying me of your desire to quit the public service, to accept a more advantageous position in civil life, and expressing regret at severing a connection of such long standing as has existed between us, is received. It is with regret also on my part that our official relations have to cease, though I am glad to believe that our personal relations will through life remain as in the past. You have my hearty congratulations that you have received so favorable an appointment. Your services in time of war and since the close of sectional hostilities, and your services in time of peace, both in a military and in a civil capacity have been of so satisfactory a nature to myself and all coming in official or personal relations with you, as to give assurance of your eminent fitness for the new and responsible trust you are about undertaking. My best wishes go with you for your success in life and for the continued health and happiness of yourself and family.

With great respect, your obedient servant,

U. S. GRANT.

To Gen. HORACE PORTER, United States Army.

New York Times, Dec. 2, 1872. On Dec. 1, 1872, Horace Porter had written to USG. "The proposition which I recently received to enter into business in civil life, is of so advantageous a nature, that I cannot help feeling that in rejecting it I should do a wrong to my family and an injustice to myself. I have, therefore, decided, with your approval, to tender the resignation of my commission. It is not necessary for me to assure you of the extreme reluctance with which I bring my mind to consent to interrupt the personal intimacy and sever the official relations which have so long existed, and the memory of which I shall always regard as the most cherished recollection of my life. For many years it has been my privilege to be a daily witness to those transcendant qualities which a grateful people have repeatedly recognized by a bestowal of the highest offices within their gift. I feel confident that a continued exercise of the same qualities cannot fail to render the remaining years of your official life as brilliant in results as your previous achievements have been fraught with advantage to the true interests of the nation. My best wishes shall always attend you, and your countless acts of kindness shall always be remembered with feelings of the profoundest gratitude and esteem. I shall always remain your obedient servant and devoted friend." *Ibid.* Porter resigned to become vice president, Pullman Car Co. See Elsie Porter Mende, *An American Soldier and Diplomat: Horace Porter* (New York, 1927), pp. 123–25. On Nov. 18, Porter had written to George M. Pullman. ". . . I am busy to day getting matters in shape for the message. If it will suit you I can run out to Chicago the latter part of this week, return the beginning of next week and put the finishing touches on the message and be perfectly foot-loose by the first Dec. As the President would rather like me to be here at the closing of the message, probably this would be a good arrangement all around. But *consult your own convenience entirely*, and I shall be ready at the crack of the whip" ALS, ICHi.

On Nov. 27, Gen. William T. Sherman, Washington, D. C., wrote to USG. "Private . . . I fear from what Mrs. Grant said here yesterday that she has set her heart on my appointing Fred. an aid on my staff, and that to accomplish it Porter will resign to give him his place &c. Ever since the Secretary of war made the Adjt. Generals Department a distinct bureau of the War Department, and made his orders to the Army direct through Genl Townsend, I have been convinced that sooner or later I would have to make the few orders which devolve on me through some other Adjt. General. I have no staff but the six Aid de Camps, allowed by law to the General of the Army, and will have to use one of them as my Adjt. General. Not wishing to make confusion in the regular series of orders, I have concluded to wait until the beginning of the New Year, and then to ask Dent and Porter to resign, when I will appoint, as aids, one Adjt. General—say Whipple—and an Engineer officer—say Poe—through whom to receive such reports as I have a right to call for, and through whom to issue such orders as I am expected or permitted to make. This will fill my personal staff to the maximum, and is, I suppose, all that I can claim as a right. I can hardly explain these matters to Mrs. Grant, and I fear she will misinterpret my meaning. I do think it would be best for Fred. to serve with his Regt. till he has done some act to make him prominent, or until he has gained real experience, when, if I have a vacancy, I will be most happy to appoint him; but meantime I would like Mrs. Grant to understand how I am situated, for I would like above all things to do her some special act of kindness to demonstrate my great respect. I have as yet spoken to no one of this proposed change, not even to the Secretary of War, but shall do so about the 1st of December, and put it into execution say about the 1st of January next." Copies, DLC-William T. Sherman. On Nov. 29, Frederick T. Dent wrote to Sherman resigning his staff position as of Jan. 1, 1873. Copy, ICarbS. On Dec. 3, 1872, Sherman wrote to Porter accepting his resignation. Copies, DLC-William T. Sherman. See Sherman to Secretary of War William W. Belknap, Dec. 2, *ibid.*; *PUSG*, 19, 143–45.

On Dec. 2, Orville E. Babcock wrote to U.S. Representative James A. Garfield of Ohio. "[Pers]onal . . . Availing myself of your kind offer of the other day relative to any suggestions, in relation to the appropriation bill for the Executive Mansion which we might desire to make, I beg to call your attention to the restriction placed upon the President in the appointment of his Assistant Private Secretary. As the law now reads, that officer must be a short-hand writer. That qualification might not be possessed by the person whom he might desire to fill that position, and as he never makes use of a stenographer, he would be pleased to have you strike out that restriction." LS, DLC-James A. Garfield. On Dec. 3, Garfield wrote to Babcock that he had made the requested change. LS (press), *ibid.*

On Dec. 2, Belknap wrote to Judge Advocate Gen. Joseph Holt. "*Confidential.* . . . At the request of the President I send you the enclosed letter of instructions in regard to Mr. O. L. Pruden. This detail becomes necessary on account of rearrangement of the clerical force at the Executive Mansion, consequent upon the resignation of General Porter. It is expected that Mr. Pruden will be appointed shortly as a permanent clerk at the White House, but for the present please continue him on the rolls of your office." LS, DNA, RG 153, Letters Received.

Draft Annual Message

[*Dec. 2, 1872*]

To the Senate, and House of Representatives.

In transmitting to you this, my fourth Annual Message, ~~to Congress~~, it is with thankfulness to the Giver of all good that, as a Nation, we have been blessed for the past year with peace at home, peace abroad, and a general prosperity vouchedsafe to but few peoples. With the exception of the recent devastating fire which swept ~~in a few days from the earth~~ from the earth, with a breath as it were, Millions of accumulated wealth, in the City of Boston, there has been no ~~widespread~~ overshadowing calamity within the year to record. It is gratifying to note how, like their fellow citizens of the City of Chicago, under similar circumstances a year earlier, the citizens of Boston are rallying under their misfortunes, and the prospect that their energy and perseverance will overcome all obsticles, and show the same prosperity soon that they would had no disaster befallen them. Otherwise We have been free from pestilence, war and calamities which often overtake nations; and as near as human judgement can penetrate the future, no cause seems to exist to threaten our present peace.[1]

With the great reduction of taxation by the Acts of Congress at its last session, the expenditure of Government in collecting the revenue will be much reduced for the next fiscal year.[2] It is very doubtful however whether any further reduction of ~~this~~ [so] vexa-

tious burthen upon any people will be practicable for the present.
At all events, as a measure of justice to the holders of the Nations
certificates of indebtedness, I would recommend that no more legislation be had on this subject, unless it be to correct errors of omission or commission in the present laws, until sufficient time has ~~been~~
elapsed to prove that it can be done, and still have sufficient revenue
to meet current expenses of Government, pay interest on the public debt, and provide for the Sinking fund established by law. The
preservation of our National credit is of the highest importance;
next to this comes a national currency, of fixed, unvarying value as
compared with gold, the standing currency of all civilized and commercial Nations.

Continue under "War Dept."

Attention of Congress will be called during its present session
to various enterprises for the more certain and cheaper transportation[3] of the constantly increasing surplus of Western & Southern
products, to the Atlantic seaboard. The subject is one that will force
itself upon the Legislative branch of the Govt. sooner or later, and
I suggest therefore that immediate steps be take to gain all available
information to insure equible and just legislation.

One route to connect the Miss. valley with the Atlantic, at
Charleston, S. C. and Savannah, Ga. by water, by the way of the Ohio
& Tennessee rivers, and canals & slack water navigation to the
Savannah &   [4] river has been surveyed, and report made, by
an accomplished Eng. officer of the Army.—A second & third new
routes will be proposed for the consideration of Congress; Namely,
by an extension of the Kanahwa & James River Canal[5] to the Ohio;
and by extension of the Chesapeake & Ohio Canal.

I am not prepared to recommend Govt aid to these or other enterprises until it is clearly shewn that they are not only of National
interest, but that when completed they will be of a value commensurate with their cost.

That production increases more rapidly than the means of
transportation in our country has been demonstrated ~~ever since the
introduction of rail roads in our country~~ by past experience. That
the unprecedented growth in population and products of the whole

country will require additional facilities, and cheaper ones for the more bulky articles of commerce, to reach tidewater and a market, will be demanded in the near future, is equally demonstrable. I would therefore suggest either a committee or commission to be authorized to consider this whole question, and to report to Congress at some future day for ~~their~~ [its] better guidance in legislating on this important subject.

In addition to these a project to facilitate commerce by the building of a Ship canal around Niagara Falls, on the United States side, [which] has been aggitated for many years ~~and~~ will, no doubt, be called to your attention at this session.

The extension of rail-roads, by private enterprise, during the last few years, to meet the growing demands of producers, has been enormous, and reflects much credit upon the ~~enterprising~~ enterprise of the capitalist and managers engaged in it.

Looking to the great future growth of the country, and the increasing demands of commerce, it might be well, while on this subject, not only to have examined and reported upon the various practicable routes for connecting the Mississippi with tidewater on the Atlantic, but the feasibility of an almost continuous landlocked navigation from Maine to the Gulf of Mexico. Such a route along our coast would be of great value at all times, and of inestimable value in case of a foreign war. Nature has provided the greater part of this route, and the obsticles to overcome are easily within the skill of the Eng.

I have not alluded to this subject with the view of having any further expenditure of public money at this time than ~~what~~ may be necessary to ~~get all the information~~ [procure & place] before Congress, in an authentic form, [all the necessary information] to enable it hereafter, if deemed ~~worth~~ practicable and worthy, to legislate without delay.

Navy

The report of the Sec. of the Navy, herewith accompanying, explains fully the ~~expenditures appropriations and~~ condition of that branch of the public service, ~~as well as the~~ its wants and deficiencies, ~~of our Navy at the present time~~ expenses incured during the past year and appropriations for the same. It also gives a complete history of the services of the Navy, for the past year, in addition to its regular service. It is evident that unless early steps are taken to preserve our Navy that in a very few years the United States will be the weakest Nation upon the ocean of all great powers. ~~upon the ocean.~~ With an energetic, driving business people like ours, penetrating and forming business relations with every part of the known world, a Navy ~~respected by others~~ is strong enough to command the respect of our flag abroad is necessary for ~~their~~ the full protection of their rights.—I recommend carefull consideration by Congress of the recomendations made by the Sec. of the Navy.

Continuation under P. O. head

for the ~~appointment~~ establishment of Post Office Savings Banks; and for the increase of the Salaries of the Heads of Bureaus—I have heretofore recommended the abolition of the franking privilege, and see no reason ~~yet why the recommendation was not worthy of~~ now for changing my views on that subject. ~~But not~~ It not ~~having~~ having been favorably regarded ~~heretofore~~ by Congress however I now suggest a modification of that privilege to correct ~~the~~ its glaring ~~and its~~ and costly abuses. ~~of it.~~ I would recommend also the appointment of a committee or commission to take into consideration the best method, (equitable to private corporations who have invested their time and capital in the establishment of telegraph lines) of acquiring the title to all telegraph lines now in operation, and of connecting this service with the postal service of the Nation.—It is not possible that this subject could receive the proper consideration during the limits of a short session of Congress; but ~~the~~ it may be initiated ~~and~~ so that future action may be fair to the ~~United~~ Government and to private parties concerned.

2 P. O. Dept

There are but three lines of Ocean Steamers, Namely: The Pacific Mail Steamship Company, between San Francisco, China & Japan, provision made for semi monthly service after Oct. 1st /73; the United States and Brazil line; monthly and the Oregon, California and Mexico line, monthly, ~~running~~ plying between the United States and foreign ~~countryies,~~ ports, and owned and ~~run~~ [operated] under ~~the United States~~ our Flag. I earnestly recommend that ~~such~~ such liberal contracts be authorized with these lines, to carry the Mails, as will insure their continuance.

If the expediency of extending the aid of Government to lines of Steamers which hitherto have not received it, should be deemed worthy of the consideration of Congress, political and commercial objects make it advisable to bestow such aid on a line under our flag between Panama and the Western South American ports. By this means much trade now diverted to other countries might be brought to us to the mutual advantage of this country and those laying in that quarter of the Continent of America.

Continuation of P. O.

The report of the Sec. of the Treas. will show an alarming falling off in our carrying trade for the last ten or twelve years, and even for the past [year]. I do not believe that public treasure can be better expended, in the interest of the whole people, than in trying to recover this trade. An expenditure of $5,000,000 pr. Annum, for the next five years, if it would restore to us our proportion of the carrying trade of the world, would be profitably expended.[6] ~~Now that prices of labor, bet in Europe are approaching what we pay and the approximate equalization of the cost of building and running ocean steams consequent thereon, between~~

The price of labor in Europe has [so much] enhanced ~~so much~~ within the last few years that the cost of building and ~~running~~ [sailing] oceans steamers, ~~built and owned~~ in the United States, is not so much greater than there that I believe the time has arrived for Congress to take this subject into serious consideration.

Territories[7] Follow Interior

Affairs in the territories are generally satisfactory. The energy and business capacity of the pioneers who are settling up the vast domains not yet incorporated into states are keeping pace in internal improvements, and civil government, with the older communities. In but one of them, Utah, is the condition of affairs unsatisfactory, except so far as the quiet of the citizen may be disturbed by real or imaginary dangr of indian hostilities. ~~by the indians.~~ It has seemed to be the policy of the legislature of Utah to evade all responsibility to the government of the United States, and even to hold a position in hostility to it.—I recommend a careful revission of the present laws of the territory by Congress, and the enactment of such a law, the one proposed in Congress at its last session for instance, or something similar to it, as will secure peace, the equality of all citizens before the law, and the ultimate extinguishment of polygamy.

Since the establishment of a territorial government for the District of Columbia the improvement of the condition of the city of Washington, and surroundings, and the increased prosperity of the citizens, ~~has been observed by all visitors~~ is observable to the most casual visitor. The Government is a large owner of property in this City. ~~and~~ I recommend liberal appropriations by Congress to keep pace along, and on, public grounds with those [improvements] made by the territorial authorities, and to bear with the citizen [of] District the Nations just share of the expense of them.

Civil Service Reform.[8]

An earnest desire has been felt to correct abuses which have grown up in the Civil Service of the country, through the defective method of making appointments to office. Heretofore federal offices have been regarded too much as the reward of political services. Under authority of Congress rules have been established to regulate the tenure of office and the mode of appointments.

But without the more direct sanction of Congress these rules cannot be made entirely effective, nor have the rules adopted entirely proven satisfactory. The method of competitive examination is not calculated to prove greatest efficiency. ~~but often the least~~ In lieu of competitive examinations I would rather approve of selection and then a thorough examination to test whether the person selected was fully qualified for the ~~for the~~ duties of his office, morally mentally and by all tests deemed proper, the nature of the examination depending on the character of the place to be filled. Higher grade of office should be filled by promotion, when practicable, but no examining board, strangers to the parties appearing before them, can any more determine the fittest man for advancement than they can go into a business establishment and inform the proprietor, by a mental examination of his employees, who are the fittest men for advancement there. With a proper selection of ~~a~~ heads of departments the ~~bes~~ most worthy promotions can be made by selection.

ADf (bracketed material not in USG's hand), DLC-USG, III. The full text is printed in DNA, RG 130, Messages to Congress; *HED,* 42-3-1, part 1.

On Nov. 26, 1872, a correspondent reported. "The rough draft of the President's annual message, though not quite finished, was read to the Cabinet to-day—all the members being present. It will be somewhat, perhaps one-fifth, longer than last year's message. . . . the President remarked that he had no objection to saying that the message would not show any change of policy on his part, . . ." *Philadelphia Public Ledger,* Nov. 27, 1872. See *Washington Evening Star,* Nov. 21, 1872.

1. A lengthy report on foreign relations follows in the printed version. On Nov. 20, Secretary of State Hamilton Fish had written to USG. "I enclose the memorandum which you requested—It is possible that despatches may be received that will require some additions, & possibly some changes—" ALS (press), DLC-Hamilton Fish. On Nov. 29, Fish wrote in his diary. "President reads his Message—very little discussion on it   He has stricken out one passage in my draft, on the relations of Spain with Cuba, wherein I say, 'the path of wisdom & of policy lies in the path of concession & of humanity &c &'   I think it interferes with the question of 'Amnesty' to the South" *Ibid.*

On Nov. 14, Amos Briggs, Philadelphia, had written to USG. "It may seem officious in me to write you in a ~~suggestive~~ way. but my excuse is the great interest I feel in the acquisition of Cuba by the U. S. It is only a question of time when it will be ours, and I know of no time so fitting and propitious as that during your second Administration   The geographical position of Cuba must ever render it a source of anxiety to our Government, as in time of war it would be the ugliest military depot against us. Its propinquity to the U. S. renders it essentially important that both should be under the same form of Government. Our people cannot longer look indifferently upon the struggle now pending there involving results so important to freedom and civilization   The policy of Nations the World over is drifting to a higher civilization than that ruling Spain and her Dependencies. With Slavery abolished in the U. S. there can be no peace with Slavery in Cuba, and without peace there, there can be no permanent security here, in view of the liability of our people becoming involved in their struggle in one way or the other. . . ." ALS, DNA, RG 59, Miscellaneous Letters. On Jan. 2, 1873, William G. Eliot, St. Louis, wrote to USG. "I do not know that a voice so feeble as mine can reach the 'President's House' at Washington, especially upon a great national topic; but I venture to make the trial in behalf of Cuba. Three years ago, in conversation with Mr Sumner, he gave me potent reasons why this country had no right in any way to interfere, but I did not half-believe them then and, at any rate, they have lost their force now by the long continuance of the Cuban struggle. If I understand it, stript of all adventitious circumstances, it is a struggle of freedom against tyranny, and we, as a free nation, ought not to stand coldly looking on. History will never cease to condemn England for her statesmanlike refusal to save Poland from its plunderers, for there are great principles of humanity which, in the long trial, become the grandest statesmanship: and if we, as a nation, permit that old oppressor, Spain, to tread down the hopes of freedom in that beautiful land, History will sorely punish us for our neglect. I know little of technical statesmanship, but believe that nations, like individuals, may do as they would be done by, and that it is our proper part to stand for the weak, who are mainly in the right, against the stronger power which is clearly in the wrong. Apologizing for my freedom, . . ." ALS, NN.

USG asked Congress for a commission to distribute money awarded to settle the *Alabama* Claims. On Dec. 7, 1872, George A. Thruston, Cumberland, Md., had written to USG. "A bill having been recently introduced into the Senate, authorising the President to appoint Commissioners, and Counsel to distribute the Geneva Award, I venture to ask of you my appointment as one of them, either as Commissioner, or Counsel—. . ." ALS, DNA, RG 59, Letters of Application and Recommendation. On Oct. 26, Robert C. Schenck, U.S. minister, London, had written to USG recommending Thruston. ALS, *ibid.* On Dec. 9, Joseph H. Mayborne, Geneva, Ill., wrote to USG asking appointment as commissioner. ALS, *ibid.* On Dec. 10, John Welsh, Nathaniel B. Browne, George W. Childs, and George H. Stuart, Philadelphia, wrote to USG recommending Frederick Fraley as commissioner. LS, *ibid.* On Nov. 14, Fraley, Philadelphia, had written to USG. "The National Board of Trade at every meeting since its organization has either formally or informally considered the expediency and propriety of establishing a Department of Trade and Commerce in our General Government which shall be equal in all respects to the Departments of the Treasury, War Interior &c. . . . Another subject I have also been requested to bring before you and that is the renewal of a Treaty of Reciprocity with the Dominion of Canada.—It has been thought that the time for enlarged Commercial intercourse with our Northern and N. Eastern neighbors has now fully come and the National Board by ~~an~~ unanimously passed Resolutions both at St Louis and New York urge the negociation of a new Treaty. . . ." ALS, *ibid.*, RG 56, Letters Received.

On Dec. 12, Ambrose E. Burnside, New York City, wrote to USG. "Personal . . . I see that a bill to form a commission to award damages to claimants under the Geneva award has been introduced in accordance with your recommendation. As one of the Commissioners I beg to recommend Mr T. P. I. Goddard of R. I, who is a most respectable, intelligent, and upright man—He has had large mercantile experience, and is in every way competent for the position—His integrity and loyalty have alwa[ys] been unquestioned— I sincerely hope the interest of the public service will allow you to make him one of the Commissioners—Senator Anthony knows him well, and will no doubt join in my recommendation—Mr Goddard knows nothing of this letter—I also beg to recommend my old Adjt Genl, Genl Lewis Richmond of R I for an appointment as Minister to some one of the South American governments, or to some of the smaller missions abroad—You will remember him no doubt. He served with me every day of the war, is highly educated, and in everyway a gentleman worthy of confidence—He formerly had the habit of occasional frolics, but of late has been perfectly correct, and I doubt not he will remain so for the remainder of his life—. . ." ALS, *ibid.*, RG 59, Letters of Application and Recommendation. On Feb. 9, 1873, Burnside wrote to [USG] recommending Lewis Richmond. ALS, *ibid.* On Dec. 9, 1875, USG nominated Richmond as consul, Cork.

On Dec. 18, 1872, John K. Sullivan, Washington, D. C., wrote to USG requesting appointment as secretary to the claims commission. ALS, *ibid.* Related papers are *ibid.*

On Jan. 7, 1873, James H. Wilson wrote to USG. "In anticipation of the action of Congress in providing for a commission to distribute the award of the Geneva Arbitrators in the matter of the Alabama claims, I take the liberty of presenting the name of Walter Evans Esqr of Hopkinsville, Kentucky, as that of a gentleman eminently fit to perform the duties of a commissioner. I do this without the knowledge or solicitation of Mr Evans, and as a matter of course could not expect the President to take any action whatever in the premises until he has satisfied himself by further inquiry and investigation of the entire fitness and acceptability of Mr Evans. He is a lawyer by profession, a member of the Kentucky legislature, and a man of standing & respectability." ALS (press), DLC-James H. Wilson. On Feb. 10, Aaron F. Perry, Cincinnati, wrote to USG. "L. H Bond Esc. of the Cincinnati Bar would accept a place on the Commission to be formed in relation to the Geneva Award. . . ." ALS, DNA, RG 59, Letters of Application and Recommendation. Related papers are *ibid.* On Feb. 20, Charles S. Hamilton, U.S. marshal, Eastern District, Wis., Washington, D. C., wrote to USG. "Senator Carpenter desires me to bring to your notice that himself & Senator Howe would present to your consideration the name of A. B. Hamilton of Wisconsin, for appointment as one of the Alabama claims Commissioners. I knew nothing of this until told by Mr Carpenter, and desire only to say, that Mr Hamilton is an able lawyer, of unquestioned integrity, & coming from a remote section of the Country, he knows none of the claimants for award, and would bring to the work an unbiased judgment & a clear head. He is an elder brother of yours most truly" ALS, *ibid.* On the same day, Isaac F. Quinby, U.S. marshal, Northern District, N. Y., Rochester, wrote to USG. ". . . While attending the U S Court in Albany in January last I several times met my friend F. A Alberger member of Assembly from Buffalo. . . . He asked me to suggest his name to you as a member of the Commission for the distribution of the Geneva Award, . . . I believe that he would be scrupulous to avoid even the suspicion of biased or unfair decisions   Further than this I have nothing to say except to regret that circumstances sometimes compel me to trouble you with letters of this kind which cannot be more disagreeable for you to read than they are for me to write. I would not have you understand however that Mr Alberger's appointment would not be gratifying to me." ALS, *ibid.*

On Jan. 24, S. M. Dent, Alexandria, Va., had written to USG. "The judiciary Committee of the Senate has reported a bill to establish a Court of Commissioners to distribute the fund under the Geneva award—The bill provides for the appointment of a clerk to the said Court of Commissioners, by your Excellency, & I respectfully solicit the appointment, feeling confident of my ability to discharge the duties in a satisfactory manner—" ALS, *ibid.*

On Dec. 17, 1872, Fish had written in his diary. "The Bill pending introduced by Senator Morton, for distribution of Geneva Award is talked of—President thinks that Insurance Cos ought not to be paid—Williams suggests that the Commission be a Court— with appeal to the Supreme Court—I object that this will cause delay, the money will probably lie idle in the Treasury—No final conclusion is reached on any point" DLC-Hamilton Fish. On Feb. 12, 1873, George T. May, "a retired Average Adjuster," Shohola, Pa., wrote to USG at length concerning proper distribution of the *Alabama* Claims award. ALS, DNA, RG 59, Miscellaneous Letters. On Feb. 27, William J. Taylor, High Bridge, N. J., wrote to USG. "As managing and principal owner of the Steamship 'Electric Spark', captured by the pirate 'Florida', I take the liberty of calling your attention to the distribution of the Geneva award. From the present outlook, I greatly fear that the present Congress will not act in the premises on account of the insurance, and other complications. Should this prove to be the case, the direst private sufferers by the guilty vessels, will feel very much aggrieved, in view of the fact that there are no differences of opinion as regards the justness of their cases, except in the matter of interest and it will seem very unjust that we should be kept out of the money due and awarded, simply because Congress can not decide as to claims of the Second Class. We think that the least this Congress can do, provided they can not decide upon all claims, is to provide for us, and to let the other claimants await the action of another Congress. Being largely interested, I have pressed this matter before Congress, but now greatly fear nothing will be done, unless you personally urge it" ALS, *ibid.* Insurance executives petitioned USG. "The undersigned, representing thousands of citizens of the United States, engaged in the lawful business of insuring the property of other citizens against the perils of the seas and the risks of war, do most respectfully appeal to you for the protection of our rights of property . . . now temporarily endangered by an Act of Congress for the distribution of the Geneva Award, . . ." DS (printed, docketed March 1, 1873), *ibid.* See *SMD*, 42-3-78; *HMD*, 42-3-97, 43-1-292. Congress declined to legislate on the subject. See *CG*, 42–3, 2170; Draft Annual Message, Dec. 1, 1873.

USG asked Congress to pass legislation upholding treaty provisions on fishing rights between the U.S. and Great Britain. On Dec. 17, 1872, and Feb. 18, 1873, Fish wrote in his diary. "I mention that opposition is manifested, as I learn in the Comm of For Affr to the bill for carrying into effect the Fisheries Articles—& suggest that it may be important that the President & Members of the Cabinet express their opinion on the importance of its passage—The President is very emphatic in his expressions" "I read a letter addressed to me by Genl Banks dated yesterday in relation to the Bill for carrying into effect the Fisheries Articles of the Treaty of Washington, alleging as the reason for not acting upon them, that the Administration men in the House, do not favour the Bill—I urge the necessity of some action, & of some influence being exerted to have the Bill passed—as I have twice before done in Cabinet—now, as then, while the subject is up, someone (no matter who) introduces some question of a minor political appointment—I recur to the question, & twice the same interruption occurs—I again introduce the subject, & the President without replying after a short pause, says he will 'have no objection to having _____ _____ appointed'—At last I secure attention to the subject, & on my suggestion the President agrees to go tomorrow about 12 to the Capitol to endeavour to secure the Bill" DLC-Hamilton Fish. On Feb. 24, USG wrote to Congress repeating his call for fisheries legislation. *HED*, 42-3-216. On March 1, USG signed a fisheries bill. See *U.S. Statutes at Large*, XVII, 482–83.

USG renewed a request that Congress fund the education of young Americans in the Far East (see *PUSG*, 22, 266). On Dec. 3, 1872, C. M. Van Valkenburgh, Atlanta, wrote to USG. "In regard to your reccommending youths in Japan &c I would humbly State my wilingness to go on this mission and recomend myself as fit canidate for the eldest of others younger who may venture . . ." ALS, DNA, RG 59, Letters of Application and Recommendation. On Dec. 5, J. E. Anderson, Lima, Ohio, wrote to USG. "In your message to Congress, I see you recommend an appropriation for the education of four young men in Japan and four in China, The said young men to be taken in to the families of our resident ministers in said countries as members there of. In case Congress should make an appropriation for said purpose I would like to be appointed as one of the four to Japan . . ." ALS, *ibid.* On Dec. 18, Charles E. Welch, Binghamton, N. Y., wrote to USG. "I address you soliciting an appointment as one of the youths to be sent to Japan, as Congress will probably act in accordance with the desire expressed in your message. I have lived in Japan more or less for three years previous to 1870 and would like to reside there. I served during the war in the 2nd Missouri Cavalry Known as 'Merrill's

Horse' and was orderly for Gen. E. A. Carr part of the time. . . ." ALS, *ibid.* On Dec. 29, Charles H. Baker, Wyandotte, Mich., wrote to USG. "In your last Message you recommended that American Youths be sent to China and Japan to be educated in those Countrys for the use of our Government. Should Congress act favorably upon your recommendation *I* would like to be one of those Youths. . . . I will be fifteen years old next May. I am in the Junior Class High School of our Public School. . . ." ALS, *ibid.* On Feb. 22, 1873, Carlos M. Browne, Oberlin, Ohio, wrote to USG. "In your recent annual message I noticed in a clause your recomendation to Congress to make an appropriation to support four American Youths in each of the foreign countries, viz. Japan and China. I will say in regard to myself that I am a *poor boy* and am slightly *colored.* My parents now reside in California and they are getting to be pretty old but are still working *hard* trying to support their only son while at college. I have been here at school about two years and if necessary can obtain an honorable dismission and recomendation to any whom I may hereafter serve. I am not tired of trying to obtain an education, but I do not wish to compel or even allow my aged parents to work themselves to death in their endeavors to have me 'go through college. And should I appear favorable in your eyes and obtain the appointment (and I suppose that I stand an equal chance with the rest) I should never be too tired or ill to study faithful concerning the language customs and manners of the natives under whom I was studying until I had mastered their language etc. . . ." ALS, *ibid.*

2. This paragraph is preceded in the printed version by tables of receipts and expenditures for the year ending June 30, 1872, as well as debt reduction figures.

On Dec. 16, Bertram H. Howell, Rahway, N. J., wrote to USG offering suggestions concerning financial affairs. ALS, *ibid.,* RG 56, Letters Received. On Jan. 1, 1873, E. D. Cornell, Boston, wrote to USG on the same subject. ALS, *ibid.*

3. On Jan. 5, Henry Hill, Tyler, Tex., wrote to USG. "Being informed that Your & Your Executive are taking an interest in the promotion of a Scheme of a Ship Canal through the isthmus of Panama or Nicarugua for the purpose of Serving the general interest of commerce, and Supplying the great wants of the western Coast of America with cheap and direct transportation. In view of this I feel it my duty to lay before You a (new principle of transportation,) upon which I have labored for over 20 years to accomplish and mature; to Supply the general want and requirements of this fast Country. . . . in plain Simple words what I propose is this: A line of communication between Some place upon the East Coast & Sanfrancisco, passing through the interior of the Country with a capacity for transporting 200,000 tons each way per day, at the cost of one tenth of cent per ton per mile, or Say $3.00 per ton from New York to Sanfrancisco, and pay upon the cost of construction, from 50 to 100 per cent per anum when in full work. This you must observe when accomplished will make the whole interior on its line equal to a Sea-port City, as the cost of transportation will not be So great as that upon the Ocean, and will naturaly make room for at least one hundred Million of thriving industrious population, where there is now little or no population. . . ." ALS, *ibid.,* RG 45, Letters Received from the President. Hill enclosed an article describing his plan to float small boats on twin graded channels across the country.

4. The word "Ocmulgee" appears in print.

5. On Dec. 13, 1872, a congressional delegation from Va. and West Va. called on USG to thank him for his support of the James River and Kanawha River canal. USG responded. "I appreciate the great importance of this work to the commercial interests of

the nation, and am glad the subject has been brought to the attention of Congress. I hope Congress will give sufficient encouragement to insure its completion. The enormous productions of the Western and Southern States interested in this route demand an outlet to tide-water and the Atlantic coast, and these interests are so important that they must ultimately compel the completion of this work in some manner." *Louisville Courier-Journal,* Dec. 14, 1872.

6. On Nov. 25, "Nathaniel McKay, Esq., of New York, and several Boston gentlemen, representing the ship-building interest," met USG, who "informed them that in the message he is now preparing he has already strongly urged the attention of Congress to this important branch of our industries, and will do all in his power to restore American ship building to the position it occupied before the war." *Philadelphia Public Ledger,* Nov. 26, 1872.

7. In 1872, U.S. Delegate Jerome B. Chaffee of Colorado Territory had written to USG requesting special attention to territorial interests in the annual message. William Evarts Benjamin, Catalogue No. 27, Nov., 1889, p. 6.

8. On Dec. 13, Orville E. Babcock wrote to U.S. Representative James A. Garfield of Ohio. "The President desires me to call your attention to the appropriation made at the last session of Congress, of $25,000, to perfect and put in force the rules adopted by him for regulating the Civil Service, and to the fact that the general law (Act of Aug. 23, 1842, sec. 2) forbids extra allowance or compensation to officers in the public service; and to say that he would be pleased, if deemed proper by your committee, to have this restriction modified so far as to enable him to use this appropriation in allowing extra compensation to the persons already in the public service employed in this work." Copy, DLC-USG, II, 1. See *PUSG,* 22, 297–98.

Also on Dec. 13, USG wrote to George Nichols, Vt. secretary of state, Northfield. "I am in receipt of your letter of the 9th instant, transmitting a Joint Resolution, adopted by the General Assembly of the State of Vermont, at its late session, approving the course of the Administration in its endeavors to reform and improve the Civil Service of the Government. Such a cordial endorsement is very gratifying to me, and I gratefully appreciate this action on the part of the General Assembly. Please accept my thanks for your kindness in forwarding the resolution." Copy, DLC-USG, II, 1. On Jan. 3, 1873, Babcock wrote a letter on USG's behalf to Garret J. Garretson, Newtown, N. Y., acknowledging similar resolutions passed by Queens County Republicans. Copy, *ibid.*

To Senate

To the Senate of the United States.

I transmit to the Senate for its consideration with a view to ratification, a Convention between the United States of America and the United States of Mexico, signed in this City on the 27th. ultimo, further extending the time fixed by the Convention between the same parties of the 4th. of July 1868, for the duration of the Joint Commission on the subject of claims.

U. S. GRANT

WASHINGTON, DECEMBER 3, 1872.

DS, DNA, RG 46, Presidential Messages. See *PUSG*, 21, 356. On Nov. 21, 22, and 23, 1872, Secretary of State Hamilton Fish wrote in his diary. "Mr Mariscal (Mexico) says his Govt desires to remove all difficulties in the way of the Claims Commission, & for that purpose proposes to negotiate a new treaty & has furnished him with full power to that effect—In answer to my enquiry how he proposes to proceed, he says to let the present Commn expire, & then make the new treaty, & appoint new Commissioners—in this way Mr Guzman will retire without any unfriendly movements toward him—I object to this—. . . He proposes to refer the Indian ~~Claims~~ Depredation Claims, to the arbitration of some third friendly power, which I decline—they are already before the Commission & have been brought there by the act of Mexico—I suggest that Nelson may negotiate for the extra time of the Commn in Mexico, & sign a Treaty in time to submit it to their Congress which he says is to adjourn on 15th Decr but may be kept in Congress beyond that time He evidently prefers signing the Treaty himself—& says that he will telegraph to Mexico, to have the Session extended to give time for the Treaty to reach there." "*Cabinet* . . . I mention Mr Mariscals proposal to extend the time fixed for the duration of the Mexican Claims Commission & President authorises me to negotiate a treaty for its extension" "Mr Mariscal (Mexico) calls at the Dept & after conference it is agreed to sign an Article extending the time of the existing Claims Convention for two years beyond the time when by the present treaty it will expire He assures me, as a preliminary to my assenting to sign an Article that Mr Guzman, will be replaced by another Commissioner, & the order of the Commission refusing the Indian Depredation Claims be allowed to go into effect" DLC-Hamilton Fish. On Nov. 27, Fish and Ignacio Mariscal, Mexican minister, signed a convention extending the commission "for a term not exceeding two years from the day on which the functions of the said Commission would terminate according to that Convention, or for a shorter time if it should be deemed sufficient by the Commissioners or the Umpire, in case of their dis-agreement. . . ." Copy, DNA, RG 46, Presidential Messages. On Feb. 6 and Nov. 23, USG had authorized Fish to negotiate extensions for the Mexican Claims Commission. DS, DLC-Hamilton Fish. After further delays and negotiations, Fish and Mariscal agreed on an amended convention that the Senate ratified on March 7, 1873. See Fish diary, Jan. 16, 29, Feb. 13, 1873, *ibid.*

On Feb. 17, USG wrote to the Senate. "In answer to a Resolution of the Senate of the 14th. instant, adopted in Executive Session, requiring of the Secretary of State information touching the business before the late Mixed Commission on claims under the Convention with Mexico, I transmit a Report from the Secretary of State and the papers by which it was accompanied." DS, DNA, RG 46, Presidential Messages. On the same day, Fish wrote to USG concerning claims made by citizens of Mexico and the U.S. LS, *ibid.* Enclosures are *ibid.* On Feb. 12, Fish had written to U.S. Representative Thomas Swann of Md., chairman, Committee on Foreign Affairs. ". . . The appropriation for the Commission, as passed by the House of Representatives, but stricken out in the Senate, will be essential in case the Commission should be revived. Should the pending Convention not be ratified, and the Commission not be revived, no part of the appropriation will be or can be drawn from the Treasury. It is very desirable to continue the Commission to save the labor thus far expended. The cases unadjusted are mostly in a state of forwardness, more or less ready for submission. Large expense has been incurred by the Claimants in the preparation of their cases and towards obtaining the evidence in their support. All this will be lost, should the Commission not be continued, or its labors in some way secured. By the terms of Article III of the original Treaty all the decisions and awards already made, will fail, unless the Commission examine and decide every claim which has been presented to them, within the time to which the Commission may be limited. . . ." Copy, *ibid.*, RG 59, Reports to the President and Congress.

To Senate

THE SENATE OF THE UNITED STATES:
I nominate Ward Hunt to be Associate Justice of the Supreme Court of the United States, in place of Samuel Nelson, resigned.

U. S. GRANT

EXECUTIVE MANSION. DECEMBER 3. 1872

DS, DNA, RG 46, Nominations. On Nov. 30 and Dec. 3, 1872, Secretary of State Hamilton Fish wrote in his diary. "Recd letter from Judge Nelson, tendering resignation of seat on bench of Supreme Court, which I take to the President He says that a year or two ago he would have appointed Ward Hunt to the place—dont know but that he will now. Asks if I think Conkling would like it—says he thinks Pierrepont would—to which I agree—. . ." ". . . President is anxious to have the nomination made before the pressure upon him is made by the friends of the various Candidates—Williams says he does not know Hunt, & asks who he is. I reply that he has been for some years Judge of the Court of Appeals in NY—He replies that is a good indorsement—Delano asks if he will be true on the Bench, & not like some lately appointed Judges—I reply that I have very great regard & Confidence in his character—that he was originally a Democrat, joined the Republican party on its first formation, & has been unwavering (The President told me months ago, that he intended to appoint Hunt whenever the vacancy should occur—& on Saturday referred to his former intention, & repeated it in effect, leaving it contingent only in case Conkling had changed his opinion with regard to Hunt) The President then directs a nomination of Hunt to be made out by Atty Genl for his signature before he leaves for New York to attend Greeleys funeral (!!)" DLC-Hamilton Fish. See Charles Fairman, *Reconstruction and Reunion 1864–88* (New York, 1971), I, 1473. Born in 1810, Ward Hunt practiced law and served as mayor of his native Utica, N. Y., and in 1865 won election to the N. Y. court of appeals. On Jan. 24, 1870, Horatio Seymour, Utica, had written to USG. ". . . As I have had a lifelong acquaintance with Judge Hunt who now holds the highest judicial rank in this State I can say with confidence that he has all the qualities and attainments which are called for in a Judge of the Supreme Court of the United States and that his selection for that office would be deemed by the Public a wise and fortunate one— It is proper I should add that my favorable opinion of Judge Hunt does not grow out of any accord in our political views—upon those we are distinctly and positively opposed" ALS, DNA, RG 60, Applications and Recommendations. Related papers are *ibid.*

On Dec. 3, 1872, John M. Harlan, Louisville, telegraphed to USG. "Papers today announce Justice Nelsons resignation allow me to recommend Bristow as preeminently qualified for a seat on supreme bench. His nomination would be a fit recognition of his talents & Be gratifying to Souther Union Men" Telegram received, *ibid.*

On Dec. 5, U.S. Senator William A. Buckingham of Conn. endorsed a letter. "Respectfully referred to the President I fully concur with Judge Shipman in recommending the Hon Lewis B Woodruff for Judge of the Supreme Court in the place of Judge Nelson resigned. The legal ability, unbending integrity & high character of Judge Woodruff commands the entire confidence of the people of Conn as well as of other states & his appointment would in my judgment reflect distinguished honor upon the Administration" AES, *ibid.* See *PUSG*, 20, 16–17.

Endorsement

Int.

Respectfully refered to the Sec. of the Int. Would it not be well to suggest this name to Mr. Brunot who is now in the city?

U. S. GRANT

DECR 7TH /72

AES, DNA, RG 48, Appointment Div., Letters Received. Written on a letter of Dec. 6, 1872, from U.S. Senators Matthew H. Carpenter and Timothy O. Howe of Wis. to USG. "We understand there is, or soon will be a vacancy in the office of Comr of Indian affairs. We recommend Hon Wm C. Allen for appointment to that office; and can most fully endorse him as to character and qualifications. Wisconsin has, as we believe, no bureau officer in the Departments. When Mr Barron, 5th Auditor resigned, we recommended Judge Allen for that place but he was not appointed. We respectfully ask a favorable consideration of Judge Allens claims for recognition, and assure you of his fitness for this place." LS, *ibid.*

On Oct. 12, Samuel F. Tappan, Shamburg, Pa., wrote to USG. "The New York Independent of the 10th inst. seems to intimate that Gen F. A. Walker contemplates an early retirement from the office of Commissioner of Indian Affairs, to accept a position elsewhere. If such is the case, and a vacancy should occur, I desire to renew my application for an appointment as Commissioner. In doing this I am prompted by a wish to aid in bringing about the incorporation of your well known and universally commended Indian policy into Law, that its permenancy may be secured and its efficiency rendered certain for all time to come. Your reelection, by the American people, upon a platform endorsing your Indian policy, and your determination to secure the equal protection of every person, will leave the law making power, no excuse, for longer delaying this matter,   that vote expresses the sovereign will of the people, that every one of whatever race may be protected alike under the law, Not excepting the Indian, who for centuries have existed under the terrible ban of outlawry and outrage. With such an endorsement you will be enabled to obtain the necessary legislation and it is my desire to aid in the consummation of this great work. In applying for an appointment I presume the utmost frankness is expected. Therefore I have to say, that the proper course for me is to refer you to my associates on the Indian Commission of 1867–68, especially to General W. T. Sherman with whom I was more intimately associated in the work of the Commission; with him I had occasion to differ, and to denounce some of his measures, to himself and to you, more, however, 'in sorrow than in anger', for I appreciated the difficulty of his position as an officer of the Army, and that he was forced to enforce a national edict as repulsive to him as it was to me, after he had failed to induce Congress to change the legal status of the Indian. I know that he is as anxious as any one to make a peace policy towards our Indian wards a success, and that they may be subjected to the law of the land, and civilized, instead of exterminated, and that he considers Law as the only remedy. He wishes the civil law to shield his much loved army from dishonorable service, in the Indian country. With his aid a Commissioner could do much, without it, and especially against his personal opposition I could not aid you, and it would be better for you to appoint some other person. I refer you to him, as to the expediency of my appointment as Commissioner of Indian Affairs." ALS, *ibid.*

On Oct. 21, William B. Allison, Dubuque, wrote to USG. "Learning that the office of Comr of Indian Affairs is likely soon to become vacant, I respectfully suggest for the place Col Geo. C. Tichener of Iowa, late Chm of our State Central Comtee. He is in every way competent to discharge the duties of the office & if apptd would ~~discharge~~ administer it in all respects with fidelity. I t[ru]st you may see your way clear to give him the appt." ALS, *ibid.*

On Oct. 30, U.S. Senator Phineas W. Hitchcock and U.S. Representative John Taffe of Neb. wrote to USG. "We respectfully suggest the name of Henry M. Atkinson to your consideration for appointment as Commissioner of Indian Affairs. Mr. Atkinson has been for several years a prominent citizen of this state; is a man of excellent character and habits, of good executive ability and a thorough Republican. This State has no appointment to any ~~d~~Department, head of a Bureau, or foreign Consulate and hence if local claims are ever to be considered can reasonably and properly claim consideration in this instance." LS, *ibid.* On Nov. 5, Robert W. Furnas, Brownville, Neb., wrote to USG. "Being advised of the probability of a vacancy in the office of U S Commissioner of Indian Affairs, and having had myself much experience with the Indians of the West, and further, an advocate of your system of dealing with the Indian race, I desire to present the name of Henry M Atkinson of this State, as a man in every respect most admirably qualified for the position named. I have had an intimate acquaintance with him for the past fifteen years, and know him to be honest and capable. He was my Adjutant in the Army, and has had much experience in the West, and with the Indians. In presenting his name for this honorable and responsible position, I feel that I am representing the views and wishes of the prominent Republicans of our State. I am authorized to say in connection, that he will be presented urgently both Senator Hitchcock and Representative Taffe. Hoping that to give this application favorable consideration, will be your pleasure . . ." ALS, *ibid.* On Nov. 8, Judge Elmer S. Dundy, U.S. District Court, Omaha, wrote to USG. "I understand that a change is soon to be made in the office of Commissioner of Indian Affairs. If that be so, it would give great satisfaction to the Republican party of this State to have you select one of our worthy citizens to fill the place soon to be made vacant. The appointment of Hon. Henry M. Atkinson to the place named would, as I think, give universal satisfaction to the great party which has given you and your administration such a generous support in this State. Mr. Atkinson is in every way worthy of the confidence reposed in him by the party to which he belongs." ALS, *ibid.* Related papers are *ibid.*

On Nov. 14, John V. Farwell, Board of Indian Commissioners, and U.S. Representative Charles B. Farwell of Ill., Chicago, telegraphed to USG. "We recommend Gen Howard for the office of Indian Commissioner" Telegram received (at 6:15 P.M.), *ibid.* About this date, Felix R. Brunot, chairman, Board of Indian Commissioners, wrote to George H. Stuart. "I do not think the President will consent to the appointment of a Commissioner of Indian Affairs without consulting the Board, and this being the case, I do not feel at liberty to ask him to consult us. I hope he will appoint General Howard, and that he may be in a position to accept the place. Should General Howard not be the man, Mr. Cree, our secretary, would make an excellent officer. He is thoroughly honest, fully in sympathy with the Indians, a true Christian, largely known in the Christian community, and has visited so extensively the Indian reservations that he has more correct ideas of what is needed than any one else I know." Charles Lewis Slattery, *Felix Reville Brunot* (New York, 1901), pp. 197–98.

On Nov. 18, Robert T. Van Horn, Kansas City, wrote to USG. "I am asked to submit my name to the President for appointment as Commissioner of Indian Affairs. Knowing the Indian policy of the Administration to be so peculiarly that of the President himself, it occurs to me that the selection of such officer would be a matter of more than mere official interest—So believing I have refused to allow my name urged in the usual manner. I have taken the liberty, then, in deference to my urgent friends, to address this to the President himself—to say that I should feel honored at the bestowal of such confidence, and thus leave the question. Should the matter come under the consideration of the Indian commission my only reference in that body is Col. Campbell of St. Louis, to whose opinion I would most cheerfully defer. I have also written the Secretary of the Interior" ALS, DNA, RG 48, Appointment Div., Letters Received.

On Dec. 24, William H. Bunting, Darby, Pa., wrote to USG. "I understand that Gen. Walker has resigned the commissionership of Indian Affairs. If you think well of it I would like to be appointed to the office. I have never solicited an office, but as I am very much interested in the Indians and having travelled through most of the Territories and California among nearly all the tribes of Indians I have considerable knowledge of their habits and wants. I have been a member of the Union League of Philada for a number of years and can refer to such men as Ferdinand J Dreer, Wm Sellers, John Thomas, Thomas J Megear, and a number of others, members of that body, who have known me for years. I am a member of the Society of Friends and have been a Republican ever since the party was first instituted. I was introduced to you at the reception of Spotted Tail and his Band by Gen. John E Smith whom I have known for some years." ALS, *ibid.*

On Dec. 26, Francis A. Walker wrote to USG. "I have the honor to tender my resignation of the office of Commissioner of Indian Affairs, which I hold by virtue of a commission from the President of the United States, under date of the 16th of December, 1871. In retiring thus from the Office of Indian Affairs, permit me, Sir: to bear my humble testimony to the fidelity with which you have maintained and carried forward the policy of justice and kindness towards the aborigines of this country, which was so auspiciously inaugurated in the earliest days of your administration, and which has already borne such abundant fruit of peace and prosperity along our once scourged and afflicted borders." ALS, *ibid.* USG accepted Walker's resignation to take effect on Feb. 1, 1873. See *PUSG*, 22, 87; *HED*, 42-3-1, part 5, pp. 391–493; Walker, *The Indian Question* (Boston, 1874).

On Dec. 30, 1872, Andreas Willmann, collector of Internal Revenue, New York City, wrote to USG. "Permit me to recommend Cap. J. C. F. Beyland for the position of Commissioner of Indian Affairs or any one of similar import at the Capital. I make free to ask this, believing that if he were in a position, that would give him influence at Washington, it would redound to the benefit of our paper the 'Oestliche Post.' It is greatly important, that the influence which the paper has over the German born citizens of New York be maintained and increased, and I believe, Captain Beylands appointment would help to do it." ALS, DNA, RG 48, Appointment Div., Letters Received. See Endorsement, March 20, 1873.

On Dec. 29, Col. Benjamin H. Grierson, Fort Gibson, Indian Territory, wrote to USG. "Permit me to present for your consideration in connection with the Appointment of a new Commissioner of Indian Affairs—the name of Henry—E. Alvord of Virginia. Mr Alvord was a Major in the Volunteer Service, and since the War—was for some years an Officer in my regiment and stationed in the Indian Territory, where he was assigned to Special duties in connection with Indian Affairs—by which he gained much valuable experience. His views are thoroughly in accord with the policy of your Administration on the Indian Question—and I am sure, as Commissioner, he would prove satisfactory to the philanthropic people, now so deeply interested in the welfare of the Indians. I know him to be strictly temperate in his habits—honest, energetic and capable. and from an intimate acquaintance of many years deem him peculiarly well fitted for the position, and therefore cordially recommend his appointment." ALS, DNA, RG 48, Appointment Div., Letters Received; ADfS, ICN. On Jan. 2, 1873, Henry E. Alvord, Lewensville, Va., wrote to USG. "Believing that I can perform the duties of the position to the satisfaction of yourself and the best friends of the Indians, generally, I have the honor to apply for appointment as Commissioner of Indian Affairs, Department of the Interior. Respectfully referring to the papers filed in connection with this application. . . ." ALS, DNA, RG 48, Appointment Div., Letters Received. U.S. Senator Henry Wilson, U.S. Representatives Henry L. Dawes and George F. Hoar of Mass. favorably endorsed this letter. ES, *ibid.* On Jan. 9, Alfred H. Love, president, Universal Peace Union, Philadelphia, wrote to USG. "Henry E. Alvord is an applicant for the office of Indian Comr made vacant by the resignation of Commissioner Walker. During his recent visit to our city having in charge the largest Delegation of Indian chiefs that have been here, I formed his acquaintance, & had an excellent oppy of learning his views on the solution of the 'Indian Question.' I do not propose, on the radical peace plane, to give an unconditional approval of any man bearing a military title, but I do say most sincerely, that Henry E. Alvord impressed me with peculiar fitness for the position named and one who would aid materially in sustaining & developing your broad humanitarian & statesmanlike Indian policy, which I may be permitted to say, has endeared you to the friends of peace. Feeling that you will excuse me for urging his appointment, because of the deep interest I have taken in this subject, & because I am thoroughly convinced that with a full & patient trial, with men of pure motives, unswerving integrity and clear judgment you will be eminently successful in this great work of your administration, . . ." ALS, *ibid.*

On Jan. 9, the Minn. congressmen wrote to USG. "The Senators and Representatives of the State of Minnesota hereby unite in recommending Dr. Thomas Foster ~~of Minnesota~~, as a man *peculiarly* qualified by general ability and *special experience* to receive the appointment of Commissioner of Indian Affairs" DS (4 signatures), *ibid.*

On Jan. 15, Brunot wrote to USG. "Just previous to the departure of the Secretary of the Interior for the South, Mr Stuart, and the chairman of the Board of Indian commissioners were consulted by him on the subject of a successor to Genl Walker in the office of Commissioner of Indian Affairs, and were informed by him that it was your desire to fill that office with an incumbent who would be entirely acceptable to the Board. The name of Mr Cowan, the Assist. Secretary of the Interior was suggested by you, among others mentioned, as a suitable person, should he be willing to accept the place. I have taken the opportunity of the meeting of the Board to state these circumstances and to consult the members on the subject; and it gives me the greatest satisfaction to say that they cordially agree as to the fitness of Mr Cowan for the place, and they instruct me to say that his appointment would be entirely satisfactory to all the members of the Board. The Board also desire me to thank you for your appreciation of our efforts to co-operate with your Indian Policy, and to assure you of our continued confidence in the successful result." ALS (misdated 1872), *ibid.*

On Dec. 13, 1872, U.S. Senator Lot M. Morrill of Maine wrote to USG. "The bearer, Mr. Weeks of New York, is so highly recommended to me by those in whom I confide, for his intelligence and integrity, as well as for his knowledge and practical experience in Indian affairs, that I have pleasure in commending him to your confidence for the trust for which he is recommended." Copy, *ibid.* On Dec. 16, Grenville M. Weeks, U.S. Indian Commission, Washington, D. C., wrote to USG. "I called to see you last Saturday noon by advice of Senators Hitchcock, Morrill of Me. and others, and with letters from leading philanthropists, clergymen and business men well known to you in their furtherance of your Indian Policy—Their letters call attention to my fitness for the Commissionership of Indian Affairs when vacated by its present worthy incumbent. When I called, a crowd was seeking your attention and Genl Dent brought word you would see me with Acting Sec't'y Cowan. The latter tells me to-day that he will at the close of the Cabinet meeting tomorrow, request you to appoint an hour most convenient to yourself when we may meet you in the matter   I take the liberty of writing this note, to keep myself in your mind with a view to your allowing this Indian Appointment to remain an open question until after the meeting proposed." ALS, *ibid.* Peter Cooper, president, U.S. Indian Commission, and eight others, petitioned USG. "We, the undersigned, being informed that a change in the Commissioner of Indian Affairs is contemplated, respectfully request that, on the resignation of the present Commissioner, Dr. Grenville M. Weeks be appointed to that position. Dr. Weeks was formerly Asst. Surgeon of the first Monitor, U. S. Navy; subsequently Surgeon U. S. Gen'l Hospital, 3d U. S. Colored Troops, and until his recent resignation Surg. 12th Inft'y, N. Y. N. G., and late President Christian Association, and Secretary of Committee of Indian Commissions. We ask his appointment for the following reasons: 1st. Because we believe him to be an honest and a capable man. 2d. Because he has lived among the Western tribes of Indians between two and three years, and we believe has made a close study of their character from a religious and moral, as well as from a psychological and physical stand-point, which his education as a physician has preëminently enabled him to do. 3d. Because he has taken the light of both our Eastern and Western civilization to guide him to the Indian's needs; has gone into their midst, lived with them as one of them, and talked with them in their own language; (for months at a time sharing their hardships in field and forest, hut, wigwam, and log-cabin; sleeping beside them in mid-winter on the frozen ground, rolled in blankets, feet to the fire, and but clouds and sky overhead.) These things should peculiarly and eminently fit him for the position of an intimate understanding of them, and do away with the objection a Westerner might, with much justifiable feeling, raise to the appointment of a man from the East, who had had no actual experience of border or Indian life, but who, on the contrary, has to rely mainly upon rose-colored theories, books, and traditions. Finally, because it should be acceptable to the Quakers and all other Christian denominations to know that Dr. Weeks earnestly desires the speediest possible Christianization of the Indian; and will also hope, pray, and strive to have his work, in their behalf, prove his faith in the broad Christian platform of the common Fatherhood of God and brotherhood of man; and, because he is in thorough sympathy and accord with the letter and spirit of your recently announced Indian policy. A more detailed showing of the ground-work upon which these reasons are based, is herewith given in the printed circular, newspaper extracts, &c., accompanying this petition." D (printed), *ibid.* Enclosures are *ibid.* On Jan. 13, Jan. 28, Feb. 1, and March 17, 1873, Weeks, Washington, D. C., wrote to USG. "As I am so much of a stranger to you personally, and have felt it out of place to allude to myself in this connection at receptions in the Executive Mansion privileging me in common with others to simply pay you my respects and give Social greeting, I will now transmit copies of Extracts from the New York Times and other papers showing somewhat my relations to Indian Affairs. I will at the same time enclose copies of letters and petitions public and private, made with a view to persuading you to appoint me eCommissioner of Indian Affairs—I send copies, lest some mischance might lose me the opportunity of presenting you the originals if you see fit to receive me with them—I hope you will not judge me by a superfluous splurginess observable in the petition—The fact of the various minor positions named as held by me and the 'hardships' &c (common to thousands,) have seemed important to certain civilians to have mentioned, though to me the allusion was as distasteful as it would be to many a manly soldier having had a similar ones. Neither are these things of themselves any proof of peculiar fitness, only so far as such intimate and common relationship with our red brothers haves given me a method of insight into their inner and home life, not attainable from the mere daily seeing of them pass the Post quarters—Neither is it attainable by mere visitation of Indian tribes, nor the witnessing the beggarly-looking painted crowds gathered at annuity payments, where their 'company manners' (?) and a certain reserve and stolidity unnatural in their daily life is misleading to their real character. Giving these hints regarding myself and views, with the assumption that I am teachable and open to every conviction that would perfect their harmony with your and my ideas of right, I will indulge in no more profuseness—Hoping to be honored with a line from your own hand granting me an interview at your convenience . . ." "Herewith I send a few papers which make favorable mention of me. The 'New-York Times' and the 'Newark Advertiser' of New Jersey, the two most influential papers in those states have two or three times also commended me to your favorable consideration as a candidate for Commis of Indian Affairs—An Object in sending you these papers is, that, if you see fit to appoint me, it may be some satisfaction to you to know that an influential part of the press of the country stand ready to approve your action, so that in selecting me you will not be put in the light of appointing a man unknown to the public in connection with Indian Affairs—Do not understand me as wishing to press my claims for merely personal reasons,—for if I am deceived, in supposing myself preeminently fitted for this office, I hope a good Providence will guide you in selecting a man who will serve the country and guard the Indians' best interests better than I could—" "I have sent to you three letters, and with one, duplicates of letters to you, from such distinguished philanthropists and divines as Peter Cooper Esq. of New York, Rev. Howard Crosby D. D. Chancellor of the 'University of the State of New York' (from which I graduated)—Rev. Henry W. Bellows D. D., who aside from his fame as a clergyman is greatfully remembered by a host of soldiers whose sufferings were greatly ameliorated by the United States Sanitary Commission of which he was president and the leading organizer,—also letters from a number of other well known clergymen and business men all urging to your favorable consideration my fitness for the position of Commissioner of Indian affairs—I refer to these things because it occurs to me that my letters may not have reached you—I trust the Statement at the close of my accompanying letter dated Jan. 28th will assure you that I am not one of that class of hungry office seekers who, I suppose, weary you with their personal and offten beggarly importunings—I say this because when I came to present in person the accompanying letter and papers for the reason therein stated I only wished to ask you if you had received my other papers and be sure that you got these, but with no desire to annoy you with requests for personal favors. It is because I valued your respect so highly that I make this effort to set myself straight before you." "The harmony of my views with your Indian Policy, and the confidence shown in the adoption by the Government of the main features of a general plan for the Indian Management, drawn up some years since by myself ~~and~~ with the approval and by the request of Peter Cooper Esq, and other well known Philanthropists, warrant me in assuming that it is not out of place to offer my services as Indian Commissioner. As an earnest of the fact that I seek no pecuniary gain I will state that I would only accept the position, if offerred, on the same basis that Mr. Brunot holds his; without moneyed compensation. My means are sufficient to enable me to donate the salary, between now and the re-assemblying of Congress either directly to the educational interests of the Indian or as an addition to the salary of some able and worthy successor commanding national respect. Such a man might then be found whose services, the present small salary could not secure, and with whom my offer might enable Government to tide matters over until Congress could see the importance of allowing eight or at least six thousand dollars a year, for the responsible and various work of the Indian Department. I have several methods in mind by which, superadded to those in force, I believe the Civilization of the Indians could be more rapidly advanced; and therefore; for their sake, should like to be put in this position where I could best set them on foot. These methods are based upon an experience of several years' intimate personal relations with the Red Maen. I write now, because I see Mr. Smith has not been confirmed by reason of contingencies of which you were not aware at the time of his nomination. Whether you see fit to favorably entertain this offer of service or not, I respectfully ask when I may speak with you a few minutes in the Indians' and not my own behalf. I have called frequently during your office hours, but press of business seemed to prevent your seeing me." ALS, *ibid.*

On March 6, Fisk Farrar, Boston, wrote to USG. "Would like the Commissionership of Indians pubished in this morning Journal   Have had charge of a large business for four years, I am familiar with Colorado Wyoming and Utah Territories and the Tribes of Indians that have reservations in these sections   Should be pleased to carry out the present ~~administration~~ Policy of the administration toward the Indians   The best of Reffrence as to past Integrity, I refer you to the following Gentlemen   Wendell Phillips Boston

Mass   Ex Gov. John Evans C̶o̶l̶Denver Col   J. H, Farrar firm of Silas Pierce & co Boston
Mass   E. L Frothingham receiver of Customs Boston Customs House," ALS, *ibid.*

On March 12, USG nominated Edward P. Smith as commissioner of Indian Affairs. On Dec. 8, 1870, USG had nominated Smith as agent, Chippewas. On March 12, 1873, a correspondent reported: "Edward P. Smith, Esq., of New-York, . . . has been long in the Indian service, and was recently agent of the Red Lake Indians. He had the indorsement of the Board of Indian Peace Commissioners, is thoroughly devoted to the humane and Christianizing policy, and comes from the Congregational denomination. He has already had much exceptional experience in the important matters of Indian management, and especially in the detection of abuses and frauds. . . ." *New York Times*, March 13, 1873. See *HED*, 42-2-1, part 5, pp. 1004–10, 42-3-1, part 5, I, 592–95; *New York Times*, Aug. 16, 1876; William H. Armstrong, *A Friend to God's Poor: Edward Parmelee Smith* (Athens, Ga., 1993), pp. 251–54.

To E. Delafield Smith

WASHINGTON, D. C., *Dec. 9th*, 1872.

MY DEAR SIR:

Your favor of the 4th instant, withdrawing your name as candidate for the office of District Attorney for the Southern District of New York, for which office you have the highest testimonials from leading citizens of the City and State, as well as my personal knowledge of your entire qualifications for the office, and your services entitling you to the most favorable consideration of the Republican party, and my own recognition of your services, was duly received, though only this moment opened.

I congratulate you on the much better appointment which you have received, and do not doubt but that it will be filled to the entire satisfaction of all lovers of good government.

Your action in this matter relieves me in the withdrawal of one good name of the number from which to select a District Attorney, several being presented with very high testimonials.

On the occasion of the appointment of the present most worthy Attorney for the Southern District of New York, I became satisfied, after tendering him the place, that you had claims to the office which I should then have recognised had the office been declined by Judge Davis.

Please present Mrs. Grant's and my kindest regards to Mrs. Smith and the children, and believe me,

Very truly, your obedient servant,
U. S. GRANT.

HON. E. DELAFIELD SMITH,
Corporation Counsel, New York City.

Copy (printed), USG 3. On Dec. 4, 1872, E. Delafield Smith, New York City, had written to USG. "The office of Counsel to the Corporation of New York having been tendered to me, I have accepted it after consulting with leading republicans and supporters of municipal reform. It presents an opportunity for honorable service to the great city in which I have lived since my early childhood. And my first official act has been to place this office in communication with Attorney General Barlow and Mr. O'Conor, in order that united action, under their lead, may be pursued against the persons charged with fraudulent conversion of public money. My name having been presented to you by judges, lawyers and mercantile men, for appointment to the office of District Attorney held by me under President Lincoln, it is now my duty to withdraw it. In doing this, I take pleasure in the humble but earnest service rendered by me to the cause which has triumphed in the strength of your name, and at the same time I am glad to relieve you from possible embarrassment by asking at your hands nothing but the high honor of your confidence and regard." Copy (printed), *ibid.* On Dec. 12, Smith wrote to USG. "Secretary Babcock's despatch is received. Mr Wm Orton, Judge Woodruff, Ex Judge Pierrepont and others all think your letter should be published, showing that my motive in accepting this office was to relieve you from embarrassment. Mr Orton and all say a few weeks will show by my acts that this office is running for good government. I enclose an exact copy of your letter, indicating two slight changes overlooked in your haste. You perceive it is entirely fit for publication, unless you think we should omit (but we do not think so) the regards to my family. It is printed for the convenience of private circulation with the printed recommendations. I *hope* you will let me publish it. Some want to build up a new Democratic Party and take Reformers with them; but letters and persons pour in upon me with assurances that only a few of our best citizens think I should resign, and most even of those declare that Mayor Havemeyer would re-appoint me. It will soon be known that O'Gorman had two years and a half yet to serve; he could be turned out only by the uncertain and slow process of legislative action; and my acceptance of the office is a public benefit. I trust you will allow me to publish your letter. It can do you no harm, and me much good. Anxiously awaiting your answer, . . ." ALS, *ibid.* On Dec. 13, Smith telegraphed to USG. "I ought to have said in my letter last night that though privately printed no copy of your letter has been given to any person and will not be till I hear from you" Telegram received, *ibid.* On the same day, USG wrote to Smith. "Personal. . . . Your letter of yesterday, asking permission to publish my letter of the 9th instant is received. While I meant all that I said in that letter, yet I did not intent it for publication as its publication might be construed into an interference in the local affairs of New York City, the appearance of which even, I would avoid." Copy, DLC-USG, II, 1. On Dec. 17 and 19, Smith wrote to USG. "Although disappointed, I appreciate the ground of your restriction. It is exceedingly kind in you to reiterate the generous expressions of your letter. My closest adviser in everything relating to this office, has been from the beginning my true friend Judge Woodruff, a man of strong sense and high integrity. If I do not misjudge, I shall so act, in relation to the entire matter, as to justify the confidence of the disinterested friends of good government, the faithful supporters of the Republican party, and the Chief Citizen of the United States." "The official recognition sought by me could not be extended without embarrassing you. The publication of your letter, which would have evinced to the public that esteem for me which the late appointment expresses for the new District Attorney, is prevented by an ephemeral local contention. I am still left the privilege of private friendship with one, whose military glory early kindled my admiration, and whose civic achievements have honored his supporters. Permit me, then, to ask that I may be pleasantly remembered in the use by you of the trifling Christmas gift which will reach you confidentially from Tiffany's with this note." ALS, USG 3. See *PUSG*, 20, 17–18.

On Dec. 14, Noah Davis, New York City, had written to USG. "Having been elected to the office of Justice of the Supreme Court of the State of New York for a term commencing on the first day of January 1873 I hereby respectfully tender my resignation of the office of United States Attorney for the Southern District of New York . . ." ALS, DNA, RG 60, Letters Received, N. Y., South. On Dec. 17, USG nominated George Bliss, Jr., to replace Davis. See letter to William F. Havemeyer, Dec. 15, 1872.

On Nov. 6, William E. Dodge, New York City, had written to USG. "Permit me to tender my congratulations at the moment when we are all rejoicing over the splendid results of yesterday—I can but feel it as a token of Gods kind Providence to the nation, any other result would have been most disastrous to all our business prospects—and been held by the disconted part of the South as evidence that they had not been well treated—Among the changes which the Election has made, will be the loss of the Honl Noah Davis as U. S. Attorney whom we have secured for the Bench of the Supreme Court. Some two years ago I had the honor of presenting for your consideration the name of Genl Joseph Jackson then the assistant District attorney, for the position since filld by Judge Davis—at that time a large number of our most influential Lawyers, Merchants, & Bankers joind in urging him for the position and the papers accompaning the application I presume are now on file in the office of the Attorney General—I have no doubt that as Genl Jackson is a great favorate with the members of the bar, and has for years been among the most active members of our 'Union League Club' & has had much experence in the office that he will be again presented to you for the office, as I know him well, as a man of high attainments of undoubted character and evry way competant for the office I venture to ask you to give to his application your favorable attention—" ALS, USG 3.

On Nov. 22, Ambrose E. Burnside wrote to USG recommending Henry E. Davies, Jr., for U.S. attorney, Southern District, N. Y.   B. Altman & Co. advertisement, *New York Times*, Dec. 15, 1974. See *PUSG*, 14, 152. On Nov. 27, Daniel R. Larned, New York City, wrote to Frederick T. Dent. "Your note to Genl Burnside was this morning received, and he desires me to say to you that the same has been destroyed, having been seen by no one but himself & myself—He begs also that you will convey to the President his thanks for the notice of his attention to his Communication—" ALS, ICarbS.

On Dec. 9, Orville E. Babcock wrote to Attorney Gen. George H. Williams. "The President directs me to say that, he thinks it advisable that a change be made in the U. S. Attorneys in Utah, and in Kings Co. N. Y. In place of the former he recommends the appointment of Wm Cary, of Salt Lake; and in place of the latter ____ Tenney of Brooklyn." LS, DNA, RG 60, Letters from the President. USG later wrote. "Advise the Atty. Gn. that I think it will be well to withdraw the nomination of Mr. Tenny as Dist. Atty Eastn Dist of New York. He will afterwards resign." AN (undated), Omaha Public Library, Omaha, Neb. On Dec. 14, Selah C. Carll, Brooklyn, wrote to USG. "Allow me as a Merchant of the city of Brooklyn to congratulate you upon the judicious choice that you have made in your selection of A. W. Tenny for District Attorney for this District—a gentleman that will give better satisfaction to the *masses* than any other man and one that is well deserving of anything that could be bestowed upon him." ALS, DNA, RG 60, Letters from the President. See *New York Times*, Oct. 21, 1881. On Dec. 10, 1872, USG had nominated Asa W. Tenney as U.S. attorney, Eastern District, N. Y.; on Dec. 19, he withdrew the nomination. On Feb. 11, 1873, USG renominated Tenney. See *PUSG*, 19, 374. For William Cary, see message to Congress, Feb. 14, 1873.

To Tomás Guardia

To His Excellency Tomás Guardia,
President of the Republic of Costa Rica.
Great and Good Friend:

I have recently received the letter of the 9th. of April, last, which Your Excellency was pleased to address to me, announcing the efforts which your Republic was making towards improving its material condition, and making special reference to the railway to the Atlantic.

I heartily congratulate Your Excellency upon the disposition shown by that Republic to which you advert, and trust that all the advantages anticipated from the enterprize adverted to may be realized, and particularly that it will tend to strengthen and improve the friendly commercial relations between our respective countries.

Your Good Friend.
U. S. Grant

Washington, December 10, 1872.

DS, Karpeles Manuscript Library, Montecito, Calif. On April 9, 1872, President Tomás Guardia of Costa Rica had written to USG. "I have had the pleasure of making the acquaintance of Mr. J. P. O'Sullivan, who has come to visit our little country. I am informed that he is highly esteemed by you, and this circumstance, together with his personal qualities, has disposed me very favorably towards him. A visit from a man of Mr. O'Sullivan's standing is a high honor to this country, and I am the first to thank him for the interest which he manifests in us. He has had occasion to see something of the efforts which we are making in order to start the Republic in the path of true progress, and he has encouraged me to address Your Excellency, as I now do, with full confidence and perfect freedom, in order to state to you what Costa Rica desires to do in order to secure her own advancement and prosperity, relying upon the powerful aid of the great nation over which Your Excellency so worthily presides, and which she wishes to imitate, following the line which your country, as an elder sister, has marked out for us. Our first desire has been to be as near your Republic as possible, in order the better to enjoy the advantages of your civilization, and the more readily to transplant to our soil the elements of your progress. To this end I have undertaken the work of our railway to the Atlantic, which will very soon enable us to enjoy these benefits, for we shall ~~only~~ be able to reach your principal cities, New York and New Orleans, in from four to seven days. Mr. O'Sullivan will acquaint you with the result of his observations in this country; and I do not doubt that you will thereby be convinced that Costa Rica, although perhaps the smallest of the nations of America, desires to appear the most prudent, in order thus to attract the attention of the world, and to gain its esteem and interest, showing itself to be the best suited to emigration, on account of the undeniable advantages which it possesses over other Spanish-American countries. I have already had the honor to address Your Excellency in relation to the important enterprise of an inter-oceanic canal through the territory of Nicaragua and Costa Rica, and to call your attention to the propriety of having the work done by American capital and under the auspices of the Government of the United States, so that the latter country may avail itself of the natural advantages to which it is justly entitled. I shall make no further allusion to this subject now, as I expect soon to visit your country for the benefit of my health, and I hope then to have the honor of becoming personally acquainted with Your Excellency, and of conferring with you in regard to the interests of our countries. Meanwhile I wish Your Excellency much happiness, . . ." LS (in Spanish), DNA, RG 59, Miscellaneous Letters; translation, *ibid.* On Nov. 19, a correspondent reported. "Mr. J. P. O'Sullivan has delivered to President Grant the translation of a letter dated Paris, Oct. 13, addressed to him by Gen. Guardia, President of Costa Rica, who desired to express his thanks to President Grant for his courteous attentions to him whi[l]e he was on a visit to this country last Summer, and also congratulations on his probable re-election to the Presidency, an event, he says, which would secure to the great American people the continuation of their colossal progress, and at the same time to the Republics of Central America the construction of an interoceanic canal as the great connecting link between the two oceans and the highway of the world." *New York Times*, Nov. 20, 1872. On Nov. 22, 1873, Cornelius Cole, Philadelphia, wrote to USG. "Allow me to suggest that in the present West India Complications, Judge J. P. O'Sullivan, whom you know personally, may be of much service to the Administration. His experience in diplomacy—particularly his experience in that portion of the world, as well as his strict honor and integrity, eminently fit him for usefulness,—besides his preferment would be highly gratifying to his many friends, . . ." ALS, DNA, RG 59, Letters of Application and Recommendation. See *New York Tribune*, Nov. 26, 1869; *SRC*, 42-2-227, III, 204–6.

On Feb. 25, 1872, Lorenzo Montúfar, foreign minister, Costa Rica, wrote to Secretary of State Hamilton Fish enclosing a confidential letter of Feb. 23 from Guardia to USG. "As Your Excellency has probably seen by the statements of the public journals of this country, I have addressed the Citizen President of the neighboring Republic of Nicaragua, with a view to the commencement of the enterprise which is most necessary for the development of the great interests of the commerce of the world, and of America in particular, soliciting his coöperation in this enterprise, which is none other than the digging of an interoceanic canal which is to traverse the territory dividing this from the neighboring Republic. The Government of Nicaragua, understanding its true interests, and the necessity under which it is of relying on the coöperation of Costa Rica in order to carry out the enterprise in question, since the canal must traverse territory and waters which are common to both Republics, is disposed to coöperate effectively. In undertaking this enterprise, I have become convinced that it can be easily carried out; I have become so from a careful consideration of the accurate examination of ~~Lake~~ the route of the cana[l] viâ Lake Nicaragua, which was made by the distinguished Mr. Belly and Mr. Davis, superintendent of the U. S. Naval Observatory. The necessary funds for its accomplishmen[t] have been offered to my Government. In taking this first step I thought at once that the great Ame[r]ican people and their enlightened Government would take such a part in the enterprise as is assigned them by their vast prestige and power on the new continent. Filled with this conviction, I instructed Mr. Henry Meiggs Keith to treat with Your Excellency, as a private commissioner, in relation to this matter, and I now address Your Excellency, for the purpose of informing you of the happy result of my conferences with the President of Nicaragua, as the first important step taken in an enterprise which I should be glad to see inaugurated during your Administration and my own. I do not doubt that your Government, to which the civilization and progress of the American world are so greatly indebted, will take a suitable part in the enterprise of the canal, and will give it the powerful support which it can and ought to give it, in view of its great power and of the no less great interest which the American Union has in our being not only masters of the new continent, but likewise of the great highway opened through its territory to the ~~to the~~ commerce of the world and to the complete civi[l]ization of the nations of America. This invitation which I have the honor to extend to Your Excellency is, I think, the more opportune, in that, the meeting of the Congress of the American Union being so near, this enterprise may be a subject of great importance in thei[r] deliberations." LS (in Spanish), DNA, RG 59, Notes from Foreign Legations, Central America; translation, *ibid.*

On Oct. 5, 1871, Guardia had written to USG. ". . . I take the liberty of requesting Your Excellency to be pleased to order a vessel of your war-navy—one of those forming the Atlantic squadron—to examine our northern coast, from the port of 'Bocas del Toro' to that of San Juan del Norte in Nicaragua. The object of this examination is to determine the ports, (or harbors) inlets or anchoring grounds on this extent of coast, and it must be made in a scientific manner, capable of deciding the views of the Government of this Republic. The British Government has anticipated the wishes of that of Costa Rica, making generous offers to it in this sense; but, while feeling grateful for this noble offer, it has wished to give the preference to an examination made by American engineers, and to be indebted for this new service to our brethren of America. Mr. Henry Meiggs Keith, who will place this letter in the hands of Your Excellency, goes as director general of the work of building the Costa Rica railway, for the purpose of engaging engineers and purchasing implements and material for the aforesaid railway. Mr. Keith is also the bearer of a special commission to procure immigrants for this country. The distinguished qualities of this gentleman, his high social position, and the glory which he has gained, doing honor to the great nation to which he belongs, render him deserving of the esteem and appreciation of every rightminded man. But if Your Excellency adds to these considerations the object of his present commission, you will understand the particular interest with which I take the liberty of recommending him. Your Excellency may be sure that I will esteem as a signal service done to my country any attention, facility or service rendered to the man who comes to open up to us the way of civilization and wealth. I feel confident, as I have already remarked, that the requests contained in this my letter will be granted, and I promise eternal gratitude on the part of the people of Costa Rica." LS (in Spanish), *ibid.*; translation, *ibid.*; copy, *ibid.*, RG 45, Letters Received from the President. See *Foreign Relations, 1871*, pp. 252–53; Watt Stewart, *Henry Meiggs: Yankee Pizarro* (Durham, N. C.,

1946); Stewart, *Keith and Costa Rica: A Biographical Study of Minor Cooper Keith* (Albuquerque, 1964).

On Feb. 22, 1872, Jacob B. Blair, U.S. minister, San José, addressed President Guardia. "In compliance with the instructions of the President of the United States. I deliver to you this autograph letter. . . ." Copy, *ibid.*, Diplomatic Despatches, Costa Rica. On Feb. 23, Blair wrote to Fish urging U.S. commitment to a canal project; on April 3, Fish wrote to Blair on the need for additional surveys. *Foreign Relations, 1872*, pp. 160–61. See Proclamation, March 13, 1872.

On Dec. 16 and 28, 1870, Fish had written in his diary. "Read a note addressed to me by Lorenzo Montugar Minister of For. Affr of Costa Rica dated San Jose Novr 7, referring to the possibility of a Canal via Lake Nicaragua, & asking that two Engineers be sent to survey, a wagon road &c—&c   President directs answer that two will be sent—to be compensated by Costa Rica &c—" "On Monday Evening President mentioned that he thought of Selecting Genl Mackenzie, as one of the officers to make a survey for a ~~possible~~ trans isthmus route by Canal or Rail way through the Territory of Costa Rica—. . . Mackenzie was dining with me (also Senator Ames when Prsdt called & President on leaving requested me to ask Mackenzie if he would like it—In reply to the Enquiry M. expressed himself much gratified by the offer—appreciated the compliment, & understood that he would receive more pay than if with his Regiment: but said that he thought his proper place was with his Regiment—that he was very young to have received the promotion & position he had recd—he thought his presence with his troops was needed— that accepting duty away from his command, would expose him to criticism, & bring him under the suspicion of a recipient of 'favoritism,' & would have the appearrance of shirking the hard duty of his command, & seeking easier or better paying duties—that he must therefore decline—He suggested Howell, of the Engineers (now in N. Orleans) Col Ruger—Lt Col Grover—&—Macfarland as persons competent for the survey—I mention to the President his decision, & the Prsdt concurs entirely in its propriety— I also name the persons suggested by Mackenzie" DLC-Hamilton Fish. On Jan. 21, 1871, Fish wrote to Blair that while the U.S. would comply with the request, ". . . the names of the engineers have not yet been determined upon and nothing is said about their compensation and expenses. . . ." *Foreign Relations, 1871*, p. 249. On March 10, Blair wrote to Fish that Costa Rica had apparently postponed the survey. *Ibid.*, p. 250.

Endorsement

Respectfully refered to the Sec. of State suggesting that the Chairman of Com. of Appropriations be requested to report favorably an appropriation sufficient to meet the sum Dr Wines has made himself responsible for.

U. S. GRANT

DEC. 12TH /72

AES, DNA, RG 59, Miscellaneous Letters. Written on a letter of Dec. 11, 1872, from Enoch C. Wines, New York City, to USG. "The late International Penitentiary Congress of London has issued its Transactions in a volume of more than 800 pages. The facts, principles and arguments embodied in the said volume are of the highest value to all students of penitentiary science and to all persons engaged in the administration of prisons. The only way in which funds could be secured for the printing of this work was by the commissioners of the several countries represented making themselves responsible for a certain number of copies. Thus the commissioners for England, France and Germany became responsible for 500 each. As representing a first class power, I assumed responsibility for an equal number of copies, in the expectation that the Government would stand behind the subscription. What, therefore, I have to ask of the President is, that he will communicate this request to the Speaker of the House of Representatives, that so it may come in an orderly manner before the Committee on Appropriations." ALS, *ibid.* On Feb. 12, 1873, Wines, Washington, D. C., wrote to USG. "I have the honor to submit to you my report as commissioner of the United States to the International Penitentiary Congress of London, together with an appendix containing summary of proceedings of the late National Prison Congress of Baltimore." LS, *ibid.* On Feb. 14, Secretary of State Hamilton Fish wrote to U.S. Representative James A. Garfield of Ohio, chairman, committee on appropriations, requesting $1,500 reimbursement for Wines. Copy, *ibid.*, Reports to the President and Congress. See *CG*, 42–3, 1990–91, 2072, 2108–9; *HED*, 42-3-185; *PUSG*, 22, 354–56; *New York Times*, July 18, Aug. 11, 1872, March 7, 1874.

On Nov. 3, 1874, Wines wrote to USG. "I have the honor to transmit to your Excellency, herewith, my report of the proceedings of the first meeting of the permanent International Penitentiary Commission, held in the city of Brussels last May. The Commission is really a continuance, for certain important ends, of the International Penitentiary Congress of London, in 1872, in the origination of which the Congress of the United States took the initiative, & at which I had the honor to represent the Government of the United States, as well as that of the Republic of Mexico. . . . Will your Excellency pardon me for adding that, if a single favorable & encouraging word could be introduced into your annual message on this question of penitentiary reform, which forms one of the leading & living questions of the day, the effect would be wonderful in drawing the attention of the world to it, in conciliating the good will and & securing the coöperaton of foreign governments, & in giving to the idea of the second International Penitentiary Congress, to be held at Rome in 1876 by invitation of the Italian Government, an *eclat* & a power which, in no other way, could it attain. . . ." ALS, DNA, RG 59, Miscellaneous Letters. The enclosure is *ibid.* On Feb. 22, 1875, USG appointed Wines a commissioner "to attend the International Penitentiary Congress proposed to be held next year at Rome." Copy, *ibid.*, General Records. See *CR*, 43–2, 995, 1155; *U.S. Statutes at Large*, XVIII, 390, 524.

On Aug. 9, Wines, Grand Duchy of Baden, wrote to USG. "One year ago the Undersigned had the honor to submit to your Excellency a report relating to the first meeting of the Permanent International Penitentiary Commission, created by the Congress of London in 1872. The Commission has just closed its second meeting in this city, having begun its sessions on the 3rd instant, and adjourned without day on the 5th. I have now the honor to offer to your Excellency a short report of the proceedings which took place on this occasion. . . ." ALS, DNA, RG 59, Miscellaneous Letters. On Sept. 15, Wines, Copenhagen, wrote to USG reporting that negotiations with King Oscar II of Sweden had resulted in an agreement "that the second International Penitentiary Congress will be held in Stockholm in the latter part of the month of August, in the year 1877. . . ." ALS, *ibid.*

On June 20, 1876, Wines, Washington, D. C., wrote to USG. "I have the honor to submit to the President a preliminary report as commissioner of the United States, appointed under a joint resolution of Congress to represent the Government in the International Penitentiary Congress to be held next year in Stockholm, together with an appendix containing a summary of the proceedings of the late National Prison Congress of New York. The document, thus submitted to the President, will be America's contribution to the studies & labors of the Congress of Stockholm." ALS, *ibid.* On June 29, Wines again wrote to USG. "The Secretary of State takes a view of the question which had not occurred to me. He thinks that the postponement ~~of the~~ to next year of the international prison congress originally fixed for this year exhausts the relation of the U. States to it, as determined by the legislation of last year, & brings the whole thing to an end, so that the paper which I submitted to the President as a preliminary report is not, in the actual state of the case, in order. The Foreign Relations Committee of the Senate voted, two days ago, to offer, as an amendment to the sundry civil service bill, the proposition" AL (incomplete), *ibid.* On the same day, USG endorsed this letter. "Refered to the Sec. of State. I see no objection to the return to Dr. Wines of the papers submitted by him." AES, *ibid.*

To Bellamy Storer

Washington D. C. Dec. 12th *1872*

MY DEAR SIR:

At the hands of Col. Robt. Harlan,[1] of Cincinnati, Ohio I am in receipt of the resolutions adopted at a Public meeting held in College Hall the evening of the 12th of November 1872, presided over by you. I heartily thank my fellow citizens of Cincinnati, who took part at that meeting, for the very flattering terms in which the resolutions are couched; and for the manner of their transmittal—engraved beautifully for preservation.

I am, with great respect,
Your obt. svt.
U. S. GRANT

HON. B. STORER PRESIDENT

ALS, Historical and Philosophical Society of Ohio, Cincinnati, Ohio. The resolutions deplored campaign attacks on USG and urged support for his second term. See *Cincinnati Commercial*, Nov. 13, 1872. Born in 1796 in Maine, Bellamy Storer settled in Cincinnati, practiced law, and served in Congress (1835–37), and as municipal judge (1854–72). On March 19 and April 11, 1873, his son and partner, Bellamy Storer, Jr., wrote to USG recommending their partner, W. Austin Goodman, as commissioner to the Vienna Exposition. ALS, DNA, RG 59, Letters of Application and Recommendation. No appointment followed.

On Dec. 14, 1872, USG wrote to John D. Caldwell, secretary, Cincinnati Board of Trade. "I have the honor to acknowledge the receipt of your kind letter of the 9th inst. with complimentary enclosures; and also of the engrossed testimonial of the warm sentiments entertained for me by distinguished citizens of Cincinnati. Please accept my thanks for these marks of esteem accompanied with feelings of high appreciation and gratitude." Copy, DLC-USG, II, 1. On May 15, 1873, Caldwell wrote to USG. "The Citizens of Cincinnati have learned with deep sorrow of the death of Capt. C. F. Hall—appointed by you in charge of the 'Polaris' Expedition. In behalf of a Citizens Committee who design to secure adequate relief for the afflicted family (Since 1860 deprived of their natural protector—by absence on arctic explorations) I wish to know what reliance may be had from any funds from the government—legitimately due under his engagement—and how long may continue the provision that furnished part of his pay, to the family. Mrs. Hall is absent in N. Hampshire attending on her aged mother—now over 90 yrs of age—The Committee directed me to obtain such information & I have this day addressed the Secy. of the Navy—Hon. Benj. Eggleston—one of the Committee—will likely call upon you in a few days—and any information pertinent to this subject will interest our citizens. Ohio feels complimented that you gave so much trust & Confidence to one of our Citizens—who entered upon his work with great Spirit, accomplished much, but has been suddenly & mysteriously cut off, when he was soon to add renewed lustre to the American name in Geographical & Scientific Discovery. England would have knighted the living successful navigator & pensioned his widow—" ALS, DNA, RG 45, Letters Received from the President. See *PUSG*, 20, 209; *New York Times*, May 11, June 18, 1873.

1. On April 18, 1871, U.S. Representatives Aaron F. Perry and Job E. Stevenson of Ohio had written to USG. "Colonel Robert Harlan is a decided Republican is Colonel of a volunteer regiment of the men of his race in Cincinnati, and by his activity and address has attracted to himself a great deal of friendship and many good wishes He is here seeking some suitable recognition His recommendation is sign by an uncommon number of our best citizens. We ask for him your kind and favorable consideration" Copy, DNA, RG 59, Letters of Application and Recommendation. On Nov. 29, Robert Harlan, Cincinnati, wrote to USG. "I have the honor herewith to transmit to you my application for the appointment of Minister to Hayti, It is rumoured that a change is likely to be made in that Office, and my Republican friends advised me to apply for the position, by sending my recommendations direct to you, the original of which is on file at the Interior Department trusting you will assign me some honorable position whenever an oppotunity presents itself" ALS, *ibid.* On Nov. 27, 1872, Governor Edward F. Noyes of Ohio wrote to USG. "Col. Robert Harlan of Cincinnati, Ohio, is an applicant for the position of Minister to Hayti, for which appointment I respectfully recommend him— Col Harlan is a Colored man of ability and pleasing address—He has seen a great deal of the world, and would as Minister to Hayti, be a dignified and reputable representative of our Government—He rendered good service to the Republican cause during our recent political campaign, and his recognition would be appreciated by the Colored race which he represents—" ALS, *ibid.* On Dec. 2, Storer favorably endorsed this letter. AES, *ibid.* On Dec. 4, Harlan wrote to USG. "I have the honor herewith to transmit to you a copy of my application for the appointment as Minister to Hayti when Mr Bassetts term expires, or any other honorable position it may please you to assign me, I forward my recommendations trusting you will look over them at your leisure, My application is signed by many of your personal friends: I expect to visit Washington some time in this

month, when you will not be so much engaged as now, and by your kind permission present my original papers in person, Trusting they may meet your favorable consideration" ALS, *ibid.* Related papers are *ibid.* On March 18 and Nov. 16, Harlan had written to USG. "I learn by telegraph that Senator Sumner desires you to decline a renomination, I beg you in the name of the colored people, not to entertain such an idea under any consideration, the people are for you, and it is only disappointed politicians who are clamoring against you, If Senator Sumner was selected in opposition to you, and no one but colored men allowed to vote, you would be elected by a large majority, The interest I feel in you reelection must be my apology for taking the liberty to address you," ALS, NN. "I have the honor to respectfully say to you that so far as my observation of the colored people extends, I am of the opinion that they do not expect of you recognition by the appointment of any one of their race in your Cabinet, as a reward for their unanimous support of you. They are satisfied with what you have done for them in the past, and are willing to trust you in the future. It affords me great pleasure to congratulate you upon your re-election by such and overwhelming majority." ALS, USG 3. On April 25, 1874, Harlan wrote to USG. "I trust your Excellency will not think me ungrateful for your kindness in the past, or for your present consideration. If it is convenient and agreeable to you I would be delighted with any recognition, which would show that my recent loss of position, was not caused by your disapproval of my official action. Whether this is done or not, I assure you personally of my continued respect and esteem for you, and that I shall never forget you kindness to me." ALS, NN. Harlan had been special postal agent. See William J. Simmons, *Men of Mark: Eminent, Progressive and Rising* (1887; reprinted, New York, 1968), pp. 613–16.

To William W. Smith

———

Washington D. C. Dec. 13th 1872

DEAR SMITH:

Can't you and Emma come a day or two before Christmas and spend a week with us? and bring the children? We will be entirely without other company and will be delighted to see you. I will be much more at leisure during Holiday week than at any other time during the Winter, and can therefore spend more time in going round. Mrs. Grant proposes having an "All Prize" raffle for her little nephews, nieces & cozins on Christmass and would like to include your children if they can be here. Let us know if you can come.

                                        Yours Truly
                                        U. S. GRANT

ALS, Washington County Historical Society, Washington, Pa. William W. Smith and family accepted this invitation. *Washington Evening Star*, Dec. 31, 1872.

To *William F. Havemeyer*

———

Washington, D. C. Dec. 15th 1872

MY DEAR SIR:

I received a letter from you while in NewYork City, attending the funeral of Mr. Greeley, and two since, in which you reflect upon the action of Mr. Bliss[1] in interfering in matters of municipal appointments in advance of the inauguration of the new Administration. I would have replied earlier but it did not occur to me that any reply was expected. I have had no conversation or communication otherwise with Mr. Bliss since the recent elections, touching NewYork City or State affairs, and cannot therefore say what he may have had to do with the appointment of a Corporation Counsel, or other City officers. It is due to Mr. Bliss however to say that I have known him very favorably for some years past, and I have attributed the fair election which you have recently had in New York,—and consequently the success of the City and State ticket— as much to the energy and efficiency of Mr. Bliss as to the labor of any other one man. I have regarded him as a man of capacity and integrity and I would be sorry to know that he had disappointed any friend. Sometimes too much zeal may lead to imprudence, which I hope will prove to be all the blame, if there is any, that can be attached to anything he has done. In regard to the Corporation Counsel,[2] whose appointment has been anticipated by the present City authorities, all I can say is that he was most favorably recommended to me for the office of Dist. Atty. at the time Judge Davis was appointed. I know however that it is natural that you should desire to appoint your own officers no matter how good the men may be who are selected by your predecessor. I have not and certainly should not counsel interference if it was a matter where I had a right to intercede, which I have not in this case.

Very Truly Yours,
U. S. GRANT

HON. W. F. HAVEMYER
MAYOR ELECT NEWYORK CITY.

Copy, DLC-USG, II, 1. Born in 1804 in New York City, William F. Havemeyer made a fortune in sugar, entered politics as a Democrat, and twice served as mayor (1845–46, 1848–49). Switching to the Republican party during the war, Havemeyer helped oust the Tweed Ring and won a third term in 1872. On Dec. 5, 1872, Havemeyer, New York City, had written to USG. "Since writing you this morning, I have learned that Bliss and Co have concocted a scheme for the Legislature to endorse, by which, all the appointments are to be placed in the hands of the Republican party by making the Pres: of Board of aldermen, the District Attorney, together with the Mayor the Board of appointment, the two first named being a Majority—will of course control. This information makes it a matter of the highest importance for you and me—that, if no impediment, other than Bliss, is in the way of Delafields appointment he should after the 6th Jany 1873, be appointed to that office—as it would shew to the people of this State and city, what I know must be the fact that you would rather favor the public interest than the schemes of politicians where they clash. Now my dear Sir I am a Grant Republican, alias a Silas Wright & Andrew Jackson Democrat   I am satisfied that the Democratic party in this country will be rebuilt ON YOU as its CORNER STONE, and I know that the more sore heads you lose from the republican Party, the better as the number of your friends from the Democratic party will be quadrupled.—Should there be no controlling objections to Delafield Smith, and he should receive the appointment, the temper of the Legislature would more conform to the wishes of the people, than if it was understood that the politicians held the power; as for myself, I shall endeavor in appointments to office to divide, what I have to give, equally among the two great parties Republican & Democratic, but the but the appointees must in every case be honorable and honest men, devoted to the work of Reform—on which question, outside of the blatant politicians on both sides, there are no differences of opinion. Excuse the liberty I have taken, in these frequent annoyances, but I see a crisis at hand which you only appear able to avert, and which if averted, will, entitle you to receive the thanks, heartfelt & earnest, of a plundered people" ALS, NN. In 1873, Havemeyer wrote a letter of introduction to USG. William Evarts Benjamin, Catalogue No. 27, Nov., 1889, p. 7.

1. Born in 1830 in Springfield, Mass., George Bliss, Jr., graduated Harvard (1851), studied law, and moved to New York City, where he became active in Republican politics and a protégé of Edwin D. Morgan.

On March 4, 1873, John Foley, New York City, wrote to USG. ". . . Two years ago the great 'Tammany' power were all confident of Success & the inauguration of Hoffman, but that famous *injunction* of 'Foley' laid out and put an end to the most corrupt Set of men known in our Country. Much excitement exists at this time all over the State because of the hasty action of Bliss & Davenport about the new *charter* for our City. If Bliss is permitted to go on He will land the Republican Party of this State just where he put Gov Morgan four or five years ago, in the *Fenton* contest. I beg you will Send our mutual friend Collector Murphy home at once. He is a practical man   If he comes without delay we can prevent the certain overthrow of our friends. I am in favor of Senator Murphy for Controller, our friends must have controll of this office." ALS, USG 3. Foley, a New York City pen manufacturer and member of the Committee of Seventy, had filed suit against city government in Sept., 1871, as part of a campaign against corruption. See Leo Hershkowitz, *Tweed's New York: Another Look* (Garden City, N. Y., 1977), pp. 183–89; *PUSG*, 22, 203.

2. See letter to E. Delafield Smith, Dec. 9, 1872.

To Hamilton Fish

———

Washington, D. C. Dec. 16th 1872.

DEAR GOVERNOR:

I would advise that a note be addressed to the Committee on Appropriations, asking an early appropriation for the Commissioners to the Texas frontier.

Either a gross sum of, say $25.000. should be asked for, to be expended on vouchers approved by the State Department, or else there should be three thousand dollars each, per annum, for transportation and traveling expenses of the Commissioners; and one thousand dollars each, for the same purpose, for the Interpreter and Secretary.

Very Truly Yours

U. S. GRANT

HON. HAMILTON FISH,
SECRETARY OF STATE.

Copy, DLC–USG, II, 1. See Proclamation, May 21, 1872.

"Col. Robb, of Georgia, and Mr. Savage, of California, two of the Commissioners appointed by the President to take testimony relative to depredations on the Rio Grande, having returned to Washington, to-day called on the President, and had a long interview. Congress, at its late session, appropriated $6000 to pay the expenses of the Commission. The President was much interested in the narration of these gentlemen (who will prepare a formal report for transmission to Congress) and was evidently gratified with the manner in which they transacted the business with which they were entrusted. . . ." *Philadelphia Public Ledger*, Oct. 11, 1872.

To Isaac H. Bailey

———

Private   *Washington D. C.* Dec. 16th *1872*

DEAR SIR:

Your letter reminding me of my engagement to be present at the Annual festival of the New England Society, on the 23d inst. was duly received. I much regret having to send my regrets. My father is very old and infirm and has concieved the idea that unless he sees me this Winter he will never see me again. I was to have gone to see him the day after Gen. Meades death. Feeling it a duty however to attend the funeral of an old comrade and personal friend I postponed my visit to my father until the adjournment of Congress for the holidays. I leave for Covington, Ky. on Friday next.[1] I am very sorry that I cannot be with the New York New Englanders on the approaching reunion, but shall hope for better luck next time.

Very Truly Yours
U. S. GRANT

I. H. BAILEY, ESQ. NEW YORK CITY.

ALS, deCoppet Collection, NjP. A native of Maine who moved to New York City, Isaac H. Bailey worked in the leather business and was active in local Republican politics. See *New York Times*, March 25, 1899.

On April 29, 1874, Bailey, New York City, wrote to USG to congratulate him for vetoing a currency expansion bill. ALS, USG 3. See Veto, April 22, 1874.

On Dec. 22, 1875, Bailey telegraphed to USG. "I rise before dawn to repeat my request that you come I don't like to face my constituency with an unredemed promise" Telegram received (at 9:35 A.M.), DLC-USG, IB.

On Dec. 6, 1876, Bailey wrote to USG. "The perusal of your last annual message impels me to tender you my congratulations upon the record you have made. Appreciating as I do the modesty which prompted the admission that mistakes have been made my faith is unshaken that fewer mistakes have occurred since your advent to the Presidency than under any preceding dynasty. I cannot think of a policy to be reversed or an act to be undone. I concur heartily in your quiet re affirmation of the wisdom of acquiring St. Domingo. Our failure in that regard *was* a mistake and I am glad the responsibility of it does not rest with the executive. I inclose my own view of the Situation, written before your message was published So much of it as relates to the party and the administration, will, I am sure by the sober verdict of history." ALS, USG 3.

1. Dec. 20. See letter to Frederick Dent Grant, Dec. 31, 1872, note 2.

To John A. McGlone

———

Washington, D. C. Dec. 18th 1872.

REV. JNO. A MCGLONE
MINNEAPOLIS, MINN.
DEAR SIR:

Mr. Dumphrey of Paterson, N. J. has just delivered to me your note of the 26th of Nov. and the magnificent gold pen voted to me by kind friends of Minn. at the Catholic Fair held in Minneapolis in

Sept. last. I shall highly appreciate the pen as a testimonial of the good opinion the donors have of my public acts. Whether it will be possible to carry out your suggestion to write my next inaugural address with this pen, or not, I cannot tell. It is so massive that to do so will insure an inaugural so short that the audience who happen to hear it read need not grow weary from the time consumed in the task.

> With great respect
> your obt. svt.
> U. S. GRANT.

Copy, DLC-USG, II, 1.

To J. Vaughan Darling

Washington, D. C. Dec. 27th 1872.

SIR:

I have the honor to acknowledge the receipt of your letter of the 12th instant, enclosing Resolutions adopted by the branch Social Science Association of Philadelphia, and to return my thanks for the very warm endorsement of my action regarding the Phila. Post Office, in the interests of reformation of the civil service of the government.

> Very Truly Yrs.
> U. S. GRANT

J. VAUGHAN DARLING ACTG. SECTY.
416 WALNUT ST. PHILA. PA.

Copy, DLC-USG, II, 1. On Nov. 15, 1872, USG had met a delegation of Pa. politicians, including U.S. Senator Simon Cameron of Pa. and Philadelphia Mayor William S. Stokley. "Mayor Stokely stated the object of their visit to be for the purpose of ascertaining whether the President intended to apply the civil service rules to the case of the Philadelphia Post-office, and of presenting certain reasons why such application should not be made. After giving his reasons at some length, he said those present had all united upon the name of an honored merchant of the city, . . . George Truman, Esq. The President's answer was very explicit. He said he knew of no reason why he should waive the regulations in this case, and he would promote to the position a person already in the office if there was one competent for it. If he was compelled to go outside for a proper person, he would appoint the gentleman recommended by those present. This will, it is understood, result in the appointment of Mr. Fairman, present cashier of the office, . . ." *New York Times,* Nov. 16, 1872. See *ibid.,* Nov. 15, 1872, Jan. 4, 1873. On Dec. 3, 1872, USG nominated George W. Fairman as postmaster, Philadelphia.

On Nov. 21, Russell A. Alger, Detroit, wrote to USG. "I commanded a regiment and brigade in the army of the Potomac. You may remember me—*I want no office.* but do want to congratulate you upon your splendid and deserved victory, and also to assure you that the solid business men of Detroit applaud your course in the Philadelphia Post-office case. Thank Heaven for your back-bone." ALS, USG 3.

On Nov. 22, George V. Dieterich, Galesburg, Ill., wrote to USG congratulating him on his election victory. ". . . The manner of your treatment of the Philadelphia Committee, recently, met with the approval of all your friends here, and forced from the opposition the meed of praise in your behalf—You settled the charge that Simon Cameron carries you in his pocket—. . ." ALS, *ibid.*

On Nov. 28, N. Y. Representative L. Bradford Prince, Flushing, wrote to USG. "I know of no more appropriate use to make of part of Thanksgiving Day, than to express to you the thankfulness which I believe the great body of the people everywhere feel over your recent action, sustaining the Civil Service Reform in the matter of the Philadelphia Post Office   To my mind, it is the great event of the year, and a greater victory on your part than those of the war;—for the pressure *here* was from friends whom it was hard to refuse, and consequently much more difficult to resist. I have never known an act give such universal satisfaction to all good men of both parties, as this. It is fair to say, that even ardent Republicans have feared that after the election, the Civil Service Reform might become a dead letter; and that there would not be sufficient 'back-bone' in the administration to resist the frightful pressure which was sure to come. . . . As a member of the Convention which nominated you at Chicago in 1868, and one on whom has devolved a leading part in the reform of the Judiciary in our own State, I feel more proud of our President, and more confident of national reform now than ever before . . ." ALS, *ibid.*

To William W. Belknap

If you see no special reason why John Collins should not receive the apt. of Sutler at Fort Laramie, or if you have no appointment which you wish specially to make your self I wish you would give it to him. The charge of Democracy against him ought not to be held as a reason for his non appointment. The family I have known from my infancy. They have always been democrats. But I have had no stronger supporter than E. A. Collins[1] & his two sons.

U. S. GRANT

DEC. 28TH /72

ANS (facsimile), John S. Collins, *Across the Plains in '64* (Omaha, 1904), pp. 66–67; re-printed (without facsimile) as *My Experiences in the West*, Colton Storm, ed. (Chicago, 1970). On Nov. 25, 1872, John S. Collins, Omaha, had written to USG. "Respectfully ask-ing your indulgence, and influence in my behalf; I desire to secure the appointment of *Post Sutler* at *Fort Laramie* in the Department of the Platte. If your personal knowledge of my fitness for the position and commercial standing will warrent you in requesting the Sec-retary of War to appoint me. I respectfully ask that you will do so. I can obtain recom-mendations from prominent commercial men of your acquaintance, Army Officers and others here and elsewhere that you will deem ample. Trusting that you will give this matter consideration at your early convenience and advise me of the result . . ." ALS, DNA, RG 94, ACP, 6191 1872. On Dec. 19, USG wrote to Secretary of War William W. Belknap. "This will introduce Mr John Collins, of Omaha, Neb., the son of my father's business partner for many years, and who I have known favorably as an honest, capable business man for years back. He solicits the apt. of Sutler at Ft. Laramie as he will explain. I can only add that I do not doubt but Mr Collins, if appointed, would prove entirely sat-isfactory to all who might have dealings with him." Copy, *ibid.* On Dec. 31, Henry T. Crosby, chief clerk, War Dept., wrote to Collins. "In answer to your letter of the 28th instant, the Secretary of War directs me to enclose to you the letter of the President rec-ommending you for the appointment of Post Trader at Laramie" Copy, *ibid.*, RG 107, Let-ters Sent, Military Affairs.

On Sept. 26, U.S. Senator Phineas W. Hitchcock of Neb., Omaha, had written to USG. ". . . I am informed that the Commanding Officer at Fort Laramie has recommended a change in the appointment of sutler at that Post. The present sutler is from this State—Was recommended by Mr. Taffe—No sutlership appointment has been made at my re-quest except the small and temporary Post at Beaver in Utah Territory—If there is to be a change at Fort Laramie it would gratify me and I think could be made servicable to the party in this State, were I permitted to suggest a successor. I have not asked a removal and make this request only upon the supposition that a change is to be made—" ALS, *ibid.*, RG 94, ACP, 5944 1872. On Dec. 28, Belknap wrote identical letters to Hitchcock and others. ". . . I have the honor to inform you that at the personal request of the President, the appointment of John S. Collins as Post Trader at Fort Laramie has been made and for-warded to him at Omaha Nebraska" Copy, *ibid.*, RG 107, Letters Sent, Military Affairs. See *HRC*, 44-1-799, 173–76.

1. See *PUSG*, 2, 44–45; *ibid.*, 18, 160–61.

To Frederick Dent Grant

Washington D. C. Dec. 31st 1872.

DEAR FRED.

Your Ma has been quite uneasy about you since the receipt of your letter from the point where you had been delayed for several days until today Gen. Babcock received a letter from your Colonel[1]

saying that you had passed Fort Richardson all well. We are all well.
I was out to Cincinnati a week ago[2] and found your GrandPa Grant
about as he was when you saw him last.

A dividend has been paid on your Adams Ex. Stock since you
left. I took your $1100 00 and put with it enough to buy you twenty
shares more of stock. You now have Seven thousand dollars worth.
I want to aid you in making it ten thousand during the next year.
After that you may feel like in investing in something else.

All send much love to you,

Yours Affectionately

U. S. GRANT

ALS, USG 3. On Dec. 20, 1872, Orville E. Babcock wrote to Gen. William T. Sherman.
"At the request of Mrs. Grant will you please inform me at what Post the Cavalry is going to rendezvous—mentioned to her in conversation last evening." LS, DLC-William T.
Sherman. On Dec. 21, Secretary of War William W. Belknap wrote to "Dear General." "I
have telegraphed to *Dennison*—the farthest point where there is a telegraph office—asking when Fred passed through & where he is at present. It may be a day or two before a
reply comes but I will notify you & Mrs. G. at once" ALS, University of Iowa, Iowa City,
Iowa. On Dec. 22, L. K. Hutchinson, Denison, Tex., telegraphed to AG Edward D.
Townsend. "Lieut Fred grant left Red River for Fort Richardson on the twelfth Inst.   was
in good health then" Telegram received (at 8:40 P.M.), USG 3.

1. Col. Ranald S. Mackenzie.
2. On Dec. 20, USG, son Jesse, and brother-in-law Alexander Sharp left Washington, D. C., on a brief visit to Covington, Ky. See letter to Jesse Root Grant, Nov. 3, 1872;
New York Times, Dec. 21, 23, 1872. On Dec. 24, USG, Mifflin, Pa., telegraphed to
Julia Dent Grant. "Detained so much by ice and snow that arrival of train will be late
tonight" Telegram received, USG 3.

Calendar

1872, FEB. 1.   William E. Chandler, Washington, D. C., to USG. "In behalf of the owners of the steamship 'Hornet,' now in Baltimore, I have to request that she may be allowed to proceed to New York City. As a condition of granting the request the Government may adopt any precautions deemed necessary to secure her arrival in New York, to answer to any charge the Government may see fit to prefer against her. The vessel cannot be sold without great sacrifice except in New York. It would be great injustice to prevent her going there, and I earnestly urge the granting of this application."—LS, DNA, RG 59, Miscellaneous Letters. See *PUSG*, 19, 545–47. Released from U.S. custody in June, 1870, the *Hornet* had left New York City in Dec. to resume insurgent operations off Cuba. By Oct., 1871, Spanish warships had trapped the *Hornet* at Port-au-Prince, and demanded its surrender. After negotiations, the *Hornet* left for Baltimore in Jan., 1872, escorted by the U.S.S. *Congress.* See *Foreign Relations, 1871,* pp. 778–91; *Foreign Relations, 1872,* pp. 256–63; *New York Times,* Oct. 22, 1871; *ibid.,* Jan. 28, 1872. On Feb. 2 and 15, 1872, Secretary of State Hamilton Fish wrote in his diary. "A communication from W. E. Chandler Counsel for the Owners of the Hornet, asking that she be allowed to be taken to NY was handed me by the Prsdt—a copy also being sent to me by Chandler—Prsdt asked if there were any reason why it could not be done—he was reminded of the reasons why it has been decided to have her taken to Baltimore, viz. that she was more likely there to obtain a fair & a speedy trial—. Williams said the crowded condition of the Courts in N. Y & the influences existing there, made it not desirable that she be tried there—Boutwell said he thought there was something in the laws which required her being tried in the district into which she first arrived—The Prsdt then said he remembered why she was brought into Baltimore & that she must await her trial there—adding that it was desirable that no unnecessary delay occur—I then read the Memorandum of the history of the transfer of the Vessel (prepared by Marquis de Chambrun) handed me this morning—& obtained Presidents authority to refer the whole case to the Attorney General for consideration, & prosecution of the Vessel if there be grounds for suspecting her of violating the Navigation laws of the U. S—" "February 15 . . . Mr Roberts, . . . enquires about the 'Hornet'—is told that she is to be allowed to go to NewYork, under bonds, & will be held there for a reasonable time for evidence & will be tried if the evidence will justify—That the Atty Genl is of opinion that the vessell cannot be forfeited under the Navigation laws, in the hands of a present owner, for a false registration in the name of a previous owner or pretended owner—He promises to furnish evidence shortly, both as to the 'Hornet' & the 'Florida'—"— DLC-Hamilton Fish.

1872, FEB. 1.   "The people of Curacao" to USG. "Whereas the always so quitly and peacefull people of this Island has been threatened on a so cruelly manner by its government under governor Herman Wagner, as killing one and wounding nineteen, and the rest of the citizens saved by the hand of our Lord; on 24th November last, and whereas on account of false and reverse report of said Wagner to our King William, we have been again bad threatened being in our fully rights, . . . we have decided to direct us to you Dear Preasident, man of rights and knowledges, to make our King know what this government of Wagner is doing with us, and also to save us of being killed by these murderers—. . . Reasons wherefore we donot sign our name is because we are afraid that afterwards they do not shoot us again but be assured if there shall be a voting here, we shall vote all to be citizens of the United States—. . ."—D, DNA, RG 59, Miscellaneous Letters.

1872, FEB. 2.   To Senate. "I transmit to the Senate, in answer to their resolution of the 16th ultimo, a report from the Secretary of State with accompanying papers."—DS, DNA, RG 46, Presidential Messages. *SED*, 42-2-28. On the same day, Secretary of State Hamilton Fish had written to USG "concerning the seizure and retention of the American steamers "Hero," "Dudley Buck," "Nutrias" and "San Fernando," the property of the Venezuelan Steam Transportation Company,—an American Corporation—and the virtual imprisonment of the officers of these vessels, who are American citizens."—LS, DNA, RG 46, Presidential Messages. In Sept., 1871, Joseph W. Hancox, president, Venezuela Steam Transportation Co., Ciudad Bolivar, Venezuela, had written to USG seeking U.S. retaliation for the seizures.—LS (docketed as received Oct. 26), *ibid.*, RG 59, Miscellaneous Letters. Printed in *SED*, 42-2-28, 14–16. See *New York Times*, Sept. 19, 1900.

1872, FEB. 2.   To William H. Shirley, clerk, q. m. dept. "I have examined the enclosed papers carefully and I would favor the extra compensation asked for if there was an appropriation out of which it could be paid, and the payment not discretionary with the War Department."—Copy, DLC-USG, II, 1. On Nov. 10, 1871, Secretary of War William W. Belknap had written to USG. "I have the honor to transmit, herewith, in compliance with your request made through W. H. Shirley, Esq., the papers relating to his claim for compensation for additional services rendered in the investigation and settlement of a/cs. for abandoned and captured property in Dept. of the South."—Copy, DNA, RG 107, Letters Sent, Military Affairs.

1872, FEB. 5.   USG endorsement. "Respectfully refered to the Sec. of War. Mr. Benton, the writer of this letter, is one of the best original Union men in St. Louis."—AES, DNA, RG 94, ACP, 38AB 1872. Written on a letter of Feb. 1 from William H. Benton, St. Louis, to USG. "This will introduce to you Mr Charles Espenschied one of the best young men of our City and the Son of one of our oldest & best respected Citizens—I have written you before respecting the application of my friend Espenschied for the position as Post trader at the Military Post established in Tularosa Valley N. M. Mr Espenschied is under the impression that his letters and recommendations have not reachd you & Concludes to Visit Washington and pay his respects to you in person—I earnestly hope you will find it agreeable to gratify his wishes and if you Can do so I will Consider it a personal favor to myself"—ALS, *ibid.* See *PUSG*, 17, 4;

ibid., 20, 220. On Dec. 27, 1871, and April 22, 1872, Benton had written USG on the same subject.—ALS, DNA, RG 94, ACP, 38AB 1872. Charles W. Ford favorably endorsed the earlier letter.—AES (undated), *ibid.* On Jan. 8, 1873, Charles Espenschied, St. Louis, wrote to Secretary of War William W. Belknap. "Company A National Guards (of which I am a member) intend to do themselves the honor of paying their respects to the President and be present at the inauguration. It would give me great pleasure to be permitted to accompany them but as the time allowed me to reach Fort Tularosa will expire about that time I will have to forego it unless I could prevail on you to allow me to place a representative there until after the inauguration & to give me time to reach there. Awaiting your answer patiently . . ."—ALS, *ibid.*

1872, FEB. 5.   Horace Porter to Mary M. Rockafellar, New York City. "The President desires me to write you and acknowledge the receipt of your letter, received by him some time ago, through Mr John L. Shoemaker. He has had it referred to the State Department, and would have had you so informed long ago, but the letter of Mr Shoemaker became mislaid & only was found again by him within the last few days."—LS, DNA, RG 59, Letters of Application and Recommendation. On Dec. 18, 1871, Rockafellar had written to USG. "The motive I have in addressing you, I feel will justify the liberty I have taken. I know it has been your *expressed* desire, to reward the wounded heroes, and as my son Col' Harry Rockafellar is one of the many, deserving ones, he threw up a lucrative situation, at the age of twenty; and went as a private in the 71st reg' NYork, the same he now commands, to defend his country; one of the first to go, and the last to leave; which he did not untill the war was ended,   wounded in the first battle 'Bull-run, first, by a bullet passing through his cheek, but he still remained in the ranks, untill his left arm was taken off, by a Canon-ball, taken prisoner, confined in 'Libby Prison,' he had been brevetted for gallantry (hence), was put with the officers, Corcoran, Wilcox, and many others, he being the youngest of ninetysix. What *his* sufferings were and *mine* I will pass over, he never alludes to them, nor have I ever heard a murmur or regret, although I *know* he suffers intensely at times, and *I* do, whenever I think of the sacrifice of my noble boy, and his dear lovely sister, whose life, also, and my own health, were given for our country. Harry's health has been delicate for the last year, his Physcian says the loss of his arm, has weakened his constitution, and reccomends change of climate, and more rest, than he now has in his present business. I am going to ask of your Excellency an appointment for him, a 'Consulship' or something of the kind, which will take him abroad,   he has energy and ability, and is qualified to fill almost any situation with honor,   he holds a high position, social business, and Military, he has hosts of friends both here, in Phil', and elsewhere, who can testify to his irreproachable character. . . . I appeal to you as a Soldier, a father, and President of this great Republic, and ask if our country was again in *danger*, would not *Mothers* be again, called upon to give up their sons. I as the Mother of one of the purest, noblest, and best, just stepping into manhood, with bright hopes for the future, reared in luxury, the idol of a widowed Mother, and sweet lovely sister, who received her death blow, when her brother was wounded, May I trust ask that *his* country, may remember *him* as he did *her* in her hour of need. You will do me a favor to hand this letter to your honored wife, she will *understand my feelings* and appreciate them,   I have heard much of her kindness of heart, and interest in the soldiers.   personally she is unknown to me, only through some friends, who spent last winter in Washington."—ALS, *ibid.* Related papers are *ibid.*; *ibid.*, RG 56, Appraiser of Customs Applications. No appointment followed.

1872, FEB. 6.   George W. Dent, appraiser of merchandise, San Francisco, to USG. "The Japanese Government having tendered to my associate Mr Hilliard M. Miller, Appraiser of Merchandise at this Port, the position of Appraiser of Customs for that Government, and having accepted the same, he has this day forwarded to you his resignation, to take effect on the 1st of March next. The necessity of having some one thoroughly conversant with the duties of Appraiser, coupled with undoubted integrity, is all important to the Government. The name of Mr Benjamin Hall is respectfully submitted for your consideration as a person suitable for the appointment. Mr Halls long connection with the Custom Department in this city at the responsible desk of adjuster of duties—his acknowledged ability—his integrity of character, and his acceptability to the Importers of this city, I trust, will sufficiently commend him to your favorable consideration. I know of no one so eminently qualified to succeed Mr Miller as Mr Benjamin Hall."—ALS, DNA, RG 56, Appraiser of Customs Applications. On the same day, Timothy G. Phelps, collector of customs, San Francisco, wrote to USG. ". . . I concur fully with Mr Dent in all that he says regarding the integrity and qualifications of Mr Hall, and only object to his appointment on the ground that he cannot be spared from the desk he now occupies (Adjuster of Duties) in the Custom House, without great inconvenience and positive danger to the revenue. The pay is the same in both positions and they are equally honorable, therefore it is no promotion to transfer Mr Hall to the Appraiser's store,   If there was any difference in the positions, I should feel that Mr Hall's long service, his integrity and abilities entitled him to promotion however great the difficulty of filling his present position. I have therefore the honor to recommend for appointment Jacob Gounter Moore, Esq.   Mr Moore is at present warehouse and withdrawal clerk. He has been a long time in the Customs Service, and is a man of fine abilities and unquestioned integrity, and has a fair knowledge of the duties which will be required of him—far better than any man who could be selected except Mr Hall, while he is a man of such untiring industry, I feel assured he would lose no time in making himself thoroughly acquainted with his new duties. Mr Moore is not as well known to Mr Dent as Mr Hall, but a two years acquaintance with both men convinces me that he will find him, should he be appointed, a no less pleasant associate, and a no less efficient officer."—LS, *ibid.* USG endorsed a docket for papers recommending Benjamin Hall. "If place is to be filled, I would prefer the apt of Jas. Coey."—Copy (undated), *ibid.*, Naval Officer Applications. On March 1, USG nominated James Coey to replace Hilliard M. Miller; the Senate did not confirm this nomination.

On Feb. 28, U.S. Senator Cornelius Cole of Calif. had written to USG. "I recommend for Appraisor, at the Port of San Francisco, in place of H. M. Miller, resigned, Eugene B. Williams, whom I know to be a suitable and competent man for the place—"—ALS, *ibid.,* Appraiser of Customs Applications. On May 27, Cole wrote to USG. "I recommend that you nominate, Matthew G. Upton, Esq, long-time Editor of the *Alta Californian*—for Appraisor at the Port of San Francisco. This will be a most judicious nomination. I cannot advise, nor can I vote for the confirmation of Mr Coey. My reasons are of a personal as well as political & public nature. Upton is a very prominent citizen & the party as well as the public owes him much."—ALS, ICarbS.

On March 18, Brig. Gen. Oliver O. Howard, San Francisco, wrote to USG. "I have written to Mr Delano giving him the result of my interview with General Schofield which he will doubtless lay before you. I have been asked to write you with reference to a gentleman who is recommended to fill the office of *Appraiser* of merchandize vice Miller resigned in case Mr Coey should not be appointed by you. This gentlemans name is *Addison Martin.* I had known him from childhood before he came to California—and I am glad to find he has ever preserved an unsullied record & character—Having been once extensively engaged as a merchant, he is thoroughly conversant with the duty required— The California delegation—at least Mr Cole & Mr Sargent will apprize you of particulars with regard to his fidelity in a political point of view; but I thought it would help you to know that he is capable honest & a Christian gentleman"— ALS, DNA, RG 56, Appraiser of Customs Applications. On Dec. 9, 1870, Howard had written to USG. "I received the enclosed from my personal friend Addison Martin Esq: of California & forward it as requested. I had mislaid the letter & hence the delay as it was written Nov. 1st 1870"—ALS (press), Howard Papers, MeB.

On June 17, 1872, Dent wrote to USG. "I received a letter today from Mr Hilliard M. Miller, from Yokohama Japan, who held the position of Appraiser at this Port until last January, when he resigned, and his resignation accepted by you. The Japanese Commission or Embasy tendered Mr Miller a position in Japan to take charge of their Customs business—hence his resignation. He has been in Japan two months and has not been assigned to duty, and says the probabilities are, that he will not be for a year to come. His wife and daughter, who accompanied him, have been quite sick since his arrival out in Japan, and he now regrets exceedingly that his resignation as Appraiser was accepted, and is desirous of returning to his old post. I have thought, Mr President, that, inasmuch as the Senate did not confirm Mr Coey, whom you appointed as Mr Millers successor and, considering the importance of the position, requiring great and particular fitness for the place, that you might re-appoint Mr Miller, who has been regarded as the best appraiser ever holding the place—and who is greatly appreciated by this community. As I have been attending to the duties of the office since Mr Miller's departure, I can so continue to do until his return which would be in about two months, and, if you think favorably of his reappointment, your action might be deferred until that time, when he could make application himself, with proper endorsements. I have a high regard for Mr Miller, and I trust Mr President, you will pardon me for thus addressing you on a matter upon which I should probably remain silent."— ALS, DNA, RG 56, Appraiser of Customs Applications.

On March 7, 1873, U.S. Senator Aaron A. Sargent of Calif. wrote to USG. "I recommend the appointment of J. B. Moore of S. F. as appraiser at San Francisco vice H. M. Miller resigned & Coey not confirmed. There is now a vacancy"—ALS, *ibid.* On the same day, USG nominated Jacob G. Moore to replace Miller.

1872, FEB. 7.   Levi P. Luckey to Secretary of the Interior Columbus Delano. "The President directs me request you to issue the necessary papers for the admission into the Insane Asylum of a lunatic, who is now in the charge of Major Richards, Chief of Police. The man claims to belong in Alabama and believes that he is the son of the President. He has paid several visits to the Executive Mansion and is a proper subject for confinement and medical treatment in the Asylum."—Copy, DLC-USG, II, 1.

1872, FEB. 8.   Maj. Gen. John M. Schofield, San Francisco, to USG. "Frederic Halverson French, a son of the General, is an applicant for appointment at large to the Military Academy. He is a promising young man, in every way worthy of the appointment. Genl French's long and distinguished services, which are well known to you, entitle him to more than ordinary consideration. He is very highly esteemed by every body here, and I am sure the appointment of his son would be very gratifying to your best and most influential friends on the Pacific Coast."—ALS, DNA, RG 94, Correspondence, USMA. Related papers are *ibid.* On March 22, U.S. Senator Cornelius Cole of Calif. wrote to USG. "I inclose letter from W. C. Ralston Esq expressing great solicitude about the appointment of Genl French's son to West Point—Judge Hoffman & many others have also applied for him."—ALS, OFH. Orville E. Babcock drafted a reply to Cole. "Young French was appointed two days since"—ADf (initialed, undated), *ibid.* Frederic H. French, USMA 1877, was the son of William H. French, USMA 1837.

1872, FEB. 9.   USG endorsement. "Respectfully refered to the Sec. of State. Should the vacancy occur I have no objection to the apt. of Mr. Hall."—AES, DNA, RG 59, Letters of Application and Recommendation. Written on a petition of Jan. 30 from U.S. Senators Zachariah Chandler and Thomas W. Ferry of Mich., *et al.*, to USG. "The undersigned respectfully request the appointment of Henry L Hall of Michigan, as Consul to the Port of Valencia, Spain in case a vacancy shall occur in said Consulate"—DS (8 signatures), *ibid.* A related letter is *ibid.* On Feb. 26, USG nominated Henry L. Hall as consul, Valencia.

1872, FEB. 9.   Secretary of War William W. Belknap to USG. "I have the honor to submit, herewith, a copy of the testimony taken and statements made relating to the trial of Sergeant William Knorr, convicted and sentenced to the penitentiary by the local courts of New Mexico, of the report of the Inspr.

General, Dept. of the Mo., and of other papers in the case, with the hope that, upon their examination, sufficient grounds will be found to justify the granting a pardon to Knorr, as recommended by his immediate superiors, the commander of his Dept. and the Lieut. Genl. of the Army."—Copy, DNA, RG 107, Letters Sent, Military Affairs. On Feb. 28, USG pardoned William Knorr, sentenced to one year in prison for "removing the cancelling marks from the postage stamps, with the intention of using them a second time . . ."—Copy, *ibid.,* RG 59, General Records.

1872, FEB. 9. Mary Woodman, Oporto, Portugal, to USG. "It is with a sad & breaking heart that I write to you. I was born in Newburyport Mass. where most of my relatives live. My father lives with a married sister in Boston, & my mother died when I was very young. My family is of great respectability Four years ago at the age of twenty-four I met & became aquainted with Mr Fletcher the American Consul now in Oporto it was in Newburyport where he was living at the time I met him—he told me the sad story of his wifes desertion & unfaithfulness.—he bewildered me with his kindness & professions of love—he was a minister & said his prayers & read his bible in my presence—he appeared like a saint & excited all the sympathy of my deep & sensitive nature—by his artfulness & with promises of marage he seduced me, then he left me to get his divorce (he told me he was free from his wife) he wrote me letters with expressions of love & promises of marage,—in some of them confessing his crime in a religious manner, he obtained his divorce in the West   after a while in a loving letter he wishes me to distroy all his letters as they would make his divorce unlawful,   I wrote him that I would not until after he had fulfill his promise to me   I met him in Newburyport before he came here   I entreated him to marey me which he promise to do if I would give up the letters first WHICH I WILL NOT DO,   he came here I wrote to him *again* & *again* in that pleading tone that only a woman with a ruined honor can write (God only knew the deep anguish of my heart when I felt that I was *lost* & *forsaken.*)   My friends knew not the cause of my sorrow. I wrote to him that I should come to Oporto   'I had lost all intrest in life, that I was *pure* before I saw him, he had ruined me & he alone could *save me.* I would seek him if I perished in the attempt to find him; for three years I have suffered in *body* & *mind.*' I started in Oct' alone for Europe   in four week I arrived at the nearest port Lisbon from there I sent him a note. I thought he would see how m[u]ch I cared for him, to take this long journey, *simple-hearted & true.* I thought he would meet me. When the steamer reached Oporto a note was given to me written in a stanger's hand, dictated by Mr Fletcher, it read thus, 'Miss Woodman, The American Consul, of Oporto, Will not see you & he will not recognise your claim.   you will accomplish nothing by staying here & this is a very expensive city.   (you of course know what by treaty are the powers of Consuls)   my advise to you is to return to the United States as soon as possible, as much of your money will be spent & you will gain nothing by it.' The Capt' took me to his friends.   he went to see the Consul who had fled; he left word that he had gone to Madrid,   he tells the Vice Consul (Mr Shore) that I am insane, & will not

see me & hides in his house. Mr Shore called to see me.   he is indignant with
him & said he should see me, for he would not 'HARBOR HIM,'—The next day
he saw me, he wished me to 'trust him a week as he wanted to PRAY over the
matter, then he would bring a pious friend, a minister, of his to see me,'   before the meeting the friend called to advise me 'to say nothing until something
was decided upon.' The next eve' I was sent for & th[ese] conditions made to
me, 'That I should not let these turms be known to any-one, That I leave
Oport[o] & go to London the next day alone, (I never was in Europe before)
That I write to no friend I have made in Oporto, That I pay his debts which is
seven hundred dollars. That his son (who left West Point) should have five hundred more & what money I have left I must give to him (I had $4800 four hun-
dred of which I have spent already   these conditions must be fulfill before he
entered the '*bonds of matrimony*' & that would be next Sept.' I assented to all,
only asking for a few days to rest before taking another voyage   at this he
started up saying, 'you have refused the conditions, I will have nothing to do
with you.' I told him I would go the next day if he would only promise before
witnesses to fulfill the conditi[on]—he told me tears & pleadings, would not
avail   that he was ~~i~~engage in a revival of religion,—that I could not come in a
worse time to INJURE, & EXPOSE him, & threatened to use his power as a Consul & force me from the city.—It was one oclock in the morning when I went
back to my friends, sick & broken-hearted.   in a few days the minister was
sent to me again—saying he was feeling more kindly towards me. I was sick,
in my bed too weak to bear any more.   then the same conditions were sent to
me with the addition that I give up all the *letters* he ever wrote to me.   he said
'his reasons for wanting the letters were 'in case I should die before Sept' when
he would fulfill his promise & if these letters were found they would injure him
I refused to give them up—then he told me that he was engage to another *lady
in America*, & coolly said I could look on him as a BROTHER. I asked him if a
brother would *ruin a sister* & begged him not to add *insult* to *injury*. Last week
I called to see him (as I am out of money, & wanted to ask him how I should
send to America for it.)   he opened the window & looked out, he would not
speak, or open the door to me, & says he will not see me. The English Consul
advised me to write to you. . . . P. S. If Mr Fletcher had only told me before I
came here, that he should treat me so, I should not have left America,   *he knew
I was coming.*"—ALS, DNA, RG 59, Letters of Application and Recommendation. On Aug. 20, William Minty, Mary Castro, and Fannie Castro, Oporto,
wrote to USG. "Miss Woodman wrote this letter last winter, but neglected
sending it hoping Mr Fletcher would soften, and she did not wish to injure
him, (she has been giving my sister and me drawing lesson's for her board)
last week we heard Mr F was going to America to be married, next month   at
first we thought Miss W would lose her reason; when she heard this, we advised her to send to America for money to go back when he went & *punish* him
by law   Mr F. is the only American in Porto. Yesterday she went to his house
to see if he would tell her how to send for it,   he said he would have nothing
to say to her if she did not wish to be insulted to leave his house,   she waited
until he had finished [his] tea, then without saying a word to her he left the

house, after telling his servant who is a Portuguen to go for the police, ard this villain would have had her carried to prison by the policeman who came, if a friend (an Englishman) had not prevented it,   we think if the United States Goverment cannot find better men than what this *coward* and *villain* is it should do without Consuls *and we do hope* that you will take notice of this outrageous treatment to an unprotected lady in a strange land."—LS, *ibid.* On Oct. 9, Woodman wrote to USG. "If it is not too much trouble will you be so kind as to read these copies of Mr Fletcher's letters to me. No one but my *Maker* knows what my poor heart has suffered by the artfulness of this man. My friends thought he was a *Christian* or they would not have advised me to go to his house instead of teaching; towards the end of August 1867; he wished me to help him pack his books which were in the house in Newburyport where we had lived; The house not being inhabited was damp, & cold. My *feet* & *hands* were cold & I had a severe headache but I worked all day with him; at night when I went home I was too sick to eat & said 'I will go to bed & if I can sleep off this headache I shall be well in the morn'   Mr Fletcher said 'I have some wiskey & will give you some   it will make you sleep;'   he made me a large tumbler full of hot wiskey & water   for the first time in my life I was intoxicated. Oh the anguish of my heart the next morn' when I found Mr Fletcher had *robbed* me of that which was dearer to me than life; for I was *proud* of my HONOR. I was *furious*   I *raved,* & *threatened him*; he begged me on his knees with tears in his eyes 'not to expose him   he said he did not intend to *seduce* me, that he was *lonely* & wanted to be near me, & would marry me as soon as he obtained his divorce,' . . . Nov 14th '/72. Since writing this letter I have been very ill; with brain-fever. Mr Fletcher was secretly married about four weeks ago; when I heard it I was almost wild for the fearful past & my *great sorrow* rushed into my mind & nearly distroyed my reason. Mrs Castro & her family did every thing to calm me. I saw Mr Shore in the afternoon & told him all I have written you; he read the letters & said 'he wished he had known it before; that I had been too merciful with him'. He asked if I had received a letter from the *Department of State*   I said 'No.'—he said Mr Fletcher came to his office about two weeks ago very much *excited,* saying 'I have a letter for Miss Woodman sent to me from Washington what *would* you do with it.' Mr Shore said, 'give it to her of course'.   he keep the letter ten days; & sent it to me the morning he was married; sent it through the Post Office & did not even pay the postage which was five cents. . . . And now in closeing let me say,—if the *crime* & the *injury* I have suffered from him is not criminal enought to *compel* him to return to the State where I can have my cause pleaded, justices done me, & the guilty punished, then I will take the *law* in my own hands. I do not say I will *kill him*; but I will leave a *fearful mark,* or *wound* upon him which he will look upon with shame: which he will carry to the grave with him. Do not blame me? for you have a daughter & may she be laid in the grave; before her pure life is blighted as mine has been . . ."—ALS, *ibid.*

In [*March*], 1869, U.S. Senators Oliver P. Morton and Daniel D. Pratt and U.S. Representative John Coburn of Ind. had written to Secretary of State Hamilton Fish recommending James C. Fletcher as consul, Naples.—LS (docketed March 29), *ibid.* Related papers, including a letter of March 15 from poet John G. Whittier to Fletcher, are *ibid.* On April 12, USG nominated Fletcher as consul, Palermo; on April 15, he changed the nomination to Oporto.

On Oct. 22, 1872, Fletcher, Oporto, wrote to Charles Hale, asst. secretary of state, denying the charges.—ALS, *ibid.*, Consular Despatches, Oporto. On Oct. [24], August J. Shore, vice consul, Oporto, wrote to Hale. ". . . In regard to the portion of the despatch from the State Department which refers to myself, I. have to reply that, the information I possess bearing on the case, is of such a private, peculiar, and delicate nature, that I should prefer not entering into the matter in an official correspondence   I think it my duty to inform you that Miss Mary Woodman is at present dangerously ill of brain fever, the result of the great mental shock she sustained in the sudden marriage of Mr Fletcher on the 22nd Inst: to Miss Frederica Smith of this city. If Mr Fletcher be not immediately withdrawn from this consulate, I shall be obliged to tender my resignation to the Department of State as vice consul for this direct. Hoping that the Department will communicate this to His Excellency the President. . . ."—LS (misdated Oct. 21), *ibid.* On Nov. 21, Morton, Indianapolis, wrote to USG. "The Rev. J. C. Fletcher—U. S. Consul at Oporto—Portugal has called my attention to certain charges that have been made against him by a woman named Woodman—While I have no knowledge of the facts in this particular case I desire to say that Mr Fletchers family is one of the oldest and most respectable in this State and Mr F. has long occupied a prominent position as a Methodist minister and so far as I can assertain no word was ever spoken against his character and should be slow to believ any acquisations against his character until the most convincing proofs were furnished"—ALS, *ibid.*, Letters of Application and Recommendation. See *DAB*, III, 465–66; Gayle Thornbrough *et al.*, eds., *The Diary of Calvin Fletcher* (Indianapolis, 1972–83), V, 500–502. On Jan. 13, 1873, USG nominated Alfred V. Dockery to replace Fletcher. For Dockery, see *PUSG*, 21, 331.

On Sept. 5, 1874, Dockery, Oporto, wrote to John L. Cadwalader, asst. secretary of state. ". . . Miss Woodman, an American subject, who has been here since the latter part of my predecessors (Mr Fletchers) term; has a lawsuit in the courts of this country, the object being to recover possession of her luggage from the proprietor of an hotel, who maintains that she has not paid her board-bill; while she says that it was paid in work; ie, she taught the proprietors daughters, music etc—. . ."—ALS, *ibid.*, Consular Despatches, Oporto. On Nov. 22, 1875, Dockery wrote to Cadwalader that Woodman had won her lawsuit.—ALS, *ibid.* On Nov. 16, Benjamin Moran, U.S. minister, Lisbon, had written to Dockery. "I have the honor to acknowledge the receipt of your Despatch of yesterday's date reporting the restoration by Mrs Castro of the property belonging to Miss Woodman which she had in her possession; and I think we may congratulate ourselves on this event. You have my entire approval of your course in the matter, as set forth in your notes to me, since I have been in the Legation; and I thank you for the wisdom and patience you have displayed in the management of what has been a most vexatious and unpleasant business. That Miss Woodman is deranged, I have no doubt; and she may yet give us trouble. . . ."—Copy, *ibid.*

On June 20, 1872, Robert C. Schenck, U.S. minister, London, wrote to USG. "I do not know whether any appointments are being made now in the Army from Civil life. If there be, I venture to recommend earnestly to your favorable notice a young friend of mine Edm[*u*]nd Livingston Fletcher for a commission as a Second Lieutenant of Infantry. This young man has strong Military tastes—is poor—dependent entirely on his own exertions for a subsistence— his father, who was a clergyman, having a consulate of $1500 a year in Portugal, & his family neither able or disposed to give him aid. He is now about 21 years old; & ought to be a graduate this year at West Point. He was a cadet there, & ought to have succeeded, but was young & got discouraged & home sick & heart sick in his first year—left—& was 'dropped' from the rolls. He has lived to regret the mistake he made, & is ambitious to amend it. He was afterwards appointed, & served through their war with Germany, a Sous-Lieutenant in the French Army; & thus has had some useful training & experience. He speaks French perfectly. This is all that occurs to me to say in his behalf, except that it will gratify me much personally, if I can, by recommendation & request of mine, help the young man himself & his family, by obtaining for him through your kind consideration, a start again in the Army, & a chance to prove himself, as I think he would, deserving of confidence & encouragement."— ALS, DNA, RG 94, ACP, 103 1873. Edmund L. Fletcher enlisted as private, 15th Inf., as of Aug. 2. On Jan. 9, 1873, USG nominated Fletcher as 2nd lt.

1872, FEB. 12.   USG endorsement. "Refered to the Sec. of the Navy."—AES, DNA, RG 45, ZB File. Written on a letter of Feb. 1 from Israel Washburn, Jr., collector of customs, Portland, Maine, to USG. "My son, Israel H. Washburn, a Lieut. in the Marine Corps, is desirous of receiving the appointment of Assistant Quarter Master in that Corps, in place of Capt. Wiley, who, he is informed, intends to resign that position very soon. My son was in the 16th Maine Regiment in 1861 & 1862, & afterwards was on the Staff of Major Genl Hiram Berry. I beg to refer you to Mr Hamlin for information in regard to the character & ability of my son."—ALS, *ibid.* See *PUSG*, 15, 269–70. On July 6, U.S. Senator Hannibal Hamlin of Maine, *et al.*, Bangor, wrote to USG. "I have been informed that there is to be appointed an Asst Quarter master in the Marine Corps; and I earnestly recommend Lt I H Washburn for that place. He is the son of Ex Gov. Washburn of this state, and I believe is well qualified for the place. I at one time conferred with you in relation to the Apt. and will very glad if you can confer it upon him"—ALS (3 signatures), DNA, RG 45, ZB File. On July 10, Mayor Benjamin Kingsbury, Jr., of Portland wrote to USG on the same subject.—ALS, *ibid.* On Jan. 6, 1873, USG nominated Capt. Horatio B. Lowry as asst. q. m., U.S. Marine Corps, to replace Capt. James Wiley.

1872, FEB. 16.   J. J. Bridges, Greensburg, La., to USG. "I address your Honor for the perpos of informeing me whither or no I can, By the law Recover a certain colored Boy By the name of Frank Bridges   he was Apprinticd to me in the year 1866 By the Honorable James Hough Suprentendent of the Freedemans Beaurough for the Parishes of St Helena Levingston St Tamona & washington for the term of 8 years   he has Been fraudulently takened from my plantation By Sum of the Democratic party which of corse Detest me and my party   he has Been Decoyed in to the State of Mississippi and is know in the possession of one M. M. Phillips   his mother is Dead and his father is un-known   he was Bourn on my plantation and I have Raised him with my owned hand   I have conculted the Lawyers on the Subject and they advised me to let him a lone   of corse they are party concerned   I am Decidedly a gainste the proceedings and I know appeele to your most noble Excilency honor & name for Jestice as the act its Self was Don By the united States its Self   I trus to allmighty God and to your moste noble magisty that the laws of the united states will Definde it   pleas answer this . . ."—ALS, DNA, RG 60, Letters from the President.

1872, FEB. 16.   C. H. Pollock, Brooklyn, to USG. "Genl Slocum and Genl Banks' remarks 'smak' of the polititian. The Brooklyn Navy Yard and property adjoining, belonging to the United States is a nuisance to the State and to the United States as a whole. It cuts off commercial communication from three very large cities viz New York, Brooklyn (Brooklyn ED) & Williamsburg The three cities occupy respectively the three corners of a right angled tri-angle and the Navy Yard occupies a position which compels commerce to run on the outer crust of a circle cutting the sides of the triangle having for its cen-tre the centre of the triangle, and converging at points entirely inadequate to the present rapidly increasing bussness of the two cities on the east side of the river. It seems to me highly expedient that the Government moves to realise on this property both for the general good and for the three great cities afore named. There are men who would manage it with honor and ability"—ALS (diagram included), DNA, RG 45, Miscellaneous Letters Received. See *CG*, 42–2, 1030–33.

1872, FEB. 18.   Sarah H. Powell, Annapolis, to USG. "I entreat you not to throw this letter aside untill you have read it through but allow me to state my case to you, Sir   I acted for three years during the war as Nurse and in other capacities in the Naval Academy while it was an Hospital, and have my dis-charge & letter of recommendation from Dr Vanderkieft and when three Nurses, my contemporaries died of spotted fever, I assisted to perform the last sad duties for them thus proving that I did not shun my duty. In Decem-ber 1865 I became clerk for Mr Swann Commissary of the Naval Academy and retained my position four years, . . . I thought I would return to Annapolis and try to get some thing to do in the yard but Sir, Mr Swann utterly refuses to employ me, and if I can't get employment in the Academy, I must sell my house and be turned out on the cold world, . . ."—ALS, DNA, RG 45, Miscellaneous Letters Received.

1872, FEB. 19.   To Secretary of State Hamilton Fish. "If there is a vacancy in the consulate at Brindisi, or to be one soon, I would suggest the transfer of Mr. Kendall now at Strasbourg."—Copy, DLC-USG, II, 1.
On Feb. 28, 1871, U.S. Senator James W. Nye and U.S. Representative Thomas Fitch of Nev. had written to USG. "We respectfully and earnestly re-

quest that Rev R S Kendall be appointed Consul at Jerusalem   Mr Kendall is a Congregational minister, a good republican and a man of ability. We would be greatly gratified if he can receive this appointment."—LS, DNA, RG 59, Letters of Application and Recommendation. Related papers are *ibid.* On April 5, Orville E. Babcock wrote to Fish. "I have not heard from you to day about the consulate for Mr Kendall. Senator Nye & Mr Kendall *the M. C* called yesterday in the afternoon to see me. Mr K. assured me that we could count on him, in case we need his help. Mr Kendall, wishes to get as near as he can to Jerusalem, in order to pursue some studies and researches. He is a true and tried republican, and ~~has~~ helped all he could in Ct. during the last campaign. Senator Nye suggested that perhaps we could transfer the man from Beyrout, and put Kendall there. I send you his papers that you may see that he is well recommended. Please do not place them on record until some place is settled upon, provided we can find a place."—ALS, DLC-Hamilton Fish. On April 5 and 6, Fish wrote to Babcock. "*Private* . . . The Consulate to which I referred yesterday is Stettin (in Germany). The Consul at Beirut has only been appointed since last July, and to disturb him would bring about our ears all the religious societies which have missionaries &c in the East. He is a competent man & I understand is familiar with the Eastern languages. There is no place in Syria and none in the Turkish Dominions, unless it be Scio, & possibly Galatza (both Consulates of fees and very small at that) to which Mr Kendall could be appointed. What shall be done? Will Stettin suit? If so I will send the name to the President—"—LS (press), *ibid.* "Private—Personal—. . . Information recd this momt seems to make necessary a change in the Consulate at Strasbourg (which is more valuable than that at Stettin—at least it was more valuable while it was part of France—the fees ranging from $1100 to—near $1500)—Perhaps Mr Kendall would prefer this to Stettin. Let me know."—ALS (press), *ibid.* On April 7, USG nominated Reuben S. Kendall as consul, Strasbourg, to replace Felix C. M. Petard. See *PUSG*, 19, 397–98. On Feb. 26, 1872, USG nominated Kendall as consul, Brindisi, to replace Samuel H. Kingman, who had died. See *PUSG*, 20, 442.

1872, FEB. 19.   James Dickey, "Grahams Saltworks," Tex., to USG. "I left ohio last fall for this place Last fall to to Erecct a Salt manufactory; And upon my arival here found So inSecure a State of affairs Existing on account of the frequent Raids of the Camanchee & Kioway Indians on the Inhabitants of this and adjoining Counties   there has not I believe been a full moon Since I Came here—they have not made a Raid Stealing Horses and in Some Instances Killing and Scalping the Inhabitants   there has been Some thousands of dollars worth of Stock driven off this winter and Several murders Committed; Some of them within a few miles of this   they made but one Raid on us Shortly after my arival here but we were well armed and Strong Enough in numbers to defeat their purpose—Indeed we have had all our work to do with our Revolvers in our belts and Rifles at our Sides—Now Im informed these Same Indians receive Rashions and farming Emplements at fort Sill and there they find in Some way a market for their Stolen Stock and Receive in Return Revolvers & Repeating Rifles of the most Improved paterns—I think the Conduct of the oficials at fort Sill Should be looked into; there Should also be a Line of Teleghaph from fort Richison to fort griffin and Sill   I do hope you will give this your Earnest attention and confer a Lasting benefit on the poor Scourged inhabitents of this part of texas or what few are Left of them—as I have not the pleasure of your acquaintanc I will Refer You to F. J. Jones Esq first audit office Treasury department washington Citty D. C to to whom I have Sent a full Statement of our greviances and asked him to use his Influance to beter our Condition also the Hon J K Moorhead of Pittsburgh Pa who is also personally acquainted with me our Post office address is fort Belknap Young County texas   we have to Send a guard 9 miles to Receive & deposit Our letters"—ALS, DNA, RG 75, Letters Received, Kiowa Agency.

On June 17, Franklin Moore, Upper Alton, Ill., wrote to USG. "I have receivd a letter which I enclose from my Cousin Enoch Moore. ~~which I enclose~~. he appeals to me for protection in behalf of his Sisterin-law. I am not able to give it and now I appeal your excelancy for the aid required. I was Captain ~~and Maj~~ afterwards Maj of 2nd Ill Cavalry. during the rebellion   give me a command and authority to rais a Regment. and in Six month there will be no more fiers of Indians murdering our friends in western Texas   I am your friend personly and politically. I refur you to Gen A. J. Smith and others of my Old commanders."—ALS, *ibid.,* Central Superintendency. The enclosed letter of June 15 from Enoch Moore, Upper Alton, to Franklin Moore, describes the murder of Enoch's brother Lorenzo by Indians on May 19 in Hays County, Tex. ". . . to you I now appeal as friend and relative to sympathise with his family for they have none to protect them from this Savage   they ~~have~~ roam in that County during the light of every full moon   they have nothing to fear; for the Citizens has no protection and of course will not for over four years longer. President Grant has been in office for more than 3 years and they have less protection at this time than when he was Inaurgerated President. I then expected much from him as a President as did my Brother   we was his Staunch friends but will he ever think of his bleeding frontier friends? I fear not—Greely I have no confidence in   he is a base Hypocrite, . . . Better Suffer I suppose under Grant a a while longer and let us suffer for it is of no use to murmer but I do most Sincerly hope that he may reconsider his policy it is murdering the frontiers. . . ."—ALS, *ibid.*

On July 15, Charles Soward, district judge, Weatherford, Tex., wrote to USG. "You will pardon me for claiming a moment of your valuable time in Considering the terrible condition of our People, (The Frontier People of Texas). For a long time have this people endured an almost uninterrupted warfare, bloody & savage, at the hands of the several bands of Indians, now *falsely said* to be upon the Ft. Sill reservation. But Sir those depredations have been growing from bad to worse, until they are perfectly alarming to our People. I might give your Excellency, scores of instances of recent date of murder, Rape and Robery which they have committed alone in the counties composing my Judicial District. It has been but a few days, since the whole Lee family, consisting of six persons were inhumanly butchered, Three of them being females were ravished murdered and most terribly mutilated. Then Mr. Dobs a Justice of the peace of Palo Pinto County was but last week murdred and scalped: his ears and nose were cut off. Then following, Mr. Peoples & Crawford of same county met the same fate   Mr. McCluskey was but yesterday shot down by those same bloody Quaker Pets upon his own threshold as he walked out in the morning. I write to your Excellency, as to one who from ~~his~~ Your Exalted Position in our nation *Can* if you *will* Protect us from this inhuman butchery. I write in the interest of our bleeding and ravished frontier—I write, as but a feeble voice from the suffering hundreds whose mouths are mute; while *men* who aspire to *rule* the land *Prate* of Peace with those bloody handed savages. I have but called your Excellencys attention to a few of the crimes which they have recently committed in this vicinity. Shall I give more instances of the victims to the *Insane 'Peace policy'* (so called). How many oh, Mr President, of our best men and women must be immolated in order to satiate this ungodly fanaticism. I am told that there is an 'Indian Ring'; that our People are butchered, burned, Ravished and Robed, that such ring may grow opulent with the *Blood money*. Can this oh! my God, be possible? Your humble correspondent believes your Excellency to be endoed with at least a moderate amount of human feeling, and a mind that cannot be trammeled by this *one Ideaed, Insane,* Pseudo humanitarian Policy: called the 'Quaker Indian Peace Policy'! Am I mistaken? Why Sir: If one of our Tooth 'Doctors' should be thrown into prison by the Spanish Authorities, Washington, and the whole country I may say, at once and in thunder tones demand redress, and and If denied, they are ready to fly to arms. How is this? What kind of Philosophy or Ethics is it, that teaches, that if our People are murdered by the scores, by savage beasts, it must be endured, and the savage beasts fed and cared for by the Government whose citizens are murdered thus; But when an enlightened christian nation of our own race, but wrongs or insults one of our citizens we ~~are ready to~~ must needs fly to arms' Hopeing that for the honor of our nation, the civilization of our Age—the lives of our common brotherhood, something will be done to stay the hands of those bloody Quakers, . . ."—ALS, *ibid.*, Letters Received, Kiowa Agency. See *HED*, 42-3-1, part 5, I, 521–23, 580–82, 612–13, 631–32; Robert H. Keller, Jr., *American Protestantism and United States Indian Policy, 1869–82* (Lincoln, Neb., 1983), pp. 99, 132–39; W. C. Nunn, *Texas Under the Carpetbaggers* (Austin, 1962), pp. 180–81. Soward had presided at the trial of Satanta and Big Tree in July, 1871. See H. Smythe, *Historical Sketch of Parker County and Weatherford, Texas* (St. Louis, 1877), pp. 275–82; *PUSG*, 22, 388–90.

1872, FEB. 22.   Governor John M. Palmer of Ill. to USG. "I would feel greatly oblig[ed] by the appointment of Hon. I A Powell of Richland County to the Pension agency in the Salem District   Dr Powell is an old and always reliable republican is entirely competent to that or any similar office and has the strongest claims upon the administration   He has freely avowed his preference for your renomination but his course has been judicious and conciliatory looking to the harmony of the party"—ALS, OFH. See *PUSG*, 20, 221. On Jan. 15, 1873, USG nominated Israel A. Powell as collector of Internal Revenue, 11th District, Ill. On Feb. 7, 1876, Powell, Olney, Ill., wrote to USG. "I notice there is a vacancy in the Commissionership of Pensions, and I write to aske you for the appointment—. . ."—ALS, DNA, RG 48, Appointment Div., Letters Received.

1872, FEB. 23.   To Frederick W. Bogen. "I have the honor to acknowledge the receipt of your book 'The German in America' and must beg you to accept my sincere thanks for it and for your kind sentiments verbal and written."—LS, Georgetown University, Washington, D. C. First published in 1851, Bogen's book introduced German immigrants to American life and served as an English primer. See *PUSG*, 19, 320–21.

1872, FEB. 24.   John D. Pope, Atlanta, to USG. "Under recent legislation certain duties are devolved on United States Attorneys which I cannot perform without great reluctance. Up to this time I have labored faithfully to discharge all these duties whether agreeable or not, but the opinions which I hold render me not a proper person to become an active agent in many prosecutions of which the United States Courts now have jurisdiction   I therefore respectfully tender my resignation of the office of 'Attorney of the United States in and for the Districts of Georgia' to take effect when my successor is appointed and qualified. I beg to assure you of my grateful appreciation of the honor which I have enjoyed at your hands."—ALS, DNA, RG 60, Letters Received, Ga. See Allen W. Trelease, *White Terror: The Ku Klux Klan Conspiracy and Southern Reconstruction* (New York, 1971), pp. 409–10.
    On Feb. 28, John H. Reece, Rome, Ga., wrote to USG. "I see from the papers that Col J. D. Pope has resigned the Attorneyship for the Northern District of Geo. Now I am a young man and not personally acquainted with you and this is the first letter I have ever written you; but I want the appointment of U. S. Attorney General for the Northern District of Geo, if no appointment has been made to fill the vacancy caused by Col. Pope's resignation. . . ."—ALS, DNA, RG 60, Records Relating to Appointments. On Feb. 29, Isaac W. Christian, Brunswick, Ga., wrote to USG asking for the position.—ALS, *ibid.* On March 1, USG nominated Henry P. Farrow as U.S. attorney, Ga.

1872, FEB. 26.   USG order. ". . . Isaac H. Sturgeon, G. M. Dodge and Geo. M. Chilcott are hereby appointed Commissioners to examine and report to the President of the United States upon the road and telegraph line of the Denver Pacific R. W. & Telegraph Co."—Copies, DNA, RG 130, Orders and Proclamations; Sturgeon Papers, MoSHi. On Aug. 29, USG issued a similar order appointing "Isaac H Sturgeon, of St. Louis, Missouri; G. W. Johnes, of Washington, D. C.; and D. H. Willard, of Lansing, Michigan," as commissioners to report on the Kansas Pacific Railroad.—Copy, *ibid.*

1872, FEB. 29.   William F. Ingram, Columbus, Kan., to USG. "My, Self together with a great maney, others who Stood Steadfast, in arms, by your, Side, During the Rebelion, are here on the So cald Neutral Lands, in Cherokee, co, Kan.   we as, Soldiers, at the Siege of vicks, Burg, Jackson, Miss, Champion Hill Ramond and a great maney other Scout and Raid two Tedious to mention, we thought them Dayes we Saw hard, Times, But it was, not like this frontier life   a great maney is a living here   you are, well a ware this land is in Dispute, and on acount of the Sutters of the land is Discouraged, and Do not No what to Do for the best   Now general as we used to call you, I am, onley gon to Speak of a fiew facts   there is a great maney here from all parts of the globe Some who was citizens during the War and Some Who was, in the Rebble, Army, and about one half in the vesinity where i live is Honerable, Bleu, Coats. Now Some cries, out, Politics Some Ses Railroad, Monopolys, Some one thing and Some, an other Keeps urs, from geting our land, as we call our claims of, 160, acres, ours. . . . we have a man at your city By the Name of Amos, Sanford, to Represent the Setlers of Cherokee, co, and there is a man from Crawford, co By the Name Lawson. Mr. Sanford rote back Some time a go that he had a Private Interview with you and he wanted the Soldiers to Petition to you. Now i Now there was Not one in ten Did at that time, for they Sed that they had Signed more Petitions than had Ever went to Washington . . ."—ALS, DNA, RG 75, Letters Received, Cherokee Agency.

On Nov. 21, U.S. Representative William Lawrence of Ohio, Bellefontaine, had written to USG. "The decision of the Supreme Court on 18th inst in the Cherokee Neutral Land Case deprives 25000 people of lands they expected to hold for homes. It is to them a greater calamity than the Boston fire to the Sufferers thereby. ~~Congress by repeated~~. The House of Representatives by repeated votes declared their opinion that the Settlers should have the right to preempt the lands. I respectfully suggest that you recommend Congress to give the Settlers a right to preempt homes in the Indian Territory   I congratulate you on your re-election   I am reelected to Congress"—ALS, *ibid.*, RG 48, Lands and Railroads Div., Letters Received.

On Dec. 21, Robert S. Stevens, New York City, wrote to Orville E. Babcock. "The Leaguers and Settlers in Southern Kansas for some time past have been threatening to burn our bridges and destroy our depots. We have found it necessary to hire men to watch the same night and day, and it is important for the preservation of the property that these guards should be armed. The Governor of Kansas has no arms under his control and none can be obtained excepting through the General Government—For this purpose, Judge Parsons, our President, on the 19th inst. telegraphed to Genl Sheridan asking if he would not give us an order upon Ft Leavenworth for Fifty stand of Arms—Enclosed I send you a copy of Genl Sheridan's reply—. . ."—LS, *ibid.*, RG 156, Letters Received. On Dec. 20, Lt. Gen. Philip H. Sheridan, Chicago, had telegraphed to Levi Parsons, president, Missouri, Kansas & Texas Railway Co., New York City. "I would do anything in the world to legally help your road but it is the duty of the Government of Kansas to provide against the riotous action of the people of the State—I have not the authority to give you arms without direction from the Secretary of War—"—Copy, *ibid.* On Dec. 23, Secretary of War William W. Belknap wrote to Babcock that the arms could be issued upon payment of a bond.—LS (press), *ibid.*

On Jan. 13, 1873, his first day in office, Governor Thomas A. Osborn of Kan. wrote to USG. "I desire to call your attention to the occupation, by United States troops, of a certain portion of this state known as the 'Cherokee Neutral

Lands' and to respectfully request that you have orders immediately issued for their removal. These troops were furnished on the requisition of Governor Harvey for the preservation of order upon these lands during the pendency of a civil action lately decided in the Supreme Court of the United States, finally settling the title to the same, which decision is fully acquiesced in by the settlers upon the lands."—LS, *ibid.*, RG 94, Letters Received, 3201 1871.

On Nov. 21, 1874, Ingram, Favor, Kan., wrote to USG. "you favored me about two and a half years ago, in regard to the title of the Cherokee Neutral Lands. I wrote a Private Letter at that time, stating, that I came here, for the purpose of securing me a home according to the Soldiers Homestead Act. And, after settling on the same Qarter Section that I now occupy, I became dissatisfied, and got afraid, that it was R. R. Land; and at that time, the occupants of said lands had brought suit against James F. Joy and the R. R. Co. I asked you in that letter if you could give me any information in regard to it. That portion of the letter requiring information of the land, you refered to the General Land Department; and in a short time, I Rec'd a letter from that office, stating that they had refered it to the Secretary of the Interior. He just stated, that if I wished to buy, any part or portion, of the Cherokee Neutral Land, I would have to purchase it from James. F. Joy his heirs or assignees. And afterward, the Supreme Court of the U. S. A. decided the land to be James F. Joys, so that let me out of a home. . . . As the Indian Nation is now being Sectionized; I wish to know, for my own special benefit, if there will be any chance in the future, for me to receive the benefit of my; Discharge from that quarter; if so, I shall be greatly pleased. If it be the contrary I shall bide by it; wishing you and the Nation honors and prosperity. Please give this letter a careful perusal, and if it be consistent with your feelings and wishes, let me hear from you on this subject, and I shall be much obliged for your kindness."—Copy, *ibid.*, RG 75, Letters Received, Central Superintendency. See *PUSG*, 20, 415–17.

1872, MARCH 1.   Sallie Gay, Philadelphia, to USG. "Since sending you a letter a few moments' since—I have had returned to me the Cols Commission from the Sec of War, saying it is incompatible with his public office to advocate any claim against the Government. I think it is a just claim—and enclose the commissions for you to see—if you think I can get it by coming to Washington, I will try to come although I cannot afford it. I am sure your kind heart— will prompt you to assist me in this matter. Although you are the Pres of the U. S. and have so much to occupy your time—you seem to be the *only one high in office*—who has any *heart* to *sympathize* with those in distress. I write to you now, feeling the utmost confidence that you will do all you can for me. I will try not to trouble you again. . . . Be kind enough to return the Commissions when you have finished with the"—ALS, DNA, RG 94, ACP, G87 CB 1869. On Jan. 16, Gay had written to USG. "The death of Col. Gay has left myself & child without other support, than such as I can provide with my needle . . . Will you be kind enough to tell me if it would be possible for me to recover the Col's back pay. He was restored with his full rank. It is a Major's pay for nine months . . ."—Copy (ellipses in original), *ibid.* On May 18, Orville E. Babcock

wrote to Maj. Asher R. Eddy, q. m., Philadelphia. "The President directs me
to say that, if you can, he will be pleased to have you employ Mrs. Sallie J. Gay,
widow of Major Gay of the Army."—Copy, DLC-USG, II, 1. On Feb. 7, 1876,
Gay again wrote to USG concerning Ebenezer Gay's back pay.—ALS, DNA,
RG 94, ACP, G87 CB 1869. See *PUSG*, 20, 349.

1872, MARCH 5.   USG endorsement. "Respectfully refered to Gen. B. F. Butler.
I believe this is an appointment made by the managers at whos head you are
and hence this reference."—AES, DLC-Benjamin F. Butler. Written on a letter
of March 4 from Bishop Matthew Simpson to USG. "Dr Wm M. Wright is
now Surgeon at the Asylum for Soldiers, near Ft. Monroe. I learn that there is
an effort for his removal. As I have known him many years as a skilful surgeon—a man of strict integrity—and intensely loyal—having been years in
the army, and having high testimonials, I wd regret to see him removed. His
family need the position, having but limited means. If possible to retain him, I
hope he will not be remvd."—ALS, *ibid.* USG served on the board of managers
of the National Asylum for Disabled Volunteer Soldiers. See *HMD*, 42-2-226,
43-1-298.

1872, MARCH 5.   Vice President Schuyler Colfax to USG. "I promised to
speak to you about the appointment of Wm H. Smith as one of the Police Commissioners of this City. There are two vacancies now, & no colored man is on
the Board. Mr Smith is a colored man of more than usual intelligence, was
President of the late Convention which elected Delegates to the National Convention, will be recommended by John F. Cook, the colored Delegate from this
District to the National Convention, Col Forney (who knew him for many years)
& others. He enjoys the confidence of the colored people here & the whites also,
as you will see by the high & responsible position he has recently held in their
Convention & I am sure would ~~make a~~ be an appt as popular as it would be meritorious. I have known him & favorably for many years."—ALS, DNA, RG 48,
Appointment Div., Letters Received. An undated petition to USG from John F.
Cook *et al.*, Washington, D. C., recommending William H. Smith, is *ibid.*
     On March 13, Henry Piper, "member elect to the House of Delegates from
9th Dist.," Washington, D. C., wrote to USG. "As the time is approaching, for
the nomination to the senate the names of persons for Police Commissioners,
and as the *race* with which I am identified has never had a representative of
their own race on that Board, I most respectfully and earnestly beg that in
making up your nominations, there for, that you will give the matter a favorable consideration and give us at least one of the number required by law to
constitute the said Board, and I would most respectfully prevent the name of
Mr Carter A. Stewart a gentleman well known by the people of this community,   He was an honorable member of the city councils under the old form of
government in this city. He is worthy and capable. Believing that the President
is willing to accord full justice to all citizens, . . ."—ALS, *ibid.*
     On Nov. 25, George P. Fisher, U.S. attorney, D. C., wrote to USG. "It af-
fords me much pleasure to recommend the appointment of George A. Bohrer

as a Police Commissioner. I have known him some eight or ten years as an upright honest man and believe him to be pure and incorruptible, just such a man
as would fill the position as it ought to be filled—honestly and for the good order and welfare of the community. He has served frequently as foreman of the
Grand Jury whilst I was on the bench and I believe him to have been the best
foreman I ever had."—ALS, *ibid.* On Dec. 13, USG nominated Smith, James G.
Berret, Henry M. Sweeney, Charles H. Nichols, and William J. Murtagh as
D. C. police commissioners. See *PUSG,* 19, 119–20.

On Oct. 13, 1871, USG had written to Murtagh, publisher, *Washington National Republican.* "It gives me pleasure to assure you of my confidence in your
integrity and honor as a public journalist, and to commend you to your brothers in the profession, whom you may meet in your travels, as a gentleman well
worthy of like confidence from them."—Copy, DLC-USG, II, 1.

1872, MARCH 5.   Joseph A. Ware, Washington, D. C., to USG. "Mr. Leo
Goldmark a German of excellent education and fine culture will be an applicant for the position of teacher of german at West Point—I am requested
by personal friends to ask you to appoint him but I am afraid I shall intrude—
I would like to know if the appointment is within the scope of your duties—If
not I shall say no more—If it is I ask to present the credentials of Mr. Goldmark in the proper quarter—He is personally known to Gen Negley M. C and
to Hillyer—If I can be of any service to him I shall be very glad."—ALS, DNA,
RG 94, Correspondence, USMA. On Feb. 26, the House of Representatives had
passed a resolution to substitute German for Spanish language instruction at
USMA. The Senate took no action. See *CG,* 42–2, 1217, 4504.

On Sept. 30, 1871, Leo Goldmark, Brooklyn, had written to USG. "Unin-
tentionally and merely per chance I became aware of the fact that heavy frauds
are to be committed on the treasury of the U. S. by a ring of unprincipled republicans, the majority of which being at present in high Office both in military and civil departments. The amount in question is at least a million of Dollars, and rather more than less, *part of it has already been drawn.* As they know
me as a true & honest republican, an admirer of yours your Government and
its unprecedented favorable results, they thought to make me safe with the recompensation of $5000—to be paid out of the earnings of their fraud by next
December. Though nothing but a poor clerk with $1500 salary and struggling
for a living, I would not accept of their offer if it was ten times as much. Since
those facts came to my knowledge I felt uneasy in my mind and did not know
to whom to confer as I was affraid it might turn a weapon against the republican party, if known by any of the democratic leaders or editors, especially now
before the manyfold republican conventions. I finally concluded to refer the
whole matter to your Excellency, feeling convinced to have it laid in the best
hands   I can give names, dates & important details, but would like to communicate only to your Excellency personally. To prevent any suspicion against my
character & integrity I sign my full name & address in addition to which I will
say that I am a brother of Dr O. Goldmark, Manufacturer of Perc: caps &
Metallic cartridges in Brooklyn in whose factory I keep a position as Inspec-

tor and Superintendend for the last five years. In conclusion I beg leave to state
that I did not hint the matter above stated to any living soul and that if your
Excellency should order mye to Washington to be personally interviewed, I
shall obey at once, if your Excellency will be so kind as to sign in your own
hand-writing."—ALS, DNA, RG 56, Letters Received.

1872, MARCH 6.   Horace Porter to Attorney Gen. George H. Williams. "The
President directs me to say that Gen. Krzyzanowski asks that the Dist. Attorney of Georgia may be instructed to thoroughly investigate his case and report
upon it; and that action be taken promptly by the Government, either to prosecute or dismiss the case according as the testimony may show to be just. He
also says he is ready to face the charges at once without delay. The President
suggests that his wish be complied with."—LS, DNA, RG 60, Letters from the
President. Indicted for fraud, Wladimir Krzyzanowski had been removed in
Nov., 1871, as supervisor of Internal Revenue, Fla. and Ga. See James S. Pula,
For Liberty and Justice: The Life and Times of Wladimir Krzyzanowski (Chicago,
1978), pp. 173–80.

1872, MARCH 11.   To House of Representatives. "I transmit herewith a report
dated 5th instant received from the Secretary of State in compliance with the
Resolution of the House of Representatives of the 28th of February ultimo."—
Copies, OFH; DNA, RG 130, Messages to Congress. *HED*, 42-2-186. On Feb.
28, the House had passed a resolution asking Secretary of State Hamilton Fish
". . . to inform the House how many of the consular and commercial agents of
the United States abroad either speak or write the language of the country in
which their districts are situated, and the language in which the commercial
business therein is chiefly carried on. . . ."—*CG*, 42–2, 1269. On March 5, Fish
reported that ". . . it is understood and believed that very nearly all of them
speak and write the language of the country in which their districts are situated. . . ."—Copy, DNA, RG 59, Reports to the President and Congress.

1872, MARCH 12.   Peter Marksman *et al.*, Washington, D. C., to USG. "We
beg to state that in the Treaty made with the Chippewa Indians at La Pointe
Wisconsin, Sept. 30, 1854, one article stipulates that 'The United States will
also pay the further sum of Ninety Thousand Dollars as the Chiefs in open
council may direct to enable them to meet their just engagements.' Now honorable Father, these engagements, on our part were fully met. Our just debts
were all paid; and we were glad to hear that a considerable sum of the Ninety
Thousand dollars remained unexpended. We have heretofore made known to
our Great Father, through his Commissioner the Hon. Geo. W. Manypenny
that we of the L'Ance bands were entitled to our just proportion in connection
with the other bands of the Chippewa Tribe; And that we desired that our own
special share might be deposited in the Treasury of the United States, where
it might remain on interest, which might hereafter prove serviceable to us. We
now desire to ascertain the state of this money. Another item which we desire
enquired into is, that when Mr. Watrous (if that is the correct spelling of his

name) was appointed agent for the Chippewas of Lake Superior and the interior, in the year 1849, our annuities for that and the two subsequent years were withheld from us, and that without our being notified by the government, or any reason being assigned for it. We were, at that time, living in peace, and in kindliness with our white neighbors and if they were present we are sure they would sustain our assertions. Our Father will we are sure, on inquiry into the facts of the case, find that we ought to receive our back annuities; And we now apply for the same"—DS (5 signatures—by mark), DNA, RG 75, Letters Received, Mackinac Agency. See *PUSG,* 21, 458–60; Charles J. Kappler, ed., *Indian Treaties 1778–1883* (Washington, 1904; reprinted, New York, 1972), pp. 648–52.

1872, MARCH 13.   Thomas Y. Mosby, Bedford County, Va., to USG. "I am, and have been connected with the Republican Party, since its organization in this State; and wish to see you reelected President for the next four years, therefore I take the liberty of writing to you to state (what in my opinion) was the cause of the failure of our Party to carry the State at the last Election. I was a candidate for the Va House of Delegates and speak from experience. The fault is in the appointments which have been made to fill the offices, the fact that most of them are filled by northern men is in itself objectionable when as good Republicans as they, might be found amongst us, . . . I have spent nearly every thing, that was left me by the war, in the party cause, have a wife & eight children, & have never asked the Government untill lately to give me a place, and would not now do so, but for my losses during the war. I have always been a Union man & expect to live & die one, and as such I take the libery of writing thus to you."—ALS, DNA, RG 56, Letters Received.

1872, MARCH 13.   U.S. Senator Allen G. Thurman of Ohio to USG. "Enclosed is a petition, signed by many of the most respectable citizens of Columbus, Ohio, and also by Govr Hays & Govr Noyes; praying for a pardon of James Fondersmith, late a soldier in Company H. 18th Inf. convicted of desertion. To which I beg leave to add my own recommendation. I thought that I had transmitted this petition to you as soon as I received it; but I have just discovered that I had overlooked it. As this negligence of mine has caused a delay of two months, I beg leave to say that it would be a personal favor to myself if the petition were acted upon, and a determination had, at as early a day as may be convenient."—ALS, DNA, RG 153, Court-Martial Case PP 1494, James Fondersmith. On Jan. 1, Samuel Galloway *et al.,* Columbus, had petitioned USG on behalf of Fondersmith.—DS (41 signatures), *ibid.* On March 15, John Potts, chief clerk, War Dept., endorsed Fondersmith's file. "So much of this man's sentence as requires that his head be shaved and he then be drummed out of service will be remitted."—AES, *ibid.*

On Aug. 1, Judge Advocate Gen. Joseph Holt wrote to Secretary of War William W. Belknap, quoting a note from Orvil L. Grant to USG. "'Doctor J. W. Baker is a personal friend of mine, and any representations made by him are reliable. If you can, consistently, pardon Jas. Fondersmith, I hope you will do so.'"—Copy, *ibid.*, Letters Sent. On Aug. 8, Belknap wrote to Orvil Grant, Chicago, declining to act in the case.—Copy, *ibid.*, RG 107, Letters Sent, Military Affairs. On Oct. 23, by Special Orders No. 262, Fondersmith's sentence was reduced by one year.—Copy (printed), *ibid.*, RG 153, Court-Martial Case PP 1494, James Fondersmith.

1872, MARCH 15.   To Congress. "I have the honor herewith to transmit to Congress a recommendation from Hon. M. D. Leggett, Commissioner of Patents for the reorganization of his office; and also the letter of the Secretary of the Interior accompanying it. I concur with the Secretary of the Interior in the views expressed in his letter, and recommend the careful consideration of Congress to the subject of this communication, and action which will secure a more efficient performance of the duties of the Patent Office than is practicable under present legislation."—DS, DNA, RG 46, Presidential Messages. *SED*, 42-2-52. In a Feb. 23 report to Secretary of the Interior Columbus Delano, Mortimer D. Leggett had proposed extensive changes to the organization and procedures of the patent office.—Copy, DNA, RG 46, Presidential Messages. On March 1, Delano wrote to USG endorsing Leggett's recommendations.—Copy, *ibid.*

1872, MARCH 15.   Charles A. Stetson, Jr., New York City, to USG. "The Regiment which I have the honor to command, (the 79th Highlanders, N. G. S. N. Y.) whose record during the war, is well known to you, being one of the very few Militia Regiments that Served throughout the war, four years, have a bill now pending in the house, remitting the customs duties on the Kilts, that portion of their uniform, which it was impossible to have made in this Country, and which they were obliged to purchase in Scotland, and which are now in the Custom House at this Port. . . ."—ALS, DNA, RG 56, Letters Received. See *PUSG*, 17, 301. On March 21, the House voted to waive duties on the kilts; on Dec. 11, the Senate declined to vote on the measure.

1872, MARCH 16.   Horace Porter to Secretary of the Treasury George S. Boutwell. "The President directs me to request you to have Charles H. Lemos, the colored man who acts as barber at the Executive Mansion and clerk in the 3d Auditor's Office, detailed for the time being at the Executive Mansion for the purpose of bringing up to date certain books of extracts from the newspapers, which clippings have largely accumulated for lack of clerical force in this office for that work."—Copy, DLC-USG, II, 1.

1872, MARCH 16.   U.S. Senator Frederick T. Frelinghuysen of N. J. to USG. "The friends of Master Robert Emmet of West Chester Co. N. Y & who was seventeen years old in Decr desire to have him admitted to West-Point—He is the grand-son of Judge Emmet of N Y. who you know by reputation—Young Emmet is I think physically intellectually & by education well qualified for the Academy & to be of service to the country—His mother is a lady of marked ability & admirable character—It may be that there are others who have claims on the appointments that are at your disposal, and if so, I desire in no way to interfere with those claims, but if you are at liberty to nominate young Emmet his friend, myself among the number, would be gratified—"—ALS, DNA, RG 94, Correspondence, USMA. Robert T. Emmet, a great-grand-nephew of Irish revolutionary Robert Emmet, graduated from USMA in 1877.

1872, MARCH 18.   Maj. Gen. John M. Schofield, San Francisco, to USG. "I beg leave to invite your attention to the claims of my old friend and classmate, Capt. L. L. Livingston, to an appointment in the Staff. He is in all respects competent and worthy and is entitled to the consideration due to ~~fourteen~~ nineteen years of faithful and efficient service, which has failed in his case, thus far, to secure the promotion obtained by the large majority of his contemporaries."—ALS, DNA, RG 94, ACP, 4130 1871. On Jan. 6, 1873, Col. Rufus Ingalls, New York City, wrote to USG. "Capt. La Rhett L. Livingston 3d Artillery is an old friend and comrade, who has served faithfully and long, but has not realized the promotion he deserved—Should promotions be opened in the Staff Corps, Capt. Livingston's friends will ask you to confer a majority in the Inspector Generals' Department on him—I cheerfully testify to his great worth as an officer and gentleman—"—ALS, *ibid.* Related papers are *ibid.* No appointment followed.

1872, MARCH 18.   J. T. Bullard, Lumberton, N. C., to USG. ". . . Cap E Thomas 4th Artillery while Stationed at this place (Lumberton) in the year 1871 duly appointed your complainant Sutler to his company and under tickets by him duly Signed this complainant furnished the members of his company with divers goods wares & merchandise to the value of $50 00 and on the eve of his departure from this place he took the tickets and promised to pay the money for them the next morning before he would leave but failed so to do and Since which time he has neglected and refused to either pay the money or return the tickets though he admits retaining the money or a portion of it from the pay of the Soldiers under his command . . ."—ALS, DNA, RG 94, Letters Received, 4107 1871. On April 2, Secretary of War William W. Belknap wrote to Bullard declining to intervene.—LS (press), *ibid.* On Dec. 8, 1871, Capt. Evan Thomas, Charlotte, N. C., had endorsed an earlier complaint. ". . . I told him I would make the men pay if possible but would not be responsible if they refused. . . ."—AES, *ibid.*

1872, MARCH 19.   To Senate. "I transmit to the Senate for consideration with a view to its ratification, a 'General Convention of Friendship, Commerce and Extradition' between the United States and the Orange Free State, signed at Bloemfonten on the 22nd of December, last, by W. W. Edgcomb; Consul of the United States at Cape Town, acting on behalf of this Government, and by Mr. F. K. Höhne, on behalf of the Orange Free State."—DS, DNA, RG 46, Presidential Messages. On March 27, Secretary of State Hamilton Fish wrote to U.S. Senator Simon Cameron of Pa. ". . . In framing the draft, the circumstance that the Orange Free State is an inland country in a similar relation to the surrounding regions in South Africa, as Switzerland is to contiguous European countries, was taken into consideration. It was consequently supposed that the Convention with the Swiss Confederation of the 25th of November, 1850 . . . would afford the most eligible materials to incorporate in the draft. That use was made of it accordingly. . . ."—LS, *ibid.* On April 24, the Senate ratified the convention.

1872, MARCH 19.   To Senate. "I nominate Francis Thomas, of Maryland, to be Envoy Extraordinary and Minister Plenipotentiary of the United States, to Peru, vice Thomas Settle, resigned."—DS, DNA, RG 46, Nominations. On July 6, Thomas, Lima, wrote to USG concerning a lack of funds to hire a secretary.—ALS, *ibid.*, RG 59, Letters of Application and Recommendation. A related letter is *ibid.* On April 18, John E. Smith, Westminster, Md., had written to USG. ". . . Whilst I was a candidate for Congress I was opposed, at the last moment by B. F. M. Hurley of Frederick who voted for my opponent   He has since been thoroughly identified with the Democratic party. He has spoken and voted for them and has denounced any man whose election has been secured by the votes of Colored people, as disgraced and infamous. I understand that this person who, apart from his political treachery, is morally and intellectually unworthy of any position of honor, or responsibility, is applying for an appointment under Governor Francis Thomas, Minister to Peru, and with a view of success has suddenly become your friend, after having denounced you and the party in unmeasured terms. . . ."—ALS, *ibid.*

On March 14, 1869, James F. Wilson, Washington, D. C., had written to USG. "Hon. Francis Thomas of Maryland, desires to represent this government near the government of Japan. He has been known in the first ranks of the public service for more than thirty years. For the six years last past he has been a member of the committee on the Judiciary of the House of Representatives, of which, during that time, I have been chairman. I well knew his history long before this association with him afforded me an opportunity to measure the real proportions, and sterling worth of the man. He is a grand American character; and deserves at the hands of your administration an emphatic recognition of his merits as a citizen and a statesman. Notwithstanding he had passed into the limits of declining life, when most men become conservative in public action, and was, when placed on the committee to which I have referred, a representative from a, then slaveholding state, he was the first member of the committee to pronounce in favor of an unconditional repeal of the 'fugitive slave law.' He has kept full measured pace with the advance of the reforms and civilization of the past eight years of our most wondrous national action. I admire the grandeur of his character, and love his devotion to the principles of this age: and do most earnestly pray that his aspirations to serve the Republic may meet with your appointing approval."—ALS, *ibid.* A related petition is *ibid.* On April 19, USG nominated Thomas as collector of Internal Revenue, 4th District, Md.

On Dec. 2, 1870, Owen M. Long, consul, Panama, wrote privately to USG seeking appointment as minister to Peru. ". . . A Pioneer Citizen of Illinois in 1832 I had the honour to serve as Surgeon in the Black Hawk War. In 1847 I was appointed by the lamented Col: Hardin of the 1st Ills: Regt: as Surgeon to Said Reg't but was prevented from serving by the unexpected and dangerous illness of my wife before the Reg't Alton. In 1861, I was Commissioned by Gov: Yates as Surgeon of the Glorious old 11th Ills: Vol: Inftry: which was so often baptised in fire and blood, . . . Being the early friend and associate of Lincoln, Douglass, Hardin, Baker, Shields, Yates, Oglesby, Logan, Palmer, Browning Richardson and many other illustrious sons of Illinois also urges me to aspire to this Place in the Gift of your Excellency. . . ."—ALS, *ibid.* Related papers are *ibid.* On Feb. 7, 1871, USG nominated Thomas Settle, former N. C. judge, as minister to Peru. On March 25, USG signed Settle's letter of credence.—DS, Gallery of History, Las Vegas, Nev.

1872, MARCH 19.   Maj. Gen. John M. Schofield, San Francisco, to USG. "My Senior Aide de Camp, Capt Wm M. Wherry is an applicant for appointment in the Adjutant General's Department. He has been with me almost constantly since 1861 and has become very familiar with the duties of A. A. G. I am sure he is thoroughly qualified for the office he seeks, besides being entitled to the consideration due to most faithful and gallant service during the War. It is difficult for me to separate my judgement of Captain Wherrys merits from my strong personal interest in his welfare, ~~for~~ but I feel sure I do not err in saying that I am acquainted with no young officer in the army more worthy than he of the appointment of Asst Adjutant General."—Copy, DLC-John M. Schofield. On June 27, 1874, Capt. William M. Wherry, San Francisco, telegraphed to Orville E. Babcock. "Is adjutant Generals dept reopened to appointment & promotions   look out for my interests   shall I come on."—Telegram received (at 8:30 A.M.), DLC-USG, IB. No appointment followed.

1872, MARCH 19.   Rear Admiral William Radford, Washington, D. C., to USG. "I respectfully request the appointment of my son Stephen Kearny Radford, who will be sixteen years of age in June next, to a Cadetship in the U. S. Military Academy, to take effect in June 1873."—LS, DNA, RG 94, Correspondence, USMA. USG endorsed this letter. "Mrs. Sherman is particularly anxious about the apt. of Geo. K Hunter, Lancaster O. His father was an Andersonville prisoner"—AE (undated), *ibid.* George K. Hunter graduated from USMA in 1877. Stephen K. Radford attended USMA but did not graduate.

1872, MARCH 19.   J. C. Helms, Howell, Mich., to USG. "as it is in your power to Do Something for a poor man as I Ha[ve] Sent all of my Boys in the field to Battle to preserve our freedom and good order   one of them Died near formington mississippi august 3d—, 1862   the other two Hast lost there Health for Life.   one of them was in the 14th infantry and one in 15th infantry and in Stead of Sending Him Home they took them the ridgement to Little Rock arkansas   there He was taken Sick and I Had to rais money to Get Him Home So you see I am lift with out any Help at all and poore   as a good many says there is no use of apliing to this Government for pay or Help for they would rather Help the Rebels than to Help a poore Soldier one who sent all the support that He Had to put Down the Rebellion and now my Health is poor and purs Emty and if you can Help me Some it will Be thankfully Received and fully Rememberd By me and others"—ALS, DNA, RG 48, Miscellaneous Div., Letters Received.

1872, MARCH 20.   To Commander James H. Gillis. "With congratulations to Commander Gillis, U. S. N., for having, with the aid of ten brave sailors, rescued from a watery grave three fellow-beings."—*HRC,* 48-1-533. On March 18, Secretary of the Navy George M. Robeson had written to Gillis, Washington, D. C., acknowledging testimonials about his rescue of foreign sailors off Montevideo in 1859.—*Ibid.*

1872, MARCH 22.   To Senate. "*I nominate* George L. Beal of Maine to be Pension Agent at Portland Maine, vice M. A. Blanchard, whose term of office has expired."—DS, DNA, RG 46, Nominations. On March 4, Frederic D. Sewall, Washington, D. C., had written to Brig. Gen. Oliver O. Howard concerning this appointment.—ALS, Howard Papers, MeB. Sewall enclosed an undated, unsigned letter to USG. "I have the honor to recommend Gen'l. Geo. L. Beal for the appointmt of Pension Agent for the Western District of Maine. Gen'l. Beal served with distinction in the late war, and is one of the representative soldiers of Maine. He is a gentleman of integrity and ability and a sound republican. His appointment would be very gratifying to the soldiers of Maine."—AL, *ibid.*

1872, MARCH 22.   Uriah Lott, Corpus Christi, to USG. "*Personal;* The act adding Starr Webb and Zapato Counties to Brazos Santiago Customs district is one of the greatest injury to the trade and people of western Texas and ought not to pass,"—Telegram received, DNA, RG 56, Letters Received. See *U.S. Statutes at Large,* XVII, 53; J. L. Allhands, *Uriah Lott* (San Antonio, 1949).

1872, MARCH 23.   To House of Representatives. "In answer to a Resolution of the House of Representatives of the 20th instant, I transmit a report from the Secretary of State, with a list of the newspapers which accompanied it."— Copies, OFH; DNA, RG 59, Reports to the President and Congress; *ibid.,* RG 130, Messages to Congress. *HED,* 42-2-219. On the same day, Secretary of State Hamilton Fish submitted a list of newspapers chosen to publish new U.S. laws.—Copy, DNA, RG 59, Reports to the President and Congress.

1872, MARCH 24.   Aaron Moody *et al.,* Old Church, Va., to USG. "we the undersighned coloured officers of our society called the Rising sons of Abraham, make this humble petition to your honourable body to give us & allows us to have side Arms that we may be able properly to celebrate all proppers days such as the fall of Richmond which is the 3rd of April and also to be able to celebrate the important Day when our beloved president was acceded to the president mansion   we also ask the honourable president to let us have a ¾ Drum any information in regard to the above petition will Please address our Treasurer Solomon Washington at the old church hanover county VA"—D, DNA, RG 156, Letters Received.

1872, MARCH 25.   USG note. "Mr. Doggett is refered to the Sec. of State for such action as he may deem proper upon the subject of accompanying letter to U. S. Minister to Great Britain."—ANS, IHi. On April 17, Secretary of State Hamilton Fish wrote to Robert C. Schenck, U.S. minister, London. "Referring to the correspondence which has taken place between this Department and the Legation, in relation to the desired exercise of clemency toward Benjamin Booth, a citizen of the United States now undergoing imprisonment in Ireland under a sentence for manslaughter, I enclose a copy of a letter of the 15th instant, from C. S. Doggett, Esqr of Wareham, Massachussetts and of the papers enclosed therewith, invoking the good offices of this Department in a renewed effort to secure a mitigation of the sentence. . . ."—Copy, DNA, RG 59, Diplomatic Instructions, Great Britain. On Sept. 23, Schenck wrote to Fish after presenting the case to Lord Granville. ". . . He had been told, he said, that, with every desire to meet the wishes of the American Government, the Lord Lieutenant of Ireland is unable, consistently with his sense of public duty, to accede to my application for the discharge of the prisoner on the condition of his leaving the British dominions and returning to the United States. His Lordship said he was further informed that nothing had occurred to justify the Irish Executive in commuting punishment inflicted for the use of deadly weapons by Irishmen returned from America, and that a recent outrage has shown the necessity of dealing firmly with that class of cases"—LS, *ibid.*, Diplomatic Despatches, Great Britain.

1872, MARCH 25.   John Cortlandt Parker, Newark, N. J., to USG. "I trust I may be pardoned for asking a favor of the Administration, since it is the first time; and is not of itself, of great magnitude, nor for myself—A connection of mine married a daughter of Col. Kinsey late U. S. A., of Chicago, Illinois. He has left a son, George Kinsey, now about 24 years old—a young man of education, capacity and character. He volunteered when only about 18 years old, and went to the war as a private—was taken prisoner and long kept in confinement. He is now solicitous of a commission as an officer in the regular army, & it is this for which I write. . . ."—ALS, DNA, RG 94, ACP, 3430 1873. On Jan. 31, George H. Kinzie, Detroit, had written to Frederick T. Dent. "I am aware that in several instances you have assisted the sons of deceased officers of the army, to obtain commissions. This emboldens me to make a personal appeal to you. My application is now on file at the War Department; at least I sent it there, but no attention has been paid to it. I am the son of the late Maj: John H. Kinzie of the Pay Department, who died in the service; my eldest brother was killed at Arkansas Post, I myself served as a private & was taken prisoner by N. B. Forrest at Memphis & was in Cahawba Prison (Alabama) two months. I think I have said enough in regard to my claims. I am young, have received a good collegiate education, and think I could make a good soldier.

Trusting you may feel disposed to interest yourself in my behalf . . ."—ALS, *ibid.* See *PUSG*, 3, 381. On Dec. 1, 1873, USG nominated Kinzie as 2nd lt. to date from Oct. 1.

On Nov. 26, 1872, Governor Cadwallader C. Washburn of Wis. wrote to USG. "I am informed that Mr. A. M. Kinzie of Chicago is an applicant for the position of Paymaster in the Army—I knew Mr. Kinzie as a Lieutenant of Vols. and should there be any vacancy in the pay Dept, I recommend that Mr. Kinzie be allowed to compete for the appointment under the established rules—"— ALS, DNA, RG 94, Applications for Positions in War Dept. On Jan. 17, 1873, Governor Richard J. Oglesby of Ill. wrote a similar letter to USG.—ALS, *ibid.* Arthur M. Kinzie did not receive an appointment.

1872, MARCH 25.   Jaris Pierce and Joshua Pierce, Cattaraugus Reservation, N. Y., to USG. "The undersigned, onondaga Indians of the Six Nations re-siding with the Senecas in Western New York, respectfully beg leave to state to you our troubles, and ask your friendly interposition in our behalf. At the original organization of the Iroquois confederacy, it was agreed, that persons belonging to any one of the Six Nations, coming to reside on territory be-longing to any other of them, should enjoy all the rights and privileges per-taining to those with whom they had come to reside. Frequent intermarriages, and the extensive commingling of the blood of the different tribes through several generations, resulted from this arrangement. This, however, so long as the Confederacy remained unimpaired, occasioned no inconvenience, because every child followed the tribal status of its mother; and though at home among the people where it was born; could be counted and represented among its mother's tribe, whenever separate tribal action might be required; and, inas-much as the territory of each nation was amply sufficient both for its own use, and that of its co-confederates residing with it, there was no occasion for the fear of being overcrowded, or for the clashing of any tribal interests. But when the different nations sold out successively large portions of their land and be-came confined to small reservations, the narrow limits of these reservations seriously modified the question of unrestricted compliance with the terms of this old arrangement. . . . Thus living together and intermarrying for three or four generations, our blood has become so mingled, that those now reckoned as Onondagas and Cayugas are really from three fourths to fifteen sixteenths Seneca. Notwithstanding this relationship, and the above-mentioned founda-tions for the claim of the other tribes to reside on the Seneca lands on equal terms with the Senecas, the latter are many of them becoming uneasy, and have caused notices to be posted up warning all not reckoned as Senecas, that, if they cut a tree on their reservations, they will be dealt with as intruders, and fined as White men would be for a similar offence,—and that if they cultivate any land, they must pay rent for it, or submit to taxation;—thus not only setting aside the agreements of the Ancient Confederacy, and the ties of blood-relationship, but ignoring also the agreements entered into by their former chiefs and Headmen, while still retaining the property which was the consideration for such agreements. They, however, justify themselves on the ground that the changed condition of the people renders the covenant of hospitality between the Six Nations inoperative . . ."—DS, DNA, RG 75, Letters Received, New York Agency.

1872, MARCH 26.   Thomas J. Petrikin, Johnstown, Pa., to USG. "By authority and through instruction of the soldiers of this City and vicinity, I am authorised to make known to your Excellency their opinions, wishes and desires, for your consideration and action thereupon, as you may deem just and right, with due regard to the public interests, and your duty as the chief Executive of the Nation, relative to a late act of Congress, and only waiting your approval, or otherwise to become a law 'granting to each honorably discharged soldier and sailor, widows and orphans and heirs and legal representatives 160 acres of the public lands, with the homestead law attached, deducting the the time of service of the soldiers and sailors from the 5 years settlement required by the homestead law to obtain a title to the lands. The soldiers claim that the law, as it stands now, is unjust and partial in its requirements and provisions, for the following reasons and facts: It is unreasonable to suppose, and utterly impossible, that soldiers who have lost both arms, who have lost both legs, who have lost both feet, who have lost both eyes, who have lost both arms, who have lost all their fingers, and all these amount to hundreds, without ennumerating the one leged and one armed soldiers, the aged Fathers and Mothers who lost all their sons upon whom they depended for support in old age, and the widows and orphans of deceased soldiers amounting to thousands in the agregate could in any way or manner whatever obtain a title to their proportion of the lands under the requirements of the law as it now stands, and it will doubtless be admitted by your Excellency, that they are, by far the most needy and meritorious claimants   The law is unjust in discriminating unfavorably between the soldiers of the late rebellion and those of our previous wars from the days of the revolution, 1812 and Mexicon wars, who were granted their 160 acres of lands, free from all restrictions or reservations . . ."—ALS, DNA, RG 48, Miscellaneous Div., Letters Received. On Nov. 22, 1869, Petrikin had written USG to urge a broader interpretation of pension laws for wounded soldiers. ". . . I have no interest in these cases and no complaint to make so far as I am individually concerned, for my son fills an honored Soldiers grave and my wife draws a full Pension, . . ."—ALS, *ibid.* On April 2, 1872, Secretary of the Interior Columbus Delano wrote to USG advising approval of the revised homestead act.—Copy, *ibid.*, Lands and Railroads Div., Letters Sent. USG signed the act on April 4. See *CG,* 42–2, 318, 483–84, 1712–13, 1883–88; *U.S. Statutes at Large,* XVII, 49–50.

On Sept. 20, John Koppitz, East Birmingham, Pa., wrote to USG. "Having been apointed by the Veteran land settling association of Pittsburgh to adress myself in their behalf to your exelency. They intend to better their condition by emigrating to the West where they may obtain their bounty land readily in one body. You will see by perusing our Constitution herby enclosed what our object is. Most of us which have joined and still are joining this sossiety, are not in prosperus circumstances, they could not muster the means to travel so far

still less to buy tools and one years provision,   for that purpose they petition
that you grant or by your Authority to have granted four passes on the R. R.
to Denver Citty for a location in those territories.   allso in a distant place we
may come in contact with the aborigeonest, we wish to live with them on a
footing of peace and equity and instruct them, but if on the other hand if they
should injure us we must atempt to repress them, therefore we pray our gov-
ernement that you would suply us with arms and amunition. Four members will
be selected right of to examine the lands and make a selection for the sossiety
before the winter sets in, we calculate the number of members will be one hun-
dert heads of families and are to move in april 1873. I wrote to Gen Sheridan
that he might indicate a location between 35 & 40 North latitude; but we had
no answer yet. On behalf of the veteran Soldiers land settling assosiation of
Pittsburgh . . ."—ALS, DNA, RG 48, Miscellaneous Div., Letters Received.

1872, MARCH 26.   J. W. H. Reisinger, editor, *Daily Republican,* Meadville, Pa.,
to USG. "The undersigned would beg leave to represent that he is personally
acquanted with Joseph T Chase of Titusville against whom a suit for Embezzlement is pending in the U. S. District Court, and that from facts known to
the undersigned he feels convinced that a further prosecution of the suit would
in no way advance the aims of justice while it would result in a lasting disgrace
to the family and friends of Mr Chase. . . ."—ALS, DNA, RG 60, Letters Received, U.S. Senate. Related papers are *ibid.* See Samuel P. Bates, *Our County
and Its People: A Historical and Memorial Record of Crawford County Pennsylvania* (n. p., 1899), pp. 740–41.

1872, MARCH 27.   Martin F. Conway, Washington, D. C., to USG. "Senator
Wilson has informed me that you have declined to afford me an opportunity of
making good the promise of my youth in the service of my country. Permit
me, Sir, to relate to you a very familiar circumstance from the History of an
ancient Republic: Aristides was the honestest man in Athens. He was os-
tracised. One day in walking the street, he was accosted by a man who wished
to cast a vote against him but could not write his name upon the shell. Not
knowing Aristides he asked *him* to write it ~~from~~ for him. 'Why do you wish to
ostracise Aristides' enquired the virtuous man. 'Because,' answered the other,
'I am tired hearing everybody call him an honest man.'"—ALS, NN. See
PUSG, 20, 451–52. On Nov. 14, 1874, Conway wrote to USG seeking an appointment.—ALS, DNA, RG 59, Letters of Application and Recommendation.
See *New York Times,* May 30, 1881.

1872, MARCH 28.   USG veto of a bill reimbursing the estate of John F. Hanks
for money seized from a New Orleans bank in 1862.—Copy, RG 130, Messages to Congress. *HED,* 42-2-222; *SMD,* 49-2-53, 378–79. See *CG,* 42–3,
697–99, 724; *HRC,* 42-3-39.

1872, MARCH 29.   Harry Hone, New York City, to USG. "If you could be
made aware of the amount of disease and death has been and is carried from the

diseased to the well, carrying the contageon so fatal to many families, I mean the dirty ragged, filthy currancy stamps that find their way into the houses of the rich and poor alike   now you should take the initiative and reccommend the abolition of it at once and let us have nickel coin instead such as our 5¢ peices . . ."—ALS, DNA, RG 56, Letters Received.

1872, MARCH 30.   Solicitor Gen. Benjamin H. Bristow to USG. "Having learned that Mr. Spencer, Assessor of Internal Revenue for the 4th District of Kentucky has tendered his resignation to take effect upon the appointment and qualification of his successor, I beg leave to recommend for the office Captain Frank Hill of Springfield, Washington County, in that District. Captain Hill served throughout the war in the volunteer service of the United States with distinction and credit; and since its close, has been a consistent and active supporter of the Republican party, having been more than once elected sheriff of his county on a popular vote. He is a gentleman of integrity and capacity and well qualified to perform the duties of the office. My information touching the resignation of Mr. Spencer comes from the Commissioner of Internal Revenue from whom I learn that an immediate appointment of his successor is desirable."—LS (press), DLC-Benjamin H. Bristow. On April 2, USG nominated Franklin S. Hill to replace William M. Spencer as assessor of Internal Revenue, 4th District, Ky.

1872, [*March*].   R. R. Finley *et al.*, Knox County, Ill., to USG. "We, the Undersigned, Respectfully Petition your Excellency—Since the Curse of Slavery has Been Removed from our Land—that all persons who, at Diffarent times did assist Slaves in making their Escape, and thereby gaining their freedom, and By So assisting Became Liable to punishment as Criminals; and were punished By Laws of the Different States; at that time in force, And as Certain ones are Still held in Imprisonment, and are Suffering Punishment for an act which could not By the present Laws Be termed a crime, therefore, we most Respectfully and sincerely ask of your Excellency to pardon, or to Do what your Excellency may think most proper to Relieve the unfortunate ones Still Suffering for that, which they Should Be Rewarded and honered for, Rather than punished."—DS (53 names, docketed March 27), DNA, RG 60, Letters from the President.

1872, APRIL 1.   USG veto. "I herewith return for the further Consideration of Congress, House Bill No 1867. 'An act for the relief of James T. Johnston,' without my approval, for the reason that ~~T~~the records of the Treasury Department show that ~~lot~~ the lot sold in the name of J. T. Johnson, situated on Prince Street Alexandria, Virginia, for taxes due the United States is numbered 162 instead of 163 as represented in this bill. With the exception of this discrepancy in the number of the lot, there is no reason why the bill should not receive my approval."—Copies, OFH; DNA, RG 130, Messages to Congress. *HED*, 42–2–239; *SMD*, 49–2–53, 379. See *CG*, 42–2, 1542, 2076, 2272.

1872, APRIL 1.   USG endorsement. "Respectfully refered to the Sec. of State."
—AES, DNA, RG 59, Letters of Application and Recommendation. Written
on a letter of March 29 from John W. Hamilton, Washington, D. C., to Secretary of State Hamilton Fish. "I desire to make application for reinstatement in
Your Department having been in employ of the Department during its administration under the Hon. W. H. Seward, and having been removed from Office
by what I deem unfair means,   The facts of my removal are simply these,
When your *Honor* took possession of the Office the number of employees & laborers were canvassed and it was deemed expedient to drop a certain number
of laborers all of whom up to that time had been under the exclusive jurisdiction of Thomas C. Cox a clerk in the office of Geo. E. Baker disbursing Agent
of the Dept, and to gratify his ambition besides it being a pecuniary matter
with him I was dropped to make place for a protegee of his by the name of Luke
Kearney who had never done a days service in the Dept although drawing a
salary for driving the said Coxs carriage from his home in Georgetown to the
Office in the morning and back again in the evening he living in the said Coxs
house and doing his personal work at the expense of the Government, . . ."—
ALS, *ibid.*

1872, APRIL 2.   To Senate. "In answer to the resolution of the Senate of the
18th of January last, relating to British light house dues, I transmit, herewith,
a report from the Secretary of State, and the documents which accompanied
it."—DS, DNA, RG 46, Presidential Messages; copy, OFH. *SED,* 42-2-57. On
the same day, Secretary of State Hamilton Fish wrote to USG transmitting
correspondence concerning the British practice of assessing merchant ships to
support lighthouses and beacons.—LS, DNA, RG 46, Presidential Messages.
Related papers are *ibid.* See *CG,* 42–2, 451.

1872, APRIL 2.   AG Edward D. Townsend endorsement. "Official copy respectfully referred to the Commanding General Military Division of the Missouri. The President directs that means be taken to prevent the setting out of
the expedition."—ES, DNA, RG 94, Letters Received, 1141 1872. Written on
a letter of March 29 from Secretary of the Interior Columbus Delano to Secretary of War William W. Belknap requesting USG's action to prevent a reported expedition into the Black Hills.—LS, *ibid.* On the same day, Francis
A. Walker, commissioner of Indian Affairs, had written to Delano. "Respectfully referring to my communication of the 26th instant, I have the honor to
inform the Department, that I am this day in receipt of a communication from
Colonel D. S. Stanley, 22nd Infantry, commanding the Middle District of
Dakota, under date of Fort Sully the 16th instant, in which Col. Stanley calls
the attention of this Office to extensive preparations being made at Sioux City
and frontier towns of Dakota, for an expedition to explore and open up to settlement the so-called Black Hills, forming a part of the general Sioux Reservation established by the Treaty of 1868. Col. Stanley expresses his belief that
'the Sioux will make bitter and continual war upon parties invading the por-

tion of their reserve these people propose to take possession of.' I have previously remarked upon the dishonorable and dangerous character of the intrigues in which certain of the Federal Officials of the Territory of Dakota are notoriously engaged. These intrigues appear to be now so near an issue in the actual organization to penetrate the Sioux Reservation, that I deem it advisable that the matter should be brought to the attention of the President and the Honorable, the Secretary of War, in order that it may be considered whether a proclamation shall issue warning evil disposed or misguided persons from joining in such an enterprise, and the commanding Officer of the Department of Dakota be instructed to stop and turn back, by force if necessary, any expedition aiming to enter the Sioux Reservation. I fully concur in the opinion of Col. Stanley that a general Indian war is certain to instantly follow the first attempt of this kind. I had occasion on my visit to Wyoming and Nebraska last autumn to become thoroughly advised of the views and temper of the Ogallalah and Brulé Sioux, in respect to the efforts of certain of the inhabitants of Dakota to reach the Black Hills. The rumors of these intrigues have kept them continually excited and alarmed, in spite of the assurances of their Agents, and the first motion to carry into execution these plans will precipitate general hostilities"—Copies, *ibid.* On April 6, Lt. Gen. Philip H. Sheridan, Chicago, endorsed papers to Townsend. ". . . steps have already been taken by the military to accomplish the object desired by his Excellency, the President."—ES, *ibid.* On the same day, Edwin S. McCook, secretary, Dakota Territory, wrote to Delano. "I have the honor to acknowledge the receipt of your letter of the 30th. of March,   In absence of Governor Burbank, and in compliance with your wishes, I have this day issued the enclosed Proclamation. I know of no organization of men in this Territory designing to invade the Black Hill Country; I believe such an organization is being perfected at Sioux City, Iowa, but from the publicity of the thing, I think it amounts to nothing. The Governor and myself have done all we could to discourage any one from trying to invade the Sioux Country, in direct violation of law, and existing treaties. I know of no Federal officials who are giving encouragement or support to this movement, as for myself I refer you to Genl. Sheridan. I have been told that parties of miners will attempt to enter the Black Hills from the Nebraska side, also from Wyoming and Montana Territories. Hoping that my course may meet with the approval of the President and yourself—. . ."—Copy, *ibid.* Related papers are *ibid.*

1872, APRIL 2.   William Breeden, clerk, Supreme Court, New Mexico Territory, Washington, D. C., to USG. "I presume that the Atty. Genl. will, present to-day, the Case of Hon. Daniel B. Johnson Jr. Associate Justice of the Supreme Court of New Mexico, whose removal from office is clearly necessary, as I believe the Atty. Genl. is satisfied. We, of New Mexico are exceedingly anxious that Hon. John D. Bail, shall receive the appointment. Mr. Bail is an honest, correct man, of good ability and would make an excellent Judge. His appointment would give great Satisfaction in New Mexico and particularly in the third Judicial District, in which he will preside if appointed and of which he is a resident.

Mr. Bail has been recommended for the place by most of the federal officers of our Territory and no better appointment can be made. During the present Administration five appointments have been made to this place, the District is very large, and the Judge who holds the courts there is required to travel more than 1500. miles every year. Each of the first four gentlemen appointed there, resigned, or declined the place after learning the extent and location of the District and I am entirely satisfied that no man really fit for the position, and not a resident there, will go there and hold the courts. The interests of the people require a resident Judge and all desire Mr. Bail's appointment because that will insure the holding of the courts."—ALS, DNA, RG 60, Records Relating to Appointments. On April 13, Breeden again wrote to USG. ". . . Mr. Bail's appointment would be exceedingly gratifying to the Republican party of New Mexico, and with the appointments of Secretary and Post-master at Santa Fé, recently made, will place the party in a position of perfect unity and harmony, and New Mexico will then have an entirely Satisfactory list of federal officers."—ALS, *ibid.* On April 15, USG nominated Warren Bristol as associate justice, New Mexico Territory. See *PUSG*, 20, 375–78; *ibid.*, 22, 307.

[*1872*], April 2. Rachel Watters, New Market, Frederick County, Md., to USG. "I address you a few lines in regard to my son Isaic   I have sent twice to the war office but as yet have not heard any thing concerning him   he has been gone seven years, last febuary and he was all my support as i am old and blind and up to this time I have not received andy assistance from the Goverment   I wrote to you once before and received the Document from the war Department which wias filled and returned to the office in Washington and since then I have heard nothing more concerning it   I send you this letter and make my appeal to you again and let me hear from the war Department in regard to my claim as it has been three months since I sent you my last letter and I have not heard any thing since   I would be glad to hear as soon as possible as I am in great meed of assistance as i am a widow and old and blind and my son Isaic Watters was all my support   he Bought me a little home before he went into the army but getting no sustenance from him and having no help to get along my home was taken from me and I was set out of doors by the man who I Bought the land from as my son was owing him a little Bill and he turned me out and took my house and lot from me and I have Been treated very Bad indeed   answer this imeadately   since i wrote you my last letter I heard of my son Isaic Death   he died in the hospital"—ALS, DNA, RG 94, Colored Troops Div.

1872, April 4. To House of Representatives. "In answer to the Res. of the House of Representatives of the 14th of January last, I transmit herewith, a Report of the Sec'y: of State"—Copies, OFH; DNA, RG 59, Reports to the President and Congress; *ibid.*, RG 130, Messages to Congress. *HED*, 42-2-244. On the same day, Secretary of State Hamilton Fish had written to USG stating that the requested report on fishing in the North Pacific had been printed as *SED*, 42-2-34.—Copy, DNA, RG 59, Reports to the President and Congress. The House had adopted the resolution on Feb. 14.—*CG*, 42-2, 1018.

1872, APRIL 6.   USG endorsement. "Refered to the War Dept. This applicant may be put on the list as an alternate next below those already named."—AES, DNA, RG 94, Correspondence, USMA. Written on papers recommending Richard S. Miner for USMA, including a letter of March 14 from Miner, Alexandria, Va., to USG. "I am anxious to obtain a cadetship at West Point, and the fact of my Congressional District (the 7th of the State of Virginia) being under the control of the Conservative party, I am precluded from any shadow of a chance from this source, and am therefore compelled to make application to you for one of the appointments at large. The record of my late Father, as well as those of his immediate family, who fell in the cause of the Union, fully attest their devotion to the great party of which you are the acknowledged chieftain. I reside in Alexandria Va. and was 18 yrs. of age on the 2nd of February last."—ALS, *ibid.* Miner did not attend USMA.

1872, APRIL 6.   James H. Smith, La Mesilla, New Mexico Territory, to USG. "I take the honor to ask you a favor to give me the appointment of Post Trader at Fort Stanton or Fort Carlen   I ask the Secretary of War about six months ago and never answered me   I am a colored man and the United States Judge Johnson tells me that I had better ask you, ~~and~~   I have soldiered two enlistments during the War,   this is the first favor that I've asked to the Government   I am in hopes you will give it to me.   you will direct my letter in care of Col. J. F. Bennett Mesilla N. M."—ALS, DNA, RG 94, Applications for Positions in War Dept.

1872, APRIL 8.   James H. Lee, Albany, N. Y., to USG. "a bill has passed both houses of Congress giving the Officers and crew of the Kearsarge prize money and not knowing whether you would sign it or not I concluded to write, and give you the facts in my case. . . ."—ALS, DNA, RG 45, Miscellaneous Letters Received. Lee had served on the U.S.S. *Kearsarge.* See *SRC*, 41-2-250, 42-2-40; *CG*, 42–2, 2297–98; *U.S. Statutes at Large*, XVII, 53; *New York Times*, Aug. 17, 1877.

1872, APRIL 9.   USG endorsement setting aside land in Washington Territory as a reservation for the Spokane, Coeur d'Alène, and other tribes.—Copy, DNA, RG 48, Indian Div., Letters Sent. *HED*, 45-3-1, part 5, I, 768, 47-2-1, part 5, II, 352; 49-2-1, part 5, I, 588; *SED*, 48-2-95, 615; *SD*, 57-1-452, I, 916. On July 2, USG modified this order. Printed in sources listed above and in *SRC*, 52-1-664. Also in 1872 USG established a reservation in Ore. "for the Snake or Pi Ute Indians"—Copy, DNA, RG 48, Indian Div., Letters Sent. USG also issued an order enlarging the Makah Indian Reservation, Washington Territory.—DS, *ibid.*, RG 75, Orders. Printed in sources listed above.

1872, APRIL 10.   Governor John T. Hoffman of N. Y. to USG. "There has been for some time an apparent necessity for a revision of the exterior pier and bulk head lines of the Harbor of New York on the Brooklyn Side; and the Legislature has requested me to apply to you, asking you to appoint three Officers of the United States service to revise such exterior lines. I enclose a copy of the resolution of the Legislature, and respectfully ask that you will appoint the board of Officers for the purpose defined in such resolution at as early a day as you may find convenient."—LS, DNA, RG 77, Rivers and Harbors Div., Letters Received. The enclosure is *ibid.* On April 22, Secretary of War William W. Belknap wrote to Hoffman naming three officers chosen for the board. ". . . I would remark, however, in this connection that as the Department has no ap[pr]opriati[on on which the] Board can draw for its expenses, the State of New York must defray them."—LS (press), *ibid.* Related papers are *ibid.*

1872, April 10.   Edward S. Tobey, Board of Indian Commissioners, Boston, to USG. "I have today signed an application for the appointment of George N Hitchcock of San Diego, California, as Collector of that port, whenever it shall be declared a port of entry. This document is also signed by several of our most prominent and influential citizens, some of whom are personally known to you as amongst your most zealous and influential political friends. Mr Hitchcock is a native of this State, & a son of Dr. Hitchcock, who is doubtless also personally known to you as one of the most steadfast & active supporters of your Administration   ~~and~~He occupies relations to the community which enable him to strengthen our political alliance. I therefore sincerely hope that you may in due time find it compatible with the public interest & your own personal views to appoint Mr H. to the office which his friends seek for him."—ALS, DNA, RG 56, Collector of Customs Applications. A petition of April 2 signed by Tobey and 19 others recommending George N. Hitchcock is *ibid.* On Dec. 19, Tobey again wrote to USG. "Mr Geo. N. Hitchcock is, as I understand, an applicant for the office of Collector of San Diego California. Although I am not personally acquainted with him, I have reason to believe that his *personal* character & entire fitness for the office will be assured to your satisfaction by parties in whom you have confidence   In that event, I trust that you may find it compatible with the public interest to confer on Mr. H. the appointment which he seeks, & which to his father Hon D. K. Hitchcock is of course an object of very deep interest. . . ."—ALS, *ibid.* On March 6, 1873, USG nominated Hitchcock as collector of customs, San Diego; the Senate rejected this nomination. On March 21, David K. Hitchcock, Bridgeport, Conn., telegraphed to USG. "Will the President Please not make another nomination till I hear from California. Reply at Boston. Hope to compromise"—Telegram received, DLC-USG, IB. On March 22, USG nominated William J. McCormick. On March 24, David Hitchcock, Boston, wrote to USG. "*Private* . . . A few months ago my son in California requested me to go to Washington and make San Diego a Port of Entry. I gladly acceded to his request, and the bill was passed, although I was assured it was so late in the session nothing could be done. My son was kindly nominated as Collector, and when it was done his confirmation was opposed, and *the* reason assigned was that one or two had not been consulted. The statement was not true for Mr Twichell, had several times as well as myself conferred with the parties as to the collectorship. The result is known, and the blow has been given to one of the dearest and best of sons.

In this great trial my loyalty and devotion to you is unchanged. Before I left your city, I was exceedingly anxious to give you my views on the subject, and I am quite sure you would have harmonised with my opinions. On reaching home my friends were of the opinion that you would speak to some of the Senators, and set this matter right as it was an act of gross injustice as well as great disrespect to yourself. I trust that they are correct & that the difficulty may be overcome   Even Mr Houghton told me that 'he should like to please the President.' Should not my son be confirmed, I would be glad to have him appointed Secretary of Legation to Berlin. It would relieve him of the unpleasant attitude in which he is placed, and at the same time it will give another demonstration of your keen sense of justice & unflinching regard for your friends . . ."—ALS, DNA, RG 59, Letters of Application and Recommendation. On the same day, Tobey telegraphed to USG. "Is it not possible that another conference with senators expressing strong personal preference may yet secure confirmation of appointment to the Collectorship in San Diego. Pardon the suggestion   I feel a personal interest in the matter. Cannot senators Conkling and Morton carry it."—Telegram received, DLC-USG, IB.

On Aug. 10, 1874, Ephraim W. Morse, "Citizen of San Diego," West Amesbury, Mass., wrote to USG. "In the event of a new appointment of Collector of Customs at San Diego I beleive it would be the almost unanimous wish of the better portion of the Republican party of San Diego, that Geo. N. Hitchcock Esq, a practicing Lawyer of that City may receive the appointment. He is a gentleman of most excellent character, promp in business and enjoys the confidence of the community in a high degree."—ALS, DNA, RG 56, Collector of Customs Applications. See *PUSG*, 21, 429. On Sept. 12, 1874, USG suspended McCormick; on Sept. 26, USG cancelled this order. Facing embezzlement charges, McCormick resigned. See *New York Times*, July 14, 1874. On Dec. 7, USG nominated William W. Bowers as collector of customs, San Diego.

On Aug. 1, 1876, David Hitchcock wrote to USG explaining past efforts to secure his son's appointment and renewing the request.—ALS, DNA, RG 56, Collector of Customs Applications. No action followed.

1872, APRIL 10.   Joseph Zeon, Chicago, to USG. "Allow me to approach you by saying that previous to the 'Great Fire' in this City, I raised and organized the First Regiment of Illinois State Militia,   the fire destroyed this organization and, I am now raising another Regiment which I have hopes will be Stronger than the first (say about 1400 Strong). I am desirous of adding to this Regiment a Company of Cavalry but Governor Palmer—whose opinions and mine are somewhat different *as Republicans*—will not afford me the aid I need. . . ."—ALS, DNA, RG 156, Letters Received.

1872, APRIL 12.   W. D. Dimon, Utila Island, Honduras, to USG. "I take the Libertey to ask you to send us hea ameditly a consel   us americans that ar Liven hear Wont american Protcton   Also our comerce stand in Nead of the same   We have a Larg trade Betweeen hear and New Orleans & Baltimor also New york and thar is No consol Nor agent on the Bay Ilands to cal on to sea that We hav our Rytes and our Constutun says that We shal Bea Protected a Brod the same as at home   i am an american Born and it Would Bea For our intrest to Let this Part of the World know that the goverment of of the united States Will giv to her citezens and comerce Protecton and Not sufer her subjects to Bea shot Down and asasanated lyke Dogs   We hav No Protecton For Life or Property unles your self Will send us hear a consul that can give you the best acount how americans ar treated hear   Even ther laws hear give us No Equal chans   hopen that you and Beaynd the hed of my goverment Will atend to the Within Ameditly . . . P S War is Declard hear Betwean Honduras Gatamela & Sant Salva   thar has First arrvd in anser an englesh Slop of War to Protect her intrest.   send us one to Protect ours"—ALS, DNA, RG 59, Miscellaneous Letters. A state dept. report advised against establishing a consulate on Utila Island.—*Ibid.* See *Foreign Relations, 1872,* pp. 302–6, 524–29.

1872, APRIL 15.   USG veto. "I return, without my approval, an Act entitled 'An Act granting a pension to Abigail Ryan, widow of Thomas A. Ryan.' The name of Mrs Ryan is now borne upon the pension rolls pursuant to an Act of Congress entitled an 'Act for the relief of Mrs Abigail Ryan', approved June 15. 1866. (U. S. Statutes Vol 14. page 590.)"—DS, DNA, RG 46, Presidential Messages. *SED,* 42-2-61; *SMD,* 49-2-53, 380. Abigail Ryan requested an increased pension to support her child. On June 8, USG approved a bill providing Ryan an additional $2 per month. See papers in DNA, RG 46, Presidential Messages; *SRC,* 39-1-99; *CG,* 42–2, 2434–35; *U.S. Statutes at Large,* XVII, 682.

1872, APRIL 15.   To Robert Patterson, Philadelphia. "I have duly received your kind letter inviting me to be present at the celebration and banquet of the Artillery Corps Washington Grays on the 19th inst., and regret that I canot gratify your wish and my own desire to be with you upon so interesting an occasion. My public duties and my recent illness both preclude the possibility of my paying a visit to Philadelphia at that time."—Copy, DLC-USG, II, 1.

1872, APRIL 15.   David R. Dillon, Savannah, to USG. "I Send you enclosd the facts of a case that, I trust you will immidiatly investigate, and assist me,   If you and my frinds do not stand by me now, in this my hour of need I may be *ruined,* by the Combinations and predjudices that exist against me here, Do Mr President, do not *neglect* this *appeal* to you, act at once, the emergency of the case demands your attention and Action, and I hope and trust to have a favourable Answer before Congress adjourns."—ALS, DNA, RG 60, Letters from the President. The enclosure is *ibid.* On April 25, Edward G. Dike, Savannah, wrote to USG. "At the request of Capt D. R. Dillon of this place, I take pleasure in stating to you that I have known him intimately since the capture of Savannah, and probably know as much about his sufferings and his losses as a Union man. I was a Capt. & A. A. G USvols and A. A. G. of the District of Savannah during the first part of 1865. Capt Dillon had a Steamer up the river and was sending in word at every opportunity for assistance to remove the torpedoes, which had been placed to prevent his boat from coming down. The latter part of February, Capt C. B. Western (now a Lieut in the Army) Provost Marshal on our Staff (Gen Grover's) was sent up on the Flag of Truce Boat 'Mayflower,' and found Capt Dillon and his Boat in charge of a Confederate guard and about 80 Bales Cotton belonging to Confederate ~~citizens~~States. Capt Dillon volunteered all the information necessary, and supplied the 'Mayflower' with fuel. Capt Western reported to me on his return, that he had told Capt Dillon to get rid of the guard as soon as possible and run for Savannah, guaranteeing him (officially) protection. About the 2d or 3d of March, the Boat was reported in sight, but when about ½ mile above the City was seized as a Prize to the Navy by Lt Comdr Luce of the Gunboat 'Pontiac.' Some sharp correspondence ensued between Gen Grover & Lt Comdr Luce in regard to the breach of faith but resulted in the Boat & Cotton being held as a prize to the Navy. Both were ordered to Hilton Head and the Cotton (which by the way was not Capt Dillons and never claimed by him) was sent to Philada and sold. It was always understood at our Hd Qrs that the Boat was his own and its safety & possession had been guaranteed him, but the Cotton (not being his) was a lawful capture to the Army. There has been great injustice done to him, for from what I can hear, he was the strongest outspoken Union man South, and when his life was threatened for his sentiments his very boldness and fearlessness carried him through. He is being sued now in the State Courts for this Cotton, which was never even claimed by him, but was brought in to be turned over to the Army as a capture. There are also several other cases pending in the State Courts and from his known sentiments, he will swear he cannot get justice except in the US Courts. I think if your Excellency understood the case you would see no difficulty in passing (or rather having passed) a law which would cover his especial case viz—to the effect that all cases coming up in regard to Capt Dillons acts during the rebellion be assigned to the US Courts, as these cases are only a portion of the persecution he has received and the true value of the cases could soon be determined by a US Court. The Hon Atty Genl under date of Apl 22d writes him, that he should consult his Attorney in Savh as to having the case transferred but there is no power here to transfer them without a special act of Congress, which is what he desires, and if it can be done, will relieve him entirely from the oppression under which he is laboring and be doing an Act of Justice to a sound lifelong Union man. Begging pardon for tresspassing on your valuable time . . ."— ALS, *ibid.* On Nov. 23, Dillon wrote to USG. "Enclosed I Send you a printed Circular, and a copy of An Act, I want passed on the Assembelling of Congress—Our state Court meets here in December is why I want it passed early—If this Act, is passed it will *releive me*, and all the friends of the Government *South*, it will put a stop to this *persecution.* Evry word is true. Ex Atty Genl Ackerman will prove that Cotton was selling at Augusta at the time mentiond at $1, to 2 per Bale—Pardon this, appeal, but it is absolutely Necessary. And one of the Strongest benefits the Govermt Can grant, I am Responsible for Evry word I hope you will give it your Especial attention"— ALS, *ibid.,* Letters Received, Ga. The enclosures are *ibid.* On Jan. 22, 1875,

Dillon wrote to USG on the same subject.—ALS, *ibid.*, Letters from the President. For reports adverse to Dillon, see *HRC*, 43-1-520; *HMD*, 45-2-4, 17–41. See also *O.R.* (Navy), I, xvi, 284–85.

1872, April 16.   USG endorsement. "No objection to this apt. to take effect July 1st"—AES, DNA, RG 60, Records Relating to Appointments. Written on a petition of April 15 from U.S. Representative William H. Upson of Ohio *et al.* to USG. "We respectfully and earnestly reccommend the appointment of Dr N B. Prentice as Marshal of the Northern District of Ohio, in place of Genl R Hastings resigned. Dr Prentice is a man of high character, strict integrity, in every respect well qualified for the position, and an active and efficient Republican. We believe that no better appointment can be made."—DS (8 signatures), *ibid.* U.S. Senator John Sherman of Ohio favorably endorsed this petition.—AES (undated), *ibid.* On April 16, USG nominated Noyes B. Prentice as marshal, Northern District, Ohio; on March 9, 1876, USG renominated Prentice.

1872, April 17.   USG endorsement. "This is forwarded in the hope that the Academic Board may find it to the public interest to recommend the restoration of Cadet Hancock to West Point, to commence with the 3d Class, after the June examination this year."—AES, DNA, RG 94, Correspondence, USMA. Written on a letter of April 16 from Achilles M. Hancock, Washington, D. C., to Capt. Robert H. Hall, adjt., USMA. "I have the honor to make the following request of the Academic Board at West Point, to be approved by the President of the United States: That the Academic Board at West Point reconsider my discharge from the Academy and permit me to return and continue with my class until the next June Examination and if I fail to be turned back into the next lower class. If this be inconsistent with the views of the Board I would most earnestly request that it consent to my restoration by the President of the United States to the present fourth Class at the commencement of the next Academic year. I promise a faithful discharge of my every duty if restored to the Academy."—ALS, *ibid.* On Dec. 7, 1874, Hancock, Union City, Tenn., wrote to USG. "Having learned that, after a class has graduated at the National Academies, it has been customary to give commissions to cadets who were found deficient during their course, should they apply, and the class to which I belonged, having graduated last June at the Military Academy, I have the honor to apply to your Excellency for a commission as 2nd Lieutenant in the Army.... There was not a graduate last examination from Tennessee, which I hope will argue in my favor."—ALS, *ibid.*, Applications for Positions in War Dept. No appointment followed.

1872, April 17.   To John James Speed Wilson. "I do not believe the country can suggest another name more capable, both by experience and qualification, than yourself, nor one who has had a larger field of operation. It was my fortune to have been thrown with you during the early part of the rebellion, when you were engaged in organizing the telegraph system for the armies; so that, although having no experience as a telegrapher myself, I had an opportunity of judging of your qualifications as an organizer."—*The United States Biographical Dictionary . . . Illinois Volume* (Chicago, 1876), p. 733. See *PUSG*, 2, 264–65; *New York Times*, Aug. 15, 1881.

1872, APRIL 18.   Secretary of War William W. Belknap to USG. ". . . As regards 'An act to remove the charge of desertion against Daniel Orner, late private in Co "H" 91st Regt. Penn. Vols.,' I have the honor to invite your attention to the report of the Adjt. General, annexed thereto, presenting certain objections to the bill, which may possibly be regarded as sufficiently grave to justify the withholding of your sanction thereof."—Copy, DNA, RG 107, Letters Sent, Military Affairs. On April 23, USG signed this bill. See *CG*, 42–2, 680, 1335.

1872, APRIL 18.   Thomas Hamilton, Toledo, to USG. "Permit me to occupy a few minutes of your valuable time, with statement of a matter which concerns myself, a host of your Mercantile & commercial constituents of this city and the party of which you are the Honored chief. By recent legislative Enactment this Port of Toledo was made full Port of Entry for Importation of Foreign Goods direct, making necessary An Officer known in the Customs Service as 'appraiser'   My friends many of them thinking I was Especially well qualified for the position from 30 years Experience in active mercantile life in a large way & life time Experience in commercial affairs—urged to become a candidate for the Office, which after consideration and assurance that probably no other candidate would be named here for the place I consented. About 20th March I wrote Hon: John Sherman Senator and Doctor Peck Representative that I would be a Candidate for the Appointment, . . . I rested secure in the Expectation that my application would be favourably acted upon in due time and left the city on a business trip of some three weeks. On my return I learned for the first time that the Petition my letters and Telegrams of leading Republicans had been entirely ignored by Messrs Peck & Sherman & the name of another party Revd Robert McCune suggested to your favourable consideration, unknown as he avers to himself and unsupported by Either Letter or Petition of any citizen merchant or Republican of this city. . . . I found letters from Messrs Peck & Sherman saying that for personal reasons & favours done by McCune for them they had united in reccommendations of him for the Office, utterly ignoring the prayer of the whole body of Merchants Importers Bankers & leading Republicans here, as unworthy of consideration as against personal favours shown them individually by Mr McCune, . . ."—ALS, DNA, RG 56, Collector of Customs Applications. On April 15, USG had nominated Robert McCune as appraiser of merchandise, Toledo.

1872, APRIL 19.   Secretary of War William W. Belknap to USG. "I have the honor to return an act to amend the 1st. Section of the act of Febry. 24. 1871, providing for the disposition of useless military reservations, and to report thereupon, that in May, 1871, the attention of this Dept. was called by the

General Land Office to a discrepancy in the act of Congress of above date in locating in Oregon the Fort Walla Walla Reservation, which was one of those it
authorized to be transferred to the Interior Dept., and that Congress was informed of the fact, and was requested to pass an amendatory act correcting the
mistake, December 15, 1871. No information has been received here of such
legislation, and as the matter now stands the act to which this communication
relates, while correct in its own phraseology, leaves uncorrected the act to
which it is an amendment. Beyond this the Department knows of no objection
to the bill."—Copy, DNA, RG 107, Letters Sent, Military Affairs. On April 29
and June 4, USG signed bills involving Fort Walla Walla, Washington Territory, amending an act concerning useless military reservations. See *CG*, 42–2,
1336, 2286–87; *U.S. Statutes at Large*, XVII, 57–58, 226.

1872, APRIL 20.   J. E. Montgomerie, Baltimore, to USG. "There appeared in
our morning papers a bill in referance to the mission to Japan, in which you are
authorized to appoint two interpreters (Students). Knowing, that in making
your appointments, your preferance leans twowards those who took part in our
late war: I concluded to transmit to you my name and to take my chances
among those who have done likewise: Should this communication be favorably
considered, and I be honored with the appointmet, I would enter upon my duties determined to discharge ~~my~~ them to the full satisfaction of our Govemnt.
From 1865—to 1868. I served on the Steam Sloop, 'Wyoming' in China and
Japan, and while out there became well aquainted with the people and country.
This is the first favor I have asked of the Govemnt, those who received boun-
ties and land grants ought to be satisfied, as for me, I have never receivd a cent
outside of my regular pay. Hoping Sir, that I have not trespassed upon your
valuable time. . . ."—ALS, DNA, RG 59, Letters of Application and Recommendation. For inconclusive congressional action to authorize a secretary and
interpreters for the U.S. legation in Japan, see *CG*, 42–2, 2985, 3661–64,
3890.

1872, APRIL 20.   P. J. Smith, Attalla, Ala., to USG. "I have the honor to say
that I edit the 'Republican Union' at this place, in the interest of the Union Republican Party, and a strong advocate of your excellency's re-election to the
Presidency—I established the 'Union' in the interest of your election in 1868,
and have stood by and advocated your Administration for the last four years
against threats of K. K. and other intimidations—and have again hoisted your
name for re-election. During the period I have been issuing the 'Union' it has
been a hard matter to sustain it—and I have now arrived at the point when I
am forced to call on the party for a small assistance in a pecuniary point of view
or let the paper go down, which will be a hard blow to the party in Ala at this
time, as it is the only Republican paper on the entire line of the A. & C. R. R. for
a distance of 200 in Ala, and supplies Republican food to a large era of country
in North Ala—I do not come to the party asking thousands of Dollars, but
simply a few hundred say ($800) which would enable me to continue through
the approaching campaign and I hope do great good for the party, by aiding in

carrying the State for the nominee of the Nat. Rep. Party, and also for State offices—I refer you to Hon. Geo. E. Spencer of the Senate, as to my standing with the party in my state   Hoping you will give this matter your attention and render me some assistance to aid me on in the good work of Republicanism—"—ALS, DLC-William E. Chandler.

1872, APRIL 22.   USG veto. "I return herewith, H. R. 622, entitled 'An Act granting a pension to Richard B. Crawford' without my approval for the reason that, said Crawford is now drawing a pension as a private soldier: the wound on account of which he was pensioned having been received before his promotion to a lieutenancy."—Copy, DNA, RG 130, Messages to Congress. *HED,* 42-2-269; *SMD,* 49-2-53, 380. See *CG,* 42–2, 148, 1881, 2100–1, 2342. On April 24, U.S. Representative Jesse H. Moore of Ill. reported a new bill to pension Richard B. Crawford, 13th Ohio. ". . . On examining the original bill the committee are of the belief that the President was misled by reason of the manner in which the original bill was drawn. It was supposed to grant an additional pension, but it was really intended to be in lieu of the pension the soldier was then receiving. Another point made in the message of the President was that this soldier was a private when he was wounded. There is the most complete testimony that could be gotten up that when he was wounded he had the commission of lieutenant and was filling a vacancy, and was in the uniform of a lieutenant. . . ."—*Ibid.,* p. 2749. See *U.S. Statutes at Large,* XVII, 725.

1872, APRIL 22.   Casper Becker, San Francisco, to USG. "You will doubtless remember your humble petitioner Casper Becker formerly of Saint Louis, Mo in the year 1859, by occupation a Carriage Trimmer, Carrondelet, with whom you done business at that time and before. In the year 1865, after the surrender of Richmond Va I emigrated with my family to California, and have followed my trade here ever since. Having applied to the Office of Chief Quartermaster Military Division of the Pacific, and having been induced to manufacture samples of seal skin Knapsacks my partner Mr Waldschmidt having delivered said skins to the Authorities, said promise has of a sudden been taken away from me and transferred to Waterlit Arsenal, after the samples manufactured by me were pronounced by Officers U. S. A a No 1. as letters in my posession will proove. If your Exellency now, will be kind enough, as I have failed in the above premises grant or see this Contract granted to me, namely the Contract for the manufacture of Knapsacks, you will conferr an everlasting favor on me and to my family, who have been suffering ever so much during & since the late war . . ."—ALS, DNA, RG 156, Letters Received.

[*1872, April 23–26*].   USG endorsement. "~~If able to attend any evening this week will send word. Am much obliged for the attention but doubt being able to accept.~~ Accept for Saturday evening"—AE (undated), IHi. Written on a letter of Tuesday, April 23, 1872, from "Messrs Simmons & Slocum," Washington, D. C., to USG. "Will you honor us by accepting a Private Box at the National Theatre any night this week to witness the Entertainment given by our

Minstrel Troupe from Philadelphia? An answer in the affirmative stating the Evening that the Box may be reserved will be fully appreciated . . ."—D, *ibid.* See *Washington Chronicle,* April 23–25, 1872; Edw. Le Roy Rice, *Monarchs of Minstrelsy, from "Daddy" Rice to Date* (New York, 1911), pp. 111, 126.

1872, APRIL 24. USG endorsement. "Let attention be called to this application after the appointment of of the present graduating class at West Point."— AES, DNA, RG 94, ACP, 4223 1872. Written on a letter of the same day from José K. Peabody, Washington, D. C., to USG. "I have the honor hereby to apply to be appointed as Second Lieutenant in the Cavalry Servis of the United States. I served during the late war for a period of four years in the Navy, and since its close, three years in the United States Army. As to my political status, trustworthiness, and capacity to honorably fill the position asked for with entire credit to the best interests of the service, I respectfully refer to Hon: Seth Wakeman, of New York, General Wm N. Grier, late Col 3rd U. S. Cavalry, and Col R. G. Usher. United States Marshal, Boston, Mass. My age is 26."—ALS, *ibid.* On Dec. 2, USG nominated Peabody as 2nd lt., 3rd Cav., to date from July 27. Peabody, who resigned in 1873, later wrote to USG requesting reappointment.—ALS (undated), *ibid.* On July 24, 1876, USG endorsed this letter. "Refered to the Sec. of War for such action as he deems proper."—AES, *ibid.* A memorandum of July 29 questioning Peabody's pay account is *ibid.* No appointment followed.

1872, APRIL 25. Millie Williams, Brunswick, Mo., to USG. "I am the widow of Watt Williams who Served and died in the Military Service of the U. S. A. during the late rebellion. I am debarred from prosecuting my claim because the adgintant Genl U. S. A refuses to give me the name of the company and Regiment to which he belonged now dear Sir beleaving that the rules of the adgitant Genl will in this case do a poor widow grate injustice and that you have it in your power to have justice done I write to you hoping that you will allow the agt Genl to furnish me the information, as with that I can fully Substantiate my clame. he belonged to 65 Regt U. S. Col. T. pleas direct answer in care of the P. M. Brunswick Chariton Co Missouri"—ALS, DNA, RG 94, Colored Troops Div., Letters Received, P121 1872. On May 11, Secretary of War William W. Belknap wrote to Williams. ". . . the ruling of the Adjutant General is in accordance with the universal practice of the Department, which cannot be deviated from in this instance. . . ."—Copy, *ibid.*, RG 107, Letters Sent, Military Affairs.

1872, APRIL 27. U.S. Senator Matthew H. Carpenter of Wis. to USG. "I respectfully recommend the Revd President A. L. Chapin of Beloit College, on the Board of Visitors to the Naval Academy Mr Chapin is a gentleman of great influence and high character No one could be appointed, more worthy of that distinction, or more deserving of any favor this administration can bestow."—ALS, DNA, RG 45, Miscellaneous Letters Received. Aaron L. Chapin served on the 1872 board of visitors to the U.S. Naval Academy.

On March 13, John C. Robinson, Binghamton, N. Y., had written to Secretary of the Navy George M. Robeson accepting a position on the board.—Copy, OFH. On Aug. 27, Robinson wrote to Frederick T. Dent. "Your letter of congratulation is received, for which you have my thanks—Our ticket is well & enthusiastically received in all parts of the state & will be triumphantly elected—Grant is gaining & Greeley is losing ground every day—I will send you a paper giving an account of the demonstration here last night—"—ALS, ICarbS. Robinson had been nominated for N. Y. lt. governor on a ticket with John A. Dix.

1872, APRIL 30. To Congress. "I have the honor to transmit herewith the annual report of the Board of Public Works of the District of Columbia, submitted to me, for that purpose, by the Governor of the Territory, in accordance with Section 37, of 'an act to provide a government for the District of Columbia,' approved February 21, 1871."—DS, DNA, RG 46, Presidential Messages. *SED*, 42-2-69. Related papers are *ibid.*

1872, MAY 1. Brig. Gen. Christopher C. Augur, San Antonio, to USG. "General Carleton, 4th Cavalry, whom you know as an old and distinguished officer, has a promising young son who is anxious for an appointment in the Army. I think I express the opinion of every officer and citizen who knows him, in saying that his appointment in the 4th Cavalry would be exceedingly gratifying to them. It certainly would be so to me, and I hope you may find yourself able to give it to him."—ALS, DNA, RG 94, ACP, 3737 1873. On Sept. 18, Speaker of the House James G. Blaine, Augusta, Maine, wrote to USG on the same subject.—ALS, *ibid.* On May 30, 1873, Sophie W. Carleton, San Francisco, wrote to USG. "I prefer addressing you as the head of the Army, rather than as President of the U. States because I can better tell you what I want and my letter being informal will reach you sooner perhaps. My husband, (the late Genl Carleton) applied last fall to have our only son, Henry Carleton, appointed ~~as~~ to the U. States Army; and he placed on file at the War Department, letters from various persons of influence asking the same favor:—the Adjutant General has them in care and will present them at the proper time—although I would prefer that my son should be appointed on the merits of his father's long and arduous services, and that of many of my relatives who served long and faithfully than by political influence. . . ."—ALS, *ibid.* On June 1, Henry G. Carleton, San Francisco, "now in the completion of my 21st year," wrote to USG requesting an art. appointment.—ALS, *ibid.* On Dec. 1, USG nominated Carleton as 2nd lt., 8th Cav. See *PUSG*, 17, 62–64; *ibid.*, 18, 73–76, 449–50.

On March 18, 1876, Sophie Carleton, Vallejo, Calif., wrote to USG. "Again I feel the desire to appeal to you in behalf of my son, hoping for success. I applied to General Townsend if possible to grant Lieut Henry Carleton, Fort Brown Texas, a leave of one month that he might go East on important business for me. I have not heard from him yet, but feel assured he will do the best he can. What I desire of you is, that my son will be assigned to duty in the Signal office at Washington. he is fully capable of performing the duties in that Department—besides having invented an automatic meteorological barometer, with self registering and multiplying attachments, which he desires to superintend, and has already sent to the Signal office. His health is not good; and he cannot long be of service in the Cavalry as a physique like his cannot long stand so much hardship—but he can be of service in any department where brain work is required of him. Henry has had the best of Education, therefore will not be out of place any where, besides having invented many useful things. I can purchase for Henry an interest in business; but if the Goverment will treat him well, i e, not make him one of the drudges of the Army, I would rather he would remain in its Service, . . ."—ALS, *ibid.* Carleton resigned as of Aug. 1. In Aug. 1885, he published "Our Captain Sleeps," a poem honoring USG.—*New York Times,* Aug. 7, 1885. See *ibid.,* Dec. 11, 1910.

1872, MAY 2.   USG endorsement. "If Barton Pratt is not appointed to West Point please call attention to this application for a Lieutenancy after the appointment of the present graduating class."—AES, DNA, RG 94, ACP, 500 1873. Written on a letter of May 1 from Col. Henry B. Clitz, Washington, D. C., to AG Edward D. Townsend. "I have the honor to apply for an appointment as Cadet at the Military Academy in the Class of 1873 for my nephew Edward Barton Pratt son of Major H. C. Pratt Pay Department U. S. A. If he should fail to receive this appointment I would esteem it a great favor if the President would grant him a commission as second Lieutenant of Infantry, after the present graduating class at West Point are commissioned in the Army"—ALS, *ibid.* On Dec. 30, 1871, Maj. Henry C. Pratt, Detroit, had written to USG. "On the 20th inst, my son (Edward B.) with my approbation applied for an appointment as Midshipman in the Naval Academy—Yesterday he received a copy of the 'Regulations governing the admission of candidates into the U. S. Naval Academy', from which he learns, that his age will prevent his admission. The application is therefore withdrawn, and I respectfully solicit from you, an appointment for him to the Military Academy."—LS, *ibid.,* Unsuccessful Cadet Applications. On Dec. 12, 1872, USG nominated Edward B. Pratt as 2nd lt. On March 5, 1873, Clitz, Springfield, Mass., wrote to USG. "I have seen my young nephew Edward Pratt who had been made very happy by the receipt of his appointment of 2d Lieutentant ~~in the~~ 23d Infantry, which ~~you~~ were kind enough to give him at my request. It may not be impossible, General, that one of these days, I may have it in my power to prove to you how grateful I am for this your kindness to me—"—ALS, USG 3.

1872, MAY 4.   John W. Hoyt, Washington, D. C., to USG. "Encouraged by the interest you have manifested in every enterprise looking to the intellectual and social progress of the American people, I take the liberty of inviting your attention to the movement now making by the National Educational Association towards the establishment of a great and true University at the National capital. The need of such an institution is recognized by leading educators in all portions of the country; and the particular plan herewith submitted for your convenient examination and criticisim has been warmly endorsed by heads of existing colleges and universities and by prominent statesmen. It is not proposed to press the measure at this time—simply to place it before Congress, and there let it await action until the people have again ordered that the enlightened policy by which your administration has thus far been characterized shall continue yet longer to govern in the management of our national affairs."—ALS, NN. For Hoyt, see *DAB*, V, 321–22.

1872, MAY 6.   USG endorsement. "Refered to the sec. of State."—AES, DNA, RG 59, Letters of Application and Recommendation. Written on a letter of May 2 from Henry Clews, New York City, to USG. "Mr. Jas A. Garguilo, is an applicant to the Dep't. of State for appointment as Secretary of Legation at Constantinople in place of Mr. Brown recently deceased. Mr. Garguilo is a native of Turkey; speaks the language of that and the neighboring Countries; has polished manners and in my judgment is a gentleman eminently fitted to do credit to the Country and Administration if appointed. Mr. G's. appointment is urged by Mr. Henry F. Vail, Cashier of the Bank of Commerce of this City, the largest banking institution in the United States with a Capital and surplus of over $13.000.000—Mr. V. is an influential member of the New York Community, and his institution, of which he has entire direction, rendered important aid in the financial conduct of the war. I believe this is the first request which has ever been made by any of the officers of that bank, and in view of what I believe will be found on examination to be the unquestioned capacity of Mr. Garguilo, and the important influence which a favorable consideration of his request would exert with the wide circle of his friends in this City, I venture to hope that unless important reasons of state should prevent some favorable action may be had in behalf of Mr. G's application. I have known Mr. Vail intimately for many years & have been acquainted with Mr. Garguilo since his residence in this Country."—LS, *ibid.* Also on May 2, Henry F. Vail, New York City, wrote to Secretary of State Hamilton Fish. "This will be handed to you by Mr Joseph A. Gargiulo, . . . He has, during his residence here been engaged in business in Wall St. with my son, who, upon visiting Constantinople some five years since made his acquaintance & that of his relatives and soon afterwards married his sister. . . ."—ALS, *ibid.* No appointment followed.

1872, MAY 6.   James W. Taylor, consul, Winnipeg, to USG. "On the morning of the 5th October 1871, before I had heard of the decisive action of Capt Wheaton in arresting the Fenian Raid at Pembina I ~~telegraphed to the State Department~~ proposed by telegraph to State Department that the U. S. Government should consent to the passage of troops ~~through~~ by Superior Canal and Northern Pacific Railroad to Manitoba. ~~and~~ By another despatch to Mr Jay Cooke, of Philadelphia, I invited his ~~attention on~~ attention to the matter: and received from him the following message in reply   (*Copy*)   At that time the Treaty of Washington was in a position, which ~~suggested to me the~~ seemed to call for the utmost vigilance against violations of the Neutrality Act. Perhaps I exerted myself more than was necessary, but the result has been that this people ~~now~~ universally attribute their exemption from civil war to the good faith of the American Government. ~~and~~ To encourage this feeling, I felt ~~to be~~ myself justified in publishing the substance of Mr Cookes despatch in a Manitoba newspaper. ~~When I~~ After my return this winter from a leave of absence, I was invited to a dinner of the Manitoba Bar, and, during the evening, was called upon to respond to a toast in your honor, which ~~was~~ had been cordially received. I ~~was not~~ did not expect [a] report of my remarks, which was published [as] follows: (Copy) ~~If I had I saw the report for the fir~~ If I had seen this report, before it was in print, I would have corrected the ~~statement~~ sentence underscored to the effect that your communication was made to the Governor General of Canada: ~~and~~ or, which ~~is what I now do~~ would have been the best thing, would have ~~in my suppressed the statement~~ suggested its omission. Yet, as a fact highly honorable to you and well-calculated to produce a warm ~~feeling~~ sentiment of gratitude and esteem among my auditors, you can readily appreciate how much I was tempted to mention ~~the fact~~ it. I now perceive, that this unlucky sentence ~~is repeated~~ has been caught up by the opposition press and may be ~~used in the~~ tortured to ~~the~~ your prejudice during the Presidential canvass. ~~I cannot~~ I think the circumstance will have an opposite effect but I cannot avoid feeling much annoyance. I hope you will pardon my indiscretion. I ~~have~~ am learning daily ~~the~~ that silence is golden, especially in a diplomatic position: although I have been ~~too~~ so long accustomed to free speech that ~~it~~ I find it difficult to make my practice conformable."—ADf (initialed), Taylor Papers, Minnesota Historical Society, St. Paul, Minn. On June 11, U.S. Senator Alexander Ramsey of Minn. wrote to Taylor. ". . . Saw Mr Fish in the Senate a day or two since & told him I would call on him so soon as we adjoured & so this moring called at the dept. & Mr Fish being out saw Mr Hale and after talkng the matter over left with him your letter addressed to the President which he read and expressed himself pleased with: and said the statemnt was satisfactory. . . ."—ALS, *ibid.* On Oct. 21, 1871, Allured B. Nettleton, Philadelphia, had written to Taylor. "*Personal* . . . Your favor of Oct. 7th to Mr. Cooke, covering copies of your dispatches regarding the Fenian demonstration, comes to my hands in Mr. Cooke's absence. Your telegram to Mr. C. was placed in President Grant's hands (as he was then in Philada.) the day it was received. We are much gratified at the prompt extinguishment of this new Fenian nuisance, and congratulate you on the prompt measures adopted by yourself to prevent a fresh cause of complaint on the part of our friends across the border."—ALS, *ibid.* See *PUSG*, 19, 466; *ibid.*, 20, 441.

On Oct. 3, 1871, and Jan. 18, 1872, Secretary of State Hamilton Fish had written in his diary concerning British anxiety over Fenian activities in Canada and the arrest of John O'Neill.—DLC-Hamilton Fish. On Jan. 22, Sir Edward Thornton, British minister, Washington, D. C., wrote confidentially to Lord Granville about a conversation with Fish: ". . . He replied to my observations that the Govt of the U. S. was most anxious to prevent violations of the Canadian Territory by Fenians from this side of of this side of the border and felt the necessity of inflicting a more exemplary punishment upon those who might be found guilty of such proceedings. He repeated that orders had been sent to re-arrest the prisoners who had been made at Pembina and had been subsequently released. He stated that they would be prosecuted, but he feared that it might be difficult to find at that place a jury who would convict them,   if however they were condemned, he could assure me that whatever the sentence might be, it would be carried out most strictly. Mr Fish added, tho' he begged me to consider the communication as most confidential, that when the President pardoned O'Neill and other prisoners who were convicted of having taken part in the raid of May 1870, the most solemn pledges were given by these men that they would never repeat their offense. The President, he said, was extremely indignant at the violation of these pledges, and he would certainly never again consent to a remission of any part of the sentence wh. in case of conviction, might be passed upon them. Mr Fish alleged that both the President and himself had been opposed to a pardon being granted to those engaged in the Raid of May 1870, but that the President had at length consented, yielding to the earnest representations of Mr Akerman, then Attorney General, accompanied by the most solemn engagements on the part of the prisoners that the crime would never be repeated. The President could not but regret that he had exercised the power of pardoning on that occasion."—Copy, Thornton Letterbook, ICarbS. See *PUSG,* 20, 222–23, 225–26.

1872, MAY 7.   To Senate. "I transmit for the consideration of the Senate, with a view to its ratification, a Convention between the United States and the Republic of Ecuador, for the purpose of regulating the citizenship of persons who emigrate from the one country to the other, which instrument was signed in this city on the 6th. instant."—DS, DNA, RG 46, Presidential Messages. Related papers are *ibid.* On May 3, USG had authorized Secretary of State Hamilton Fish to negotiate a naturalization treaty with Ecuador.—DS, DLC-Hamilton Fish.

On Dec. 3, USG transmitted "a Treaty between the United States of America and the Republic of Ecuador, providing for the mutual surrender of fugitive criminals, signed at Quito on the 28th. of June last."—DS, DNA, RG 46, Presidential Messages. Related papers are *ibid.*

1872, MAY 7.   To House of Representatives. "In answer to a Resolution of the House of Representatives of the 15th of March last, I transmit herewith a Report of the Secretary of State and the papers which accompanied it."—Copies, DNA, RG 59, Reports to the President and Congress; *ibid.,* RG 130, Messages to Congress. *HED,* 42-2-292. On the same day, Secretary of State Hamilton Fish had written to USG recommending "reasonable compensation" to the owners of the steamer *Aroostook* for salvage work following the wreck of the *Oneida* at Yokohama.—*Ibid.* See also *ibid.,* 41-2-236.

1872, MAY 7.   C. A. Buck, Holmes County, Miss., to USG. "I now in my feeble manor & feeble Health Send personally to your Honor and ask your good will toward me and mine in useing your influence and assisting me petitioning aid of the u states Goverment,   Please find inclosed a Duplicate copy of a letter which was written & handed me by Col P. F Winslow In memphis Tenn in

Aug 1864 when on my way to Lexington Miss, via Vicksburg, To try to re-cover the remains of my Husband, and also some of our lost estate, But was re-fused to pass through the Confederate lines by Gen Wert Addams who was at that time campaining at Jackson Miss,   I will now relate to your Hon General The circumstances of my true situation, Trusting that this petition may meet with the approbation of your Honorable benevolence,   My Husband J, N, Buck of Holmes, Co, Miss, was a devoted friend to the united states, Gov, and for being such & for aiding the Fedrals, he Suffered death,   In a short time af-ter my unfortunate Husband was executed, The Confederate Souldiers Come to my House, and ordered me to leave, Stating that they had, for my husband's aiding the Fedrals, ~~that they~~ ordors, by Confederate orthorities, to ordor me to leave the Confederate lines, & to take every thing that was on our premisis or that we had that would do for the use of their army, & to burne the balnce, I was hurried off, and of course could take but little with me, as I had to travel the distance of two hundred & fifty miles, in a Small waggon & poor Team,   We were permitted passes from the Court Hoouse at Lexington, & also through the Confederate lines To Tennessee,   Some time after arriveing in Tenn I went To Memphis, and There to the Fedral orthorities I made known my sit-uation,   I asked the Fedral orthorities to render me protiction and aid. when they adviseed me to make out my Petition Stateing domages received by Confederate Souldiers, with a view of receiving aid as soon as The war ques-tion was settled. I had a petition made out by congressman, David Nunn of Brownsville Tenn. Stateing particulars, &c estimating our damageis at ten Thousand dollars and recorded by Mag Genl C C Washburne, in 1865, (& I Think in Feb or march)   The Confederate's had our House sold for Confeder-ate Tax had used ~~all~~ and distroyed all of our Stock, and every thing that we had, including Four hundred & thirty bales of cotton,   To your Hon General I now state or Testify that I have no means of support and myself & children are suf-fering really for the necessarie's of life,   Trouble, Hardship's, & Deprivation's, have brot on bad Health, and I have been suffering from a pulmonary disease since Nov 1870   The milinary buisiness of which I have been at work at work at for some time I am not able to work at now attall, only being able to sit up a portion of the day only,   as I am not able to work, I am not able to rent a house to live in, as I have had to do since 1863,   My oldest daughter Emma C Buck, fourteen years of age has been afflicted all of her life, Is not able to work but very little, my youngest daughter, Fannie M Buck 12 years of age, is not stout, . . ."—ALS, DNA, RG 94, Letters Received, 2062 1872. The enclo-sure is a letter of Aug. 3, 1864, from Col. Edward F. Winslow, 4th Iowa Cav., Memphis, to Maj. Gen. Henry W. Slocum, Vicksburg. "I very respectfully ask your good will towards Mrs John Buck, wife of late John Buck Esqr, Lexing-ton Miss—Mr Buck acted as guide for me during an expedition made in au-gust 1863, from Big Black River to this city via Grenada, Returned with my command to Vicksburg, Started for his home and was caught just outside our lines, with protection papers and a pass given by Maj Genrl W D Sherman, He was at once token to Brig Genl Whitfield's HdQrs, near near Vernon, and by his direction or connivance hung without form of Trial—Mr Buck was

charged with being a union man & with guiding my column! . . ."—Copy, *ibid.*
On June 25, 1872, Maj. Henry Goodfellow, judge advocate, wrote to Buck that
"only the Legislative & not the Executive branch of the Gov. has power to
afford relief."—Df, *ibid.* On July 16 and Aug. 31, Buck wrote to USG seeking
assistance with an appeal to Congress.—ALS, *ibid.*

1872, MAY 7.   William Hunter, North Lewisburg, Ohio, to USG about obtaining arms for veterans staging "Sham fights" at annual reunions.—ALS,
DNA, RG 156, Letters Received. On May 17, Secretary of War William
W. Belknap wrote to Hunter. "The President has handed me your letter of the
7th. inst., asking his friendly offices in procuring for yourself and comrades an
hundred muskets from the Columbus State Arsenal. The Federal authorities
have no control over the property of individual States and therefore the State
of Ohio cannot be compelled to loan you the desired arms. I regret to say that,
under existing laws and circumstances, the arms cannot be loaned to you from
public stores."—LS (press), *ibid.*

1872, MAY 8.   Joseph R. McCready, Boston, to USG. "I have been sending you
my paper since its first publication. I supported you at the last Presidential
election, and have always been a devoted Republican. The '*Protestant*' circulates
in nearly every State in the Union, and it is the organ of the 'American Protestant Association' and the 'Loyal Orange Institution of the United States. Our
Order has never taken a public stand in reference to politics, but we have
worked *secretly.*—I have sacrified myself to maintain my paper to its present
position. I have a large bill to meet in a short time and I respectfully request
your Excellency to send me a donation. It is in a good cause—I refer to
Hon G. Twichell. Hon. S. Hooper. Hon. H. Wilson Hon. B. F. Butler Hon. W. Cla-
flin. Hon. A. H. Rice."—ALS, OFH. See John Higham, *Strangers in the Land:
Patterns of American Nativism 1860–1925* (New Brunswick, N. J., 1955), p. 61.

1872, MAY 9.   H. L. Mellen, Brookfield, Mass., to USG. "I have a Son (Albert
H. Mellen) at West Point Military Academy, who for some misdemeanor last
autumn was punished by being deprived of his furlough the coming summer
the boy has suffered severely by it—Now Sir knowing that you understand the
situation perfectly, will you be so kind as to grant him a pardon . . ."—ALS,
DNA, RG 94, Correspondence, USMA. Albert H. Mellen, punished for hazing
new cadets, graduated from USMA in 1874.—D (undated), *ibid.*

1872, MAY 9.   U.S. Senator John Sherman of Ohio to USG. "I enclose to you
at the request of the signers this appeal for the appointment of Rev. Garland
H White (colored) of Toledo Ohio to some appointment under the Gov't. and
ask for it your favorable consideration . . . He would be an excellent Chaplain
for a Col'd Reg't."—ALS, DNA, RG 94, Applications for Positions in War
Dept. Enclosed are two petitions, including one of May 4 from F. A. Stevens &
Co., *et al.*, Toledo, to Sherman commending Garland H. White, former chaplain, 28th Colored, as a Republican speaker. ". . . We the ever devoted friends

to the party that freed us & made us men—has but one request to ask of the administration & that is to appoint our Rev & Worthy leader to Some office from Which he can be at once detailed & enabled to go among the masses of the colored people—. . ."—DS (29 signatures), *ibid.* No appointment followed. See Edward A. Miller, Jr., "Garland H. White, Black Army Chaplain," *Civil War History,* 43 (Sept., 1997), 201–18.

1872, MAY 11. USG proclamation authorizing consular jurisdiction for Sweden and Norway over crews of their vessels in U.S. waters and ports.—DS, DNA, RG 130, Presidential Proclamations. *Foreign Relations, 1872,* pp. 1–2.

1872, MAY 11. Eli T. Tappan, Washington, D. C., to USG. "As I am leaving this City for Ohio, I have received the inclosed letter from Governor Hayes, relating to the matter which I brought to your attention to-day."—ALS, DNA, RG 59, Letters of Application and Recommendation. The enclosure is a letter of May 8 from Rutherford B. Hayes, Cincinnati, to USG. "I write to recommend for appointment in the Diplomatic service of the Country Mr Eli T. Tappan of this State. He is the President of Kenyon College, . . ."—ALS, *ibid.* No appointment followed.

1872, MAY 13. Secretary of the Treasury George S. Boutwell to USG. "I transmit herewith for your signature a document removing Thomas H. Barzin, Local Appraiser of Merchandise, at the Port of Charleston, in the State of South Carolina, subject to the advice and consent of the Senate of the United States. This action is in pursuance of the authority in you vested by the 1st Section of the Act of Congress approved April 5th 1869. The officer above mentioned, has repeatedly been guilty of neglect of duty on account of intoxication."—Copy, DNA, RG 56, Letters Sent. On Aug. 3, 1869, U.S. Representative Christopher C. Bowen and U.S. Senator Frederick A. Sawyer of S. C., Charleston, had written to USG. "The undersigned respectfully recommend the suspension of Messrs. B. J. Parker and David Barrow, appraisers at this Port, and the appointment of Messrs. Thomas H. Bazin and Michael H. Collins to said offices. The name of Mr. Collins has already been presented for one of these places, strongly endorsed, and though some opposition was made to his appointment, by interested parties, we have seen no reason to withdraw our approval. These gentlemen are as good candidates as we can present for the places. Either is much more competent than Mr. Barrow, and Mr. Parker is a person whose relations to the Confederate government should have prevented his qualifying."—LS, *ibid.,* Appraiser of Customs Applications. On Dec. 7, USG nominated Thomas H. Bazin and Michael H. Collins as appraisers of merchandise, Charleston. After Bazin's removal, Collins was the only appraiser.

On Nov. 25, 1873, U.S. Senators John J. Patterson and Thomas J. Robertson of S. C. wrote to USG. "We respectfully recommend Honl Jas T. Greene of Charleston S. C. for the appointment of Appraiser of Merchandise for the Port of Charleston S. C. in place of M. H. Collins resigned."—LS, *ibid.* On March 24, 1874, USG nominated Alexander Lindstrom as appraiser, Charleston; on May 23, he withdrew this nomination. On May 26, USG nominated James F. Green. On March 23, 1869, Sawyer, Robertson, Bowen, and U.S. Representative B. Frank Whittemore of S. C. had petitioned USG to select Lindstrom for a consulship in Germany.—DS, *ibid.*, RG 59, Letters of Application and Recommendation.

1872, MAY 13.   J. D. B. Cook, Lincoln, Calif., to USG. "Trusting that you will pardon the liberty I now take in addressing a letter to you, but desireing to see you get the Nomination at the Philadelphia convention, and to be our President for another four years, which I trust you will, for I think the man that accomplished so much during War, is able to accomplish more in peace, I am induced to write to you and enclose a fiew articles cut from some of our California Republican Newspapers, so that you can see the feeling of the Republicans here upon the appointment of Thos B. Shannon to the Collectorship at at San Francisco. . . ."—ALS, DNA, RG 56, Collector of Customs Applications. The enclosures are *ibid.* On May 1, USG had nominated Thomas B. Shannon as collector of customs, San Francisco. On July 5, 1876, U.S. Senator Aaron A. Sargent and U.S. Representative Horace F. Page of Calif. wrote to USG recommending Shannon's reappointment.—LS, *ibid.* On July 11, USG renominated Shannon.

On Dec. 9, 1869, James Genning, San Francisco, had written to USG. "Being informed that General Miller Collector of this Port is at Washington, endevoring, to get appointed to the same office another term, I beg to inform you that. by removeing him and Thos B. Shannon, who is Surveyor of the port, the Government will be the gainer of over one Million of Dollars, which will help to pay, our national debt   this money is taken from the Government by these men and the men they have employed, on the ships and on the Wharfs.   they are smuggling the goods on the steamers from China, Japan from the Isthmus, and also from Alaska and there is no way to get rid of this evil, but ~~to not~~ give Miller or Shannon ~~an~~ no appointment, and by this means you break the ring of thieves, that are engaged in this scheme   some of the Members of Congress &c who have their sons under Millir and Shannon will no doubt urge thier rea appointment   to show you I am Correct I send you the statements and remarks that have been passed here lately, and Knowing you are in favour of redeeming our Country and get it out of debt I Consider it my duty as a Citizen to inform you of this fact. . . . P. S. No matter who you appoint to the Positions of Collector & Surveyor It will Change the evil & break up the Ring."—ALS, *ibid.* The enclosed clippings are *ibid.* On Jan. 26, 1870, John F. Miller, Washington, D. C., wrote to USG. "Having been intimately acquainted and officially associated with Hon Thomas B. Shannon, Surveyor of Customs at San Francisco Cal. for the past four years I beg leave to state to your Excellency, that I have always found him honest faithful and intellegent in the discharge of the arduous duties of his office. In truth, I have never known a more competent energetic or exemplary officer. He is exceedingly popular with the best class of our citizens and is one of the leading Republicans of California. He has been true to the principles and policy of our party in all these years of strife. While many others were wavering and undecided, he was firm and earnest. In 1868 he labored with great zeal and energy for the success of our cause and contributed freely of his means to aid in carrying on that memorable campaign. His political influence is great and he is an ardent supporter of the present administration—even enthusiastic. Although poor and having a large family dependent upon him for Support he boldly denounced the bad measures of Andrew Johnson regardless of personal consequences. No man whether in office or out of office was more outspoken in his denunciations of Johnsons policy. I mention this to show that he is a man of courage and firmness & honest in his convictions of right. His reappointment will I am sure be eminently satisfactory to all classes and factions of the Republican party in California. For this and other reasons I earnestly hope your Excellency may decide to reappoint Mr Shannon for another term of four years."—ALS, *ibid.* On March 20, 1869, Thomas D. Johns had written to USG requesting appointment as collector of customs, San Francisco.—ALS, *ibid.* In Jan. 1870, U.S. Senator Cornelius Cole of Calif. wrote to USG. "I recommend the Hon. Chansellor Hartson of Napa, California, for Collector of Customs, at San Francisco, California—He is a good lawyer, a good business man, a good friend of true Republicanism & free from all 'entangling alliances.'"—ALS, *ibid.* See *PUSG*, 19, 503–4; *ibid.*, 20, 373.

1872, MAY 15.   Governor Ridgley C. Powers of Miss. to USG. "Learning that an effort is being made to secure the removal from office of Mr. J. C. Jacobson U. S. District Atty for the Southern Dist of Miss. I desire respectfully to protest against such action being taken. From my own personal observation, I kow Mr Jacobson has been an earnest, industrious and faithful officer. The vigor he has exhibited and the promptness with which he has acted in prosecuting Ku Klux has been of great service to me in protecting the lives and property of many citizens within his District. His removal at this time would be construed by the Klans as an abandonment on the part of the Government of vigorous prosecutions. A large number of cases with which he is familiar, are now pending in the Dist. Court, and, in my opinion, the Government would lose by turning thim over to a new appointee. I have no knowledge of the character of the charges preferred against Mr. Jacobson nor do I know by whom they have been presented. I believe him to be a faithful and valuable officer, and until he is fairly convicted of some offence, I trust you will sustain him."—ALS, DNA, RG 60, Records Relating to Appointments. On May 21, U.S. Senator James L. Alcorn of Miss. wrote to USG. "I have the honor to herewith enclose a letter directed to my care by Governor Powers of Mississippi with the request that I should present the same,   The statements made in regard to the fitness of Jacobson for his place I fully endorse. And I will add in addition the fact, that I am in receipt of a letter from Jacobson himself,   he state the fact to be, that although he advertised for the prosecution of Claims against the Governmt he has not in truth taken a single case and will not do so. I trust Mr President, that you may consider the continuance of Mr Jacobson in his office proper, under the circumstances surrounding his case, & that he may not be removed."—ALS, *ibid.* On May 7, Benjamin H. Bristow, solicitor gen. and

act. attorney gen., had written to U.S. Senator Adelbert Ames of Miss. "In view
of certain information which has come to the knowledge of the President
touching the conduct of the Attorney of the United States for the Southern
District of Mississippi, he thinks it desirable that a change should be made in
that office. I will be pleased to have you call or to hear from you, in reference
to the appointment of a suitable person for that position. I have addressed a
similar letter to Senator Alcorn."—Copy, *ibid.*, Letters Sent to Executive
Officers. On May 15, S. Jones, Jackson, Miss., wrote to Ames. "On receipt of
information that there is on hand a Progick to remove, E. P. Jacobson from his
position as U. S. District Attorney. I hasan to trespas upon your time, for the
following reasons. We are about entering a campain this fall for the Presidency
and Members of Congress, which canvas will be very clost at best. In my
judgement his removal will lose the State to Grant,   When he commenced the
duties of his office we had nothing but insobordination and defiance of law,
now from his vigerous prosicution it has decreased Since the last term of the
U. S. court to all most nothing which goes lorgley to his credit, and Should he
he removed the K K K would take it as a disapproval of his corse in said prosicution,   Therefore it is to us in this State all important, that he be retained
untill after the Eliction or So long as he desiers to *keep it.* . . ."—ALS, Smith
College, Northampton, Mass. See *PUSG,* 19, 430–32; *SED,* 42-2-41, part 11,
pp. 53–60; William C. Harris, *The Day of the Carpetbagger: Republican Reconstruction in Mississippi* (Baton Rouge, 1979), pp. 404–5, 718.

On April 16, 1873, E. Philip Jacobson, U.S. attorney, Jackson, wrote to
USG. "My recent resignation of the Office of U. S. Attorney will render the appointment of a successor to me necessary. Of all the applicants for the Office I
consider Mr. Felix Brannigan as most entitled to your consideration. He is my
present Assistant, by appointment of the Attorney General, and fully familiar
with the duties and the business of the Office. He has been my assistant for a
year and a half. He served in the Union army during the late war, and I am able,
from personal observation, to testify to his gallantry. Mr. Brannigan has enjoyed the confidence of the Government ever since in various official situations
and is well and favorably known to the Solicitor of the Treasury and the Comp-
troller."—ALS, DNA, RG 60, Records Relating to Appointments. Related papers are *ibid.* On April 21, Judge Robert A. Hill, U.S. District Court, Miss.,
Oxford, wrote to USG recommending Arthur R. Yerger.—ALS, *ibid.* On the
same day, Charles T. Clint, Jackson, wrote to USG requesting appointment.—
ALS, *ibid.* On Dec. 2, USG nominated Felix Brannigan as U.S. attorney,
Southern District, Miss.

1872, MAY 15.   C. S. Winstead, collector of Internal Revenue, Greensboro,
N. C., to USG. "If the Judicial bill, now pending before the Senate, becomes a
law, I know of no one better suited, or who will make a more efficient District
Attorney, than Hon. A W Tourgee, now one of our Circuit Judges for the
State, and I would therefor most respectfully recommend his appointment."—
ALS, Chautauqua County Historical Society, Westfield, N. Y. In an undated
letter, Judge Albion W. Tourgee, N. C. Superior Court, Greensboro, wrote to

USG. "I have the honor to be an applicant for appointment as District Attorney for the Western District of North Carolina. As regards my fitness for this position I beg to refer you to the accompanying letters of prominent Republicans and petitions of the citizens of several counties of the District recommending my appointment. I also enclose petitions from two counties opposing my appointment on the ground that the subscribers desire that I should remain in my present position. So far as I am aware, the only objection against my appointment is that urged by Senator Pool in the letter enclosed, to wit: That I am a resident of the same city with Hon. Robt P Dick whom he presumes will be appointed Judge of said District. Whether Judge Dick shall be so appointed or not, I would respectfully submit whether the neighbor-ship of so good a man, should of itself absolutely disqualify one for the position of District Attorney. Hoping that my application may receive such consideration as it may deserve, . . ."—ALS, DNA, RG 60, Records Relating to Appointments. Related papers are *ibid.* On June 7, USG nominated Robert P. Dick as judge, Western District, N. C.

On June 4, U.S. Senator John Pool of N. C. wrote to USG. "I beg leave most respectfully to recommend the appointment of Virgil S. Lusk, of Asheville, N. C. as District Attorney for the Western Judicial District of North Carolina. Mr Lusk has been acting as Assistant District Attorney, for some time, & has given great satisfaction by his energy & ability. He is a gentleman of most unexceptionable character, & his appointment is recommended by many of the most eminent & worthy lawyers of the State, whose letters & petitions I inclose herewith."—ALS, *ibid.* On June 7, USG nominated Virgil S. Lusk as U.S. attorney, Western District, N. C. On June 27, 1876, Lusk, Asheville, wrote to USG accepting recommission.—LS, *ibid.*, Letters from the President. See Gordon McKinney, ed., "The Klan in the Southern Mountains: The Lusk-Shotwell Controversy," *Appalachian Journal*, 8, 2 (Winter, 1981), 89–104.

1872, MAY 16. USG endorsement. "Will the Sec of the Treas. please see Mr. Colgate, bearer of this, and hear his argument against the decission that 'borrowed money is taxable capital.'"—AES, DNA, RG 56, Letters from the President. Written on a letter of May 10 from Levi P. Morton, New York City, to USG. "Will you allow me to present Clinton G. Colgate, Esq; who has been authorized by a vote of the New York Stock Exchange to request in its behalf a modification of the rule taxing borrowed money as capital. Mr Colgate desires to make some statement of facts to you personally with reference to the petition of the New York Stock Exchange on this subject, and I shall be gratified if you can give him a hearing—"—LS, *ibid.* On Feb. 14, 1873, Clinton G. Colgate testified before the Ways and Means Committee concerning his lobbying for the New York Stock Exchange and meetings with USG and Secretary of the Treasury George S. Boutwell.—*HMD*, 42-3-98.

1872, MAY 16. Erastus C. Gaffield, Montreal, to USG. "The Distillery run by Mr Oscar King corner of Kent & Division Avenues Brooklyn NewYork, is now and has been during the last three years conducted in violation of act of

July 20. 1868. In consequence of which violation a sum equal to $1200.00 pr
diem has been lost to the Government. I have reason for doubting the integrity
of certain parties detailed to investigate the matter in 1870. There is one
Officer however connected with the Customs department whom I know to be
above reproach and in whom I have reasons to believe the Govt may safely
place the matter. To him I will give such positive evidence as cannot fail to
secure a conviction, provided he is permitted to assume complete control of the
case. That gentleman is Norman W Bingham of Boston   I take the liberty of
addressing you privately hoping this letter may come under your special notice"—ALS, DNA, RG 56, Letters Received. On Feb. 21, a case against Oscar
King had been settled for $9,500 in taxes plus costs.—*Ibid.* On March 2, 1869,
Thomas Russell, collector of customs, Boston, had written to USG. "Learning, that N W. Bingham Esqr is a candidate for the office of Commissioner of
Customs, I take pleasure in stating, that in my official intercourse with him as
Special Agent of the Treasury, I have had occasion to admire his integrity, his
skill, his energy, intelligence and fidelity. His appointment would be a severe
blow to smuggling, and a benefit to the revenue."—ALS, *ibid.*, Appointment
Div., Letters Received. Related papers are *ibid.* Norman W. Bingham remained
a special agent, Treasury Dept.

1872, MAY 17.   USG endorsement. "Let special attention be called to this ap-
plication after assignment of the present graduating class at West Point."—
AES, DNA, RG 94, ACP, 2694 1873. Written on a letter of May 15 from
U.S. Senators Simon Cameron and John Scott of Pa. to USG. "We most re-
spectfully request that you confer upon Harry C. Johnson, Son of Henry
C. Johnson, of Meadville, Pennsylvania, an appointment as a Lieutenant of
Cavalry, Artillery, or Infantry in the Army of the United States. This young
Gentleman is now twenty-two years of age, is cultivated and refined, and seeks
the position in the military service of his country as a matter of taste. His
Father is a Gentleman of prominence and great influence in the Republican
party of Pennsylvania, and enjoys an enviable reputation as a citizen of that
State. . . ."—LS, *ibid.* On Dec. 2, USG nominated Harry C. Johnson as 2nd lt.,
2nd Inf., to date from July 27.

1872, MAY 17.   Pinkey Hall, Salisbury, N. C., to USG. "I would most respectfully make application for the position as keeper of Soldiers' Cemetery at
the above mentioned place. All the facts have been forwarded to Mr John Poole
to whom with Senator Abbot, Representative Cobb, Gov Holden, I can refer
you for recommendation. My name has been forwarded three different times
and I respectfully submit myself as an applicant for the position. The present
keeper is making death-blows to my people."—ALS, DNA, RG 94, Applications for Positions in War Dept. See *SED,* 43-2-28, 56–57.

1872, MAY 21.   To House of Representatives. "In answer to the resolution of
the House of Representatives of the 14th inst. requesting information in regard to commerce between the U. S. and certain British Colonial possessions,

I transmit a report from the Secretary of State, and the documents by which it was accompanied."—Copies, DNA, RG 130, Messages to Congress; *ibid.*, RG 59, Reports to the President and Congress. On the same day, Secretary of State Hamilton Fish had written to USG transmitting correspondence related to commerce with Australia and New Zealand and the establishment of a U.S. naval station in the Pacific.—Copy, *ibid.* HED, 42-2-319. On May 28, USG again wrote to the House transmitting a report from Postmaster Gen. John A. J. Creswell concerning mail contracts with Australia and New Zealand.— Copy, DNA, RG 130, Messages to Congress. HED, 42-2-319, part 2.

[*1872, May 22*].   Speech. "I am thankful to you for your kindness, and also to all the members of your profession. Of course I know nothing of homeopathy, but I recognize the fact that we may learn something in the future, and may find something that is better than that we had in the past. I return thanks for this visit."—*Washington Evening Star*, May 22, 1872. USG spoke at the White House to delegates attending a homeopathic convention.

1872, MAY 22.   Secretary of the Navy George M. Robeson to USG. "I return herewith the Bill for the relief of H. C. Christopher, G. W. Beard C. A. Uber, Edward Stiles and N. H. Lamdin and have the honor to state that I know of no reasons why this Bill should not receive your approval."—LS, NHi. On May 23, USG signed the bill assigning these men the rank of 2nd asst. engineer in the navy. See *CG*, 42–2, 1898; *U.S. Statutes at Large*, XVII, 662–63.

1872, MAY 23.   To Senate. "I have the honor to transmit herewith, in answer to the resolution of the Senate of March 12th. requesting to be informed of 'the amount of money expended by the government of the United States during the last three years for telegraphing by Ocean cables,' reports from the different departments of the government, to which the resolution was referred."—DS, DNA, RG 46, Presidential Messages. *SED*, 42-2-82.

1872, MAY 23.   John Callanan, Brooklyn, to USG. "I mailed a memorial to you on the 16th of April last   up to this date I got no reply   I also mailed a note to you on the 27th ult calling your attention to the memorial of the 16th ult up to this date I *got no reply*   Fearing the former memorial may be mislaid I send a Copy   This matter is of Considerable importance to me   The interest of the Commonwealth of this Republic is very seriously Concerned in the Charracter and Conduct of the men appointed to fill the important offices in the government and the honest and faithful discharge of their duties to the Citizens by those men   It is therefore that I ask your Ecellency to order this inquirie   no PAUPER politicians should be appointed as heads of departments   Men of this Class defy a like public opinion and the Civil laws of the Country and Cover themselves under their official Cloaks   If suid in a Court of law and Judgment is had against them they know well the sherriff Can get nothing for the order he holds against them as outside of their offices they stand on their pauper positions   Waiting a reply . . ."—ALS, DNA, RG 60, Letters from the

President. Enclosed is another letter dated May 23 from Callanan to USG. "As a Citizen of this Republic I deem it my duty to Call your Excellencys attention to the Conduct of Mr Sharp the united states marshal in New york. I ask your Excellency to order a sworn inquirie into the manner and System adopted by this Mr Sharp and his deputy to cover their FRAUDS and THEFTS in the managment of the duties of the very important office you have intrusted him with For several weeks Mr Sharp as united states marshal had possession of the property of the Bankrupt who was proprietor of the metropolitan Hotel on Broadway New york City   Mr Sharp as such marshal offered those goods for sale by auction   I attended that sale and bought several lots as per Catologue and paid the required deposit   I paid my bill and took away one load of the goods   I returned for a nother load of the goods   Mr Sharps deputy would not allow me to take them and threatened me with violence if I attempted to remove the goods   I called on Mr Sharp at his office and stated to him what his deputy did   Mr Sharp said he would ~~he~~ see the auctioneer about those goods that evning and asked me to Call on him the next day   I did Call on him as requested   he said he had not time to see the auctioner and requested me to Call the next day   I did Call and receivd a similar answer each day till the time for removing the goods expired   on this last day I Called and waited to see Mr Sharp   he sliped out of his office and went to the metropolitan Hotel I followed him and saw him inside   I attempted to enter the Hotel   His deputy threatened to shoot me if I did so   I heard and belive that Mr Sharp sold my goods and *converted* the *proceeds to his own use* as well as the *money* I *paid for them*   The Goods are value to me for the sum of five hundred and fortyfive Dollers   I also bought goods from Mr Sharp at the Park avenue Hotel a good part of which were stolen while in the Charge of his deputiees   I hope your Excellency will order this inquirie to be made as my Case will appear more fully before such a Court,   By doing so your Excellency will show the heads of departments appointed by you that they cannot ROB *or* DEFRAUD the Citizens with impunity Under Cover of their official positions"—ALS, *ibid.* On May 24, 1876, Callanan, New York City, testified before a congressional committee concerning his grievance against George H. Sharpe, U.S. marshal, Southern District, N. Y.—*HRC*, 44-1-800, 42–43.

1872, MAY 25.   William S. Godbe, Salt Lake City, to USG. "The sutlership at Beaver, Beaver Co: in this Territory is I learn in ~~in~~ your bestowal,   If you will make the appointment in my favor, believe me your kindness will be appreciated and nothing shall be left undone on my part to fill the position in a way that will in every respect prove creditable and satisfactory. . . ."—ALS, DNA, RG 94, Applications for Positions in War Dept. See *DAB*, IV, 337–38.

1872, MAY 27.   Horace Porter to Secretary of the Navy George M. Robeson. "The President directs me to say that, the several departments of the government will be closed on the 30th. inst. in order to enable the employees of the government to participate, in connection with the Grand Army of the Republic, in the decoration of the graves of the soldiers who fell during the rebellion"—LS, DNA, RG 45, Letters Received from the President. On the same day, Porter sent an identical letter to other cabinet members and heads of depts. On May 30, USG attended ceremonies at Arlington Cemetery.

1872, MAY 28.   USG note. "Endorse on Capt. Thos. H. Carpenter's applicatio[n] for army apt. to be aptd. in July unless reason of record in the War Dept. exist against such apt."—AN, DNA, RG 94, ACP, 463 1871. On May 15, Thomas H. Carpenter, Washington, D. C., had written to USG. "Believing myself entitled to a share of the patronage of your administration, having served through the whole of the late War as a Captain in the 17th U. S. Infantry and relying on my Military record as such, I respectfully ask to be commissioned to any vacancy now existing in the Army. Having had great opportunities and believing myself a thorough horseman, should prefer the Cavalry arm of the service."—ALS, *ibid.* On Aug. 16, Carpenter, Kittanning, Pa., wrote to AG Edward D. Townsend. "The President having on the 25th of May last, ordered my appointment to such vacancy as might exist on the first of July past—Provided there was no reason shown by the War Dept. why such appoinmtment should not be made. Having your own admission that my 'Military reccord was without a blemish,' I am at loss to know why this appointment has not been made. The President having assured me at his residence on the 10th of July, that it would be forthcoming on or by the 15th of said month Any information on the subject would be thankfully received."—ALS, *ibid.* Related papers are *ibid.* No appointment followed. See *SRC*, 46-3-770.

1872, MAY 28.   To House of Representatives. "In answer to the resolution of the House of Representatives of the 7th instant requesting copies of correspondence in regard to an Extradition Treaty with Belgium I transmit a report from the Secretary of State and the documents by which it was accompanied."—Copies, DNA, RG 130, Messages to Congress; *ibid.*, RG 59, Reports to the President and Congress. *HED*, 42-2-323. On the same day, Secretary of State Hamilton Fish had written to USG transmitting materials.—Copy, DNA, RG 59, Reports to the President and Congress.

1872, MAY 28.   Benjamin H. Bristow, solicitor gen. and act. attorney gen., to USG. "I have the honor to acknowledge the receipt of a note from General Porter, calling my attention by your direction, to the resolution of the Senate of the Senate of January 24. 1872, asking for information relative to the amount of the receipts and expenditures of the Government since March 4, 1869, and requesting that my reply be furnished with as little delay as possible. . . . under the act to establish the Department of Justice, approved June 22d 1870, there has necessarily been considerable increase both in the number of persons employed and of the expenses incurred in this Department. That act having cut off the power of the Department to employ special counsel and pay fees, and devolved upon this Department the duty of furnishing and compensating such counsel whenever requested, a large amount of expense heretofore falling on other Departments has now been imposed on this and is payable out of its ordinary appropriations."—Copy, DNA, RG 60, Letters Sent to Executive Officers. On Jan. 24, U.S. Senator Roscoe Conkling of N. Y. had introduced a resolution requesting information on government expenditures and losses.—D, *ibid.,* RG 59, Miscellaneous Letters; *CG,* 42–2, 546. USG never officially answered this resolution. On Jan. 20, a correspondent had reported from Washington, D. C. ". . . It has become a common thing for politicians and self-styled 'Reformers' to declare that this is the worst period that the civil service ever saw; that it has steadily gone on from bad to worse for the past three years; and that embezzlements and defalcations are more frequent now than ever before. They never stop to inquire into the facts, . . ."—*New York Times,* Jan. 22, 1872.

1872, MAY 28.   U.S. Representative Peter M. Dox of Ala. to USG. "In common with others who have had an opportunity of judging of it's national importance, I have taken the greatest interest in the projected Water Communication between the Atlantic & the Mississippi which contemplates utilizing the Tennessee & Coosa Rivers, and finding it's Eastern terminus at Brunswick, or Savannah, in Georgia. . . . The Rail Road combinations of the Country, with the short sightedness so common to cupidity, will, no doubt, oppose this great national enterprize; but, I cannot doubt that, sooner or later, the people of the West will appreciate the project as furnishing not only the readiest, but their *only* relief from the monstrous tribute which is now exacted by rail road monopolies, in the interest of greedy capitalists. I have as little doubt, that you already appreciate the magnitude & the national importance of the work. Adding, therefore, my own testimony to that of others in it's behalf, I invoke for it, so far as can be consistently given, your friendly interposition."—ALS, Duke University, Durham, N. C. On May 31, Horace Porter wrote to Secretary of War William W. Belknap. "The President directs me to enquire whether you have yet received from the Chief of Engineers the report in regard to the construction of a canal to connect certain rivers in Georgia. If received, the President requests that it may be sent to him as soon as possible, in order that he may forward it to Congress."—Copy, DLC-USG, II, 1. See *HMD,* 42-2-41; *HED,* 42-3-1, part 2, II, 59–60, 509–35; *SMD,* 43-1-73.

1872, MAY 29.   USG endorsement. "Refered to the Atty. Gn. Application to be regarded as for Territorial Judgship."—AES, DNA, RG 60, Records Relating to Appointments. Written on a letter of the same day from U.S. Representative Alfred C. Harmer of Pa. to USG urging appointment of his friend Henry W. Bach "in New Mexico, or some Western Territory" as "all important to the Success of the republican cause in my District."—ALS, *ibid.* Related papers are *ibid.* No appointment followed.

1872, MAY 29.   Governor Preston H. Leslie of Ky. to USG requesting extradition of Anderson Branch from Canada.—ALS, DNA, RG 59, Miscellaneous Letters. Leslie enclosed an indictment from the Grand Jury of Woodford County, Ky. ". . . The said Anderson Branch on the 2nd day of October 1871, in the County aforesaid did wilfully feloniously and of his malice aforethought Kill and Murder Michael Lindsey (colored) . . ."—Copy, *ibid.* A related affidavit is *ibid.* On June 5, USG issued a proclamation authorizing W. S. Worsham to return Branch from Canada to Ky.—Copy, *ibid.,* General Records.

1872, MAY 30.   U.S. Representative John W. Killinger of Pa. to USG. "Dr Parry, & his father Hon Edward Owen Parry, of Pottsville, Pa, are anxious to have yr favorable decision upon the application for the Doctors restoration. There are many similar cases of restoration, though not one of more merit. Begging yr attention to the papers on file before Congress adjourns, . . ."—ALS, DNA, RG 94, ACP, P874 CB 1865. On May 13, Secretary of War William W. Belknap had written to USG concerning Henry C. Parry.— LS (press), *ibid.* On March 20, 1869, Edward O. Parry, Pottsville, Pa., had written to Secretary of War John A. Rawlins asking him to assist his son.— ALS, *ibid.,* Letters Received, 116R 1869. Papers authorizing leave for Parry in 1868 on account of "recurrent attacks of neuralgia attended with nervous prostration" are *ibid.,* 166P 1868.

On Dec. 9, 1873, Nathan D. Morgan, Brooklyn, wrote to USG requesting a review of his friend Parry's case.—ALS, *ibid.,* ACP, P874 CB 1865. On June 20, 1874, Belknap wrote to USG. "I have again examined the case of Henry C. Parry M. D. late Assistant Surgeon U. S. A. The status of the officer appears to be that of a man who is entirely out of the service, and as much a citizen as though he had never been in the army. Under these circumstances he can only be restored to a position in the army by appointment of the President and confirmation by the Senate; and I find no good or sufficient reason to recommend him for reappointment."—LS (press), *ibid.*

On Feb. 15, 1877, Killinger wrote to Secretary of War James D. Cameron about Parry.—ALS, *ibid.* On Feb. 20, AG Edward D. Townsend endorsed papers to Cameron. "H. C. Parry, late Ass't Surgeon U. S. A. was tried by Court Martial in Oct. 1868, and sentenced to be Cashiered. . . . A number of appeals have been made to the President for his re instatement, upon the claim, strongly urged, that the Board was in error in its conclusion, and that the disability *was* incident to Service. The claim of Dr. Parry was examined by the Secretary of War in 1874, by direction of the President, and the Secretary of War reported that the claimant was lawfully out of the service, and a civilian, and therefore could not be reinstated by Executive action, and that he found 'no good or and sufficient reason to recommend him for reappointment.'. . ."— AES, *ibid.* For a favorable assessment of Parry's case, see *HRC,* 43-2-130.

1872, MAY 30.   Capt. Charles W. Thomas, Washington, D. C., to USG. "On the 23rd5th of January last I tendered my resignation to take effect May 1. 1872, with the verbal assurance from the Hon. Secretary of War that if, by that time, I furnished a satisfactory explanation with regard to the discrepancy which existed in my accounts it would be returned to me—Within the time specified I furnished an explanation which I trusted would be satisfactory—I understand that it has not been so considered by the Quartermaster

General and that he has advised that my resignation take effect from the thirty first of May, the time to which it was so kindly extended by yourself—I now most respectfully ask that my resignation be cancelled and returned to me or at least extended until you can exaime the case yourself, after the adjournment of Congress, and that I may be allowed to make such further explanations as may be required by the Quartermaster General   In making this request I do not think that I am asking more than I am entitled to after seventeen years faithful service in the Army, eleven of which have been spent in the Quartermaster's Department, and disbursing upwards of twenty one millions of dollars. In conclusion I have to remark that I have deposited in the Treasury the full amount charged against me on account of the errors made in my accounts and that I am not indebted to the United Stat[es] in any sum whatever—"— ALS, DNA, RG 94, ACP, 139 1871. Charles Thomas, retired col., q. m. dept., father of Capt. Thomas, favorably endorsed this letter.—AES (undated), *ibid.* Thomas, USMA 1855, resigned as of May 31.

1872, JUNE 1.   USG endorsement. "Respectfully refered to the Sec. of War. If Capt. Gill can be restored legally I have no objection to his restoration, or to his apt. subject to confirmation by the Senate. This is supposing of course that his record is good."—AES, DNA, RG 94, ACP, G149 CB 1870. *SRC*, 46-2-560, 47-1-3; *HRC*, 46-3-254, 47-1-57. Written on a letter of May 31 from U.S. Senator James Harlan of Iowa to USG in support of William H. Gill, who had resigned as of Dec. 16, 1870.—ALS, DNA, RG 94, ACP, G149 CB 1870. Gill was reinstated as of March 25, 1882.

1872, JUNE 1.   Albert Summerville *et al.*, Nashville, to USG. "We the Under-Signed Citsen of the Staite of Tennessee Pray Your Honrable Bordy to gave ous the A Porer to Rais A Compneay of hom gards   We Wosh the gard to Be Arm By the Govment. With Musket Soe As toe Orginyzin Grant Clubs And Labor Union in the Entres of the Republincen Party"—DS (40 signatures), DNA, RG 94, Letters Received, 2401 1872.

1872, JUNE 3.   C. Pinkham, San Francisco, to USG. "In the early days of California, a Friend of mine, buried some money on Angel Island, in San Francisco Bay,   When he came to die (which was very sudden) he described the Signs by which to find it. I went over and found some of the signs. But the main one was gone, As the Island was claimed by a man afterwards who built a little house and cleared of a few acres, choping down trees &c, When he sold out his right to the Government,   There is now about 100 Soldiers stationed on the Island under Gen Wilcox. And Gen. J M Schofield, is the Commander over the Pacific Coast. I spoke to them about a permit to dig and take up treasures, If I could find any, But getting no satisfactory answer, I wrote the Secretary of War with no better results. Now I wish to apply to you. . . . I am now 51 years of age, and a Preacher of the Gospel, of Jesus, Christ, to the best of my Gifts and ability, and should I find any treasures, I should spend largely for the poor, and the Education of the poor young, . . ."—ALS, DNA, RG 94, Letters Received,

1767 1872. On Feb. 19, 1873, Pinkham wrote to USG. ". . . Your answer through the Secretary of War, Caused Gen Schofield to grant me the permit to dig, but to have to run my risk of getting it away, if I found it,   But as the treasure lays near the Reverand Mr Reynolds, House, And he having procured a little Dog, so as to give the alarm, It is doubtful whether it could be moved without somebody knowing it, . . ."—ALS, *ibid.*

1872, JUNE 5.   Secretary of the Treasury George S. Boutwell to USG. "I have the honor to say that there appears to be no objection to bill H. R. 2937."— ALS, OFH. This bill authorized the transfer of appropriations between pension funds. See *U.S. Statutes at Large,* XVII, 230.

1872, JUNE 6.   William M. Graham, Adairsville, Ga., to USG. "I am now in my 59th year. At the commencement of the war in 1861, I was opposed to the rebellion, and did all in my power to prevent it. I have always been a union man. I committed no act of hostility against the U. S. government during the war, nor sympathysed with the rebels at any time   The Federal army under Genl Sherman took every thing I had & reduced me to poverty. I have had Paralysis since 63. *I have made out my claim against the Government and it is now on file in Washington City* amounting to some $1400 00 and upwards. . . ."—ALS, DNA, RG 94, Letters Received, 2509 1872.

1872, JUNE 11.   Solicitor Gen. Benjamin H. Bristow to USG. "I hand you herewith a dispatch just received from Judge Gresham of Indiana, requesting the appointment of Captain Samuel Montgomery of New Albany as Supervising Steamboat Inspector for that District. I do not know Captain Montgomery personally, and Judge Gresham is as well known to you as to myself and needs no endorsement from anyone."—LS (press), DLC–Benjamin H. Bristow.

1872, JUNE 11.   Levi P. Luckey to John W. Owen, Newtown, Va. "The President directs me to acknowledge the receipt of your letter of the 3rd inst: and to convey to you his thanks for the kind sentiments which it contains, and the offer to perpetuate the republican party and all it has secured alike to the colored and white man."—Copy, DLC–USG, II, 1.

1872, JUNE 12.   USG endorsement. "The Adjt Gn. will please refer to Gn. Sheridan with instructions (to take such measures as he deems expedient, with the force at his command, for the protection of the Citizens of Colfax Co, N. M."—AES, DNA, RG 94, Letters Received, 2360 1872. Written on a letter of May 28 from Governor Marsh Giddings of New Mexico Territory to USG. "I have the honor to inform you that for many months there has been forwarded to me complaints from Colfax County in the Northern portion of this Territory showing that their exists in that vicinity a band a band of marauding robbers, cattle thieves horse thieves, and murderers who have ever since last September, and I think before that time been committing the most outrageous murders thefts and robberies, and putting and keeping in fear of utter destruction the whole population of the County. . . . If the general government could furnish a company or even fifty men (soldiers) for 30 days to aid the civil authorities in arresting the criminals and securing the stolen property most of it within 40 miles of Cimarron as I am informed & believe, then I think with this aid the criminals could be mostly arrested and sentence of the law be executed upon them. Without such aid from the government, unmitigated calamity is likely and almost inevitably will fall upon the people of that county. The laws of this Territory seem to have been framed so as carefully to exclude any executive action whatever on the part of the Governor of the Territory, and he has not as much actual authority to meet such an emergency as has the sheriff of any county, or perhaps even a constable. . . ."—ALS, *ibid.* Related papers are *ibid.*

1872, JUNE 14.　U.S. Senator Oliver P. Morton of Ind., Indianapolis, to USG. "*Personal* . . . I am advised by General Browne the District Attorney for Indiana, and Republican candidate for Governor, that he has forwarded his resignation as U. S. District Attorney to you; and I desire to recommend for appointment in his place—Nelson Trusler of this city. Colonel Trusler is a lawyer of ability and high character, who served as Secretary of State in this state for four years, elected by the Republican party, and served in the Army for three years with distinction as Colonel of the 84th Indiana Regiment. He is an excellent man and a hard worker, and has borne his full share in every campaign for the benefit of the Republican party. I do not think a better appointment can be made and I earnestly recommend him for the position."—LS, DNA, RG 60, Records Relating to Appointments. Related papers are *ibid.* On July 18, Thomas M. Browne, Winchester, Ind., wrote to USG resigning his office.—ALS, *ibid.*, Letters from the President. Browne narrowly lost the election to Thomas A. Hendricks. On Dec. 2, USG nominated Nelson Trusler to replace Browne.

1872, JUNE 19.　Orville E. Babcock to Samuel D. Greene, Chelsea, Mass. "The President desires me to acknowledge the receipt of your letter and of the book which you were kind enough to send him for which he wishes me to convey to you his thanks. In reply to your question, he instructs me to say that he is not a mason."—Copy, DLC-USG, II, 1. Greene had written *The Broken Seal* (Boston, 1870), an anti-masonic tract about the alleged 1826 murder of William Morgan.

1872, JUNE 28.　Grenville M. Dodge, Marshall, Tex., to "General," possibly USG. "I learned today that Governer Davis had gone East—I have had an excellent opportunity to observe him in this state and I desire to say that he is a *true honest* man and has done great good in Texas—And I am confident you can rely upon him—I have never met him but once a year ago—and I write this to you knowing how difficult it must be to keep well informed of matters so far away—I write this without the Governers knowledge and dont know as you will see him　I gave 'White' position on the Pecos Division"—ALS,

CSmH. 2nd Lt. Ulysses G. White resigned as of July 31, 1873, to serve under Dodge as civil engineer on the Texas Pacific Railroad. See *PUSG*, 18, 150–51.

[*1872*], JUNE 30.   [*James V.*] Chilton, Warrenton, Va., to USG. "I am an earnest cooperator with Col Mosby in the effort of securinge the vote of the Southern Whites [f]or your election. You must emphatitcally give the South and your friends in the south some evidence of a desire for the Southern White vote. I believe you an undisputeded friend of the southern peopeopel at heart. Give some call for a preference in your favor from the Southern Whites against Horace Greeyly   Unless you do it the ~~g~~Greely Enthusiasm will prevail . . . I refer you to Col Mosby   P S. If you think it advisable you can answer this letter"—ALS (misdated 1871), NN.

1872, [*June*].   USG endorsement. "Refer to Sec of State. Leave it to the judgement of the Govr whether the parade should be interdicted."—AES (docketed June 20), DNA, RG 59, Utah Territorial Papers. Written on a letter of May 25 from Governor George L. Woods of Utah Territory to USG. "There is some reason for believing that the Mormons will undertake to bring out the Militia Organization known as the Nauvoo Legion, for Parade on the coming 4th of July as they did on the 4th of July 1871. I need not state you that it is an organization without the authority of Law, hitherto exercising its powers, without, and in defiance of the authority of the Governor of the Territory. In my Judgment, it ought not to be permitted to parade   But as I do not wish to take any Steps which might embarrass the Administration without first consulting you, I write to you for instructions. . . ."—ALS, *ibid.*

1872, JULY 1.   USG pardon. "Whereas, on the 20th day of July, 1871, in the Supreme Court of the District of Columbia, one Septimus T. Shuman was convicted of manslaughter and was sentenced to be imprisoned for two years and six months; And whereas, Doctor D. W. Bliss, C. C. Cox, and J. H. Thompson, Rev. J. P. Newman and other highly respectable citizens petition for his pardon; And whereas, Judge Humphreys, before whom he was tried, and the jurors on the case strongly recommend that his pardon may be granted: Now, therefore, be it known, that I . . . do hereby grant to the said Septimus T. Shuman a full and unconditional pardon. . . ."—Copy, DNA, RG 59, General Records. Dr. Septimus T. Shuman had been tried for the death of Henrietta Paddon, who sought his care after she had attempted an abortion. See *Washington Evening Star*, July 19, 20, 1871.

1872, JULY 3.   Horace Porter to Orville E. Babcock. "Strictly confidential . . . You are designated by the President, in connection with Hon. Wm A. Richardson and Capt. Thos O. Selfridge U. S. N. to examine the Rebel records recently purchased and compare them with the schedule. You will be prepared to certify to your report as to the character and reliability of the records and how they compare with the schedule."—LS, USG 3. On July 12, Levi P. Luckey wrote to "Genl." "The papers & records were all Examined and found to compare with the Inventory, with the single exception of a private letter of Hotze, consular agent at London, marked as No 15 on the list, & which is noted on the inventory as missing. Capt. Selfridge thinks this may have been lost when he first Examined the papers, as a gust of wind came in the room & scattered the papers all about. He supposed he gathered them all up, but as these letters are on tissue paper this one may possibly have blown out of the window—. . ."— ALS, *ibid.* On July 13, Commander Thomas O. Selfridge, Washington, D. C., wrote to "Dear General." "All the papers have been returned to the boxes, & the latter Sealed up with a seal of Mr. Luckey's—They are in every respect correct according to the Inventory, except No 15 private correspondence of Mr. Hotze rebel Agent in London, which could not be found, & no doubt was mislaid when I overhauled these papers in Canada—I expect to leave town tonight—My address is Portland Maine, and you can send me to that place the report to sign after Judge Richardson has overhauled them—The original inventory & the Thompson paper are in the large trunk near the door marked (diplomatic)."—ALS, *ibid.* For political use of these "Rebel Archives," see *New York Times,* July 20, 25, Aug. 1, 1872. See also *U.S. Statutes at Large,* XVII, 350; *O. R.* (Navy), II, iii, 16–17; James Morton Callahan, *The Diplomatic History of the Southern Confederacy* (1901; reprinted, Springfield, Mass., 1957), pp. 13–22; Dallas D. Irvine, "The Fate of Confederate Archives," *American Historical Review,* XLIV (July, 1939), 826–27; Henry Putney Beers, *Guide to the Archives of the Government of the Confederate States of America* (Washington, 1968), pp. 75–76.

1872, July 3.   William S. Young, Lockport, N. Y., to USG. "I have for some months been aware of heavy smuggling from the Frontier from 5 mile meadows below Lewistown and at Fort Schlosser, above the falls. Since I have talked with Deputy marshall Danl Tucker., Capt Flagler. Capt Ellsworth & 2 other officials at the bridge, not a team has passed my place since. I live 1½ miles west of this city, it has been usual for the team to go past quite regular about 2 o'clock a. m   I have sent a man to Chippeway as spy to get a starting point— contraband goods from Schlosser above niagara Falls & 5 mile meadows below Lewistown are the points for smugglers. I would like a *position* as *detective* and then I will try my skill ~~in trying~~ to capture. I am warmly interested in maintaining your cause and will do all I can, but the contrast between yourself & Greely, I scarcely argue with any one, as I consider him an embodyment of abstractions & his criticisms in ~~the~~ time of the late war as well as his tariff dogmas are worth but little attention; a Philanthropist to every thing & every body is nobody, and I am opposed to him & ever shall be."—ALS, DNA, RG 56, Collector of Customs Applications.

1872, July 5.   James P. Newcomb, Tex. secretary of state, to USG. "When in Washington last I presented to you an application from Willis S. Walker, asking a cadetship in West Point.—Young Walker is the son of Judge M. B. Walker who served gallantly as a volunteer officer during the war and is now on the retired list because of wounds received on the field of battle,—Judge

Walker is one of our Supreme Judges.—The applicant graduated at the Military Institute here with the first honors, and in recommending him I feel confident he will not disappoint his friends, if he receives the favor at your hands."—ALS, DNA, RG 94, Correspondence, USMA. On July 13, Moses B. Walker, Austin, wrote to USG enclosing additional recommendations. ". . . There may be some irregularity about this application, but I cannot ask either of our Congressmen to nominate my Son, on account of political difer- ences, between us. I have not had a Son, or brother educated at the point. I am retired from active service—on account of wounds received at the Battle of Chickamauga Sept 20th, 63 . . ."—ALS, *ibid.* No appointment followed. Walker had served as col., 31st Ohio.

1872, JULY 6.   U.S. Representative John B. Hawley of Ill., Rock Island, to USG. "I have the honor to recomend for appointment 'at large' as a cadet to West Point, Master Frank Stevens of Dixon Illinois. He is a very worthy young man and I believe well fitted for the place. His Father was a soldier in our Army, was wounded at Shilo and died a few days thereafter."—ALS, DNA, RG 94, Correspondence, USMA. Related papers are *ibid.* No appointment followed. See *Illinois State Journal*, Oct. 17, 1939.

1872, JULY 8.   "John Ward," Benicia, Calif., to USG. "As the time is Approch- ing for the next Presidential election I would respectfully call your attention to matters at Benicia Arsenal   There is a large appropriation granted for for this Arsenal and there will be a great many men employed at the works,   those men will be influenced to vote against you at the next election if you dont have Col McAlister removed from this place   he is over five years in command here and that is one year over his term   it is true that Benicia is a small place but under present circumstances every vote will be wanted that can be obtained. both McAlister and his Superintendant are opposed to your re-elecction"— AL, DNA, RG 156, Letters Received. On Aug. 1, Maj. Julian McAllister, Beni- cia Arsenal, endorsed this letter. ". . . The letter sent to the President is, in re- ality, anonimously written, and the falsity of the implications it contains is proved by the fact that Mr John. C. Stone, the master workman, or as he is called in the letter the superintendent at this arsenal, is a delegate from this town to the Gant [Re]publican convention of the county. [E]very commanding officer of a post, [w]ho deals with contractors and discharges incompetent workmen is subject [to] similar anonimous mis-representations."—ES, *ibid.*

1872, JULY 9.   George A. Black, secretary, Utah Territory, to USG. "I have the honor to enclose herewith letters which were published in the 'Salt Lake Herald' of 7th inst., and to say to you that they furnished me the first informa- tion I had of the existence of any such Mining Bureau. My name was used without my sanction or knowledge, and I take this means of informing you that I am not now, *and never have been*, in any way connected with it."—ALS, DNA, RG 59, Utah Territorial Papers; (press) Utah Archives, Salt Lake City. The enclosures include a printed letter dated May 18 from Governor George L.

Woods of Utah Territory to the *Times* (London) representing Black as secretary and himself "as manager of the Utah branch of the Mining Bureau of the Pacific Coast, established in California by Colonel J. Berton, Vice-Consul of France at Sacramento, . . ."—DNA, RG 59, Utah Territorial Papers; *Times* (London), June 12, 1872. On Aug. 29, Secretary of State Hamilton Fish wrote in his diary. "President signs a Warrant for payment to Govr Woods of Utah of $498 50 of secret service money—he having summoned him to Washn in reference to some statement in relation to attempts to influence the Sale of Mining lands, in Europe &c"—DLC-Hamilton Fish.

1872, JULY 10. Agustin Aspiazu, La Paz, to USG. "I make it my duty to transmit to your Excellency a copy of my work entitled 'Dogmas of International Law.' . . ."—ALS (in Spanish), DNA, RG 59, Miscellaneous Letters; translation, *ibid.* See *Dogmas del Derecho Internacional* (New York, 1872).

1872, JULY 10. C. D. Nicholas, Philip Joseph *et al.*, Mobile, to USG. "The people of Mobile instructed their Delegate to Philadelphia, that on his return from the Convention, he should call on your Excellancy and the Honorable Secretary of the Treasury, and complain, that, Republican Conventions and primary meetings are interfered with, and broken up in riots; their officers murderously assaulted and the people menaced by a regularly organized mob, of Federal office holders and their subordinates in this City. Owing to your absence, and that of the Honorable Secretary of the Treasury, the Representative of the Republicans of this District and Representatives from other parts of the State, were not afforded the opportunity to lay these matters plainly before you. The Representative Colored men, impelled by a sense of indignation over the wrong, injustice and outrages continually perpetrated upon the people;— by the agents of the Government, assembled in mass Convention from all parts of this County, and delegated the undersigned to address this communication to your Excellancy; demanding that the Administration take such steps as will restrain the present Collector of the port, Post Master, Collector of Internal Revenue, Assessor of Internal Revenue, U. S. Appraiser of Merchandise, their Deputies and Subordinates, in their unholy work of Terrorism in this City and County. . . ."—DS (8 signatures), DNA, RG 56, Letters Received. A related clipping is *ibid.* On July 31, John T. Foster, collector of Internal Revenue, Mobile, wrote to USG. ". . . In reply to the above charge of terrorism let me state the truth that I nor any Deputy of mine have even been present at any meeting, political or otherwise, where a riot occurred. I have not, nor has any subordinate of mine, aided in getting up any riot either directly or indirectly. And that I have never seen any spirit of strife and insubordination manifest itself in any Republican meeting in Mobile except that manifested by Philip Joseph himself. . . . In my humble judgement there are no men in this community who have wrought so hard to destroy the true (Grant) Republican party as Philip Joseph & Willard Warner. And it is believed by a great number of true Republicans here that this whole tissue of falsehoods has been gotten up and placed in form, by these two men. I have no confidence in them at all, politically or otherwise. The other names attached to this address, besides Philip Joseph, I do not know, personally. This address to you says; 'in conclusion that positions have been tendered to prominent and influential Republicans of this county, by the officials herein complained of, and in every instance they have declined to accept the offices.' Well so far as my Knowledge & belief goes, this last is a monstrous lie. . . ."—ALS, *ibid.* Joseph edited newspapers in Ala. and served as delegate to the 1868 and 1872 Republican national conventions.

In an undated petition, John Elliott, president, and George E. Yarrington, vice president, Republican Central Council, wrote to USG. "Your Petitioners, citizens and Republicans of the City and County of Mobile, would respectfully show unto your Excellency that the interests of the Republican Party demands the revision of appointment to Federal Offices in Mobile County. The present incumbents in said Offices have in every instance used the patronage and influence acquired by them from their positions, to the great detriment of the Republican party. . . . The course of action then pursued by these men, has produced the following results: First. The defeat of five Republicans for the Legislature from Mobile County. Second. The defeat of a Republican for the United States Senate from Alabama. Third. The driving from our midst of a great number of good true and capable Republicans, by the appointment of Democrats to subordinates Federal positions. Fourth. A general despair among colored men of Republican success, and an idea among them that no white man is to be trusted. From these facts and deductions your petitioners are forced to the conclusion that the interests of the Republican party demands a revision of Federal appointments in Mobile County. Wherefore they pray that your Excellency will, in accordance with the powers vested in you by the Constitution, remove from Office all the Federal appointees in Mobile County with the Exception of Dr. Moore, Receiver of U. S. Land Office, Mr. C. T. Stearns, Register U. S. Land Office and Dr. Foster Collector of Internal Revenue for the first District of Alabama, and they further pray that you will cause to be appointed in their places, good and true Republicans, who will use their positions for the interests and advancement of the party."—DS, *ibid.*, Appraiser of Customs Applications. See *PUSG*, 21, 18.

1872, July 15.   Albert S. Rosenbaum, New York City, to USG. "The Undersigned, engaged in the Tobacco trade in San Francisco since 1850—an adherent to the party you represent, has been placed in a very precarious position by the ruling of Comm. Douglass. A very large amount of manufactured Tobacco shipped from Eastern bonded warehouses and factories during the month of May arrived in San Francisco after June 6th and were duly bonded, which are now tied up,   we are unable to get possession of this our property unless we pay 12¢ more Tax than the Law requires. This ruling of your Commissioner will without a doubt create a great many enemies to the party. I flatter myself to have worked for you as much as any man in the U. S. I got up Labels on Tobacco and on Cigars in Havana and the U St. /: Gen. Grant :/ and distributed them all over the Union, directly after my interview at Willards Hotel in Washington with you, where I was introduced to you by Senator Conness. It cannot be equity for the Pacific States to pay 32¢ pr pound on Tobacco on account of the distance they live in, whilst on the Antlantic they pay but 20¢ pr pound. *The intent of the ta[x] could not bear such.* Your answer will be no [d]oubt /: if your eyes meets this :/ this is not my function, nevertheless, all Merchants on the Pacific look upon you as the Head of the Executive Department, to have at least, an opinion or decision of Atty Gen. Williams in regard to this, to us so vital question, pronounced. Awaiting anxiously that some step of relief may be taken in this matter . . ."—ALS, DNA, RG 56, Letters Received. Letters from Watson Van Benthuysen, New Orleans, to USG criticizing the tobacco ruling are *ibid.* For Rosenbaum, see *New York Times*, Feb. 18, 1894.

On March 20, a "committee of colored men who labor in the Virginia tobacco factories" had presented USG with a petition "signed by twenty-five hundred working men in the tobacco manufactories of Richmond, Petersburg and other Virginia cities, favoring a uniform tax of sixteen cents on tobacco."—*Philadelphia Public Ledger*, March 21, 1872.

1872, JULY 18.   James F. A. Sisson, Atlanta, to USG. "I am an ordained minister of the African Methodist Episcopal Church, and am pastor of Ringgold Circuit, of the said Church; my residence and Post office address being Ringgold, Catoosa Co, Ga. My pastorate began May 23rd 1872, from that date, to this, whenever I have walked the streets of Ringgold I have been insulted, by the white people, without provocation; the insults consisted of all kinds of noises, hideous to the ears even of those that did not know the cause of their being made: such as mule noises, mocking persons blowing the nose, vomiting, Sneezing, yelling, Indian war whoop, and indescribable noises, too numerous to be counted. Indecent epithets have been applied to me, with snaping of the fingers close to my head, in the Post office, and upon the Streets Strings of bells—Cow, and Sheep—have been rung near my person, as I passed through the Streets, and once violently rung at the Post office door, while I was in the said office. Bricks and stones have been frequently thrown at me, while I have been passing through the Streets of the town aforesaid. Threats have been made to ride me on a rail, to drive me out of town, and to kill me. A man ordered me to leave the end of the town in which the Western and Atlantic Rail Road Depot is situated, and stated with oaths that he would whip me if I ever visited that part of the town again. Another man ordered me to leave town. At the instance of evil minded white men two members—not officers—of my church were induced to have me arrested on a Justice's warrant, under the false pretense that they, the two colored men, were Trustees of St Johns African Methodist Episcopal Church, under my charge. I was arrested as, and treated as a criminal until I was released: the case was a civil one, the actual trustees claiming their right to hold in trust the Deed of the said St Johns African Methodist Episcopal Church, one of them, Anderson was promised prior to the court that the Deed should be placed in his hands, the court was a perfect farce; Anderson's Lawer was insulting to me, while I was pleading for the church aforesaid: and the whole affair plainly revealed to me thate fact that justice cannot be served in that town. As many as a hundred persons have, frequently, at one and the same time engaged in the treatment given to me, following me, &c. Threats have been made to break up my church, and day school. It is important that I should be in Ringgold at once, that I may attend to my official duties: but it is certainly not safe for me to return for one hour without the defence of united States Troops that are so thoroughly tried that it is morally certain that the officers, and privates cannot be successfully bribed. I have made official, and unofficial appeals to the commissioners of the town, through my church officers, repeatedly, for an estopal to the conduct mentioned above: but: notwithstanding this course has been taken, they, with the town marshall have daily been eye-witnesses to these gross outrages, neither they, nor he have taken a single step toward quelling the difficulties: hence: I say: they approve the acts refered to. I have not asked for the action of the state, or United States authorities—civil—at this point: because all precidents I know of confirm me in the opinion that such efforts would be futile. I called to-day at the office of Capt. Kline in command of United States Troops in this city who refered me to United States civil authorities, with the assertion that the matter ~was~is out of his jurisdiction. I deem the lives of the colored people, at large, in Ringgold, in jepordy. I most respectfully petition for Troops to be sent immediately to Ringgold; and suggest that not less than a full company be sent: and that they have all the power martial that can be placed at their disposal. I may add that my day School teacher has been pushed off of the Rail Road Verander, and hit in the head by the fist of a white man, without provocation: the teacher has also been bricked, and stoned, when alone, & when in company with the writer. I am allowed to refer you to Hon. T. G. Campbell, Sen. (now in this city:) whom I have consulted in the subject matter of this letter, if you desire to know more of my status, officially, morally &c; &c. Please address me at Willingham House Atlanta Ga. I enclose a certified copy of a letter from the Post Master at Ringgold."—ALS, DNA, RG 94, Letters Received, 3177 1872. The enclosure is *ibid.*

1872, JULY 19. USG endorsement. "Respectfully forwarded to the Sec. of State. I think it will be well to apt. Mr Dabney."—AES, DNA, RG 59, Letters of Application and Recommendation. Written on a letter of July 17 from Alexander H. Rice, Boston, to USG, Long Branch. "Mr Cover, U S. Consul at Fayal, Azores, has just died, and the Consulate there is consequently vacant. His predecessor, Mr Dabney, held the position many years with credit to himself and honor to the country. It would gratify many of our merchants who have business at the Azores, and many of our citizens, if Mr Dabney Jr, could succeed his father in this appointment. Mr Dabney is qualified for the place in every particular; and is a gentleman universally respected and esteemed by his acquaintances. The compensation is only $750—per annum, and therefore cannot be very attractive to those seeking places for pecuniary emolument."— ALS, *ibid.* Related papers are *ibid.* On July 23, USG appointed Samuel W. Dabney. See *PUSG,* 19, 512–14.

On July 19, L. Mayer, Hartford, wrote to USG. "I read in last nights paper that the Consul for the U. S. at the Azores Mr J. C. Cover has died and if agreeable to you I should like the appointment very much, I am a german by birth and in the Country twenty five years and am well versed in the three leading languages of the age and as far as being competent or having deserved the position I can refer you to our Governor Mr M Jewell whose Surgeon Gen. my brother has been for a number of years, in fact since his election, The german population we controle to a considerable extent, myself acting secretary generally to most of their political meetings. If you wish recomendations I am fully able to furnish them from our leading men here who side with you Please give this your attention as we germans have had very little favors so far in the east from the government"—ALS, DNA, RG 59, Letters of Application and Recommendation. On the same day, George D. Sidman, Bay City, Mich., wrote to USG. "Having fought under your command in the Army of the Potomac during the late war, and at present fighting under your command in the war for Grant and Wilson, I have taken the liberty to ask your consideration of my application for the office of Consul to Fayal, Azores. I fought four years in the war for the Union, and bear three honorable wounds as proof of my fidelity, at the close of the war I came home and commenced the study of law, the year following I was appointed Asst. Assessor of Int. Rev. for this Dist. and in 1867, (unknown to myself,) upon the reccommendation of Sec'y Seward I was nominated by the President, and confirmed by the Senate, as Consul to Schwerin, Germany but I could'nt 'Swing around that circle' so I resigned.— Having a desire to see more of the world, I shipped on a Whaler for a voyage in the Atlantic, and Pacific, and after a year's hard service, I ran away from her in Fayal, secreting myself in the mountains until my ship had set sail for the South Pacific, when I came down and gave myself up. Having money of my own, I preferred remaining on the Azores, and the Consul gave me an appointment as 'Act'g Vice Consul at Santa Cruiz, on Flores, where I remained nearly a year, making myself acquainted with all the business of that Consulate, which on account of the laws for Whalers being different, necessarily makes the duty double, and more complicated for an inexperienced person, After leaving the Azores I went to China and was employed at the Consulate of Shanghai for a short season, after which I was employed by the Chinese government as guard in a silk boat up the Canton River, afterward I set sail for Bombay India where I remained a year in the employ of the British Government, and finally came home in 1871—Since which time I have been in the U. S. Detective Police Force.—I am now anxious to change, and with the knowledge I have of the Azores, and the duties of that Consulate, I think I am better fitted for it, than, perhaps, any other man in America, If any Boards of examination have been formed since the passage of the Civil Service Reform bill, and it is necessary for me to pass an examination, I am ready at any moment to report, you may deem best, or may advise me of, Trusting this may meet your favourable consideration, . . ."—ALS, *ibid.* No appointment followed.

1872, JULY 19. Judge Richard Busteed, U.S. District Court, Ala., to USG, Long Branch. "Accompanying this you will find a copy of a communication addressed by me to Judge Richardson, Assistant Secretary of the Treasury. I leave for Europe, for a short stay, tomorrow, in quest of health and quiet. My judicial labors for the last few months in Alabama, have made sad inroads upon both. The matter of Mr Blakes removal from the South to the North, or Northwest, as suggested in my letter to Judge Richardson, conserns my wishes and feelings very greatly, and I pray you, as a personal favor to me, that you add to my request the weight of your recommendation. You will bear me witness that I have not troubled you by any former application for favors."—ALS, DNA, RG 56, Letters Received. Enclosed is a letter of July 16 from Busteed, Jamaica, N. Y., to William A. Richardson, asst. secretary of the treasury, requesting a new assignment for James Blake, special agent, Treasury Dept.— Copy, *ibid.*

1872, JULY 19.   John B. Mhoon, Washington, D. C., to USG. "Believing that the Petition of Buenaventura Pareda, to which I had the honor of calling your attention on Monday July 15th Inst, had been referred in accordance with the assurance you were then pleased to give me, to the Honorable Secretary of State, I, to day called on him with the original papers in the case, and in a note addressed to him, formally asked to have them placed on file in the State Department. After listening to a very brief statement of the case, the Hon. Secretary informed me, that Pereda, the Petitioner, being a foreigner, his petition, in order to be considered, must come through the accredited representative of his native Country; that although he had filed his Declaration of Intention to throw off all allegiance to the King of Spain, and become a citizen of the United States, he must still look to the Spanish Minister for protection against wrong and outrage, even though he suffers that wrong and outrage on American soil and under the shadow of the American flag—. . ."—LS, DNA, RG 59, Miscellaneous Letters. Papers related to the arrest and detention of Buenaventura Pereda, a Spanish army deserter who fled from Cuba to San Francisco, are *ibid.*

1872, JULY 23.   USG endorsement. "Let the land office described within be located at Gainesville Florida as recommended by the Secretary of the Interior."—Copy, DNA, RG 48, Lands and Railroads Div., Letters Sent. On July 11, Secretary of the Interior Columbus Delano had written to USG. "I have the honor to recommend that the office of the recently created land district in Florida be located at Gainesville, Alachua county, in said State. This recommendation is rendered necessary by the fact that, owing to a clerical error, the act reads *Jaynesville*, whereas there is no town of that name in Florida. The Hon. J. T. Walls, member of Congress from that State, informs me that *Gainesville* is the place in which it was the intention of the act to locate the office."—Copy, *ibid.* See *CG*, 42–2, 3553; *U.S. Statutes at Large*, XVII, 335.

1872, JULY 23.   To Secretary of State Hamilton Fish. "The nomination for the office of Coiner United States Branch Mint Carson City, Nevada, having been erroneously submitted and confirmed during the last session of the Senate. I have to request that a temporary commission be issued for Chauncey N Noteware vice Granville Hosmer resigned:"—Copy, DLC-USG, II, 1. On the same day, Secretary of the Treasury George S. Boutwell had written to USG. "... Mr Noteware, was erroneously nominated and confirmed during the last Session of the Senate as Chauncey E. Noteware."—Copy, DNA, RG 56, Letters Sent.

On March 29, 1873, U.S. Senators John P. Jones and William M. Stewart of Nev. twice wrote to USG. "We desire a change in the office of Coiner of the Mint at Carson Nevada—We recomend William H Doane for that place,   We are Confident that the public service will be promoted by this Change" "We desire a change in the office of melter and refiner at the mint in Carson Nevada & recommend the appointment of G. W. Bryant for that place. We feel sure that the public interests require & that the public service will be promoted thereby"—LS, *ibid.,* Asst. Treasurers and Mint Officials, Letters Received. On April 4, "Officers and Employees in the Mint of the United States at Carson City" petitioned USG protesting "against the removal of C. N. Noteware from the Office of Coiner, and also against the removal of R. P. Andrews from the Office of Melter and Refiner, for the reason that we believe such removals will result in disaster to a much needed public institution."—DS (21 signatures), *ibid.* On May 15, Henry F. Rice wrote to USG resigning "as Superintendent of the Carson Mint" because of disagreement with recent removals and appointments.—ALS, *ibid.* On Dec. 1, USG nominated Frank D. Hetrick as superintendent, William H. Doane as coiner, and George W. Bryant as melter and refiner, U.S. Mint, Carson City.

1872, JULY 23.   To Col. William B. Hazen. "I have the honor to acknowledge the receipt of the very handsome volume of your work, 'The School and the Army in Germany and France', which you were good enough to send me. Please accept my sincere thanks for the book and for the kind remembrance."—LS, DLC-George Dewey. See Hazen, *The School and the Army in Germany and France, With a Diary of Siege Life at Versailles* (New York, 1872).

1872, JULY 23.   "Mrs. Dr. A. M. Heistand," Mount Joy, Pa., to USG. "I have had the duty imposed upon me of soliciting donations toward the liquidation of the debt of the Methodist Church of this place. We have been struggling for eight years, and I have canvassed the country from Harrisburg to Philadelphia; but have not yet succeeded in obtaining the small sum of $2,000, (the portion required of me by the trustees) after giving the very last doll[ar] out of my own pocket. We have been unfortunate as a Church losing many of our most substantial men during the ~~w~~War. I am some what ambitious in this matter and am ready to do anything that is honorable to accomplish this project   I learn through the public press that you are overwhelmed with letters from politicians and office seekers, therefore do not consider it necessary to go into detail with regard to our trouble; but will simply say we will be thankful for any donation you may feel disposed to give, and in return we will do all we can for the candidate of the Presidency. We do not expect large sums anything from $10.00 to $1000. ~~For~~As the truth of the matter I refer you to Rev W. Boole of Brooklin N. Y. If you have any doubts, I will refer you to some of our leading

men of Lancaster Pa A. Herr Smith D. W. Patterson Att'y at Law. Nathaniel
Elmaker or John W. Geary Gov. or Thomas. A Scott from whom I received a
donation a few weeks ago."—ALS, NjP. USG endorsed this letter. "Answer
donation are asked from every section of the country and it is impossible
to respond to them or even to answer the majority of these appeals."—AE
(undated), *ibid.* On July 30, Orville E. Babcock wrote to Heistand. "The President desires me to acknowledge the receipt of your letter, and say that he
would be very glad to be able to comply with your request but he is in receipt
of similar appeals daily from every section of the country, and it is imposibl to
respond to them, or even to answer the majority of the letters. It is a source of
regret to him that he cannot respond in such cases."—Copy, DLC-USG, II, 1.

1872, JULY 24.   USG pardon. "Whereas, on the 23d day of February, 1864, in
the Supreme Court of the District of Columbia, holding a criminal term, one
Jeremiah Hendricks was convicted of murder, and was sentenced to suffer
death by hanging, which sentence was afterwards commuted to imprisonment
for life; And whereas, he has now been imprisoned over eight years; And
whereas Judge Olim, District Attorney Fisher, ten of the Jurors who found
him guilty and other citizens of Washington, believing, in view of his former
good character, that he has been sufficiently punished, recommend his pardon.
Now, therefore, be it Known, that I . . . do hereby grant to the said Jeremiah
Hendricks a full and unconditional pardon. . . ."—DS (partial facsimile), Remember When Auctions, Inc., Catalog No. 43 [1998], no. 1498; copy, DNA,
RG 59, General Records. See *National Intelligencer*, Feb. 25, April 2, 1864.

1872, JULY 24.   Attorney Gen. George H. Williams to USG. "I have the honor
to acknowledge the receipt by reference from you, of a letter addressed by the
Hon. Secretary of the Interior to Henry Sherman Esq. respecting an application for an order directing the District Attorney of Utah to commence a suit
in the name of the United States on behalf of Joseph W. Haskins to set aside
a patent issued to the Salt Lake Mining Company . . . I cannot in view of the
letter of the Secretary of the Interior advise favorable action by the President
upon the application of Mr. Sherman."—Copy, DNA, RG 60, Letters Sent to
Executive Officers. On Aug. 16, Henry Sherman, Washington, D. C., wrote to
USG. "Referring to our interview of yesterday, in which I had the honor to call
your attention to the Petition of J. W. Haskin in relation to the Flagstaff Mine,
Utah, and the Patent to it, I beg leave further, respectfully, to submit, That after a full and careful investigation of all the facts, I am persuaded that the Patent was improperly issued, and that it was procured by fraudulent representations by which the holders of it are now profiting to the extent of at least some
ten thousands daily to the loss of my client. Secretary Delano has orally expressed his entire willingness to have proceedings commenced to vacate the
patent, or test the title to it, as petitioned for; And the Attorney Genl has so
far signified his doubts of its validity, as to say, that he is willing, if so requested
by the Secretary or, so di directed by the Executive, to institute such proceedings, as pray'd for. . . ."—ALS, *ibid.*, Letters Received, D. C. On Dec. 9, 1872,

and Dec. 22, 1876, Sherman wrote to USG concerning this case.—ALS, *ibid.,*
Letters from the President.

1872, JULY 27.   Orville E. Babcock to Henry Kramer, Bay St. Louis, Miss.
"The President directs me to say in reply to your letter that, he was not in
Galena until 1860, except for a few hours one day in 1850."—Copy, DLC-
USG, II, 1.

1872, JULY 27.   Orville E. Babcock to Otto Rothlender, "City Hospital,"
St. Louis. "The President directs me to say in reply to your letter that he never
was in Benton Barracks during the war nor after; never had a veterinary surgeon attend his horses during the war, and never had Col: Fitz Henry Warren
directly under his command."—Copy, DLC-USG, II, 1.

1872, JULY 28.   Horace Porter, Long Branch, to Secretary of State Hamilton
Fish. "The President directs me to say that Col. Thomas A. Scott has written
an urgent private letter asking that the within named appointment be made,
and to request you to appoint Mr. Macmanus, if the vacancy, as represented,
exists."—ALS, DNA, RG 59, Letters of Application and Recommendation. On
Dec. 3, USG nominated George L. Macmanus as consul, Chihuahua. For con-
troversies involving this consulate, see files for William H. Brown, Charles
Moye, and Joseph F. Bennett.—*Ibid.* See also *O.R.,* I, iv, 147.

1872, JULY 30.   Albert G. Bonsall, Philadelphia, to USG. "Having been summarily dismissed from the naval service of the United States, by order of the
Secretary of the Navy, dated January 12, 1866, and having been peremptorily
refused, before witnesses, a court-martial which was demanded by me in person as my right under the law of March 3, 1865, as soon as I could get to Washington from Norfolk, Va., I hereby renew my application in writing for a
court-martial, to comply with all the requirements of the law, the former application having been a verbal one."—*HMD,* 44-1-170, part 5, 482 (Appendix).
For Bonsall's continuing demand for a court-martial, see *ibid.,* pp. 691–92.

1872, JULY 30.   Mary A. Derby, Paris, to USG. "Having just made an application to the Secretary of War for a Cadetship for my son—may I appeal to the
old friend of his Father in his behalf? Gen. Sherman has just told me that you
have 300 applicants and only ten appointments to make   rather discouraging,
I must confess but I will not despair—George has just passed the examination
for the Polytechnic and taken the second prize ($20) altho he has been study-
ing english but ten months. I kept him in Europe until he was fourteen and so
favorable was the opinion entertained by his Profr of his mental abilities that
he offered to give him the most finished education that could be given in Europe and not charge a sous, if I would give him the absolute control of his
studies—His physical qualifications are all that you require—now may I not
hope that he ~~may~~will be among the favored? I could have applied through political friends but, I preferred to be indebted to *you*—It was a great dis-

appointment to me not to see your daughter—I hear she is lovely and very accomplished—I congratulate you upon possessing such a treasure—Love to your wife—. . . We sail for America, in October and hope to have the happiness of congratulatg you as our future President—You have never seen my California Daisy—we shall make a flying visit to Washington and I will present my daughter (remarkable in size if nothing else)."—ALS, DNA, RG 94, Correspondence, USMA. Letters from George W. Fishback, Robert Campbell, and William H. Benton to USG recommending George M. Derby are *ibid.* Appointed from Mo., Derby graduated from USMA first in his class in 1878. See *PUSG*, 12, 412.

1872, Aug. 5.   Robert R. Barrow, New Orleans, to USG. "I view it as important to the masses in the United States to write you the following and solicit your answer. You may recollect during the war your calling on me in the St Charles Hotel, and making enquiry about your relations and friends, Hewitt and Norton, I am the person you addressed. . . . I wish to know of you, for the good of the mases of more than 40 millions of people, if the Democratic party will drop Greeley and vote for you and elect you as President, will you act as Millard Fillmore did—do justice to all North, South, East and West, black and white, rich and poor. . . ."—Printed broadside, DLC-Andrew Johnson.

1872, Aug. 5.   Robert T. Lyons, Washington, D. C., to USG. "I have the honor most respectfully, to make application for an appointment in the regular Army as second Lieutenant. In 1861 I enlisted in the U. S. Army at the age of fifteen years, and was wounded three times. I served in the 1st Delaware Infantry, and in the 2nd U. S. Cavalry, and also in the 5th U S Cav, being transfered by your order to this latter Regiment in 1867, from the frontiers, reporting to Major Leet for duty. I served at your Headquarters in this City until June 1868 at which time I was honorably discharged from the service, by your order. As to my faithful services in the U. S. Army, I would respectfully call your attention to my papers herewith enclosed together with letters of recommendation from Ex. U. S. Officers and gentlemen well known in public life. Should I be so fortunate as to receive an appointment I shall always endeavor to discharge the duties of the office, with honesty and fidelity. I am 26 years of age was born in Ireland, and emigrated to this country with my parents at the age of 5 years. Am a resident of the State of Delaware, and at the present time a clerk in the Treasury Department. Hoping this, my application will meet with your kind consideration and approval, . . ."—ALS, DNA, RG 94, ACP, 204 1873. On Aug. 8, George P. Fisher, U.S. attorney, D. C., wrote to USG. "The bearer R. T. Lyons I have known from boyhood. I knew his father. In 1861 at the outbreak Robert went into the army enlisting under Lt. (now Genl) Woodall) of the 1st Del. Vols. His father came to me & I had the boy released. But in a short time he ran off and enlisted again & remained. His father was a redhot democrat & for this offense disinherited the boy who I know to be of more worth than all his other sons. He is sober upright honest and loyal. He now wants to be appointed a 2d Lt. Will you not do me the favor to appoint him?"—ALS, *ibid.* USG wrote an undated note enclosed with these letters. "The Sec. of War may appoint R. T. Lyons a 2d Lt. of Infy"—AN, *ibid.* On Dec. 17, USG nominated Lyons as 2nd lt., 17th Inf.

1872, AUG. 6. Luisa M. de Zenea, New York City, to USG. "Permit an afflicted widow, the widow of an American citizen, an American citizen herself, and the mother of an orphan girl who according to the American law enjoys the privileges of the American citizenship, to apply to you directly in search of justice and protection. . . . my husband, an American citizen since 1852 was shot in the island of Cuba, in violation of all laws and treaties, and of the safe-conduct given him by the Spanish Minister in Washington, *in the name of the Regent of Spain and of the Spanish nation, . . .*"—ALS, DNA, RG 59, Miscellaneous Letters. Zenea sought aid in presenting a claim on behalf of her husband, Cuban-born poet Juan Clemente Zenea, shot at Havana on Aug. 25, 1871. See Alfred Coester, *The Literary History of Spanish America* (New York, 1938), pp. 409–13; Enrique Piñeyro, *Historia de la Vida y Escritos de Juan Clemente Zenea* (Paris, 1901); *SED,* 50-1-93.

1872, AUG. 6. James E. Yeatman, St. Louis, to USG. "My esteemed friend Geo K McGunnegle, who is and has been one of your zealous supporters, has asked me to write and request as a favor, th[e] assignment of his son in law Lt Col J W Davidson 10th Cavalry, to duty in the recruiting service at the arsenal in this city, at the expiration of the term of the present officer—. . ."—ALS, DNA, RG 94, Letters Received, 3174 1872. No action followed. See *PUSG,* 17, 377–78.

1872, AUG. 17. To Christian IX of Denmark, acknowledging the recall of Danish minister Frantz E. Bille.—Copy, DNA, RG 84, Letters Received, Denmark.

1872, AUG. 17. William H. Dove, Wilson, N. C., to USG. "I write to you to see if you would be so kind as to aid me in going to West Point, as I am very anxcious to be a learnéd Sodier my native home is in the city of New Berne N. C. But I am working in Wilson county trying to accumulate some money to go with, But wages are very low here. If you will be so kind as to aid me in going, I will work for you or repay you after I graduate. Thinking that you were a friend to the colord people is what induced me to write. Please look over all mistakes from your humble and Obedient Servant."—ALS, DNA, RG 94, Unsuccessful Cadet Applications. On March 21 and Nov. 18, 1873, Dove wrote to USG on the same subject.—ALS, *ibid.*

1872, AUG. 19. James B. McKean, chief justice, Utah Territory, Salt Lake City, to USG. "General Ord has furnished me with the following extract from one of his orders:—'. . . If it shall become absolutely necessary, Col. Morrow is authorized to call on the citizens and miners in the vicinity of the hostile Indians, for such aid, not to exceed one hundred scouts, as they can promptly furnish. He can provide them with rations and ammunition.' General Ord deems the emergency such that he desires to lay these instructions before you, Mr. President, and ask your ratification thereof, by means more direct and expeditious than those of the usual military channels. . . ."—ALS, DNA, RG 94, Letters Received, 2770 1872. On Sept. 26, Lt. Gen. Philip H. Sheridan, Chicago, endorsed this letter. "Respectfully forwarded for the information of the General-in-Chief. I have only to say now what I have said heretofore that the expedition to the San Pete Valley was an error of judgment. Gen. Ord I think now realizes fully the indelicacy of asking Judge McKean to communicate with the President outside the regular military channels."—ES, *ibid.*

On July 12, Orville E. Babcock had written to Secretary of War William W. Belknap. "The President directs me to request you to direct Gen. Sheridan to give such force, when called for by the Secretary of the Interior, as may be necessary to compel Indians in Utah to go upon reservations."—LS, *ibid.* See *HED*, 42-3-1, part 5, I, 481, 678–79.

1872, Aug. 21.   G. Sontheimer, Stuttgart, to USG. "Excuse the liberty of addressing you.—I am a Banker of this city and in course of business. I recommended also the Georgia Aid Bonds. The last mail from the States brought the sad tidings, that the Comittee appointed by the last legislature of Georgia to investigate reported to declare the Brunswick and Albany (Georgia Aid Bonds) illegaly issued. Reviewing the report of that Committee, they did not have a single moral or legal right, to ask of the Legislature to repudiate them, except the obligation they entered into with the Bondholders to pay the interest when due, & which they wish to avoid now. . . ."—ALS, DNA, RG 60, Letters from the President. See Alan Conway, *The Reconstruction of Georgia* (Minneapolis, 1966), pp. 204–7.

1872, Aug. 22.   USG note. "I concur with Mr. Blow in the view that the location of the Custom House in st. Louis should be postponed until after the meeting of Congress."—ANS, ICHi. On March 27, USG had signed a bill authorizing $500,000 to purchase a building site in St. Louis.—*U.S. Statutes at Large*, XVII, 43–44. Henry T. Blow, Elias W. Fox, John F. Long, Constantine Maguire, and James Richardson served on a commission to select the site, a process that degenerated into public dispute amid charges of conflict of interest. See *Missouri Democrat*, Aug. 16, 17, 19, Sept. 3, 4, 1872; *CG*, 42-3, 911.

1872, Aug. 22.   "I. O. U.," Washington, D. C., to USG. "Had Caesar read the *'private note'* or *letter* addressed to him, a few days before the 'ides of March,' he would have lived longer and proved, by his future course, that *he did not* desire *to be made King*! Pard[on] this introduction,—*the writer is your friend,* (faithful and just to you).—he desires an interview, at some day—'the sooner the better,' he thinks, for the interests of the American people. . . . PS. The best of references can be given both in Church or State as to our character— loyalty &c &c—*address, please—as above. If no answer* is recd within 10 days, *this note* will be returned to the P. O. Department, Washington D. C.   'There are more things occurring in Heaven and Earth, than are dreamed of in *thy* philosophy O Horatio!"—AL, OFH.

1872, Aug. 26.   To Secretary of the Navy George M. Robeson. "Revoke order sending Mid Webster to duty and extend leave six months   notify him by telegraph."—Telegram received (on Aug. 27), DNA, RG 45, Letters from the President. On March 4, Joseph D. Webster, assessor of Internal Revenue, Chicago, had written to USG. "My son Lewis D. recently promoted to Lieutenant in the Navy, has leave of absence for 3 months, with a promise of extension for an equal period 'if his services can be spared.' The first leave expires on the 20th inst. and I very much desire the extension. Some pressing family reasons make it very necessary. One of them is that my second daughter is now very dangerously ill and should she not recover it will be most desirable to send Mrs. W. to So. Carolina to escape our spring winds. And should she be spared to us she should go soon as possible. I want Lewy to go with them, as I cannot well leave for so long a term as would be necessary. Other reasons there are but I need not trouble you with them. Tho' I certainly hope Lewy is a good officer I cannot believe that his services cannot be spared for three months longer. Indeed I would think it very possible to spare him for *six* months now 'without injury to the service'! Will you add to your many kindnesses by doing what may seem right to foward my wishes in this matter, *and that without prejudice to the standing of my son at the Department.* His application for the desired extension will go to the Department tomorrow. He tells me that one of his classmates, who has not been at sea so long as he has has *a year's* leave, as have many others. If Lewy could have six months additional it would be very grat[i]fying."—ALS, *ibid.*, ZB File. On March 7, Orville E. Babcock endorsed this letter to Robeson. "This is an old friend of the President—The President has not seen the lettr"—AES, *ibid.* On Dec. 20, 1871, Frederick T. Dent had written to Robeson. "The President directs me to say that, when Lieut. Lewis D. Webster, U. S. N. applies for a leave of absence, he will be pleased to have such leave granted."—Copy, DLC-USG, II, 1.

1872, Aug. 29.   USG endorsement. "Refered to the Sec. of War. Let special attention be called to this application when further apts. are made in the Army."—AES, DNA, RG 94, Applications for Positions in War Dept. Written on a letter of Aug. 29 from William Dulany, Baltimore, to USG. "I would respectfully make application for the appointment of Second Lieutenant in the U. S. Army. I am twenty Seven years of age, a native of Maryland and a son of the late Colonel Wm. Dulany, U. S. Marine Corps who served his Country for over half a Century and was a warm friend of General Grants. Will your Excellency permit me to remark that almost Every Officer of my father's Standing & Service, has a son in either the Army or Navy, whereas of four Sons of my father two of whom served during the [war] not one of them has a commission in either branch of the Service. I trust you may take this application into favorable Consideration, and assure you should you see fit to appoint me I will endeavor to do my duty as a soldier. I have served in two branches of the

Service."—ALS, *ibid.* On Nov. 11, Dulany wrote to USG. "I have the honor to enclose a letter from Judge D. K. Cartter recommending my appointment to a Second Lieutenantcy in the Army. I neglected to hand you this letter upon the occasion of my interview with you on the 9th Inst. . . ."—ALS, *ibid.* The enclosure is *ibid.* On Dec. 12, USG nominated Dulany as 2nd lt., 5th Cav.

In an undated letter to USG, Dulany's mother had sought assistance for another son, Tasker B. Dulany, an applicant for the U.S. Marine Corps.—ALS, *ibid.*, RG 45, ZB File.

1872, AUG. 29. To U.S. Representative J. Lawrence Getz of Pa. "I have the honor to acknowledge the receipt of your very kind invitation to attend the 18th Annual Fair of the Berks County Agricultural Society, commencing on the 10th of next month. I must beg you to accept my thanks for the kind remembrance, and the assurances of my sincere regret that my engagements are such that I shall not be able to comply with your wish, and be present and meet the citizens of Berks County. Please convey my thanks to the other Officers of the Society associated with you."—LS, Gallery of History, Las Vegas, Nev.

1872, SEPT. 1. William H. Cornell, St. Louis, to USG. "In compliance with your instructions I delivered to General A. J. Smith (in person) those documents entrusted to my care—and up to the present date, no visable action has been taken by Genrl Smith towards obeying the instructions contained therein,   at all events, the person contemplated in those papers, has not been removed, but still retains his position as Assistant Post Master, and that to the detriment of the Republican party. Since my return from Washington, Messrs. Smith, Walsh, & co. have indulged in several spasmodic attempts to *Whitewash* themselves into acknowledged republicans, but the coating was so thin, that the cloven foot was easily seen,   enclosed please find a speech, delivered by General A. J. Smith on the evening of August 25th 1872. at a Grant and Wilson Flag-raising in the 2d Ward, it speaks for itself. I am informed that General Smith made this speech, at the solicitation's of Con, McGuire, Ferdinand Meyer, and several other of his Liberal and Democratic advisers, for the purpose of making it appear that they was in perfect harmony with the Administration party, and were doing all in their power to advance and promote the political interests of Grant and Wilson,   But, Mr. President, to use a homily western phrase, *They are not Clean Cats*, they wont do to bet on, if a man deceives me once, it is *his* fault, But if he deceives me a second time it is *my* fault, for I should not have trusted him—and these parties feeling that Liberalism is at a discount in Mo. and that your re-election is a foregone conclusion, are now anxious to secure an identity with the winning party for the sake of the loaves and fishes,   I have been advised by well known Republicans, to make the following statement to you. One year ago last August, I called the first meeting, and organized the first Council of the Native American element in Mo. My efforts have been crowned with entire success, and now the councils are numerous, and its membership runs high into the thousand's,   being a true blue republican myself, I have laboured constantly to instil into the minds of our converts Republican ideas, as most of my recruiting has been done in the Democratic rank and file. I have taken the bone and sinouw out of the old Democratic Carcass, until there is nothing left of it in Saint Louis County, but a mass of corruption,   I also extended my labours among our colored brethren, and to day their councils are a unit in support of Grant and Wilson Mr President, I have laboured unceasingly for the past year, for the advancement of republicanism in Mo. I have defrayed my own expenses thus far, and have been rewarded with the knowledge that I have prevailed upon several thousand Democrats to forsake the evil of their ways, and openly declare themselves in favour of Grant and Wilson. Our friends advise me, now to apply to you for the appointment of United States Marshal, for the Eastern district of Mo.   they advise me to take this step for two reasons, the first is, that C. A. Newcomb (the present encumbant) is a candidate for Congress, the second reason is, that when Judge Newcomb was appointed, I was endorsed for the same position by every Officer of the State of Mo. from Governor McClurg down, togeather with nearly every republican member of the then Legislative Assembly,   my papers were forwarded to Carl Schurz. (when he was thought to be upright and honest) and I was informed by him, that they were on file in the Attorney General's Office, but I never could find them,   I desire the above appointment if consistant with your views, But Should you determine otherwise, then I hope your Excellency will not discard me entirely, but give me some other appointment where I can still be of service to the present Administration,"—ALS, DNA, RG 60, Records Relating to Appointments. Also in 1872, Andrew J. Smith, postmaster, St. Louis, wrote to USG about the formation of a local Native American organization.—William Evarts Benjamin, Catalogue No. 28, Jan., 1890, p. 6. On May 5, 1873, Cornell wrote to USG. "Enclosed you will please find an additional recommendation for a Consular Appointment, signed by the Merchants of St. Louis (On Change) irrespective of Political Affiliations, Also by Hon's C. W. Ford C. A. Newcomb, E. W. Fox and Chauncy, I. Filley—Mr President, *I need the appointment*, my political enemies in Mo. have driven me from one position to another, until they have accomplished my ruin pecuniarially. I trust Your Excellency will favourably consider my application, and give me an appointment. I will not disgrace the position, or betray the confidence reposed in me. Hoping to meet with success, . . ."—ALS, DNA, RG 59, Letters of Application and Recommendation. Related papers are *ibid.* On Oct. 1 and Nov. 6, 1875, Cornell, clerk, St. Louis Post Office, wrote to USG requesting appointment as marshal.—ALS, *ibid.*, RG 60, Records Relating to Appointments.

On Feb. 8, 1873, Chester H. Krum, John McDonald, William McKee, Charles W. Ford, and William Patrick, St. Louis, had written to USG asking the reappointment of Carman A. Newcomb as marshal, Eastern District, Mo.—LS, *ibid.* Related papers are *ibid.* See *PUSG*, 20, 284–85. On March 7, USG renominated Newcomb.

1872, SEPT. 2.   William A. Richardson, act. secretary of the treasury, to USG, Long Branch. "Reduction of debt, past month, nearly eleven million."— Copy, DNA, RG 56, Telegrams Sent.

Probably in Sept., [*1870*], USG wrote to Richardson. "We leave here on Monday morning next for Boston to put my son at college and my daughter at Farmington on the way back. As I will have so much family with me, however, and as Mrs. Grant will be very busy during the only day we expect to spend in Boston furnishing Ulysses' room, she thinks we had better stop at a hotel."— Goodspeed's Book Shop, Inc., Boston, Mass., Catalogue 369, [1943], no. 1089. See *PUSG*, 20, 278; *ibid.*, 21, 28.

1872, SEPT. 2.   William Sumner *et al.*, Nashville, to USG. "We the collored People of Davidson and Suronding Counties haveing Seen in Sevral papers that thire is to be appoint An Agt to Pay off the Bountyies and Back Pay of Collored Solgiers and widows and as We have never asked for any thing from you before and thinking that we ought to Have Same of the offices from the Goverment and as duty bound Shall Ever pray for the Same we now ask you to appoint Wm Lyton a collored man who lives in Nashville and one that has Sated in the Bureau of R. F. A. L. For Six years with Credit to him Self and Race and that We know of no orther man So worthy of it as Mr Lyton and his appointment will not only be sattiesfactrey to the People but ad Strenk to the Republican Party here and Els where and as thire Is a great many here that have not drawn thire bounty and as Mr Lytton is A Grant & Wilson man it will be a means of bringing A great many weak minded cold man to his duty . . ."—DS (42 signatures), DNA, RG 105, Bureau of Refugees, Freedmen, and Abandoned Lands, Letters Received.

1872, SEPT. 3.   USG note. "Refered to the Post Master Gen.l."—ANS, RPB. USG endorsed this note. "Gen. Babcock will please retain this until I return to Washington"—AE (undated), *ibid.*

1872, SEPT. 4.   USG proclamation establishing reciprocal trade with Japan.—DS, DNA, RG 130, Proclamations. *Foreign Relations, 1872*, p. 2.

1872, SEPT. 4.   USG endorsement. "This applicant for pay due, and pension, lost his arm in battle no doubt, but from his wound taking him from his regiment, and through ignorance how to proceed, he has never received the proper discharge. I wish the Adjt Gen would cause the proper investigation to be made to secure him the pay and allowances due him."—AES, DNA, RG 94, Colored Troops Div., Letters Received. Written on an undated letter from Joseph J. McIntire, Long Branch, to AG Edward D. Townsend. "I, Joseph Jackson McIntyre, was speaking to President Grant about my pension, and he commanded me to go to you in Washington, to tell you how I entered into the services of the United States, under Captain Fautz, at Lake Providence Mississippi. Served under him as much as a year, exchanged from him into the charge of Captain McKnelly, Col. Tittermann, Commanding Officer. Served under that capacity, until I lost my arm, 18 miles from Savannah Georgia, sent to Beaufort, South Carolina Ward L. Hospital under Dr Buck Assistant Surgeon, Dr Whitmore, sent from there to David's Island, New York Harbor where I stayed in Hospital about a year. Sent from there to Fort Schuyler, N. York Har-

bor. Served altogether 3 years, from 1863 to 1866. & only received 1 month's
pay, as I did not wish to draw it all at once. The number of my regiment was
110. United States, Colored Troops, Company C. I was a slave in Louisiana,
Bunch's Bend, before the war. I want my discharge & my pension & if it is
worth while for me to go to Washington to see you, please write me, as I would
not want to go to the expense for nothing—. . . The above was dictated to
Miss Hosack by the colored man, McIntyre—"—L, *ibid.* On Sept. 30, Secretary of War William W. Belknap wrote to USG. "In accordance with your endorsement, of the 4th instant, of the application of Joseph Jackson McIntyre
for the pay and pension that he may be entitled to, an investigation of the case
has been had, and I have the honor to inform you that, as shown by the records,
the above named man was received as a recruit for Company C. 110th. U. S.
Colored Troops, and rejected by the mustering officer, January 14th. 1864, as
unfit for service. Not recognized as a soldier, or borne on the rolls as such, he
appears to have accompanied the command as an officer's servant, or camp fol-
lower until wounded, about December 28th. 1864—under circumstances not
shown by the records—when he was sent to hospital and received the necessary treatment, and finally disappeared from hospital and from military control without a discharge certificate or other authority. Not having been in the
military service of the Government, he is not entitled to a discharge or to the
pay or allowances of a soldier."—Copy, *ibid.*, RG 107, Letters Sent, Military
Affairs.

1872, SEPT. 6.   A. B. Goodwin, Lima, S. C., to USG. "I am a poor young man
but respected and lixed by my neighbors   I have a desire to go to Africa as a
mishionary though I am not a preacher but simply a member of the Baptist
Church. I wish to go to the coast of guinea probably to the slave coast in Da-
homey. I wish to use my influence as an American Cittzen to promote our
National interest as well as the common benefit of humanity among this dark
and benighted people   But as I am poor I respectfully ask is it possible for
me to be appointed an American Consul to this place with a small salary   If
this petition should meet with your Excellency's approval I will give you such
reference that your Excellency will not doubt my good character. I am now
25 years old—my health is not good—I have to go on crutches—I my af-
flictions are White Swelling & Chronic Rheumatism but both are better—a
warm climate suits my health &c. Dear Sir I humbly ask that you will not make
this note public. May the great God bless our National Executive and the
people of our Glorious Union."—ALS, DNA, RG 59, Letters of Application
and Recommendation.

1872, SEPT. 7.   USG endorsement. "Refer to the Sec. of the Treas. I remember Mr. Gilmer's letter and that the Sec. of the Trea. took some action in regard to the recommendations though he & I thought it not advisable to make
removals at this time."—AES, DNA, RG 56, Letters Received. Written on a
letter of Sept. 3 from John H. Gilmer, Richmond, to Frederick T. Dent. "I had
hoped, in some form, to have received a reply to my letter to the secretary at

War—but designed for the eye of the President. I wrote in perfect candor—
and for the special interests of the President. I wish to ascertain whether
any thing is to be done—not that it will abate *my* interests—or, in the least,
limit *my* exertions. This state—can be carried for General Grant—with the
proper exertions—if not *too* heavily weighed down—by the worse than dead
weight—of the Custom House men—in this City. If not freed from this
terrible incumbrance—and that soon—I shall feel compelled—to assail the
men—who are so odious to their own party—in order to disencumber myself—from the odium attached to the entire set. I shall be pleased to hear from
you—at your earliest convenience."—ALS, *ibid.* See *PUSG*, 18, 379; *ibid.*, 20,
345–47.

On Nov. 8, Gilmer wrote to USG. "Next to the general results, of this Presidential election, allow me to congratulate you and the whole country, on the
electoral vote of thise state of Virginia. I regard this fact as one, indicating a
'new departure' in the policy for a sure and rapid development of the agricultural, mineral and commercial interests of the Northwestern states and Virginia. I earnestly hope that the James River and Ohio canal, so promptly considered and anxiously pressed upon the country by Gel. Washington, will, at
your hands, receive the crowning act of success—and thus cluster around your
administration, the grand results, awaiting the successful completion of this—
the most important inter-state—enterprise of the age—on American Soil."—
ALS, USG 3.

1872, SEPT. 10, 1:00 A.M.   Speaker of the House James G. Blaine, Augusta,
Maine, to USG, Long Branch. "We have carried the State for Gov. Perham by
more than 15,000 majority, a net gain of 5,000 on last year's vote. We have carried all the Congressional districts the closest by well 2,000 majority. We have
carried every county in the State, something we never achieved but once before; have elected every Senator, and chosen more than four-fifths of the House
of Representatives. Our victory is complete and overwhelming at all points,
and insures you more than 25,000 majority in November."—*New York Times*,
Sept. 10, 1872.

1872, SEPT. 11.   To Augustus Hageboeck, Davenport, Iowa. "I have the
honor to acknowledge the receipt of your letter of the 2nd inst:, and the arrival
of the pen-picture which you were kind enough to send me. It is a very commendable piece of penmanship, and I must beg you to accept my thanks for it,
as well as for the very kind sentiments expressed in your letter."—Copy, DLC-
USG, II, 1.

On March 17, 1876, Ulysses S. Grant, Jr., wrote to Hageboeck. ". . . The pen
you wish was never his own. It was sent to him simply to write his approval on
the bill appropriating money in aid of the Centennial Exhibition and passed
out of his hands into those of the owner upon the writing of such approval. It
is not known where the pen now is, though were it his own he would have had
much pleasure in forwarding it to you to be used in the very patriotic way you
propose."—Copy, *ibid.*, II, 3.

1872, SEPT. 12.   Orville E. Babcock to Charles Hale, act. secretary of state.
"The President desires me ask you to please let him know if there is any vacant consulship in Europe at this time. Also, if Mr Johnson, appointed consul
at Tampico, has yet left for his post. He would be pleased to know if Mr Ames,
our commercial agent at San Domingo, has sent in his resignation. If he is not
to return soon, the President will name his successor."—LS, DNA, RG 59,
Miscellaneous Letters. For Edmund Johnson, see *PUSG*, 21, 386; for Fisher W.
Ames, see *ibid.*, p. 491; *ibid.*, 22, 26–27. On Sept. 13, Babcock twice wrote to
Hale. "Before leaving last night, the President directed me to request you to
send to this office, for his use, a copy of, or if more convenient, the volume containing, the correspondence between Hon. E. D. Morgan on behalf of the W. U.
Telegraph Co. and the Secretary of State relative to Hon. C. M. Clay, then Our
minister to Russia." "The President directs me to say that, he will be pleased
to have you write to Dr Ames, who is now at Covington, Ky, and inform him
of the necessity of his returning to his post, and if he is not soon to return that,
the President will be pleased to appoint his successor."—LS, DNA, RG 59,
Miscellaneous Letters.
    On Nov. 15, 1873, David R. Locke, editor, *Toledo Blade*, wrote to USG.
"Mr. Paul Jones of this city desires th appointment of Commercial Agent of th
United States at San Domingo. Mr Jones has resided on th Island, is entirely
familiar with th country and its people and would doubtless make an efficient
representative of our commercial interests. He was for many years a prominent
banker in this city and is a man of ability, and, what is not altogether useless in
an official, of integrity   I should verry much like to have him appointed to th
place"—ALS, *ibid.*, Letters of Application and Recommendation. Related papers are *ibid.* On June 16, 1874, USG nominated Paul Jones for promotion
from commercial agent to consul, Santo Domingo, after Congress upgraded
the post.

1872, SEPT. 13.   Governor Ozra A. Hadley of Ark. to USG. "On the 31st ultimo I addressed a letter to Hon: Geo H Williams Atty General,—A copy of
which is herewith enclosed, asking his opinion, as to the effect of the 'Enforcement act' in certain cases. I also send you a copy of his reply. If you will have
the kindness to ask him to give his official opinion as requested in my letter at
his earliest convenience, you will confer a great favor upon the people of this
State"—ALS, DNA, RG 60, Letters Received, Ark. The enclosures are *ibid.*
Hadley sought an opinion on a recent federal amnesty act that had strengthened Democrats in Ark. See Proclamation, June 1, 1872.
    On Nov. 2, Horace Porter wrote to Hadley. "Your letter of the 24th ultimo
is received and the request contained in it for the presence of a company of Infantry to preserve the peace during the election at Little Rock, was brought to
the notice of the President and the Secretary of War. The number of troops
now in Louisiana is very limited and appeals are constant for the sending of
more. As none could be sent it seemed inexpedient to take any away and make
a movement of the kind immediately before an election. New Orleans has so of-

ten been the scene of bloodshed, that the troops at this time there, will be scarcely able to preserve the peace. I hope you may a quiet and free election and with a favorable result."—Copy, DLC-USG, II, 1.

On Nov. 13, U.S. Senator Powell Clayton of Ark., Little Rock, wrote to USG. "*Confidential* . . . Gov. Hadley visits Wash. to confer with you in relation to Arkansas affairs, He will ask to have the Garrison at this place strengthened with an additional force of U. S. Troops I fully concur in his views and earnestly ask that his recommendations be adopted. I believe that timely action in this direction will have a most salutary effect, and will prevent the inaugeration of the revolutionary proceeding which a set of desperate and unscrupulous men are now attempting to put on foot. The Governor will inform you fully of the situation which I consider very grave and threatening"—ALS, USG 3. On Nov. 12, Stephen R. Harrington, U.S. attorney, Eastern District, Ark., Little Rock, had written to Hadley. ". . . I deem it my duty, as well as privilege, to advise you of some of the plans about to be resorted to, by Senator Rice and others, to bring about, by force, the inauguration of Mr Brooks as governor. . . ."—ALS, *ibid.* On Nov. 26, Hadley, Washington, D. C., wrote to Secretary of War William W. Belknap. "Having obtained reliable information that the managers of the party opposed to the National Administration in the state of Arkansas, are contemplating a revolutionary movement ~~to~~by attempting to install men as officers who were repudiated by the electors on the 5th inst. (A portion of the information I have received is now in the hands of Genl Horace Porter), I earnestly request that an additional force of U. S. troops be immediately ordered to Little Rock to aid the State authorities in the preservation of peace and the enforcement of the law. In my opinion one regiment of infantry is sufficient."—ALS, DNA, RG 94, Letters Received, 5020 1872. On Dec. 18, Belknap wrote to USG. "I have the honor to transmit, herewith, a communication from the Committee on Military Affairs of the United States Senate, submitting for the views of this Department a Resolution proposed by Senator Rice requesting the President to furnish information in regard to an application for troops to be sent to Arkansas. The 4th Infantry has been sent to Little Rock, Arkansas, from Kentucky, for the present; its ultimate destination being up the Arkansas River."—LS, *ibid.* For continued post-election turmoil in Ark., see *SMD,* 42-3-4, 42-3-14; *SRC,* 43-1-771; *HRC,* 43-2-2, 43-2-127; letter to Elisha Baxter, April 22, 1874.

On Dec. 2, 1872, USG nominated William A. Britton as marshal, Western District, Ark.; on Feb. 3, 1873, the Senate rejected the nomination. About this time, William M. Fishback *et al.* petitioned USG. "The undersigned members of the Bar of the Western District of Arkansas, now in attendance upon the United States District Court at Fort Smith in said State, and of both political parties, would respectfully call to the attention of your excellency a few facts connected with the conduct of Wm A Britton, the Marshal of this District, during and since the recent elections in this State, which has a tendency to render the Said Court, instead of a source of protection to the citizen, a standing menace to his liberties and a merely political machine rather than a court of

Justice and Law! . . . In the interest, therefore of peace, and in the name of that essential right of the freeman—the right to his ballot, the undersigned would most earnestly appeal to your excellency not to permit the courts of our common country to be made, by its officers, the instruments of our oppressors and of our oppression. . . ."—DS (20 signatures—undated), DNA, RG 46, Nominations. The petition charged that voters had been illegally dropped from registration rolls. On March 17, USG nominated John N. Sarber in place of Britton.

1872, SEPT. 13.   Merced Vidal, New Orleans, to USG, seeking to claim the estate of her father, Nicolás María Vidal, Spanish lt. governor of Louisiana.— L, DNA, RG 59, Miscellaneous Letters.

1872, SEPT. 17.   To Hollis C. Pinkham, Mass. constable, Boston, authorizing the extradition of Charles H. Foster, Montreal, wanted for forgery.—DS, DNA, RG 59, Miscellaneous Letters. Related papers are *ibid.* Foster was jailed in Boston on Dec. 26.

1872, SEPT. 18.   U.S. Representative Aaron F. Perry of Ohio, Cincinnati, to USG. "Charles. B. Wilby Esq, is a young gentleman, who studied law in my office; is a graduate of Harvard, a member of the Cincinnati Bar, and a man of good abilities and character. As such I commend him to confidence and kindness."—ALS, Cincinnati Historical Society, Cincinnati, Ohio.

1872, SEPT. 20.   Governor John W. Geary of Pa., Erie, to USG. "You have doubtless, ere this, been informed of the melancholy death of Lieut Reid T. Stewart, 5th Cavalry U. S. A. slain by Indians, on the 27th day of August last, in Arizona Territory. In behalf of my esteemed friend, Dr. Stewart, the father of Lieut. S., and in behalf of the people of this city, I most earnestly endorse the request of the Mayor and Councils of this city to the Secretary of War, that the remains of Lieut. S. be forward at as early a time as practicable for interment here. . . . Lieut Stewart graduated in the same class with you son at West Point. . . ."—ALS, DNA, RG 92, Consolidated Correspondence, Reid T. Stewart.

1872, SEPT. 20.   Grace Greenwood (Sara Jane Clarke Lippincott), Manitou, Colorado Territory, to USG. "I yesterday took the liberty of telegraphing you, requesting you to honor the recommendation of my husband Mr. L. K. Lippincott, for the position of Recorder of the General Land Office,—made to you, by the Commissioner. Allow me to say that Mr. Drummond has done this without any solicitation whatever—indeed the act is a surprise to us—though I know he regards Mr. Lippincott very highly, as a man who has made himself very useful in the Department, and has done very good work for very poor pay. Indeed, the insufficiency of his salary as a clerk in the Land Office, though often having charge of the Division—has compelled me to work harder than ~~than~~ is justified by my frail health. In short, my dear sir, if you will make this appointment, you will do a great kindness . . ."—ALS, DNA, RG 48, Appointment Div., Letters Received. On Dec. 2, 1873, USG nominated Leander K. Lippincott as recorder, general land office.

1872, SEPT. 25. Daniel Wyman, Somerville, Mass., to USG. "Having been employed at U. S. Arsenal at Watertown Mass for a number of years I wish to inform you of the state of affairs existing there at this time. Mr Dennis Phalon Supt. there & Thomas Walsh & Patrick MacLaughlin of the machine department being very strong Greely men will not employ men of the opposite party. I being a very strong man of the other party, I wish to be reinstated & I appeal directly to you. believing I have as good a right to be employed there as they. Taking a very active part in the coming election I hope you will reinstate me for I am sure we shall be successful."—ALS, DNA, RG 156, Letters Received.

1872, SEPT. 26. Secretary of the Navy George M. Robeson to USG, Long Branch. "Telegram received and young Hoyt appointed. To what address shall I send permit?"—Telegram sent, DNA, RG 45, Letters Sent to the President.

1872, [*Sept.*]. Mrs. Frank Hamilton, Maumee, Ohio, to USG. "I seat myself to ask a great favor of you and I shall have to say as I do to my Savior I have no where else to go as no one has the power to grant my request but you I entreat you to send me a pardon for my son . . . my son *Deserted* (there the dreadful word is written) he was in the war the last year and a half got an honorable discharge at that time he was not yet Eighteen so course he was in love with Army life and again enlisted in the regular army at Fort Wayne Detroit Mich he was there most two years and was liked by his Col (I know because the Col *wrote me so*) but in an evil hour he drank to much and did quarrelled with an officer and so he done the deed I have named after two years he wrote me and I went to see him I found him grieving sore that he had so disgraced his Country and himself . . ."—ALS (docketed Sept. 5, 1872), DNA, RG 153, 1034 BMJ 1872. On July 20, 1875, Henry T. Crosby, chief clerk, War Dept., wrote to Hamilton. "In reply to your letter of the 4th. instant, to the President, asking for the pardon of your son Curtis J. Orcutt, a deserter from Co. G, 4th. Artillery, you are respectfully informed that no action can be taken in the case while the man continues, as at present, a deserter at large."—Copy, *ibid.*, RG 107, Letters Sent, Military Affairs.

1872, SEPT. Malcolm Livingston, Mount Vernon, N. Y., to USG, alleging mistreatment from Thomas H. Dudley, consul, Liverpool.—Copy, CSmH. Also in Sept., Thomas H. West, Haverhill, Mass., wrote to USG. "As there is a Remonstrance against retaining T. H. Dudley as Consul at Liverpool. I would say, that should the Administration conclude to make a change therein, I have or had an application in the State Department for that Consulate, based upon a letter from John G. Whittier and endorsed by the late Governor Andrew, and the then mayor of Boston . . ."—ALS, DNA, RG 59, Letters of Application and Recommendation. See *PUSG*, 19, 424–26.

1872, OCT. 1.   To David McConaughy, Gettysburg. "I have the honor to acknowledge the receipt of your letter informing me of my election as an honorary director of the 'Gettysburg Battle field Memorial Association', for which
compliment I beg that you will accept for yourself and associates my cordial
thanks, and my best wishes for the Association."—LS, Gettysburg College,
Gettysburg, Pa.

1872, OCT. 2.   U.S. Senator Hannibal Hamlin of Maine to USG. "Capt Lewis
H Sanger late of the 17th U. S. Infantry has been dismissed the Service upon
the finding of a Court Martial. The charges against Capt Sanger, the finding of
the Court and the approval of the Secretary of War are all on file at the War
Department. Capt Sanger was a good officer and did good service during the
late war. He feels that he has been harshly delt by, and that the evidence in the
case dose not justify the finding of the Court. Such too is the opinion of those
who have carefully examined the case. Now in simple justice to Capt Sanger,
we respectfully ask that you will order Judge Advocate Holt to carefully review
the case, with a view to restore Capt Sanger to the Army, if it shall be found
that the decision of the Court is unjust and not warranted by the evidence"—
ALS, DNA, RG 94, ACP, 115 1873. U.S. Representatives John A. Peters and
Eugene Hale of Maine favorably endorsed this letter.—AES, *ibid.* On Oct. 21,
Louis H. Sanger wrote to USG presenting his service record, denying allegations that he had seduced a woman, and charging his accusers with perjury.—
ADS, *ibid.* Sanger was reinstated as of Jan. 6, 1873.

1872, OCT. 3.   E. D. Carnahan, "Late of Co "E" 139th Regt Pa Vols.," Chicago, to USG. "I venture to address you in my own behalf. I have no influence
that I can bring to bear on the subject on which I address you. I enlisted when
only fourteen years of age, and was made a cripple for life at the battle of the
Wilderness where I was the first to receive a bullet in that campaign. I desire
to ask your excellency to appoint me to something in your gift whereby I can
support my young wife and Babies. Can give testimonials in regard to character and ability. Hoping I have not tired your patience . . ."—ALS, DNA, RG
107, Appointment Papers. No appointment followed.

1872, OCT. 4.   A. Ludlow Case, act. secretary of the navy, to USG. "I have the
honor to return herewith the letter of Mr Lathrop, referred by you to this Department, relative to his claims for services rendered in the capture of the
blockade-runner 'Emma,' by the steamer 'Arago' in which he was a passenger.
A similar letter from Mr Lathrop was referred to this Department in May last
by the Secretary of War, and I have the honor to enclose a copy of the reply of
the Secretary of the Navy, dated the 31st of that month."—LS, OFH. See
O.R. (Navy), I, xiv, 399.

1872, OCT. 7.   James N. Muller, Baltimore, to USG. "Allow me the honor to
write this Letter to you, and to say—In view of the probable change to be
made in the Collectorship at Balt, in consequence of the long affliction of the

present incumbent—and perhaps death, or, by reason of your second term *which is certain*—with a purpose to make certain changes—In such an event occurring—please allow me. Honord Sir, to present to your favourable consideration the name of *Robert Turner* Esqr. A *merchant* of High and long standing in the City of Balt, Well Known in the Mercantile community for his honor and integrity—also buisness qualities—and merits as a Gentleman of fine moral principles, A member of the M. E. Church, well Known in all classes of our city. He is not a Politician in the common use of that term, yet a thorough Union Lincoln and Grant Advocate, . . . By strict attention and integrity to his buisness as a merchant—he has amassd a fortune of upward of One hundred thousand $100,000 dollars—hence he is not beholding to seek for a position   Further in his appointment—He would make subordinate selections out of good sober honest material—which would reflect credit to all concerned in the Government Employ—which is—which is far from being so at the present in many respects—. . ."—ALS, DNA, RG 56, Collector of Customs Applications. On Oct. 14, Horace Porter wrote to John L. Thomas, Jr., collector of customs, Baltimore. "The President directs me to request you to call upon him at the Executive Mansion either to-morrow or Wednesday."—Copy, DLC-USG, II, 1. See *PUSG*, 19, 339. On Nov. 6, Thomas wrote to USG. "Although prevented from participating in the glorious result of yesterday by a severe illness, which commenced in July last, and has not yet ended, I nevertheless crave the liberty of Congratulating you on your triumph over your enemies. No campaign has been more bitter, No vindication more complete. I have only to add that I sincerely hope the success of your new administration, may be as grand in its results as the one about to close and that you may long live to enjoy the love and gratitude of your Countrymen"—LS, USG 3.

On March 8 and 15, 1873, Thomas again wrote to USG. "I learn, to day, for the first time, that in a conversation you had with Mr Washington Booth, some weeks ago, you told Mr Booth, that you had determined on my removal from the position I now, hold under your administration, and expressed the wish, that Mr Booth would communicate this fact to me, together with your desire, that I would send you my resignation. Not being aware of any cause for my removal I had supposed that in the spirit of the Civil Service rules, there would be no action necessary, on my part, other than to make an application, for reappointment, at the proper time—my commission not expiring until the middle of April, next, and by which time, I expect to be fully able to be in attendance, at the Custom House. I cherish a sincere desire for the success of your new administration and, if my reappointment is calculated to embarrass you, in the least, I have no desire to hold on to it, and by indicating to me, that you wish to make a change, my resignation will be placed in your hands. Hoping to hear from you, before you take final action, in the matter, . . ."—LS, DNA, RG 56, Collector of Customs Applications. "Having learned from a reliable source that the report that you had made up your mind to remove me from the position I now hold under you. has no foundation in fact—I have the honor to make application for re-appointment at the expiration of my present official term—. . . For the past seven months, I have been sorely afflicted with a malady which at times threatened my life—but during the whole of that period—I was able to attend to all of my official duties—except—being in attendance at the Custom House. . . ."—ALS, *ibid.* Related papers are *ibid.*

On March 18, A. M. Hancock and three others, Bel Air, Md., telegraphed to USG. "The republicans of this town & the Co of Harford are averse to the Retention of Jno L Thomas as Collecter of Customs at Balto   public sentiment here endorses The appointment of Washn *Booth* for that Place and general *King* for the naval office   with the gentlemen at head of affairs We may hope to carry the State next fall   without them the Result is Doubtful"—Telegram received, *ibid.* Related papers are *ibid.* On the same day, James M. Deems, Baltimore, wrote to USG. "As a Union man of 1861 and a soldier of the Army of the Potomac (having commanded 1st Md cavalry as Lt Col.) in all those heavy battles before the battle of Gettysb[ur]g.) I take the liberty of asking you to consider well before you place such an important office as Collector of this Port in the hands of a Catholic—I am not pleading for Mr Thomas, he has given satisfaction to the merchants generally; but, if you do make a change let the appointee be a protestant, as we have not twenty Catholic Union men in this city, or even in the state—they are almost to a man against us. Mr Booth holds a high place as a gentleman and merchant—but he can not influence ten Catholic votes, as they vote as the Priest tells them. This city and also the state are controlled by Catholics who hold three forths of the offices. Mr B. was brought out on our ticket for Congress by our wire pullers who expected to get the Catholics to vote for him; but he badly beaten when scarcely half the votes were polled. He has had two of his friends appointed in the Custom House—both are Catholics—one a Democrat who was turned out of a city office. I am not opposed to any religion but you must know the bad use made by Catholics to carry their point. Thanking you again, for the kind appointment of my Son Clarence to a Cadetship—he is now 3rd sergeant—"—ALS, *ibid.* On March 19, A. D. Evans, Baltimore, wrote to USG. "You will please pardon this intrusion as I had long since determined never to interfere with official appointments. only where I feared that the true interst of the whole country would likely be injured by impoper persons beng apponted   it is this fear that prompts me to write these few lines. I have watched carefully for these many years the pertenacious manner in which that certain Class of persons in our land press their claims for office *particularly* where there is PATRONAGE, that Class are Jesuits Catholics, who as a people were disloyal to our goverment 900 out of every 1000 in our land and to day are organising religous political Societys under all kinds of names and instituting unions to the exclusion of protestants, and also organsng armed Soldiers in Maryland all Catholics. So that in a few years the nearly the whole Malitu of the State will be Foregen Catholics   it is they and a few Short Sighted protestants who are urging the appointment of *Mr Booth* for Collector of the Port of Baltimore—I write this in the interst of no one in particular but to warn you against one of the Agents of a Society which is in opposition to YOU and OUR GOVERMENT. Prince Metternech of Austra said all the Factions of Europe emminate either directly or indirectly from the FREE STATES of NORTH AMERICA AND THEY MUST BE

PUT DOWN   Our people must emigrate in larger comunities haveing there own Priests and teaches that there childen may be kept from the Contamnating influence of the REPUBLICANS THEY go AMONGST. YOU WILL PLEASE PONDER on these thoughts and facts."—ALS, *ibid.* On March 20, USG nominated Washington Booth as collector of customs, Baltimore. See *New York Times,* March 20, 1873.

On March 3, Daniel C. Bruce, collector of Internal Revenue, Cumberland, Md., had written to USG. "I would most earnestly recommend to your favorable consideration the appointment of Col Chas Gilpin as Collector of the Port of Baltimore . . ."—ALS, DNA, RG 56, Collector of Customs Applications. Related papers are *ibid.* On Dec. 1, USG nominated Charles Gilpin as surveyor of customs, Baltimore.

1872, OCT. 9.   U.S. Senator William P. Kellogg of La., New Orleans, to USG. "I beg to invite your special consideration to the name of Master William Carey Jones which was sent you sometime since, as an applicant for a cadetship at West Point. Master Jones is the son of a widowed daughter of Colonel Thos. H. Benton who struggling under pecuniary difficulties and is very desirous that her son should receive a Military education. Master Jones is a young man of promise and possesses the requisite qualifications for admission. I would be gratifying to myself and other friends of yours if an appointment could be given him"—LS, DNA, RG 94, Correspondence, USMA. A related letter is *ibid.* No appointment followed. See *National Cyclopædia of American Biography* (New York, 1929), XX, 252.

1872, OCT. 10.   USG endorsement. "Respectfully refered to the Atty. Gen. for his recommendation. Dr. Crumley, the ~~Comm~~ U. S. Commissioner is anxious to see early action taken for reasons which he will explain."—AES, Gallery of History, Las Vegas, Nev. Written on a letter fragment containing an endorsement of Oct. 7 from James L. Orr. "I concur fully in the recommendations of Dr J. L. Crumley U. S Comr for the pardon of Moore & Gaines. They are in my judgment fit subjects for Executive clemency."—AES, *ibid.* On Nov. 25, USG pardoned John A. Gaines, convicted of liquor tax evasion and sentenced to six months in prison with a $1,000 fine, "on account of his feeble health."—Copy, DNA, RG 59, General Records. On April 3, 1873, USG pardoned John L. Moore, convicted on Jan. 5, 1872, of conspiracy and sentenced to eighteen months in prison; on Jan. 15, 1874, USG pardoned Walker Moore, convicted on May 1, 1872, of conspiracy and sentenced to eight years in prison with a $100 fine.—Copies, *ibid.* Gaines and the Moores had been convicted in S. C.

1872, OCT. 10.   USG note. "The Sec. of War may call special attention to the application of E. P. Eckerson for a 2d Lt' apt. when civil appointments come to be made next."—ANS, DNA, RG 94, ACP, 5185 1872. On June 11, Edwin P. Eckerson, Chester, Pa., had written to USG. "I most respectfully apply for an appointment as a Second Lieutenant in a regiment of Infantry, Cavalry or Artillery. I am twenty years of age, was born and brought up in the army, and have been through a course of instruction at the Military Academies of the country for four years past, the last three of which at the Pennsylvania Military Academy. . . ."—ALS, *ibid.* On Dec. 12, USG nominated Eckerson as 2nd lt., 5th Cav.

On Aug. 21, 1875, AG Edward D. Townsend wrote to USG, Long Branch. "Referring to your telegram of the 4th instant; I have the honor to transmit herewith, a copy of the report of the Judge Advocate General of his re-examination of the Proceedings of the General Court Martial in the case of 2nd Lieut Edwin P. Eckerson, 5th Cavalry together with a copy of the General Court Martial Order, from which it will be seen that Lieut. Eckerson ceased to be an officer of the army July 15, 1875. The additional charges (which are in possession of the Adjutant General) referred to in the report of the Judge Advocate General were forwarded by Lieut. Eckerson's company commander and have not been tried, but show that subsequent to his trial he has been guilty of a further violation of his pledge to abstain from the use of intoxicating liquors, and also of a repetition of boisterous conduct while under the influence of liquor."—Copy, *ibid.*, Letters Sent. On Nov. 19, Secretary of War William W. Belknap wrote to Eckerson. "The argument submitted by you *against your sentence by General Court Martial, and requesting re-instatement by a new appointment* in the 5th U. S. Cavalry at the foot of the list of Second Lieutenants, having been referred to this Department by the President, I have respectfully to inform you that after comparing the comments upon the testimony in in your printed argument with the testimony itself in the record, no sufficient ground is discovered for modifying the unfavorable conclusions already arrived at in your case. . . . This decision is arrived at, after an elaborate report by the Judge Advocate General, which has been submitted to the President and he concurs in it."—Copy, *ibid.*, RG 107, Letters Sent, Military Affairs. On Feb. 7, 1876, Capt. Theodore J. Eckerson, Fort Adams, R. I., wrote to USG. "My son (Edwin P.) has suffered much since his dismissal seven months ago, and the lesson has been a severe and salutary one. Can he not be now appointed to a vacancy in the 7th Cavalry? I am confident he would now make a good officer— his field record being already unexceptionable. He would even then lose three years of promotion."—ALS, *ibid.*, RG 94, ACP, 5185 1872. On April 12, USG nominated Edwin P. Eckerson as 2nd lt., 7th Cav.

On Sept. 9, Capt. Eckerson, Newport, R. I., wrote to USG. "The appointment of my son, Theodore H. Eckerson, to a Second lieutenantcy in the Army, was received a few days since. I will not essay to describe, nor can you ever know, what gladness has been brought to the hearts of my family by your generous action in his case, and in that of his brother in June last. Out of the goodness of your heart you had appointed my two sons, Theodore and Edwin, to Commissions in the Army; but in an evil hour (too young properly to appreciate the positions and favors thus bestowed,) they suffered themselves to be deprived of these appointments, plunging those nearest and dearest to them into affliction of mind from which for a time there seemed no way of escape, and frustrating what had been one of the dearest objects of parental existence. To your kind offices I had been largely indebted in obtaining my first Commission in the Army, in 1853. Again in 1865, through you alone I obtained my present Commission; and when in 1870 you gave my eldest boy a cadet-ship at West Point, and afterward, in 1872, gave his brother a Commission in the Cavalry, our cup of happiness was indeed full! Since then we have been called upon to suffer much, and our only ray of consolation was found in the fact that these sons, although unwise, had not been criminal. They too suffered,—for, born and brought up in the Army, they realized that they had thrown away their occupation,—that they were unsuited to any other profession, and that a spirit of forgiveness more than human could alone restore them to the positions they had so foolishly parted with. But this letter is not written to describe past troubles, which are only referred to here as showing the 'depths' out of which we have been raised by your action. We desire to express to you our boundless and undying gratitude for the restoration of these sons to the service, and for our consequent restoration to happiness. They, as well as the rest of my family, have entreated me to write to you, and this must be my apology for this intrusion. General: The *desire* to do good to others is in itself always a source of happiness, which all can taste and enjoy; but when to this desire is added the *power* to do good and the *will* to exercise that power,—who shall attempt to measure the happiness of him who has thus been favored by the Almighty for the benefit of his fellow-men? That the same good God who watched over you in battle both in youth and in riper years, and placed you as the Head of a mighty Nation, where your course has been marked by thousands upon thousands of instances of goodness such as I have feebly attempted to acknowledge, may still keep you in the hollow of His Almighty Hand, is the prayer we unceasingly offer up,—in which we are joined by millions of true hearts."—ALS, USG 3. Theodore H. Eckerson, USMA 1874, had resigned as of Sept. 15, 1875; on Aug. 11, 1876, USG nominated him as 2nd lt., 5th Cav.

1872, OCT. 10.   D. Eglinton Barr, Washington, D. C., to USG. "In accordance with your instructions received yesterday, I submitted your endorsement on a Petition signed by gentlemen of New Orleans, to the Sec.y of War. As he stated that the Endorsement did not amount to any thing, & did not meet the case, or words to that effect, and declined to read the Petition which your Excellency was pleased to read;—I have the honor to submit to the President of the United States the cause of the pressure leading to my resignation, & the ample testimonials of character & usefulness rebutting the charges; . . . Awful as the charges are, yet considering that they are made against a Chaplain, the only wonder is that they are so few, for the document appears imperfect without embracing Adultery & horsestealing & a service of years at the Penitentiary. Each Specification in this false paper is directly or virtually contradicted by some name or names given as witnesses testifying to their high respect for my Christian characte[r] & usefulness & selfdenial for the good of others:—extending my labours beyond the duties assigned me of instructing the Coloured troops, and, in addition, wherever I was stationed, inaugurating successfully the Public Free School system on which greatly depends the preservation of the liberty so triumphantly achieved by the Sword. I have the honour of inviting attention also to the Endorsement of Col. Andrews, refusing me the privilege, when placed in arrest, of temporarily going beyond the narrow limit assigned me intending to see the parties said to be my accusers: . . . This *pun- ishment* of an *Officer* by a Post Commander, so unnecessary & oppressive, it is hoped will lead to just action in my behalf, taken in connection with my long uninterrupted services as Senior Chaplain in the Army, under Col. Gaskill 81st U. S. C. I. under Generals Mower & Wheaton of the 39th U S C. I having been appointed from the 81st U. S. C. I, & continuously after the consolidation un- der Gen. Hinks & Col. Bliss, the last of whom is still in the 25th Regt & whose testimonial I enclose as one of the old officers of General Mower's command in the city of New Orleans. And now Mr President, I have the honor to request that your endorsement on the Petition from New Orleans be carried into ef- fect, & that I be reinstated in such way & at such time as in your wisdom may be deemed expedient & just, so that, meanwhile these testimonials may be al- lowed their full weight of influence in correctly exhibiting my record of duty on the frontier, and the estimation in which I was held."—ALS, DNA, RG 94, ACP, 4671 1872. No reinstatement followed.

1872, OCT. 12.   J. Haydon Burns, Cincinnati, to USG. "An unknown and humble boy writes to you to ask a favor of you. Will you grant it? Will you do me the great favor to appoint me to the U. S. M. Institute at West Point as a Cadet. I was born in Richland County Ohio on the 5 of February 1853   I am 5 feet 5½ inches in height light hair and blue eyes. My Father is a minister at Chagrin Falls Ohio and was during the war of the Rebellion Chaplain of the 65th O V I Harker, Col   Four Brothers of mine also served in the Union Army . . ."—ALS, DNA, RG 94, Correspondence, USMA. On March 13, 1873, Burns, Chicago, wrote to USG. "I see by this mornings 'Tribune' that you have appointed me a Cadet at West Point. Allow me to thank you, from the bottom of my heart, and to assure you that by my course of action, I will endeavor faithfully, to deserve the honor, you have confered on me,   For my dear old Father I thank you again"—ALS, USG 3.
     On July 1, 1875, Burns, Long Branch, wrote to Secretary of War William W. Belknap seeking reinstatement to USMA.—ALS, DNA, RG 94, Correspon- dence, USMA. Burns did not graduate.

1872, OCT. 12.   U.S. Senator Henry W. Corbett of Ore., Portland, to USG. "I have been informed that a petition is in circulation asking the removal of my friends from office viz those who stood by me and advocated my re-election. If such be the case, I trust that no such step will be taken   I do not know of one that is not an advocate for your re-election. All kinds of falsehoods have been used for my defeat & perhaps may be used to remove good republicans from office; I should personally return to Washington to prevent this, were I not de- sirous of remaining here to do what I can to aid in carrying our state for Grant & Wilson. I desire the success of our ticket here and should regret to see any step taken that would in any way distract our party. I write you thus early to apprise you and prevent any unwise step of which you may not be fully advised. I regard the state sure for our ticket"—ALS, USG 3. Rival Republican factions in Ore. contested Corbett's reelection. See *New York Times*, Sept. 26, Oct. 12, 1872.

1872, OCT. 14. USG pardon. "Whereas on the 25th day of June, 1872, in the Supreme Court of the District of Columbia, one Robert Williams was convicted of bigamy, and was sentenced to be imprisoned for two years; And whereas, it is represented that he is an ignorant man—formerly a slave—who had committed this offence entirely without criminal intent, or knowledge that he was violating the law;—And whereas, Judge Humphreys, before whom he was tried, and the jurors on the case, strongly recommend his pardon;—And whereas, District Attorney Fisher joins in this recommendation: Now, therefore, be it known, that I, . . . grant to the said Robert Williams, a full and unconditional pardon. . . ."—DS, Roosevelt University, Chicago, Ill.

1872, OCT. 14. To Thomas Murphy *et al.*, New York City. "I take great pleasure in introducing Mr J. Parker Jordan of Norfolk, Virginia a loyal man and staunch supporter of the Government who thinks of moving to New York City to commence the practice of his profession."—Copy, DLC–USG, II, 1. On Nov. 15, J. Parker Jordan, New York City, wrote to USG. "Will you allow an humble friend—One who admires you for your sterling worth—and not for the tinsel which adorns the Office—to congratulate you—tho late—upon the Success of the Republican Cause, of which you are the living embodiment You will remember I gave you on every occasion we met—the earliest opportunity being in last March—in your reception room in the presence of our friend Platt & others from Norfolk—the opinion that we should Carry Virginia! I know our friends were not so sanguine as I was, and that as late as Nov 1—Mr Chander told me Mr Platt & our friends at Washington doubted it—Well it is glorious news I write tho particularly to thank you with a heart warm with generous emotions—for your kind letter introducing *me* to Mr Thos Murphey—It *has done* me *great* good—the war broke me up—I had made 100,000$ by my practice—I come here to get clear of the infernal persecution for opinions sake—My prospect is bright. If *at any* time an opportunity offers to speak a kind word to our friends *here* on my behalf it will not be forgotten by one who is an enthusiastic admirer of your unpretending ability and modest worth . . . P. S. Mr Platt & others knows my ability & if the U States should need the services of a Special attorney I would be glad to accept the employment."—ALS, USG 3. On March 20, 1873, Jordan, Washington, D. C., again wrote to USG. "You know I am now living in NY City—Rebel persecution was too much to bear—I want no office, nor ask any—; but inf our friends in NY City could understand it would be agreeable to the legal advisers of the Government to invoke my ability in the prosecution of claims professional or otherwise it would touch me with a gratitude I have no language to express Judge Underwood I feel certain will both endorse my ability as a lawyer & honesty I am poor—lost over 100,000 by war in Slave property to the *War*—Have been loyal Since /65—Could you aid me in this way I will repay it with a thousand impulses of my generous nature . . . PS. Came here purposely to see you but cant wait 2 days"—ALS, DNA, RG 60, Letters from the President.

1872, OCT. 15.   Joshua Ashworth, former private, 7th Pa. Veteran Cav., Oregon Hill, to USG. ". . . I was Born in England 1831   I Landed the united States 1849   I took the enlisting Oath *Sep* 1 in witch i pledge my Live property and Sacred honner to Defend the union against all foes   October 12th 1861 at Harrisburg camp Cameron the Enrollment Oath in which I pledge myself against all foes Both foreign and Domestic   I have fullfill these pleges on many a Battle field   Now General Does Not the oaths which I Give to the State and to the united States Give me a right to vote   in what firmer Way cud I Show my Layality to this goverment then meet all her foes Both Foreign And Domestic in mortal combat . . . it Seem hard to me Who had Borne the Brunt of Battle to Stand Back and see Deserters vote   Now I See in the tioga Agitator that No Deserter as a right to vote   if that is so tell Me . . ."—ALS, DNA, RG 59, Miscellaneous Letters.

1872, OCT. 15.   Henry O. Dwight, "formerly Adjt 20th Ohio Infty (Vet. Vols) & A. D. C. to Maj Gen. Force," Bible House, Constantinople, to USG. "Allow me to express to you the infinite satisfaction the news from the October elections, has caused with us, as showing that the people at large have taken in hand the answering of the wild statements which have been scattered ofver the country so freely within the last year in regard to yourself. It would have pleased you I think have seen the enthusiastic manner in which the news was received at this building by the little group of Americans who happened to be present. . . ."—ALS, USG 3.

1872, OCT. 16.   USG endorsement. "Let special attention be called to this application when appointments are made."—AES, DNA, RG 94, Correspondence, USMA. Written on a letter of Oct. 12 from Col. Henry W. Benham, Boston, to USG. "I would respectfully request for my son Henry Hill Benham, one of the appointments within your gift to cadetships at West Point, for entering in the year 1874. I would state that my son is now in the last half of his 15th year, . . ."—LS, *ibid.* On April 5, 1873, Benham wrote to USG. "I wrote you on the 1st instant, acknowledging your kindness in the appointment of my son to a cadetship for the year 1874,—an acknowledgement that had been delayed a few days by a severe illness from rheumatism from which I had suffered greatly. At the letter I also referred to the few months that would be wanting at the date of his commencing his studies, of the age of 17, which to my surprise I found as a requirement in the form of acceptance—as I had supposed it as it had been for so long,—to be 16 years; his age having been candidly stated both in my letter to yourself—and in the form of acceptance. . . ."—LS, *ibid.*

On Dec. 27, 1873, and Jan. 30, 1874, Benham wrote to USG again requesting his son's appointment to USMA.—LS and ALS, *ibid.* Henry H. Benham entered USMA in 1875. On Aug. 19, 1876, Benham telegraphed to USG. "Will you be kind Enough to have the acceptance of my sons Cadetship resignation delayed till you receive my Letter or he can see you   he has leave on

Good standing as to Conduct—"—Telegram received, *ibid.* On the same day, Elizabeth Ann Benham, Boston, telegraphed to USG. "Please accept my sons resignation and refuse him a reappointment"—Telegram received, *ibid.* Henry H. Benham, who did not graduate from USMA, was appointed 2nd lt. in 1879.

1872, OCT. 16.   R. Woods, Cincinnati, to USG. "I left my home at Midway Ky some 2 months since & came here to assist the True Republican party. I labored hard & as we thought to best interest of the cause but see how we were fooled in our calculations here in the city & county by those who betrayed their Savior the Jews   The firm of Trounstine, & Co a Wholesale cloth House here took it upon themselves to visit secretly every Jew in the city & county exhibiting your Order against them during the War & advising them to go against you & your Administration that in the event of your reelection you would endeavor to drive them from the country   But as things were now promised & in the event of your defeat they would be enabled to smuggle in everything desired for their welfare   I am satisfied from good authority that the House of T. & Co are smuggling many goods through Canada, &c   Cloths, Laces, Jewelery &c are here that come through in way. I wish it were in your power to banish them all from our country. The skies I think & hope are brightning for the Ides of Nov & without a great unforseen change in the Political world your Election is sure. I shall remain here & fight for you & cause until the Election   Hoping you every success &c . . . Be of good cheer"—ALS, DNA, RG 56, Letters Received. See *PUSG*, 7, 53.

1872, OCT. 17.   John D. Harrington, Div. Superintendent's Office, Erie Railway, Jersey City, to USG. "When out of situation and in trouble some months ago I did myself the honor to write you asking your valued influence towards procuring me some position on a line of Railway &c   My letter must have been overlooked by you or perhaps never presented to you by your Secty. I now write to say that I am the Council & recognised head of over Seven thousand men in this state, and one of the Council of 20, who govern some 50.000 men in the state of N. Y.   I have never asked for a dollar nor shall I now for any services on my part but must say that had I had a few thousand I could make more use of it in the Coming Contest than any fifty men who are now Conducting the Campaign. I dont write you as a politician but as a man of Character & honor, having the welfare of my Country at heart   Should you cause to furnish me with the sinews of war, I can get a weeks leave of absence, and will then at once visit my several Presdts, & other influential members of the Associations who will at once act—(as they must) as I will instruct them. As to character, principles &c &c I refer you to Genl A S Diven, Vice Presdt. Erie Ry. Mr Presdt. I am as certain of gaining 10,000 Votes if the needful is supplied me as I am of now writing this hasty scrall   A good friend of yours that has Caused me to write you. Please let me hear from you thru' one of your Sectys as early as possible"—ALS, DLC-William E. Chandler.

1872, OCT. 19.   USG endorsement. "Respectfully refered to the Sec. of State. If there is any Consulship vacant in the West Indies, Central or South America, I have no objection to Mr. Frank having, it, supposing of course his record while in Japan to be satisfactory to the Dept."—AES, DNA, RG 59, Letters of Application and Recommendation. Written on a letter of Oct. 9 from Andreas Willmann, New York City, to USG. "Allow me to introduce to you the bearer, Genl Paul Frank, who served with distinction during the whole war and at the close of it, was sent to Yokahoma, Japan by Secretary Seward as U. S. Marshall. At the opening of the port of Hiago he was temporarily assigned as Consular Agent. The last year and a half he acted as Vice Consul at Hiago, for T. Scott Stewart   Through the climatical influences in that Country, together with the exposeures, and the wounds received by him during the late war, his health is almost utterly ruined and the Doctors say that his life is in danger here every day, and urge him to go to Havana where he can regain his health   As he has not the necessary means to go there, he would respectfully apply for some position there, whatever you see fit to give him   I take the liberty to recomend him to you, as I know him to be worthy and deserving."—LS, *ibid.* Related papers are *ibid.* No appointment followed.

1872, OCT. 22.   USG pardon. "Whereas, on the 12th day of August, 1872, in the Police Court of the District of Columbia, one Charley Brown was convicted of engaging in an affray, and was sentenced to be imprisoned for one hundred and eighty days;—And whereas, on account of his general good character and behaviour, District Attorney Fisher, and many other citizens of Washington, believe that his offence was not of an aggravated nature, and recommend his pardon. Now, therefore, be it known, that I . . . grant to the said Charley Brown, a full and unconditional pardon. . . ."—Copy, DNA, RG 59, General Records. A similar pardon for "Charles Brown" dated Oct. 7 is *ibid.* The arrest followed a dispute between a pavement contractor and black laborers over pay. See *Washington Evening Star,* Aug. 12, 1872.

1872, OCT. 22.   To Secretary of War William W. Belknap from New York City. "Please grant extension of leave to Lieut Alexander M, Wetherill to accompany sick sister to Europe,   Application he says has been forwarded,"—Telegram received, DNA, RG 94, ACP, W1225 CB 1867. On the same day, Belknap telegraphed to USG. "No application received yet from Lt. Wetherill, but order will be issued granting the extension."—ALS (telegram sent), *ibid.,* RG 107, Telegrams Collected (Bound). On Nov. 16, T. D. Wetherill, Philadelphia, wrote to Dr. William Keating, Philadelphia. "My brother A. M. Wetherill desired me to tell you that he had some difficulty about his leave of absence. Genl Grant, gave him an extension of one year but through some mistake at Washington the paper was made out for only four months   Zandy said that if you spoke to Mr. Borie he would have it arranged. . . ."—ALS, *ibid.,* ACP, W1225 CB 1867. USG endorsed this letter. "Refer to Sec. of War with direction to extend leave to Oct, if no good reason exists for changing it."—AE (undated), *ibid.*

1872, OCT. 26.   Horace B. Sargent, Boston, to USG. "I take the liberty to send to you a copy of an address delivered before the Society of The Army and

Navy of The Department of The Gulf. If you should be able to read it, I should be highly gratified. It does not claim your attention from its merit.—I desire to lay it before you, because in it I endeavor to maintain the proposition, of infinite importance to the Executive energy of the Nation, that our civil war has, without any revolutionary action upon the constitution, but simply by a return to first principles, destroyed the Jeffersonian theory of interpretation and established, for the future, the broader National meaning that Washington, and Hamilton, and Madison before he became infected by Jefferson's views, intended. If my view is correct, as some of our best legal minds think, it is a most happy coincidence, that—at the same time with this change of constitutional theory, Society should be toned up by the return of a million of men, accustomed to energetic subordination;—and, that the chief executive authority rests in hands so National and determined as your own. We can be a *Nation.* This theory of the National authority by which I mean Nationalization not centralization, is far more extensive than it seems, and touches vast interests of liberty and Law, that have hitherto been dwarfed into mere matters of *local* concern, over which the Jeffersonian school denied any authority to the Government, of which you are the Head. This century sees the great movement— begun. It seems to me, General, that Mr. Greely's election would be a *fatal* reaction, because it would be a step back to National impotence, where we have been grounded for seventy five years. And I believe, that you have the grand opportunity of taking up this Government where Washington left it. With my own and my daughter's Congratulations on the safe return of Miss Grant to Her Father's Home, and Her Mother's arms, . . ."—ALS, DLC-USG, IB. See also *New York Times,* Aug. 28, 1872.

1872, Oct. 28.   Richard H. Young, Washington, D. C., to USG. "I am Now Repliing to you for my Rights   I has Receved my goverment But Bounty Not my State Bounty   I am Looking to you for it.   you are my portaction   I has Never got it   you Said that you Ware going to Show me Justdus   I am A man Who Will Show him Self to Be as Just man to mr Grant   Richard H young 38. co D U S c Trups E Street Bet 3. 4½ 334 South Side   Return a answer as Soon as you Received Dis"—ALS, DNA, RG 105, Letters Received. Endorsements related to Young's loss of his army discharge are *ibid.,* RG 107, Register of Letters Received.

1872, Oct. 29.   USG endorsement. "Refered to the Sec. of the Treas."—AES, DNA, RG 56, Letters Received. Written on a letter of Oct. 18 from Francis D. Connelly, clerk, 2nd Auditor's Office, "in behalf of Fifty other Pennns," probably to U.S. Senator Simon Cameron of Pa. "We are just informed by *our Auditor* (Hon E. B. French) that the *Secry of the Treasy,* has just given *orders* that no further *Election* leave be given to *Penna clerks in his Dept*! Will you not try to have this order riscinded? We all want to roll up the majority in our good old State to the highest possible figures. I have written to Col Dickey to the same effect, & hope that you may influence the rescinding of the said order, and that we may yet get the customary time for voting for our honored Prest—" —ALS, *ibid.* Cameron endorsed this letter to USG.—AES (undated), *ibid.*

1872, OCT. 30.   USG proclamation reimposing discriminatory duties on certain imports arriving on French ships after France had reimposed comparable duties on goods arriving on U.S. ships.—DS, DNA, RG 130, Presidential Proclamations. *Foreign Relations, 1872*, pp. 3–4. On June 12 and Nov. 20, 1869, USG had abolished these duties after France had taken similar action.— DS, DNA, RG 130, Presidential Proclamations. On Sept. 22, 1873, USG again abolished these duties, following a similar declaration by France.—DS, *ibid. Foreign Relations, 1873*, I, 29–30.

1872, OCT. 30.   Jasper M. Whitty, Washington, D. C., to USG. "The undersigned would respectfully and humbly beg to invite your attention to the following statement:—On the 26th inst., I had the honor of an interview with your Excellency, in which I stated to you, that I had been sick and unemployed since May 1st, 1870, and consequently my family were suffering for the necessaries of life. You were so kind as to tell me to 'see the Secretary of War, and ask to be enlisted in the general service, and that you would see the Sec'y afterwards.' I saw the Secretary of War, this morning, and was informed, that owing to my absence from duty while a clerk in the Q. M. G. Office, he could not recommend me to your Excellency. I would beg to state, that my absence from duty, was caused by sickness, over which I had no control, and in each case was verified by a certificate of the attending physicians, setting forth the nature of my disease. Two years and six months having elapsed since my discharge, and my health now, being fully restored, I do think that it should not be a bar against my earning a living for my wife and little ones; or that I should be compelled by necessity, to place my children in an Asylum, send my wife adrift upon the world and myself enter a Soldiers Home, there to eat the bread of charity.—I would further beg to state, that on the 20th of April 1861, I entered the military service as a Lieut. of Co. "C" 69th Reg. N. Y. S. Militia, and was honorably mustered out Aug. 3rd, 1861. I then raised a company ("C" 69th Reg. N. Y. Vols.) and was commissioned Captain, October 4th, 1861. I have a bullet remaining in my body, lost my right eye and received a severe wound in my left hip. I subsequently commanded my regiment in the field before the enemy. The neglect of my business occasioned by my service in the army, left me a poorer man by over five thousand dollars, than when I entered the service, and I trust that your Excellency will not regard my past sickness, (diagnosed by Doctor Norris, U. S. A. as typhoid condition,) a sufficient cause to deprive me of an opportunity to earn bread for my family, now that my health is fully restored. I enclose a Surgeons certificate as to my present health. Begging your Excellency's pardon for trespassing upon your attention, on the plea of dire necessity."—ALS, DNA, RG 107, Appointment Papers. USG endorsed this letter. "Sec. of War"—AE (undated), *ibid.* Wounded at the battles of First Bull Run and Antietam, Whitty petitioned Congress in 1876 for restoration of his pension and an artificial eye. See *CR*, 44–1, 1998; *HRC*, 44-1-602.

1872, OCT. 31.   USG endorsement. "Respectfully refered to the Sec. of War. Please call special attention to this application when Civil apts. are again made to the Army."—AES, DNA, RG 94, ACP, 4543 1872. Written on a letter of Oct. 20 from Thomas L. Alexander, USMA 1830, Louisville, to USG. "As my Son, Lee Alexander, is going to Washington City, I write this to be handed You by him. He is extremely anxious to obtain the appointment of 2nd Lt in the Cavalry Service, for which I wrote you some two months ago, enclosing the strong endorsements of Genl Terry & many other Officers, Friends of yours, stationed here. As I have been nearly forty three years in the service, and shall soon pass off the Stage, should it be in your power to grant his request, I will esteem it a person favor to myself."—ALS, *ibid.* Related papers are *ibid.* On Dec. 12, USG nominated Richard H. L. Alexander as 2nd lt., 7th Cav.

1872, OCT.   Lewis W. Drennen, St. Joseph, Mo., to USG. "I have the honor to address you Exelency in behalf of my famly which is loil and always has ben and myself also . . . two years ago I bought me an extry team an started for the Solaman valley to look up a homested   I left my famly in brown Co Kansas with one horse for my boy to cultivate some rented ground and I took three horses waggon & Breaking plow & other farming material and went out to the folks of the Solaman thair found two of my old nabors and I took a Clame jorning them on Oak Creek   my Clame had 40 acrs of timber   I sent to Junction City to file on my Clame so as to enable me to hold it till I mooved my famly as I intended to have don in Sept   Junction City was over one hundred miles from my Claime   I Commence improvements by braking some acrs of land and Commence to build a house but the Indians becum so hostile thay Kild three men in may 1870 on limestone 8 miles distant and on the 29 Day of may 1870 the Indians Came in on the war path and took my three horses . . . I staid till the last day of June then I was ablidge to go back to Brown County ware my famly was   I had to leave every thing out thare   I wanted to moove out in Sept but my famly was not willing to go out thair . . . I Concluded to go to Pottawatomie County Kansas and take a homested   I don so took one withoutought timber   Ɨ our legislature past an act to create a commission of three men to be appointed by the Governer to send for pursons & papers and to investagate and ardet all just Claims & Memorilesed Congress to make some provision to pay said claimes out of Indians funs   the clames is Cald the Kansas Indian depredation Claimes   my Clame was alowed for fore hundred & fifty (4,50,00) Dollars   thay have not ben paid yeat   they ar still at the propper Dept at Washington, D. C.   I have onley 18 acrs broke on my homested   I am not able to improve it for wont of means . . ."—ALS (docketed Oct. 17), DNA, RG 75, Letters Received, Kansas Agency. See *SMD*, 41-2-56, 41-2-59, 41-2-60, 43-1-76, 44-1-78.

[*1872, Oct.*].   Wah tah in kah, or Wah-Ti-An-Ka, to USG. "We a portion of the Cheifs of the Osage Nation of Indians have for a long time been anxious to communicate with you, but have been able for we have no way only through an agent whom we dont like.—He has never treated us like free men who have rights but like children or some thing worse. We think an agent should try to prove himself a friend and not a master—We have not been used to it and are

not willing to submit to it. Though he has shown his disposition continually
to pet up an interpreter an one or two cheifs so as to get some backing among
Osages then to entirely slight and disregard the wishes and interests of the
great body of Osages—we will mention only one thing. That is his habit of
continually intermedling in the internal affairs of the Osages—and trying to
dictate even who we shall have for cheif—The term of office of our head cheif or
govenor had run out—The agent was busy trying to put a cheif over us whom
he keeps in his employment and petted up so that he would agree to any thing
the agent might want. About ten days ago we met at the agency—the whole
Osage Poeple—We Cant write and hold elections like the cherokees or the
white poeple but we have a right to our choice—so we did it in our own way—
we cut two long poles—we named one Joe Paw ne no pa she—our candidate,
& told the agents pets to name their candidate—the said they would run
Alexcy Beatt—so we named their pole 'Beatt.' Each voter took a stick in his
hand—The poles were stuck up in the open prarie and the voters assembled
divided each going to the pole standing for the candidate he prefered and laid
by the pole a stick or rod about a foot long—as his vote—We ~~afterward~~ then
examined the piles of sticks in the presence of all the assembled chif's and
voters—and found four men had voted for Beatt—and the rest of the Osage
poeple en mass had voted for Joe—All the Bands of both great and little
Osages were present—also the agent—Alexcy Beatt is the interpreter of the
agent entirely under his influence—and we have no confidence that the truth
will ever reach the Indian Department—or the President in relation to this
election if it has to go through the agent so we have [a] cherokee to write this
down for us and send it through the mail   Another thing. We lately agreed in
council to allow white men to make a stock road through our country—We
were unwilling to it. Not because we were unfriendly to the whites no because
we were stingy of our grass, but because white poeple and especially stock
drivers mistreate our poeple and get into dificulties with our young men and
when they get into our country on any pretence they begin to try to take our
country from us.—But we were told by Our agent and the Rail road man, who
was there that the President wanted us to agree to it and would be angry if we
did not agree to it and they threatened that if we did not agree to it the President would send soldiers down among us and make us do so—So we agreed to
allow them drive for one year only—paying five cents per head for cattle—We
care not much for the five cents—we would rather keep troublesome poeple
out of our country—We have no confidence in our half breeds or our agent—
Direct your answer to the Osage cheifs care of Lewis Downing cheif of the
Cherikees Chouteau—Cherokee Nation—I your friend write this by authority of the Head cheifs and Council of the Osage Nation—"—L (docketed
Oct. 31, 1872), DNA, RG 75, Letters Received, Neosho Agency. In March,
1873, Thomas Mosier, Bird Creek, Indian Territory, wrote to "Hon Sir," probably USG. "It is with respect, I, drop you, these few lines, knowing the circumstances we are in. Sir, I am a half, Breed Osage, belonging to the Great &
little Osage Indians, I take the responibility on myself of writing. We are a Nation of people unaware of our interests, and, welfare,   we have an agent, with

us, but the general run of the Indian for, some cause, or other do not like him, . . . they have I suppose or will have in time, vast, amount of money, due them, they are sometimes destitute of provisions and other nesaries of life, but nevertheless they are in eager earnest to try to become civilized   it is not on the part of the Agent, that they will work, and farm, they have done the like before the war, commens   I have seen full blood Indian, living, then at that time in good (log houses) ful, of furniture of they best kind, had plenty of cattle, hogs, & chickens, in large quantity, and even till now they have commenced in like manner, they have little farm opened, and raising some cattle and hogs again, but I tell you the Agent, is not taking the right course to bring them to civilization,   they need some help and, assistance to commence on, . . ."—ALS (docketed March 24), *ibid.* See Frank F. Finney, "The Osages and Their Agency During the Term of Isaac T. Gibson, Quaker Agent," *Chronicles of Oklahoma*, XXXVI, 4 (Winter, 1958–59), 416–28.

1872, Nov. 4.   R. Beverly Frayser, Point Caswell, N. C., to USG. ". . . Greely will get the thinest vote here than any candidate ever did get who was supported by the Democratic party—His professions are all esteemed as hollow and insincere; made only to secure self aggrandizement—indeed he is called by many ~~the~~ a 'Political prostitute'—oblivious of all things else except place, power and emolument—His career though for a number of years bright, glorious and important, will terminate, on the 5th Nov to his utter disgrace and ruin, politically as well as Socially—for who can honor and respect a political renegade at a time like this in our history? . . ."—ALS, USG 3.

1872, Nov. 5.   Capt. Henry Johnson, medical storekeeper, San Francisco, to USG. "I have the honor to ask for an appointment for my Son Henry Johnson to the West Point Military Academy. Please accept my hearty congratulations for your reelection to the Presidential Chair."—ALS, DNA, RG 94, Correspondence, USMA. Related papers are *ibid.* On Dec. 13, 1875, USG nominated Henry Johnson, Jr., as 2nd lt., 8th Inf., to date from Oct. 15. See *PUSG*, 16, 433.

1872, Nov. 5.   George B. Loring, chairman, and George S. Merrill, secretary, Republican State Central Committee, Boston, to USG. "'Peace hath its victories no less than war.' Four years ago, Massachusetts enwreathed the victorious general with seventy-seven thousand majority. Today, with eighty thousand she crowns the successful President. The Republicans of the Old Bay State, the home of Henry Wilson, send cordial greeting; and in their behalf we congratulate you and the country upon your triumphant reëlection, securing continued peace and prosperity throughout the land."—*Boston Transcript*, Nov. 6, 1872. Probably on the same day, USG received a copy of a telegram dated 6:30 P.M. from William W. Clapp, editor, *Boston Journal*, to O. K. Harris, Washington, D. C. "Gooch carries every town & city in his district but one. Banks is defeated in his own town of Waltham. Benjamin W. Harris is elected in the Second Congressional District by 5000 majority. There are republican gains of Senators & Representatives."—N (undated, unsigned), ICarbS.

1872, Nov. 7.   James F. Casey, New Orleans, to USG. "Herewith enclosed I
have the honor to hand you a communication from leading Republicans of this
State, asking that Mr. A. J. Cassard be appointed to a Consul's position either
in Mexico or Central America, and in forwarding the same I can heartily endorse all that it contains. Mr. Cassard is a personal friend of mine—a thorough
going business man—acquainted with the peculiarities of the countries named,
by residence and travels therein and the appointment of him as requested
would be looked upon by favor by all our best citizens with whom he is well
known   I hope the recommendation will meet with favor and attention at your
hands."—LS, DNA, RG 59, Letters of Application and Recommendation. Related papers are *ibid.* On Dec. 19, USG nominated August J. Cassard as consul,
Tabasco, Mexico.

1872, Nov. 7.   Gideon J. Pillow, Memphis, to USG. "I am happy to congratulate you—(on what is now apparent, from the telegraphic intelligence, from
all parts of the country—) *your triumphant* re-*election*—The results in this city
& state, has surprized even your Friends—It is certain that Judge Barbour
Lewis is elected   You had thousands of Friends here & all over the country,
who were not known to each other, as your Friends—In the face of all efforts
and threats, I voted with an open ticket for you, & now I find myself in the majority, and I am congratulated that I stood *firm* and acted upon my *own convictions,* of duty to the country—Allow me Mr President to express the hope that
you will *conquer* the *prejudices* of your *enemies* & will *winn* over to your support, the great '*rebel Element*' of the south, by acts of justice & manifestations
of *interest* in, and sympathy for this section of the country. If you will but give
those of that class who were *friends,* your *confidence,* and extend to the southern people, who have been so utterly ruined by the war, *evidences* of *sympathy,*
and of a desire to do them justice, their *prejudices,* which impelled them into a
folly, which was *stultifying* to themselves & to all calm lookers on, will bring
them almost in a body to the support of your administration. Instead a *senti-
mental* '*closing* of the *bloody chasm*' that will *practically* close it over, with *restoration* of the *good fruits* of reconciliation   With my best wishes for your happiness & the success of your admiration for the next four years . . ."—ALS,
USG 3.
    On July 26, Pillow had written to Horace Porter. "I acknowledge with the
pleasure the reception this morning of your letter of the 12th Inst—written by
direction of the President. The object of my visit to Washington was to see the
President & to bring to his attention a Petition which I had forwarded to the
War Department for remuneration for a large lot of mules taken from me 1862
and My *right* to this *remuneration,* under late *decisions* of the *supreme court,* & to
invoke, his *love* of *justice* in my behalf—. . ."—ALS, Aurora College, Aurora, Ill.
See *PUSG,* 18, 360–61. On Aug. 14, Attorney Gen. George H. Williams wrote
to Secretary of War William W. Belknap rejecting Pillow's claim for mules allegedly taken from his Ark. plantation.—*Official Opinions of the Attorneys-
General,* XIV, 103–4.

On March 21 and May 31, 1873, Pillow wrote to USG. "On my return to this City yesterday I found your letter of the 16th Inst—addressed to me at the Arlington Hotel. I left Washington the evening I called with my wife, to pay you our respects. I need not my Dear Sir, say I was gratified by your kind invitation to myself & Mrs Pillow, to visit you *socially.* Nothing could have afforded both myself and Mrs Pillow, more pleasure than it would have done to have accepted your invitation. I regretted to leave Washington without an opportunity of a *conference* with you   I am your Friend & the friend & supporter of your administration. I am identified with the Southern people & I have so conducted myself since the war as to retain their *confidence* & *respect*, and yet I have been, as you know, true in my *allegiance* to the Goverment of the U. S. I was known all over the country in the late canvass to be for you over Mr Greely,—and though strong appeals were made to me—through the Press & by letters, in all parts of the South—not to seperate myself from the great body of the Southern people, yet I remained *steadfast* and *immoveable* in my support of yourself & voted for you with an open ticket, yet so great was the respect for me, that *no word* of *censure* or of reproach, was cast upon me for so doing. Being called to Washington by a matter deeply interesting my wife— (to whom I was but recently married) she was most anxious to go with me to pay you, her respects & to know you personally—(whose election she had herself as a Lady warmly espoused) I confess to you, that I felt that our reception was not what I expected, in the short & formal interview, with which we were honored. Still I was disposed to ascribe it, rather to your pressing engagements, than to intentional indifference. Hence you can see Mr President, the pleasure your kind and considerate letter afforded both my wife and myself. Though somewhat disappointed in the reception we met, yet permit me to assure you, that we are deeply recompensed in the fact, that you suspended your pressing public duties, in order to address us, a kind, friendly *private* letter, giving us an invitation to spend a social visit of an hour with yourself and Mrs Grant. We take pleasure Sir, in acknowledging the Honor thus conferred upon us, and for which, we make you our grateful acknowledgements & tender to you our best wishes & prayers for your long life & successful administration of the affairs of this great nation. While at Washington it was my purpose— had I have had an opportunity to do so—to have conferred with you in regard to the *condition* & *mind* of the Southern people. To win back the *heart* of the southern people—so as to bring them again into the great national Famaly, in true *allegiance* and *love* to the Goverment, all *patriots must feel* is the *wisest*, & only true *policy.* A Father, whom a sense of duty impels to chastise a rebellious son—until *humbled*, would naturally by *kindness* & *sympathy*, seek to restore the child *so humbled* to his natural affection for the Parent. The Parent should no longer cherish *resentment* to the son—nor *distrust him.* Every Parents heart would prompt that as the *wise course*, and as the natural one, by motives of love. Such a course on the part of the Goverment of the U. S. will bring back, in true allegiance to the Goverment, the great body of the southern people. The southern people are impoverished & ruined by the war. They have been

embittered by the many acts—in the shape of public laws—imposed upon
them by Congress. I do not mean to say that these people have been, in their
conduct blameless—and that Congress has been, without provocation, *harsh,*
but I think a milder course on the part of Congress—with gentler measures,
& with the manifestation of some *sympathy* & *respect* for the souther people—
in their ruined condition, & with some allowance for the irritation growing out
of the great civil war—in other words, the Goverment having triumphantly
maintaned its authority and dominion over a people, who had—from misguided *political teachings,* rebelled against it—could have well afforded to be
magnanimous to so brave & chivalrous a portion of its people. By so doing it
would *greatly have strengthened* its own powers, by winning back that people—
in love to duty. Such Mr President are my views, of the policy which this goverment ought to have adopted towards the south—As far as possible the work
of restoration to a proper legal status, of the southern State Goverments
should have been left to the southern people themselves. If the U. S. Govt will
confide in them and trust them, they will not prove *treacherous* or *false* to it.
A people so brave & gallant as they have shewn themselves to be, will not—
(after laying down their arms) prove false to their own honor, nor in the duty
of allegiance to their Goverment. In the late Presidential election, it is aston-
ishing how general a disposition was shewn by the people to support you,
against all the efforts of a most powerful public Press, which bitterly opposed
you. Kindness & confidence in them, on your part—and the manifestation of
sympathy & respect for them, will bring to your support the great body of the
intelligent souther white population. The *political atmosphere* of the north, is
still *cold,* & *harsh,* & *embittered,* towards the south. The *brave officers* & *soldiers*
of the army which fought us, is not so, but the controuling influence at the
north is the POLITICAL element. That is not as much *tempered* down as as wisdom should have dictated. You Mr President can controul & bring back to the
support of the Goverment all the *brave men,* whom your greatness as a military
commander, subdued in arms. If your Policy as the chief executive of the Nation should be as wise, as was your talants skill and success as a General in the
Field successful—then indeed, will you deserve to rank with *Washington,* in
greatness and *glory,* and you will fill the place ~~in the place,~~ in the hearts of sixty
millions of people, which he filled in the hearts of six millions—It is *you,* and
you alone, ~~that~~ who can acheive this *great result.* Your subordinates in the Administration of the Govt cannot be trusted with political power, as your subordinates could in military command. The rigid exactions, & reins of *account-
ability,* in military command, afforded an assurance of *promptitude* & *fidelity* in
military Goverment, which cannot be had, or expected in political Goverment.
I fully believe you are *equal* to the *greatness,* & to the *success* which are indicated in these remarks. To settle the *jars* & *conflicts,* which *exists* ~~in some~~ in
some of the southern states—growing out of the corrupt *political Factions*—
which have sprung up & out of the war, is the *first* and *perhaps* the most difficult
and important of your public duties at present. This can best be done, by setting aside both *Factions* & letting the popular voice be heard. The whole south-

ern people will support you in the steps necessary to accomplish *this end.* You
have a clear right to send your own *special Agent* to these *distracted* states, with
orders to report *facts* to *you,* & to recieve your orders in *return,* & to *ignore,* &
recognize, as your sense of duty and judgement shall dictate as proper—& to
see in the end, that *Political fraud* & *corruption* shall not be sanctified by your
action, and to see that the people of each state, *has,* what the Constitution,
guarantees, that is, a Republican Goverment IN FACT—as well as in theory. You
have *sufficiently* the *confidence of the* country to do this, & you have the power
under the Constitution, and the duty under that instrument, to do it. & you can
best do it by the selection of some sensible & prudent southern Friend of your
own—(not *politician*)—as your agent. The country will sustain you and Congress will sustain you, & make the necessary appropriations—such an agent
should have your full confidence, and should be armed with large discresion,
& should be identified with the people whose rights are to be thus settled, &
whose *political relations* are to be thus made, in *Harmony,* with their duty, to
the Federal Govt   If you do not do something to restore peace, as against
these political Factions, they will involve the people of these states in state civil
war—when the General Goverment will be obliged to *interfere,* ~~with~~ by the
exercise of *armed* military force, which the Political power of the Federal Goverment could now prevent. I was anxious to have had a conference with you on
these matters when I was in Washington. But as you know, I did not have an
opportuty to do so.—To place myself right before you, and to releive my motives in these suggestions, I desire to say that I seek *no place*—but am content
to work on in private life as I always have done & thus make my living—I feel
that to you Mr President I can claim to have given, proofs of love of country
and of patriotism, in other days, which none can doubt. To this knowledge my
character I appeal, now, to *vindicate* my *motives* for making to you *these suggestions,* and as proof, that they are not made from venal or selfish considerations. My wife, who returned Home from Washington sick, desires me to make
to you & Mrs Grant, her kindest acknowledgements, for the Honor of your invitation to spend a social evening with you and Mrs Grant, and to express the
regret she feels, that our departure from Washington before your invitation
reached us, deprived her of the pleasure she should have felt in its acceptance.
With my apology Mr President for troubling you with this long letter . . . Allow me Mr President to ask your attention to the matter of my wife, referred
to in her letter"—ALS, University of Tennessee, Knoxville, Tenn. "If deemed
worthy the confidence of the Goverment, and possessed of the requisite qualifications, I should feel very much gratified to recive from the President, any
appointment, the salary of which would yield me a support. You are so well acquainted with my past History & character, that I consider it unnecessary to
procure expressions of popular opinion in my favour. I am a Lawyer by profession, of 40 years experience & practice, and should feel most grateful for the
appointment of Judge on the Supreme Bench of the U. S. I suppose it would not
be deemed *indelicate to me,* to say that I suppose there is no southern Lawyer,
who would be more acceptible to the southern people, and I am pursuaded that

the people of the whole country, who know of my past services to the country, would be satisfied with the appointment. If you should be of opinion that the south, should not have a representative on the Supreme Bench, or that the part I bore, in the late unhappy civil war, should *debar* me, from that, or any other place, under the Goverment, I should be content. As a soldier and Patriot you have know me Mr President. Two years ago my name was spoken of, for the Supreme Bench of Tennessee—I enclose to you a series of *Editorials* which appeared in the leading news papers of this city. I declined to allow my name to be used as a candidate for that place then, as I should now, but I would, in my advanced age, feel highly complimented and gratified, with an appointment at your hands for the place indicated. If you desired recommendations and testimonials of my fitness, furnished by the Bar, I am pursuaded that they could be furnished in any quantity and to any extent. With my best wishes Mr President for the success of your adminstration & for your health and happiness . . ."— ALS, ICarbS. No appointment followed. See Nathaniel Cheairs Hughes, Jr., and Roy P. Stonesifer, Jr., *The Life and Wars of Gideon J. Pillow* (Chapel Hill, 1993), pp. 313, 315–17.

1872, Nov. 8.   William Jackson, Alexandria, Va., to USG. "This letter will be unexpected to you Sir. I am a colored man now confined in the Alexandia Jail I have taken this liberty to write to you, to let you know where I am. I have voted for you when I was at liberty. I am very sorry that I could not vote for you this time   I have prayed to God for your sucsess and I thank God you have been sucsessfull   I was with you around Petersburgh va and I hope you will remember me in my trouble. I am innocent of the crime that I am charged with—. . ."—ALS, DNA, RG 60, Letters from the President. Charged with murdering his wife, Jackson was sentenced to hang.—*Washington Evening Star,* Nov. 12, 14, 18, 1872.

1872, Nov. 8.   John H. Purnell, Opelika, Ala., to USG. "Ere this you have undoubtedly heard 'the news.' Allow me therefore one among thousands to congratulate you. The Republican party of this state has done her whole duty. . . ."—ALS, USG 3. On Dec. 16, Purnell wrote to USG requesting an appointment as navy paymaster.—ALS, DNA, RG 45, Miscellaneous Letters Received. No appointment followed.

1872, Nov. 9.   Caroline V. D. Chenoweth, Ebbitt House, Washington, D. C., to USG. "The Hon. Secy. of State refuses to consider for a moment the question of appointing a woman to any Foreign Consulate. He kindly admits that I mastered the duties of the Consulate at Canton while I had charge of that Office, but while he does not doubt my ability to perform the regular consular work would oppose such an appointment upon the ground that questions are liable to arise which it would be improper for a woman to discuss.—In answer to my plea that such questions had never yet arisen, he replied that they might. Upon this remote possibility I am set aside, and am left to wonder why I need be denied this position under a Government which it has already been proven

I can intelligently serve—and for whose sake the life so necessary to myself and family was cheerfully sacrificed. Am I to consider that Mr Fish's views decide my final answer, or may I still leave my application before yourself with permission to resume it should a more favorable opportunity ever offer."— ALS, DNA, RG 59, Letters of Application and Recommendation. See *PUSG*, 9, 644–45; Frances E. Willard and Mary A. Livermore, eds., *A Woman of the Century* (1893; reprinted, Detroit, 1967), pp. 172–73.

1872, Nov. 12.   Henry Bergh, president, American Society for the Prevention of Cruelty to Animals, New York City, to USG. "I beg permission to invite your attention to the atrocities which are spoken of in the accompanying letter. The world is beggining to appreciate the value of the inferior animals, and to accord to them a share of human justice. I have been instrumental in causing some twenty States and Territories of our Union, to enact laws similar to those of this State for the prevention of Cruelty to dumb animals; and have aided their citizens to organize kindred Societies. These humble creatures, which feed, clothe and work for us; have the right to be treated mercifully, while useful; and when no longer so, have accorded them a speedy death. I feel that I may confidently rely on your Excellency's interposing your high and humane authority, in the matter to which I refer at this time; . . ."—ALS, DNA, RG 94, Letters Received, 164 1873. Enclosed is a letter of Oct. 20 from Charles L. Smith, Santa Fé, to Bergh complaining that worn out "horses and mules belonging to the U. S. Government" were sold at auction and then maltreated rather than "mercifully destroyed, which would be but a trifling loss to the government and a great saving of misery to those poor creatures."—Copy, *ibid.* On Dec. 21, Lt. Col. Frederick Myers, deputy q. m., Santa Fé, endorsed these papers. "I have made inquiry at the only Hotel in this place, and of all the merchants and others, and have as yet been unable to find a single person who ever met or heard of Chas. L. Smith. I therefore am of the opinion; that said name, 'Charles L. Smith,' is assumed, in order to shield himself from detection and exposure. His statements are erroneous, and most of them are false, . . ."— ES, *ibid.* Other endorsements are *ibid.*

1872, Nov. 13.   To Samuel T. Spear, Brooklyn. "I have the honor to acknowledge the receipt of your kind letter of congratulation and beg you to accept my sincere thanks for the kind sentiments which you express. Such evidences of kindly feeling and good will are truly gratifying."—Copy, DLC-USG, II, 1. On Nov. 9, Spear had written to USG. "I drop this note to you to congratulate you on the verdict which the people have rendered by your re-election. Having conducted the political discussion in your behalf in the columns of the *Independent,* as the political, commercial, & financial Editor of that paper, & being a Grant man up to the hub, I naturally feel much gratified with the result. I have no favors to ask, as I am not an office-seeker; yet I am willing that you should know that there is such a man in existence, & that I have done what I could to secure your re-election. Now, Mr President, if you can spare time enough to send me a brief reply that I may have your autograph in my posses-

sion, I shall be much gratified. Wishing you a successful administration, &
suggesting that the overwhelming triumph of the Republican party is now its
greatest peril, . . ."—ALS, USG 3.

1872, Nov. 14.   To V. C. S. Topsöe, Copenhagen. "I have the honor to acknowledge the receipt of your very kind letter of the 23d ultimo, together with
the copy of your interesting work on America which you were good enough to
send me. Please accept my sincere thanks for your kind attention."—Copy,
DLC-USG, II, 1. See Topsöe, *Fra Amerika* (Copenhagen, 1872), especially
pp. 210–15.

1872, Nov. 15.   USG endorsement. "Acknowledge receipt. Letter for my signature"—AE, IHi. Written on a letter of Nov. 7 from A. Jay Smith, New York
City, to USG. "I take pleasure in forwarding to Your address a box containing
a bag of coffee, which has been remitted to me for that purpose by Count
Manuel Rocha Leao, of Rio Janiero, Brazil. This coffee is a part of a crop
grown by him, which has obtained great celebrity, some of which was exhibited at the Expocicion Universalle at Paris, and received the Gold Medal Prize.
None of this crop has ever been sold, but has been kept for his own use, and for
presents to his friends. Having as he expresses it conceived a high admiration
for the Victorious General, and able Ruler of the United States, General Grant.
He begs you will accept this trifle, as a small token of his esteem and admiration. Should the offerring meet with your approbation it would afford me great
pleasure to convey to him Your acceptance of the same."—ALS, *ibid.*

1872, Nov. 18.   USG endorsement. "Dr. McKeon would like a clerkship in
the Custom House at Chicago or New York City. The Collector is requested to
answer Dr. McKeon at his home in Cleveland."—Copy, DLC-USG, II, 1. Cop-
ied in a letter of Dec. 13 from Orville E. Babcock to Richard C. Parsons, marshal, U. S. Supreme Court. "The President wishes me to say that at the time
Dr. McKeon called, he made the following endorsement upon the papers:— . . .
This endorsement was made and the papers mailed to the Collector of
Customs at Chicago, on the 18th of last month. The President supposed that
Dr. McKeon had received word from it before this."—Copy, *ibid.* On Oct. 19,
Patrick E. McKeon, "M. D. (Bar. at Law)," Cleveland, had written to USG. "I
beg leave to seek at your hands the appointment of *Consul* at one of the Ports
of the British Provinces; but if there should be no vacancy among those, then
at some European Port—and I have the honor to enclose herewith my testimonials as to fitness to discharge the duties &c"—ALS, DNA, RG 59, Letters
of Application and Recommendation. On March 6, 1873, McKeon, Chicago,
wrote to Secretary of State Hamilton Fish. "Placed in the Chicago Custom
House, through the prompt kindness of our good President, *en attendant* a
place in the Consular Service; I am praying for you, in this 'Holy season,' all the
time; and that you may, one day, place me *en rapport* with your Department."—
ALS, *ibid.*
    On April 10, 1875, McKeon, editor, *Northwestern Chronicle*, St. Paul,
wrote to USG. "Referring to the *enclosure*, I feel impelled by an unwavering

admiration, already known to you, to solicit your just judgment of the grievances herein set forth. I am not presently an applicant for office, but I should
be happy to lay down my editorial pen, and present 'practice,' to become your
Inspector of Indian Agencies, to the end that these complaints may cease, & the
illustrious record your name adorns, remain unsullied by false friends & fanat-
ics. I pray you consider my proposition: Senator McMillan whom I know &
esteem, would, I am sure, be happy to urge it."—ALS, *ibid.*, RG 48, Appcint-
ment Div., Letters Received. The enclosed editorial alleged government bias
against Catholic Indian missions.—*Ibid.*

On March 31, 1876, McKeon wrote to USG urging early passage of an immigration bill.—ALS, *ibid.*, RG 59, Miscellaneous Letters.

1872, Nov. 18.   To J. Robley Dunglison, Philadelphia. "I have the honcr to
acknowledge the receipt of your letter of 9th inst: together with the copy of
your volume which you were good egnough to send me, and beg you to accept
my sincere thanks for your kind attention."—Copy, DLC-USG, II, 1. USG
probably acknowledged a book by Dunglison's late father Robley, *History of
Medicine from the Earliest Ages to the Commencement of the Nineteenth Century*
(Philadelphia, 1872).

1872, Nov. 19.   USG endorsement. "Respectfully refered to the Sec. of the
Navy."—AES, NNP.

1872, Nov. 19.   To Thomas Street, New York City. "I read with much pleasure your very kind letter of congratulation which reached me in due time, and
desire to express my sincere thanks for the kind sentiments and wishes you express. I trust I shall have the continued prayers of all good people to guide me
in doing my whole duty in the responsible position I now hold."—Copy, DLC-
USG, II, 1. In an undated letter, Street, "Pastor of North Presb. church," had
written to USG. "With my heart full of gratitude to God for his goodness to
our nation by leading it to your reelection to the high office you have so faithfully filled and in granting to you so marked a vindication from the aspersions
of your political opponents, and Such an overwhelming approval of your administration—I cannot refrain from the liberty of calling to your mind the
subject I had the honor to present before you, last Summer at the religious
Service on Mr. Pulman's Island. My text then was 'What I do thou knowest not
now but thou Shall know here after' and I took occasion to show that though
it may be necessary for us to meet with heavy opposition and endure the malignity of others even while we are endeavoring to do our best—Yet time will
cause all this to be dissipated and we shall in the Divine wisdom be lifted to our
true place and Stand all the firmer and grander in the reaction—This has been
signally manifest in recent events concerning Yourself, and I desire with the
thousands who have supported and defended you to tender you my congratulations upon the result. Allow me to say that you are borne daily in the hearts
and upon the prayers of Christian Pastors and people to the theme of God and
His blessing invoked upon you that your life and health may be very precious
in his sight and that your future may be marked by the wisdom prudence and

success which have characterized your past services—Trusting Dear Sir that you will pardon my presumption on the ground of my profound personal regard . . ."—ALS, USG 3.

1872, Nov. 22.   Orville E. Babcock to U.S. Representative James A. Garfield of Ohio, chairman, Appropriations Committee. "Your letter relative to our Contingent Fund is received and I thank you for making the inquiry. I have consulted with the President and he would be glad to have it increased so that the fund might furnish books for the library and current magazines. The appropriation asked for, for the past four years, has been but $4000. out of which amount stationery and office furni[ture] has been purchased [and it] has been felt to be a limited amount. While $10.000 would be very acceptable, $6.000 would be highly appreciated. I know of nothing else to suggest in this connection."—LS, DLC-James A. Garfield; copy, DLC-USG, II, 1. The appropriations bill enacted March 3, 1873, designated $6,000 for "contingent expenses of the executive office, including stationery."—*U.S. Statutes at Large,* XVII, 491.

1872, Nov. 25.   To John S. Crocker, warden, D. C. jail. "Whereas, one Barney Wood was, on the 19th day of October, in the year eighteen hundred and seventy-two, convicted in the Supreme Court of the District of Columbia of the crime of murder, and sentenced to suffer death therefor, and Wednesday, the 27th day of November, instant, was appointed as the time of the execution of said sentence; And whereas, the friends of the said Barney Wood desire that he may have further time for preparation for death;—You are, therefore, hereby informed that the execution of said sentence has been, by me respited and delayed until Friday, the sixth day of December, next, on which day you are authorized and directed to carry said sentence into effect, in manner and form as therein prescribed. . . ."—Copy, DNA, RG 59, General Records. On Nov. 9, Mary Woods appealed to USG. "I am the unhappy wife of Barney Woods, now awaiting execution under sentence of death in this District. I am the mother of four small children. I sat by my husband through his recent trial, heard the verdict against him, awaited and hoped until the motion for a new trial was denied and now as soon as I recovered from the blow I bring the case to the executive and earnestly implore that my husband's punishment may be commuted to imprisonment. My husband by nature is a kind, just and true hearted man, and when himself never injured a living thing. He has been for some years subject to fits, which latterly have been aggravated by his unfortunate habits of drink, . . . On the trial I could not be heard as a witness for my husband, and I make this statement under the solemnities of an oath."—*Washington Evening Star,* Nov. 13, 1872. Albert G. Riddle, counsel for Barney Woods, endorsed this statement. "Mrs. Woods' first husband served in the war, and she devoted herself for most of the time to the care of our soldiers in the hospitals and in aiding loyal refugees."—*Ibid.* Riddle also wrote to USG that this "case was tried under great disadvantage to the defendant. A great number of homicides had been committed recently, and his was one of seven or eight cases coming on for trial, and in addition to the necessary and excusable alarm in the public mind, there was a strong prejudice bearing against him individually. . . ."—*Ibid* On Nov. 27, Barney Woods spoke to a reporter. "'Yes, I feel thankful to our worthy and kind-hearted President for giving me a few more days to prepare. . . . and perhaps he may yet commute my sentence.'"—*Ibid.*, Nov. 29, 1872. On Dec. 6, Woods was hanged for murdering a man who had purchased the ice co. where he worked and then fired him. See *ibid.*, Aug. 13–14, Oct. 9–12, 19, Nov. 22, Dec. 6, 1872; *PUSG*, 18, 86.

1872, Nov. 25.   Joseph A. Chipley, McGaheysville, Va., to USG. "i Will caul youre attension to my sad condishon that i am now placed under.   i have dunn all in my power for you and have bene treted badley for the Same.   i resited i augustay County near Staunton Va at the time of the Presidenttual Electtion. i lecttioneard for you and got a great meny vots for you. Whill all the time Wars Scorned and allmost trampeld under the feet of those of the opposet side. the Roat A great meny letters to mee thretning to destroy every thing i posest and to merder mee and my Wife if i did not turn my Corse and Chang my princiable   those letter wier writen without eny name. sined to them But i Sood up for you and would Not change my princiabl and and would not go back on my word. and in too days after the the Electtion i receved a letter to leave the contry i the next day or i would bee hanged. But deturmned to Stand to my perfesion i Would not move A peg. and that night my house and barn and every thing i persest under the heavens Wars Set on fire and burned up.   my Wife and child made A narrow escape—and allso my Self but as for my Self i card nothing and now i am left without A muth full of bred for my family or a seckond Sute for them to war. and have no A comodagions for every one seames to rejoice at my fallen condishon and with out helpe from some sose my family must undoutably suffer. and this is why i call on you to help me for i have no other friend near mee that is able help me—and i implore you to help me   i dont like to call on eny one to help mee but now i A blige to ask for help. if you will Send me money enough to tak me and my family out of this place i Will never bee dunn giving my thanks to you   the lord will reward you for it. Just Please send me A nough to take me amoungst friends Whar i can get work to doo that i may suport my family for hear i Can not get A days work to doo and So i can not help my family hear nomore than if i had no Aistance in the world.   pleas Send mee money Enough to take mee A way   i can make A rais A gain and will pay you youre money back   if i am out of the cluches of theas tyrants i can soon come out of this.   i no you have a heart of kindness and money is no object with you and heaven will reward youre kind deeds—. . . Pleas let me hear from you soon"—ALS, DNA, RG 60, Letters from the President.

1872, Nov. 25.   C. M. B. Thurmond, Memphis, to USG. "Instead of sending you an imposing array of names recommending me to your consideration, I am prompted by some spirit—'black or white, *blue* or *gray*—to approach you directly and apply for an appointment—suiting your convenience and opportunity, of course—to the Consulate at Callao, Peru, or to Rio De Janeiro, Brazil—I am a native Missourian,—was first a private, then a captain of the line in the Confederate army, was wounded at Franklin Tenn—and imprisoned at Fort Delaware—Release was several times tendered me, (in consideration, I suppose, of my precarious condition,) but I declined to accept terms until Genl Kirby Smith surrendered—From an anxious sense of duty and a profound sentiment of honor I adhered to my allegiance, and stood to my flag so long as it waved over an army in the field. Immediately upon the final loss of our cause—when the star I followed had set forever in a sea of blood, in the same spirit, I adapted myself to the new order of things, renewed my allegiance to the Government in good faith; and my published letters and public speeches subsequently were in advocacy of reconcilliation—leaving the dead past to bury its dead. Since the war my occupation has been that of a student and attorney at law. I am an advocate of the Constitution and laws under all circumstances—in the spirit of Henry Clay—looking to them as our constant guide, whatever might be my individual convictions on subordinate questions—I am in favor of utilizing and protecting the new element in our citizenship—. . ."—ALS, DNA, RG 59, Letters of Application and Recommendation. No appointment followed.

1872, Nov. 26.   Anthony W. Faulkner, New Orleans, to USG. "I have the Honer to apply for an appointment, as Diplomatic agent, of the Government, or as Commissioner, or on a special Commission, to the Governments of Spain, or Mexico—or to some of the South American Governments, as may seem best.   as for services I have rendered—in aiding the Establishment of the National Republican Party, the following endorsements is the best voucher I could present,—"—ALS, USG 3. The signatures of Pinckney B. S. Pinchback, William P. Kellogg, and 28 others are appended. Faulkner also wrote an undated memorandum, probably to Richard M. Corwine. "I have just seen Genl Dent after leaving you, he is my Friend, and will help you. I told him you had the application, so you see him early to morrow [morn]ing—or at least see the President—and File the Application, if neither of the places can be h[a]d alluded to, and the California Surv[e]y Bill passed—which I believe did, the appointment on that Commission will do, as that would not prevent me, carrying out our affairs in person, and still could afford to—allow you, your $1000— or I believe this would be best—You and Genl Dent divide—that is I would compliment you and he with $500, each, for the Genl—is glad to help me, in any way,   Make the point that, Louisaniania has had no appointments, and my & John Rays—sustaining always—Col Casey—I want you to drive this matter right up—whether I accept the Office or not, I am going to make money, and am not a going to let—your, and my interest suffer under any circumstances"—ADS, *ibid.* Born in Ohio, Faulkner had owned slaves and served in the C.S. Army. Letters recommending his amnesty are *ibid.* No appointment followed.

1872, Nov. 26.   James Hall, "of Balto, M'd," Kingston, Jamaica, to USG. "On the Subject of the Annexation of Santo Domingo—& ultimately other Islands of the West Indies to the United States, the writer feels justified in tendering his opinions. And this, from having devoted forty years of his life to the service of the African Race, having founded and for several years governed the American Colony of Cape Palmas, in Liberia, & laboured in the cause of African Colonization, until the final & general emancipation of the Slaves in our Country. Since which period the writer has spent the winter seasons in several of the W. I. Isles, & has labour'd to inform himself of the condition of the Africans resident therein. In the mean time he is familiar with arguments used by your Excellency; & the members of congress & the press favourable to scheme of annexation; also with the objections against it, urged by Mr Sumner in the Senate chamber & elsewhere, & by Mr Gerritt Smith in a pamphlet: & also by the opposition press. All of which he forbears to repeat or comment upon; but he believes he is able to add some testimony in favour of annexation that has not been fully set forth. During the period the purchase of St Thomas was pending in the Senate, the writer was residing or journeying amongst the English Windward Islands & became familiar with the feeling of the Coloured population in regard to that measure. It was hailed by all as a Second emancipation. It fed the strong hope entertained, that once begun a general annexation must sooner or later follow—Again, Ere the final rejection by the Senate of the Treaty [w]ith St Domingo, the same feeling was excited, and not only multitudes of Labourers from other Islands were prepared [to] emigrate but men of capital & energy both from the Islands [a]nd Central America were ready to invest in business, planting, [s]team navigation &c &c—Any where said they, that a stable [g]overnment is established & property secure.—Even in this Island the most valuable of the British Islands [&] loyal to the crown, the feeling among the labouring class is decidedly for annexation. Only last winter one of the richest [l]and owners here, yet residing in England, Col. Dawkins, of the Coldstream Guards, boldly advocated annexation in one of the daily papers of this city. The Cause of this feeling among the labouring class is very apparent, viz, *free labor,* which they do not & cannot enjoy under European rule— Plantation labour in the English Islands is fixed at the minimum, barely sufficient to sustain life. One Shilling per day, with no provision of food or shelter. In the Danish Islands, one half that price with an allowance of six qurts of meal & two pounds of meat or fish pr week—In fact, as a general rule, all the Colonial Legislation tends to operate in favour of the property holders & to depress the interests of the labouring class, as would have been the case in our Southern States but for the late amendments of our Constitution. The welfare & improvement of the African race, to advance [&] guarantee which, seems to be the destiny of the government [o]f the United States, demands the annexation of St Domingo as the first step, leaving future policy to be shaped by events. To one familiar with the condition of this people in these Islands that policy is clearly foreseen. Ten years after annexation, under our system of free labour, protection, & security of life & property, it would be safe to prophecy an [a]ddition of half a million of people to its present population, [f]rom other Islands alone—to say nothing of the influx of capitalists requiring their labour—The writer forbears any allusion to the advantages sure to accrue to our Government & people, from this measure, he urges it solely for

the benefit of the African race in these Islands—"—ALS, DNA, RG 59, Miscellaneous Letters. See Penelope Campbell, *Maryland in Africa: The Maryland
State Colonization Society 1831–1857* (Urbana, Ill., 1971).

1872, Nov. 27.   USG endorsement. "Grant the permission."—AE, IHi. Written on a letter of Nov. 16 from Amanda E. Pomeroy, New York City, to USG.
"I take the liberty to address you to ask permission to use your name as a reference in a school which I am about to open in Monroe Orange Co. N. Y. As
Miss Nellie was under my instruction at Mrs. Buel's, I have thought you would
be willing to allow me to make use of such a privilege. With great respect for
your self and family, and much pleasure for your triumph in the late election . . ."—ALS, *ibid.* See Orville E. Babcock to Pomeroy, Nov. 27, 1872, copy,
DLC-USG, II, 1. On June 3, 1876, Mary J. R. Buel, Philadelphia, wrote to
USG requesting a clerkship. ". . . You will remember the appointment to Liege
Belgium, of C. W. Kleeberg to whom I loaned the sum of $500 to enable him
to pay the passages of himself & wife, that he might enter upon the duties of
his station, which he never refunded,   This loan, foolishly made I confess, (but
I had confidence in his integrity) was the first cause of my ill health and subse-
quent embarrassment, which obliged me to close my delightful School in
Washington   I have since made two attempts to teach but find my strength
unequal to the wear of the school-room. . . ."—ALS, DNA, RG 59, Letters of
Application and Recommendation.

1872, Nov. 27.   To Peter Cooper, New York City. "I have the honor to acknowledge the receipt of your kind letter of the 18th inst, and must beg you to
accept my sincere thanks for your kind congratulations and good wishes. In return allow me to wish you many more years in which to continue the good
work of your life. With sentiments of sincere respect . . ."—LS, Columbia University, New York, N. Y. In 1870, Cooper had written to USG concerning patronage in N. Y.—William Evarts Benjamin, Catalogue No. 27, Nov., 1889, p. 6.

1872, Nov. 27.   To F. Reinecke, Pyrmont, Waldeck, Germany. "I have the
honor to acknowledge the receipt of your letter of the 3d inst. I must beg you
to accept many thanks for your beautiful work, for the receipt of which I have
supposed an acknowledgement was sent you. I regret exceedingly that you
have not received a reply to your former very kind letter. Again thanking
you, . . ."—Copy, DLC-USG, II, 1.

1872, Nov. 27.   John H. Conlee, Vesta, Johnson County, Neb., to USG. "allow
me to Congratulate you on your Success the Second Time to the high Position
That you now Ocupy   allow me to ask you a favor. I would Like the marshal
position of this State if you can Confer Such a favor   I Concluded that I would
write Direct to you in Sted of through Mr Tipton our Representative as he
worked hard for greely and I and him are Political Enemyes   you no Dought
will Rember me   I was Sheriff of JoDaviess County Ills when you Resided
in galena   I Could Refer you to many Persons in galena and other Places

E B Washburn and B H Campell J E Smith W. R. Rowley are old friends   three of my Sons Served in the army   I Stayed at hom and done my Part to feed the War widows."—ALS, DNA, RG 60, Records Relating to Appointments. No appointment followed.

1872, Nov. 28.   U.S. Senator Simon Cameron of Pa., Harrisburg, to USG. "I cordially endorse Mr John Hall of Washington Co Pa as a candidate for appointment as US Marshal of the Western District of Penna. He is a gentleman of ability, character, and influence, and his appointment would give general satisfaction to the only influence I am desirous of obliging—the Republican Party."—ALS, DNA, RG 60, Records Relating to Appointments. On Dec. 14, Judge William McKennan, U.S. Circuit Court, Washington, Pa., wrote to USG. "It affords me especial gratification to join in the recommendation of the appointment of Capt. John Hall to the office of Marshal of the Western District of Pennsylvania—I have known him for many years, and can, therefore, speak of his personal character and his special fitness for the office with the confidence of positive knowledge of both. . . ."—ALS, *ibid.* Related papers are *ibid.* On Dec. 16, Alexander Murdoch, Pittsburgh, wrote to USG resigning as marshal, Western District, Pa.—ALS, *ibid.* On Dec. 18, USG nominated Hall. On Nov. 16 and Dec. 11, 1876, McKennan, Pittsburgh, wrote to USG recommending Hall's reappointment.—ALS, *ibid.* On Dec. 6, USG renominated Hall.

1872, Nov. 29.   To Samuel B. S. Bissell, Norwalk, Conn. "I have the honor to acknowledge the receipt of your very kind letter of the 27th inst: and beg you in return to accept my sincere thanks for your kind thoughtfulness in writing it, and for the good wishes you express."—Copy, DLC-USG, II, 1. Born in 1812 in Westport, Conn., and educated at Yale and Princeton Divinity School, Bissell had ministered to slaves in Va. and worked as an agent of the American Tract Society. See *New York Times*, Aug. 24, 1894.

1872, Nov. 29.   John M. Read, Pa. Supreme Court, Philadelphia, to USG. "Personal . . . General Collis has told me, of the very complimentary manner in which you spoke of my son, and I am much gratified to know that his official conduct has won your approval. I feel assured, that when a fitting opportunity occurs, you will testify the administration's appreciation of his services, during a most eventful period, by such advancement as may be practicable. I need not say, that such an endorsement will be personally gratifying to me.—"—ALS, DNA, RG 59, Letters of Application and Recommendation. Related papers are *ibid.* See *PUSG*, 19, 330. On Oct. 21, 1873, Secretary of State Hamilton Fish recorded in his diary a discussion with USG. "I stated that I had received from Mr. Francis, Minister to Greece a letter stating that he would not be able to return and suggested that it would afford a good opportunity to send General J. M. Read to Greece, transfer Torbert from Havana, to Paris, and appoint Hall Consul General at Havana; he remarked that it wd be a great disappointment to Dr. Howe not to be appointed Minister to Greece. I asked him whether Mr. Francis had said anything to him on the subject of Howe representing the

Government at Athens. He answered Yes, but that objection seemed to be in Mrs. Howe   I referred to Mrs. Hill's large school and said the personal relations between Mr. Hill and Dr. Howe were not good and that Mr. Francis thought the appointment would entirely break up the Mission School: I referred also to some exception taken by Greeks to Dr Howe's administration of the fund raised at the time of the Cretan revolt: after some hesitancy he said 'well I suppose we may have to send Read to Greece.'"—DLC-Hamilton Fish. See *PUSG*, 21, 138; letter to Michael J. Cramer, May 11, 1875. On Dec. 2, 1873, USG nominated John Meredith Read, Jr., as minister to Greece.

On March 25, Joseph H. Ramsey, Albany, N. Y., had written to USG. "As Gen Read our present able Consul General at Paris, will probably soon be called to represent the Goverment. in some more responsible position, the friends of *Mr Franklin Olcott*, desire to present his name to the President as his successor,   Mr Olcott was apppointed a consular clerk in 1866 and has since that time served in that capacity in Montreal and Frankfort and for the last five years at Paris, and is at present the vice consul General at that place,   During the siege of Paris by the Prussians in the recent war, and through the whole of the time when that city was in the hands of the Communists, Mr. O. remained at his post, and with his family, passed thro' all the dangers and privations of that eventful period, . . ."—ALS, DNA, RG 59, Letters of Application and Recommendation. Related papers are *ibid.* On Dec. 2, USG nominated Franklin Olcott as consul, Nantes.

1872, Nov. 29.   Thomas B. Shannon, collector of customs, San Francisco, to USG. "The signers to the Enclosed petition are business men and Merchants of this City, of good standing, and I have no doubt that the facts as stated are true—A steamer regularly plies between this Port and San Blas, and the trade, therefore is becoming extensive and important—I have no hesitation in saying, that there should be some person residing there, clothed with Authority to Act, and represent the interests of the Citizens of the United States; I therefore most respectfully join with the petitioners in their request and hope it may be granted"—ALS, DNA, RG 59, Letters of Application and Recommendation. The enclosed undated petition from San Francisco merchants to USG recommending Manuel Garfias as "Consul or Commercial Agent at Tepic for the Port of San Blas" is *ibid.* On Nov. 18, George W. Perkins, Oroville, Calif., had written to U.S. Representative Aaron A. Sargent of Calif., Nevada City, concerning "Manuel Garfias, a citizen of the United States, a resident of Los Angeles, where his family resides. This gentleman is very intelligent, having received a regular military education at the college of Chepultepec, and is a relative of Gen. Porfirio Diaz. He was in 1851 County Treasurer of Los Angeles County. For two years past he has been in Mexico, acting under the appointment of Presdt Juarez as agent of the Government, to inspect the Custom houses of the Pacific Coast from La Paz to the extreme Southern limits of that government. That agency is nearly concluded, and he is willing to accept such appointment as that of Consul at Tepic, under Gen. Grant's Administration; he being a great admirer of the General, having at both the presidential elections most assiduously worked among the Mexican population of this State for his election, and having voted on each occasion for Gen. Grant's election."—ALS, *ibid.* On Jan. 7, 1873, USG nominated Garfias as consul, San Blas.

1872, Nov. 30.   Governor David P. Lewis of Ala. to USG. "Legislature at Court House recognized by the Governor as the General Assembly of Alabama. Law passed by Recognized Legislature and approved by Governor asking protection by National Government against domestic violence and raising committee to present memorial to National Government. Suspension of opinion respectfully asked on any representations by Capitol Assembly, until Committee arrives. Sheriff with United States troops as posse will preserve peace unless force comes from other places here. Everything quiet."—Copy (telegram received), DLC-William E. Chandler. On Nov. 18, following the Nov. 5 election, the Ala. legislature had convened in two competing bodies; Republicans met at the U.S. District Court House. See Sarah Woolfolk Wiggins, *The Scalawag in Alabama Politics, 1865–1881* (University, Ala., 1977), pp. 82–86. On Dec. 5, Levi P. Luckey wrote to William H. Smith, Robert M. Reynolds, and Benjamin W. Norris. "The President directs me to say that he is in receipt of your letter of this date requesting an interview to lay before him the memorial and Joint Resolution of the General Assembly of Alabama, and in reply to inform you that he prefers that you will lay the matter before the Attorney General of the U. S. first."—Copy, DLC-USG, II, 1. The memorial from the Republican legislature is in DNA, RG 60, Letters Received.

On Nov. 30, Ala. Senator Peter Hamilton and seven other members of the rival legislature petitioned USG. ". . . Since the adjournment of this General Assembly on yesterday, a body of United States soldiers has been brought from a distance to this city, and are now stationed within sight of the Capitol of Alabama, though not within the Capitol enclosure. These soldiers are not here at the request or with the concurrence or knowledge of this General Assembly. . . ."—Copy (printed), *ibid.* On Dec. 9, Brig. Gen. Alfred H. Terry, Louisville, telegraphed to AG Edward D. Townsend. "An officer was sent from Huntsville to Montgomery, Alabama, with orders to ascertain if any troops, had been, or were at that place, for what reason: and by whose authority,   The following is his Telegraphic report, 'Capt Weir and thirty men of Company "D" Seventh Cavalry, from Opelika, are here, encamped about two hundred yards from the Capitol,   these Troops came here on a Telegram: from the Governor of Alabama, based upon a request from the Sheriff of Montgomery County, to be at hand in case of a breach of the Peace,   they have taken no part in the political difficulties here nor have they as yet been needed, to prevent violence.   full report by mail, (signed) H. CATLEY, First Lieutenant Second Infantry.' The detachment moved to Montgomery without orders from me, or instructions from the asst Adjutant General of these Headquarters, Capt. Weir has been ordered to return to his proper Post."—Copy (telegram sent), *ibid.*, RG 94, Letters Received, 4927 1872. On Dec. 10, Secretary of War William W. Belknap wrote to Gen. William T. Sherman. "The President directs that if Genl. Terry be instructed *not* to relieve the Company from Montgomery, if they have not left, under the order referred to in Genl. T's telegram."—ADfS, *ibid.*

1872, DEC. 1.   To James Ormond Wilson, D. C. Superintendent of Public Schools. "I regret that I shall be unable to be present, in accordance with your very polite invitation, at the formal opening and dedication to morrow of the Jefferson School Building. The cause of Education is one in which all good citizens must take great interest, and the praise worthy efforts in behalf of that great object made by the District of Columbia can but be a source of great gratification to its citizens & reflect much credit upon the officers in charge of the work. It would afford me much pleasure to be present to-morrow if my public engagements would allow, and I beg you to accept my thanks for your kind invitation."—Copy, DLC-USG, II, 1.

1872, DEC. 2.   USG endorsement. "Respectfully refered to the Sec. of State."—AES, DNA, RG 59, Letters of Application and Recommendation. Written on a letter of Nov. 29 from Anthony J. Drexel, Philadelphia, to USG recommending Robert M. Hooper for a European consulate.—ALS, *ibid.* George H. Stuart, George W. Childs, Adolph E. Borie, and others favorably endorsed this letter.—ES, *ibid.* On Nov. 24, Borie had written to USG. "I cannot well refuse to send you the enclosed, confirming what is said in it."—ALS, *ibid.* The enclosed letter of Nov. 22 from Henry M. Philips to Borie described Hooper's financial losses in the stock market and from the Boston fire.—ALS, *ibid.* On Dec. 3, Hooper, Washington, D. C., wrote to USG. "Pardon me for again troubling you, but I feel it to be my duty to make you an explanation. Since my troubles I have suffered from nervous prostration, & yesterday when you kindly granted me an interview, I was so very nervous I hardly knew what I did, when I asked you if I should call on Mr Secty Fish, my only object was to save you trouble, I can assure you Mr President on my honor. I have spent several years in Europe & have been actively employed in business for 25 years, and feel I could do justice to any appointment you might entrust me with   I leave my application in your hands hoping for your kind consideration & a favourable reply"—ALS, *ibid.* On March 11, 1873, Hooper wrote a similar letter to USG.—ALS, *ibid.* On Feb. 13, 1874, Hooper was appointed deputy consul gen., Paris.

1872, DEC. 3.   To Congress, transmitting the State Dept. report on consular fees collected in 1871.—Copies, DNA, RG 59, Reports to the President and Congress; *ibid.*, RG 130, Messages to Congress. *HED,* 42-3-25.

1872, DEC. 3.   To Senate. "I transmit for the consideration of the Senate, with a view to ratification, a Convention between the United States and His Majesty the King of Denmark, relating to Naturalization."—DS, DNA, RG 46, Presidential Messages. On Jan. 13, 1873, the Senate ratified the treaty.

1872, DEC. 3.   Samuel B. Gibson, Canton, Mo., to USG. ". . . One of my Brothersinlaw, *Major Barnibas B. King,* Fell at the Battle of Shiloh, april 6th

1862   he was major of the 21st Regt Missouri Infty Vols Col. David Moore
Commanding. My other Brotherinlaw John W. Carnegy, was murdered by a
Band of Bushwhackers, who Came Into Canton on the 29th day of august 1862,
under the Command of one Franklin Martin E. Green and Ralph Smith. So
you See dear general, that we have Suffered In the flesh and I do assure you that
We have Suffered greatly in the pocket In Consequence of that most infamos
Rebellion, . . . I recollect of Seeing you upon an occasion in Palmyra Missouri
While in Command of Some Illinois Regt, During the first of the Rebellion, but
never Had the pleasur of your personal Acquaintance,   Now dear Genl, If you
have anything to give in the way of an office or any favor To Confer upon any-
one, please remember me and my family, for I do assure you That we are in
great want and That your favor whatever it may Be will be Kindly received and
remembered, . . ."—ALS, DNA, RG 59, Letters of Application and Recommendation. See *PUSG*, 2, 69; *O.R.*, I, xiii, 533–34.

1872, DEC. 3.   Baldwin D. Spilman, Warrenton, Va., to USG. "I respectfully
request an appointment at large as Cadet at West Point. I refer you to Col
Jno. S. Mosby as to my qualifications."—ALS, DNA, RG 94, Correspondence,
USMA. John S. Mosby endorsed this letter. "I take great pleasure in recommending the above application to the favor of President—The favor of the
Government could not be bestowed on a more worthy young man—I first suggested to him to apply for the place—"—AES (undated), *ibid.* On Dec. 15,
Mosby, Warrenton, wrote to Frederick T. Dent. "I endorse the application of
young Spilman for the cadetship at West Point—I hope the President will give
him the place—it will not only be a favor to me in justifying my support of
Genl. Grant but also to a talented young man who makes the application by my
advice—I hope you will do what you can to forward ~~the~~ it—There is now a
perfect revolution here in sentiment towards the Administration—Our people
are not only reconciled to the result of the election but those who were the
strongest for Greely now say that his defeat was a blessing—"—ALS, *ibid.*
Spilman graduated USMA in 1878.

1872, DEC. 4.   Orville E. Babcock to Christopher C. Andrews, U.S. minister,
Stockholm. "The President desires me to acknowledge the receipt of your letter of the 3rd of Oct. and of the acorns, which you were kind enough to gather
and send to him. He wishes me to convey you his sincere thanks. He has had
them sent to his farm near St Louis, with instructions to plant them as you direct in your letter."—Copy, DLC-USG, II, 1. On Oct. 28 and Nov. 26, Andrews
had written to USG concerning Swedish press coverage of the U.S. campaign
and election.—ALS (press), Andrews Papers, Minnesota Historical Society,
St. Paul, Minn.

1872, DEC. 5.   USG endorsement. "Refered to Sec. of War. Please let this case
come up to-morrow with other recommendations for apts. to the Army."—
AES, DNA, RG 94, ACP, 349 1873. Written on a letter of Nov. 5 from
William H. Kell, Lebanon, Ohio, to USG. "Desiring again to enter the Military Service I made application for a Lieutenantcy of Infantry in the Army. I

entered the army early in 1861 in the three months service, and reinlisted for
three years in the 2nd Ohio Infantry of which my Father was Colonel, and who
was killed at the Battle of Stone River. I served through the war from the first
battle of Bull-run to that of Nashville. I was born in Steubenville O in 1841 and
am now 31 years of age"—ALS, *ibid.* Related papers are *ibid.* On Dec. 12, USG
nominated Kell as 2nd lt., 22nd Inf.

1872, DEC. 5.   USG endorsement. "If vacancy exists in Sept. please call special attention to this application."—AES, DNA, RG 94, Correspondence,
USMA. Written on a letter of June 13 from Gerrit Smith, Peterboro, N. Y., to
USG. "My friend, Rev. Dr Tryon Edwards, is a highly esteemed Minister of
the Gospel in Hagerstown, Maryland. Mr Edwards desires from me a letter of
introduction to you. He visits you in behalf of his son William, who is a remarkably promising youth—"—ALS, *ibid.* On June 7, 1873, Smith again
wrote to USG. "This day's mail brings me a letter from Rev. Dr T. Edwards of
Maryland (Hagerstown, Md)   I wrote you, a year ago, in behalf of his son's
application to fill a vacancy at West Point. The Doctor called on you in person,
soon after. As so much time has elapsed, he fears you may have forgotten the
encouragement you then gave him. I trust it will be in your power to gratify
him & his promising son. I judge from the newspapers that you are enjoying
good health. Very glad should I be to have you, when you shall again visit this
section of the country, spend a day or two at my pleasant & healthful home—"—
ALS, *ibid.* William Fitzhugh Edwards, great-great-grandson of Jonathan Edwards, did not attend USMA.

1872, DEC. 5.   Eugene Field, Nice, France, to USG. "I am a young man
twenty years of age, who have come to this country to perfect myself in the
modern languages and acquaint myself with the politics and literature of Continental Europe. I am desirous of obtaining permission to inspect libraries in
the different cities and gain admittance to various institutions which are not
easy of access, on account of their privacy. I am a native of St Louis, Missouri,
and am personally acquainted with William McKee Esqr, the editor of the
daily GLOBE, who has advised me to apply to you for a letter of introduction
to American consuls in Europe and to 'all whom it may concern'. Such a letter
would be of great value to me and I trust you will see fit to favor me with it.
Mr. Ford has promised to introduce me to you and I send this letter to you by
him."—ALS, DNA, RG 59, Miscellaneous Letters. Related papers are *ibid.* See
Slason Thompson, *Life of Eugene Field: The Poet of Childhood* (New York,
1927), pp. 40–44.

1872, DEC. 6.   De Witt C. Whiting, chairman, Ala. Republican State Executive Committee, Montgomery, to USG. "This will introduce to your acquaintance Hon. J. J. McLemore of Alabama   Mr McLemore is the official bearer
of the Electoral vote of this State to Washington. He was one of the Republican Electors in the recent canvass; and by his able and eloquent speeches
contributed very largely to our brilliant triumph. Any kindness shown to

Mr McLemore by your Excellency will be highly appreciated by the Republicans of this State—"—ALS, DNA, RG 60, Records Relating to Appointments. On Dec. 1, 1873, USG nominated Whiting as appraiser, Mobile. On Dec. 17, 1872, J. J. McLemore, La Fayette, Ala., wrote to USG requesting appointment to a territorial judgeship.—ALS, *ibid.* On Dec. 19, U.S. Senator George E. Spencer of Ala. favorably endorsed this letter.—AES, *ibid.* On March 31, 1873, McLemore wrote to USG. "The maintenance and education of six daughters occasion me to forget or ignore proprieties and earnestly yet most respectfully request your personal inspection and consideration of an application and letter of recommendation in my behalf now on file in the Office of the Attorney General, . . ."—ALS, *ibid.*, Letters from the President. McLemore served as postmaster, La Fayette, from April 16, 1875.

1872, DEC. 9.   To Senate. "In answer to the resolution of the Senate of the 5th instant, I transmit herewith a report from the Secretary of State."—DS, DNA, RG 46, Presidential Messages. *SED*, 42-3-10. The Senate had requested information on British efforts to suppress the African slave trade. See *Foreign Relations, 1872*, pp. 208–15.

On Nov. 27, Joseph Cooper, London, had written to USG. "At the request of the British & Foreign Anti Slavery Society, I take the liberty to forward the Enclosed Address.—As Sir Bartle Frere with the other members of the Commission have already set out for Zanzibar, the Anti Slavery Committee would feel very grateful to you, should kindly see your way to take action in the matter at a very date."—ALS, DNA, RG 59, Miscellaneous Letters. The enclosure is a letter of Nov. 21 from Cooper and three others to USG. "The Committee of the British and Foreign Anti-Slavery Society respectfully entreat the attention of the President of the United States, to a subject which has to them, for many years been one of deep anxiety and concern.—They have repeatedly called the attention of their own Government to that great branch of the Slave-trade which is carried on in the vicinity of Pemba and Zanzibar on the Eastern Coasts of Africa, by which vast tracts of the interior are laid waste and many of the Native tribes are destroyed, and they rejoice that now at length, the public interest in this Country is roused, and in consequence the British Government is disposed to take immediate steps for its total extinction. This is to a large extent due to the letters of Dr Livingstone, so happily discovered and relieved by your intrepid Countryman, Mr Stanley   You are probably aware that our Government has appointed a Commission to proceed to Zanzibar at the head of which is Sir Bartle Frere, a Gentleman highly respected in this Country. Our object in addressing you at the present time is respectfully but earnestly to solicit your aid in this great work of humanity. We venture to express our ardent desire that you may see it right to instruct your Consul at Zanzibar to afford every assistance in his power to aid the objects of the British Commissioners in their efforts to bring this great evil to an end   And seeing that the existence of the Slave-trade is everywhere a consequence of the institution of Slavery, we earnestly desire that the influence of your Great Republic may be exerted in favor of its extinction in the Mohammedan Nations of the East and wherever else it may still continue to exist. We feel the less hesitation in addressing you on this great subject in consequence of your noble utterances on the subject of freedom, and your desire that Slavery may disappear from every part of the World"—DS, *ibid.* See *Foreign Relations, 1873,* pp. 430–31.

1872, Dec. 9.   To Frederick G. Gedney, New York City. "In response to your letter of the 22d of Nov. I herewith enclose you an engraving of myself, with autograph, to be placed in the Album to be presented to the Hon. A. B. Cornell, by admiring friends, as a token of their high regard for him personally, and of his eminent services in the late political campaign. No one has a higher appreciation of Mr. Cornell's worth as a citizen and friend than I, nor has he a more sincere well wisher for his future success and prosperity."—Copy, DLC-USG, II, 1. See *New York Times,* Jan. 2, 1873; *ibid.,* Feb. 25, 1899; *PUSG,* 20, 252.

1872, Dec. 9.   John H. Foraham, Charleston, S. C., to USG. "I am a Freedman who write to you wishing you to aid me by putting me in a Military School, or Naval Accademy, to be servicable to the U. S. I. have no friends to help me, for full well you know that the people of So. Ca will not help one colord boy to obtain an education. I have no help nor money only making out to live. I have studied Geography, Arithmetick,—Davies & Felters Gram' Schools, Algebra,—Davies Elementary, Geometry—Davies Legendre,—Latin— Principea Latena, Rhetorick, a little of Mineralegy, Grammar, &co. Please to write to me soon."—ALS, DNA, RG 94, Unsuccessful Cadet Applications.

1872, Dec. 9.   Stephen A. Hurlbut, Belvidere, Ill., to USG. "Profr. Haskell of Aurora, desires to receive an appointment in the Diplomatic service, prefrably to Greece or Turkey. I take pleasure in *strongly recommending* him to your favorable considration as a gentleman of large experience of the world, of thorough education and of a most blameless and Christian life. . . ."—Copy, IHi. No appointment followed. A list of letters returned to Thomas N. Haskell is in his file in DNA, RG 59, Letters of Application and Recommendation.

1872, Dec. 9.   Mayor Franklin Wood of Petersburg, Va., to USG. "James M. Donnan. Esq. Attorney at Law—Cashier of the People's Savings Bank and Member of our City Council, has expressed a desire to serve as a Consul, for the United States—to one of the Ports of Scotland; and it is both a pleasure and an honor to recommend—a gentleman so fully qualified by character, social standing—educational capacity—as well as by firm adhesion and long advocacy of the principles of the present national administration, for a position in the Civil Service of the government."—ALS, DNA, RG 59, Letters of Application and Recommendation. On April 7, 1873, John S. Mosby, Warrenton, Va., wrote to Secretary of State Hamilton Fish. "A few days ago when I had an audience with you, you asked me if I knew anything of Mr Donnon of Petersburg who is recommended by Platte & others for a Consulate. On inquiry I learn that he is an old & highly respectable citizen of Petersburg Va—& a member of a leading law firm of that City. From all I can learn of him I think his appointment would be highly satisfactory to the Va people as well as creditable to the government. . . ."—ALS, *ibid.* Related papers are *ibid.* On Dec. 2, USG nominated James M. Donnan as consul, Belfast. On Jan. 18, 1376, Mary H. W. Donnan, Belfast, wrote to USG concerning her fears that Democrats in Congress would legislate lower salaries for her husband and other consuls.—ALS, *ibid.*, Miscellaneous Letters.

On Dec. 24, 1872, Robert C. Schenck, U.S. minister, London, had written to USG. "Doctor McDermont of Ohio is an Applicant for a Consulate. He is one of the best & fittest men in the state for such an appointment. I say this confidently from long personal acquaintance with him. His faithful service during the war, & since as Surgeon of the Soldier's National Asylum at Dayton & at Hampton Virginia, entitle him also to the most favorable consideration. Doctor McDermont would, for many reasons, prefer an appointment at Belfast in Ireland; and to this I do not hesitate heartily to recommend him—not merely on account of his own deserving, but also because I am of opinion that the public service might be benefitted much by the removal of Mr Rhea the present consul at that place."—ALS, *ibid.*, Letters of Application and Recommendation. On March 12, 1873, Clarke McDermont, Hampton, Va., wrote to Secretary of the Interior Columbus Delano. ". . . The hitch in my appointment seemed to be, that I was from Ohio, which already has more than her share of foreign place—To meet this, I obtained recommendations from Mr. Platt the Rep. from this District and good endorsements from Senator Lewis Ex. Gov. Wells, Mr. Stowell of the 4th dist & other Virginians, who are willing to have me credited to Virginia—Mr. Platt is said to favor my appointment very strongly because it will make room for another of his constituents who is anxious to get my place—Gen. Eaton had a talk with the President who said if I could be charged to Virginia it would be satisfactory to him. Some reluctance was indicated to sending naturalized citizens to the country of their birth, . . ."—ALS, *ibid.* Related papers are *ibid.* No appointment followed.

On Feb. 1, James Martin, St. Louis, had written to USG. "Your petitioner would respectfully represent, that he is a citizen of St Louis, an Irishman by birth and a Republican in politics. He is anxious to obtain the appointment of Consul to the city of Belfast, or if that is not obtainable, to some other city in Ireland, where he could be of service to the land of his adoption."—ALS, *ibid.* John F. Long, Charles W. Ford, and six others favorably endorsed Martin.—ES (undated), *ibid.* No appointment followed.

On July 30, U.S. Senator John A. Logan of Ill. wrote to USG. "I write merely to say that the removal of Dr Ray as Consul to Belfast, was a Surprise after Secty Fish stating to me that he made a first class officer. I have recd several letters from travelers in Ireland (amongst whom iswas Mr Chandler, formerly Asst Sec of Tres), who speaks highly of him, and say that the assurance that he would be retained, caused him to purchase property, which he can not dispose of and is ruinous to him   he is a poor man but deserving. I understand he was removed for making so many speeches.   he did make some speeches that is true but they were good ones and certainly complimentary to this Ad-

ministration. I am truly sorry that it has been thought best to sacrafice as good
a man as Mr Raey, and hope at least that his case may be reconsidered"—ALS,
ibid. On Dec. 20, James Rea, Washington, D. C., wrote to USG concerning his
dismissal as consul, Belfast.—ALS, *ibid.* On Jan. 10, 1874, Logan wrote to
USG. "I would most respectfully represent that Dr Rea, is in very embarrassed
circumstances, and could you give him any position that would enable him to
make a subsistence for his family I would be pleased to see him placed in such
position"—ALS, *ibid.* Related papers are *ibid.* No appointment followed.

1872, DEC. 11.   George P. Hachenberg, Rochester, N. Y., to USG. "I am at
this time making another attempt to bring Musical Telegraphy before the
public, in which I receive considerable encouragement from the Centennial
Commission who wish to make it one of the features of the Centennial Celebration of 1876. Prof Henry of the Smithsonian Institution speaks favorably of
the practicability of the enterprise. I am the inventor of this Mus. Tel. and have
kept it before the public for many years. In order to keep myself in readiness
to give attention to this important affair, will you please favor me with some
position in the Gov. service, either in Washington or Phila or if possible a position in immediate connection with the Cent. enterprise itself. Since I left the
U. S. Army where I served as surgeon, I lost my property through the unfortunate management of parties having my property in charge, and not having
recovered my professional business I make this application in order to secure
an immediate competency for myself and family. In 1869 on my return from
the Army in Dakota I had an interview with you at the White House soliciting a German Consulship. I then candidly told you that I was seeking the position in order to favor my Mus. Tel. in Europe, as I saw no chance to put it
through in this country. You may remember I then came to Washington not for
the Consulship alone, but to meet some gentlemen with a view of consulting on
the enterprise to constructing gas works in the Cumberland Mts for supplying
some of the eastern cities with gas. The liberal spirit you manifested in your
last message towards national improvements, prompts me to make this application. Should you act favorably act in this matter, you will not only do me a
great favor; but perhaps deside the fate of one of the greatest inventions of the
age."—L, DNA, RG 59, Letters of Application and Recommendation. Related
papers, including a circular describing Hachenberg's invention, are *ibid.* On
March 11, 1873, Hachenberg, Philadelphia, wrote to USG on the same subject.—L, *ibid.,* RG 56, Letters Received. No appointment followed.

1872, DEC. 12.   Julia Berard, West Point, N. Y., to USG. "With this letter you
will receive the formal application for an appointment to a cadetship at the
Military Academy made by my brother John Berard. Upon my return to West
Point, I spoke to Prof Church on the subject of obtaining the signatures of
some of the Professors here to such an application, according to your suggestion. Prof Church expressed the kindest interest in my brother's success, but
told me that he, in common with the other members of the Academic Board,
deemed it best to hold aloof from anything like a recommendation of any can-

didate for this Institution, and on this ground alone he felt obliged to decline my request. In any other way that he could further our wishes he very kindly and warmly expressed his willingness to do so. Thanking you very sincerely for your kind reception of my request and in earnest hope that it may result in the appointment we so much desire for my brother . . ."—ALS, DNA, RG 94, Correspondence, USMA. Appointed at large to USMA in 1874, John H. Berard did not graduate. See *PUSG*, 16, 62–63.

1872, DEC. 12. William H. F. Hall, Greenville, Ga., to USG. "The undersigned would respectfully solicit the Governorship of one of our Territories, a Consulship, or a position in one of the Departments in Washington. . . . P. S. Perhaps he may, with propriety, say that he is one of the few white men comparatively, in the 'black belt,' that actively aided your re-election."—ALS, DNA, RG 59, Letters of Application and Recommendation. On Nov. 30, Dawson A. Walker, unsuccessful Republican candidate for governor, Dalton, Ga., wrote. "I am well acquainted with Hon. W H F Hall of Meriwether Co Ga. and regard him a man of integrity & capacity. He has served with honor in the Georgia Legislature and is I think worthy of employment"—ALS, *ibid.* As of Sept. 30, 1875, Hall served as storekeeper, Internal Revenue, Pueblo, Colorado Territory.

1872, DEC. 14. USG endorsement. "The present incumbent tenders his resignation to take effect on the 31st of this month, in favor of the within named applicant for his place, who is most highly spoken of by the Com. of Int. Revinue, Mr. Douglass. I approve the appointment."—AES, DNA, RG 59, Letters of Application and Recommendation. Written on a letter of Nov. 25 from John C. Hilton, Erie, Pa., to USG. "I have the honor to apply for the position of Consul at Port Mahone, Manorca Islands; In a recent conversation with the Rev. J. H. Whallon, I causually remarked that such an appointment would suit me very much. Mr. W. said he would resign if he thought I needed and wanted the place, therefore I ask that my claims may receive due attention; placing my claims on the following reasons; I entered the army as a private in Aug. '62 and was promoted until I commanded the company—was in active service all the time—wounded at Frederreksburg Va Dec 19. '62 and at Gettysburg Pa July 2d 1863. met with the loss of my right leg, and am using an artificial leg to supply my loss. Was a candidate in 1869 for the Post Office in this city, but the Administration saw fit to give it to the present incumbent, and since that time I have been acting in the capacity of clerk, yet the confinement will soon compel me to seek other employment. . . ."—ALS, *ibid.* On Dec. 14, James H. Whallon, Erie, wrote to USG recommending Hilton.—ALS, *ibid.* On Dec. 19, USG nominated Hilton as consul, Hesse-Darmstadt. On Jan. 14, 1873, USG withdrew Hilton's nomination pending examination by the Civil Service Board.—Hamilton Fish diary, Jan. 14, 1873, DLC-Hamilton Fish. Hilton was not renominated; Congress discontinued the consulate.

On April 19, 1869, USG had nominated Aaron Seeley as consul, Hesse-Darmstadt. On July 5, 1872, John H. Vincent, New York City, wrote to USG introducing "the Rev. Dr J F. Hurst now a professor in Drew Theological Seminary Madison N. J. and for years a resident and theological professor in Germany."—ALS, DNA, RG 59, Letters of Application and Recommendation. On July 9, John F. Hurst, Madison, N. J., wrote to USG that ". . . Mr J. P. Jackson, is every way worthy of your confidence, and what he says concerning Mr Seeley may be credited fully, and is confirmed by what I myself heard repeatedly when resident there. It is my impression that the continuance of Mr. Seeley in the office would be injurious to our interests now in his keeping. Mr Jackson words his communication strongly, but I know that he speaks without temper or any interested motives."—ALS, *ibid.* On June 10, J. P. Jackson, Frankfurt-am-Main, had written a letter accusing Seeley of misusing funds.—ALS, *ibid.* On Aug. 29, USG suspended Seeley. On Jan. 21, 1873, Secretary of State Hamilton Fish wrote in his diary. "The President says that a letter has been read to him stating that Seeley, Consul at Hesse Darmstadt has seduced the daughter of a respectable American lady who has been spending some time there."—DLC-Hamilton Fish.

On Dec. 3, 1872, USG had nominated Philip Figyelmesy as consul, Hesse-Darmstadt. Figyelmesy declined the appointment. On Jan. 25, 1870, Figyelmesy, consul, Demerara, had written to Fish asking for a consulship in Hungary.—ALS, DNA, RG 59, Letters of Application and Recommendation.

In an undated note, USG wrote. "Mr. Scofield asks the apt. of Isaac S. Alden to Hesse Armstead or elswhere. Speaks highly of his capacity and qualifications"—AN, Columbia University, New York, N. Y.

1872, DEC. 14. Charles Dunham, Washington, D. C., to USG. "I behalfe of the merchants & the Police force of this city I would humble sugest a benevolent act on your side for their protection   1, for the protection of the trade, to recoment to Congress to repeal the Law, sentencing to the penitentiary for stealing to the amount of $35.00 *value stolen* and to reduce it to $5 or $10., this act has been adopted for the reason that the many futgitives from the south came here &, not being employment enogh here, the consequenses had to be 'stealing' & under the old law the penitentiaris of the whole country would not been sufficient to mentain them,   now, is plenty work and all can make an honest living if they are willing. Now it is hard for the merchants here to make a display of their goods out side, as the many pilferers know that they get off with a light punishment—2, To protect the police force, is to give us at better Judge of the police Court. The desperatos fight the officers, in the discharge of their dudies & they get of to easy, as you (will see in last friday's star, (a *slip you find inclosed*)   instead to send such cases to the grand jury he encourages them to repead it when the short term is out. This is the sentiment of an old colored citizen who likes the reputation of the colored race promoted"—ALS, DNA, RG 60, Letters from the President.

1872, DEC. 17. To Francis A. Eastman, Chicago. "I have the honor to acknowledge the receipt of your letter, which has just reached me, tendering your resignation of the Postmastership of Chicago, to take effect on the 14th of Feby. next. In accepting your resignation I wish to thank you for the kind sentiments which you express in your letter towards myself and to assure you of my appreciation of the ability with which you have carried on your office since your appointment a part of which period was made particularly difficult by the great fire of 1871, and to wish you all success in your future undertakings."—Copy, DLC-USG, II, 1. On Dec. 18, USG nominated John McArthur as postmaster, Chicago.

1872, DEC. 18.   USG endorsement. "If the Sec. of State sees no objection to the change I am willing to see Col. Stewart appointed Consul to Bordeaux vice Clinch."—AES, DNA, RG 59, Letters of Application and Recommendation. Written on a docket listing letters from Ohio Republican congressmen endorsing James E. Stewart. On Dec. 16, U.S. Representative John F. McKinney of Ohio had written to USG. "Col. James E. Stewart, the bearer hereof, is an editor of the Springfield Republic, a daily and weekly Republican paper published in Springfield, Ohio. I take great pleasure in being able to indorse Col. Stewart as a gentleman of education and refinement, and by extensive business experience, well qualified to render valuable service to the Government in any position that may be assigned him. Being opponents in politics, I know Col. Stewart to be a party enemy to be feared and respected. If thorough qualifications to discharge the duties of office, and fealty to his party are to be regarded, I am sure his claims will be favorably considered. By conferring on Col Stewart the favor asked, the Government will have a faithful and efficient officer, and will be doing partial justice to a worthy citizen and soldier."—ALS, OFH. On Dec. 15, U.S. Representative Ozro J. Dodds of Ohio, also a Democrat, had written a similar letter to USG.—ALS, *ibid.* On Jan. 3, 1873, Secretary of State Hamilton Fish wrote in his diary. "Call Presidents attention to endorsement on an application of Jas E. Stewart of Ohio for the Consulate at Bordeaux—& advise that no change be made—the reasons would be misunderstood—he assents"—DLC-Hamilton Fish. See *PUSG*, 19, 417–18.

On April 10, Stewart, Springfield, Ohio, wrote to USG. "I am just in receipt of information from the State Department, ignoring my claims upon the Consulate at Bordeaux. I at once referred the communication to Mr. Shellabarger, who was much surprised and disappointed at the course things had taken. With the strong recommendations I presented, and your own assurances to Mr. Shellabarger and myself, I likewise am much disappointed. Mr. President, I served my Country at the front for nearly four years—was a prisoner of war—and have been a faithful Republican—is there nothing now you can grant me?"—ALS, DNA, RG 59, Letters of Application and Recommendation. On April 14, USG endorsed this letter. "Refered to the Sec. of State. I have no recollection of the promise spoken of within."—AES, *ibid.* On April 10, Stewart had written to William H. Crook, White House clerk, asking that his letters of recommendation be returned.—ALS, *ibid.* USG endorsed this letter. "I have no objection to Mr Stewart being permitted to withdraw his recommendations for a consular appmt from the State Depmt."—Copy (docketed April 16), *ibid.* On Dec. 2, USG nominated Benjamin Gerrish, Jr., as consul, Bordeaux.

1872, DEC. 18.   Charles S. Russell, St. Louis, to USG. "Congratulating you upon your re-election, I venture to make our former acquaintance and association the basis of a favor I have to ask, not for myself but in behalf of a very good and worthy friend of mine. I refer to Mr. Jame N. Norris of the firm of Norris Taylor & Co of this City . . . I lately heard that he was negotiating with some one who had a 'permit to trade' to take charge of such business at some distant military post, and it was indeed this fact that suggested to my mind this application to you, for if he himself could through you obtain such a 'permit' he would then have *all* the benefits and profits, instead of performing the same labor for some one else for a mere salary . . ."—ALS, DNA, RG 94, Applications for Positions in War Dept.

1872, DEC. 19.   George D. James, Washington, D. C., to USG. "The undersigned Commissioner on the part of the Chickasaw Nation, in obedience, to instructions from Cyrus Harris Governor of the said nation, copy of which is herewith enclosed and begs leave most respectfully to present Preamble and Resolutions passed by the Legislature of the Chickasaw Nation during its late Session September 24th 1872, . . ."—ALS, DNA, RG 75, Letters Received, Choctaw Agency. The enclosed resolutions asked USG to settle a dispute between the Chickasaw and Choctaw Nations concerning land allotment under an 1866 treaty. See *PUSG*, 20, 315–16; M. Thomas Bailey, *Reconstruction in Indian Territory: A Story of Avarice, Discrimination, and Opportunism* (Port Washington, N. Y., 1972), pp. 127–28. Also on Dec. 19, James wrote to USG forwarding a protest against congressional measures to open the Indian Territory to white settlers.—*HED*, 42-3-141.

    On Feb. 17, 1874, William Bryant, principal chief, Choctaw Nation, wrote to USG. "You will please permit me to have the honor to invite your attention to the following, Resolutions passed by the general council asembled in extra session, of the choctaw Nation in January last, Protesting against the allotment of lands in the chickasaw District as provided for by a Resolution of the chickasaw Legislature, approved the 24th day of september 1872.   also a resolution passed at the same time protesting in the name of the Choctaw people against any territorial form of government to be extended over them against the wish of the choctaw people, which I transmit herewith certified copy of the Resolution which was passed at the extra session of the general council of the choctaw Nation, which I will beg leave of you to permit me to request of you to submit the same to congress, with favorable recommendations   also you will permit me to implore for you the continued presence and blessing of Almighty God,"—ALS, DNA, RG 75, Letters Received, Choctaw Agency. The enclosures are *ibid.* See *Calendar*, Dec. 5, 1873; *HED*, 43-2-1, part 5, I, 380–81.

1872, DEC. 20.   Margaret R. Clune, Yankton, Dakota Territory, to USG. "I beg of you to forgive the great liberty I take in addressing you, and sending it to your Wife to deliver. I am very poor, and need your aid if it be just, and right you should d give it to me. My Husband W. H. Clune inlisted in the 6th Iowa

Infty'—was promoted Lieutenant Colonel just before the close of the War. Was wounded at Griswoldville Ga. but died very suddenly after the close of the War in Galveston Texas. I wish for the sake of my only child a boy (George H. Clune) to have a bill pass Congress for a pension in his, or my behalf. . . ."—ALS, DNA, RG 233, 43A-D1. A lengthy letter of Dec. 17 from Clune to Julia Dent Grant is *ibid.* On Feb. 12, 1873, Orville E. Babcock wrote to U.S. Representative Jesse H. Moore of Ill. "Mrs Grant desires me to write you this letter and say that a pension bill before your Committee, H. R. 3339, for Mrs. Margaret Clune, widow of the late Col. W. W. Clune of the 6th Iowa Vol. Inf. is in behalf of a lady whom she knows well, and knows to be very deserving. She wishes me to say that she will be very glad if you will give the case special attention and thus insure its becoming a law."—Copy, DLC-USG, II, 1. See *HRC*, 43-2-68, 49-1-2538, 56-1-829; *SRC*, 56-1-1331.

1872, DEC. 20.   George A. Halsey *et al.*, Jersey City, to USG. "The undersigned, members of the Republican State Committee of New Jersey, respectfully recommend for a Consular appointment Mr. Francis W. Potter, Editor of *the Newark Evening Courier.* . . ."—DS (7 signatures), DNA, RG 59, Letters of Application and Recommendation. Similar petitions are *ibid.* On March 14, 1873, USG nominated Francis W. Potter as consul, Marseilles.

On Dec. 23, 1872, Eliphalet M. Brown, Jr., "Flagship 'Wabash,'" Villefranche, France, had written to Frederick Dent Grant. ". . . Having heard, incidentally, that the present Consul at Marseilles intended returning to the United States in the coming spring, I wished you to ask your father to give me the appointment, . . . You may perhaps remember that, before you left us at Gibralter, you said if I was ever in want of anything in which you could render me assistance you would do so—and now I earnestly request your good offices in my behalf—I am getting *pretty well* along in years—find that a sea-life is not the most congenial one for me—and I would like to settle down into something humanizing—. . ."—ALS, *ibid.* On Nov. 28, 1873, Brown, New York City, wrote to USG requesting appointment to a European consulate and citing his long service in the U.S. Navy, including duty as an artist on Perry's expedition to Japan.—ALS, *ibid.* No appointment followed. See *HRC*, 36-1-208.

On Jan. 27, Lycurgus Edgerton, Washington, D. C., had written to [USG]. "*Colonel Milton M. Price*, United States Consul at Marseilles France, who has held the appointment for four years—has written to the Honourable William A Dart, United States Consul General in Montreal Canada, proposing to him to arrange for an exchange of positions; . . . Mr Price is a resident of the State of *Iowa* where he has interests in Railways and in other properties, which are suffering from his absence, and if he could receive an appointment in Canada—within 48 hours time of his home—it would enable him to take a more immediate supervision of his affairs than he can now do, so far away.—*I am an applicant for the Consulate at Marseilles.* . . ."—ALS, DNA, RG 59, Letters of Application and Recommendation. On Feb. 15, Edgerton wrote to USG on the same subject. ". . . my cooperation in aid of the negociation of the 'refunding loan', now being floated in Europe, is deemed to be desirable, especially with the Messrs deRothschilds in Paris, and with their *confreres* in Frankfort; and, my presence there, might effectively promote the pending negociations; and it is thought that the *prestige* of the Office for which I am an applicant, might strengthen my position and influence with the financial group of which they are the centre; . . . I trust that the President will pardon the liberty I am taking in bringing this subject to his notice, and also permit me to assure him that my views will be sustained by Govenor Cooke and by his brother Mr Jay Cooke, who are deeply concerned in the success of the negociation of the new loan. . . ."—ALS, *ibid.* Related papers are *ibid.*

On April 1, Hiram Price, Davenport, Iowa, telegraphed to USG. "News papers say my Son has been removed as consul at Marseilles France, and left without an appointment   is this true   Please cause an answer to be sent me and confer a favor . . ."—Telegram received, *ibid.*, Miscellaneous Letters. On April 19, Price, St. Louis, wrote to Secretary of State Hamilton Fish. "I had a conversation here this day with the President in reference to the removal of my Son as Consul at Marseilles, France, and learned for the first time that he had been removed for cause. I am well Satisfied that there is Some mistake about it, and I write now at the Suggestion of the President to ask of you the favor, to Cause to be Sent to me, a copy of the charges and the names of those who make them, So that my Son if innocent may be heard in his own defence even at this late day—. . ."—ALS, *ibid.*

1872, DEC. 20.   Santiago Martin *et al.*, "officers and principal men, of the Pueblo of Taos," New Mexico Territory, to USG. ". . . Our Pueblo is one of the most populous of the ten or twelve Pueblos in this Territory; and is situated in a densely settled valley; and from its proximity to the settlements of the whites; we are continually entangled in difficulties and endless litigation, concerning the rights, titles &c. to the lands, that we now occupy and possess, under and by virtue of the Land Grant or Reservation, set apart and confirmed to us, by the Government of the United States of America: We have often and repeatedly, represented, our grievances, and brought them to the knowledge of our present United States Indian Agent, John O. Cole Esq; as well as before other agents, that have preceded him, in the Pueblo Indian Agency of this Territory; but as yet, none of them have listened to our many complaints, much less, render us, the necessary assistance in holding our lands, against the pretended claims of Mexicans . . . In view of the many facts, herein set forth and of the great inconveniences under which labor: we most respectfully, beg of your Excellency, to remove the 'United States Pueblo Indian Agency' from Santa Fé, N. M. and cause the same to be permanently established at Fernandes de Taos, N. M. and also, pray to have the present incumbant of said Pueblo Indian Agency, John O. Cole Esq., removed; and have Major Ferdinand Maxwell, of this place, appointed in his place and stead: Major Ferdinand Maxwell, . . . has been strictly tried in the capacity of U. S. Indian Agent, for the Mescalero Apaches, during the years 1861, 2 & 3; which duties, he most honorably fulfilled, to the entire satisfaction of the United States Government.

Hoping that our prayer may be heard and answered favorably, . . ."—DS (23
signatures, by mark), DNA, RG 48, Appointment Papers, New Mexico Territory. On Dec. 22, Ferdinand Maxwell, "formerly of old Kaskaskia Randolph
County Illinois," Taos, wrote to U.S. Senator John A. Logan of Ill. asking him
to forward the petition.—ALS, *ibid.* Related papers are *ibid.* On Dec. 2, 1873,
USG nominated Edwin C. Lewis as agent, Pueblo Agency.

On March 29 and May 5, William H. Henrie, St. Louis, had written to USG.
"I respectfully submit to you this my application for the office of Indian agent
of the Pueblo Indians of New Mexico. I have resided twenty seven years in New
Mexico a near neighbour of the Pueblos all of whose head men I personally
Know, . . ." "On the 12th Ultimo I called at the white house, and having sent up
my card accompanied with letters from Mr W. McKee of the Globe and
Hon E. O. Stanard, had not the honnor of Seeing your Exelency, but was told
that my letters and aplication would be refered to Hon C. Delano. I was informed that there would be no probability of anything being done, in my case,
untill the next following monday, and my means being very limited I was compelled to leave the next day without seeing either yourself or Mr Delano, . . ."—
ALS, *ibid.* Related papers are *ibid.*

1872, DEC. 24.   Col. Israel Vogdes, Charleston, S. C., to USG. "I have
the honor, respectfully, to request the favor of an appointment at large to
a Cadetship at the United States Military Academy of my son Charles B.
Vogdes. . . ."—LS, DNA, RG 94, Correspondence, USMA. On Jan. 8, 1873,
Col. Rufus Ingalls, New York City, wrote to USG. "I take the liberty to add my
recommendation in behalf of the Son of General Vogdes for a Cadetship in
1874—Since you know General Vogdes' whole career as intimately as any can,
it will be unnecessary to recall it—I hope you will find it easy to confer the
appointment."—ALS, *ibid.* On April 15, 1876, Vogdes, Fort Adams, Newport,
R. I., wrote to USG on the same subject.—LS, *ibid.* On June 13, Vogdes again
wrote to USG. "I would respectfully request an appointment for my son
Charles B Vogdes. ~~in~~ as 2nd Lt. in the 7th Cavalry—I was in hopes of getting
an appointment ~~in~~to West Point for him but have hitheto been unable to do so.
If you will be kind enough to recall an interview that I had with you during my
last visit to Washington—I mentioned that I might make an application for
such an appointment,   you seemed disposed to to give a favorable consideration. Should you be able to grant my request I will be much abliged. One of my
sons served througout the war. And my own services should have some consideration"—ALS, *ibid.,* Applications for Positions in War Dept. Charles B.
Vogdes graduated USMA in 1880.

1872, DEC. 26.   USG endorsement. ". . . [the] Sec. of War. Let special attention be called to this applicati[on] when apts. come to be made."—AES (torn),
DNA, RG 94, Unsuccessful Cadet Applications. Written on a letter of Dec. 11
from George E. Maney, Nashville, to USG. "I most respectfully apply for appointment of my son *James A Maney* as a cadet to the U. S. Military Academy
at West Point. The party applied for is Seventeen years of age and possessed of

all qualifications requisite for appointment. His Post office *Nashville Ten-nessee*"—ALS, *ibid.* James A. Maney graduated USMA in 1877.

On April 14, 1873, George Maney wrote to USG recommending "Genl A. C. Jones for a position in connection with Indian Affairs. . . . I know Genl Jones to be a gentleman, not only of liberal education but liberal views also. He was one, of the not too many with his antecedents, who supported your election. . . ."—ALS, *ibid.*, RG 48, Appointment Div., Letters Received.

On Sept. 23, 1874, Maney, Nashville, wrote to USG. "I would most respectfully represent that Genl Pennypacker, who was recently ordered, from command at this place to duty in Louisiana, had during his assignment here, not only made quite extensive acquaintance with this People and their local affairs, but also decidedly impressed many good citizens, friends to the Government, with conviction of his capacity for usefulness in the position. For these reasons if this Post is to be continued I very earnestly suggest that he be returned to its command so soon as exigencies in Louisiana may permit. While on this subject let me congratulate your Excellency upon adoption of such action as on both principle and expediency must be overwhelmingly sustained by the Nation. Rash effort even reaching the momentary overthrow of an existing State-government by unusual means had reduced a Party to the legitimate absurdity of claiming with only, credentials of force, and violence, recognition by the Supreme Goverment, a *prime* duty of which is to prevent and suppress such force, and violence, Such attempts in a matter so solemn must always shock both the intuition and reason of an enlightened Self governing People. May not however an election be obtained *during* the necessary presence of military force in Louisiana which in its fairness will *compel* Public satisfaction and at same time secure Officers to the State who will afford *support* and *strength* in place of embarrassment to the National Administration? . . ."—ALS, *ibid.*, RG 94, Letters Received, 4096 1874.

1872, DEC. 27.   Governor Marshall Jewell of Conn. to USG. "I have not yet noticed the appointment of Mr. Bailey as I had hoped to have done. So I fear there is some hitch in it tho I understood from you that unless the Civil Service rules applied in this case that he would be appointed. May I not ask for his sake, an early decision as any thing is better than suspense   My only excuse for taking any interest in this matter is that Mr. Bailey is one of my oldest & best friends and would in my opinion make a most excellent officer."—ALS, OFH.

1872, DEC. 29.   Maj. Alexander J. Dallas, Camp Lowell, Arizona Territory, to USG. "I have the honor to request the appointment of the Rev. Antoine Jouvenceau of the Roman Catholic Church, as Chaplain in the U. S. Army, for duty in this Department. A large proportion of the enlisted men stationed in Arizona are Catholics, and have to my personal knowledge expended several hundred dollars to procure from time to time the ministrations of a clergyman of their own church, the diocese being a missionary one and too poor to furnish the same gratuitously. The gentleman mentioned above is eminently qualified for the duty, is an excellent linguist, and has proved heretofore acceptable to all; he is beside the only clergyman his Bishop can spare   This request is made at the desire of the Rev. Antoine Jouvenceau, and with the approval of Bishop J. B. Salpointe of Arizona. His address will be Tucson, A. T."—ALS, DNA, RG 94, Applications for Positions in War Dept. On June 23, 1873, Dallas, Washington, D. C., wrote to USG on the same subject.—ALS, *ibid.* No appointment followed.

1872, DEC. 30.   Orville E. Babcock to John M. St. John, Chicago. "The President desires me to acknowledge the receipt of your kind letter of the 23d instant and the carvings you were good enough to send him. He was very greatly pleased with them, and as an evidence of his appreciation of your skill in carving and your kind & thoughtful attention in sending him the ingenious specimens of such skill, he wishes me to send you the enclosed pocket knife with his thanks & best wishes for your success."—Copy, DLC-USG, II, 1.

1872, DEC. 31.   Milton J. Durham, Danville, Ky., to USG. "Mr Wm Stewart of Columbia Ky I learn is an applicant for a judgship in some one of the Western Territories. I have known him for several years   He is a good Lawyer a man of sobriety honesty and good conduct. His age, learning experience, and high moral integrity, make him well qualified to fill the highly responsible position of judge   Although I differ with Mr Stewart in *politics* I bear testimony cheerfully to his worth as a gentleman, a scholar and a Lawyer."—ALS, OFH. No appointment followed. Durham had been elected U.S. Representative in Nov.

1872, [*Dec.*].   James Sloan, "St Louis Mo. Medical College," to USG. ". . . I feel it my duty to appeal *somewhere* for those who have befriended me & were I to neglect them, now that they are so persistently set upon by those bent upon their ruin, I should be ungrateful. I mean the Indians. I have been among them Long enough to have become acquainted with them, & I can say that though there are a few of their own people who desire to sell their land, the majority cannot bear the idea. There is not much of it at most, & even if there is five or six Hundred acres apiece for each Indian, it should be theirs & their heirs for all time, & would then be but a tithe of that vast territory once *all* theirs. Many of our anglo saxon white citizens own extensive tracts of land, & no objection is made to it, why should these fast fading memorials of a once powerful race, be denied the *poor privelege*, so dear though to them, of dying in what is now but a shadowy imitation of of their former unfenced & unfettered freedom. *Do* let them have the satifaction of tending their stock & burning their prairie for *one* generation more, one generation is all they ask! They know very well that their prestige has gone! that civilization is absorbing them! & they long ago submitted & threw themselves, upon the clemency of a Government whos integrity is their only hope now. President Grant ~~your~~ your crowning glory will be to guarentee ~~these~~ Government pledges to these people. Every Newspaper is filled with new schemes, of powerful parties in-

deed, but not in the interests of the rank & file of our country, the farmers
the true defenders & vindicators of their country, for the acquisition of the
Cherokee lands. It is my individual prayer & hope that *you* will interpose. I have
not a single acre of land yet; but I am going to settle my soldiers homestead
which I am glad to see Congress has donated, but I do not want to take these
lands from the Indian.—This from one who was a soldier & knows the loyalty
of those for whom he is petitioning—"—ALS (docketed Dec. 18), DNA,
RG 75, Letters Received, Cherokee Agency.

Index

All letters written by USG of which the text was available for use in this volume are indexed under the names of the recipients. The dates of these letters are included in the index as an indication of the existence of text. Abbreviations used in the index are explained on pp. xv–xix. Individual regts. are indexed under the names of the states in which they originated.

Catacazy, Constantin de (Russian minister), 90*n*, 91*n*, 239*n*, 240*n*
Catholics, 133*n*, 135*n*, 136*n*, 221, 226*n*, 236*n*, 276*n*, 285*n*, 330–31, 430–31, 451, 474–75
Catley, Henry (U.S. Army), 459
Catoosa County, Ga., 408
Cattaraugus Reservation, N.Y., 365
Cattell, Alexander G. (U.S. Senator), 29*n*
Cattle, 80 and *n*, 81 and *n*, 401, 442, 443
Cayugas, 365
Cedartown, Ga., 69*n*
Cemeteries, 78, 394, 396–97
Census, 212*n*
Centennial Celebration, 423, 466
Central Pacific Railroad, 141*n*
Céspedes, Carlos Manuel de (Cuban president), 210*n*
Cessna, W. K. (Fla. representative), 260*n*
Chaffee, Jerome B. (U.S. Delegate), 306*n*
Chagrin Falls, Ohio, 434
Chambrun, Marquis de, 337
Champion's Hill, Miss., battle of, 352
Chandler, William E. (Republican official), 169*n*, 243*n*, 257*n*, 337, 435, 465
Chandler, Zachariah (U.S. Senator), 122*n*, 195*n*, 243*n*, 342
Chapin, Aaron L. (Beloit College), 381
Chaplains, 388–89, 433–34, 474–75
Chapultepec, Mexico, 458
Chariton County, Mo., 381
Charleston, S.C., 138*n*, 296, 389–90, 464, 473
Charlotte, N.C., 360
Chase, Joseph T. (of Titusville, Pa.), 367
Chatham County, Ga., 24*n*
Chattanooga, Tenn., 67*n*, 216–17, 217*n*, 223–24, 224*n*
Chautauqua County Historical Society, Westfield, N.Y.: document in, 392
Cheatham, William S. (of Nashville), 67*n*–68*n*
Chelsea, Mass., 402
Cheltenham Academy (Pa.), 221*n*
Cheney, Edward (of Fla.), 256*n*
Cheneyville, La., 102*n*
Chenoweth, Caroline V. D. (U.S. vice consul), 448–49
Cherokee County, Kan., 352–53

Cherokees, 96, 97*n*–99*n*, 145, 272*n*, 442, 476
Chester, Pa., 431
Chester County, S.C., 65
Chesterfield County, S.C., 65
Chew, Robert S. (State Dept. clerk), 157*n*
Cheyennes, 124*n*
Chicago, Ill.: collector appointed, 4, 4*n*–5*n*, 148, 149*n*, 450; West Division Railway Co., 5*n*; fire in, 27*n*, 295, 374; conventions in, 117, 162*n*, 332*n*; USG visits, 118*n*, 272*n*; U.S. Army in, 124*n*, 126*n*, 370; business activity in, 294*n*; postmaster, 468–69; mentioned, 23*n*, 33*n*, 34*n*, 54*n*, 92*n*, 97*n*, 131*n*, 157*n*, 176, 185*n*, 204*n*, 205*n*, 207, 219*n*, 243*n*, 244*n*–45*n*, 249*n*, 272*n*, 311*n*, 353, 359, 364, 365, 417, 418, 428, 434, 475
Chicago Historical Society, Chicago, Ill.: documents in, 6*n*, 46–47, 50*n*, 144*n*(2), 164*n*, 165*n*, 243*n*, 294*n*, 417
Chicago Tribune, 3*n*, 244*n*, 434
Chickamauga, Ga., 272*n*, 405
Chickasaws, 470
Chihuahua, Mexico, 414
Chilcott, George M. (railroad commissioner), 352
Childs, Emma (wife of George W. Childs), 263*n*
Childs, George W. (friend of USG): recommends appointments, 10*n*, 302*n*, 460; letter to, April 1, 1872, 57; asked to invest, 57; praises Nellie Grant, 249
Childs, Orville W. (engineer), 49*n*
Chile, 138–39, 139*n*
Chilton, James V. (of Warrenton, Va.), 403
China, 75*n*, 134*n*, 202, 298, 304*n*–5*n*, 379, 390, 410
Chipley, Joseph A. (of McGaheysville, Va.), 453
Chippewas, 316*n*, 357–58
Chiricahua Reservation, Arizona Territory, 186*n*, 187*n*, 190*n*
Chisum, Jeff, 127*n*
Chittenden, Simeon B. (of New York City), 284*n*
Choctaws, 272*n*, 470
Chouteau, Indian Territory, 442

ried, 221*n*; may travel with USG, 279; educated, 421, 456; mentioned, 192*n*, 291, 345

Grant, Frederick Dent (son of USG): travels in Europe, 20*n*, 82, 82*n*–85*n*, 91*n*, 140, 141*n*, 142*n*, 159, 172, 238, 471; portrait painted, 117*n*; letter to, April 28, 1872, 82; travels with USG, 200, 201*n*, 279; serves under Philip H. Sheridan, 221*n*, 249; visits Washington, Pa., 263*n*; seeks staff appointment, 294*n*; letter to, Dec. 31, 1872, 333–34; serves in West, 333–34, 334*n*; graduated USMA, 426

Grant, Jesse Root (father of USG): letter to, June 2, 1872, 159–60; receives family news, 159–60; USG visits, 197*n*; as postmaster, 214*n*; must resign office, 245 and *n*; letter to, Nov. 3, 1872, 279; USG plans to visit, 279, 280*n*, 329–30, 334 and *n*; business partner, 333*n*; mentioned, 268*n*

Grant, Jesse Root, Jr. (son of USG): opposes third term, 118*n*; with Conkling family, 201*n*; at school, 221*n*; hikes to Pa., 221*n*; travels with USG, 279, 334*n*; mentioned, 82, 159, 160, 166*n*, 196, 197*n*

Grant, Josiah (of Ga.), 30*n*

Grant, Julia Dent (wife of USG): misses Nellie Grant, 20*n*, 263 and *n*; concerned about Frederick Dent Grant, 82 and *n*, 83*n*, 85*n*, 294*n*, 333, 334*n*; receives statue proposal, 105*n*; praises USG portrait, 132*n*; receives jewelry, 132*n*; urged to support suffrage, 168*n*; attends dinner with USG, 174 and *n*; extends invitation to Long Branch, 177; letter to, July 2, 1872, 183–84; USG reports plans to, 183–84; telegram to, July 2, [1872], 184*n*; writes to Cyrus B. Comstock, 220, 221*n*; may travel with USG, 279; acknowledges Horace Greeley's death, 291; Christmas plans of, 326; praised, 340; receives pension appeal, 471; mentioned, 19, 121, 122, 140 and *n*, 154*n*, 160, 164*n*, 166*n*, 190, 191*n*, 192*n*, 196, 199, 200, 201*n*, 233, 238, 249, 268*n*, 284*n*, 317, 415, 421, 439, 445, 447

Grant, Mary M. (wife of Orvil L. Grant), 4

Grant, Orvil L. (brother of USG), 4, 4*n*–5*n*, 205*n*, 358–59

Grant, Ulysses S.: advocates Civil Service reform, 3, 61–62, 62*n*–63*n*, 306*n*, 331, 331*n*–32*n*; embarrassed by brother, 4, 4*n*–5*n*; and Philadelphia patronage, 5, 6*n*–11*n*; negotiates *Alabama* claims, 11, 11*n*–15*n*, 22 and *n*, 76, 77*n*, 119–20, 120*n*, 122*n*, 142, 143*n*, 144*n*, 156 and *n*, 157*n*–59*n*, 233, 235*n*, 303*n*; invests in quarry, 18–19, 21*n*–22*n*; ill, 20*n*; and Ga. patronage, 23, 23*n*–32*n*; welcomes Japanese embassy, 35–36; administers Indian policy, 40–41, 46*n*, 123, 124*n*, 144–46, 146*n*–48*n*, 184 and *n*, 188*n*, 189*n*, 190*n*, 270, 271*n*, 278*n*, 288*n*, 309, 309*n*–10*n*, 350, 351, 369–70, 417, 470, 472–73; orders Isthmian canal survey, 46–47, 319, 322*n*; owns St. Louis farm, 51–52, 60 and *n*, 80, 80*n*–81*n*, 81, 120–21, 250–51, 254, 461; owns horses, 51–52, 95, 120–21, 414; administers Rawlins fund, 52–53, 53*n*, 175–76, 176*n*–77*n*, 199, 207–8, 215–16, 216*n*, 217–18, 219, 220*n*, 264, 264*n*–66*n*; administers Reconstruction, 64–66, 155, 211, 228–29, 229*n*, 231*n*, 258*n*, 289–90, 459–60; supports soldiers' monument, 78; issues pardons, 79 and *n*, 247 and *n*, 343, 403, 413, 431, 438; comments on politics, 81, 95, 117–18, 118*n*, 139–40, 195, 200, 201*n*, 238; enforces eight-hour-day law, 85, 86*n*–87*n*, 103–4, 104*n*; vetoes bills, 94 and *n*, 108, 152–53, 155*n*, 367, 368, 375, 380; cannot attend army reunions, 95–96, 173, 173*n*–74*n*, 246; upholds civil rights, 99, 100*n*–101*n*, 289–90; seeks Senate advice, 105–6, 106*n*–7*n*; recommends aid for immigrants, 109–11; opposes persecution of Jews, 115–16; portrait of, 132*n*; transmits Samoan treaty, 134–35, 135*n*; and John A. Rawlins statue, 149–50, 150*n*; statue of, 151*n*; threatens to extend congressional session, 160; renominated, 161, 161*n*–68*n*, 191*n*–92*n*, 197*n*, 241*n*; in Vanderbilt tax dispute, 163*n*–64*n*; on